Holt, Rinehart '25/94

Market Segmentation

Concepts and Applications

Market Segmentation

Concepts and Applications

Edited by

James F. Engel
The Ohio State University

Henry F. Fiorillo
Canadian Breweries, Ltd., University of Toronto

Murray A. Cayley
Imperial Oil, Ltd.

HOLT, RINEHART AND WINSTON, INC.
New York Chicago San Francisco Atlanta
Dallas Toronto Montreal London Sydney

Copyright © 1972 by Holt, Rinehart and Winston, Inc.
All rights reserved
Library of Congress Catalog Card Number: 79-167809

ISBN: 0-03-088082-3
Printed in the United States of America
2 3 4 5   090   1 2 3 4 5 6 7 8 9

To Sharon, Chris, and Barbara

Editor's Foreword

The Advisory Editors of the Holt, Rinehart and Winston Marketing Series are pleased to publish the first volume completely devoted to the important topic of market segmentation. James F. Engel, Henry F. Fiorillo, and Murray A. Cayley have gathered within the covers of a single volume the best readings that have appeared on the subject. The readings are organized in a logical sequence and aided by essays and editorial introductions of considerable merit in themselves. The readings reflect the economic, behavioral, mathematical, and managerial facets of market segmentation—a topic which is becoming increasingly viewed as a key construct in marketing science.

PAUL E. GREEN
PHILIP KOTLER

Preface

Since World War II marketing has emerged as the focal activity of the business firm. The emphasis, by necessity, is placed on adapting the output of a firm to the expressed needs and desires of the market. Success, in turn, is increasingly determined by the ability of management to uncover demand variations within segments of the overall market and then to achieve a competitive edge by producing, pricing, promoting, and distributing a product that meets these demands. As a result, *market segmentation* has come to be recognized as a key to profit in a volatile competitive environment.

Not surprisingly, the marketing literature contains a growing volume of articles and research reports on this subject. There is, however, no one source which attempts to view it in a comprehensive and integrated manner. Consequently those interested in acquiring the necessary background in concept and applications are forced to consult a widely scattered and frequently inaccessible literature. It is the purpose of this book to provide a single source whereby both management in the business firm and students of marketing in colleges and universities can readily grasp concepts, methods, and applications of market segmentation.

We have attempted to provide a wide range of articles so that the needs of all users will be met. Not all contributions, of course, will be of equal value to all readers. For those primarily interested in business applications, it is recommended that special emphasis be placed on the starred readings in the table of contents. Other readings delve more deeply into details of technique and applications.

We have provided suggested readings at the end of each major section for those interested in further background. Also, an exhaustive bibliography is included after the last reading.

It is with genuine thanks that we acknowledge the willingness of the many authors and publishers represented here to have their efforts reprinted in this form. Our editors, Paul E. Green of the Wharton School of Finance and Commerce, University of Pennsylvania and Philip Kotler of Northwestern University, deserve special thanks. Others have also helped in various ways, especially Ian Christensen from the University of Manchester and Martin Murenbeeld of the University of California, Berkeley, both of whom have read the entire book and offered a number of useful insights. In addition, Sarah McCutcheon of the *Montreal Gazette,* Montreal, has done much to make this a readable manuscript. Our thanks also go to Christine Fiorillo, who typed much of the manuscript and assisted in the preparation of the bibliography.

Assembling the volume has been an exciting experience for us in many ways. Certainly we have learned much. Our joint association over several years as management and consultant has enabled us to extend many of the concepts encountered in the readings, both theoretically and practically. In total we have seen payout in application of market segmentation in business policy and decision-making.

Columbus, Ohio   JAMES F. ENGEL
Toronto, Ontario   HENRY F. FIORILLO
November 1971   MURRAY A. CAYLEY

Contents

PART FOUR   NEW ANALYTICAL TECHNIQUES IN MARKET
             SEGMENTATION ANALYSIS   383

PART FIVE   A LOOK TO THE FUTURE   457

      References in Market Segmentation   469
      Index of Authors   485

Market Segmentation
Concepts and Applications

PART ONE

INTRODUCTION
AND OVERVIEW

IN RECENT YEARS research into marketing methods has proceeded at an unprecedented rate, particularly in those areas amenable to computer analysis. We have witnessed, for example, the development of models for sales forecasts, sales analysis, brand performance analysis, test market selection, and evaluation of product alternatives. These systems, of necessity, produce vast amounts of data which, unfortunately, tend to be enshrouded in novel vocabularies that hide the significance of results from the uninitiated. Truly, the marketing manager is in danger of being overwhelmed by this information explosion without gaining an improved understanding of his market place.

It may justly be argued, however, that every marketing manager can, and should, understand the notion of market segmentation. Formulated by Wendell Smith in 1956, this concept has prompted much discussion and publication. When thoroughly comprehended, it offers substantial benefits in understanding the market and how to relate marketing decisions to that market.[1]

The concept of segmentation is based on the proposition that *consumers*

---

[1] Wendell R. Smith, "Product Differentiation and Market Segmentation as Alternative Marketing Strategies," *Journal of Marketing*, Vol. 21 (July 1956), pp. 3–8. This article is Reading 1.

are different. It is often easy to measure these differences in terms of age, income, education, ethnic background, race, religion, and position in the life cycle. It is not always easy to measure how consumers differ in terms of needs, personality, motives, and perceptions. Nevertheless, the basic fact remains that consumers exhibit differences that in many instances are measurable.

A second proposition underlying the concept of segmentation is that *differences in consumers are related to differences in market demand.* It is often useful only from a practical viewpoint to know that possession of a characteristic and subsequent behavior are related. This point is elaborated later.

That *segments of consumers can be isolated within the overall market* is a third proposition. The consumer differences of greatest interest are those which reveal or reflect basic underlying differences in consumer needs, wants, and product preferences. When differences in consumer product preferences are considerable, it is unlikely that one product can satisfy the wants of all. In a situation of wide customer preference differences that are being met by only one product that seeks to be all things to all people, it is not difficult to imagine the existence of a sizable unsatisfied group. Often, this minority of consumers can be distinguished from other consumers of the basic product in terms of their product needs, their preferences, or their personal characteristics. When they are so isolated, these consumers may be considered as one or several potential submarkets worth cultivating. Through a process of adapting to the buyer needs of carefully researched and defined segments, marketers can gain substantial competitive advantage over other firms which may still be pursuing a broad approach to the market.

BENEFITS OF THE SEGMENTATION CONCEPT

Why should a marketer cut up or segment his market? The first reason for not ignoring the diversity in markets is simply because it would be unrealistic. Not all consumers are alike, and their differences can have a profound effect on market demand. The second is that the presence of unfulfilled consumer needs provides a market opportunity. New products offer potential for growth and profit. More specifically, a segmentation outlook offers, among others, the following benefits:

A segmentation perspective leads to a more precise definition of the market in terms of consumer needs. Segmentation thus improves management's understanding of the customer and, more importantly, *why* he buys.

Management, once it understands consumer needs, is in a much better position to direct marketing programs that will satisfy these needs and hence will parallel the demands of the market.

A continuous program of market segmentation strengthens management's capabilities in meeting changing market demands.

Management is better able to assess competitive strengths and weaknesses. Of greatest importance, it can identify those segments where competition is thoroughly entrenched. This will save company resources by foregoing a pitched battle with locked-in competition, where there is little real hope of market gain.

It is possible to assess a firm's strengths and weaknesses through identifying market segments. Systematic planning for future markets is thus encouraged.

Segmentation leads to a more efficient allocation of marketing resources. For example, product and advertising appeals can be more easily coordinated. Media plans can be developed to minimize waste through excess exposure. This can result in a sharper brand image, and target consumers will recognize and distinguish products and promotional appeals directed at them.

Segmentation leads to a more precise setting of market objectives. Targets are defined operationally, and performance can later be evaluated against these standards. Segmentation analysis generates such critical questions as these: Should we add another brand? Should we drop or modify existing products, or should we attempt to reposition a faded and obsolete brand image?

It is clear that market segmentation can offer significant advantages as a competitive strategy and as a guide to market planning and analysis. For segmentation to be effective, however, the commitment of senior marketing management to such a policy is an absolute must. The reason for this, of course, is that attention to previously unrecognized market opportunities will usually require the appropriation of additional company resources. Often it will demand that the company move in a direction different from that currently being taken. In fact, it often provokes a serious questioning of what business the company is actually in. Therefore, unless the approach is well understood and the modes of segmentation appreciated, application of the strategy could have only minimal results.

USING SEGMENTATION ANALYSIS

The nature of marketing is to satisfy consumer wants at a profit. In doing this, the firm engages in a number of activities. Functionally, these have been categorized as developing new products and services for new markets, new products and services for old markets, and so on. It is imperative that the firm constantly keep the consumer in mind—and this is the essence of the marketing concept that has been successfully adopted by the most progressive business organizations.

In pursuing a marketing strategy, firms, whether they recognize it or not, conceptualize a model of the consumer. This model is then used to guide subsequent planning decisions with respect to product quality, product features, model line, product lines, brand names, packaging, media selection, price levels and changes, and distribution mix decisions. The firm's model of the consumer is, in effect, a portrait, a picture of the consumer in the marketplace. The picture may be explicitly stated in the formal objectives of a marketing plan or program, or it may be implicit, and inferred from external observations of the firm's marketing strategy.

Three Simple Consumer Models

Marketing managers usually group consumers for the purpose of marketing strategy into three classes:

1. *Similarity.* All consumers are basically similar. Although differences exist among consumers (for example, age, income, and so forth), these differences are not thought to be important in affecting the purchase of their specific product class. A standard product will essentially satisfy the large majority of consumers.
2. *Unique.* All consumers are unique. The differences among consumers (for example, age, income, needs, preferences, and so forth) make a standardized product or service unacceptable. Market offerings must be tailored specifically to the needs of each individual consumer.
3. *Difference/Similarity.* Consumer differences and similarities exist and are important sources of influence in market demand. Such differences can be regarded as differences in consumer needs and wants. These differences and similarities facilitate the grouping of consumers into aggregates or *segments* according to their needs and wants and the degree to which they are present. Marketers using a segmentation approach adopt marketing programs to match the peculiar need combinations of each of some market segment.

Three Alternative Marketing Strategies

In pursuing marketing programs, managers have available three alternative marketing strategies—market aggregation, extreme market segmentation, and partial market segmentation.

Market Aggregation

All consumers are treated as being similar.
A standard product is presented with very few real differences from other products in the company's line to serve the needs of all consumers.

Heavy use is made of promotional resources to distinguish one company's product from another, with emphasis on *product distinctions.*

The objective of promotional campaigns is to create the image of overall "superiority" in appealing to the broad needs of all consumers.

This approach is usually selected when dealing with a commodity item, that is, products which are basically alike (for example, salt, coal, wheat, gasoline, flour).

not to customers.

Market aggregation pays relatively little attention to differences in consumer preferences or needs; hence, it results in the bending of demand to the will of supply. Firms which successfully differentiate themselves from competitive firms often strive to do this through psychological differentiation, that is, by creating a strong image. However, this does not imply segmentation since it is supposed that such advertising will appeal to the whole market, not just several segments. Two firms with essentially the same product and marketing programs may be perceived differently if advertising has successfully shaped consumer perceptions.

The dangers of pursuing a strategy of market aggregation when consumer needs are distinctly different comes from the market opportunities available to competitors following a segmentation approach. New entrants to the market as well as existing competition can quickly capitalize on unfulfilled consumer needs and obtain significant competitive advantages.

Extreme Market Segmentation

All customers are treated uniquely.

This approach is not usually found in mass marketing of low-cost consumer goods.

Many examples exist in industrial marketing (for instance, specially designed machinery for capital goods industries). Examples in consumer marketing include custom-built homes, cars, furniture, some luxury goods.

Extreme market segmentation is not usually considered to be a practical marketing strategy. It has obvious disadvantages in that products, prices, promotion, and distribution must be tailor-made to customer requirements. This prevents use of, and subsequent economies to be gained through, standardized production runs, advertising media, and so forth.

Partial Market Segmentation

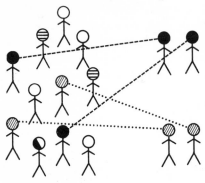

Clusters or segments of customers are assumed to exist with high intra-cluster similarity and low inter-cluster similarity.

Only selected segments are chosen as market targets.

This approach is essentially a merchandising strategy—"Sell what the customer needs." The emphasis is principally on customer needs and wants.

Promotional material is used to guide product appeals to designated market targets.

Partial market segmentation leads to a more precise fit between consumer needs and company products. In other words, product lines are developed to parallel market wants. With improvements in production technology, economies of scale allow standard products to be developed for submarkets which are much smaller in scope than the broader market.

In pursuing a strategy of partial market segmentation, the firm chooses to serve only one or a few of the possible segments that might be cultivated. As is often the case, participation in one segment may involve foregoing other segments. This occurred in the case of a major western brewer who had built a strong franchise in the young beer-drinking segment and then attempted to cultivate the middle-age market. The net result was a rapid loss of favor with members of the first segment; it did not seem possible to maintain both segments with the same product. Another example of partial segmentation is given by Sony in the field of television. The Sony Corporation has concentrated its marketing efforts on that segment of the television receiver market which shows a strong preference, above all else, for portability. In automobiles, Volkswagen and Toyota have concentrated on that segment of the auto market which wants cheap, economical transportation, with a low initial investment.

The disadvantages of a partial segmentation approach usually center around the loss of large purchase economies from buying advertising on a national basis. Similarly, production costs may increase when companies produce for submarkets which are often considerably smaller than the broad national market. Organization costs may also increase should additional staff be required to handle the marketing duties for new brands. Finally, a partial market segmentation approach can lead to increased marketing research costs because implementation and maintenance of a segmentation program requires considerable research effort.

The important point is that firms must balance the increased costs of doing business, both in terms of the short and long run, against the increased returns that a segmentation approach could offer. Maximum use of segmentation will involve cultivating all major market segments rather than just one or a few. In other words, the firm is preparing to outflank competitors by participating in every segment worth cultivating.

Not all firms, however, can pursue this strategy because, for example, participation in one segment may prevent development of a closely allied segment. Firms must consider questions of compatibility of market segments, the value of each, and the capabilities and strengths of competitors and themselves in meeting certain consumer needs.

Criteria for Market Segments

For usable segments to be developed (1) the segment should be of sufficient size and market potential to warrant the expenditure of marketing funds, (2) it must be possible to reach the segment through available media, and (3) the segment should show clear variation in market behavior in comparison with other segments.

Size. A leading manufacturer of paper products faced the problem of size when a new and demonstrably different crayon was introduced in eleven test markets. While the product appealed to a certain segment of users more than to others, it appeared that only 2 percent of a $30-million market could be captured. Thus, sales revenue did not warrant the necessary expenditures to produce and market the product.

Reachability. Frequently, measurable differences in consumer attributes do exist, but the segments thus isolated cannot be reached feasibly through promotional efforts. An excellent example is provided by a series of studies on the personality trait that has been termed "persuasibility."[2] It has been established experimentally that some people are more resistant to communication influences than others. This conclusion led to a series of studies on the correlates of persuasibility. It has been demonstrated that women are more persuasible than men, that intelligence and persuasibility are not related, that feelings of social inadequacy underlie persuasibility, that behavior is guided

[2] See James F. Engel, Hugh G. Wales, and Martin R. Warshaw, *Promotional Strategy*, rev. ed. (Homewood, Ill.: Richard D. Irwin, Inc. 1971), Ch. 9.

by external standards, and that conformity is the rule. Self-esteem is the personality trait most frequently correlated with persuasibility.

These data are interesting for marketing, but their relevance for marketing planning is not evident. It is by no means clear that those low in self-esteem and hence high in persuasibility possess unique needs to which appeals can be directed. Of even greater importance, there is no reason to expect differences in media exposure patterns among those who are persuasible and those who are not. Hence, there is no good way to reach the persuasible without considerable waste. Persuasibility as a segmentation variable, therefore, has not proved to be a way to isolate reachable segments.

Variations in Market Response.   Segments that show no clear variations among themselves in response to changes in the marketing mix are, for most practical purposes, not meaningfully defined. Where price is an active ingredient in stimulating consumer purchasing, price insensitive segments should not change significantly when price levels are altered. If they do show a change, the segment is not clearly defined. Similarly, deal-prone customer segments should react more actively to a promotional campaign offering "cents off" or "two for one" packages.

Using Segmentation in Market Planning Decisions

Whatever action the firm engages in will automatically lead to the attraction of some consumers and the repulsion of others. Marketing managers, however, can first identify customer groupings in the market and then alter the different elements of the marketing mix so as to differentially match the needs of various customer groups.

Broadly speaking, marketing mix planning decisions fall into four functional areas:

1. Product line planning
2. Promotional planning
3. Pricing
4. Distribution

Some of the decisions necessitated in each category are designated below:

Product Line Planning
   1. Product use
   2. Product quality and features
   3. Number of products in the line
   4. Number of brands
Promotional Planning
   1. What advertising appeals?

a. To what needs?
b. To what segments of the market?
2. Brand names
3. Package designs
4. Point of purchase
5. Media selection
a. What media (radio, TV, magazines, newspapers)
b. Reach, frequency and cost

Pricing
1. Price levels
a. Penetration pricing
b. Cream skimming
2. Price changes
a. Size
b. Timing
c. Duration
d. What products
e. Against what competitors

Distribution
1. Channel decision (that is, where should the product be sold?)
2. Shelf policy
3. Inventory policy

In determining the importance of knowing ahead of time what the consumers' likely reaction to changes in the marketing mix will be, management must rely heavily on the expertise of the market research function.

The function of the market research department is to improve management's understanding of the marketplace. Solid results will be achieved if management and research participate jointly in structuring the marketing problem. By so doing both parties gain a better understanding of each others function and, hence, can develop a more creative segmentation program. In this process management supplies experience, feel, and intuition; market research can offer a creative approach to problem formulation, technical expertise to carry out the sophisticated analysis, and the measurements usually required in a segmentation study.

Involving the researcher in the problem definition stage ensures that the best possible approach to information gathering is achieved. An understanding of what decisions are to be made and how the information will be used allows research to approach data collection and analysis systematically.

Because customer needs, tastes, and preferences are constantly changing, market segments do not remain stable for any great length of time. Thus, market segmentation must be a continuous process that involves research in keeping track of dynamic changes in the market. Competitors' marketing programs will similarly be undergoing constant change. New strategies will be implemented, and new marketing tactics developed. The market research department must be aware of what competitors are doing and how this in itself alters the market structure.

In addition, the firm's capabilities are constantly changing. New production techniques are developed, and new production economies become possible. Through the interaction of changing technology, buyer expectations, needs and preferences, and a changing competitive environment, the company becomes a different entity over time. Research data that documents how the company is being perceived must continuously be available. Finally, new techniques, theories, and propositions are becoming part of the marketing lore. For example, powerful analytical tools are now available for the analysis of marketing data that involve many consumer dimensions (called "multidimensional" data). Consequently, part of any segmentation program within the firm will involve acquainting managers with the use of the new technology, at least to some extent. Some understanding of the process of identifying market segments will ensure a more "comfortable" feeling when managers are called upon to make decisions using the results of data and analytical techniques with which they are scarcely familiar.

MARKET SEGMENTATION ANALYSIS

Market segmentation analysis is a systematic method of studying markets, how markets are related to consumer characteristics, needs, wants, and preferences, and how products fit into those markets in the process of satisfying consumer wants.

Two Approaches to Market Segmentation

Figure 1 summarizes the discussion thus far. In addition, it shows that there are two ways to isolate segments within a market environment characterized by consumer dependent differences—(1) analysis of consumer characteristics (attribute differences) and (2) analysis of consumer response (behavioral differences). Each approach offers certain advantages and disadvantages; therefore, it is impossible to generalize with respect to an ideal approach. Each problem situation should be approached in the light of its particular circumstances. Through imaginative research and creative planning it is possible to identify potentially profitable groupings that lie beneath the surface of the market. Usually, it will be necessary to utilize a wide battery of measures of both consumer characteristics (age, income, education, social class, personality variables, and so on) and behavior (attitudes, perceptions, product usage, and so on). The primary method of data collection will be the market survey. Considerable use can also be made of internal company sales data.

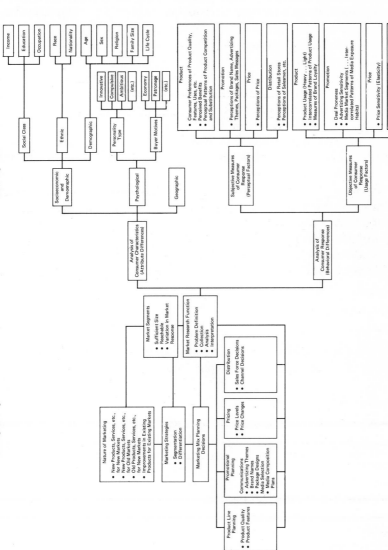

Figure 1. Market Segmentation in Marketing Planning

It is essential that correct statistical techniques be employed. A wide variety are applicable including cross-classification with chi square analysis, multiple regression, multiple discriminant analysis, factor analysis, and non-metric multidimensional scaling, to mention only a few. Many practical applications of each of these techniques are given elsewhere in the book. Consequently, further discussion of these methods is reserved for later sections.

When one attempts to segment the market by the *analysis of attribute differences,* the usual procedure is to measure a number of consumer characteristics, such as personality, attitudes, age, income, social class, position in the family life-cycle, and so on. Then, determination is made of the extent to which variations in these characteristics relate to (and are thereby assumed to predict) variations in market behavior (that is brand use, shopping patterns, media selection, and so on).

A different approach is the *analysis of behavioral differences.* The investigator begins with observed variations in behavior or stated preferences (the end point in the above approach) and works backward to variations in consumer attributes within the segments which result. An example is given later in which the market for Flavorfest, a condiment, is segmented initially into three different classes based on frequency of purchase:

1. Heavy users
2. Light to moderate users
3. Nonusers

Then it was found that housewives within these segments differed widely in such terms as age, education, geographic location, and personality.

Bases for Segmentation

A great variety of factors can be used to segment a market, and many of these are itemized on the right-hand side of Figure 1. The most widely used bases fall into five basic classifications, each of which is discussed in this section:

1. Socioeconomic and demographic
2. Geographic
3. Psychological
4. Product usage
5. Perceptual
6. Brand loyalty

Socioeconomic, Demographic, and Geographic Bases. The most useful dimensions of socioeconomic and demographic classification are (1) income, (2) education, (3) occupation, (4) social class, (5) race, (6) nationality,

(7) ethnicity, (8) age, (9) sex, (10) religion, (11) family size, (12) position in the life-cycle.(family life cycle)

These variables can provide rich insights into important behavioral and motivational differences between segments. Income, education, and occupation are often usefully combined into an index of social class. This composite measure of social groupings can be employed as a variable to separate groups of consumers to observe variations in their purchase behavior and product preferences. In addition, the market planner can learn much about the probable life style and behavior of a segment once he has found it to be defined, for example, as consisting of young families, located in midwestern rural areas, with incomes under $10,000, and with occupations that fall mostly into the white-collar category.

In general, the primary usefulness of socioeconomic, demographic, and geographic variables is in the selection of mass communications media. Mass media circulation figures are commonly maintained by the type of reader reached (that is, young, old, high, low income, and so on) as well as by geographic distribution. By identifying market segments in terms of the same variables which describe media reach, a more precise fit between media and segment occurs. It is obviously a more efficient allocation of company resources, resulting in less waste circulation.

Geographic variables can also provide a useful basis for determining relative sales potential from one geographic area to the next. For example, if a product is sold nation-wide, should twice as much effort be placed in the Chicago market as compared with the market served by Columbus, Ohio? Or should Columbus receive an equivalent allocation of promotional funds? Such questions can be answered only when market potentials are computed for each market area.

Psychological Bases. In recent years personality variables have been used extensively to predict brand preference, brand loyalty, store preference, and other types of buyer behavior. With few exceptions, these attempts have proved to be discouraging. Ronald E. Frank reports, for example, that only 1 percent of the variation in brand loyalty for beer from one household to the next is associated with personality and socioeconomic characteristics *combined*; an even weaker relationship was discovered for coffee and tea.[3]

The negative findings to date, however, may simply have resulted from the statistical tests used. The true underlying relationships may be more positive. Frank M. Bass, Douglas J. Tigert, and Ronald T. Lonsdale[4] have presented

[3] Ronald E. Frank, "Is Brand Loyalty a Useful Basis for Market Segmentation?" *Journal of Advertising Research,* Vol. 7 (June 1967), pp. 27–33.

[4] Frank M. Bass, Douglas J. Tigert, and Ronald T. Lonsdale, "Market Segmentation: Group Versus Individual Behavior," *Journal of Marketing Research,* Vol. 5 (August 1968), pp. 264–270. This article is reprinted as Reading 18 of the present volume.

convincing evidence that a reanalysis of the data using simple cross-classification analysis often results in high positive relationships between personality, socioeconomic status, and consumer behavior.

Much more positive results may also be generated by utilizing more appropriate personality measures. The tests used in published studies have, for the most part, been borrowed directly from the psychological clinic. It may be asking too much for a test designed for individual diagnosis to prove useful in a marketing context. It may be far more appropriate to design a personality scale for the specific problem, in the hopes of obtaining measures that relate to the behavior under analysis. Irving S. White, for example, employed a series of questions that isolated a housewife's attitude toward cleaning and the extent to which it relates to her concept of herself as a wife and mother.[5] He found two segments: (1) housewives who are "emancipated" and do not judge their worth by cleaning and activity in the home and (2) housewives who feel that their personal worth is judged by prowess in cleaning and home maintenance. Members of these groups, in turn, showed very different preferences for a particular type of cleaning product.

Product Usage Bases.   Sometimes it is useful to segment consumers into nonusers, light users, and heavy users and then to assess consumer attribute differences within each class. Some feel that the best strategy is to avoid the first two segments and to aim marketing efforts largely at the heavy users. For example, the so-called "heavy half" of the beer drinkers' market (17 percent of the total) consumes 88 percent of all beer; the heavy half in the market for canned hash (16 percent of the total) consumes 86 percent of the product sold.[6] The assumption is that the heavy half is the most productive segment and, hence, should be the target of most marketing efforts. Concentration on this segment has been made much more feasible by use of data provided by the Brand Rating Index (BRI), a syndicated service which shows the extent of product and brand consumption by the audiences of various advertising media.[7]

Efforts should not be concentrated on the heavy half, however, unless there is firm evidence documenting that it is not feasible to turn nonusers into users and light users into heavy users. There should be an inquiry into why these segments buy or do not buy, what the product means to them, and other related questions. It may be found that distinct sales increases are a possibility.

[5] Irving S. White, "The Perception of Value in Products," in Joseph W. Newman, ed., *On Knowing the Consumer* (New York: John Wiley & Sons, Inc., 1966), pp. 90–106.
[6] See Dik Warren Twedt, "How Important to Marketing Strategy Is the 'Heavy User'?" *Journal of Marketing,* Vol. 28 (January 1964), p. 72.
[7] Norton Garfinkle, "How Marketing Data Can Identify Your Target Audience," address given to Eastern Regional Convention of the American Association of Advertising Agencies, October 1966.

An example[8] of such an inquiry is illuminating. The Flavorfest Company (the company name is fictitious) manufactures and distributes a well-known bottled condiment product. The firm has long dominated the market for this product, with its share of the market approximately 85 percent. Its product line also includes spices and seasoning items. Flavorfest management, in searching for a better understanding of the marketplace, undertook a segmentation study in cooperation with the market research department of the company. Research disclosed three distinct market segments, each of which offered very different prospects for marketing success. A summary of the research findings appears in Figure 2.

Figure 2. A Summary of Research Findings on the Market for Flavorfest

I. *Heavy Users* (39 percent of the market)
   a. Demographic attributes—housewives aged 20–45; well-educated, higher-income categories, small families with most children under 5, concentration in Northeast and Midwest and in suburban and farm areas.
   b. Motivational attributes
      1. Strong motivation not to be old-fashioned, and a desire to express individuality through creative action and use of exciting new things.
      2. The traditional role as a housewife viewed with displeasure, and experimentation with new foods done to express individuality—not to please the family.
      3. Exciting and exotic taste suggested by the image of Flavorfest. Favorable reaction in terms of taste, appearance, and food value. Highly prized in experimental cooking. Hence, substantial compatibility between values of the user and product image.

II. *Light to Moderate Users* (20 percent of the market)
   a. Demographic attributes—housewives aged 35–54: large families with children under 12, middle-income groups, location mostly in Southeast, Pacific states, and Southwest.
   b. Motivational attributes
      1. A strong desire to express individuality through creative cookery, but constrained somewhat by a conflicting desire to maintain tradition and subordinate herself to the family's desires.
      2. The desire to experiment with new foods constrained by a lack of confidence in the results of experimental cooking.
      3. Favorable image of Flavorfest. The product liked in all respects, but confined largely to use with one type of food. Viewed as unacceptable in other uses. Hence, vision limited regarding new uses for Flavorfest.

III. *Nonusers* (41 percent of the market)
   a. Demographic attributes—older housewives: large families, lower-income brackets, location mostly in the eastern states and some parts of the South.

[8] Used by special permission from Engel, Wales, and Warshaw, *op. cit.*

b. Motivational attributes
1. A strong motive to maintain tradition and emotional ties with the past; identification with her mother and her role in the home.
2. A conservative nonventuresome personality.
3. Experimental cookery discouraged by self-concept of role as a mother and housewife. Flavorfest thus regarded unfavorably. Exotic flavors and a degree of modernity, which is unacceptable, connoted by the image of Flavorfest.
4. No interest expressed in new uses and experimentation with Flavorfest, for the product not representative of the values embraced by these housewives.

From this research it is clear that there are important demographic differences between users and nonusers (the classification "user of product but not brand" was not employed here because there are no important directly competitive products). Therefore, it is possible through skillful use of advertising media to avoid certain segments if this is deemed to be desirable.

The heavy-user segment of Flavorfest is relatively large and the product is well regarded by these buyers. Because of the product's use in experimental cookery and its role in expressing individuality, the potential exists for stimulating greater use. The nonuser segment, on the other hand, presents a different situation. While this segment tends to be large, it is comprised mostly of those with relatively little purchasing power, living in areas where population growth is stagnant. In addition, the potential for stimulating use of Flavorfest is not at all favorable. The existence of strong negative values raises the probability of selective perception of any type of persuasive message and there would seem to be no opportunity for successful promotion aimed at this group.

The segment including the light-to-moderate users perhaps represents the greatest opportunity for increased sales. The desire for creative cookery is present, but it is constrained by a desire to maintain tradition and a lack of confidence in results of experimental efforts. Yet, the product is liked in nearly all respects. In view of this the company may have a good opportunity to attack the constraining forces. Lack of confidence, for example, may be minimized by stressing recipes with "nonfail" features. The interest in pleasing the family can be shown as compatible with creative cookery by stressing favorable family reaction to new tastes and recipes. Finally, Flavorfest can be featured as an ideal accompaniment for a variety of foods. Obviously, there is no certainty that greater inroads can be made into this market, for the chances of success lie in the amount of strength of opposing values and attitudes. Yet, there appears to be no reason why some experimental promotion should not be tried. Whatever the strategy to be used, it is clear that an appeal with one message to a nonsegmented mass market would be totally inappropriate. Such a mistake could easily have been made if the research data had not been available.

Brand Loyalty Bases. Frequently, and especially in the case of convenience goods, an obvious marketing problem centers around brand loyalty. Marketers through promotional strategy seek to build brand loyalty among current users of the brand and to switch away customers from competitors' brands.

The measurement of brand loyalty can be achieved in two ways. First, loyalty can be thought of as a measure of attitude toward the brand. The segmentation objective is then to array market segments with respect to strength of brand attitude. Another way of looking at brand loyalty is in terms of the sequence of brand purchases. Purchase sequences such as the following, XXXXY, can be contrasted with one of XXYYX for another household. Customer segments can be grouped around households with common purchase patterns. Research can then attempt to determine the reasons for the different patterns. Subsequently, advertising may be directed at households which show little brand loyalty [that is, the probability of purchasing Brand X at purchase time $(t + 1)$ is low] in an attempt to convert these individuals into loyal users [that is, the probability of purchasing Brand X at purchase time$(+ 1)$ is high].

Perceptual Bases. Two approaches included under the heading Perceptual Bases are finding increased use. The first, known as "benefit segmentation," attempts to classify the market in terms of values or benefits that consumers desire in a product.[9] Factor and cluster analysis are used extensively in such studies.

The second approach to analyzing consumer preferences—nonmetric multidimensional scaling—involves a set of analytical procedures that can be used to develop a "perceptual space" to represent the market structure.[10] The axes or dimensions that describe the product space are believed to be the attributes of the product class which influence consumers' judgment of the market offerings. A more detailed examination of this approach is reserved for the later chapters.

The first stage of a benefit segmentation study is to obtain detailed data on consumer values systems, which is typically done by having a representative sample of consumers rate the importance of those benefits or values which they desire in the product. These ratings are then factor analyzed to assess which patterns of benefits are associated. In Figure 3 the results of a hypothetical benefit segmentation of the under $50 camera market are shown.

[9] See Russell Haley, "Benefit Segmentation: A Decision-Oriented Research Tool," *Journal of Marketing,* Vol. 32 (July 1968), pp. 30–35, in this volume Reading 12; and Robert N. Reitter, "Product Testing in Segmented Markets," *Journal of Marketing Research,* Vol. 6 (May 1969), pp. 179–184, in this volume, Reading 14.
[10] Lester A. Neidell, "The Use of Nonmetric Multidimensional Scaling in Marketing Analysis," *Journal of Marketing,* Vol. 33 (October 1969), pp. 37–43. See reprint of this article in this volume, Reading 25.

Figure 3. A Benefit Segmentation of the Under $50 Camera Market

The "Do-It-Yourselfer" (25 percent)
    Great pride in good pictures.
    Gratification from making settings and adjustments.
    Pride in a complex camera.
    Regards a good picture the result of his expertise.
The "Black Box User" (40 percent)
    Taking pictures considered a necessary evil.
    Little pride expressed if the picture is good.
    Desire for camera to be as simple as possible.
The "Timid Photographer" (35 percent)
    Great pride in good pictures.
    High perceived risk that the picture will not be good.
    No confidence in ability to manipulate camera and settings.
    Desires camera to guarantee a good picture without his effort.

Three segments emerge which are labeled the "do-it-yourselfers," "the black box users," and the "timid photographers." Do-it-yourselfers take great pride in their pictures and strongly prefer a camera that allows them to make all necessary settings and adjustments. The black box user, on the other hand, prefers an instrument that he can aim and shoot with no difficulty. Finally, the timid photographer shares the do-it-yourselfer's concern over high picture quality but lacks confidence in his ability to manipulate settings and gadgets. He wants a high-quality, completely automatic camera which almost guarantees a perfect picture.

At the present time the do-it-yourself market for under $50 cameras is not being adequately supplied as is illustrated by the continued sale of used Kodak Pony cameras, which, until recently, featured full settings and adjustments. Thus, a real market opportunity appears to exist for an enterprising firm. (It was this type of analysis in the automobile market, for example, that led to the introduction and successful sale of the Ford Mustang and Maverick.)

Other segments of the camera market are being satisfied by a variety of product alternatives. Promotional strategy, of course, should be oriented to these segments. The desired benefits can readily be highlighted and amplified in the creative message and the opportunity exists to present the company's offerings in terms of these stated preferences. The timid photographer could be appealed to, for instance, by demonstrating that the only requirement is to "aim and shoot."

SUMMARY AND OVERVIEW

The intent of this chapter has been twofold. First, market segmentation was discussed as a systematic way of improving management's ability to understand the market environment. Accordingly, the propositions underlying the concept of market segmentation were outlined, and the use of market segmentation as a management strategy described. Second, an introduction to the all-important subject of classification of market targets was presented. Two main approaches to market segmentation analysis were discussed, and a number of segmentation bases were described, including socioeconomic, demographic and geographic variables, personality, brand loyalty, product usage, and consumer perceptions.

It must be stressed that no single approach is ideally suited for all purposes. The final selection of methods will be the responsibility of the particular research department, and the outcome will in some measure be dependent upon creative imagination. When imagination is well applied, the result will frequently be the uncovering of profitable market segments that might otherwise have been overlooked. In addition, the market researcher will find firm indications as to how this new market may be successfully approached.

Let us now turn to the remainder of the book. Part Two is concerned with illustrating segmentation as a management concept and with outlining its possible uses as a management strategy. The first paper formalizes the concept, distinguishes it from product differentiation—a major alternative—and discusses possible strategy implications. In section B the papers suggest how a segmentation approach can be used successfully as a competitive strategy. Many illustrations of practical applications, drawn from a wide variety of problem situations and industries, are cited.

Also included in Part Two are papers that deal with such questions as: When is it appropriate to follow a segmentation approach? When is a differentiation strategy best suited? What factors must be considered in selecting either strategy? One paper considers the important question of integrating planning and research. Unless each function harmonizes with the other, it will probably be difficult to achieve maximum effectiveness from a segmentation approach. Finally, an overview is presented of recent research findings on the usefulness of socioeconomic, demographic, and personality variables as bases for segmenting markets.

Part Three is concerned with the use of segmentation analysis in product and promotional planning. The papers in the part on product planning deal with approaches which have been used successfully for guiding a wide number of product planning decisions. Then the question is raised as to how a segmentation approach could be followed in allocating media funds to the most promising market segments.

Part Four contains three papers which discuss the most recent analytical techniques. Comparison among techniques are made, advantages and disadvantages described, and limitations of each are outlined. The book concludes with a look at the future.

PART TWO

MARKET SEGMENTATION IN MARKETING MANAGEMENT

CONCEPTS AND THEORY

THE FIRST two papers in this part lay the foundation for the detailed discussion of the new marketing concept of segmentation. The first, "Product Differentiation and Market Segmentation As Alternative Marketing Strategies" by Wendell Smith, is generally considered the classic statement in the marketing literature on the topic.

The economic theory of market segmentation evolved from the pioneering work in the 1930s of Joan Robinson and Edward Chamberlain. In revitalizing classical and neoclassical theories of perfect competition they provided a more adequate explanation of the contemporary business society. Homogeneity of supply and demand, the typical feature of American business life in its early stages, had now been replaced by an increasing diversity of supply and demand.

Despite the increasing variety in the output of goods and services, market segmentation as a management strategy was still not an especially vital consideration in planning in the 1930s. Although there may have been heterogeneity in the market in terms of desires and product preferences, it was frequently possible to ignore these differences. This was permissible because the environment often was characterized by a lack of aggregate demand during the depression years. Thus, while firms had the ability to produce, individual household buying units did not have much in the way of discretionary buying power. Hence, for many producers, it made little sense to treat the market in other than an undifferentiated manner.

In the immediate post World War II era American business continued to be dominated by a production orientation. Aggregate demand, pent up during the war years, was unleashed with a tremendous force. Manufacturers of the first electric refrigerators and television sets could, for example, sell their entire output without consideration of consumer preferences for colors, sizes, and the other bewildering array of options and features that became *characteristic* of the American business scene of the late 1950s and 1960s.

However, in the early and mid 1950s the situation did show signs of change. American business, having broken down the technological barriers to mass production, began to face a waning demand. Industry became increasingly competitive. Firms were no longer finding themselves able to produce large volumes of goods without consideration to the needs of the consumer. Bulging warehouses often stored the unsalable output of firms that failed to heed the needs of the market. It was the realization of these needs which led to the new marketing concept in the early 1950s. Firms now began to look more closely at the buying side of the market and to gear their production accordingly.

Under the prevalent conditions of imperfect competition the usual approach to the diversity apparent in markets was for the firm to adopt a strategy or program ". . . designed to bring about the convergence of individual market demands for a variety of products upon a single or limited offering to the market."[1] This was the strategy of *product differentiation* or *market aggregation*. In using this strategy, marketing managers may recognize the diversity in consumer wants, but they prefer not to react to these differences. Instead all consumers are treated as being similar, and a standard product is presented with very few real differences from other products in the company's line. Heavy use is made of promotional resources to distinguish one product from another, and emphasis is placed on product distinctions. The objective then of promotional campaigns in the 1950s was to create an image of "overall superiority" in appealing to the broad needs of all consumers. The strategy of product differentiation, in short, was considered to be the marketing counterpart to standardization in mass manufacturing.

It was not unexpected that American business, only newly acquainted with the marketing concept in the early 1950s, should be slow to recognize the inadequacies of a product differentiation strategy for certain marketing situations. While changing production economies, brought about by technological advances, made smaller production runs feasible, marketing managers were required to undergo a second change in their conceptualization of market

---

[1] See Wendell Smith, "Product Differentiation and Market Segmentation as Alternative Marketing Strategies," in this volume, Reading 1.

demand in less than a decade. This fact, in part, explains the init
acceptance of segmentation as an important marketing strategy tool.

As early as 1956, Smith correctly stated that for certain marketing
"it is better to accept divergent demand as a market characteristic and
adjust product lines and marketing strategy accordingly." This implies ability to *merchandise*[2] to a heterogeneous market by emphasizing the precision
with which a firm's products can satisfy the requirements of one or more
distinguishable market segments. The strategy of product differentiation here
gives way to marketing programs based upon the measurement and definition
of market differences."[3]

The notion of market segmentation radically altered the thinking in the
area of marketing strategy. While lack of homogeneity in consumer demand
had been recognized before, little had been done to cater to the varied needs.
Now marketers were being told to shape marketing programs to fit the needs
of submarkets based on these differences. Substantial benefits to firms following a segmentation approach were suggested. Firms were advised that a
"rational approach to minimizing of total costs must take precedence over
separate approaches to minimization of production costs on one hand and
marketing costs on the other."[4]

Smith's early contribution to the development of marketing theory was in
recognizing the basic difference between product differentiation as a promotional strategy, which emphasised product differences on the one hand, and
market segmentation as a merchandising strategy on the other, which emphasized demand-related differences in consumers. Smith also clearly pointed
out the "disaggregative" nature of segmentation. In other words, marketers
were alerted to recognize the existence of several demand schedules rather
than one schedule as before. With the notable exception of Henry J. Claycamp
and William F. Massy's paper "The Theory of Market Segmentation" in this
part and those papers devoted to the description of management applications
of a segmentation strategy, most, if not all, the subsequent literature concerned
with market segmentation and marketing management is devoted to the
measurement of consumer differences and the identification of previously
unrecognized market targets. Accordingly, we have attempted to organize this
collection around concepts, management applications and the measurement
of consumer differences.

In the second paper of Part Two, Claycamp and Massy present a normative theory of market segmentation that considers major implementation
problems. Claycamp and Massy examine the criteria that must be satisfied in
order to arrive at market segments. Obviously, if market segmentation is to
be realistically employed it must be possible to determine which are the

[2] Smith, p. 30 in this volume. Italics added.
[3] *Ibid.*, p. 30.
[4] *Ibid.*, p. 31.

thermore, it must be shown how each segment varies in
inputs from other mutually exclusive groupings. In
of response elasticities that the most challenging
ave been encountered. Segments which show no clear
es in response to changes in the marketing mix, for
s, are not meaningfully defined.

in in defining market segments, as Claycamp and Massy
, is due to the information constraints facing the researcher and
anager. As we shall see later, in the review of segmentation research by
Ronald E. Frank, attempts to find relationships between socioeconomic and
demographic variables and brand purchasing behavior have been discouraging. While it is true that the negative relationships to date may have resulted from the statistical tests used, a point argued by Frank M. Bass,
Douglas J. Tigert, and Ronald T. Lonsdale in a later paper, it is also true
that marketers must employ more sophisticated measuring instruments which
relate to the purchasing behavior under analysis. However, even if relationships between brand purchasing and consumer characteristics are established
at some point in time, the fourth problem area which Claycamp and Massy
discuss—institutional constraints—may prevent full utilization of an effective segmentation strategy. For example, media market segments may not
correspond to underlying segments based on consumer preferences and thus
prevent a selective promotional approach.

The primary goal of the Claycamp and Massy paper is to extend the
microeconomic theory of market segmentation. This goal is achieved through
the development of a multistage mathematical model which includes the extreme possibilities (from a perfectly discriminating monopolist to a mass
marketer) open to a would-be segmenter. The model considers only price and
promotional variables but, as the authors suggest, could be revised to consider other elements of the promotional mix. The model is aggregative: stages
1 and 2 consider individual units as segments, stage 3 aggregates consumer
units into microsegments, stage 4 aggregates microsegments into larger groupings, termed macrosegments, and stage 5 is the mass market stage or final
aggregation of consumers. This aggregation approach then views segmentation as process of successive building up rather than of breaking up as much
of the marketing literature appears to imply. Thus, the would-be segmenter
is advised to start from the point at which institutional and informational
constraints are first felt (that is, the individual level) and then move up to
form larger macrosegments.

MARKET SEGMENTATION AS A MANAGEMENT STRATEGY

After the management reader has examined for himself the theoretical
and conceptual foundations for market segmentation, he is likely to ask: How
can I apply the strategy of market segmentation? The primary purpose of the

readings in this section are to give to the management reader ample illustration of how a segmentation strategy can be creatively applied for greater profits.

Application of a segmentation approach calls for much more than the basic research findings which indicate a positive correlation between some consumer characteristics and purchasing. Development of a segmentation strategy must be a creative blend of management intuition and systematic analysis. Frequently, management expects that segments will suddenly emerge because the research department is employing a new computer algorithm which they have been told will be useful in market segmentation studies. More often than not, this approach can lead to disappointment and disillusionment with a tool that could potentially do much for the firm.

On the other hand, management which carefully sifts through the research findings by employing a conceptual framework of the type advocated by Nelson N. Foote in his paper "Market Segmentation as a Competitive Strategy" will find the going much easier and much more profitable. Foote views the process of market segmentation as "a tripartite matching of customers and offerings and the array of competitors in the market, as seen from the standpoint of any one competitor within this constellation."[5] His case is well illustrated by examining Zenith's approach to the television receiver market. Zenith's success resulted from its realization that consumers considered it an exemplar of product reliability. By catering to this want Zenith was able to carve itself a sizable portion of the television receiver market.

Management's frequent failure to employ a systematic method of handling research findings is often parallelled by the failure to consider segmentation as a continuous process. Both consumers and competitors change. Therefore, it is only logical that a firm should continuously strive to keep in touch with the tempo of the market.

While it may first appear from the first three articles in this collection that market segmentation is the only viable alternative to a product differentiation strategy for marketers seeking to grow and expand, this is not the case. In a vein closely approaching Theodore Levitt's classic "Marketing Myopia,"[6] Lee Adler discusses the segmentation approach as one of a dozen strategic tools available to marketers. Application of these tools, however, is often complicated by a lack of vision and self-imposed limitations. Drawing upon examples from many consumer industries (including tobacco, beverage, detergent, beauty aids, and brewing), Adler illustrates how companies have successfully employed each strategy.

Industrial marketing offers many fine examples of segmentation. Capital equipment, for example, is usually made to fit the precise specifications of

[5] See Nelson N. Foote, "Market Segmentation as a Competitive Strategy," in this volume, Reading 3.
[6] Theodore Levitt, "Marketing Myopia," *Harvard Business Review,* July–August, 1960, pp. 55–68.

the buyer. Similarly, as in the case of sheet steel, the output of the rolling mill is consumed by thousands of secondary manufacturers across the country. How far should a steel producer go in customizing or standardizing his output? Obviously, each alternative requires a trade-off. Marketing decisions such as these are amenable to a segmentation approach as Alan R. Roberts illustrates in the case of American Agribusiness in his paper "Applying the Strategy of Market Segmentation."[7]

One of the most commonly asked questions by marketing executives newly acquainted with the strategy of selective marketing is: How do I determine whether I should use a segmentation or a differentiation strategy for my product? From the discussion thus far it is obvious that selection of a particular strategy is a function of a number of factors that impinge upon the marketing of a product. Smith, Claycamp, and Massy note such factors as consumer response elasticities, size of market, and type of product. Foote mentions customers, competitors, and firms' capabilities in particular.

It is the function of R. William Kotrba's paper, "The Strategy Selection Chart," to provide a conceptual model which considers the interaction of relevant factors in the selection of a segmentation versus a differentiation strategy.

PLANNING AND RESEARCH

Since World War II increasing competition and a growing consumer affluence, which extended consumer choice considerably, resulted in more and more firms adopting the new marketing orientation. We have witnessed this in the growth of the number of firms adopting a segmentation approach to the market. With the increasing attention firms are giving to consumer preferences and the like, planning for markets has emerged as a formidable function of marketing management. It is becoming evident, however, that while many firms pay homage to the rule of planning, few firms are entirely successful in this activity. For those firms where planning has been instrumental in attaining marketing objectives, the planning effort has been characterized by an acceptance of the need for, and a top management commitment to, this activity. In addition, successful planning requires a set of procedures which permits finding of answers to such critical questions as: Who are our customers? Whom do we want to have as customers? What needs are we now satisfying, and what needs will we be required to satisfy in the future? What strategies are we using to generate demand? What strategies will we need in the future? How are we now reaching these customers? How should we be reaching them in the future?

The purpose of including the two papers that deal with planning in a

[7] See Reading 5 in this volume.

collection of readings on market segmentation should now be obvious. William J. E. Crissy and Robert M. Kaplan's paper, "Matrix Models for Marketing Planning," illustrates a solid method for improving the planning process to reach desired customer targets. In particular, the Crissy and Kaplan approach is entirely consistent with the normative theory of successive aggregation, outlined in the earlier paper by Claycamp and Massy. The importance of the research function in marketing management has parallelled the growing role of planning in many firms. This is primarily the result of the new marketing orientation since the early 1950s. Research departments which once were only relied upon to collect, analyze, and report often unrelated facts to management are now asked to share in the problem definition and decision-setting functions of the manager. Marketing research has been called upon to go further and extend its analyses beyond mere fact gathering. Recently developed marketing information systems call for greater participation in the planning systems of the firm.

In "Phasing Research into The Marketing Plan" Lee Adler cites past obstacles to progress and how these can be overcome to successfully phase the research function into the marketing planning activity.

Ronald Frank's extensive examination of segmentation research is presented as the last selection of Part Two. While Frank, in this paper, reports almost entirely negative results to date, he does illustrate the type of methodologies and statistical techniques employed thus far by researchers seeking to find relationships between consumer characteristics and purchasing behavior.

NOTE ON THE BIBLIOGRAPHY

The reader is directed at this point to the extensive bibliography appearing at the end of this book. While an attempt has been made to include a relevant cross-section of the literature related to either market segmentation theory, concepts, applications, or research, it is by no means an exhaustive listing. In addition, the classification system used in the bibliography bears some resemblance to Figure 1, in Part One developed as a conceptual model for viewing segmentation within the firm. Finally, in the Readings appearing at the end of each major section references are made to larger works that serve to expand and relate the main topics of the section to other areas of the marketing process.

Readings for Part Two

Adler, Lee, ed. *Plotting Marketing Strategy*, New York: Simon and Schuster, Inc., 1967.

Alderson, Wroe, and Paul Green. *Planning and Problem Solving in Marketing,* Homewood, Ill.: Richard D. Irwin, Inc., 1964.

Boulding, Kenneth. *Economic Analysis*, New York: Harper & Row, Publishers, Inc., 1955, pp. 608–615.

Chamberlain, E. H. *Theory of Monopolistic Competition*, Cambridge: Harvard University Press, 1933.

Engel, J. F., H. G. Wales, and M. R. Warshaw. *Promotional Strategy*, Homewood, Ill.: Richard D. Irwin, Inc., 1967.

Kotler, Phillip. *Marketing Management: Analysis, Planning and Control*, Englewood Cliffs, N.J.: Prentice-Hall, Inc., 1967. See especially Chapter 3.

Levitt, Theodore. *The Marketing Mode: Pathways to Corporate Growth*, New York: McGraw-Hill Book Company, 1969.

Myers, John G. *Consumer Image and Attitude in Marketing*, Research Program in Marketing, Berkeley: Graduate School of Business Administration, University of California, 1968.

Robinson, Joan. *The Economics of Imperfect Competition*, London: Macmillan & Co., Ltd., 1954, pp. 179–188.

A. The Concept

1.

Product Differentiation and Market Segmentation As Alternative Marketing Strategies

Wendell R. Smith

During the decade of the 1930's, the work of Robinson and Chamberlin resulted in a revitalization of economic theory. While classical and neoclassical theory provided a useful framework for economic analysis, the theories of perfect competition and pure monopoly had become inadequate as explanations of the contemporary business scene. The theory of perfect competition assumes homogeneity among the components of both the demand and supply sides of the market, but diversity or heterogeneity had come to be the rule rather than the exception. This analysis reviews major marketing strategy alternatives that are available to planners and merchandisers of products in an environment characterized by imperfect competition.

DIVERSITY IN SUPPLY

That there is a lack of homogeneity or close similarity among the items offered to the market by individual manufacturers of various products is obvious in any variety store, department store, or shopping center. In many cases the impact of this diversity is amplified by advertising and promotional activities. Today's advertising and promotion tends to emphasize appeals to *selective* rather than *primary* buying motives and to point out the distinctive or differentiating features of the advertiser's product or service offer.

The presence of differences in the sales offers made by competing suppliers produces a diversity in supply that is inconsistent with the assumptions of earlier theory. The reasons for the presence of diversity in specific markets are many and include the following:

From Wendell R. Smith, "Product Differentiation and Market Segmentation as Alternative Marketing Strategies," *Journal of Marketing,* Vol. 21 (July 1956), pp. 3–8. Published by the American Marketing Association. Reprinted by permission.

1. Variations in the production equipment and methods or processes used by different manufacturers of products designed for the same or similar uses.
2. Specialized or superior resources enjoyed by favorably situated manufacturers.
3. Unequal progress among competitors in design, development, and improvement of products.
4. The inability of manufacturers in some industries to eliminate product variations even through the application of quality control techniques.
5. Variations in producers' estimates of the nature of market demand with reference to such matters as price sensitivity, color, material, or package size.

Because of these and other factors, both planned and uncontrollable differences exist in the products of an industry. As a result, sellers make different appeals in support of their marketing efforts.

DIVERSITY OR VARIATIONS IN CONSUMER DEMAND

Under present-day conditions of imperfect competition, marketing managers are generally responsible for selecting the over-all marketing strategy or combination of strategies best suited to a firm's requirements at any particular point in time. The strategy selected may consist of a program designed to bring about the *convergence* of individual market demands for a variety of products upon a single or limited offering to the market. This is often accomplished by the achievement of product differentiation through advertising and promotion. In this way, variations in the demands of individual consumers are minimized or brought into line by means of effective use of appealing product claims designed to make a satisfactory volume of demand *converge* upon the product or product line being promoted. This strategy was once believed to be essential as the marketing counterpart to standardization and mass production in manufacturing because of the rigidities imposed by production cost considerations.

In some cases, however, the marketer may determine that it is better to accept *divergent* demand as a market characteristic and to adjust product lines and marketing strategy accordingly. This implies ability to merchandise to a heterogeneous market by emphasizing the precision with which a firm's products can satisfy the requirements of one or more distinguishable market segments. The strategy of product differentiation here gives way to marketing programs based upon measurement and definition of market differences.

Lack of homogeneity on the demand side may be based upon different customs, desire for variety, or desire for exclusiveness or may arise from basic differences in user needs. Some divergence in demand is the result of shopping errors in the market. Not all consumers have the desire or the ability to shop in a sufficiently efficient or rational manner as to bring about selection of the most needed or most wanted goods or services.

Diversity on the demand side of the market is nothing new to sales management. It has always been accepted as a fact to be dealt with in industrial markets where production to order rather than for the market is common. Here, however, the loss of precision in the satisfying of customer requirements that would be necessitated by attempts to bring about convergence of demand is often impractical and, in some cases, impossible. However, even in industrial marketing, the strategy of product differentiation should be considered in cases where products are applicable to several industries and may have horizontal markets of substantial size.

LONG-TERM IMPLICATIONS

While contemporary economic theory deals with the nature of product differentiation and its effects upon the operation of the total economy, the alternative strategies of product differentiation and market segmentation have received less attention. Empirical analysis of contemporary marketing activity supports the hypothesis that, while product differentiation and market segmentation are closely related (perhaps even inseparable) concepts, attempts to distinguish between these approaches may be productive of clarity in theory as well as greater precision in the planning of marketing operations. Not only do strategies of differentiation and segmentation call for differing systems of action at any point in time, but the dynamics of markets and marketing underscore the importance of varying degrees of diversity *through time* and suggest that the rational selection of marketing strategies is a requirement for the achievement of maximum functional effectiveness in the economy as a whole.

If a rational selection of strategies is to be made, an integrated approach to the minimizing of total costs must take precedence over separate approaches to minimization of production costs on the one hand and marketing costs on the other. Strategy determination must be regarded as an over-all management decision which will influence and require facilitating policies affecting both production and marketing activities.

DIFFERENCES BETWEEN STRATEGIES OF DIFFERENTIATION AND SEGMENTATION

Product differentiation and market segmentation are both consistent with the framework of imperfect competition.[1] In its simplest terms, *product*

---

[1] Imperfect competition assumes lack of uniformity in the size and influence of the firms or individuals that comprise the demand or supply sides of a market.

differentiation is concerned with the bending of demand to the will of supply. It is an attempt to shift or to change the slope of the demand curve for the market offering of an individual supplier. This strategy may also be employed by a group of suppliers such as a farm cooperative, the members of which have agreed to act together. It results from the desire to establish a kind of equilibrium in the market by bringing about adjustment of market demand to supply conditions favorable to the seller.

Segmentation is based upon developments on the demand side of the market and represents a rational and more precise adjustment of product and marketing effort to consumer or user requirements. In the language of the economist, segmentation is *disaggregative* in its effects and tends to bring about recognition of several demand schedules where only one was recognized before.

Attention has been drawn to this area of analysis by the increasing number of cases in which business problems have become soluble by doing something about marketing programs and product policies that overgeneralize both markets and marketing effort. These are situations where intensive promotion designed to differentiate the company's products was not accomplishing its objective—cases where failure to recognize the reality of market segments was resulting in loss of market position.

While successful product differentiation will result in giving the marketer a horizontal share of a broad and generalized market, equally successful application of the strategy of market segmentation tends to produce depth of market position in the segments that are effectively defined and penetrated. The differentiator seeks to secure a layer of the market cake, whereas one who employs market segmentation strives to secure one or more wedge-shaped pieces.

Many examples of market segmentation can be cited; the cigarette and automobile industries are well-known illustrations. Similar developments exist in greater or lesser degree in almost all product areas. Recent introduction of a refrigerator with no storage compartment for frozen foods was in response to the distinguishable preferences of the segment of the refrigerator market made up of home freezer owners whose frozen food storage needs had already been met.

Strategies of segmentation and differentiation may be employed simultaneously, but more commonly they are applied in sequence in response to changing market conditions. In one sense, segmentation is a momentary or short-term phenomenon in that effective use of this strategy may lead to more formal recognition of the reality of market segments through redefinition of the segments as individual markets. Redefinition may result in a swing back to differentiation.

The literature of both economics and marketing abounds in formal definitions of product differentiation. *From a strategy viewpoint*, product differentiation is securing a measure of control over the demand for a product by advertising or promoting differences between a product and the products of competing sellers. It is basically the result of sellers' desires to establish firm market positions and/or to insulate their businesses against price competition. Differentiation tends to be characterized by heavy use of advertising and promotion and to result in prices that are somewhat above the equilibrium levels associated with perfectly competitive market conditions. It may be classified as a *promotional* strategy or approach to marketing.

Market segmentation, on the other hand, consists of viewing a heterogeneous market (one characterized by divergent demand) as a number of smaller homogeneous markets in response to differing product preferences among important market segments. It is attributable to the desires of consumers or users for more precise satisfaction of their varying wants. Like differentiation, segmentation often involves substantial use of advertising and promotion. This is to inform market segments of the availability of goods or services produced for or presented as meeting their needs with precision. Under these circumstances, prices tend to be somewhat closer to perfectly competitive equilibrium. Market segmentation is essentially a *merchandising* strategy, merchandising being used here in its technical sense as representing the adjustment of market offerings to consumer or user requirements.

THE EMERGENCE OF THE SEGMENTATION STRATEGY

To a certain extent, market segmentation may be regarded as a force in the market that will not be denied. It may result from trial and error in the sense that generalized programs of product differentiation may turn out to be effective in some segments of the market and ineffective in others. Recognition of, and intelligent response to, such a situation necessarily involves a shift in emphasis. On the other hand, it may develop that products involved in marketing programs designed for particular market segments may achieve a broader acceptance than originally planned, thus revealing a basis for convergence of demand and a more generalized marketing approach. The challenge to planning arises from the importance of determining, preferably in advance, the level or degree of segmentation that can be exploited with profit.

There appear to be many reasons why formal recognition of market segmentation as a strategy is beginning to emerge. One of the most important of these is decrease in the size of the minimum efficient producing or manufacturing unit required in some product areas. American industry has also established the technical base for product diversity by gaining release from some of the rigidities imposed by earlier approaches to mass production. Hence, there is less need today for generalization of markets in response to the necessity for long production runs of identical items.

Present emphasis upon the minimizing of marketing costs through self-service and similar developments tends to impose a requirement for better adjustment of products to consumer demand. The retailing structure, in its efforts to achieve improved efficiency, is providing less and less sales push at point of sale. This increases the premium placed by retailers upon products that are presold by their producers and are readily recognized by consumers as meeting their requirements as measured by satisfactory rates of stock turnover.

It has been suggested that the present level of discretionary buying power is productive of sharper shopping comparisons, particularly for items that are above the need level. General prosperity also creates increased willingness "to pay a little more" to get "just what I wanted."

Attention to market segmentation has also been enhanced by the recent ascendancy of product competition to a position of great economic importance. An expanded array of goods and services is competing for the consumer's dollar. More specifically, advancing technology is creating competition between new and traditional materials with reference to metals, construction materials, textile products, and in many other areas. While such competition is confusing and difficult to analyze in its early stages, it tends to achieve a kind of balance as various competing materials find their markets of maximum potential as a result of recognition of differences in the requirements of market segments.

Many companies are reaching the stage in their development where attention to market segmentation may be regarded as a condition or cost of growth. Their *core* markets have already been developed on a generalized basis to the point where additional advertising and selling expenditures are yielding diminishing returns. Attention to smaller or *fringe* market segments, which may have small potentials individually but are of crucial importance in the aggregate, may be indicated.

Finally, some business firms are beginning to regard an increasing share of their total costs of operation as being fixed in character. The higher costs of maintaining market position in the channels of distribution illustrate this change. Total reliance upon a strategy of product differentiation under such circumstances is undesirable, since market share available as a result of such a promotion-oriented approach tends to be variable over time. Much may hinge, for example, upon week-to-week audience ratings of the television shows of competitors who seek to outdifferentiate each other. Exploitation of market segments, which provides for greater maximization of consumer or user satisfactions, tends to build a more secure market position and to lead to greater over-all stability. While traditionally, high fixed costs (regarded primarily from the production viewpoint) have created pressures for expanded sale of standardized items through differentiation, the possible shifting of certain marketing costs into the fixed area of the total cost structure tends to minimize this pressure.

CONCLUSION

Success in planning marketing activities requires precise utilization of both product differentiation and market segmentation as components of marketing strategy. It is fortunate that available techniques of marketing research make unplanned market exploration largely unnecessary. It is the obligation of those responsible for sales and marketing administration to keep the strategy mix in adjustment with market structure at any point in time and to produce in marketing strategy at least as much dynamism as is present in the market. The ability of business to plan in this way is dependent upon the maintenance of a flow of market information that can be provided by marketing research as well as the full utilization of available techniques of cost accounting and cost analysis.

Cost information is critical because the upper limit to which market segmentation can be carried is largely defined by production cost considerations. There is a limit to which diversity in market offerings can be carried without driving production costs beyond practical limits. Similarly, the employment of product differentiation as a strategy tends to be restricted by the achievement of levels of marketing cost that are untenable. These cost factors tend to define the limits of the zone within which the employment of marketing strategies or a strategy mix dictated by the nature of the market is permissive.

It should be emphasized that while we have here been concerned with the differences between product differentiation and market segmentation as marketing strategies, they are closely related concepts in the setting of an imperfectly competitive market. The differences have been highlighted in the interest of enhancing clarity in theory and precision in practice. The emergence of market segmentation as a strategy once again provides evidence of the consumer's preeminence in the contemporary American economy and the richness of the rewards that can result from the application of science to marketing problems.

2.

A Theory of Market Segmentation

Henry J. Claycamp
William F. Massy

INTRODUCTION

One of the most striking developments in marketing is the amount of interest shown in market segmentation strategy. Nearly every issue of major marketing journals includes discussions of it and its implications for marketing management.

Despite the attention devoted to this topic, little progress has been made in developing a normative theory of the segmentation process. Most articles on segmentation tend to be either general discussions of the basic concept or research reports showing differences in consumption patterns among specific consumer groups. The *strategy* of segmentation often seems to be roughly equated with the *act* of defining subparts of some total market. As a result, considerable controversy—and perhaps some confusion—exist about the strategy's implications for the optimal allocation of scarce marketing resources and the requirements for effective implimentation.

This article takes a fresh look at the theory of market segmentation and its implications for marketing management. Although the article is intended as a contribution to marketing theory, we believe it also has implications for the practice of market segmentation. In the following sections we will (a) briefly review the theoretical foundations of the segmentation strategy and identify the major barriers to effective implementation, (b) develop a normative theory of the segmentation process that recognizes major implementation difficulties, and (c) investigate some of its operational implications.

THE ECONOMIC THEORY OF SEGMENTATION

The concept of market segmentation was developed in economic theory to show how a firm selling a homogeneous product in a market character-

From Henry J. Claycamp and William F. Massy, "A Theory of Market Segmentation," *Journal of Marketing Research,* Vol. 5 (November 1968), pp. 388–394. Published by the American Marketing Association. Reprinted by permission.

ized by heterogeneous demand could maximize profits.[1] The theory shows that optimal profits can be achieved if the firm uses consumers' marginal responses to price, i.e., price elasticities, to define mutually exclusive segments and sets price (or output) so that marginal profits achieved in each segment are equal. Extension of these results to include other marketing variables (besides price) is easily done.

Since there seems to be little doubt that marketers are interested in the segmentation concept because of its profit implications and because the economic theory model shows how the concept is related to profit maximization, it can be considered as an "ideal" or "optimal" approach.

Although optimal segmentation is a simple and appealing concept, at least four kinds of problems can be identified that make it exceedingly difficult to utilize:

1. Problems of defining mutually exclusive market segments
2. Problems of measuring response elasticities on a segment by segment basis
3. Information constraints that affect the possibility of reaching segments selectively (i.e., the marketer ordinarily has only socioeconomic or demographic information about audiences reached by promotional media or areas covered by distribution outlets, and it is usually difficult to find relationships between these variables and marginal response differentials)
4. Institutional constraints that limit the ability to use existing means of reaching segments with the desired degree of price or promotional selectivity.

The economic theory of segmented markets does not deal with these problems. If the obvious advantages of optimal segmentation are to be realized, we need to extend the theory to include fundamental problems of implementation. The primary purpose here is to present an extension of the segmentation process as a mathematical model.

A MULTISTAGE THEORY OF MARKET SEGMENTATION

As indicated, our goal is to extend the classical microeconomic theory of market segmentation to take account of problems in defining segments, and the existence of institutional and informational constraints on managers' ability to design promotional strategies that will reach specified segments. The problem of using demographic, socioeconomic, or other "practical" variables to describe consumer groups will also enter the analysis. Although our model uses only price and promotional variables, it could be revised to include any of the marketing mix elements.

We assume a market with firms sufficiently decoupled such that strategies can be planned without direct reference to problems of possible competitive

[1] See [7] for example.

retaliation, at least in the short run and for some marketing variables. The analysis considers profit maximization strategies for a single product. The model will be developed in five stages, representing successively more aggregative and easier to apply approaches to market segmentation. Though each stage is best considered separately, we emphasize that we are not presenting five different models of market segmentation. Our "final" model is represented by Stage 4. Stage 5 shows how the procedures developed in Stages 1–4, if carried to the limit, lead logically to a nonsegmentation or "mass market" strategy.

Stage 1: Segmentation by Perfect Discrimination Among Customers

Suppose that a firm attempts to market its product to N customers, each with the demand function:

$$d_i = f_i(p_i, x_i), \qquad i = 1, \cdots N,$$

where p_i is the price and, x_i a vector of m nonprice promotional variable offered to the ith customer. If the unit cost of distribution (not including promotion) to the ith customer is c_i, the firm's gross revenue equation can be written as:

$$R = \sum_{i=1}^{N} (p_i - c_i) d_i = \sum_{i=1}^{N} (p_i - c_i) f_i(p_i, x_i).$$

The firm's cost equation, also easily defined, includes the costs of supplying and promoting the product:

$$C = g \left\{ \sum_{i=1}^{N} d_i \right\} + \sum_{i=1}^{N} q_i,$$

where d_i is the product demand and q_i is the total cost of implementing the promotional package, denoted by x_i, both for the ith customer. The function $g\{\cdot\}$ is the typical cost function of manufacturing the product (a function of the sum of all customers' demands) and any fixed costs of operating the firm; it does not include distribution or promotion costs, which are handled elsewhere in the model. The cost equation is best rewritten as an explicit function of the controllable variables in the marketing mix, p_i and x_i. Let v_i^1 be the vector of per unit costs of promotion to the ith customer so that $q_i = v_i^1 x_i$:

$$C = g \left\{ \sum_{i=1}^{N} f_i(p_i, x_i) \right\} + \sum_{i=1}^{N} v_i^1 x_i.$$

Given revenues and costs, we can write the following profit equation for the firm:

$$(2\text{--}1) \quad \Pi = R - C = \sum_i (p_i - c_i) f_i(p_i, x_i) - g \left\{ \sum_i f_i(p_i, x_i) \right\} - \sum_i v_i^1 x_i.$$

The firm's optimal marketing mix will be obtained when Equation 2–1 is maximized with respect to p_i and the elements of x_i (for $i = 1, \cdots N$).

By differentiating (2–1) partially with respect to each of the controllable marketing variables and setting the derivatives equal to zero,[2] we get the familiar decision rules:[3]

(2–2)
$$(p_i - c_i - MC) \frac{\partial f_i}{\partial p_i} = -f_i, \qquad i = 1, \cdots N,$$

$$(p_i - c_i - MC) \frac{\partial f_i}{\partial x_{ij}} = v_{ij}, \qquad \begin{matrix} i = 1, \cdots N \\ j = 1, \cdots m; \end{matrix}$$

where MC is the cost function derivative with respect to total demand. This development is a direct descendent of the microeconomic model of the perfectly discriminating monopolist (see [7] for example), generalized to include both price and nonprice competitive variables. The $(m + 1)N$ equations must be solved to determine the optimal price-promotional mix for each market (here, an individual customer) supplied by the firm.

This model represents the market segmentation strategy in its extreme form. Each customer is identified as a segment in his right because each person's demand function may be at least slightly different from his neighbor's.

Besides the obviously severe computational problems that are likely involved in solving (2–2), other problems ordinarily preclude this approach in practical situations, that is:

1. Marketers are rarely to know the form or parameters of individual customer's demand functions. When such knowledge must be obtained by statistical methods, it is almost always necessary to deal with customer groups rather than individual customers.
2. It is rarely possible to pinpoint promotional efforts to specific customers or to maintain perfect price discrimination strategies. Marketers are faced with legal constraints on pricing and price leakage for resale by customers. For promotion, they must usually use standing promotional vehicles, such as advertising media, with predetermined audience characteristics.

The model must be generalized to account for difficulties. We will deal with Point 2 first because it will provide the groundwork for analyzing Point 1.

Stage 2: Customer Segmentation with Institutional Constraints

Suppose that the firm faces a fixed set of promotional vehicles through which it must exercise its nonprice marketing efforts. The fixed set of pro-

---

[2] Second-order conditions will be ignored here.
[3] Profit maximization subject to a constraint on the total promotional budget would lead to slightly different decision rules but would not change the conclusions drawn from this or any of the following models.

motional vehicles will be denoted by the vector y_i, y_2, $\cdots y_n$, which we shall call "media." Thus, there are n media to reach the firm's N customers. We would expect $n < N$—though the model does not specifically require this relation. Now, the elements of the nonprice promotional vector for the ith customer can be related to the media by the set of equations:

$$x_{ij} = \Psi_i(y) \; j = 1, \cdots m; i = 1, \cdots N.$$

We shall assume that the Ψ-functions are all linear (a reasonable assumption, as demonstrated by the following example). Thus, we may write

$$x_{ij} = \sum_{k=1}^{n} b_{ijk} y_k,$$

where the "media characteristic parameters" b_{ijk} represent the contribution of the kth kind of promotional input for the ith customer. The above is more concisely written in matrix form:

(2–3) $$\qquad\qquad x_i = \underline{\underline{B}}_i y, \qquad i = 1, \cdots N,$$

where $\underline{\underline{B}}_i$ is the $m \times n$ matrix of media characteristic parameters. Equation 2–3 implies that when the firm sets the variables' values in the media vector y, it determines the level of all nonprice promotional variables for the customers. Thus the y's, instead of the x's, should be seen as the controllable marketing variables.

We can clarify the meaning of (2–3) by using a simplified numerical example. Suppose that the market consists of three customers: one with high, one with middle, and one with low socioeconomic status. Now, assume there are two forms of nonprice competition (magazine ads and the amount of shelf space the retailers allocated to the brand) and three media available to the manufacturer (a "class" or prestige consumer magazine, a "pulp" or low-status consumer magazine, and a trade newspaper read by retailers). Assume also that all three customers shop at the same retail outlet. (These assumptions are made only to simplify the example; they are not an essential part of the model.) Table 2–1 gives the matrices $\underline{\underline{B}}_i (i = 1, 2, 3)$ that might be expected to occur in the kind of situation just described. The matrices indicate that the high-status customer reads Magazine A, the low-status customer reads B, and the middle-status customer reads neither. Also, retailers are assumed to adjust shelf space in response to advertising in both the prestige consumer Magazine A and the trade paper, though the last is ten times more effective in this regard than is the first. The level of the nonprice competition vector x, e.g., the number of advertising exposures or shelf facings, that stimulate each customer can now be determined by Equation 2–3, using the matrices in the table.

Before changing the profit equation developed in Stage 1 to include the existence of promotional media with specific characteristics, we will invoke two simplifying assumptions. Suppose that for legal reasons, the firm decides not to follow a strategy of price discrimination. That is, the price to each customer is to be the same so that $p_i = p$ for all i. Suppose also that the distribution costs are the same for all customers so that $c_i = c$ in all cases. These assumptions are made only for convenience (the notation is simpler if the subscripts on p and c are omitted). The model's development does not depend on these assumptions, nor do we suggest that they are realistic.

Table 2–1
Hypothetical Media Characteristic Matrices for Two-Variable,
Three-Media, Three-Customer Example

Customer (N = 3)	Nonprice competition variable (m = 2)	Media (n = 3)		
		Consumer magazine A (prestige)	Consumer magazine B (pulp)	Trade magazine
Customer 1 (high status)	Advertising exposures	1.0	0.0	0.0
	Shelf space	0.1	0.0	0.0
Customer 2 (middle status)	Advertising exposures	0.0	0.0	0.0
	Shelf space	0.1	0.0	1.0
Customer 3 (low status)	Advertising exposures	0.0	1.0	0.0
	Shelf space	0.1	0.0	1.0

Recall from the numerical example that the elements of the media vector y are dimensioned in physical terms, e.g., number of exposures or number of shelf facings. Let the vector $w' = w_1, w_2, \cdots w_n$ be the per unit costs of using the media. For example, if $w_1 =$ one cent, a one-unit "buy" in medium 1 (the high-status magazine in the example) will cost one cent per exposure or ten dollars per thousand. Substitution of Equation 2–3 for x_i, w' for v'_i, and setting $p_i = p$ and $c_i = c$ in Equation 2–1 yields the following Stage 2 profit equation:

$$(2\text{–}4) \quad \Pi = R - C = (p - c) \sum_i f_i(p, \mathbf{B}_i y) - w'y - g\left\{ \sum_i f_i(p, \mathbf{B}_i y) \right\}.$$

Equation 2–4 must be maximized with respect to p and the n elements of y.

Differentiation with respect to price leads to a simple aggregation of the first part of Equation 2–2.

$$(p - c - MC \sum_i \frac{\partial f_i}{\partial p} = - \sum_j f_i.$$

(This relation is the same for all subsequent models and will not be considered further.) The derivative with respect to a given medium variable y_k is:

$$\frac{\partial \Pi}{\partial y_k} = 0 = (p - c) \sum_i \sum_j \frac{\partial f_i}{\partial x_{ij}} \frac{\partial x_{ij}}{\partial y_k} - w_k - MC \sum_i \sum_j \frac{\partial f_i}{\partial x_{ij}} \frac{\partial x_{ij}}{\partial y_k}.$$

Transposing and recognizing that $\partial x_{ij}/\partial y_k = b_{ijk}$, we have the following set of decision rules for media:

$$(2\text{--}5) \qquad (p - c - MC) \sum_i \sum_j b_{ijk} \frac{\partial f_i}{\partial x_{ij}} = w_k, k = 1, \cdots n.$$

This result differs from the one for Stage 1 (the second part of Equation 2–2) because weighted averages of the response derivatives $\partial f_i/\partial x_{ij}$ are used in aggregated equations, instead of individual terms in individual equations.

Stage 2 accounts for what might be called *institutional constraints* that restrict the marketing manager's freedom of action. Note, however, that the information requirements for Stage 2 are even more demanding than they were in Stage 1. Besides knowing all individual response derivatives $\partial f_i/\partial x_{ij}$, the manager must get estimates of the parameters of the media transfer functions $\Psi_i(y)$.

Information at the required level of detail is rarely available even for widely researched mass media (possibly except for certain industrial buying situations). Instead of relating to individual customers, audience data are usually broken down by demographic and socioeconomic variables, or at the very most, coverage may be reported by consumption level for certain key product classes [4]. Therefore, we must extend our Stage 2 model to account for these information constraints.

Stage 3: Microsegmentation

Suppose that media circulation is known only for a total of M mutually exclusive and exhaustive consumer classes, which are defined by socioeconomic, demographic, or similar variables. (These classes will be called *media descriptor classes* or, alternatively, *microsegments*.) The media characteristic coefficient matrices now refer to the descriptor classes rather than to individual customers—we have $\underline{B}_l$, $l = 1, \cdots M$, where, for example, a given matrix might refer to "high-income, high-educated persons over 65." In principle, these matrices can be determined from audience survey information.[4] Introducing descriptor classes leads to the following modification of the Stage 2 decision rule presented in Equation 2–5:

$$(2\text{--}6) \qquad (p - c - MC) \sum_j \sum_l b_{ljk} \sum_{i \in l} \frac{\partial f_i}{\partial x_{ij}} = w_k; k = 1, \ldots n,$$

where the notation $i \epsilon l$ means all persons within the lth descriptor cell.

It is obvious from Equation 2–6 that the constraint on media audience information leads to equal weighting of all members in each media descriptor class. The term $\Sigma_{i \epsilon l} \partial f_i/\partial x_{ij}$ represents the aggregate marginal response to be

---

[4] This model implicitly assumes that media cover a given descriptive class homogeneously, i.e., problems of audience accumulation and duplication are ignored.

expected from all persons in descriptive cell *l*. Thus, imposing a constraint on media information automatically relaxes the information requirements with respect to the individual response derivatives.

We have named the segmentation level represented by Stage 3 *microsegmentation* because segmentation by media descriptor classes is the least aggregative degree of promotional discrimination possible given existing institutional constraints and media research methods.

Stage 4: Macrosegmentation

Now let us consider the problem of estimating the marginal response of sales to promotion. It seems likely that purely judgmental methods will be insufficient to determine the demand functions or their derivatives. Some kind of empirical approach is needed if we are to obtain estimates of the response derivatives in (2–6).

Empirical analyses of sales response to price or promotional variables may be discussed in terms of either individual or aggregative demand functions. The first approach is very difficult. The only substantive effort to deal with individual demand functions of which we are aware is included in Duhammel's study [1]. Though the results were interesting, they do not give us confidence in the practical efficacy of a fully disaggregative approach. If we are to conduct more aggregative statistical demand analyses, however, we must decide how much to aggregate and on what variables the process should be based. Equation 2–6 gives an immediate answer—at least in part. According to the results of Stage 3 we can always aggregate to the level of the smallest microsegment for which media information is commonly available.

But aggregation to the level of (6) may not be enough. Demand function analysis involves estimation of the change in sales to be expected per unit change in promotion, but media audience research concerns average audience levels for descriptor classes. If we consider data sources for these analyses, it becomes apparent that sample sizes sufficient to measure the elements of B_l for a given descriptor class, with reasonable degree of accuracy, may be insufficient to measure $\Sigma_{i\epsilon l} \partial f_i/\partial x_{ij}$. As Frank and Massy [2, 3], and others have shown, the estimation of response coefficients is not easy. Even if the analysis is based on time series data, the time series must be based on the buying behavior of a sufficient number of families to avoid gross instabilities.

Since the sample sizes necessary to estimate response sensitivities for a given microsegment must often be rather large, the researcher is faced with two alternatives: (1) using the maximum number of descriptor cells, and hence a very large overall sample size, or (2) aggregating over descriptor classes to form a smaller number of new classes with adequate numbers of respondents in each, while keeping the total sample within bounds. The total sample size for a study is often fixed (as when working with syndicated panel data), in which case the second alternative is the only feasible one. Or perhaps the cost of data collection precludes using a large overall sample size. Finally, the cost of audience research is usually absorbed by the media (or agencies), suggesting that larger sample sizes will be possible there than for product or brand specific sensitivity analyses, if only because the costs can be divided among many users.

This reasoning implies that aggregation beyond the minimal descriptor class sizes dictated by available media audience statistics will be the rule rather than the exception if statistical methods for estimating demand sensitivities are to be used practically. How should the aggregation be performed? Given the potentialities of media research for dealing with relatively disaggregative microsegments, it seems reasonable to use these media descriptors to build more aggregative demand descriptor classes. Therefore, we define a *macrosegment* as follows: macrosegment h consists of the customers in media descriptive cells $l \epsilon h$. This definition ensures that it will be possible to make media decisions for each segment. Since media characteristic coefficients can be found for each microsegment l, the media characteristics for macrosegments h can be found by simple aggregation.

The promotion rule for Stage 3 (Equation 2–6) is easily modified to accommodate the higher level of aggregation.

$$(2\text{–}7) \quad (p - c - MC) \sum_j \sum_h \{ \sum_{l \epsilon h} b_{ljk} \} \left\{ \sum_{l \epsilon h} \sum_{i \epsilon l} \frac{\partial f_i}{\partial x_{ij}} \right\} = w_k, k = 1, \cdots n.$$

The sensitivity term $\{\Sigma_{l \epsilon h} \Sigma_{i \epsilon l} \partial f_i / \partial x_{ij}\}$ might be written simply as $\partial f_h / \partial x_{hj}$ to emphasize that it refers to the aggregate demand function for the hth macrosegment.

Stage 5: The "Mass Market" Concept

It will be useful to present another generalization of our market segmentation model, this one corresponding to the case in which no segmentation strategy is practiced at all. Profit maximization without segmentation leads to the following decision rule for promotion:

$$(2\text{–}8) \quad (p - c - MC) \sum_j \left\{ \sum_{l=1}^{M} b_{ljk} \right\} \left\{ \sum_{l=1}^{M} \sum_{i \epsilon l} \frac{\partial f_i}{\partial x_{ij}} \right\} = w_k, k = 1, \cdots, n,$$

where the first term in the brackets represents the total impact of medium k in terms of promotion type j for all numbers of the population, and the second term is the derivative of the total market demand function. As easily recognized, (2–8) is the same as (2–7) if there is only one inclusive macrosegment.

SOME IMPLICATIONS OF THE THEORY

The theoretical models presented in the preceding section have several implications for both the philosophy and practice of segmentation.

First, it seems clear that segmentation should be considered as a process of *aggregation* rather than *disaggregation*. For example, recall that the theory's five stages dealt with the full range of segmentation possibilities. That is Stages 1 and 2 treat individual consumer units as segments; Stage 3 deals with aggregation of consumer units into microsegments; Stage 4 considers aggregations of microsegments into larger groups (macrosegments); and Stage 5 deals with the mass market or complete aggregation of consumers.

It should be obvious that if consumers have different responses to the firm's marketing variables and if there are no scale diseconomies in fitting specialized programs to individual consumers, segmentation at the level of individual consumer units (the case of the perfectly discriminating monopolist) would yield maximum profits. However, this discussion showed that even if the dubious assumption of no scale economies in the marketing mix is valid, other constraints typically preclude this form of segmentation. For example, lack of information about the response characteristics of groups reached by promotional media and institutional constraints on the flexibility of their use require aggregation at least to the level of microsegments (Stage 3). Additional aggregation to macrosegments—or ultimately to a single segment—may be required because of difficulties in measuring response differentials for specific groups.

It is easy to see that addition of the successive constraints and corresponding higher levels of aggregation must reduce the level of the firm's profit. (This statement ignores research costs required to implement a given level of segmentation.) That is, the application of Stage 1 segmentation yields more profit than Stage 2, Stage 2 more than Stage 3, etc. This is a direct result of the mathematical properties of constrained versus unconstrained maxima. Thus the fundamental problem of market segmentation can be characterized as finding the point at which the marginal reduction of profits caused by the imposition of another constraint, or level of aggregation, is just balanced by the marginal reduction in research and administration costs made possible by the constraint.

We argued earlier that this balance will likely occur at the macrosegmentation stage. Thus the basic resource allocation problem in segmentation involves finding the values of the controllable marketing variables that bring the decision rule in (2–7) to equality. The problem of finding the solution to (2–7) can be handled with standard mathematical programming procedures when the necessary data have been collected and the macrosegments have been defined. Though the problems of finding a solution are not trivial, they will not be explored here.

The concept that segmentation is a process of aggregation implies building to a viable segmentation strategy rather than tearing a market apart to find one. This may be a fine point in regard to the philosophy of segmentation, but it appears to be important for the implementation of the strategy. It is impossible to form meaningful market segments without making institutional and information constraints into account and this means building from the point at which the constraints are felt, namely from persons to microsegments to macrosegments.

Criteria for Forming Macrosegments

Let us now consider some implications of the theory for the formation of meaningful macrosegments. In particular, we consider the question of how media descriptor cells (microsegments) should be allocated to macrosegments.

It is clear that if the response derivatives for all microsegments included in each of the macrosegments are identical, Equation 2–7 is merely a factored form of Equation 2–6. For the jth type of nonprice competition we have:

$$\sum_l b_{ljk} \sum_{i \in l} \frac{\partial f_i}{\partial x_{ij}} = \sum_h \left\{ \sum_{l \in h} b_{ljk} \right\} \cdot \left\{ \sum_{l \in h} \sum_{i \in l} \frac{\partial f_i}{\partial x_{ij}} \right\}, \qquad k = 1, \cdots n,$$

if

$$\sum_{i \in l} \frac{\partial f_i}{\partial x_{ij}} = \sum_{i \in l*} \frac{\partial f_i}{\partial x_{ij}} \qquad \text{for all } l, \, l* \epsilon h.$$

(Recall that we can do nothing about any possibility that the $\partial f_i \partial x_{ij}$ are heterogeneous within a given microsegment without changing audience research procedures.)

This consideration suggests that for a given kind of competitive activity it will be useful to form segments such that

$$\text{variance} \qquad \left\{ \sum_{i \in l} \frac{\partial f_i}{\partial x_{ij}} \right\}, \qquad \text{for } l \epsilon h,$$

is as small as possible for each of the macrosegments. This means that microsegments (l) should be assigned to macrosegments (h) in such a way that the within-group variances of microsegment response coefficients are as small as possible relative to the between-group variance.[5] (The media characteristic coefficients b_{ljk} are not included in the variance formula because the macrosegments must be developed before a specific promotional program is chosen.)

Macrosegment formation requires grouping microsegments by similarities among their promotional responses. How can information on the response derivatives for each microsegment be obtained? It will generally be necessary to determine the kind of promotional variables that are likely to be used in

---

[5] The average within-group variance will surely decline as more macrosegments are permitted, assuming that optimal allocations are made at each stage. As noted earlier, the question of determining the optimal number of segments must be resolved by analyzing the trade-off between costs of research and marketing administration (which rise with the number of segments considered) and the gains to be expected from reductions in within-group variance. The analysis will depend on factors specific to problem and product class and is beyond the scope of this article.

the marketing mix and define specific response variables for each of them. (The change in the buying probability caused by an additional advertising exposure would be one such measure.) Often it will be necessary to use surrogates for the response variables, as when the response of consumer attitude or awareness measures to changes in advertising are used in place of the sales response.

Looser response measures, e.g., less adequate surrogates, will more usually be dictated when working at the microsegment level than will subsequently be used when dealing with macrosegments. This will occur because of the many microsegments for which response measures must be estimated and the difficulty of obtaining data on individual microsegments. However, this difficulty will be reduced because the response measures will be reestimated at the macrosegment level.

The last problem raised by the theory is to find a method for optimally grouping microsegments into macrosegments, assuming that information on the relevant response derivatives is available for each microsegment. That is, we want to make assignments such that the resulting macrosegments consist of microsegments with large within-group and small between-group homogeneity of response derivatives.

Making such assignments is a problem in optimal taxonomy, also called cluster analysis.[6] It is fortunate that such programs have recently been developed, because without them macrosegment formation would largely be guesswork. Although many detailed problems in using these procedures must be solved by future research, we conclude that the data sources and research methods now available are sufficient to permit their application. The value of our theory of market segmentation will be proved if it leads researchers to experiment with these techniques that allow a systematic attack on the practical problems of segmenting markets.

References

1. William F. Duhammel, "The Use of Variable Markov Processes as a Partial Basis for the Determination and Analysis of Market Segments," Unpublished doctoral dissertation, Graduate School of Business, Stanford University, March 1966.
2. Ronald E. Frank and William F. Massy, "Marketing Segmentation and the Effectiveness of a Brand's Price and Dealing Policies," *Journal of Business,* 38 (April 1965), 186–200.
3. "Estimating the Effects of Short-Term Promotional Strategy in Selecting

---

[6] For a description of one optimal taxonomy procedure, see [8]. For an application of the clustering method to a marketing problem, see [5]. Claycamp and Massy are doing research on using the Rubin cluster analysis program to form macrosegments as indicated above. Results will be in a future article.

Market Segments," in Patrick J. Robinson and Charles L. Hinkle, eds., *Sales Promotion Analysis: Some Applications of Quantitative Techniques,* Philadelphia: Marketing Science Institute, [1969].

4. Harper W. Boyd, "Correlates of Grocery Product Consumption Rates," *Journal of Marketing Research,* 4 (May 1967), 184–90.

5. Paul Green, Ronald Frank, and Patrick Robinson, "Cluster Analysis in Test Market Selection," *Management Science,* 13 (April 1967), B387–400.

6. William F. Massy, "The Cost of Uncertainty in Advertising Media Selection," Graduate School of Industrial Administration, Carnegie Institute of Technology, Working Paper No. 2, December 1966.

7. Joan Robinson, *The Economics of Imperfect Competition,* London: Macmillan & Co., 1954, 179–88.

8. Jerrold Rubin, "Optimal Classification into Groups: An Approach for Solving the Taxonomy Problem," International Business Machine Corporation, New York Scientific Center, May 1965.

3.

Market Segmentation as a
Competitive Strategy

Nelson N. Foote

Let us assume we have made the discovery that consumers of ice cream differ significantly in their preferences for chocolate, strawberry, and vanilla. And let us assume that these flavor preferences are not distributed randomly among all kinds of people, but are differentially associated with some other characteristic of customers for ice cream, such as hair color, and that these associations are substantial in degree and practical to ascertain. For example, let us say that brunettes tend strongly to like chocolate, redheads to favor strawberry, and blondes, vanilla. Finally, let us imagine that this pattern is just that simple and orderly—product differences nicely match customer differences.

Then what?

What is the businessman who wants to sell ice cream in this market to do about our findings? Is he to conclude that he should offer all three flavors, the same as the rest of the industry, lest he forego any important source of sales? Or should he try to serve only blondes and brunettes, since there are not enough redheads to make serving them profitable? Or should he seek to establish a reputation as the producer of the finest Dutch chocolate ice cream, so that he captures nearly all that segment of the market? Or should he go after the great mass of vanilla fans, by upgrading this lowly flavor with a French accent? Or should he take account of his newness or smallness in the industry and challenge the incumbent giants of the trade by introducing pistachio or frozen custard? Or should he offer the normal product line of his industry, but allow some major chain of retail outlets to apply its store brand to his product? Should he go after the door-to-door trade with a very short line—like Neapolitan only—or open his own chain of soda fountains with 28 flavors? Or should he be creative and try to think up some utterly new way to exploit his knowledge of differing customer preferences, since all these strategies—and more besides—are already in use today in the ice cream business?

From Nelson N. Foote, "Market Segmentation as a Competitive Strategy," in Leo Bogart, ed., *Current Controversies in Marketing Research* (Chicago: Markham Publishing Company, 1969), pp. 129–139. Reprinted by permission.

Plainly, even if one knew far more than is known already about patterns of correlation between product and customer differences in any particular market, it takes a lot of thinking and doing before this knowledge can be turned into a calculated competitive strategy. Meanwhile we find examples of marketing managers who have very successfully employed a strategy of market segmentation, quite without the resources of detailed information that as professional marketers we like to think are indispensable to decision-making in matters of such complexity and risk.

It seems important throughout discussion of market segmentation to recognize that the main source of interest in the concept is its potential value as a competitive strategy. There may be quite a number of people whose interest is in promoting the sale or purchase of data regarding the "stratigraphics" of consumer choice. But unless these data can be put to practical use in improving or defending the market position or profits of their user, only the data seller will benefit, and he not for long. So my self-chosen assignment here is to bear down on the task of thinking out the use of such data in actual marketing management. Although I make my living as a marketing researcher, I think that we need more thinking on this matter as much as we need more research.

Immediately, however, the question arises of who is going to discuss competitive strategy in public—especially in the presence of competitors of his own firm—save in empty generalities. A salesman of research data, or representatives of advertising agencies or media, might set forth some hypothetical tactics of market segmentation as a means of soliciting business. But other than personal vanity or the desire to solicit another job, what would induce someone connected with a manufacturer or a retailer to disclose his thinking about competitive strategy? The incentives of professional exchange of technique or the teaching of younger members of the fraternity are not sufficient justification. Many kinds of professional know-how are properly kept proprietary by the firm which paid for their development. If market segmentation is to be analyzed publicly and candidly from the standpoint of an actual competitor in a market, it has to be justified by some benefit that it will bring to this competitor. If it were not my conviction that in fact it is to the benefit of every competing firm that market segmentation be discussed publicly in terms of its implications for competitive strategy, you would not be listening to these words at this moment.

Moreover, we can go one step further and declare that market segmentation as a competitive strategy is also in the interests of customers. If it were not—if it did not offer customers a firmer base for choice among competing offerings and a wider array of genuine choices—it would not work as a competitive strategy. Like any deal, market segmentation is good business only when both parties to the transaction benefit. Market segmentation is thus in effect a logical extension of the basic principles of marketing.

The process of market segmentation, however, when approached as a task of formulating and executing a marketing strategy, involves matching not merely customer characteristics and product characteristics, but a tripartite matching of customers and offerings *and* the array of competitors in the market, as seen from the standpoint of any one competitor within this constellation. If we think of offerings by competitors as expressions of their differing *capabilities,* it will not only be easy to remember the three C's—*customers, competitors,* and *capabilities*—but the full task of developing a strategy is more clearly pushed into view.

Let me illustrate concretely by referring to one of our most respected competitors in the Chicago area, the Zenith Radio Corporation. Zenith won a preeminent position in the television receiver market some ten years ago by becoming established in the minds of consumers as the leading exemplar of product reliability. Its policy of manufacturing products of good workmanship goes back many years, but during the middle fifties many consumers became quite concerned to identify the set that would, they hoped, give them the least trouble from breakdown. That was when Zenith's market share soared, until it surpassed the erstwhile industry leader. Servicemen and the radio-TV specialty stores with which they are associated lent vigorous aid. Zenith's management and its advertising agency pressed the opportunity that had widened for them. But Zenith had not adopted product reliability as a self-consciously opportunistic, short-term tactic. As far as known, Zenith's strategy was not derived through marketing research, although marketing research by competitors soon verified its efficacy. After some delay, other competitors raised their quality control standards, but none has been able, coming in later on a me-too basis, to emulate Zenith's success. One could quibble about some details of Zenith's reputation—whether hand-wiring is in fact more or less reliable than printed circuits, whether reliability has not been confused to some extent with repairability, whether Zenith sets any longer enjoy the lowest breakdown rate—but from the marketing standpoint, Zenith remains king among that segment of the set market which emphasizes reliability above other virtues when buying sets. The quality standards of the whole industry were forced up by Zenith's success, an outcome of obvious benefit to the consumer, but of at least equal benefit to all the other competitors in the industry, whose personnel devote their whole lives to their industry and much prefer feeling proud of their occupation to feeling ashamed of it.

The meaning of the Zenith example would be very incomplete, however, if we paid attention only to the success story and failed to note that there are many other virtues in television sets which consumers prize besides reliability. If there were not, it would be hard to explain why the Zenith brand share at its zenith rose barely above a fifth of the market. To be sure, Zenith may have preferred its profitability to the greater volume it may have deliberately foregone by upholding a price premium. On the other hand, maybe not; a price premium is just about the loudest advertisement for quality there is.

Meanwhile Zenith's major rival did not simply decide it had to emulate Zenith, but staunchly pursued its strategy of industry statesmanship through the introduction of color, achieving handsome victory and reward from matching its offering with the rising wants of all those customers who were reaching for color in magazines, movies, photography, and other visual media. Alongside these two industry leaders were certain other manufacturers, one of whom has done well by stressing portability and personalization, another by treating the television set as a major piece of furniture, and so on. What is important here is that several competitors held their own or improved their position, even during the period of greatest success by Zenith and RCA, not by seeking to manufacture some hypothetically optimum television set, but by addressing themselves to some substantial segment of the market which *they saw themselves as peculiarly fitted to serve.* The firms which got shaken out during the past dozen years—among which some were big for a time—or which severely lost position can best be described as undistinguishable in their capabilities and offerings, hence undistinguished by consumers.

Now what has been added to the understanding of market segmentation by the example of television receivers? What has been added that is indispensable is the element of competitive capability—a virtue that one particular competitor preeminently possesses—which matches a substantial or rising consumer want. In colloquial terms, what have I got that the other guy hasn't, and which the customer wants badly enough to walk a mile for it?

A few years back, we looked at some commonplace demographic characteristics of television customers arrayed by the brands they tended to favor. When we looked at these demographic characteristics simultaneously, certain results were far more revealing in combination than singly. Only a limited example—because here we are indeed verging on the disclosure of competitive intelligence: we found that one highly meaningful segment of the market—meaningful in terms of sensitivity of discrimination among brands—consisted of households below the median in years of schooling but above the median in income. For convenient reference we called them merely the new-rich, obviously an inexact term. One particular brand seemed to be designed and advertised and priced—properly overpriced, as it were—specifically for this segment, and in fact it enjoyed at that time an inordinate share of their set-buying. Now that company has not noticeably changed its offerings during recent years; they still seem pointed toward the new-rich segment; but its brand share has dwindled substantially. It appears that people with more money than schooling nonetheless are able to learn from experience and do upgrade their taste, given a little time.

The moral of this example is that market segmentation has to be viewed as a continuous process, and marketing strategy has to keep in step with the changing structure of the market. While this implication is probably obvious, perhaps less obvious is the corollary that, just as consumers learn, it is necessary for competitors to learn to exercise differing capabilities from those which may have won them success in the past. And here we come to a matter which lies beyond not only research but also ordinary logic and in the realm of managerial will. Who is to tell a manufacturer that he is capable of doing something he has not done before, and of doing it better than any of his other competitors? By definition, the ordinary kinds of evidence are lacking because there is no past experience to be projected forward.

In the course of interpersonal relations among individuals, a teacher or a parent may tell a child that he possesses talents he did not previously recognize; the child may then adopt this observation as a conviction about himself which empowers him to demonstrate that it is true. All of us are familiar enough with instances of this outcome not to need to debate whether they occur. The faith of a coach in an athlete, of a critic in a writer, of an employer in an employee, of a wife in a husband, is often the ingredient which brings out a latent capability. Because so little is understood about the process, we cannot make it happen on demand. We are fortunate to recognize it when it does happen, even more so when we spy the opportunity beforehand and do not waste it, for ourselves or for others. Even further beyond present understanding is the possibility of specifying here a reliable formula whereby the management of a company can truly discern those latent talents in its own organization which can be mobilized more effectively by itself than by any of its competitors to satisfy some important emerging customer want.

I do know this, however: recognition of such a talent feeds on itself; it is a cumulative process, a benevolent spiral. I am positive that when the management of Zenith found itself being recognized by consumers for its virtues of good workmanship, it was immensely stimulated to push further in that direction. Thus one of the most valuable functions of marketing research in implementing a strategy of market segmentation is to listen to what is being said about a company by its customers in terms of recognizing its special talents. Developing something that is already there—watering a plant that is already growing, to mix a metaphor—is surely much easier and more likely to succeed than trying to create new capabilities out of whole cloth or, for that matter, borrowing the garments of others, in the sense of imitating or acquiring another company and offering that as an expression of one's own capability.

Part of the growing sophistication of consumers is their increasing interest in the character of the organization they are dealing with. At General Electric we are acutely conscious that certain of our competitors, whose products are no better and sometimes not as good as ours by any measure of product quality, nonetheless enjoy the preference of certain customers. This problem repeatedly confronts the manufacturer who finds himself in competition with retailers who handle only store brands. The whole fascinating issue of what is going to emerge as private branding widens its sway is too vast to open up here. Yet it deserves mention here as constituting market segmentation on an utterly different axis from market segmentation on the axis of product features and brand images.

Segmentation varies in degree as well as in kind. The famous case of the ordinary salt which "rains when it pours" illustrates a valued product feature which has maintained for a particular brand a large and stable market share for many years, while conferring on consumers a valued satisfaction for which they are quite willing to pay a price premium and a rewarding degree of brand loyalty. Many such product features are easily imitated, however, and the reputation for distinctiveness originally achieved may dissolve in the minds of consumers despite advertising. The impermanence of minor product features as a source of competitive distinctiveness and effective market segmentation is a conspicuous failing of the current picture in package goods competition. Like rock-and-roll music, there is too little difference between the new ones and the old ones to make much difference. The proliferation of trivial product differences which appeal to trivial differences among consumers and represent trivial differences among the capabilities of their makers is in effect a mockery of the theory of market segmentation. This proliferation of trivial differences provokes denunciation by producers, retailers, and consumers alike as market fragmentation rather than segmentation and makes an industry vulnerable to the outsider who commences to segment on a different axis. The effective response to the trivialization of market segmentation, however, is not to abandon it as a strategy. To do that would be to abdicate all initiative to competitors. The way out of the expensive waste of trivial segmentation is to engage in serious segmentation, which means segmentation on a larger scale or even on another axis.

Serious, large-scale innovation seems often to come from outside an industry rather than inside. Examples like General Motors in locomotives, Volkswagen in autos, IBM in typewriters, Corning in housewares, Lestoil in detergents, come to mind. Rivalry within a going constellation of competitors seems often to lead to implicit imitation, even when everyone involved is convinced that he is trying to be different from everyone else. How this result occurs is not hard to discern. Close rivals tend very easily to magnify the importance of small differences, whether initiated by themselves or others. If created by another, a close competitor often feels he must come up with a rival innovation but only of corresponding scale.

One detects nothing very distinctive about Silvertone television sets, to mention another respected Chicago competitor. Viewed as manufactured products, they are close to the industry's average line. But where Zenith stresses the reliability built into the product, Sears stresses the services offered by the stores in which Silvertone sets are bought—the promptness of repair service, the easy credit, the ample parking, the special sales well advertised in local newspapers or by direct mail. That is, Sears segments the market on another axis than Zenith. But thus far, Silvertone has encroached far less upon Zenith's clientele than upon the portions of the market occupied by companies whose offerings are less distinctive.

We shall come back to this intriguing question of how far the competition of store brands with manufacturer brands may go before some equilibrium is reached. Some companies as yet have a less urgent private-brand problem anyway, like the auto and gasoline firms and the sellers of services—insurance, banking, air travel, lodging, dry cleaning—which distribute through their own exclusive retail outlets. So for some moments longer, let us stay within the sphere of competition among manufactured products and nationally advertised brands.

Assuming this sphere, we can now state our main hypothesis in further detail: Market segmentation works best as a competitive strategy, i.e., contributes most to the success of competitors and the satisfaction of customers, when product and brand and maker are closely identified in the minds of all concerned.

If we were to assume that one by one more competitors in a market choose to attract particular segments of customers on the basis of correct appraisal of their own special capabilities to satisfy these segments, then the competitors who do not make such deliberate choices will find themselves increasingly confined to the miscellaneous and dwindling residue. As alluded to in our first example, such a development is to some extent a description of what has already happened in some markets, so we may be prophesying simply an intensification of current tendencies rather than anything new under the sun. In other words, self-conscious segmentation may become not only a means of success but the price of survival in a market.

Beyond the ordinary criteria of survival or success as measured in profitability and market share, however, are some other benefits of segmentation to an industry and the various competitors in it. We have mentioned the feeling of pride in their occupation and the quality of its products which most people desire in their life work. Some other benefits of belonging to an industry which steadily adds to the values it offers its customers also deserve explicit recognition. They include the fact that being bested by a competitor whom one respects is easier to accept than being bested by a competitor whom one does not respect. There is a good deal of satisfaction to the producer as well as the consumer in seeing an industry progress over time through advanced applications of science and technology. In an industry plagued with cut-throat price competition instead of value competition, imitation is almost inevitable, because no one can afford the research and development required for innovation. In the vicious downward spiral which obtains in such an industry, jobs are insecure because companies are insecure; and morale and morality seem to decline together. Enough examples spring to mind. An industry trapped in such a spiral, worst of all, has rarely been able to reverse it without outside help, as from major suppliers. DuPont, for example, has struggled quite nobly to raise the plastics molding industry from its swamp. Customers themselves, especially in recent years, have some-times under these conditions willingly paid substantial premiums for quality and reliability, and this has brought a turnabout, but not before the damage became painful to all concerned.

Both competitors and customers share the benefits of stabilized markets wherein strong degrees of mutual loyalty exist between particular companies and particular segments of customers. Distribution and advertising costs are significantly lower under conditions in which repeat sales make up a high proportion of total sales. The model line of any competitor can be shorter, yet his volume nowadays may be higher, than when he tries to carry every-thing everyone else in the industry offers. All phases of marketing are much more intelligently, effectively, and efficiently conducted when companies and customers, having chosen each other with care and sophistication, can rely on each other's growing discrimination and sympathetically anticipate the orderly, developmental unfolding and matching of their future wants and capabilities. Some marketing researchers even envision a paradise in which companies will spend as much money in listening as in talking and will make more money doing so.

Let us commence to summarize while injecting a few additional elements into this consideration of market segmentation as a competitive strategy. Our first proposition was that any approach to market segmentation which dealt only with matching customer characteristics with product features was seriously incomplete. The very incentive for exploring market segmentation is to gain advantage—to seek some basis for customer preference—against the array of other competitors and their offerings in a particular market. If one plays only with customer characteristics and product features, he may arrive at the notion of some optimum product for an average customer, in effect, a recipe for reducing his product to commodity status, hence the very opposite of market segmentation, which implies product differentiation. But if he goes to the opposite extreme and tries to equal or surpass the total array of differing products offered by all competitors to all segments of his market, he courts the usual fate of me-too-ism, while suffering impossibly mounting marketing costs. Hence he must seek to identify those offerings which most appeal to some desirable segment of the total market and simultaneously express those capabilities in which he is strongest. The problem of choice here is analogous with that of the boy who must seek distinction from a brother who excels him athletically and another who excels him academically: what talent can he develop which, though different, will seem equivalent in the eyes of those whose approval he seeks? To be all things to all people, to excel in every virtue, is impossible; to be average in all means indistinguishability. Achieving only trivial distinctiveness is a barely veiled form of imitation, although it can immensely add to promotional expense in an industry. Hence the evolution of a criterion for selecting which customer segments and matching product distinctions to pursue must come from and be disciplined by correct identification of the real strengths and weaknesses of the company itself, as compared with other competitors in its market.

Companies, like individuals, sometimes involuntarily suffer crises of identity, as when merged with other companies. A company embarking upon market segmentation as a competitive strategy is deliberately precipitating a crisis of identity. In place of identity, however, which seems to apply only to the maker of a product rather than to a triple set of interrelations, I believe the concept of theme is more applicable and explanatory of the common element which has to be discovered or invented to match customer characteristic with product feature with company capability. The so-called total marketing approach in its sophisticated form seems finally to come forth with such recognizable themes. The theme of *ease of use* of essentially highly technical equipment has served Kodak for generations and recurs in numerous notable expressions—from the Brownie to the Instamatic, from the ubiquitous yellow box to the universally recognizable name itself. It illustrates how versatile in its manifestations a theme can be.

But just as product innovation can be trivialized through pointless small variations which make no real contribution to anyone, the concept of theme can be trivialized also, and in fact is, whenever some advertising agency tries to adorn an advertiser with a superficial image that has no real structural relationship to customer segments, competitive constellation, or company capabilities.

The concept of theme is useful in teaching marketing and market segmentation to managers whose experience has been in more exact fields. It helps to avoid the mental blocks that arise when segmentation is grasped as a series of pigeonholes in which various kinds of customers are filed for separate treatment, whereas the manager is eager for all the sales he can get from any source whatever, and finds it hard enough to devise one marketing strategy without having to devise many. To return to our main example, the television receiver market, the theme of reliability can be applied by one manufacturer to all the models in his line and throughout all the functions of marketing in his total marketing program. But the same manufacturer could hardly pursue simultaneously with equal thoroughness and equal success such contrasting themes as modern and traditional cabinetry, portability, technical innovation, and retail convenience, although he may keep pace with the industry average in these respects. Market segmentation does not deal with water-tight compartments, but with emphases sufficiently simple and distinctive to win notice and preference among customers to whom they are important, without alienating customers by being deficient in the other virtues which they more or less take for granted.

In terms of demographic and other statistical dimensions by which customers and products may be differentiated, the possibilities for market segmentation are troublesomely infinite. But when the problem of choosing a theme to emphasize is disciplined by attempting to match customers, competitors, and capabilities, these troubles are usually reduced to very few choices that are actually open to a particular firm—though hopefully at least one. The real difficulties of choice are not statistical but spiritual—the anguish of facing up to the fact that if a company is going to move in one direction, it must forego moving in all the others. Such a decision comes especially hard in diversified companies, yet some diversified companies have achieved real synergy through this discipline.

Once this clarifying commitment has been made, its effect on everyone in the organization is to release spontaneous ingenuity in its implementation. A good theme stimulates numberless applications and suggestions, furnishes a guide in numberless subordinate decisions, and eases numberless chores of communication, both inside and outside.

Not only does a positive theme help to mobilize an organization in pursuit of its marketing objectives and heighten their satisfaction, but it wins respect from competitors, even while strengthening and securing its position against them. Spirit is harder to imitate than matter; hardware is easy to copy, but the spirit of a whole organization is not. The competitor who wishes to emulate the success of a competitor's dominant theme must, instead of echoing it, come up with an equivalent theme that uniquely fits himself to his situation, that matches his own three C's.

When my wife was forced to listen to the draft of this paper, her first reaction was that there is much more to marketing than she had previously realized. But there is bound to be more than she or we realize even now. Imagine, for example, how much thicker the atmosphere would get if we tried to push onward into the problems of market segmentation faced by such diversified companies as General Electric which sells many products under mainly a single brand, General Motors which sells mainly one product under several brands, and General Foods which sells many products under many brands but now seems bent on making the customer aware of the identity of the maker. To add General Mills to this list might also be instructive, if we recall its brief effort to diversify by getting into the electric iron market. There are limits to diversification, at least in consumer markets which are set not only by internal considerations of manageability but externally by the market itself.

We did promise to come back before closing to that matter of competition between the retail sphere and the manufacturing sphere, as an example of market segmentation along radically different axes. It was partly a matter of convenience to set this question aside and partly a matter of conviction. One observes that retailers, regardless of size, seem to want to sell what their customers want to buy. If these customers show no very pronounced preferences among the offerings of various manufacturers, it is probably because there is no very pronounced basis for preference among the competing products. And when this is so, the manufacturers of these more or less indistinguishable commodities are most vulnerable to the substitution of store brands for manufacturer brands. Retailers can compete with retailers in the sale of commodities, by offering store values instead of product values; manufacturers cannot. But when a real basis for product preference exists, the preferred brands either show up on the retailer's shelves, or the retailer is forced to forego substantial business to his competitors who will stock the preferred products. A&P is not about to discontinue Campbell's soup or Heinz ketchup or Jello or other items of this character.

Competition is far from dead among retailers. And as long as competition among retailers exists, manufacturer brands which offer distinctive values to customers will find their way to those customers, if not through one channel, then through another. In a competitive society, the customer will not be denied his choice between less satisfaction and more.

Hence the problem of the manufacturer in confronting the rise of private branding is only in part a task of confronting changes in his environment. The other half of the task is to confront himself and his need for continuous learning and development of his own distinctive capabilities. It is the birthright of the manufacturer to determine the character of his product.

Nowadays we have the phenomenon of the publisher who dreams up an idea for a book and then hires someone to write it. Such offerings by publishers, however, are so poorly received by critics and readers that they have become known as non-books. In the same sense, we might speak of products which no longer portray the identity of their makers as non-products. But the consuming public will always remain more responsive to the author than to the publisher—to the manufacturer than to the middleman—if only the maker will put himself into his product.

4.

A New Orientation for Plotting Marketing Strategy

Lee Adler

Since World War II ever intensifying competition and the need for profits have prompted alert companies to forge a number of new and productive marketing strategies, concepts, and tools. Unfortunately, however, there are signs that a grave illness affects many managements, preventing their effective use of these modern marketing instruments. Among the symptoms are:

1. A tendency to engage in bloody, knock-down-drag-out fights with entrenched competitors. Examples abound, especially in the packaged goods industries.
2. Haphazard or sophomoric application of theoretically sound marketing strategies—market segmentation, selection of companies for merger or acquisition and, above all, product differentiation. Products without truly demonstrable points of difference meaningful to the consumer are legion. Ask any advertising agency copywriter.
3. Devoted marriage to an existing business pattern despite evidence that it is in a declining phase. In the beauty aids business, for example, a famous company jealously guarded its department and drug store trade while sales volume in their product categories relentlessly shifted to supermarkets. To make matters worse, this company persisted in holding onto its older customers, despite ample evidence that women under thirty-five are the heavy users and are also becoming a larger proportion of the entire female population.
4. Emotional attachment to products that have outlived their viability. Take the case of the packaged breakfast food. It had been the foundation item in the original line, and, though tastes in breakfast foods had shifted and new products had been successful competitors for years, its manufacturer,

like an indulgent parent, could find no fault with it. Or, when pressed to justify its continued existence, the company rationalized that the brand was a symbol for the company and that its old-time trade was still loyal to it.

5. A passion for the cachet conferred by volume without reckoning the cost of attaining that volume. This bit of irrationality leads to a drive for volume for the sake of volume, rather than volume at a profit.

6. Failure to consider alternate routes to profitable volume. Thus, some companies continue to regard the United States as their sole territory while their peers are also vigorously expanding abroad where product potentials are easier to tap. Similarly, some marketers maintain safe advertising-to-sales ratios in fields where advertising makes a powerful contribution to total sales effect. In the meantime, their rivals have learned not to regard advertising as a cost, an inhibiting, negative viewpoint, but rather as an investment that can produce fabulous returns.

MARKETING VISION

What is the nature of this illness that so inhibits creative marketing effort? Levitt called it "marketing myopia."[1] He argued that failure to define a business broadly enough leads to premature senescence. Levitt noted four conditions which tend to foster decay in the midst of apparent bounty: reliance on population growth, confidence in the infallibility of one's current product, reliance on the cost efficiencies of mass production, and "preoccupation with products that lend themselves to carefully controlled scientific experimentation, improvement, and manufacturing cost reduction."[2]

Several other considerations that seem also to interfere with the achievement of marketing breakthroughs can be added to Levitt's discussion. The concern here is not so much with a whole industry as with the growth of individual companies, divisions, and brands.

Trapped in the Square

The problem is basically lack of vision and self-imposed limitations. There is no better analogy than to the nine-dot square, the familiar puzzle requiring the player to connect all nine dots arranged in the form of a square with no more than four lines, without lifting his pencil from the paper.

[1] Theodore Levitt, "Marketing Myopia," *Harvard Business Review,* XXXVIII (July–August, 1960), pp. 47–48.
[2] "Marketing Myopia," pp. 47–48.

Figure 4–1.
(Solution to puzzle on p. 66)

Most players don't succeed at first because, even without being told, they think that they have to remain within the square. It's only the bolder and more deeply reasoning who immediately realize that they must go outside the square in order to succeed.

Another factor responsible for this nearsightedness is the overdetailing of objectives. It used to be that if a man was asked what his business goal was, he would say, "to make money." More likely, he wouldn't even have been asked the question in the first place. A corporate manager today will give some fancy responses, such as:

> To implement the marketing concept
> To build my share of market by five percentage points by January, 1966
> To assure maximum use of our manpower, financial, and productive resources
> To widen our distribution to 90 per cent of all supermarkets
> To achieve an advertising penetration of 62 percent by the end of the campaign, and so on.

It is vital to have goals. A steady parade of marketing experts are calling for businesses to lay down both broad corporate and divisional goals, and specific marketing objectives. But we should be aware of a danger inherent in setting objectives. To be workable a given objective must be concretized and aimed at a single target. While doing so, however, one tends to block his broader thinking. Thus, the objective of building Brand X's share of market from 18 per cent to 23 per cent within two years leaves out such other considerations as, "Maybe we should launch another brand in this market," or, "Would franchising help broaden our market, lessen our competitive burden?" or, "Our technical people say they can obsolete our brand and those of our competitors with a radically new idea. Should we market the idea, or suppress it for the time being?"

Although the process of detailing objectives is necessary, it tends at the same time to scatter objectives. The setting of numerous, detailed targets for an existing business bearing on advertising, sales management, sales channels, expense control, and so on, may not add up to an integrated system of goals leading to market breakthroughs. On the contrary, this process may perpetuate the status quo because it obscures the need for fresh approaches, because its benchmarks and building blocks all emerge from the existing situation, and because it administratively entangles marketers in today to the neglect of tomorrow.

Two other factors abet this tendency to blind business vision. The first is ~~pseudo~~ decentralization. Not decentralization itself, to be sure, for when unit managers are given the freedom and responsibility to operate, the spirit of innovation often flourishes. The trouble is with those managements who cannot keep their hands off the divisional steering wheels and insist that profit responsibility belongs to headquarters. When only lip service is paid to decentralization, both practical and psychological obstacles are raised to the free-thinking of divisional personnel.

The brand manager system, with all its merits, is an even worse offender in this respect. While acceptable in concept, in practice brand managers are often turned into production schedulers, inventory controllers, budget preparers, sales analysts, and expense control clerks. They are so busy with the mechanical details of their jobs that they have no time for its vital aspects—market planning, improving the creativity of their advertising, expanding their brands' domains. The growing roles of marketing consultants, package designers, sales promotion creators, and other outside business services testify to the sterility inside.

This problem is a serious one. It leads to such ill-advised actions as discordant mergers, copy-cat brands, and futile attacks on well-fortified positions. Or it leads to no action at all. The results are failure to grow and to manage change, and increased vulnerability to competition. This is a useless waste when powerful and proven marketing weapons are waiting to be deployed.

Breaking Out of the Square

To take advantage of opportunities, management needs a vision of the business.[3] This vision, McKay observes, should be spelled out in terms of (a) customers and markets, (b) products and services, (c) technology and production capability, and (d) corporate personality and character—all geared to the satisfaction of customer wants and needs.

Development of this vision enables a company or a division to apply

---

[3] Edward S. McKay, "The Marketing and Advertising Role in Managing Change," in an address before the 54th meeting of the Association of National Advertisers, November 10–13, 1963.

marketing strategies in an orderly, consistent manner. It helps to plan and program marketing innovation. In a more detailed fashion, it guides the selection and use of each marketing weapon geared to the desired direction, pace, and timing of growth.

Put another way, this vision helps marketers break out of their nine-dot squares. It arises from a wholistic view of a business' *raison d'etre*, a return to fundamentals. And of all the fundamentals, the most basic is: a company is in business to make money by providing consumer gratifications. Within reason, it does not matter how the company makes money. No law says it must make money with Brand A if Brand A simply no longer has the capacity to make money. Brand B might do a much better job. Or, similarly, if Market C is exhausted, Market D may be wide open.

The vision necessary to grasp this fundamental reality has two dimensions. For breadth, according to Levitt,[4] industries should define their spheres broadly enough to assure continuing growth and to head off competition or, at least, to be fully prepared to deal with it. Thus, it is not sufficient for an oil company to conceive of itself as being in the oil business; it is far healthier if it regards itself as being in the fuel or energy business, or in the even broader petrochemicals business.

The second dimension is depth. Every company has an essential being, a core, the commercial equivalent of a soul. Deep-thinking managers learn to look for, identify, and capitalize on the essence of a company—that which gives it vitality and makes the crucial difference in dealing with rivals and making money.

Consider the Coca-Cola Company. It can be described as a manufacturer of a popular soft drink, or, more correctly, as the manufacturer of syrup used as the base of the soft drink. Or, more recently, as the parent of a whole line of soft drinks—Coca-Cola, Tab, Sprite, Fanta. But a definition of the Coca-Cola Company as a remarkable distribution network may be much closer to the truth. The company's great leader, Robert Woodruff, laid down the policy in the 1920's of putting Coca-Cola "within an arm's length of desire." Today, Coca-Cola is distributed in 1,600,000 outlets, more than any other product in the world. Every kind of retail outlet carries the brand. It is put into these outlets by over 1,000 local franchised bottlers in the United States. Because these bottlers, guided by the parent company, have created this extraordinary distribution, it is easier for the company to market new brands. So, with increasing competition on all sides, the heart of this success is the means of achieving widespread availability.

Procter & Gamble Company furnishes another good example. Sure, P&G manufactures soaps and detergents. To define their business in broader terms, as they keep adding products by internal development and by acquisition, P&G is in the household cleaner business, the food business, the health and

---

[4] "Marketing Myopia," pp. 52–53.

beauty aids business, or in short, in the personal and household products business—a broad enough definition to keep even P&G going for years.

But P&G can also be viewed as a marketing management philosophy embodying such vital elements as careful market testing, the assurance of genuinely good products, a high order of merchandising skill, and well-supported brand managers. The application of these elements in a determined and unified manner brings marketing success whether the product is a detergent, a dentifrice, or a decaffeinated coffee.

Still another example is the Alberto-Culver Company, a manufacturer of hair preparations that has lately been broadening its line to include a headache remedy, a first-aid item, a dentifrice, and so on. Its president, Leonard Lavin has said: "If you judge us to be successful (the company went from sales of $400,000 in 1956 to over $80,000,000 in 1963), chalk it up to innovator products, excellent packaging, premium pricing, hard-driving promotions, and heavy TV backing of effective creative commercials."[5] Many marketers have innovator products and excellent packaging, and the rest, but not many have the kind of heavy TV backing Lavin refers to. For in my opinion the essence of Alberto-Culver is really a courageous media investment policy that results in their profit rate outdistancing their sales rate. The company has said as much: "We have found an astounding fact: the more we invest in advertising, the less our advertising-to-sales ratio becomes. The sales for our established brands are growing at a greater rate than their substantial advertising budgets. Where a million dollars in advertising used to buy for us $1 to $2 million in gross sales, for our leading brands it now buys added millions of dollars worth of sales, and the ceiling hasn't been reached. Our aggressiveness continues with the added incentive that once we get a brand off the ground, its ability to grow and return profits to the company accelerates at a much greater rate than the increased advertising expenditure."[6]

A company's definition of itself is at the root of marketing success. Only the company with unobstructed vision can use the marketing weapons with maximum effect.

MARKETING WEAPONS SYSTEM

There are an even dozen marketing weapons and together they make up a weapons system. They have been isolated by a qualitative analysis of the operations of many firms, mainly in the consumer nondurable packaged goods industries. Utilization of one or more of these marketing weapons was found to run as a common thread through the marketing practices of the successful companies in these fields. But these weapons were not used in a

[5] Address before the New York Marketing Executives Association, April, 1962.
[6] John S. Lynch, "Turmoil in Toiletries—the Rise of Alberto-Culver," *Food Business* (November, 1962), p. 19.

vacuum. Rather, an underlying philosophy gave them power and impact. By contrast, haphazard utilization of these weapons consistently characterized the less able marketers.

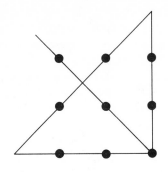

Figure 4–2.
(*Solution to puzzle on p. 62*)

The End Run

The purpose of the end run is to avoid unnecessary, costly, time-consuming, or otherwise undesirable battles with entrenched competitors or other nearly insuperable obstacles. The objective is to create the arena rather than uncritically accept one made by the competitor. The following examples show how to do battle in one's own arena.

Those tobacco companies that are outflanking the serious problem of government regulation, public outcries and negative publicity revolving around the health issue are practicing the end run. A number of possible end runs are available to the industry. Defining oneself as being in the tobacco business, not just the cigarette business, leads to more vigorous activity in cigars and pipe tobaccos, which do not have the serious problem of cigarettes. The self-definition can refer to a technology-based firm using the tobacco plant as raw material. R. J. Reynolds' development of a fertilizer from tobacco stems is a step in this direction. The next step is to become a chemical processor of other vegetable matter.

Increased overseas marketing to escape or soften the strictures of the U.S. scene is another illustration. So, too, is a tobacco company's viewing itself as an expert in mass distribution rather than as a cigarette manufacturer. Philip Morris exemplifies this approach, as shown in their acquisition of Burma-Vita Company, American Safety Razor Company, and Clark Chewing Gum Company, all different products that rely on the same channels of distribution.

During the late 1940's and early 1950's, Lever Brothers Company made a number of unsuccessful assaults on P&G's solid position in the heavy-duty detergent field.[7] Finally, in 1957, Lever acquired "all" from Monsanto for the automatic washing machine market. In this way, Lever succeeded in out-flanking P&G in a high-volume segment of the laundry market.

Not to be outdone, P&G counter-attacked "all" frontally with Dash. This tactic worked for a time, but by 1961 "all" had regained its lost ground. Then P&G launched its own end run—Salvo low-sudsing tablets. What P&G could not accomplish directly, it accomplished indirectly. Between Dash and Salvo P&G won half the low-sudsing business in several years. By 1963, P&G was well ahead of Lever with a 16.1 per cent share of the heavy-duty soap and detergent market with two brands as against only 12.7 per cent for Lever's "all" and Vim low-sudser combined.[8]

Thus, acceptance of the boundaries of a marketing battlefront, or of the weapons to be used, does not nurture the development of competitive advantage. But a penetrating vision of one's business strips away these restrictive definitions and leads to refreshing new horizons.

Domination

The principle of domination calls for sufficient concentration of effort, funds, manpower, or creativity (within the limits of one's resources) in one area to "own" that area rather than to spread oneself thin over a wider sector. Application of this principle calls for realistic self-perception. For example, one manufacturer of deodorants recognized that in his field, crowded with multimillion dollar advertisers relying heavily on television, his own modest resources would be insufficient. He therefore elected to use a medium then largely ignored by his competitors—radio. Put into radio, his budget was large enough to make him the dominant deodorant brand for radio listeners. This advertiser understood that it was not absolute dollars only that mattered but *share* of dollars too. Moreover, he saw that domination brought not only extra dollar volume but important psychological advantages in leadership and in the surety of a solid position, as well as a good jumping-off point to seize another segment of the business.

Market Segmentation

The concept of market segmentation is well known, and need not be discussed here. Its purpose is to identify and concentrate on fractions of a total market capable of yielding a disproportionate volume and profit. The key point of focus is on the skill with which factors that truly divide markets are identified, vital target groups are defined, marketing programs are tailored

---

[7] Spencer Klaw, "The Soap Wars: A Strategic Analysis," *Fortune,* LXVII (June, 1963), p. 123 ff.
[8] *The Gallagher Report,* XII (May 13, 1964).

according to their motivations and needs, and segments harmonizing with a company's own talents are selected.

Some companies in the cosmetic industry, for instance, have developed an almost uncanny skill at grasping the psychology of beauty-conscious American women. The essence of their business is selling beauty rather than certain chemicals made up into cosmetics. "In the factory, we make cosmetics," says Charles Revson, president of Revlon, "in the drugstore, we sell hope." The subtle sale of hope has led to a profitable segmentation of the total cosmetics market.

Other companies have developed a flair for segmenting markets on a price basis. The heart of their business is efficient, low-cost production combined with low-margin marketing effort. Price segmentation also works at the other end of the scale—some firms have the taste for opulence that leads to success in "class" selling.

In this manner, insight into the heart of a business leads to use of the principle of market segmentation in ways that are uniquely right for the individual marketer. Market segmentation is no longer necessarily an unenlightening slicing of populations in terms of demographic and socioeconomic characteristics. It becomes a creative approach to markets that leads to real benefits.[9]

Consider what manufacturers of makeup and skin care preparations have achieved. Once upon a time there was a simple product called cold cream. Segmenting in terms of specialized consumer needs and desires, manner and occasion of use, age, motivation, and attitude, cold cream manufacturers now market foundation, cleansing, vanishing, nourishing, conditioning, hormone, astringent, lanolin, marrow, and wrinkle creams.

The vision of a business as a money-making operation also helps to secure concentration on key target groups, rather than dissipation of effort over a broad front. And so beauty aids companies zero in on young women, beer marketers direct their attention to young men, laxative and tonic producers to older, lower-income people, soft drink bottlers to teen-agers, floor wax makers to suburban housewives, cigarette manufacturers to men, and so on through all the heavy users in each field.

At the same time, this vision of a business reduces the dangers of the misuse of market segmentation. Three misapplications frequently observed are described below.

Pursuing the Wrong Segment.   One Western brewer, having won a good hold on the heart of the beer market—younger, lower-income male drinkers —aspired to win the favor of a more elegant, upper-income audience. Not

[9] Daniel Yankelovich, "New Criteria for Market Segmentation," *Harvard Business Review,* XLII (March–April, 1964), pp. 83–90.

only did his effort fail, but he also managed to alienate his original market. Contrast this with the case of other brewers who appeal to different social class and price segments with different brands. Thus, Anheuser Busch now offers two premium beers, Michelob and Budweiser, and one popular-priced brand, Busch Bavarian. Schlitz has two regional popular-priced brands, Burgemeister and Old Milwaukee, along with its premium-priced Schlitz.

Oversegmentation. This phenomenon manifests itself in more specialization than the market requires. The deodorant industry is a case in point. Until the mid-1950's, women were the heart of the market and all products were named and promoted with feminine appeal uppermost. Men used womens products. By the early 1960's the female market was saturated and much had been done to evolve brands with a masculine appeal. Gillette's Right Guard was a prominent example. Then Gillette discovered that other family members were using Right Guard, too. Now the brand is being promoted for the whole family. Since men are willing to use "women's" deodorants and women are willing to use "men's" deodorants, one wonders whether segmentation by sex may not be overdone.

Overconcentration. Sometimes companies, indeed whole industries, learn to concentrate too well. The brewery industry, for instance, has concentrated for many years on young men and justifiably so, in light of their heavy usage. But this has led to a sameness in advertising themes and subjects, media, and sports associations, and to near maximum penetration of the young male market at the expense of other segments worthy of further development. This may help to explain a static per capita level; annual gallons consumed per person were 18.0 in 1946, 16.8 in 1952, and 15.1 in 1962.

In the malt beverage field additional cultivation could include many other segments. The segments suggested in Table 4–1 are necessarily an incomplete catalog and do not purport to be a set of recommendations to brewers. Rather, they are cited to demonstrate the potential in building new segments where competition is low-key or nonexistent, while not neglecting established segments.

Soundly used, with guidance provided by a vision of the business, market segmentation is a creator of new markets rather than a constrictor of established markets.

Market Stretching

New markets are created in many different fashions; the one a business uses depends on how it identifies itself. For example, it is becoming more common for industrial chemical producers to "go consumer." This can

Table 4–1

Possible Malt Beverage Market Segments for Additional Cultivation

Upper social class, "snob" appeal	via	Ale, imported beers
"With-meals" market	via	Advertising and store promotions depicting with-meals use
With snack foods	via	Promotion such as Coca-Cola's "Nothing beatsa Coke n' Pizza," or "Coke n' Burger" promotions
Women	via	Feminine appeal brand name, small package sizes, recipes using beer, as the wine industry does*
Those who prefer strong beers	via	Malt liquor, some imports
Draught beer lovers	via	Bottled draught beer (for example, Michelob)

* These measures would be introduced to foster greater consumption of beer by women, in addition to the fact that they buy most of the beer in grocery stores (now over 40 per cent of total beer volume—and growing steadily) as their families' purchasing agents.

only come about from a redefinition of a business. Dow Chemical Company, for example, has broadened its horizon with plastic food wraps, oven cleaners, even Christmas tree decorative materials, among a long list of consumer products. A number of makers of hair care products have gone consumer another way; specialists serving the beauty salon trade, Helene Curtis, Rayette, Ozon, Breck, Clairol, and VO-5, have all made their mark by selling direct to the consumer.

Paradoxically, market segmentation can lead to the broadening of markets. Zealous specialization evokes a countervailing force: a strong desire is born for all-purpose products sold to and used by practically everyone. The detergent industry is ripe for one; now there are specialized products for heavy-duty laundering, fine laundering, manual dishwashing, automatic dishwashing, cleaning floors, kitchens, bathrooms, and so on. As a result, uses for even the most general cleansers are narrowing. The floor wax business is also setting the stage for an all-purpose product with its profusion of pastes, waxes, polishes—including a product that removes the other products. In this context, the recent burgeoning of one-step cleaning and waxing in floor waxes and one-step dusting, waxing, and polishing in furniture waxes may be the industry's way of broadening user segments. Thus, the sharp strategist recognizes when the time has come to throw the gears into reverse and use the tool of product or line simplification.

Multibrand Entries

Underlying this marketing strategy is a basic premise: two brands tend to capture more of the available sales than one. Marketers with a broad conception of their business have learned to overcome their passionate devotion to one brand. Their vision grants them detachment; they can see that their role in life is not to nurture their brand regardless of cost, but rather to maximize profitable volume. They can then also see that there will always be a few contrary consumers who will persist in buying a rival brand. So they reason that the other brand might just as well be theirs too. They know there may be some inroads into sales of the original brand, but that there will be a *net* gain in volume with two brands instead of one.

Many packaged goods industries provide examples of the application of this strategy. In deodorants, Bristol-Myers has four brands and seven product variants: Ban (roll-on and cream), Mum (including Mum Mist and Mum Mist for Men), Trig, and Discreet. In soaps and detergents and tobacco products, examples of this strategy abound. Alberto-Culver has enunciated multibrand competition as a policy, and has begun to send second brands into markets in which they already compete.

Perhaps the shrewdest extension of this strategy, particularly applicable when a company is first with a truly new product and can realistically anticipate competition, is to lock out rivals by bringing out multiple offerings at the time of product introduction. One food manufacturer used this approach recently in a product category segmented by flavor. Similarly, a housewares producer applied this strategy to preempt the key position with different-featured models in a market that segments by price. The cigarette field also furnishes current examples: Philip Morris brought out no less than four new charcoal filter brands virtually at the same time—Philip Morris Multifilter, Galaxy, and Saratoga; and Liggett & Myers introduced two—Lark and Keith.

Brand Extension

Marketers' emotional attachment to products often includes the brand name. With brand extension strategy, too, a wholesome and realistic view of the business precludes the imposition of artificial and unnecessary limitations on the use of brand names. There is nothing holy about a brand name and if extension of it can bring about marketing good, while not discrediting or cheapening the original product or confusing the consumer, then extension can serve as a potent instrument. Thus, Dristan, first a decongestant tablet, is now a nasal spray, cough formula, and medicated room vaporizer. Lustre Creme, in addition to ignoring the literal meaning of its name and coming out as a liquid and a lotion shampoo, is now also a rinse and conditioner and a spray set. Ivory, as homey and hoary a brand name as any, is as vital as ever in Ivory Flakes, Ivory Snow, Ivory Soap, and Ivory Liquid.

Product Change

As in the case of market segmentation, the crucial importance of product innovation is so clear and so well understood that it requires no description here. Product change lies at the heart of many market strategies and is capable of application in a marvelous variety of ways. The essential prerequisite is a conception of a business that permits free scope to product change and, indeed, urgently demands ceaseless product change. The exact form and pattern of change will be conditioned by the nature and goals of the individual business.

End run candidates—and the concomitant avoidance of me-tooism—are evident in the development of essentially new products such as cold water detergents, hair sprays, electric toothbrushes, low-calorie foods and beverages, sustained-release cold tablets.

Flank attacks are also possible by what might be called extra benefit innovation, as contrasted with straight innovation. The typical example is in the use of an additive, for instance, lanolin, hexachlorophene, fluoride. The less typical example is the double-duty product; shampoos may also provide a color rinse, such as Helena Rubinstein's Wash 'n' Tint.

Product differentiation is the usual means of seeking a demonstrable point of difference. Taste, packaging size, and ways of using established products are the customary variations, as in orange-flavored analgesics for children, spray antiseptics, aerosol oven cleaners, liquid aspirin, mint-flavored laxatives, roll-on lipsticks, powdered deodorants, and travel-size packages of dentifrice.

To outflank competition or to carve out new segments, the ultimate in products must come from a policy of deliberate obsolescence. But this policy is applied reluctantly, and as a result, change is forced on companies by bold innovators, or by new competitors who have no vested interest to preserve. P&G changed the detergent industry with the introduction of Tide synthetic detergent in 1946, and thus widened the future of its own soap brands. Armstrong Cork Company entered the consumer field with a one-step floor cleaner and wax and had no compunctions about upsetting the established order. Gillette joined the stainless steel razor blade fray to protect its enormous franchise; because it was less than enthusiastic about it, the firm also demonstrated the high cost of being late.[10]

Overseas Expansion

Not only can the definition of a business be product-based, saying, "We are in the railroad industry, not the transportation industry," or conceptual in foundation, believing, "The strength of our company lies in the skillful use of media of communication rather than in our experience in this or that segment of the food trade," but the definition may also be geographic. Therefore, the vision of a business can also be liberating in this respect. Most American companies have, until recently, regarded themselves as serving the American market. The foreign market was truly foreign to their thoughts.

[10] Walter Guzzardi, Jr., "Gillette Faces the Stainless Steel Dragon," *Fortune,* LXVIII (July, 1963), p. 159 ff.

In contrast, companies that have the vision to see both the vast potential of the foreign market for basic goods, and their own role in supplying it, have profited enormously. In the case of Colgate-Palmolive, for instance, while its headquarters happens to be in New York, its spirit is global. This self-image is reflected in its sales and profit story. Faced with savage competition in most of its markets in the United States, Colgate has pushed its business abroad. Thus, its 1952 foreign sales were 36 per cent of its worldwide total; by 1962 this ratio had risen to 51 per cent. But the profit contribution from abroad soared from 45 per cent of total earnings in 1952 to a whopping 89 per cent in 1962. True, Colgate's overseas divisions do not have to absorb any of the costs of product development and testing, all which are borne by the U.S. division. Nonetheless, the disproportionate overseas profit role is eloquent testimony to the benefit of this liberating vision. Another kind of corporate vision is working here in providing the extra margin necessary to overcome cost differentials, tariff barriers, and so forth, permitting overseas business to become feasible.

Investment Philosophy

The packaged goods world provides a sad, almost daily spectacle of products being sent into ferociously competitive markets by their loving or niggardly, but niggardly parents. To prevent nearly certain slaughter, products, especially new ones, require continued substantial support. But again it takes a certain vision to see beyond the tendency to hold down on spending and seek as rapid as possible a return on investment. The vision includes a financial aspect in seeing the company as investor, not spender, and a temporal aspect in realizing that the company is going to be around for a long time and, if necessary, can wait for its money. It is surely going to have to wait longer as marketing rivalries intensify and greater resources are brought to bear. In the packaged goods field, a realistic vision is frequently identified by three policies:

Heavy weight in advertising, sales promotion, merchandising, and distribution-building, particularly in the introductory phase

Substantial share of weight in whatever media and segment(s) one competes in

Prolongation of payout periods from a "traditional" three years to four or five years, where necessary, while maintaining a firm hold on future profit by sharp sales forecasting and margin control. (Obviously, this can't be done in fields where product life cycles are growing shorter.)

To challenge so well-established a brand as Listerine is a formidable undertaking. When Johnson & Johnson entered the market with Micrin, their investment in traceable advertising expenditures alone gave evidence of their awareness of these realities of the marketplace. Similarly, a deodorant brand of fairly recent vintage bought position by both heavy weight and deferment of profit taking to four and one-half years after launching. As the president of Alberto-Culver has observed, very heavy advertising appropriations build volume and market share to the point where, in that rarefied atmosphere where few marketers venture, the return becomes disproportionately higher than dollars invested, and the advertising-to-sales ratio actually drops.[11]

Distribution Breakthroughs

Almost as limiting in its effect on the vision of a business is being wedded to a given distribution system. It is also almost as frequent a manifestation of marketing backwardness because the forces of inertia, tradition, and myopia all exert their pull in the same direction. Helene Curtis' acquiring Studio Girl and Bristol-Myers' acquiring Luzier to tap the rich house-to-house sales channel are positive examples. So, too, is Chock Full o' Nuts' signing up local licensees for door-to-door selling. Cosmetics lines nationally sold to main-line department stores, and Class A drug stores that have now extended distribution to grocery stores are also cases in point. (Indeed, one must credit supermarkets more than manufacturers for breaking out of the traditional mold of being only food outlets and creating a vast enterprise in health and beauty aids and in packaged household necessities. Moreover, one must credit retailers in general for the positive effects of scrambled distribution in all manner of goods.) If a national beer brand were to franchise local brewers, taking a leaf from the book of the parent, soft drink companies, they would be acting on this principle.

Merger and Acquisition

The growing tide of mergers and acquisitions testifies to industry's awareness of the potential benefits of corporate marriages. Yet many curious matings raise questions about the vision of the corporations initiating them. This is not to argue against a most unlikely merger of a business whose vision is management talent for buying depressed situations and upgrading them or a business whose core is financial wizardry. But these are special circumstances. For most companies, mergers are a serious drain on manpower, time, and resources. Blind worship at the shrine of the Great God Diversification may hinder or arrest opportunities to blend the benefits of diversification with logical extensions of a business. Sound mergers take sound vision.

Chiclets are quite different from Bromo-Seltzer, Richard Hudnut Shampoo, Anahist, and DuBarry cosmetics, yet the purchase of American Chicle by

---

[11] Leonard Lavin, in an address before the New York Marketing Executives Association, April, 1962; and Alberto-Culver's 1963 annual report, p. 4.

Warner-Lambert marries dissimilar products with similar characteristics of packaging, rapid purchase-repurchase cycles, channels of merchandising, and advertising response. By the same principles, the subsequent merger of American Chicle with Smith Brothers cough drops is a further logical development of the Warner-Lambert vision.

The merger of Coca-Cola with Minute Maid and Duncan Coffee simultaneously with soft drink line extensions in different flavor categories with Sprite and Fanta and the low-calorie category with Tab represents the application of a two-fold vision of the business. One aspect of the vision has already been noted—an extraordinary distribution skill that Coca-Cola management can contribute to the acquired companies, though outside the bottler network, of course. The second is the definition of the firm as being not in the carbonated cola beverage field, nor even in the soft drink field, but rather in the refreshment business, or indeed, in the beverage business. To these instances of horizontal mergers can be added vertical ones, such as cosmetics companies acquiring chemical interests or, more frequently, chemical and ethical drug producers entering cosmetic and proprietary drug fields. Philip Morris has effected mergers in both directions—horizontally with shaving cream and razor blades and vertically with Milprint.

Moreover, creativity and imagination in realizing a business' vision can lead to interesting symbiotic relationships. (Here I borrow the concept of symbiosis from biology where it refers to the living together of two dissimilar organisms in a mutually beneficial relationship.) International Breweries, for example, has undertaken to manufacture the product requirements of a small Cleveland brewer at one of International's own plants. The added volume will help amortize a goodly share of plant overhead and, at the same time, the Cleveland firm will become the distributor in that market for International's brands. The two companies remain independent while enjoying the benefits of a merger.

Iconoclasm

One of the hallmarks of practical application of a creative vision of a business is a willingness to depart from customary ways, to seek unorthodox solutions to orthodox problems. This iconoclasm runs as a common thread through the success stories of the period after World War II. Icon-breaking is necessary even in applying the most sophisticated marketing strategies. For example, it is by now axiomatic to concentrate on heavy users; yet this is not always the wisest strategy. In the wine industry, for example, a careful analysis of the characteristics of heavy users reveals a diverse assemblage of consumer segments. Marketing to each segment requires different tools and can be quite costly. Moreover, many confirmed users require only reminder advertising, but it is well worth promoting to the occasional user who can be cultivated to a greater frequency of usage.

To illustrate further, it is customary for national marketers to have advertising agencies serving them nationally. But Carling Breweries chose a quite different method to help bring the company from forty-ninth place to fourth place between 1950 and 1960. Reasoning that much of the beer business is local in character and competition, and that local advertising agencies are best suited to understand local circumstances, Carling worked up a network of eight local agencies, each of which serves the brewer in one of its marketing divisions, and is coordinated by the agency in the home city.

The advantages of marketing vision should be apparent. It is a mind-opening, horizon-stretching way of business life, keeping industries in the growth camp or converting them into growth situations. It fosters industry leadership, enabling companies to bypass competition and to manage change rather than to be managed by it. It helps decentralization to live up to its promise. Moreover, in providing a systematic framework for exploring new profit avenues, marketing vision is especially valuable in fields with built-in limitations. Some industries have trouble in new product development. Dentrifrice manufacturers, for example, despite many efforts to give tooth-paste companions in powder, liquid, and tablet forms, still find the paste in the collapsible tube owning the business. In their case, marketing vision found its practical expression in additives, including chlorophyll, antienzymes, hexachlorophene, and, most recently, the brilliantly successful fluoride development.

For another field, marketing vision might call for overseas expansion, diversification, or new distribution channels. But for each industry, for each company, for each division, and for each brand or line there is often one success factor that is more appropriate than any other. The utilization of these marketing weapons cannot be generalized. What works well for one business will not work for another; what works well for one set of competitive circumstances will not work for another. Also, what works well at one point in time will not work at another. On the other hand, in some situations, two or more strategies at work in a multidivision, multibrand company might present a most haphazard appearance and yet make sense for each unit and harmonize with over-all corporate goals. To exemplify this point, Table 4–2 shows the strategies at work over a recent five-year period for some of the components of one company. Some of these strategies can be developed within a brand management group; others, for example the acquisitions, have been worked out by top management.

It should be evident that these marketing strategies *interlock*. Segmenting a market helps one to dominate it. Product change is often an essential for segmentation. Brand extensions can lead to new distribution channels. And, in the final analysis, all other strategies are end runs, and all break with the rhythm and style of the past. It is the systematic yet bold imposition of a fresh image of a business that provides insurance against decay and a foundation for growth.

Table 4–2

Multibrand Deployment of Marketing Strategies

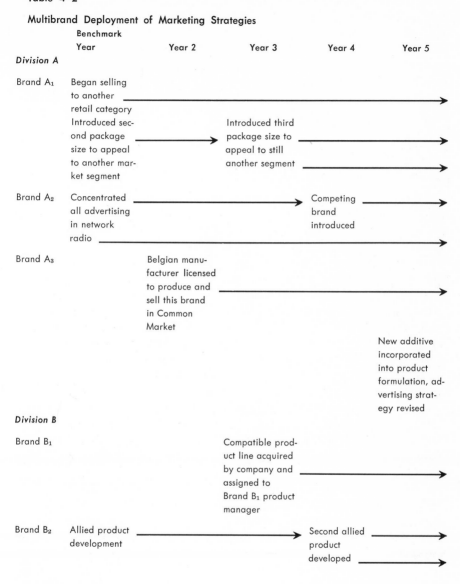

	Benchmark Year	Year 2	Year 3	Year 4	Year 5
Division A					
Brand A_1	Began selling to another retail category Introduced second package size to appeal to another market segment	→	Introduced third package size to appeal to still another segment	→ →	→
Brand A_2	Concentrated all advertising in network radio	→		Competing brand introduced →	→
Brand A_3		Belgian manufacturer licensed to produce and sell this brand in Common Market	→		New additive incorporated into product formulation, advertising strategy revised
Division B					
Brand B_1			Compatible product line acquired by company and assigned to Brand B_1 product manager	→	
Brand B_2	Allied product development	→		Second allied product developed →	→

5.

Applying the Strategy of Market Segmentation

Alan A. Roberts

Market segmentation is the strategy of dividing markets in order to conquer them. Its philosophy is "something for everybody," within practicable limits. As a defintion, this is less formal but more useful than those found in marketing textbooks.

Textbooks define a market segment as any subsection of a total market that is worth cultivating. They add that in order to implement a strategy of segmentation a firm must first identify the segment and then take marketing action based upon that identification. Unfortunately, bookish definitions like these do not cast much light upon the process whereby businessmen decide whether a segment worth cultivating truly exists. Moreover, they seldom give a basis for relating the single decision of whether or not to segment a market to any dynamic, over-all corporate strategy that implies continuity in this decision-making process.

It is well known that all companies more or less segment their markets. What we are interested in is this: Are the company's criteria for deciding whether a submarket is worth cultivating so general that the decision to segment is frequently made, or are they so specific that the company seldom moves in this direction? Looking at the same set of objective marketing facts, one firm may decide to segment progressively, while another firm may decide not to segment at all, depending on their relative enthusiasm for segmentation as general strategy behind their marketing approach. Moreover, marketing action, following the decision to segment, may take different forms.

AGGREGATION V. SEGMENTATION

Perhaps the best way to understand this concept and its implications is to consider simultaneously the approach and the rationale of each of these opposite strategies. The opposite of market segmentation could be called market aggregation, suggesting the policy of lumping together into one mass market many groups of buyers who might otherwise be marginally differentiated one from another into smaller submarkets.

The strategy of market aggregation is sometimes related to such considerations as cost of production, warehousing, and transporting. The idea here is that long production runs are more economical than short runs, that inventory costs may be minimized if fewer lines are offered, and so forth. Another set of reasons supporting market aggregation focuses upon measurements of the buying efficiency of promotional funds. Within certain dollar ranges, at least, the efficiency of promotional budgets may respond elastically to changes in size. That is, each dollar added to the promotional investment in a single product may result in a proportionately larger increase in promotional efficiency. The explanation of this lies in the basic per-thousand costs of advertising media. Media costs tend to follow this law: The larger and more general the medium, the smaller the cost per thousand; the more limited or specialized the medium, either geographically or by editorial or audience appeal, the greater the cost per thousand. The more that markets may be aggregated, the lower the cost per thousand in buying advertising to reach that mass market, at least within the range of certain promotional budgets.

For the major consumer advertisers, however, promotional budgets frequently pass the range of efficiency discussed above. The size and diversity of the mass-consumer markets require supplemental advertising investment in local and/or specialized audience media. The latter then become an important part of the company's total national advertising program. At this point, one rationale for the strategy of aggregation tends to disappear; indeed, national advertisers move toward segmentation strategy in proportion to their targeting of selective local and/or specialized markets.

The strategy of market segmentation suggests a continuous policy of looking for differences, geographical or otherwise, in the total market, and the continuous exploitation of these differences. Often they are quite marginal, and their exploitation may require imaginative thinking on merchandising and promotion. Thus, some of the finest examples of market segmentation entail really creative actions. These may be the creation of new buyer needs, or at least the crystallization of needs previously felt only vaguely or to a slight degree. The effective crystallization of such needs in the minds of some consumers invokes demand for a new specialized product where previously there was reasonable satisfaction with a more generalized product.

Segmentation may also be practiced in many facets of marketing other than the product mix—for example, the penetration of new markets for existing products through sales force specialization, or the greater diversification of distribution channels.

As a consistently practiced strategy, segmentation seems to be oriented toward high sales volume, more so than the opposite policy of aggregation. It is ordinarily demonstrable that total sales may be increased with a more diversified product line sold through more diversified channels. The operative consideration is, traditionally, whether the line can thus be expanded profitably. This in turn may lead to the weighing of average unit profits versus marginal unit profits. These are always changing relationships, but important secular trends seem to be altering the equation in favor of market segmentation as more generally advantageous strategy.

Some of these trends relate to simple demographic factors, which tend to make markets larger and more segmentable. Such factors include increased population, income, leisure time, home ownership, educational level, and so forth. A perhaps less obvious factor in increasing the acceptance of market segmentation as a corporate strategy has been the advance of technique in market research, which always seems to be finding better ways to identify consumers and their buying motivations.

Common Examples

All around us we can see the fruits of market segmentation as practiced by major national manufacturers of consumer goods. Taking the period just before World War II as our reference point, we find everywhere examples of companies that have followed a pattern of progressive segmentation of their markets. Remember when most cigarette smokers were users of only four brands, all standard size, soft-packaged, nonfilter, nonmentholated? Cigarettes are perhaps a noteworthy example, but they are surely not unique. Package foods, cosmetics, soaps, liquor, and automobiles are other obvious examples.

Some consumer product-line manufacturers have practiced segmentation so assiduously over so many years that they are now in danger of losing their corporate identity in the minds of consumers. Even the most confirmed segmenters acknowledge that the "family of products" effect can be beneficial. It is then that they turn to umbrella devices, like the Betty Crocker name and the spoon on the General Mills packages.

Few companies that have chosen the strategy of market segmentation, however, have reached such a point. For most would-be segmenters the immediate problem is how to diversify rather than unify their offerings. They tend to use corporate emphasis only for special purposes—on a temporary basis when introducing a product or at trade rather than at consumer promotional levels.

Management's widespread adoption of segmentation—made obvious by the postwar boom of new brands and sales outlets—must be recognized as a marketing strategy that takes account of more than just simple economic or demographic changes in American life. For example, as consumers and as businessmen, we are subject to a constantly increasing volume of advertising messages. So great is the total number of advertising messages with which we are daily bombarded that this fact alone tends to outmode one implication in the strategy of market aggregation. The marketer who formerly preferred to concentrate his promotion on a tightly limited product line had in the back of his mind that he could, perhaps, overwhelm his buying public with the sheer volume of his repeated advertising messages. This has become an impossibility in recent years.

More and more the successful advertiser has to depend on the uniqueness of his selling message in order to win consumer interest. And product differentiation, however marginal, is one of the more obvious ways of finding a unique selling message. Even the Coca-Cola Company, that steadfast proponent of market aggregation that has been in the mind of man and boy one brand, one product, and one bottle, has in recent years edged slightly toward segmentation with its multisized bottles, and thus has found new selling appeals.

Sociologists and others have commented on the increasing sameness in many aspects of American life. The other side of this coin of sameness is that it forces us as consumers to distinguish ourselves from our development-housing neighbors, increasing our demand for at least minor distinctions in the products that we consume. This, of course, plays right into the hands of the market segmenters.

The postwar onset of television has furnished a most convenient springboard for market segmentation as a strategy to be more widely and systematically applied. In the introduction of new products, a regular condition of life for thoroughgoing market segmenters, a common approach is market-by-market. Spot TV is a powerful, well-adapted medium for promoting new products in selective markets. Another recent development in advertising—the multiplication of state and regional editions of magazines formerly available only as single national buys—may be understood both as an applied form of market segmentation by the magazines and a stimulus toward the strategy of market segmentation on the part of advertisers.

BUSINESS AND AGRIBUSINESS

Leaving the more familiar realm of consumer goods, we encounter dramatic insights into segmentation strategy everywhere in industrial marketing. Recently, a manufacturer of industrial metal buildings, aiming to sell store buildings to large retail chain organizations, shifted its tactics to allow its dealer organization to carry the ball in promoting such national construction contracts. Previously, this manufacturer had tried, not too successfully, to handle these retail chains as house accounts, and to offer them a standardized, prototype building. The dealer organization was finally recognized as the key to unlocking this market, because dealers are better able to tailor their product offering to the buyers' local needs, even when the buyer is a large national chain. In other words, what had been considered as a single aggregated market proved through hard experience to be more correctly defined as a segmentable market.

Another broadly segmentable market is represented by American agribusiness in its role as purchaser of numerous production inputs. Despite some widespread stereotypes about agriculture—as in the expression "the farm problem," which implies that agriculture could be considered as a unit—today's agricultural organization is rich in variations. It actually makes segmentation strategy mandatory for suppliers who would penetrate agricultural markets in any depth. In agriculture, the problem for marketers is not whether to segment this vast buying potential, but how and to what degree. In the last analysis, no two farms are precisely the same in their significant demand characteristics, nor do they have precisely the same enterprises. As in consumer marketing, the firm selling in agricultural markets must aggregate its final customers at least to the extent of dealing with groups rather than individuals. There is no point in analytically subdividing agriculture into purposeless fragments, or even going beyond some of the broader, more obvious subdivisions.

Since the tree of agriculture has too much foliage for us to examine every leaf, we propose to strip back the bark from just one branch, and see how the sap runs.

The two most basic branches in agribusiness are crop production and livestock-poultry production, although the interrelations and overlappings between the two are so complex that their presentation as a dichotomy could mislead. Of these two, the livestock-poultry sector is the more important in terms of total income to farmers. Moreover, secular trends in American consumption patterns toward higher protein diets indicate even greater future importance for this sector. In general, livestock-poultry is a more dynamic and challenging example for the purposes of this article.

LIVESTOCK CHEMICALS

Among the most important of the industrially purchased inputs used for livestock-poultry production are fine chemicals and drugs. Indeed, the annual expenditure of $250 million for these represents about 1 per cent of all farmers' total reinvestment in productive goods and services. A shortened term for this particular reinvestment volume is the market for livestock chemicals.

The balance of this article will focus on experience gained by companies that are trying, in various ways, to segment the market for livestock chemicals, and generalized conclusions will be developed from their experiences.

The Structure: Submarkets

One consideration in focusing upon the marketing of livestock chemicals is that it involves definite submarkets that are representative of (1) quasi-professional or ethical product marketing; (2) industrial bulk product marketing; and (3) quasi-consumer packaged product marketing. These natural submarkets are briefly explained below.

The Licensed Veterinarian. When compared with the professional marketing of drugs for humans, the marketing of livestock drugs through professional veterinarians offers points of both similarity and dissimilarity. The essential difference, of course, is that the veterinarian operates on an economic rather than a humanitarian rationale. Nevertheless, veterinarians are motivated to some extent at least by a service concept, and they tend to be quite "touchy" about their professional status. In short, veterinarians think of themselves, and foster an image of themselves, in ways to set them apart as a distinct submarket and an obvious target for segmenting strategy by chemical and drug manufacturers.

The Feed Industry. In selling to major feed manufacturers, the appropriate marketing mix is that required in many industrial marketing situations, such as the selling of bulk chemical intermediates. It happens, however, that concentration in the feed industry is very low, compared with other basic manufacturing industries. More than 50 per cent of total manufactured feed volume is accounted for by some 5,000 small operators. At the lower end of the feed-tonnage spectrum, these 5,000 merge into the manufacturing retailers, who sell over the counter in package form many of the same drugs that they buy in bulk for mixing in their registered and/or custom feeds.

Over-the-Counter Packaged Products. Some 25,000 assorted drugstores, feedstores and mills, country elevators, hatcheries, cooperatives, farm-to-farm salesmen, and other retailers sell livestock chemicals over the counter in both feed and nonfeed forms. Drug promotion to farmers through these unrestricted channels simulates consumer goods marketing, with manufacturers using all the techniques of mass promotion and advertising. This occurs despite the fact that the products involved are production inputs and should (theoretically) be bought by the farmer not in his capacity as consumer but as purchasing agent for his livestock enterprise.

Before analyzing how manufacturers have implemented their identification of these three segments of the livestock-chemicals market, we should understand that many firms limit themselves agriculturally to a cream-skimming operation, confined to a single submarket. For example, a large variety of firms—some not essentially chemical or drug companies such as distillers, brewers, Eastman Kodak, Borden's, and others—simply sell bulk vitamins or antibiotics to the commercial feed industry. For them, as well as for other firms that confine their involvement to the veterinarian submarket (as do some ethical drug manufacturers) or to the over-the-counter package goods submarket, the opportunities to practice market segmentation are much fewer. Our main interest here is in approaches employed by those firms that aim for substantial operations in all three of the major submarkets of the live-stock-chemical industry.

Implementation

Marketing management's problems begin, not end, with the identification of the above three submarkets. Complications arise from the fact that they overlap. Broadly speaking, drug and chemical manufacturers have sought to segment these submarkets through two approaches:

1. Sales force separation, which, carried to its logical conclusion, entails operating in each submarket through quasi-independent, differently named corporate subsidiaries
2. A less formalized approach, with somewhat lower-key emphasis on product-line multiplication under one label and one management.

Firms that have sought to keep their marketing efforts in each of the three submarkets completely separate have commonly used the cover device of different corporate names. Partly, they aim for greater sales and deeper penetration by fostering specialization; the marketing effort of each subsidiary is tightly compartmentalized to one or, at the most, two of the major submarkets. Their aim is also to prevent one submarket—especially the veterinarian segment—from knowing what happens in another. For example, Vick splinters off the veterinarian submarket for development by its Jensen-Salsbery subsidiary, while its Hess & Clark subsidiary operates over the counter; American Home Products markets ethically as Fort Dodge Laboratories, and over the counter as Wyeth; Lilly appears as Corn States to veterinarians, but sells to the feed industry under the Lilly name, Elanco division. There are numerous other examples.

A special consideration for some human drug companies, which are greatly concerned with maintaining a 100 per cent ethical image in the eyes of druggists, is that they wish to sell farmers packaged animal-health products while avoiding the hurly-burly of shelf competition within the drugstore itself. With retail druggists controlling about 25 per cent of the packaged animal-health business, this image is hard to maintain without benefit of a cover organization. Schering handles this by selling its own labeled animal-health products through licensed veterinarians, while its American Scientific subsidiary sells through unrestricted channels, including drug outlets.

The other general approach to market segmentation—emphasis on product-line diversification under one label—is the favorite of the large companies that have entered agriculture from fine chemicals. The idea here is to offer the same basic product in a wide array of forms, package sizes, "formulas," and convenient combinations. The objective is to cover by product: all species of livestock and poultry; all routes of entry into the animal; types that typically move over the counter (such as growth stimulants); and types that are usually distributed to veterinarians (such as certain biologicals). All are under one corporate name and/or umbrella-brand label. Because the three submarkets tend to blend together in certain areas, this approach permits the same salesman to "sell everybody in town," while the advertising "gets more mileage." Heavy consumer and trade promotion is a concomitant of this species of market segmentation, which relies on the pulling power of advertising to compensate, in some instances, for loss of veterinarian and/or dealer incentive to push merchandise.

In other words, the product-line diversification approach can be developed to modify or even overcome the traditional attitudes held by some veterinarians, druggists, and other retailers who might expect local "exclusives" in animal-health products. Merck, American Cyanamid, and Pfizer have all been notably successful in operating on this basis. Pfizer, for instance, has been most ingenious in multiplying its brand of oxytetracycline into a profusion of forms, package sizes, combinations, and special formulas, some rather marginally differentiated one from another, and then backing all this up with a saturation distribution and promotion program to farmers and to all three of the submarkets.

Evaluation of Techniques

The separate sales force approach, institutionalized into operation through differently named corporated subsidiaries, is firmly rooted in the traditions and predilections of veterinarians and, to a lesser extent, of druggists and feed manufacturers.

For the many manufacturers that so far have made only a token entry into livestock chemicals, this particular segmentation route undoubtedly offers interesting possibilities for achieving wider and deeper market penetration. It does suffer, however, from the ultimate limitation of being oriented toward the *status quo* of the agribusiness. With the organization of American livestock and poultry production rapidly moving toward thoroughgoing specialization, larger unit size, and more integration—both horizontal and vertical—these changes are being reflected in the relative importance of various channels in distribution of livestock chemicals.

In Western commercial cattle feedlots, for instance, veterinarians are tending toward more specialized diagnostic-advisory functions with less dispensing, and with control (particularly application) of health products passing heavily into the hands of laymen. Even in the Midwest, hypodermic syringes, ownership of which was once the hallmark of the professional veterinarian, are now in the hands of one-third of all livestock farmers. More than 50 per cent of all large animal injectable products are estimated now to be applied by farmers themselves.

Developments such as these, plus the already mentioned dispersal of the feed industry, create difficulties for the segmentation approach based on separate subsidiaries operating in rigidly defined submarkets. Within the parent corporation, need may frequently arise to arbitrate jurisdictional problems caused by these shifting areas between submarkets

In contrast, the segmentation approach, which is based mostly on product diversification, allows more flexibility in the matching of products to channels. The trade classifies itself, so to speak, with minimum intraorganization friction and with no bases left untouched. It is easy, then, to handle the many overlapping trade classifications, such as the integrated broiler organization, or the veterinarian in the wholesale feed supply business. No matter what buyer wants a particular drug in whatever form, quantity, or package size, any of the manufacturer's territorial salesmen can service the account. The extreme diversity of production patterns in different species of livestock and poultry, and in the various regions, is reflected by how producers buy livestock chemicals. It puts a premium on flexibility of the marketing organization in firms that would sell livestock chemicals in great volume.

Thus, the most generally successful approach to segmenting the market for livestock chemicals appears to involve (1) a single marketing management; (2) multiplication of product offering to suit the needs of every major type and size of buyer; and (3) full-line offering in the field. This is recognized as a somewhat less aggressive response to the segmentation possibilities inherent in the three major submarkets than its alternative—split operations through quasi-independent corporate subsidiaries.

The latter approach seems, eventually, to become a type of overresponse to the inherent segmenting possibilities. This conclusion suggests that there is an implied time dimension in identification of market segments. In the short run, before deep market penetration can be programmed, market segments can be identified by their close correspondence to prototype. In the long run, after enough time has elapsed to sell a market segment in real depth, this deeper penetration takes the marketer past the clear-cut, close-to-prototype customers, and into the areas populated by cross-over customers who are only partly in that segment. It is not a matter of the market segment becoming illusory; these are real concepts. Rather, it is a case where the validity limits of the segment identification have been finally reached.

In contrast, the more flexible approach toward segmenting the livestock chemical submarkets—exemplified by Cyanamid, Merck, and Pfizer—represents a more mature form of segmentation strategy, in this industry at least. A view of the organizational history of these firms tends to verify this thesis. At one point or another in the past, all three of these firms have had marketing organizations that incorporated some of the philosophy of the completely separate-sales-force-*cum*-different-label approach. For example, the licensed veterinarian submarket was, in the past, singled out by Cyanamid to sell under the Lederle label, by Merck under the Merck-Sharp & Dohme label, and by Pfizer under a special brown label. In time, however, with deeper market penetration accompanied by a stream of new products, these special submarket labels were sloughed off as the present segmentation strategy crystallized and emphasis shifted to offering many products tailored to submarkets under one corporate label and one marketing management.

Market segmentation is the strategy of divide-and-conquer, and its implementation takes many forms. Like Molière's character who had been speaking prose all his life without realizing it, all firms practice market segmentation to some degree, mostly without conscious formalization of it as corporate strategy. In order that market segmenting action by any firm qualify as part of a general strategy, there should be a background of a more or less *continuous* search for identifiable submarkets plus *continuous* exploitation of them.

In their purest form, segmentation actions require imagination and creativity but are compensated for by higher sales volume. The operative criterion, however, in weighing such segmenting action as product-line diversification has traditionally been profitability. Numerous examples from everyday life suggest that secular trends are altering certain equations in favor of more extensive segmentation as the profit-maximizing strategy for more and more firms. A few of the postwar demographic, sociological, and business factors contributing to this development were mentioned.

The livestock-chemical industry was analyzed for applications of segmentation strategy. Three major submarkets were described. Companies broadly involved in livestock chemicals were found to practice two kinds of market segmentation: one based on sales force diversification, which in its purest form is operation under differently named quasi-independent subsidiaries in each submarket; the other emphasizing product-line diversification under one label and one marketing management. While the first approach is widely used, and undoubtedly is a promising avenue of expansion for firms now only modestly involved in livestock chemicals, it was concluded that long-run sales maximization in the interrelated and shifting livestock-chemical markets requires the greater flexibility of the second approach. The area of cross-over products and mixed channels of distribution emphasize the need for flexibility, in order to be sure that all bases are covered—by product as well as by field sales effort.

It was concluded that the other market segmentation approach in livestock chemicals, based on split operations through separate corporate subsidiaries, becomes in the long run a form of overresponse to the segmenting possibilities inherent in identification of the three sub-markets. This conclusion led to the suggestion that there may be a time dimension implied in the identification of any market segment. In the short run, a firm can identify a market segment by the close correspondence of customers to a prototype. In the long run, after that market segment has been sold in depth, the marketer works himself into areas populated by crossover customers who are only partly true to prototype. Thus, the validity limits of the segment are finally reached. And it is at that point that a too rigid marketing organization, one that attempts to institutionalize segmental distinctions, becomes an instrument of less than optimum efficiency.

6.

The Strategy Selection Chart

R. William Kotrba

Two questions are increasingly crucial to marketers of both local and national consumer products:

1. What alternatives are available to "individualize" a product and thus boost its market visibility?
2. What product, market, and competitive factors influence the selection of a particular marketing program?

TWO ALTERNATIVES

Most consumer advertising messages appeal to selective rather than to primary buying motives, as each firm strives to emphasize the distinctive features of its own products or services. And successful product "individualization" is no longer an easy task in today's competitive marketplace. In fact, almost all businesses are offering so many new products that the problem is largely one of individualizing products, so that each new product has "some discernible difference from other products."[1]

Traditionally, sellers have strived to create distinctiveness for their products through two basic marketing programs—product differentiation and market segmentation.

Product Differentiation

A marketing approach that is dependent upon the promotion of product differences, whether they are actual or imagined, is that of product differentiation. Neither the most expensive nor the least expensive product is always the most appealing. "Difference (or differences) in the product itself may be in the package, or in the advertising and promotion which give you

[1] Steuart Henderson Britt, *The Spenders* (New York: McGraw-Hill Publishing Co., 1961).

From R. William Kotrba, "The Strategy Selection Chart," *Journal of Marketing,* Vol. 30 (July 1966), pp. 22–25. Published by the American Marketing Association. Reprinted by permission.

an 'image' of the product as being different. But in any case, the seller's objective is for you to discern a difference, or feel that you discern a difference."[2]

Product differentiation is highly dependent on some unusual aspect of the seller's product, advertising media, selling message, package design, or selling location. Sellers who favor the promotion of product uniqueness believe that consumers are pleased to learn of these differences and will buy products on account of them, even if actual differences are slight. They conclude that so long as people *believe* things to be different, then they are different.

Market Segmentation

The second concept, market segmentation, is believed by some marketers to be the more modern strategy alternative. Market segmentation is "based upon developments on the demand side of the market and represents a rational and more precise adjustment of product and marketing effort to consumer or user requirements."[3] Unlike product differentiation—with the implication that any particular market consists of a homogeneous or a *typical* group of buyers—market segmentation is characterized by a recognition of wide diversity in demand. Since the seller adapts his product or service to suit the distinct wants of selected groups of buyers, this approach is highly dependent on the existence of some demonstrable uniqueness or difference in the seller's product.

Sellers who favor market segmentation commonly criticize the product-differentiation strategy because they believe promotional emphasis is placed on trivial product differences. They argue that the sheer volume of product-differentiating messages is overwhelming, and thus that it is more difficult than ever to get the consumer's attention and persuade him to buy.

STRATEGY DIFFERENCES

The marketer employing the strategy of product differentiation tries to build sales by offering a product that can be easily distinguished from similar products, and usually directs his marketing efforts at the typical consumer in the group of potential buyers for his product. The product differentiator searches for unusual or distinctive ways to promote his product, in an effort to convince consumers to buy his product rather than those of competitors.

The marketer who segments the market of potential buyers for his product directs his marketing effort at exclusive consumer groups or submarkets. He

[2] Same reference as footnote 1.
[3] Wendell R. Smith, "Product Differentiation and Market Segmentation as Alternative Marketing Strategies," *Journal of Marketing,* Vol. 21 (July, 1956), pp. 3–8, at p. 5.

believes that each group of consumers probably will buy that product which best satisfies their particular needs. Therefore, he searches for a means to present his product in a form which better satisfies these needs.

This means that the "product-differentiators" are more sensitive to product characteristics, and the "market-segmenters" more sensitive to consumer characteristics.

Simultaneous Use

Neither strategy is likely to be employed exclusively; in practice, marketers often employ them simultaneously, or in sequence in response to dynamic market conditions.

For example, if a manufacturer views the market for his product as comprised of several consumer groups or submarkets, each requiring a slightly different product and selling approach, then he is practicing market segmentation. However, as his market is divided into submarkets and these submarkets into sub-submarkets, he realizes that at some point differences in consumer wants become negligible. If a number of firms already are selling a similar product to a particular group of consumers in which variations in product desires are indistinguishable, then imaginative thinking is required to stimulate demand for the *brand* rather than for the *product class* in general. Thus, the manufacturer must develop unusual or unique packaging, advertising, or selling techniques in order to set his product apart from those of competitors.

An example of the active relationship of the differentiation-segmentation marketing alternatives is found in the change of strategies of automobile marketers during the past 10 or 15 years. Automobile manufacturers have been increasing the number of models available, in order to satisfy better the wide diversity in consumer demand—for compact cars, sports cars, convertible cars, two-door cars, economy cars, luxury cars, and so on. These changes have been consistent with a strategy of market segmentation, and advertising campaigns have been aimed at supporting this strategy.

However, in 1964 the manufacturers reduced the number of car models available. As a result, the promotion of cars within the same model-class (for example, Ford's Mustang and Chrysler's Barracuda) increasingly depended upon a product differentiation strategy. Under such conditions, differences in techniques of advertising, selling and public relations ultimately determine the distinctiveness which a product will achieve in the minds of consumers.

STRATEGY SELECTION FACTORS

Faced by the challenge of selecting a marketing strategy for a new product, decision-makers need a feeling of confidence. But frequently this feeling never comes.

When is a differentiation policy appropriate? When is a segmentation policy appropriate? Or would a combination of these alternatives be best?

Since conditions are constantly changing, certain factors need to be reviewed at each launching of a new marketing program. Although the following list of factors can be revised, readjusted, and refined, it illustrates a specific concept of strategy selection.

1. *Size of Market.* Selection of a marketing strategy for a product involves estimating the number of consumers who might purchase it. When the total number of available buyers for a product is already small—as defined demographically, sociologically, or psychologically—segmentation of this market is undesirable. For example, the market for hearing aids is small and cannot easily be segmented, while the market for cameras can and has been successfully segmented. Low-, medium-, and high-quality cameras are being produced to satisfy a broad range of distinguishable variations in consumer demand.

2. *Consumer Sensitivity.* Does consumer sensitivity to product differences exist, or can it be easily stimulated? In this sense, differences refer to variations in the package, selling message, media, and so on. Some product categories are so dull or uninteresting to consumers that people are insensitive to any form of product differentiating efforts, even with exposure to vigorous marketing campaigns. Detergents represent a product class in which certain consumers are always interested in learning something new or different; and differentiation can be successfully employed. If sensitivity to product differences is low, as for garden rakes, then segmentation is more appropriate than differentiation.

3. *Product Life-cycle.* Every product has a life-cycle: introduction, growth, maturity, and saturation. The stage at which a new product enters the market place directly affects the marketing strategy selected for it. For example, a firm introducing a product in a market where similar products are in their introduction stage should attempt to develop or reinforce primary demand for the product, knowing that there is time later for modifications which will better satisfy particular market segments.

In contrast, a product being introduced in a market where similar products have reached their saturation stage might best be marketed by applying a market segmentation strategy. Once primary demand for a particular product class is established, it becomes practical for a firm to produce the additional product versions required by a strategy of market segmentation. This is the case with color television sets.

4. *Type of Product.* Most products are included in one of two major product categories: *distinct items* and *commodities.* A distinct item refers to any type of product for which significant changes or revisions can be made. For example, an automobile is a distinct item because it is possible to change or

modify it significantly. A commodity refers to a product for which it is difficult to find ways to modify it; examples include cinnamon, sugar, and white gasoline.

Since commodities tend to be basically alike, a consumer is less likely to perceive differences among them. Accordingly, marketers must rely on a strategy of product differentiation. In contrast, a distinct item lends itself to a market segmentation strategy which requires that some recognizable and useful product variation be made available to the consumer. The refrigerator is an example of this type of product.

5. *Number of Competitors*. As the number of firms selling a particular product increases, it becomes difficult for any single firm to differentiate successfully or to distinguish its product from others. Only in rare instances has a manufacturer been able to "hold" a large consumer group as the number of new competitive products increased. Vaseline probably is an example of a product in this category. Under such conditions, the better marketing strategy is market segmentation, directed only at those groups of consumers who respond most fully to the firm's products or services.

6. *Typical Competitor Strategies*. What is the typical marketing strategy of competitors? When the majority of competitors are applying a segmentation policy, it becomes difficult for a firm to compete with a differentiation policy. The reverse is true when the majority of competitors are applying a differentiation policy. In other words, there may be value in applying a strategy similar to that employed by competitors.

The relationships of these six factors and their effects upon marketing strategy selection is illustrated in the *Strategy Selection Chart*. See Figure 6–1.

SELECTING A MARKETING STRATEGY

Typically, the Strategy Selection Chart would aid the marketing executives in answering the question: *Is my product best suited to the application of a differentiation or a segmentation strategy; or is it suited to both?*

Among the almost infinite list of product categories which might be tested are such items as lipsticks, sleeping bags, cameras, flyswatters, chewing gum, vegetables, china, eyeglasses, fireplaces, air-conditioners, tennis rackets, magazines, pie-tins, chairs, dictionaries, and coffeemakers.

To determine whether or not any one of these products might best be marketed using a differentiation or a segmentation strategy can be "tested" with the chart. By deciding upon the effect of each factor and checking the one of the ten positions along the factor-continuum which best describes the market, product, and competitive conditions for the type of product being tested, the predominant strategy alternative can be selected.

	Apply Product Differentiation	Apply Market Segmentation
	Strategy emphasis should be on promoting product differences.	Strategy Selection Factors	Strategy emphasis should be on satisfying market variations.

Market Factors

Size of Market — Narrow (1) ... Broad (10): O at 3, X at 6

1	2	3	4	5	6	7	8	9	10
		O			X				

Consumer Sensitivity to Product Differences — High (1) ... Low (10): O at 4, X at 5

1	2	3	4	5	6	7	8	9	10
			O	X					

Product Factors

Product Life-Cycle — Introduction Stage (1) ... Saturation Stage (10): O at 6, X at 8

1	2	3	4	5	6	7	8	9	10
					O		X		

Type of Product — Commodity (1) ... Distinct Item (10): O at 3, X at 8

1	2	3	4	5	6	7	8	9	10
		O					X		

Competitive Factors

Number of Competitors — Few (1) ... Many (10): X at 4, O at 6

1	2	3	4	5	6	7	8	9	10
			X		O				

Typical Competitor Strategies — Differentiation Policy (1) ... Segmentation Policy (10): O at 1, X at 8

1	2	3	4	5	6	7	8	9	10
O							X		

Figure 6–1. Strategy Selection Chart

The writer chose rocking-chairs as a test product; and he has indicated his judgments of the influence of each factor by the X's shown on the continuums in Figure 6–1. These judgments strongly favor *market segmentation*.

Another product, flyswatters, was tested with factor judgments designated on the chart by O's. These judgments favor *product differentiation*.

Other marketers should test a number of products for themselves, to determine the appropriate strategy suggested by the chart.

This formal arrangement of factors and effects is not intended to imply that these relationships are precisely known. After all, such an expression can be no more exact than existing ability to come to an accurate determination of the factors involved. Also, the question of factor-weightings purposely has been neglected, in order to illustrate clearly the basis of a chart selection procedure.

While it is possible that the influence of any single factor may favor the opposite strategy, it is the *average* effect that is indicative of the strategy alternative to be employed. For a number of products, a sharp strategy disagreement may occur among some of the factors. Normally, products of this type might be successfully sold through either marketing strategy, or through a combination of strategies. Such a combined-strategy approach is not at all uncommon; such products as cola, cigarettes, and soap appear to fall into this category.

C. Planning and Research

7.

Matrix Models for Marketing Planning

William J. E. Crissy
Robert M. Kaplan

It is axiomatic that the success of the effort expended on marketing by a company hinges upon the soundness and thoroughness of the marketing planning involved. This relationship holds whether consideration is given to the total market place, to a geographic segment such as a sales district, or indeed to the marketing plan for a single account. If such planning is to be effective, there is need for current, accurate, and complete answers to the following four interrelated questions:

1. Who are our customers? Whom do we wish to have as customers?
2. What needs and wants of theirs are we now satisfying? What needs and wants of theirs do we wish to satisfy?
3. What demand-creating forces are we now using? What demand-creating forces should we be using?
4. What methods or channels of distribution are we currently using? What methods or channels of distribution should we be using?

THE FOUR MIXES

An analytical answer to the first question provides the marketing planner with a picture of the sources of existing and potential business. Only when customers and prospective customers are known and classified does the firm have a target for its marketing effort. This target is its *customer-prospect mix*. Answering the second question forces the firm to perceive its products of want-satisfiers is the company's *product-service mix*. The firm's answer to the third question involves a critical review of currently used demand-creating forces as well as ones that might be added. The ultimate objective is to marry the customer-prospect mix to the company's product-service mix.

From William J. E. Crissy and Robert M. Kaplan: "Matrix Models for Marketing Planning," pp. 48–67, *MSU Business Topics* (Summer 1963). Reprinted by permission of the publisher, Division of Research, Graduate School of Business Administration, Michigan State University.

This interactive combination of such marketing forces as personal selling, advertising, sales promotion and the like is the *promotional mix*. Finally, as the firm answers the fourth question, it comes to grips with that important aspect of marketing—getting the goods and services to the right place, at the right time, in the right sizes and assortments, in the right amount and by the most efficient means. This is the domain of physical distribution. The combination of channels which the firm uses, or contemplates using, to get its product-service mix to the customer-prospect mix is the *distribution mix*.

While these four questions remain constant, clearly the answers to them are dynamic and changing for each company. The quality of the answers hinges upon a continuous input of trustworthy and relevant marketing information. This must encompass the on-going study of customers and prospects as well as competitive activity. Figure 7–1 is an attempt to graphically portray the interrelationships among the four mixes described above.

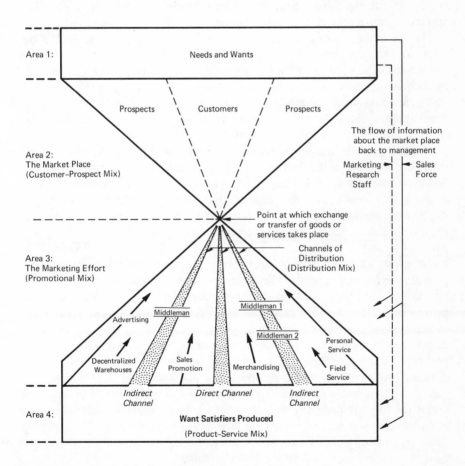

Figure 7–1. The Four Mixes

Area 1 at the top of the figure represents the needs and wants of the customer-prospect mix for a particular firm. Just below, in area 2, is the mix of customers and prospects who have the above needs and wants. They comprise the market place. Note specifically the location of the customer section in this mix. This position serves to emphasize the fact that the customers of a firm should be front and center to the marketing or promotional effort (represented by area 3). The company cannot afford to desert present customers in its attempt to acquire new customers unless, of course, it is changing its marketing targets. By devoting primary attention to the present customers, a firm should be front and center to the marketing or promotional effort (represented by area 3). The company cannot afford to desert present customers in its attempt to acquire new customers unless, of course, it is changing its marketing targets. By devoting primary attention to the present customers, a firm may get some prospects as customers through referrals and word-of-mouth advertising. Also a firm should be cautious and not outrun its talent and money resources in its quest to broaden its customer base.

The marketing management of a firm must have a means of finding out what are the needs and wants of the customers and prospects, where they are located, and what are their buying habits and motives. This can be done by the market research facilities, augmented by observations of the field sales staff. This dual source of market information is represented by the two lines running down the . . . side of the diagram. The information received from these two marketing intelligence arms has two primary applications, to the product-service mix and to the promotional mix. Additionally it may contribute to decisions about the distribution mix. Notice that the product-service mix is depicted by area 4, while the promotional and distribution mixes are in area 3. From this information the planners can design a program of marketing the product-service mix to the customer-prospect mix. The marketing program will involve the use of some demand-creating forces such as advertising, personal selling, merchandising, sales promotion, field service, decentralized warehousing, etc.—the promotional mix. The vectors pointing up from the product-service mix represent the elements of the promotional mix that will be used by management to marry the product-service mix to the customer-prospect mix. The vectors vary in length because the elements will be used to different degrees and in different proportions. For example, a company may spend 50 percent of its marketing budget on personal selling and 25 percent of it on advertising. As can be seen in Figure 7–1, all the vectors are directed toward the customer-prospect mix and the point at which the exchange of the goods or services takes place. The combination of promotional forces used by the company will, it is hoped, be an *optimum* one, i.e, maximum benefits will accrue for the money and effort expended. This promotional mix, then, would be the most efficient combination to use considering the customer-prospect and product-service mixes.

The fourth is the distribution mix, commonly known as the channels of distribution used by the firm. This mix represents the marketing institutions through which the product-service mix flows to reach the point of exchange with the customer. It is represented in Figure 7–1 by the pathways or channels in area 3 running from the want-satisfiers or product-service mix up to the customer-prospect mix. Three possible channels are represented in this diagram. Channel 1 is the direct method of distribution, from the manufacturer directly to the user. The second channel in area 3 of Figure 7–1 might depict the use of a supply house by the manufacturer in the case of industrial goods, or the use of a retailer in the case of consumer goods. The third channel represents the use of more than one middleman by the manufacturer to get his product to the consumer. A specific firm may use more than one channel to market its goods and indeed it may even use different channels for the same product.

The Place of Competition

Admittedly, this schematic approach (Figure 7–1) is an oversimplification; it does not portray competition. Competition could be depicted through an additional lower half—areas 3 and 4—for each competitor. These competing firms would be using their own promotional efforts to market their products and services to a common market place. Indeed, one firm's customers may be another firm's prospects. Managements are not likely to perceive promotional efforts in the same way as competitors. For example, the management of Hershey Chocolates Corporation does not place the same emphasis on advertising as a demand-creating force for its chocolate bars as the management of the makers of Peter Paul Mounds.

MIX INTERRELATIONSHIPS

The models and discussions which follow are concerned with the interactions of the four mixes—customer-prospect, product-service, promotional and distribution—and how they combine synergistically to make up the marketing plan for the entire enterprise.

Consumer-Prospect Mix and Product-Service Mix

In answering the first question set forth in the introduction of this paper, a multidimensional classification problem exists. Two factors bring about this classificatory problem—the *number* and *diversity* of customers and prospects. The peculiarities of the customer-prospect mix of the particular company will dictate which variables are relevant in classifying the market place. For example, size of account (volume), geographical location, frequency of purchase, short and long range trends, and above all else communality of needs and wants are all acceptable criteria to use. Each resulting category of customers and prospects becomes a relatively homogeneous marketing target. Thus the idiosyncrasies of each sub-group may be handled on a more individualized basis than if all customers were dealt with in the aggregate.

Consider an example of the possible groupings of a marketer of industrial goods such as wood products: (1) wholesalers; (2) large retailers and chains; (3) industrial accounts, e.g., furniture manufacturers; and (4) contractors. Illustratively, the marketing intelligence information indicated the key wants of each group. The wants of the wholesalers may be to have a wide variety of sizes and grades and the chance to purchase "mixed cars." The wants of the retailers may be to have the goods nicely packaged and readily displayable. The industrial accounts may be more concerned with rapid delivery and the sales engineer's technical advice on his problems. The contractors will probably be more concerned than the other customer categories with materials handling on the job and other means of reducing their on-the-site labor costs. But all of the customers within a particular market segment have something in common.

An example of customer-prospect mix classification or market segmentation for a consumer goods marketer may be a grouping of his accounts by volume: e.g., accounts having (1) $100,000 sales per year and over, (2) $50,000 to $100,000, (3) $25,000 to $50,000, (4) $10,000 to $25,000, and (5) under $10,000. It is very likely that different emphasis on promotional tools would be used in each of these volume categories. Or the classification could have been by geographic areas. When geography becomes the prime classification criterion, it is most likely that there will not be much variation between categories for promotional tools used, but the main effect will be upon the channels or distribution mix.

The customer-prospect mix should be an optimum function. By this is meant that the market place should not become too wide or too narrow. Profits may suffer as distribution costs increase because of too wide a market place, or production costs may increase because of too limited a market place and relatively low volume. A firm may place too many of its eggs in one basket, in terms of a narrow customer-prospect mix. In extreme cases, if most or all of its production is taken by one large account, the firm then puts itself at the mercy of the customer. If the customer has a bad year, the sales of the supplier will decline; if the customer chooses to change suppliers, the producer may be caught without an outlet for his production. At the other extreme is the firm that tries to increase the size of the customer-prospect mix and in so doing spreads itself too thin for its resources of money and manpower. This is an illustration in the market place of the old saying, "biting off more than one can chew."

Administrative feasibility of the segmentation of the market place is another consideration. If a company divides its customer-prospect mix into too many categories, planning may become too time-consuming and expensive. In contrast, if the categorization is too coarse, it may become increasingly difficult to set specific marketing objectives and programs for achieving them.

The product-service mix can be conceptualized as a want-satisfier system. Here, too, the classification problem is multi-dimensional. Communality of needs and wants becomes the prime classifying variable here as it does in the customer-prospect mix. Additional variables may include common ingredients or components, common production processes, or frequency of demand. For example, the wood products firm might have a product-service mix such as: (1) lumber, (2) plywood, (3) pre-cut building components, and (4) siding and shingles, together with the services related to each category.

Matrix Analysis.   Clearly there is an interaction between the customer-prospect mix and the product-service mix. This can be shown as a multi-dimensional space by the use of a matrix model. Figure 7–2 is such a matrix.

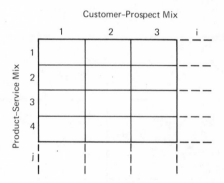

Figure 7–2. Interaction of Customer-Prospect
and Product-Service Mixes

The horizontal axis represents the customer-prospect mix divided into a finite number of groups. The vertical axis, also divided into a finite number of groups, represents the product-service mix for this company. As noted before, the number of categories on each axis should be optimum for the company.

As a part of market planning, a company is often faced with the question of whether to open up a new market segment, or less frequently, to close down a market segment which seems no longer to be profitable. Decisions like these affecting market diversification must necessarily be interrelated with decisions regarding product diversification. Thus, as part of its marketing planning, a company is also often faced with a decision on introducing a new product or product line or on removing a product from the line. These decisions and actions in the domain of product diversification cannot be coped with independent of considering their implications for market diversification. Ideally, a company wishes to cultivate market segments which will purchase as full a product line as possible. Hence, as we look down each column in Figure 7–2, it would be ideal to find many, if not all, of the cells containing profitable sales or profitable potential sales. Similarly, looking across each row in Figure 7–2, it would be desirable to find each product or product group having sales or potential sales in most if not all of the market place segments.

Cell Analysis.   Once the marketing planner has identified, analyzed, and classified his customer-prospect mix and product-service mix, and placed them on a matrix like Figure 7–2, he should then analyze each cell of the matrix in order to understand more clearly the situation in the particular market place segment for the particular product or product group. Figure 7–3 is useful in making the necessary analysis. In this case, just one segment (cell 2:2 of Figure 7–2) is blown up to illustrate how this analysis could and should be made for all cells within the matrix.

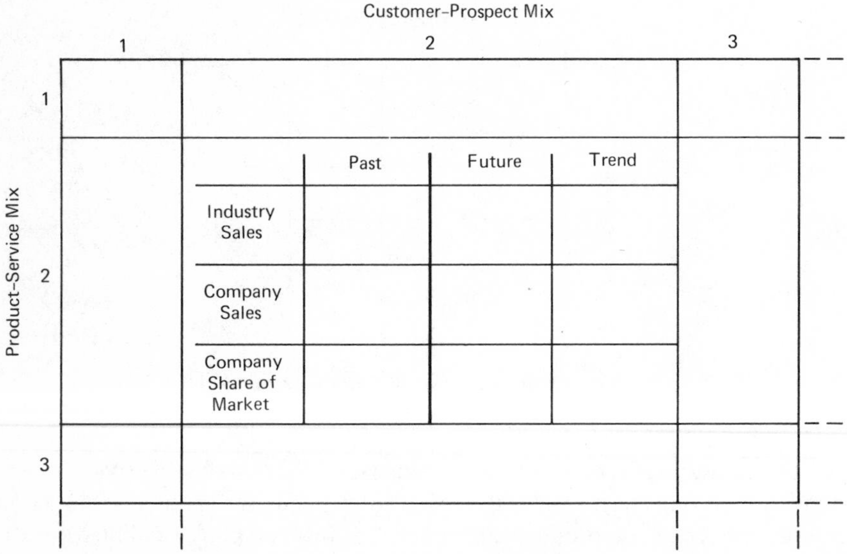

Figure 7–3. Segment Analysis

Figure 7–4 is a blow-up of cell 2:2 from Figure 7–3. Observe the horizontal axis. Attention is directed from the past up to the present: the first column represents the past sales record for the industry, the company, and the company's market share for this product-service group in a particular customer-prospect category. This record of sales could be for the previous six months period, a year, or even longer depending upon the nature of the product and the customer. The heavy line represents the present. Sales up to now are considered as past sales, and sales in the next short while will be referred to in the figure as future. The next column represents future sales. Here management needs as accurate predictions as can be made regarding industry sales and company sales. This time period may be short or long depending upon the nature of the product, the customer, how long the company has been selling this product-service to the customer-prospect mix, competition, and a host of other variables. The actual time period chosen will be by management decision. Obviously the length of time chosen for the past period will be constant in analyzing both the industry and company sales, as will the future time period. But the time period used for the past can, but need not, be the same as that used for the future.

	Past	Future	Trend
Industry Sales	Market	Potential Market	Up or Down
Company Sales	— —	Potential Sales	— —
Company Share of Market	— —	Potential Market Share	— —

Figure 7—4. Segment Analysis

The third column along the horizontal axis, headed *Trend*, takes the past sales per period and compares them with the future sales per period. From this comparison, one can easily see if sales in this product group are increasing, remaining constant, or decreasing over time in this particular market segment.

Changing perspective, attention is now directed to the vertical axis. The first consideration is the industry, composed of all the firms competing in this market segment with similar want-satisfiers. The past and future sales of the industry and the trend of these sales should be considered. Accurate information about the company's past and future sales and the trend of these sales should be considered next. Finally the company's share of the market must be scrutinized. This is computed by dividing the company sales by the industry sales, both for the past and future. From this information the trend of market penetration can be determined. Generally speaking, the noncomputational entries, in order of decreasing accuracy, are likely to be: past company sales, past industry sales, future company sales, and then future industry sales.

Figure 7–5 is an example of an analysis like the one made in Figure 7–4, but in this instance the company is not yet selling in a specific market segment and has obviously not made any penetration.

	Past	Future	Trend
Industry Sales	Market $	Potential Market $	Increase, decrease or no change
Company Sales	Sales $	Potential Sales $	Increase, decrease or no change
Company Share of Market	Market Share %	Potential Market Share %	Increase, decrease or no change

Figure 7–5. Segment Analysis

For marketing managers, the importance of this type of diagram is that it will set forth the record of each element of the product-service mix in each segment of the customer-prospect mix, stressing both its past performance and the best possible indication of what to expect in the future. A new enterprise is likely to have more 7–5 type cells than 7–4 type, while a well-established firm is likely to have more 7–4 than 7–5 type. Obviously, too, nearly every company is likely to have some cells that are blocked out: they are not selling a particular product or product-group to a particular market segment. Regardless of how effective marketing planning is, it is unlikely that a company can deal only with customers and prospects who will buy the full line of goods and services.

Value of the Analysis. If a company summarizes relevant marketing information in the fashion suggested by these figures, it will be able to focus in its planning upon each segment of the market place and upon each category in its product line. Where trend data indicate a leveling off or a decline in sales for the industry, withdrawal may be considered. Where the industry trend is toward sharp growth, increased marketing effort may be dictated. When trend in sales is viewed in a frame of reference of industry trends, management has an index of marketing effectiveness and can also avoid the delusion that any given increase in sales can be equated with marketing success. If industry sales are up 20 percent and the company sales have increased only 10 percent, remedial actions rather than congratulatory behavior may be in order.

A further advantage of the diagrammatic analysis set forth in Figure 7–2 is that it suggests a need for a system of checks and balances in marketing management. For example, good management will fix responsibility for the firm's marketing effort for each market segment on some specific department or individual. Thus, the sum of each column entry in Figure 7–2 becomes a key datum in evaluating how each market segment is being managed. An illustration of the application of this principle could be a hypothetical pharmaceutical firm. The columns in Figure 7–2 might correspond to such market segments as wholesale sales, hospital and institutional sales, dispensing physicians, etc. Presumably this firm would have someone in its marketing staff responsible for penetration in each of these segments. Conversely, as part of the scheme of checks and balances, the firm might have a manager in charge of each product or product group, a "product manager." Thus, the sum of each row in Figure 7–2 would give corporate management a prime tool for assessing the effectiveness with which any given product or product group had been managed.

Product-Service Mix and Promotional or Marketing Mix

Marketing planning should be carried out segment by segment for the total market place. The company's overall marketing plan should be an aggregate of these sub-plans: the total plan should be built up brick by brick once the objectives in each segment are known. It should not be built by arbitrarily allocating a certain percentage of gross sales to, say, advertising or merchandising, without knowing what the needs are or what the job to be done is. There is, of course, the danger of each segment building up the costs without regard for the total budget. If the aggregate requests are grossly out of line with management's thinking, a reconciliation or compromise may be necessary—but it can be accomplished under more enlightened conditions.

Knowing which ingredients of the product-service mix are now being sold in a given market-place segment, or are being considered as sales possibilities there, management must decide on the demand-creating forces to be used in order to most effectively promote its products and services to these particular customers and prospects. Figure 7–6 is the now-familiar Figure 7–2 with one of the customer-prospect segments subdivided into a number of columns in order to show how the customer-prospect category is held constant while the interrelationship between the promotional mix and the product-service mix is analyzed. Each customer-prospect mix has a similar breakdown, but for the sake of simplicity and expediency only one market segment is analyzed here. The procedure and analysis would be the same for each category of the customer-prospect mix.

Note that in Figure 7–6 the entries on the horizontal axis within the one customer-prospect segment are demand-creating forces: advertising, personal selling, merchandising, sales promotion and field service. Note also that the vertical axis reflects the *product-service mix* categories of the firm being considered for this customer-prospect segment. The reason for making these sub-divisions within each mix category is that each product-service group will have its own promotional campaign to each specific market segment. The components used in the campaign may include advertising, personal selling, etc. Likewise, each market segment may have a unique campaign even for the same product.

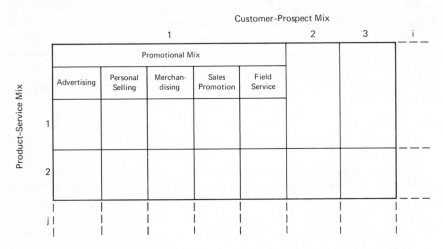

Figure 7—6. Interaction of Promotional and Product-Service Mixes

Customer-Prospect Mix and Distribution Mix

By using a similar figure to that used to show the two previous relationships, we can now hold the product-service mix constant and show how each product might use even more channels of distribution to move to a specific market segment or customer-prospect group.

An example of the use of different channels in order to reach a market segment could be a breakdown of the market by institutions. These institutions may be widely dispersed geographically. If such is the case, a food processor may have his house sales force sell directly to the retailers within a 100 mile radius; he may use wholesalers to sell to retailers more than a hundred miles away in less populated areas; food brokers or even his own decentralized warehouse to sell to large accounts in heavily populated areas more than 100 miles away from his plant.

Obviously the planning and execution of sales through the different channels make different demands on the firm's resources of time, talent, and money. Hence these channels of sales should be separated and handled in terms of the specific situation.

Promotion Mix and Distribution Mix

Since the different channels of distribution will require different emphasis and use of promotional tools even though the same product may be heading for the same market there will be an interaction between the promotional mix and the distribution mix. This interaction can also be shown on our matrix diagram by superimposing cell 1:1 of Figure 7–7 onto cell 1:1 of Figure 7–6. The resulting diagram would be Figure 7–8.

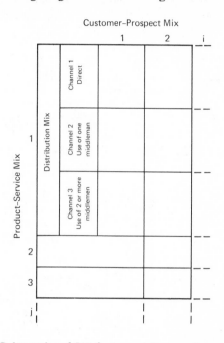

Figure 7–7. Interaction of Distribution and Customer-Prospect Mixes

Figure 7–8 shows that for each category of the customer-prospect mix and for each product or product group, there will be a choice of channels through which the product could travel to reach the customer and there will also be a choice of the tools available to management with which it could promote the product to the customer. In many cases this fine a stratification of the channels or promotional tools will not be necessary, and the job of using the matrix model will be less complicated. For example, in the case of a given product the manufacturer may not wish to use the direct channel to the market. Then it can be left blank on the analysis or not included. Also there will be a number of the sub-cells left blank because some channels may not require the use of certain promotional foods. For example, merchandising may not be used if channel 3 (two or more middlemen) is used.

SUB-CELL PLANNING

Figure 7–8 gives us the final breakdown to show the interrelationships among the four mixes. Now each sub-cell in Figure 7–8 must be analyzed regarding the objectives and targets that management would like to achieve for each product to each customer or prospect type, with each promotional tool, via each channel of distribution. Therefore all the components of the interactions should be viewed in relation to the other components and not just by themselves. One method which has been found effective in planning and analyzing each sub-cell is to use a diagram similar to Figure 7–9.

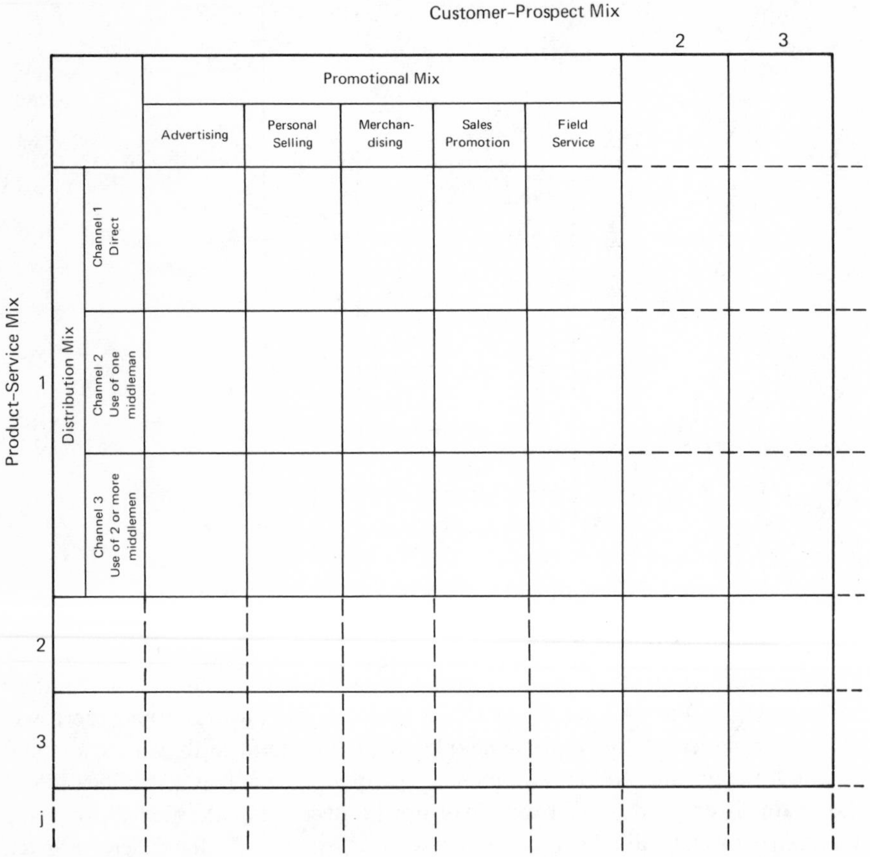

Figure 7—8. Total Interaction

Each sub-cell entry in Figure 7–8, if enlarged, would become a Figure 7–9. It would show specific objectives, the program to achieve these objectives, the contemplated plan of execution, and an evaluation of the expected results compared to the resources expended to achieve them.

The Steps in Planning

The first step in using Figure 7–9 is to decide on the *Objectives* or results desired from the promotional tool for this product-service group to the specific market segment. Step two would be to plan a program that would facilitate the achievement of the objectives. The elements of the program should be arranged in a time sequence with the phase that will be executed first at the top, then the next phase in time, etc. These are represented in Figure 7–9 by *a, b, c,* etc. under the heading of *Program.*

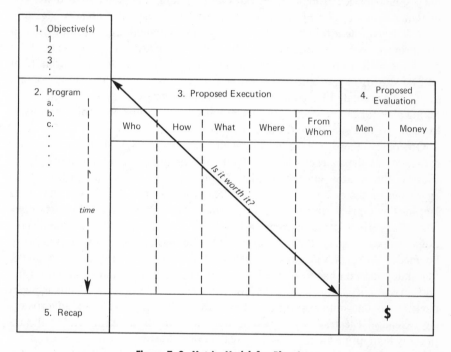

Figure 7–9. Matrix Model for Planning

The third step in planning is to decide on how each phase of the program will be executed—the *Contemplated Execution*—who will do it, how it will be done, what will be done, where it will be done, and who will be informed of the progress. The fourth step is the *Evaluation of the Program* in terms of energy and dollars expended in order to achieve the objectives set forth as step one. This evaluation can be boiled down into the elements of manpower and money. When these elements are totaled, the gross figure should be compared to the return that will be received for the expenses incurred. If a company has as one of its objectives a 10 percent net return on all investments and the rewards from the execution of a certain plan only yield 8 percent, then the question "Is it worth it?" is answered in the negative.

The diagram in Figure 7–9 shows how each sub-cell of Figure 7–8 can be analyzed, and when this is completed each column in Figure 7–8 should be summed up. This will give the whole plan for that particular demand-creating force used for the product-service mixes directed to the specific customer-prospect segment. As each row is summed up within each customer-prospect category, it will show the total marketing or promotional plan for a particular product group to that market segment and for that specific channel of distribution used. The total marketing plan for each market segment for all the product-service groups can be built up by adding the plans in each sub-cell in the columns of the promotional mix, within the specific market segment. This will give the total effort expended by each demand-creating tool used in the promotional mix directed to this customer-prospect group. The total plans for each promotional mix element, e.g., advertising or sales promotion, will be shown at the bottom of the respective columns. When these column totals are summated horizontally, the resultant figure will show the total marketing plan for all the want-satisfiers produced by this firm and sold, or offered for sale, to this specific customer-prospect segment.

Obviously, there will be as many of these segmental plans as there are categories in the market place (refer to the horizontal axis of Figure 7–2). Finally, the master marketing plan for the entire company consists of an aggregate of these segmental plans. Clearly, there are interactions and over-lappings as entries are made and as actions are contemplated. For example, when the various demand-creating forces for each marketplace segment have dollar values assigned them in terms of budgeting, compromises may have to be made. Also, in the case of certain demand-creative forces, a molar or "Gestalt" decision has to be made regarding the use of certain tools employed, and on the allocation of cost, as, for example, in the case of a management decision to do some institutional-type advertising. This type of advertising, e.g., General Electric's "Progress is our most important product," will supposedly help all or most of the product-service categories in all or most of the customer-prospect segments.

The Advantages

Notwithstanding these difficulties and complexities, it is far sounder to formulate plans segment by segment and aggregate them than to proceed as some companies are prone to do: from the total market place back to the various segments, with an *a priori* notion of the number of dollars available for advertising. It would certainly appear to be sounder to aggregate all contemplated advertising needs for all marketplace segments across all products and product groups and then to find out how many dollars will be required to do the job. Similarly, a company sometimes arrives at capricious decisions with regard to a total promotional budget available for a given product or product group. It would seem wiser to determine which segments of the market place are users or potential users of the products and services. Then decisions can be made concerning which demand-creating forces are best calculated to move that product or product group into those marketplace segments. Finally, estimated costs can be aggregated and weighed relative to potential profits.

In summary, the models suggest the need to build the marketing plan from sub-plans rather than to begin planning on the basis of the total market place. Moreover, they provide an easy-to-use flexible method for such planning.

MATRIX MODEL USE

An illustration of how these models can be used in industry may be helpful in clearing up any reservations the reader may have regarding their application and usefulness. A lumber producer and marketer sells its products world wide. Because of the different marketing techniques used for different geographical markets, the first segmentation of the customer-prospect mix is on a geographic basis. For example: (1) The North American market (United States and Canada), (2) The European market, (3) The Far Eastern market, (4) The remainder of world markets (Australia, New Zealand, South Africa, etc.). Although this division appears influenced by geographical factors only, there are other secondary bases for these divisions such as the products sold, the promotional tools used, and the channels of distribution employed in each market. This company then makes a further breakdown within each geographical area. If we take one of these areas—say North American sales—there is a further sub-division according to export or domestic sales. Taking just the U.S. market, a customer-prospect mix stratification would be: (1) wholesalers, (2) large retailers and chains, (3) industrial accounts, (4) contractors. These four categories are placed along the horizontal axis of Figure 7–2 for the U.S. sales department of this company as the most useful customer-prospect categories. [See Figure 7–10.]

The Examples

The answer to question 2 at the beginning of this article, what want-satisfiers is this company producing, would be: (1) lumber, (2) plywood, (3) shingles and siding, (4) pre-cut building components. These categories represent the vertical axis of the matrix in Figure 7–2 and serve somewhat differentiable wants in each customer-prospect segment.

Each cell within the array should now be analyzed in accordance with Figure 7–3. For example, the cell 2:1, the selling of plywood to the wholesalers, may look as in the accompanying example, within the context of the more encompassing diagram.

Customer–Prospect Mix

	(1) Wholesalers	(2) Retailers and Chains	(3) Industrial Accounts	(4) Contractors
(1) Lumber				
(2) Plywood				
(3) Shingles and Siding				
(4) Pre-cut Components				

Product–Service Mix

Figure 7—10. Example of the Use of Figure 7—2

Customer–Prospect Mix

	(1) — Wholesalers				(2)	(3)
(1)						
(2) Plywood		Past Sales (1 yr.)	Future Sales (1 yr.)	Trend		
	Industry Sales	*1,000,000 units*	*1,100,000 units*	*Up*		
	Company Sales	*100,000 units*	*120,000 units*	*Up*		
	Company Share of Market	*10%*	*10.9%*	*Up*		
(3)						
(4)						

Product–Service Mix

Figure 7—11. Example of the Use of Figure 7—3

Once this general overall picture is secured for all the cells within the array, the management is in a good position to analyze and plot the courses of action that it should take.

The next step in the analysis would be to use the answers to question 3 about demand-creating forces; these comprise the horizontal axis for each market segment. In other words, each segment of the customer-prospect mix is held constant. A promotional mix is developed for each product-service segment. The demand-creating or promotional forces that the company uses to promote the product groups to a market might be: (1) advertising, (2) personal selling, (3) merchandising, (4) sales promotion, (5) field service. Arranged schematically, the equivalent of Figure 7–6 for this company would appear as in the example.

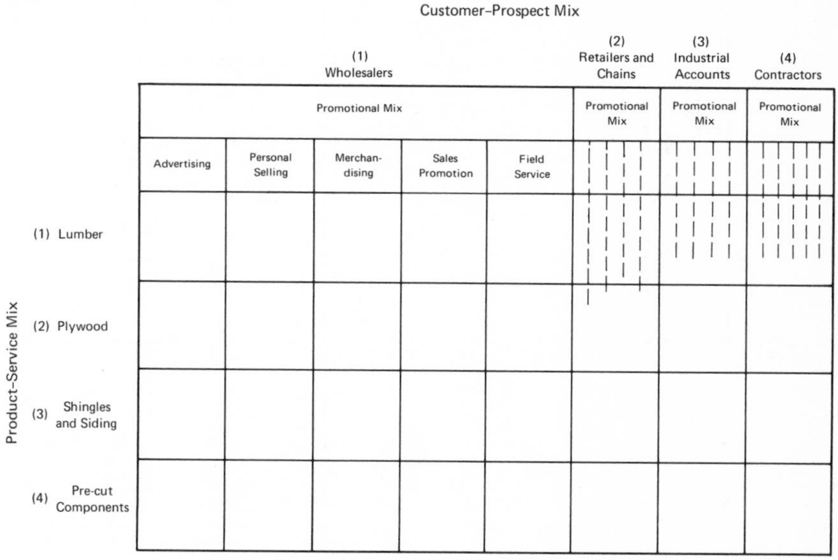

Figure 7–12. Example of the Use of Figure 7–6

Following the analysis used in the body of this article, the firm should next make a detailed study of the distribution channels which it uses for each product-service group to each segment of the customer-prospect mix. Staying with the example of selling plywood to wholesalers, this firm uses a direct approach, i.e., company house salesmen for large wholesalers located within a radius of one day's automobile travel time from the head office. For the smaller accounts within this geographical area the company uses manufacturers agents. The rest of the country is reached through company-owned decentralized warehouses. Thus this company uses three distinct channels of distribution. This would be shown on the diagram of Figure 7–7 for plywood to wholesalers as in the example detailed in Figure 7–13.

The final picture of the matrix analysis for this case would appear in Figure 7–14, considering only the selling of plywood to wholesalers.

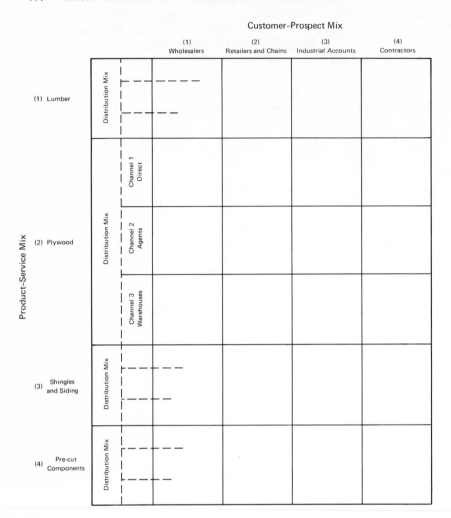

Figure 7—13. Example of the Use of Figure 7—7

Within each one of the sub-cells of Figure 7–8, there will be the equivalent of Figure 7–9, which will explain the objectives of, say, advertising of plywood to the wholesalers via the direct channel of distribution. Similarly there will be a Figure 7–9 for each other sub-cell within the diagram.

Once this analysis is made, management would then be in a position to evaluate the marketing program for each promotional tool used in presenting each product-service category to each market segment via each channel of distribution. For example, management would be able to see the objectives, the program, the proposed execution and the proposed evaluation for advertising plywood to wholesalers when using the direct channel.

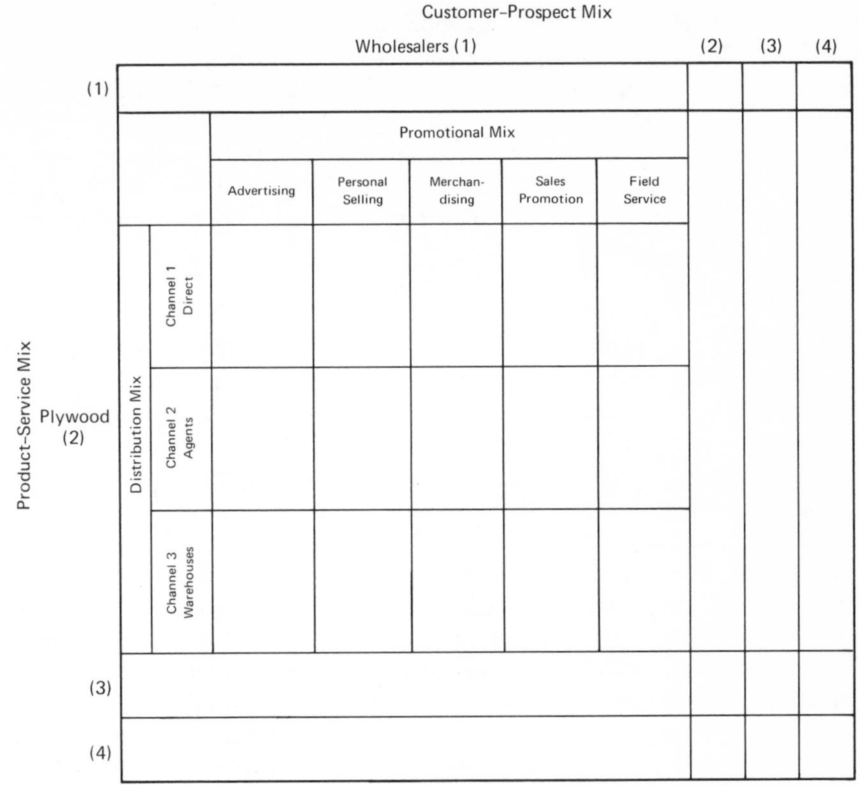

Figure 7—14. Example of the Use of Figure 7—8

Segment by Segment

These plans should then be aggregated into sub-groups which would tell the story of the use of all the promotional tools to be employed for the marketing of plywood to wholesalers through each channel. Carrying the analysis further, the same procedure should be done for all the product-service categories to all the customer-prospect segments. Once all these sub-groups are combined, management will then be able to evaluate the programs of selling each product to each market, the total effort put into one market segment (e.g., wholesalers for all product categories—lumber, plywood, shingles and siding, and components), and the total effort for each product (e.g., plywood to all market segments—wholesalers, retailers, industrials and contractors). The gross figure arrived at in our example will show the total cost of marketing—via the tools in the promotional mix—for all the product-service categories of lumber, plywood, shingles and siding, and pre-cut components to the four market segments of wholesalers, retailers and large chains, industrial accounts, and contractors for the United States market.

This analytical treatment of plywood and other product groups in the frame of reference of the total market and of the company's own sales is likely to be very helpful to the plywood products manager as well as to the general marketing management of the firm.

It can be seen, from this overly-simplified example, how the marketing plan for the U.S. sales department should be built up brick by brick, segment by segment, in order to arrive at a meaningful and useful total marketing plan.

CONCLUSION

Every company operating in the field of marketing, regardless of size, should concern itself with the management of its marketing effort. The program of market planning presented above gives a basic pattern that can be used by most companies. By using the matrix models the management team will be able to plan, execute, and control its marketing program efficiently. The advantages of using such a procedure are numerous but the two main ones are the flexibility of the model, which allows it to be adapted to any size company selling any product or products to any market or market segment; and the simplicity of the plan and of its components, which allows for a lot of the work to be delegated, and which means that, in aggregating, the total picture is easily comprehended from the summation.

Clearly, modern industry has reached the stage where production is not the major problem. It is almost platitudinous now to say that we no longer live in an age of scarcity but instead in an age of abundance. Therefore, the emphasis of corporate management should be on how to market most efficiently the goods that can be produced. To neglect this function is to cut off the life-line of the company.

8.

Phasing Research into the Marketing Plan

Lee Adler

Because of its preoccupation with gathering unrelated facts, the pressures of day-to-day business, and other unfortunate tendencies, marketing research today tends to be out of phase with other marketing operations.

The key to a larger and more important role for research is a systematic effort to design individual studies so that they not only contribute useful knowledge for short-term marketing needs but also help in the development of a long-range departmental program.

In making research planning effective, it is important to set up the work so that a series of studies can "feed in" to the needs of the marketing department as a whole.

Firms that have successfully used research planning have discovered in it a variety of important advantages, ranging from more sophistication and economy in the design of studies to better anticipation of marketing problems.

In the past few years there has been much talk about the creation of a unified concept of marketing research that would make it possible for researchers to grapple with marketing problems as seen by top management. Unfortunately, to date, this idea has remained talk more often than it has become action. As a consequence, marketing research is not helping to solve management's problems as it might.

If research executives want to assume more responsible positions in the corporate structure, they will have to find ways of increasing the contribution of their groups to the successful implementation of the marketing concept. By "marketing concept" I refer, of course, to the idea of customer rather than factory orientation, and to the idea of making integrated use of all the tools of marketing.

OBSTACLES TO PROGRESS

Success for the research executive is not likely to come easily. He inherits a legacy of practical difficulties. In company after company a gap exists between marketing research needs and fulfillment. Breakdowns of communication occur between researchers and marketing management. And many researchers' studies—prettily bound and lavishly illustrated with charts—gather dust.

Why? One reason looms large. The problems that marketing management must deal with are broad-scale and complex. But the problems that are defined for investigation by researchers are so delimited that the findings made either deal with too small a piece of the total problem or cannot be easily related to other aspects of the total problem. They lose their link with reality as the top marketing executive sees it.

What accounts for marketing research being out of phase with marketing in so many firms? There are, I believe, five principal reasons:

(1) *Preoccupation with the gathering of unrelated facts.* On the whole, American marketing researchers are busy collectors of isolated bits and pieces of information, but they pay scant attention to constructing bodies of knowledge. In part, this tendency derives from the history of research in the United States. Still in its formative years—50 years old altogether—the marketing research function has enjoyed substantial growth only since World War II. As a result, expectations from research have been modest. Many a corporate executive, if he authorizes research at all, has not looked for—and still does not look for—more than a mechanical assemblage of "facts" which he may or may not apply to the problem at hand. Accompanying this limited role for research have been limited budgets, staff, and time for doing a job thoroughly.

It is not surprising, then, that it is only accident when several studies in a field can be related to each other so that the whole is greater than the sum of the parts, or even as great as the sum of the parts.

(2) *Pressures of day-to-day business.* The competitive pressures of American business result in a demand for concentration on urgent, immediate problems to the exclusion of the more leisurely contemplation of broad problems. Of course, it is understandable that *some* short-range assignments of applied research cannot be readily integrated into any larger scheme. But to the extent that today's frantic drive to solve short-range problems deflects attention from the more fundamental and thornier problems of the long term, the urgencies of the market place do disservice to broader scale research.

This failing is not entirely the responsibility of researchers themselves. If pressing problems need solution, they must be solved, whether or not they contribute to a system of hypotheses for longer range study.

(3) *Insistence on rigorous methodology.* Robert K. Merton has noted that "the American [researcher] raises aloft the standards of affirming adequacy

of empirical data at any price, even at the price of surrendering the problem which first led to the inquiry."[1]

A case in point is the work of David Riesman. His studies have appeared to many to offer significantly new ways of looking at the American way of life, with important consequences for marketing management in his analysis of our consumption-oriented economy.[2] Yet the ardent defenders of rigorous methodology have criticized Riesman for his relaxed, impressionistic approach to his studies. The trouble is that the socio-psychological well-springs of our culture do not readily lend themselves to multiple correlation analysis. How can Riesman possibly cite levels of significance in his discussion of the "other-directed" personality?

Our culture is so complex and the forces prevailing on American consumers so numerous and subtle that a technician has trouble getting at them. By contrast, an approach which permits a freer play to imagination and a broader sweep to an investigation than statistical designs will allow stands a better chance of showing a more complete view of our society.

(4) *Tendency to specialize.* Applied research also mirrors the specialization of knowledge and function that characterizes American civilization. To a certain extent, the researcher and his work exemplify the popular observation that excesses of specialization result in "knowing more and more about less and less."

(5) *Recurring love affairs with new techniques.* In a curious way, the very advances made in marketing research contribute to the trend toward specialization by leading to a preoccupation with technique instead of content.

For example, during the past decade more and more behavioral scientists have joined the ranks of business researchers. And these men have had a healthy effect in broadening the horizons of applied research; they have made available entirely new dimensions and tools for solving problems. But instead of these welcome additions to the armory of researchers being integrated into a battery of weapons designed to combat problems in their totality, they have helped fragment research even more. The spotlight has played around on the methods, leaving the problems themselves partly in the dark.

Again, the injustice of pointing accusing fingers only at the researchers must be emphasized. As marketing management has become increasingly enamored of the new disciplines, it has created a demand for applied sociological and psychological research. And in research, too, the customer is always right.

Take motivation research. From being virtually unknown in the 1940's, the technique blossomed into the research giant of the late 1950's. Rightfully, the behavioral scientists insisted on documenting William I. Thomas' observa-

[1] *Social Theory and Social Structure* (Glencoe, Illinois, The Free Press, 1949), pp. 205–206.
[2] See *The Lonely Crowd* (New Haven, Yale University Press, 1950); and *Faces in the Crowd* (New Haven, Yale University Press, 1950).

tion that if men define situations as real, they are real in their consequences.[3] So the psychologists proceeded to demonstrate that products have not only rational meaning and serve utilitarian purposes for consumers, but also have symbolic and emotional meanings. Then, not so long ago, when there was great fascination with the discovery that men unconsciously regarded their cars as surrogates for the mistresses they enjoy in their fantasy lives, it was almost forgotten in Detroit that a more basic *raison d'être* for the automobile is to get people from one place to another at fairly reasonable cost. The stage was set for sexless and inexpensive foreign cars to have a field day.

The foregoing is, of course, oversimplified, and it is not intended as an attack on motivation research, already much maligned. I simply want to stress that new methods have succeeded too well in making American researchers and their clients technique-oriented instead of problem-oriented. A few years ago, probability samples were all the rage. Today it is fashionable to use the semantic differential technique. Preoccupation with any one method hurts marketing.

MEETING THE CHALLENGE

All this puts the research director in a tough spot. If, bowing to the needs and pressures just outlined, he designs and carries out studies dealing with very narrow problem areas, his findings will not fully meet the needs of marketing management. But if he goes to the other extreme and examines general, abstract questions, his data may have no validity at all for a particular firm in a particular situation. Somehow he must define his problems concretely enough to be manageable.

Is there a way out of this dilemma? I believe that there is. It seems to me that the solution lies in the formulation of an *over-all, long-range research program for each firm and for each market.* This program would be used to guide the design of individual studies so that they not only contribute knowledge for the short term but also contribute the evolution of a unified body of information needed to implement the marketing concept over the long term.

There is a common expression among advertising men about the need to "see the big picture." What they mean by this expression is, of course, the importance of having a framework of knowledge about their clients' problems, including every step involved in getting the product from the factory into happy and repeated use by the consumer. Having this framework, they can then relate individual bits and pieces of information to the whole. Short-range problems are seen for what they are. The day-to-day concerns of advertising the product do not become confused with the total problem of marketing it.

[3] William I. Thomas and Florian Znaniechi, *The Polish Peasant in Europe and America* (New York, Alfred A. Knopf, Inc., 1927).

What the alert advertising man does more or less impressionistically (or through disciplined intuition) when he looks at "the big picture" provides the key to the kind of research approach that is needed. Essentially, this approach calls for the prior or simultaneous formulation of long-range marketing objectives and the spelling out of the plans, policies, and programs calculated to reach those objectives through the use of the appropriate marketing tools. Describing these goals and plans in detail inevitably exposes the need for certain data which, in turn, leads to a listing of research projects over the same term as the marketing plan. It also suggests a priority order for their completion.

Here, in outline form, are the major steps that some progressive companies are taking in building long-range research programs which develop concurrently with, which parallel, which inform and are informed by the master long-term marketing plan:

1. Decide on long-term marketing objectives.
2. Enumerate in detail the policies, plans, and programs needed to attain the objectives.
3. Identify roadblocks barring progress toward goals and specify the areas where further information is necessary.
4. Define what and how the marketing research function can contribute to information gathering and problem solving.
5. Obtain the agreement of all members of the marketing team to objectives, plans, and programs.
6. Set up a priority order and timetable for the research projects.
7. Allocate the necessary budget, personnel, and facilities for implementing the program.

DEVELOPING THE PROGRAM

Defining a company's long-range goals is a painful, soul-searching process. But, as we have all learned by now, these goals should be as concrete as possible; this helps both in setting up plans and in assessing performance after the programs go into effect. Obvious as this seems, it is surprising how many companies continue to define an objective as "to boost sales" when more down-to-earth statements of sales targets are needed, such as:

Increase unit sales
Sell the whole line, not items
Improve share of market
Concentrate on key accounts
Introduce new products successfully
Gain greater immediate profitability
Open new territories

Such objectives, alone or in combination, are specific enough to help in the choice of tactics to implement the master marketing plan. In the assignment of sensible goals, research can help by turning up data on such questions as:

What share of market is rightfully ours?
What payout period on investment should we strive for?
Are we going after the best markets?
Should we be in this business in the first place?

For example, the marketing plan of a producer in the transportation field was predicated for many years on the oversimplified sales goal of selling as much of its service as possible. This firm believed that all men were potential customers. Hence, the only criterion available to it for the proper use of such tools as advertising copy and media selection was that of reaching adult males. Later, marketing research showed that there was an enormous concentration of potential customers among businessmen who traveled considerably. The sales goal was then defined more specifically so as to concentrate marketing efforts on this crucial market segment. As a result, it was possible to reach the market more effectively and economically.

Team Activity

Effective long-range planning is necessarily a team activity. In addition to the immediate members of the marketing team, headed up by the marketing vice president or his equivalent, many companies have found it wise to have production, finance, and control men participate sufficiently so that (1) they understand and accept the marketing targets established and (2) the marketing goals harmonize with the over-all corporate objectives. In a framework of this kind the researcher can contribute more than he himself is able to see. The value of his data is not limited to what he can infer from it.

The responsibility of marketing to develop such a role for research is exemplified by Westinghouse Electric Corporation's philosophy: "The entire organization (research, engineering, production, and marketing) must work together to determine what the customer wants, how best to produce it, how to motivate its sales, and how to deliver it."[4] To achieve this over-all goal, each division of the Westinghouse organization is bound into the over-all plan and its contributions clearly delineated. Simultaneously, marketing and product research are specified at each phase of the cycle leading from initial customer indications of what they want to their ultimately being sold what they want. Each individual research study is coordinated with the other elements of the program and becomes a part of the whole structure of marketing knowledge.

[4] James Jewell, vice president of marketing, Westinghouse Electric Corporation, in an address before the Marketing Committee of the National Association of Manufacturers, Spring, 1958.

PROBLEMS AND SOLUTIONS

To understand the planning approach better, let us turn now to some concrete problems. These will help to show the kinds of alternatives that confront managers wishing to make research an integral part of marketing, and the kinds of decisions that contribute to progress.

Media Selection

A good type of problem to begin with is media selection because, for many firms, it is a vital part of the larger problem of developing a unified marketing strategy. Moreover, not only do considerations of product, budget, market position, marketing objectives, and creative strategy affect media choice, but it is also influenced by numerous psychological and personal factors, by the diverse selling activities of media themselves, and by the various individuals in companies and advertising agencies who participate in buying space and time. Figure 8–1 represents an attempt to portray these relationships schematically. Now here, briefly, is an illustrative case history:

In 1958 the Market Planning Corporation (now Marplan) was commissioned by *Printers' Ink* to assess the forces which affect media selection and to show how advertisers' decisions in this area are reached. One of the alternatives considered by the research team assigned to conceptualizing the problem was to isolate one or two crucial variables and intensively analyze their influence on media selection. Here are three examples of what might have been done:

1. It would have been legitimate for a researcher to design a study to explore the awareness of and attitudes toward media's own marketing activities (advertising, direct mail, research, personal selling, and so on) on the part of advertisers and advertising agency executives.
2. It would have been equally proper for a researcher to design a study to investigate the range and differential roles of personnel at advertising agencies and their clients in selecting media.
3. A technique-oriented motivation researcher might have concerned himself with the unconscious reasons affecting the selection of some media and not others, the correlation between certain personality types and choice of certain media, and the influence of prestige, habit, and other emotion-laden factors.

Another approach would have been to design research which would come to grips with *all* phases of the problem. It was foreseen that a narrowly designed project would preclude obtaining sufficient information by which to judge the relative importance of the factors analyzed compared with others known to exist but not investigated. However, this alternative presented the difficulty of sorting out numerous factors and, in all likelihood, the disadvantage of being unable to make precise statements about the findings.

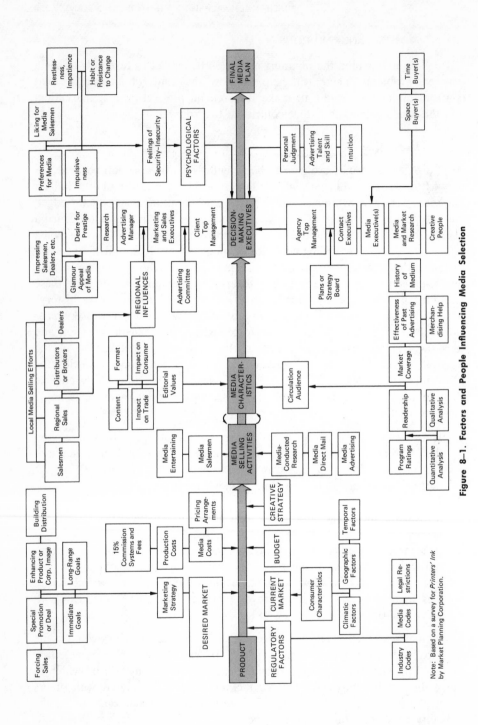

Figure 8–1. Factors and People Influencing Media Selection

Note: Based on a survey for *Printers' Ink* by Market Planning Corporation.

At first, therefore, the research team appeared to have a choice between dealing with a small problem with a high degree of scientific rigor or dealing with a large problem with only moderate scientific rigor.

It was then recognized that the advantages of the two research philosophies might be well mated in the form of a plan which would allow enough breadth for rich hypothesis formulation, on the one hand, and means for quantifying some of the findings, on the other hand.

The techniques chosen reflected this hybridization approach, too. For instance, the major instrument of research was that of the "depth" interview, using the "probes" of the psychological researcher to dig deeper after the respondent had exhausted his spontaneous comments, but the interviews were sufficiently structured by question guides to follow a broad outline and thus allow for systematic analysis.

As a result, it was possible to reach conclusions that would not have emerged from a one-dimensional study of one aspect of the problem. If, for example, the study had been more narrowly conceived and been an analysis of reactions to the various tools used by media men to sell space and time, it would have yielded data on how to strengthen media's selling approach— useful but of tactical value only. As it was, the broader approach covered the roles of various executives in decision making, and this produced data of a more basic nature, with more implications for management. Among other things, it was learned that a far greater number of men exercise some influence than had been hitherto suspected, ranging from the lowliest media clerk at the agency up to the chairman of the board of the client firm. This suggested the need for media to reach *every* decision-influencer, not just the media buyer, the account executive, or the advertising manager.

"Feed-In" Process

To make planning effective, it is important to conceive of and set up programs so that a series of research studies can feed into the picture.

In the case just described, for instance, the first research project was followed up by a second designed to probe even more deeply into the factors affecting the selection of major media classes: newspapers, radio, magazines, television, and the business press. Still other studies were projected to evaluate the problems of more specific media groups, such as station representative firms and news magazines. In other words, the over-all, long-range plan was being used to guide the development of individual studies so that they would not only contribute knowledge needed for immediate decisions but would also be helpful in constructing a theory of media marketing that would be useful for the long term.

There is no one rule for systematizing this "feeding-in" process. To a considerable degree it depends on the nature of the problem. For example:

In the case of a firm planning a new product, the research process might last at least several years and go from initial consumer research through product testing, analysis of the most suitable channels of distribution, test marketing, and then repeat consumer research to check on product satisfaction and use—with each study being atomistic in design and yet contributing to the over-all picture.

By contrast, in the study of media selection just described, "feed in" occurred in two ways: (a) the first study was broad-gauge enough so that its separate parts contributed importantly to the desired whole, while (b) later studies were planned to add more brush strokes to the picture.

A New Product

Let us turn now to a more detailed problem in new product marketing. The case I shall describe here concerns a leading manufacturer of consumer durables. Since the innovation represented a radical departure from the proven product in its field, the company felt the need for considerable research. As Figure 8–2 shows, the research followed a logical sequence (dates and some of the details of the plan have been disguised):

Phase I. As soon as the technical feasibility of making the new item was determined, but before the company had committed any significant funds to the idea, consumer and dealer attitudes were sought. Was there enough dissatisfaction with the current product to create a solid foundation for marketing a new one? Would dealers carry and support such a product? What ideas did consumers and dealers have that might improve on the proposition?

Phase II. The response to these questions being encouraging, the company authorized product development and laboratory tests. The latter were conducted both by company personnel and, later on, by an outside testing firm.

With product development proceeding favorably, research went into high gear early in 1958. The marketing research director designed a consumer usage test to measure product performance under normal conditions. As soon as findings became available from this research to serve as guidance, a test was conducted to select the name that would best convey a favorable image of the product. Next several package designs and dealer sales promotion and merchandising materials were prepared and tested. Each research project was feeding into the succeeding one as the marketing mix for the new product took shape.

In the meantime, the consumer survey had pointed up a possible problem involving one product feature. The problem was referred back to product development and testing; a modification in the design was made, and a special consumer test was conducted to check the acceptability of the revised feature to consumers. The funds for this research were drawn from a reserve set aside at the initiation of the whole plan for unforeseen problems.

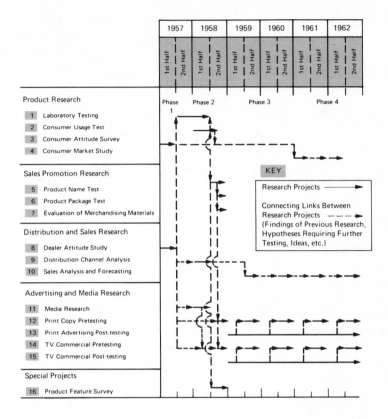

Figure 8—2. Six-Year Marketing Research Plan for a New Consumer Product
(Market Introduction—Spring 1959)

During Phase II the marketing research department also analyzed its dealer organization to help sales management choose the broad classifications of dealers and also the individual dealers particularly well qualified to get the product off to a good start. This step was especially important since there were not enough units produced initially to supply all retailers. As the exhibit indicates, the earlier dealer attitude study was useful in selecting trade channels.

Media research was also undertaken to answer the questions: (1) which media classes to use and (2) which specific media to use. As soon as it was decided that consumer magazines and spot television would be the principal media, the agency began to prepare advertising. The consumer surveys were used extensively in determining creative strategy. Ads and commercials were then pretested to ensure that the most effective appeals possible would be used.

Phase III. During this stage, the company instituted what were to become *continuous* research projects. These projects included pretesting new printed and broadcast advertising, as well as tests of advertising after it had appeared, using regular rating services for this latter work. The exhibit indicates that the findings from "post-testing" were used to improve the ads subsequently designed and pretested.

Simultaneously, the company began a program of *continuing* sales analysis, which included breakdowns of sales by categories of retail trade, salesmen, price lines, geographic areas, and so on. This activity was designed to lead to annual sales forecasts that could be used to formulate more accurate production and marketing plans. Territorial sales analysis is also being used to assess salesmen's performance and to set up area potentials, sales quotas, and a sales incentive program.

Phase IV. The company is now in this phase. A large-scale consumer survey is planned for two years after market introduction. Management expects that by this time there should be sufficiently broad distribution and consumer experience with the new product to make such a study informative and practicable from a cost standpoint.

For succeeding years, the firm's marketing research director has recommended repeating from five to ten of the key questions of the large-scale consumer study, either in a mail survey among members of a consumer panel or as part of another national study. The purpose of this continuing research is to trace trends in product penetration and acceptance at low cost.

IN RETROSPECT

Marketing research planning—particularly the long-range variety—is not easy, and the approaches to it contain various pitfalls. But five important advantages of planning show that it is worthwhile to cope with the problems and circumvent the pitfalls.

1. *Those firms which have most successfully used this kind of planning have discovered that it not only helps to pinpoint areas of needed research but contributes to far more sophisticated research.* For instance:

In 1957 a major oil company defined its marketing objectives for the following decade with a view to maximizing its share of the market in each of the states it served. In detailing its plan, it was recognized that more knowledge would be necessary in numerous areas. (There were wide variations in marketing opportunities and in the company's status in each state, which complicated the planning picture considerably.)

Accordingly, demographic and automobile ownership and expenditure trends in each state were studied; trends in public and private transportation and highway growth were considered. Many other questions were examined— for example, the pricing structure of the industry; practices in service station ownership, operation, and personnel; changes in consumer shopping habits;

the rising influence of private brands; and pertinent developments in such other fields as highway retailing.

In effect, a study of nearly every factor that conditioned the firm's marketing effort was built into the over-all research program. From a management viewpoint, this resulted in more useful findings than could have been obtained by "bits and pieces" studies of the diverse facets of petroleum marketing.

2. *Another common benefit is a multidimensional quality to the research.* It may have breadth; that is, it may cover different sectors of the marketing front. It may also have *depth*; that is, more than one type of research may be used in a sector over a period of time. Thus:

In the case of a whiskey brand, motivation research was utilized to explore attitudes toward the product. This qualitative study furnished insights of considerable value in planning the creative strategy for the promotion of the brand. Subsequently, it became important to determine exactly how widespread these consumer attitudes were, both geographically and among socioeconomic groups. Accordingly, the attitudinal data were quantified through the use of a structured questionnaire and a large nationwide probability sample.

Market analysis, employing secondary data from trade and government sources, then documented the size, character, and potential of given markets, while a briefer study among liquor retailers identified their reactions to the brand.

Strengthening the multidimensional character of this research was the use of parallel questions to cement the separate studies together. Thus, in the consumer studies respondents were queried about a unique product characteristic. The counterpart of this question was then put to dealers. By relating the findings from both surveys, important conclusions were reached leading to better promotion.

Thus, it was learned that retailers had not been sufficiently motivated (in terms of higher markup, local advertising, special merchandising aids, and so forth) to learn the whiskey's unusual sales appeal, let alone use it to push the brand to their customers. It was thus logical to recommend stronger preselling to consumers coupled with a promotional "deal" for retailers which made it worthwhile for them to stress the brand's unique sales story.

All in all, the sum of this research in terms of value was greater than the mere addition of its parts.

3. *Long-range research planning is economical.* By taking inventory of research needs, it is occasionally possible to combine what would otherwise be two studies into one, with consequent savings. An industrial goods manufacturer achieved such an economy in this way:

His sales department was concerned about negative attitudes on the part of the firm's wholesalers toward a new functional discount policy. The sales manager was interested in having research conducted on this matter. In the meantime, the head of the public relations department was evolving a new campaign and required knowledge of wholesalers' attitudes in the industry. As a result of joint planning, these respective needs were made known, and the research manager was able to map out one trade survey to fill both needs.

Economy also results from the fact that research is permitted a more logical and useful sequence of development.

4. *Planning tends to assure greater application of research to marketing problems.* Fewer reports wind up gathering dust. The reason is plain: by building research into the plan, making it an integral part of marketing activity, and obtaining greater acceptance for it by members of the marketing team, it can be brought to bear on problems far more effectively. Also, of course, a project is likely to be more useful if it has its birth in marketing problems or information deficiencies. Technique is not confounded with problem solving, and research becomes more sensitive to the needs of management.

5. *More marketing problems are anticipated.* This means that research can be provided in sufficient time to eliminate some of the "firefighting" that characterizes the operations of so many companies.

Pitfalls to Avoid

As with any other relatively new procedure, there are "bugs" in long-range research planning which need to be eliminated. The hard lessons from experience of companies in the vanguard of planning can be summarized briefly like this:

1. Do not leave the planning to the director of marketing research alone. He is only one of the marketing team; the procedure requires a joint effort to be successful. The research director's contribution during the planning stage is:

To help isolate problems amenable to research and delineate fuzzy information areas.

To outline the scope and method of research which will prove most effective.

To indicate the contribution research is expected to make.

To furnish time, cost, and personnel estimates to help in setting up timetables, budgets, and staff requirements.

2. Do not attempt to incorporate too much detail into the plan, particularly for any period more than a year away. The usual consequence is to become bogged down in details that lead to frustrations, delays, and, at worst, abandoned plans.

3. Modify the plan as often as market and other conditions dictate. The very life and value of a program stem from its flexibility and responsiveness to the market place. A static plan soon becomes a worthless plan.

4. Formalize the plan by committing it to paper and distributing copies to all of the individuals involved in its development and use. Although this may sound a bit naive, it is amazing how many hours are spent in meetings creating a long-range plan without an official record being compiled of the decisions reached. It is also valuable to have responsible officials initial the document. Psychologically, it builds up their stake in the plan's soundness and success.

5. See that there are sufficient funds, personnel, and facilities for the marketing research department to carry on the bigger job called for by thinking ahead.

CONCLUSION

To serve management better, marketing research must become broader gauge. It must escape its preoccupation with narrow investigations of limited utility. It is true that broad definitions of problems often make for unmanageable research projects, but this is not a major obstacle. The solution suggested is to devise long-range research plans so that they will guide the design of individual studies. Research can then furnish data needed for today's decisions *and* contribute to the accumulation of information needed for making long-range decisions.

To begin, marketing management must be able to define its long-range goals and detail the action programs necessary to attain those goals. This detailing of plans inevitably highlights problems and information gaps. Marketing research should then be called on to map out long-range plans to solve the problems and fill the information gaps. A timetable should be agreed on, and the plan implemented with the help of the necessary budget aid, personnel, and facilities.

Operating executives in marketing are not the only ones to gain from planning. Research practitioners themselves stand to benefit considerably. We are all familiar with such epithets for researchers as "residents of ivory towers," "the slide rule brigade," and so on. The images thus created, right or wrong, have helped relegate the research function to a position of limited stature. The planning concept, with its emphasis on what research can do for departmental operations, can help to change all this.

It can be reasonably anticipated that the hunger for certainty in marketing operations will result not only in more calls for helpful facts but in increasing demands for measures of marketing effectiveness. The opportunity for research executives is exciting. To the extent that they are able to see a marketing problem in its totality, they will be seeing it as top marketing executives do. By thus being alert to general management needs, they will have won half the battle for greater recognition and acceptance.

9.

Market Segmentation Research: Findings and Implications

Ronald E. Frank

The strategy of market segmentation is defined as the development and pursuit of different marketing programs by the same firm, for essentially the same product, but for different components (for example, heavy versus light buyers) of the overall market. The logic underlying this strategy is deceivingly simple and straightforward. Presumably the market for a product is made up of customers who differ either in their own characteristics or in the nature of their environment in such a way that some aspect of their demand for the product in question also differs. The strategy of market segmentation involves the tailoring of the firm's product and/or marketing program to these differences. By modifying either of these, the firm is attempting to increase profits by converting a market with heterogeneous demand characteristics into a set of markets that although they differ from one another, are internally more homogeneous than before.

For example, a cereal manufacturer may choose to develop products especially tailored to the younger set such as sugar-coated or alphabet-shaped cereals. Another example of segmentation is the attempt by many manufacturers to aim their promotion disproportionately at the heavy buyer of a product by choosing media that have a particularly strong appeal to this group.

The concept of segmentation was first articulated in a pioneering article by Wendell Smith in 1956 [31]. Since its publication, this concept has permeated the thinking of managers and researchers alike as much, if not more, than any other single marketing concept since the turn of the century. The importance of segmentation as a source of increased profits was highlighted in *Grey Matter*:

> Markets of the future will not only be segmented but each segment will be fragmented. Even fragments will offer great profit opportunities because of our

From Ronald E. Frank, "Market Segmentation Research: Findings and Implications," in Frank M. Bass, Charles W. King, and Edgar A. Pessemier, eds., *The Application of the Sciences to Marketing Management* (New York: John Wiley & Sons, Inc., 1968), pp. 39–68. Reprinted by permission.

mushrooming population, expanding affluence, and spreading education. Advertisers who see the future clearly and develop the skill to cultivate *diverse segments and fragments* will sharpen their competitive edge [18, p. 4].

According to Smith:

> The phenomenon of market segmentation suggests that, even in an economy characterized by imperfect competition, a drift toward equilibrium in market segments is discernible. It is worthy to note that the emergence of market segmentation as a strategy once again provides evidence of the consumer's preeminence in the contemporary American economy . . . [30, p. 3].

In other words, to the extent that firms take advantage of existing opportunities for market segmentation, their actions are apt to benefit not only themselves but also their ultimate consumers. On the other hand, the choice of segmentation as a strategy, when in fact it is unwarranted, can result in losses to both groups.

Marketing management is faced with two crucial decisions with respect to segmentation:

1. To what extent should the firm pursue a strategy of market segmentation?
2. If the market is to be segmented, upon what basis (or bases) should it be segmented?

It is normal to answer the first question in the affirmative if it can be shown that, on the average, certain segments (groups) of people buy more of the product under consideration than do other groups.

These customer segments are usually classified in terms of socioeconomic, life-cycle, or locational characteristics, although other dimensions such as personality variables may also be used. Groups for which the *average purchase rate* is high are identified as "target" market segments. Presumably, if average purchase rates were equal among all groups of a product's customers, segmentation would not be a profitable strategy.

How can we judge the validity of this conclusion? Are there criteria, other than the existence of differences in average purchase rate among various groups of customers, that are associated with opportunities for profitable market segmentation? The following section presents a conceptual framework for determining whether market segmentation will, in fact, result in higher profits. As we shall see, differences in average purchase rates are only one of several demand criteria for judging opportunities for profitable market segmentation.

This section is followed by a review of research on the usefulness of household socioeconomic, personality, and purchasing characteristics as bases for segmenting a wide range of grocery product markets. The majority of the work reported consists of investigations that I conducted with William

Massy and Harper Boyd, Jr. This chapter concludes with a discussion of the implications of our work, to date, together with some suggestions for further research.

CRITERIA FOR SEGMENTATION

Management needs criteria for determining the extent to which segmenting a market would place it in a more beneficial position than would treating it as a homogeneous entity. What should these criteria be? Presumably a firm desires to achieve increased profits through segmentation. Under what conditions can these be obtained?

If the incremental costs of serving different customers in a market are the same, then there is only one condition under which a firm can achieve greater profitability through market segmentation: different groups of customers must have different responses to changes in the firm's marketing program. Consider, for example, a market in which some customers are very likely to switch brands in response to a cut in price while others are more sensitive to changes in national advertising. If we could identify these segments and find a way to reach them separately, greater profits could probably be achieved by charging somewhat different prices and aiming different levels of advertising at each group.

This idea can be restated as follows. "In the language of economics, segmentation is *disaggregative* in its effects and tends to bring about recognition of several demand schedules where only one was recognized before" [31, p. 5].[1] A demand schedule is simply an expression for the quantity of a product that is demanded at each of the number of different price or promotional levels.

Suppose, for example, that a firm is spending the same amount of promotional funds on all of its customers. Furthermore, suppose that it is trying to sell as much output as possible, in light of its promotional budget. An increase in promotional expenditures is contemplated. Should the firm extend the offer to all of its customers? If management knew that a particular identifiable group of customers (a market segment) would increase its expenditures on the product by $10 per unit sold, whereas other customers would tend to increase their total expenditures by only $5 per unit, it clearly would be better off if it cut its prices to the first group, thereby selling an increased proportion of its output to that segment. This would continue until the incremental revenue associated with the sale of an additional unit was the same for the two groups. This is a well-recognized principle in the field of economics.

In other words, one crucial criterion for determining the desirability of segmenting a market along any particular dimension is whether the different

---

[1] For a more detailed statement of the logic underlying this point, see Ref. 29.

submarkets have different elasticities with respect to the price and promotional policies of a firm. An elasticity is simply a summary measure that relates a percentage change in quantity demanded to the associated percentage change in some casual variable, such as price.

Where there are differences in the incremental costs involved in serving customers in the different submarkets, these cost differences should be matched against the effects of price and promotion upon demand in order to arrive at a criterion for judging the desirability of market segmentation. The treatment of costs in market segmentation is beyond the scope of this chapter; the important point for our purposes is that, whether costs are equal or not, the degree to which the demand elasticities in the various submarkets are different from one another remains a crucial criterion for market segmentation.[2]

In spite of the importance of response differences as a criterion for judging the appropriateness of market segmentation, only three studies have (1) reported results bearing upon this problem and (2) illustrated techniques for operationally defining the magnitude and nature of these differences [12, 14, 25]. All three of these studies have appeared in the literature since 1963. Variations in the response of customers to promotion, although not the only criterion for evaluating a given strategy of market segmentation, is the most neglected in the literature.

The most commonly discussed criterion is the extent of differences in the average purchase rate among various customer segments. It is frequently the practice in empirical research dealing with the demand for a given brand in a product class (for example, the Del Monte brand of canned corn) to base elasticity estimates on the response of the brand's market share to changes in pricing, retail advertising, and similar things. Although these response estimates are useful, they do not take into account differences in the average purchase rates for the various segments. Therefore, both elasticity and average purchase-rate criteria are required for an analysis of the usefulness of a given scheme of market segmentation.

In addition to these criteria, effective segmentation depends (in part) on the ability to communicate separately with whatever segments are of interest. To the extent that the segments are identical with respect to such characteristics as their socioeconomic status, personality, and media habits, the effectiveness of segmentation is severely constrained.

Summary of Criteria

We have found it useful to think of these criteria in terms of the following questions.

---

[2] For a discussion of the relationship between costs and promotional sensitivities, see Ref. 1.

1. To what extent can members of each segment be identified in terms of characteristics such as socioeconomic status, personality, and media habits?
2. What is the degree of variation in the average level of customer demand for the product from one segment to another?
3. What is the degree of variation in customer sensitivity to changes in the firm's promotional policies as well as those of competitors? That is, do customers in one segment respond to a greater or lesser degree than those in another to changes in such promotional inputs as the rate of dealing and retail advertising as well as price level?

If customers belonging to different segments (for instance, high- and low-brand loyalty) have virtually identical incomes, personalities, and media exposures, then the effectiveness of segmentation based on this dimension is severely constrained because there is no way to tailor promotion to any one segment. Instead, segmentation must be directed at the entire population of customers.

In addition, if the average level of customer demand and customer sensitivity to changes in promotion is the same for all segments, there are no incremental profit opportunities to provide motivation for segmenting the market along the dimension being considered.

In contrast, where differences in average demand levels or sensitivities do exist, there is the possibility that segmentation will lead to increased profits. Whether increased profits are, in fact, associated with segmentation also depends on the magnitude of any incremental costs that are incurred in the tailoring of the marketing program to each segment.

SOME RESEARCH FINDINGS

The most frequently used bases for defining the market segments to be considered as targets for promotion are these household bases:

1. Demographic and socioeconomic characteristics, occasionally together with personality traits.
2. Purchasing characteristics, especially the total consumption of a product (that is, heavy versus light buyers) and brand loyalty.

In the following two sections of this chapter, each of these bases for segmentation is evaluated in terms of the three previously mentioned criteria. Although the findings presented do not completely resolve the issues that are discussed, they nevertheless provide a somewhat better basis for evaluation than has been previously available in the literature.

Demographic, Socioeconomic, and Personality Characteristics as Bases for Market Segmentation

The evaluation of demographic, socioeconomic, and personality characteristics as bases for market segmentation rests primarily on the answers to questions 2 and 3 in the preceding section; that is, the extent to which these characteristics are associated either with differences in *average purchase rates* or *responses* to the firm's promotional activities. The problem of identifiability is of somewhat less interest, since it is (in part) built into the definition of the segments. For example, obviously high- and low-income segments can be identified in terms of income.[3]

Average Purchase Rate Differences.   The most extensive investigation of the relationship between household purchase rate and demographic-socioeconomic characteristics was conducted by Frank, Massy, and Boyd [15]. Their study was based on *Chicago Tribune* panel data for 1961. These authors obtained a complete purchase history for 491 households for each of 57 product categories. The categories ranged from food products (such as regular coffee, carbonated beverages, margarine, and peanut butter) to household products (such as liquid detergents, scouring cleaners, toilet tissue, and food wrappers).

For a particular product category, we have a record of each individual purchase made by every household in the panel. The record of an individual purchase includes the brand purchased, the date of the transaction, the quantity, the package size, the total cost, the source from which the purchase was made, and whether a deal was associated with the transaction. A deal was defined as some special inducement to purchase (for instance, a 5¢-off label), a coupon allowing some reduction of price, or the inclusion of a premium with the purchase. (Many of the studies reported in this work were based on panel data. Although the panel involved differed from study to study, the type of data available did not. Thus, this description will not be repeated.)

Separate multiple regression analyses were conducted for each of the product categories. The dependent variable was the quantity of the product purchased by the household during 1961, while the independent variables were fourteen socioeconomic characteristics (for example, size of family, income, occupation, education, and so on).

[3] The question of identification might be further pursued in this context by an analysis of the intercorrelations existing between demographic, socioeconomic, and personality characteristics. The interrelations between the demographic and socioeconomic variables used in the results to be reported are relatively small. An analysis of the relations between these variables and personality characteristics is in progress, although results are not as yet available [24].

The multiple R^2's associated with each of the 57 regressions provided a measure of the proportion of variation in purchase rate from household to household that was accounted for by the net effect of the fourteen socioeconomic characteristics.

The highest proportion of variation in the quantity of product purchased from household to household was 0.29 for rice cereals. In 46 of 57 product categories, the proportion of variation explained was less than 0.20. In addition, less than 10 percent of household variation in consumption was explained in about one half (25) of the categories.

In 1961, Koponen published a study (based on J. Walter Thompson's panel data for 12 household products) that, although the products were not all identified, consisted of more than one grocery product [22]. The data base comprised purchase data for the 12 products (for an unspecified period of time), a record of household socioeconomic characteristics, and the results of the Edwards personal preference schedule for both the husband and wife in each household. The Edwards schedule generates measures of 15 personality traits for each individual (see Table 9–1 for a list of the measures). Most of Koponen's presentation was based primarily on two-way cross-classification analysis, which makes it virtually impossible to separate the effects of personality and socioeconomic characteristics on the expected household purchase rate for a product. Two products were singled out for regression analysis, neither of which were identified. In one analysis, only 100 households were included (out of 5000). There were 19 independent variables, 4 of which were socioeconomic, and 15 of which were personality (no indication was given of which 15 out of the 30 possible variables). In the case of the other product, the regression included all households in the panel. There were 20 independent variables (which were not defined). At any rate Koponen reports that, in the case of the first product only 13 percent of the variation in total household consumption was explained whereas, in the second regression, only 6 percent of the variation was explained. Neither household-demographic, socioeconomic, nor personality characteristics were highly associated with the amount of a product purchased by a household.

A subsequent study, using the same panel (JWT) that Koponen used, was conducted by the Advertising Research Foundation (ARF) [21]. The ARF study is based on toilet tissue purchasing behavior for 3206 members of the J. Walter Thompson panel in 1956. For each household, the ARF had a record of 15 socioeconomic characteristics and the results of the Edwards personal preference schedule for both husband and wife.[4]

---

[4] Twelve measures for both husband and wife were included. Three measures (achievement, dominance, and heterosexuality) were excluded because of the high level of multicollinearity associated with their presence in the equation.

Table 9–1

---

1. Achievement: to do one's best, to accomplish tasks of great significance, or requiring skill and effort, and to do things better than others.
2. Deference: to get suggestions, follow instructions, do what is expected, accept leadership of others, and conform to custom.
3. Order: to have work neat and organized, make plans before starting, keep files, and to have things arranged to run smoothly.
4. Exhibition: to say witty things, tell amusing jokes and stories, talk about personal achievements, and have others notice and comment on one.
5. Autonomy: to be able to come and go as desired, say what one thinks, be independent in making decisions, and feel free to do what one wants.
6. Affiliation: to be loyal to friends, do things for friends, form new friendships, make many friends, and to form strong attachments.
7. Intraception: to analyze one's motives and feelings, observe and understand others, analyze the behavior of others, and predict their acts.
8. Succorance: to be helped by others, to seek encouragement, have others be kindly, to receive affection, and have others feel sorry when sick.
9. Dominance: to be a leader, to argue for one's point of view, make group decisions, settle arguments, and persuade and influence others.
10. Abasement: to feel guilty when wrong, accept blame, feel need for punishment, feel timid in the presence of superiors, and feel inferior.
11. Nurturance: to help friends in trouble, treat others with kindness, forgive others, do small favors, be generous, and show affection.
12. Change: to do new and different things, to travel, to meet new people, try new things, eat in new places, and live in different places.
13. Endurance: to keep at a job until finished, work hard at a task, keep at a problem until solved, and finish one job before starting others.
14. Heterosexuality: to go out with opposite sex, to be in love, to kiss, to discuss sex, and to become sexually excited.
15. Aggression: to tell others what one thinks of them, to criticize others publicly, to make fun of others, and to tell others off.

The ARF conducted a multiple regression analysis aimed at determining the degree of association between household personality, socioeconomic characteristics, and total units purchased. Separate analyses were made for both one- and two-ply tissues.

The total predictive efficacy, as measured by the square of the multiple correlation coefficient, was 0.12 for one-ply tissue and 0.06 for two-ply tissue. The ARF results were quite consistent with those reported in the two preceding studies.

Massy, Frank, and Lodahl also conducted an analysis of the association between total household purchases and demographic-socioeconomic-personality attributes [26]. Their data base was the same as that used by the ARF (J. Walter Thompson panel data) except that they analyzed beer-, coffee-, and tea-purchasing behavior instead of toilet tissue-purchasing behavior.

Table 9–2 presents separated analyses for each of the three product categories and, within each category, for two different measures of total household purchases. The two measures are:

1. A total purchases factor score.
2. Total number of units purchased by a household.

The principal measure of total household purchases used by Massy, Frank, and Lodahl was the factor score. For each household in a given product category, a score was generated as a result of a factor analysis conducted on 29 measures of household-purchasing behavior. The 29 variables consist of measures of the rate of household consumption, the degree of brand loyalty, the degree of store loyalty, and the extent of dealing engaged in by the household. One of the factors that clearly stood out as a result of the analysis was total purchases. The total purchase factor scores, generated for each household, can be viewed as weighted averages of the 29 dimensions upon which the analysis was based, where by far the highest weights are given to measures such as the total number of units purchased, the number of shopping trips, and the like. The factors scores were used as dependent variables in place of these raw purchase variables.

The results are based on a multiple regression analysis that included 24 personality measures from the Edwards test and five household socioeconomic characteristics. For each combination of product and total purchases measure, three statistics are reported:

1. The square of the correlation coefficient (R^2) which measures the extent to which the 29 variables are associated with the particular measure of total purchases under study.
2. An F-ratio that provides information as to the extent which the observed degree of association is due to chance (F).

Table 9–2
Massy, Frank, and Lodahl Study Results: Total Household Purchases

	R^2	F	F-ADD	Number of Households
Beer				486
Factor score	0.07	1.25	0.80	
Number of units purchased	0.07	1.25	1.25	
Regular coffee				1283
Factor score	0.06	2.69[a]	1.61[a]	
Number of units purchased	0.07	3.04[a]	2.30[a]	
Tea				900
Factor score	0.07	2.18[a]	1.18	
Number of units purchased	0.07	2.31[a]	1.19	

[a] Significant at the 5% level.

3. An F-ratio that measures the extent to which knowledge of husband and wife personality characteristics contribute to our ability to predict total household purchases once socioeconomic characteristics are known (F-ADD).

At best, only 7 percent of the variation in total household purchasing for a product is accounted for by the net effect of household demographic, socio-economic, and personality characteristics. These results are not encouraging when considering these characteristics as bases for market segmentation. Based on this analysis, the heavy-buying household apparently has a profile of demographic, socioeconomic, and personality characteristics that is virtually identical to that of households exhibiting a lower rate of purchasing. Furthermore, the fact that the only two of the $F = $ ADD ratios are statistically significant means that the little degree of association that does exist is predominantly due to the demographic and socioeconomic (as opposed to personality) characteristics.

The last study to be described was conducted by Tucker and Painter [32]. They administered the Gordon personal profile test to 133 male marketing students at the University of Texas. The test was used as a basis for generating measures for four traits; that is, ascendancy, responsibility, emotional stability, and sociability. Separate analyses were conducted of the relationship between an individual's score for each trait and his consumption of headache remedies, vitamins, cigarettes, mouthwash, alcoholic drinks, deodorants, automobiles, and chewing gum, as well as his acceptance of new fashions. Tucker and Painter generated 36 two-way cross-classification tables (9 product categories $\times$ 4 personality traits). Of these, 13 were statistically significant at the 0.05 level or less. Although a high proportion of the observed relationships were statistically significant, the degree of association observed was nevertheless quite modest. In addition, the 36 sets of results were based on a set of independent variables, some of which (as the authors note) were intercorrelated. Nothing in the investigators' analytical procedures explicitly took into account these intercorrelations (for example, they might have used multiple regression or discriminate analysis). Thus, their procedures probably tend to overstate whatever effects are actually present.

Household demographic, socioeconomic, and personality characteristics appear to have, at best, a relatively low degree of association with total household purchases of any particular grocery product.

Customer Sensitivity to Promotion.   The effect of demographic and socioeconomic characteristics on customer response to promotion was the subject of only one investigation, which was conducted by Frank and Massy [12, 25]. The investigation was based on household purchasing behavior for a single food product in one major metropolitan area over a 101-week period.

The analysis was focused on the effect of demographic and socioeconomic characteristics on customer response to the pricing, dealing, and retail advertising activity of one particular brand (hereafter called brand M) as well as on that of competing brands.

The product in question is used by the vast majority of families in the United States. Purchases occur at the rate of several a month for many users. The product is sold through supermarkets and receives a significant amount of promotion at both the manufacturer and retailer levels.

Two sets of data are used in the analysis:

1. The purchase records of several hundred households who were members of the Market Research Corporation of America's Consumer Panel.
2. A sample of retail advertising lineage for the product covering every brand in the market. The sample included approximately 90 percent of the food lineage placed in the market during the 101-week period of the investigation

Income, household size, wife's age, wife's employment status, and wife's education are used as a basis for defining market segments. Income and education are surrogates for social class, while wife's age and family size are related to the household's stage in the life-cycle. Occupation, which is also related to social class, could not be included in the analysis because the distribution of households across the categories by which social class was defined did not permit breaking them down into meaningful groups.

Separate analyses were conducted for each of the five characteristics. In each case, the sample of households was divided into two groups on the basis of their relative standing on the socioeconomic dimension being investigated. The definitions of the groups are shown in Table 9–3. For example, all families who earned more than $6000 a year were assigned to the "high-income group" and, conversely, families earning equal to or less than $6000 were assigned to the "low-income group." For each group, Frank and Massy next computed a weekly time series of M's market share, its price relative to the prices of competing brands, the magnitude of its dealing relative to competing brands, the extent of its dealing coverage, and the magnitude of its retail advertising as well as that of competitors. Using econometric techniques (based on multiple regression analysis), these two sets of time series were used as the basis for estimating the *current* and *long-run* effects on weekly market share for M of the changes in the pricing, dealing, and retail advertising activity of both M and its competitors.

The current effect of brand M's relative price was defined as the association between the relative price and M's current market share, while holding the effects of dealing and retail advertising constant. The long-run effect of price took into account not only its *current* effect but also the *carry-over* effects of past relative price levels (that is, the effects of M's relative price in the preceding two weeks on its current market share combined with the assumption that the effect of a given level of relative price declined exponentially over time). Analogous definitions pertain to both dealing and retail advertising. There were two sets of retail advertising variables. One set provided a measure of the current and carry-over effects of *nonfeature* (small-size) ads, while the other set of variables measured the effect on M's market share of varying the total amount of space in a given week devoted to feature (large-size) ads.

Table 9–3
Break Points, Percent of Households, and Ounces in Low Segment
for Each Socioeconomic Characteristic

Socioeconomic Characteristics	Break Point	Low Percent[a]	Low Households Percent
Income	$6000	38.8	48.5
Household size	2 persons	61.5	58.5
Housewife			
Age	42 years	45.4	45.8
Employment	0[b]	69.7	69.0
Education	12 years	73.6	70.0

[a] Households belonging to the low segment have a value in terms of the relevant socioeconomic characteristic equal to or less than the one stated in this problem.
[b] "0" (zero) stands for a household with an unemployed wife while "1" is the code for a household where the wife is employed.

Correlations Between the Segments.   In analyzing the segmentation results, it is relevant to inquire whether the five pairs of equations tend to be orthogonal to one another. For example, the data might indicate that nearly the same set of families would be included in the "high-income" and "high-education" groups. If this were the case, we should expect that the regression results for these two groups would be nearly the same, just because of the overlap between the two data bases. Conversely, if the two groups are found to have fewer families in common, we are justified in making separate interpretations of the price, dealing, and advertising elasticities. Separate interpretations are valid only if the various pairs of groups are fairly orthogonal to (uncorrelated with) one another.

We might expect that some of the household traits included in this study would be correlated in the general population. In the data upon which the study was based, these traits were independent enough to justify separate analyses. The highest simple R between any pair of the five was 0.48, which was the degree of association between household size and age of housewife. The highest multiple R between any one of the five characteristics and the remaining four was 0.57 for age of housewife.

A factor analysis containing the five socioeconomic characteristics was performed to see if the nature of the intercorrelations of the characteristics led to any natural groupings with better orthogonality than the original five. The analysis generated four varimax factors. The only two variables that did not appear as separate factors were size of household and age of housewife. Therefore, Frank and Massy concluded that there was no need to revise their socioeconomic definitions.

The principal findings resulting from their analysis were the following.

1. *Housewife education.* For the most part, differences in the response pattern of low- versus high-education households were consistent with the notion that higher levels of education tend to be associated with both a faster rate and a greater degree of adaptive activity in the face of change. The long-run effects of changes in brand M's pricing, dealing, and feature retail advertising activity were greater for the highly educated market segment. In addition, the current response to market share in the highly educated market segment to changes in pricing, dealing, feature, and nonfeature retail advertising was consistently greater than that for the low-education segment.

The differences in the responses of these two groups to promotion, while not significant at the 0.95 level, were significant at the 0.90 level, so that we may be fairly confident that the two education groups respond differently (though the differences involved are slight).

2. *Housewife employment.* Households with unemployed housewives were more responsive to both current and long-run changes in price. Unemployed housewives may be more interested in the home, better informed, and in a more flexible position to spend the shopping time necessary to take advantage of price offers. There appears to be no clear-cut pattern to the current and carry-over effects of dealing. It seems as though the impact were some number close to zero with sampling variability accounting for the fluctuation in the observed direction of the effects.

Although the differences between the responses of the two groups are not significant at the 0.90 level, yet there is a fairly good chance that these differences, like those for education, are real but small in magnitude. This same argument pertains to the results for the income segments that are discussed in the next paragraph.

3. *Income.* We might expect that the lower a household's income the more sensitive it would be to changes in the offers made by manufacturers, especially changes in relative price. Although, at first, the results seemed to be inconsistent with this expectation in that the long-run elasticity with respect to price is greater for the low-income market segment as opposed to the high-income market segment (thus, confirming the hypothesis), the opposite was true of the current price elasticities. However, it may well be that high-income families do more stocking up in response to price changes than do their low-income counterparts, thus making the high-income families appear

to have a greater price sensitivity in the short run. In other words, both inventory practices and sensitivity to price may vary by income.

The differences in response to dealing appear to have no consistent pattern, whereas the low-income elasticities for nonfeature advertising were consistently lower than those for the high-income segment. The responses of the two groups tend to converge when we look at feature advertising effects. It may be that low-income households have a higher threshold of response to retail advertising than do their high-income counterparts.

4. *Household size and age of housewife.* The observed differences with respect to segments formed on the basis of either household size or age of housewife were so slight that they did not justify detailed interpretation.

The two least-important socioeconomic characteristics, in terms of response differentiation, are household size and housewife age. Both of these characteristics are associated with the concept of life cycle. Education, income, and employment, relatively speaking, are more effective bases for segmentation. Education, income and, to a lesser extent, employment are associated with the definition of social class. In other words, in terms of response differentiation, social class seems to be a more important basis for market segmentation than does life cycle for the product under study.

Based on the research reported in the preceding sections, for the most part socioeconomic characteristics are not particularly effective bases for segmentation either in terms of their association with household differences in average purchase rate or in response to promotion.

Household Purchasing Characteristics

The total amount purchased by a household and the degree of brand loyalty exhibited are used more often than any other household purchasing statistics as bases for market segmentation. Marketing literature abounds with references to contrasts involving each of the dimensions. It is often argued that two of the most valuable market segments to penetrate are the "heavy half" and those households that exhibit a high propensity to be brand-loyal. In the two sections that follow, each of these bases for segmentation is evaluated in terms of the three criteria previously mentioned.

Total Household Purchases

By definition, the segmenting of a market in terms of heavy and light customers results in between-segment differences in average household purchasing rates (the second of the three-evaluation criteria). Thus, the discussion that follows is focused exclusively on the extent to which customers in the different segments can be identified in terms of other characteristics (for example, socioeconomic and personality traits) as well as the extent to which the *responses* to promotion differ from one segment to another.

Identifiability.   The issue of identifiability is of particular interest because different assumptions with respect to the nature and extent of differences between heavy and light customers can lead to quite different media-selection procedures.

Suppose that a manufacturer wants to concentrate his media budget on the "heavy half." For many promotional vehicles (newspapers, magazines, and TV shows), data are available concerning audience socioeconomic characteristics. It is often the practice to use this information as a basis for media selection. The implicit (at times explicit) assumption underlying this practice is that there is a correlation between various demographic and socioeconomic characteristics and total consumption for the product in question [34, 35].

Recently, this assumption has been questioned by Twedt [35] who also has suggested an alternative media-selection procedure. He asserts that household demographic and socioeconomic characteristics are not useful surrogates for total purchases for a broad range of grocery products. Assuming that this is true (he indicates, without presenting any data, that research confirms his assumption), Twedt then concludes that various media should collect audience purchase data for grocery products. He shows [35] how a media schedule for bacon (based on purchase data for a number of media) differs from those schedules that are based on demographic and socioeconomic profiles.

The same studies used to evaluate demographic and socioeconomic characteristics (in a preceding section of this chapter) as a basis for segmentation are relevant for evaluating average purchase rate as a basis for segmentation. To what extent can households with different average purchase rates be *identified* by using demographic and socioeconomic data?

Without repeating the review, let us repeat the conclusion: demographic and socioeconomic characteristics have only a relatively modest degree of association with household purchase rate for a wide range of grocery products.

This *conclusion* therefore supports Twedt's position.

Customer Sensitivity to Promotion.   A second assumption that under-lies the singling out of the "heavy half" as a special market target is that customers in this segment have different responses to promotion than do customers whose relative consumption is lighter. Only one investigation of response differences is reported in the literature. The results are from the same study (by Frank and Massy) discussed in the preceding section on demographic and socioeconomic characteristics as segmentation bases. The only difference is that, in this case, the customer segments were defined in terms of their purchase rates instead of in terms of their demographic and socioeconomic characteristics.

Light users of the product are defined as those households who purchased less than or equal to a certain specified annual rate during the period of the investigation. Heavy buyers are correspondingly those that purchased more than the rate specified. The rate is set so that approximately one-half the number of ounces purchased in the market during the 101-week period are purchased by those households that are defined as light users.

What differences in response characteristics with respect to pricing, dealing, and advertising might we expect when contrasting light and heavy buyers?

On the average, light buyers buy less often than do heavy buyers. The per capita consumption rate for light-buying households is lower than that for the heavy-buying category. It is reasonable to assume that light-buying households tend to be less interested and less well informed with respect to current price, dealing, and advertising conditions in the market, let alone with respect to changes in these conditions over time. Probably a greater proportion of the purchases of light-buying households are accounted for by special needs such as entertainment. In fulfilling these needs, more attention is probably paid to the nature and immediacy of the occasion than to the offers made by alternative brands.

These characteristics lead us to expect a lower proportion of the week-to-week variation in demand for brand M to be accounted for in the case of light buyers as opposed to heavy buyers. The results are consistent with this expectation. The proportion of variance in M's market share explained in the heavy-buyer segment is 0.59, while in the light-buyer segment it is 0.50.

In addition, light buyers are probably less sensitive to long-run changes in pricing policy. They are probably also less responsive to current price changes and tend to do less stocking up. Their results are consistent with this assertion. The current effect of a 1-percent cut in price on M's market share is greater for heavy buyers than for light buyers. However, the carry-over effects are also greater for heavy buyers. Heavy buyers apparently stock up more than light buyers. In spite of this difference in stocking up, the long-run sensitivity of heavy buyers to changes in relative price is still greater than that for light buyers.

The pattern of effects for dealing among heavy buyers is similar to that for pricing. The rationale is the same as that previously discussed.

The long-run effect of feature advertising is greater for light buyers than for heavy buyers, but the opposite is true for nonfeature advertising. Possibly a feature-sized ad is required to affect the awareness of a substantial proportion of light buyers. Small ads may tend to be selectively screened out by light buyers, leading to a considerably smaller net effect of market share. The change from a nonfeature ad to a feature ad accomplishes little by way of increased response among heavy buyers as opposed to light buyers, because of what is probably the already high level of their knowledge and awareness.

In spite of the fact that the observed differences in response between the heavy- and light-customer segments are consistent with expectations, these differences nevertheless are not significant at the 0.95 level. However, there is still a fair chance that there is a real (although modest) difference in response between the two groups.

Summary.   There is some support for total consumption as a basis for market segmentation, especially as a basis for media selection, if more media take on the responsibility of collecting purchase data from their respective audiences.

Brand Loyalty

The relevance of "brand loyalty" to the formulation of a profitable program of market segmentation has stirred the imaginations of practitioners and scholars alike ever since pioneering work by George Brown [4] and Ross Cunningham [5, 6] in the early 1950's. In contrast to the previously discussed bases for market segmentation, there has been considerable uncertainty expressed as to how brand loyalty should be defined as well as to the extent to which it actually exists. Before evaluating brand loyalty as a basis for market segmentation in terms of our three criteria (identifiability, average rate of purchase, and response to promotion), its definition and existence will first be discussed.

Definition and Degree.   The discussion of the definition and degree of brand loyalty is based on the results of five investigations. Each investigator uses a slightly different definition of brand loyalty.

The first study, by George Brown [4], is based on the purchase histories of a sample of 100 households from the *Chicago Tribune* panel for 1961. The 9 product categories included are listed in Table 9–4. Although Brown experimented with a number of measures of brand loyalty, the one upon which he placed primary emphasis is as follows.

> Any family making five or more purchases during the year was placed in one of four basic categories, depending upon the purchase pattern shown . . .:
> 1. Family showing undivided loyalty bought brand A in the following sequence: AAAAAA.
> 2. Family showing divided loyalty bought brands A and B in the following sequence: ABABAB.
> 3. Family showing unstable loyalty bought brands A and B in the following sequence: AAABBB.
> 4. Family showing no loyalty bought brands A, B, C. D, E, and F in the following sequence: ABCDEF [4, January 26, 1953, p. 75].

The results of applying this classification scheme are reported in Table 9–4. A majority of customers concentrate their purchases on relatively few brands and, consequently, by Brown's definition, exhibit brand loyalty. This is a particularly striking fact because customers are often exposed to as many as 10 or 15 brands in each of the categories included. In addition, week-to-week fluctuations in brand pricing and dealing are relatively substantial in most of the markets. There does appear to be some tendency for customers to stay with a particular set of brands even in the face of changing competitive conditions.

Table 9—4
Brown's Brand-Loyalty Analysis

Item	Undivided Loyalty	Divided Loyalty	Unstable Loyalty	No Loyalty
Margarine	21.1	13.8	27.5	37.5
Toothpaste	61.3	6.5	17.7	14.5
Coffee	47.2	18.1	29.5	5.2
All-purpose flour	73.2	7.1	14.1	5.6
Shampoo	44.0	10.4	12.3	33.3
Ready-to-eat cereal	12.5	22.7	18.2	46.6
Headache remedies	46.1	23.1	5.8	25.0
Soaps and sudsers	16.8	20.0	26.2	37.0
Concentrated orange juice	26.8	7.0	39.4	26.8

Ross Cunningham published an analysis of brand loyalty based on a 66-family sample from the *Chicago Tribune* panel covering their purchase histories for 7 product categories (toilet soap, scouring cleanser, regular coffee, canned peas, margarine, frozen orange juice, and headache tablets) from 1951 to 1953 [5, 6]. Cunningham defined brand loyalty in terms of the proportion of purchases that a household devoted to the brand it purchased most often. In the case of all 7 product categories, at least 50 percent of the households concentrated 43 percent or more of their purchases on the brand most often bought. For headache remedies, the percentage reaches a high of 72 percent, while the 43 percent figure pertains to toilet soap; scouring cleanser falls in the middle of the 7 categories with more than one half of the customers concentrating 53 percent of their purchases on the brand bought most often [5, p. 122].

Both Brown and Cunningham measured brand loyalty in terms of the extent to which customers tend to concentrate their purchases on a relatively few brands in a given product category. In contrast, studies by Guest [19, 20] as well as by Massy, Frank, and Lodahl [26] examine the stability of house-hold brand loyalty over time.

In 1941, Guest measured the brand preferences (the favorite brand) of 813 public school students for 16 product categories. Twelve years later (in 1953), he obtained preferences from 165 members of this group for the same products. Four of the 16 categories were food products, that is, coffee, cereal, bread, and gum. The percentage of respondents whose present and past preferences agreed are 35, 23, 31, and 29, respectively. In addition, a comparison was made between present use and past preference, which resulted in these percentages of agreement: 33, 25, 23, and 28. Considering that the results were based on the stability of individual behavior over a *12-year period,* they provide further evidence of the existence of "brand loyalty."

Massy, Frank, and Lodahl [26] based their analysis on the J. Walter Thompson panel data for regular coffee from July 1956 to June 1957. These authors split the purchase histories for each of the 670 households included into two 6-month time periods. Households making fewer than 6 purchases during the year were excluded from the analysis. They measured the share of purchases devoted to the brand bought most often in each of the two time periods (Cunningham's measure of brand loyalty). They also measured the number of brands bought by each household in both time periods. Split-half correlation coefficients between the first and second time periods were then computed for each of these statistics. Thus, the coefficients measure the degree of association between a household's brand loyalty in one time period and that in the next time period. The coefficient for Cunningham's measure was 0.69, while that for the number of brands was 0.76.

Tucker [33] constructed an experiment as a vehicle for studying the formation of brand loyalty. Each of 43 housewives was presented 4 alternative brands of bread on each of 12 consecutive household deliveries. The loaves were virtually identical except that they had 4 different "brand names" (L, M, P, and H). Based on Tucker's definition, if no brand loyalty were present, we should expect 25 percent of each housewife's purchases to be made for each brand. More than one half of the respondents developed a higher degree of allegiance to 1 of the 4 brands than would be expected on the basis of this chance model. A number of customers became brand loyal even though there was no difference between the brands other than the "brand name" itself.

Whether we look at the concentration of household purchases among brands at a point in time or at its stability over time, there is marked evidence that brand loyalty is a "real" and reliable phenomenon—a phenomenon the understanding of which is a challenge to managers and researchers alike.

Identifiability

To what extent can brand-loyal customers be identified in terms of some subset of their personal attributes? Four investigations are either published or (in the case of one) are about to be published. All four analyze the relationship between the degree of brand loyalty exhibited by a household and its socioeconomic and personality attributes. The first two studies (by the ARF and Massy, Frank, and Lodahl) were described in a preceding section of this chapter, and therefore their full description will not be repeated.

The first of these is the ARF study based on household toilet tissue purchasing behavior. Separate analyses were conducted for both one-ply and two-ply tissue. In each case, a multiple regression analysis was conducted to measure the net degree of association between household brand loyalty and demographic, socioeconomic, and personality characteristics. Household brand loyalty was defined as the proportion of purchases devoted to the brand purchased most often.

The total predictive efficacy, as measured by the square of the multiple correlation coefficient, was 0.05 for one-ply tissue and 0.07 for two-ply tissue. In other words, they found virtually no association between personality, socioeconomic variables, and household brand loyalty.

Massy, Frank, and Lodahl [26] also conducted an analysis of the association between household brand loyalty and socioeconomic-personality attributes. This analysis was included in the previously mentioned study that used J. Walter Thompson panel data and was based on household purchases of beer, coffee, and tea.[5] Table 9–5 gives separate analyses for each of the three product categories and, within each category, for three different measures of household brand loyalty. The results are directly comparable to those given in Table 9–2.

Table 9–5
Massy, Frank, and Lodahl Study Results: Brand Loyalty

	R^2	F	F-ADD	Number of Households
Beer				486
Factor score	0.08	1.43	1.27	
Percent favorite brand	0.09	1.61[a]	1.41	
Number of brands	0.10	1.70[a]	1.40	
Regular coffee				1283
Factor score	0.05	2.42[a]	1.63[a]	
Percent favorite brand	0.05	2.05[a]	1.09	
Number of brands	0.07	3.13[a]	1.39	
Tea				900
Factor score	0.04	1.38	1.14	
Percent favorite brand	0.05	1.46	1.30	
Number of brands	0.05	1.70[a]	1.40	

[a] Significant at the 5% level.

At best (for beer), only 10 percent of the variation in brand loyalty from one household to another is associated with personality and socioeconomic characteristics. Coffee and tea did only about one half as well. In any case, the results are not encouraging from the standpoint of developing a profile

[5] Discussion of the split-half correlations in the preceding section was based only on coffee because the purchase rates for tea and beer are too low.

of the brand loyal customer. Based on this analysis, the "high brand-loyal" household apparently has a profile of personality and socioeconomic characteristics that is virtually identical to that of households exhibiting a lower degree of loyalty. Furthermore, the fact that only one of the F-ADD ratios are statistically significant means that the little degree of association that does exist results predominantly from the socioeconomic characteristics (as opposed to the personality characteristics).

A recent study published by Farley [8, 9] focused on the prediction of household brand loyalty separately for each of 17 grocery products. The data covered 197 households belonging to the Market Research Corporation of America's consumer panel in 1957; the households were residents of one market area. Attempts were made to predict two measures of brand loyalty (number of brands purchased and whether the household switched favorite brands from the first to the second 6-month period) based on knowledge of household income and size as well as the quantity of the product consumed by each household. The prediction of number of brands purchased was based on a multiple regression analysis. Of the 17 multiple R^2's that were generated, 11 were less than 0.04. The prediction as to whether a household switched favorite brands from one 6-month period to the next was based on a two-way multiple discriminant analysis. The results of both Farley's discriminant and regression analyses were quite consistent in that neither provides any managerially significant basis for identifying brand loyal customers.

In 1966, Frank and Boyd published an investigation of household brand loyalty to private brands [11]. The study is based on the purchasing behavior of 492 households who were members of the *Tribune's* panel throughout 1961. The investigators studied the association between the proportion of purchases a household devoted to private brands in a particular product category (for example, margarine, canned corn, potato chips, and regular coffee) and its socioeconomic characteristics, store shopping habits, and the total amount of the product purchased during the year. Separate analyses, based on multiple regression techniques, were conducted for each of 44 product categories.

Frank and Boyd found virtually no differentiation between private and manufacturer brand customers based on socioeconomic and total consumption characteristics. For 13 of the 44 products, the resulting squared correlation coefficients were 0.00, while for 32 of the products they were less than 0.23. Store shopping habits were correlated with private branding; however, this comes as no surprise. A customer who shops in the A & P or Jewel stores is much more likely to buy private brands than a customer who shops in the smaller chains or in an independent food store.

In spite of the reliability that households exhibit with regard to brand loyalty, research efforts aimed at identifying the brand-loyal customer have been notably unsuccessful.

Average Level of Customer Demand.   For each of the seven products included in Cunningham's analysis [5], he computed rank correlation coefficients between the quantity consumed by each of the 66 households and its level of brand loyalty. The coefficients are reported in Table 9–6. The highest, which is only 0.195, is for canned peas. There appears to be little relationship between purchasing activity and brand loyalty.

Table 9–6
Cunningham's Average Level Purchased, and Brand Loyalty Rank Correlation

Item	Correlation Coefficient
Toilet soap	0.109
Scouring cleanser	0.089
Regular coffee	0.003
Canned peas	0.195
Margarine	0.133
Frozen orange juice	0.028
Headache tablets	0.102

Massy, Frank, and Lodahl also examined this relationship. In addition to the brand loyalty factor generated by the factor analysis mentioned in the preceding section, a total activity factor was also identified. Scores for each household for both the brand loyalty and the activity factors were correlated. The resulting correlation for coffee was only 0.00, while those for tea and beer were 0.36 and 0.09.

Based on an analysis of frozen orange juice purchases from 1951 to 1953 for 650 households from the *Chicago Tribune* panel, Kuehn found that brand loyalty (as measured by the tendency for customers to repeat their purchase of the brand bought previously) was higher for heavy purchasers as opposed to light purchasers of the product [23]. These results are not consistent with those reported in either of the other studies. Kuehn's methodology is considerably more sensitive than Cunningham's; thus, we might place more weight on his results.

However, this does not explain the difference in conclusions reached by Kuehn and by Massy, Frank, and Lodahl. For two of the products studied, their results were consistent with Cunningham's conclusion, whereas for tea there did appear to be some association between activity and brand loyalty.

One possible explanation of the difference between these studies might be the products involved. For example, at the time of Kuehn's study, frozen orange juice concentrate was a relatively young product category. It may be that with respect to a new product, so closely tied to health, heavy users occur disproportionately in cases where a household feels that it has found a definitely superior brand. This effect might tend to disappear as the product becomes better established.

Customer Sensitivity to Promotion. The effect of brand loyalty on customer response to promotion is the subject of only two investigations. The first of these was the Frank and Massy study [12, 14, 25] of the response of brand M's market share in selected market segments to changes in its pricing, dealing, and retail advertising levels (described in a preceding section of this chapter).

The investigators computed the share of purchases that each household devoted to brand M as well as to competing brands. Those households that bought brand M more often than any other brand are called "loyal" and those that bought it less often "nonloyal." Frank and Massy then computed a weekly time series of brand M's market share, its price relative to the prices of competing brands, the magnitude of its dealing relative to competing brands, the extent of its dealing coverage and the magnitude of its retail advertising as well as that of competitors. Using econometric techniques (based on multiple regression analysis), these two sets of time series are used as the basis for estimating the current and carry-over effects on M's weekly market share of the changes in the pricing, dealing, and retail advertising activity of both M and its competitors.

These authors found no statistically significant difference between the price, dealing, and retail advertising elasticities for families who are loyal to brand M and those who are not. If loyalty were successful in building up the resistance of buyers to switch to other brands in the face of changes in market conditions, we might expect that the elasticities for loyal buyers would be less than those for the nonloyal group. However, this was not the case.[6]

The second investigation by Frank Massy, and Morrison [25, 26] consisted of a study of the introduction of Folger's coffee into the Chicago regular coffee market. The data base consisted of *Chicago Tribune* panel data for 538 households from 1958 through 1960 for regular coffee as well as data covering 88 other food products for which *Tribune* records were kept for the same households from January to April, 1961.[7] The investigators estimated the extent to which household socioeconomic and purchasing characteristics (for both regular coffee and total household consumption of all food products reported by the panel members), during the 62-week period prior to Folger's introduction, predicted whether a household would either buy Folger's coffee more often than any other brand or not at all. Five socioeconomic and 15 purchasing characteristics are included in the two-way multiple discriminant analysis upon which their results are based. One of the

[6] For more detailed discussion of the rationales underlying this loyal-nonloyal analysis, see Refs. 12, 14, and 25.

[7] The four-month 1961 household purchase data had been previously obtained for use in another study. Ideally, we would have preferred to have this information as of 1958; however, it is unlikely that the Folger's introduction affected patterns of overall consumption in a way that would tend to confound the results.

purchasing characteristics is Cunningham's measure of brand loyalty (the proportion of purchases devoted to the brand purchased most often by a household during the period prior to Folger's introduction). Brand loyalty was associated with a resistance to adopting a new brand. The effect of loyalty, while it is probably "real," is nonetheless quite modest.

Summary.   The pattern of results for brand loyalty as a basis for market segmentation in food products is not encouraging. Brand-loyal customers almost completely lack identifiability in terms of either socioeconomic or personality characteristics. With the exception of one study by Kuehn, brand-loyal customers do not appear to have different average demand levels than nonloyal ones. Loyal customers do not appear to have economically important differences in their sensitivity to either the shortrun effects of pricing, dealing, and retail advertising or to the introduction of new brands.

THE NEED FOR FURTHER RESEARCH

Neither the socioeconomic nor the purchasing characteristics that have been discussed appear to be particularly effective bases for market segmentation. Although most of the results consisted of only modest differences between segments, nevertheless these "negative findings" do have a positive value. For some of us, they add to the weight of evidence favoring what we already believed, while for others they may have had a somewhat greater surprise value.

Many practitioners have expressed doubt as to the usefulness of socioeconomic characteristics as bases for market segmentation [36]. In general, our findings are quite consistent with this conclusion. In contrast, the consistently negative character of our findings regarding brand loyalty comes as a surprise. In spite of the fact that brand loyalty appears to be a real, persistent phenomena, our research thus far has provided little insight into the process that generates loyalty proneness. Results, to date, contradict what we might expect.

The case for total consumption as a basis for market segmentation is somewhat stronger than that for brand loyalty as, by definition, different market segments contain customers with somewhat different demand characteristics. However, even in this case, the response to pricing, dealing, and retail-advertising differences between heavy and light market segments (although their directions were reasonably consistent with expectations) appear nonetheless to be of only a modest magnitude. This finding raises some doubt as to the usefulness of even this approach.

Although many of the results that have been discussed are quite provocative, they nevertheless are fragmentary in character. Clearly, there is a need for more research if we are to gain sufficient understanding of the determinants of customer purchasing behavior in order to be able to design more effective programs based on market segmentation.

At the very least, there are the following needs.

1. We should replicate the study of differential response of socioeconomic market segments to policy variables, over a wide range of product categories. (The results reported in this chapter are based on only one product category.)

2. We should extend the response models beyond pricing, dealing, and retail advertising to cover instore promotion as well as manufacturer spot television, radio, and newspaper coverage.

3. We should replicate the differential response analysis for both socioeconomic and purchase variables for the same product class in several different market areas. For example, we might work with market areas in which (1) there are different levels of total retail advertising, dealing, and pricing for the product in question (the response differences across customer segments may depend, in part, on the total level of industry promotion for the product as well as on the brand's relative position), and (2) the brand under study has quite different market shares.

4. We should replicate studies of the correlates of brand loyalty across a broader range of product categories while at the same time experimenting with alternative definitions. For example, studying products with high prices as opposed to low prices per unit might reveal differences in the process by which brand loyalty is formed, as might a contrast of a product that usually has a low degree of personal risk associated with use versus a product with a high risk level.

5. We should conduct a more penetrating analysis of the association between psychological and sociological characteristics of buyers and the degree of brand loyalty they exhibit. It may be that the psychological dimensions that are idiosyncratic to the particular category being studied as opposed to, say, personal characteristics that are presumably enduring characteristics of the individual (that is, that are common to many, if not all, of the decision problems faced by the individual) are important determinants of brand loyalty.

6. We should extend the analysis of response differences to include the effects of variation in product characteristics. For example, we might study the extent to which different brands of cereals appeal to different customer segments. (In my opinion, this form of marketing effort can also be embraced by the concept of market segmentation. However, this view is not shared by some [28].)

In addition to these suggestions, there is a need to investigate systematically a much broader range of alternative bases for segmentation than have been considered thus far. One of the most promising attempts at achieving this objective has been launched by Pessemier, Teach, and Tigert [27]. These authors plan to investigate the relationship between household purchasing behavior in a number of grocery-product categories. They also plan to investigate household characteristics such as, for example, family and individual activities, brand preferences, and self-perception of risk involved in purchase, in addition to the more traditional socioeconomic characteristics. Their results are not yet available. Clearly, more work of this type is essential.

References

1. William Baumol and Charles Sevin, "Marketing Costs and Mathematical Programming," *Harvard Business Review*, **35(5)**, 52–60 (September–October, 1957).
2. Kenneth Boulding, *Economics Analysis* (New York: Harper and Bros., 1955), pp. 608–615.
3. Brand Rating Index, *Report on the Marketing Value of Media Audiences,* March 1965.
4. George Brown, "Brand Loyalty—Fact or Fiction?" *Advertising Age* **23,** 53–55 (June 19, 1952); 45–47 (June 30, 1952); 54–56 (July 14, 1952); 46–48 (July 28, 1952); 56–58 (August 11, 1952); 80–82 (September 1, 1952); 82–86 (October 6, 1952); 76–79 (December 1, 1952); and **24,** 75–76 (January 26, 1953).
5. Ross Cunningham, "Brand Loyalty—What, Where, How Much," *Harvard Business Review*, **34(1),** 116–128 (January–February, 1956).
6. ———, "Customer Loyalty to Store and Brand," *Harvard Business Review*, **39(6),** 127–137 (November–December, 1961).
7. ———, "Measurement of Brand Loyalty," *The Marketing Revolution,* New York: American Marketing Associaton (December 27–29, 1955).
8. John Farley, "Brand Loyalty and the Economics of Information," *Journal of Business*, **37(4),** 370–831 (October, 1964).
9. ———, "Testing a Theory of Brand Loyalty," *Proceedings of the American Marketing Association Winter Conference*, pp. 308–315 (December, 1963).
10. Ronald E. Frank, "Is Brand Loyalty a Useful Basis for Gorcery Product Market Segmentation?" mimeographed (December, 1965).
11. ——— and Harper Boyd, Jr., "Are Private-Brand-Prone Food Customers Really Different?" *Journal of Advertising Research*, **5(4),** 27–35 (December, 1965).
12. ——— and William Massy, "Estimating the Effects of Short Term Promotional Strategy in Selected Market Segments," *Market Response to Sales Promotion*, a volume to appear in the Marketing Science Institute Series (New York: McGraw-Hill) [1969].
13. ———, "Innovation and Brand Choice: The Folger's Invasion," *Pro-

ceedings of the American Marketing Association Winter Conference,
pp. 96–107 (December, 1963).

14. ———, "Market Segmentation and the Effectiveness of a Brand's Price and Dealing Policies," *Journal of Business,* **38(2),** 186–200 (April, 1965).

15. ———, William Massy, and Harper Boyd, Jr., "Correlates of Grocery Product Consumption Rates," mimeographed (April, 1966).

16. ——— and Donald Morrison, "The Determinants of Innovative Behavior with Respect to a Branded, Frequently Purchased Food Product," *Proceedings of the Winter Conference of the American Marketing Association,* pp. 312–323 (December, 1964).

17. Norton Garfinkle, "A Marketing Approach to Media Selection," *Journal of Advertising Research,* **3(4),** 7–15 (December, 1963).

18. Grey Advertising Agency, "Herd Hysteria: a Mounting Marketing Hazard," **36(5)** (May, 1965).

19. Lester Guest, "A Study of Brand Loyalty," *Journal of Applied Psychology,* **28,** 16–27 (1944).

20. ———, "Brand Loyalty—Twelve Years Later," *Journal of Applied Psychology,* **39,** 405–408 (1955).

21. Ingrid Hildegaard and Lester Krueger, "Are There Customer Types?" *Advertising Research Foundation,* New York (1964).

22. Arthur Koponen, "Personality Characteristics of Purchasers," *Journal of Advertising Research,* **1(1),** 6–12 (September, 1960).

23. Alfred Kuehn, "An Analysis of the Dynamics of Consumer Behavior and Its Implications for Marketing Management," unpublished Ph.D. Dissertation, Carnegie Institute of Technology (May, 1958).

24. Thomas Lodahl, William Massy, and Ronald Frank, "The Intercorrelation Between Demographic, Socioeconomic, and Personality Characteristics," *Journal of Advertising Research,* Vol. 9, No. 4, Dec. 1969, pp. 15–24.

25. William Massy and Ronald Frank, "Short Term Price and Dealing Effects in Selected Market Segments," *Journal of Marketing Research,* **2(2),** 171–185 (May, 1965).

26. ——— and Thomas Lodahl, "Buying Behavior and Personality," Graduate School of Business, Stanford University, working paper (forthcoming, June, 1966).

27. Edgar Pessemier, Richard Teach, and Douglas Tigert, *Consumer Behavior Research Projects,* Purdue University, Krannert Graduate School of Industrial Administration (August, 1965).

28. Willam H. Reynolds, "More Sense About Market Segmentation," *Harvard Business Review,* **43(5),** 107–114 (September–October, 1965).

29. Joan Robinson, *The Economics of Imperfect Competition* (London: Macmillan, 1955), pp. 179–188.

30. Wendell Smith, "Imperfect Competition and Marketing Strategy," *Cost and Profit Outlook*, **8(10)** (October, 1955).

31. ————, "Product Differentiation and Market Segmentation as Alternative Marketing Strategies," *Journal of Marketing*, **21(1),** 3–8 (July, 1956).

32. W. T. Tucker and John J. Painter, "Personality and Product Use," *Journal of Applied Psychology*, **45,** 325–329 (1961).

33. ————, "The Development of Brand Loyalty," *Journal of Marketing Research*, **1(3),** 32–35 (August, 1964).

34. Dik Warren Twedt, "How Important to Marketing Strategy is the 'Heavy User'?" *Journal of Marketing*, **28(1),** 71–72 (January, 1961).

35. ————, "Some Practical Application of 'Heavy Half' Theory," *Proceedings of the 10th Annual Conference of the Advertising Research Foundation* (October, 1964).

36. Daniel Yankelovich, "New Criteria for Market Segmentation," *Harvard Business Review*, **42(2),** 83–90 (March–April, 1964).

PART THREE

SEGMENTATION AND THE
MARKETING MIX

P ART TWO examined the concepts and uses of segmentation. The purpose of Part Three is to show how advances
have been made in the measurement of consumer needs and wants as they
relate to the four decision areas—price, product, promotion, and distribution—
of the marketing mix. Creative applications of segmentation analysis can mark
the beginnings of a sound segmentation strategy. It is here that clues as to
how the market will respond to changes in the firms marketing mix may be
obtained. Underlying all carefully thought-out segmentation strategies is the
attempt to gain differential advantage through some means of adapting the
firm's marketing program to the needs of the market. This involves making
critical decisions with respect to the firm's product, pricing, promotion, and
distribution policies. To date, the bulk of the literature in market segmentation analysis has been concerned primarily with the areas of product and
promotion decision-making and the response elasticities of consumers to
these variables. Relatively little work has been done in the area of pricing or
distribution channels as they apply to the strategy of segmentation.

As we shall see in the papers in this part, segmentation analysis has profited
greatly from an improved understanding of consumer behavior. As a preface
to this section, it is worthwhile to examine some of the significant developments in the field since 1955.

We already noted in Part Two that the new marketing concept fostered a consumer orientation in American industry which previously was dominated by a production and financial management flavor. This development occurred in the early 1950s and began to emerge as a significant area of marketing inquiry by the late 1960s. Growing interest in this field first brought together economists, psychologists, and sociologists whose studies were variously related to the consumer. Often, however, their methods and models were found lacking in providing an explanation for some aspect or another of consumer choice as it related to the product or brand. As a result, marketers primarily interested in these questions borrowed heavily from the behavioral sciences and synthesized the literature that dealt with those aspects of the buying process. In the early 1960s, as more and more researchers were trained in the behavioral sciences, the field of consumer behavior took on a new light. By the second half of the decade comprehensive models of buyer behavior which attempted to depict a structure of the various influences on the consumer decision process began to appear.[1] Together, these models view brand choice as a dynamic decision process rather than a static reaction of the consumer to one or another ingredient of the firm's marketing mix. In the years ahead new developments in the theory and measurement of consumer choice, as it relates to the product, will surely produce greater insights for market planners.

SEGMENTATION IN PRODUCT LINE DECISIONS

A significant impact of the developments taking place in the field of consumer behavior research has been felt in the area of product planning. Both the planner and marketing director have learned that successful implementation of marketing strategy requires answers to the following critical questions: Who is my customer? Why does he buy from me? Why does he not buy from me? What amount of our product and which brands does he buy or not buy? Where and when does he buy from us? What influences his purchasing process? What media is he exposed to?

It is, or should be, obvious that answers to questions such as these have strong implications for the marketing decisions made by a firm. Assume, for example, that a company identifies those beliefs held by nonusers of its products that influence them to refrain from purchasing the company's product. For simplicity, let us imagine that research shows that the firm's product, call it Brand A, is seen as being a general-purpose product with no particular

---

[1] See, for example, F. M. Nicosia, *Consumer Decision Processes: Marketing and Advertising Implications* (Englewood Cliffs, N.J.: Prentice-Hall, Inc., 1966); J. F. Engel, D. T. Kollat, and R. D. Blackwell, *Consumer Behavior* (New York: Holt, Rinehart and Winston, Inc., 1968); and J. A. Howard and J. N. Sheth, *The Theory of Buyer Behavior* (New York: John Wiley & Sons, Inc., 1969).

strengths and weaknesses. Through research, a sizable potential submarket is identified within the overall market for that product class. Research also shows that this submarket is being tapped heavily by Brand X, which is getting 85 percent of the sales to this subsegment. What course of action should the marketer of Brand A take?

It is clear to the company's marketing director that he cannot expect to participate in this segment with his present brand. For one, Brand A is poorly perceived by the nonusers. They recognize it simply as indistinguishable from other all-purpose products. This subgroup, however, has certain preferences and desires for this type of product which tend to influence their choice of Brand X. Management of Brand X, realizing that this subgroup has needs that are not being met by the current market offering, strives to develop a specific brand to meet these needs. Thus by astute marketing it is now enjoying overwhelming success in appealing to this group and is thereby yielding greater volume than would otherwise be attainable from a thin slice of the larger market.

Turning back to the marketing director of Brand A, we find a course of action open. The marketing director may decide that what he needs is a new brand marketed specifically for this subgroup. Recent advances in product development methods offer vastly-improved capabilities to enable marketers like Brand A's to make a more precise fit between product attributes and consumer preferences than already exists. Choice of such a product strategy approach to problem solving is a realistic way of meeting the real needs of the market.

It was not easy, however, for many firms to adapt their thinking to this new approach. For years firms had been accustomed to using "natural" socioeconomic and demographic methods of segmenting markets. It was easy, for example, to segment the national United States or Canadian market in terms of geographic areas. Thus, marketing managers often thought in terms of customers from "our western region" or "our southern region." Later, developments in the field moved in a direction of a heavy reliance on demographic methods of segmentation. Soon marketers were classifying their customers as high or low on the income scale, upper, middle, or lower in social class, older or younger on the age scale, highly educated with college degrees, and so on. At first these often provided more meaningful and useful insights into understanding the market than were previously available.

Soon, however, limitations to demographic analysis were discovered. Quite often these variables could not provide direction to the marketer who needed to know what features his product should offer or what set of end-benefits it should portray to the consumer. Demographic methods often failed in answering why consumers bought the product or why they did not. These were the limitations which prompted marketers to look elsewhere for guidance to the problem of identifying consumer wants and benefits and which could aid in the area of product strategy decisions.

In Section A of Part Three we present studies that examine several of the new directions marketers have moved to overcome this obstacle. In the first paper, "New Criteria For Market Segmentation," Daniel Yankelovich explores seven different modes of nondemographic segmentation in the context of ten consumer and industrial markets. Yankelovich's approach is typical of the careful and systematic analysis needed to ensure a thorough knowledge of consumer wants, how these wants are related to other consumer characteristics, and how products fit into those markets in the process of satisfying these consumer wants.

In "Market Segmentation and Food Consumption" Leslie A. Beldo presents a somewhat similar approach to that of Yankelovich. Beldo attempts to translate nondemographic market segmentation into a more realistic context —that of new product concept development and from there to a product communications strategy. Beldo's article also provides an extension of the basic conceptual positions of segmentation by defining some new conceptual categories termed structural, functional, interpersonal, and intrapersonal forms of segmentation. His example deals specifically with functional segmentation, which he defines as "a subset of a market universe that is differentiated or differentiable by attitudes, life style, interests and values generating varying subjective product requirements."[2] He then discusses the marketing implications of this approach.

In our third article Russel I. Haley suggests an approach called "benefit segmentation" whereby customer groupings are identified according to causal rather than descriptive factors. Haley believes that it is the benefits that people are seeking in the consumption of a given product that give rise to the existence of true market segments.

Where Yankelovich, Beldo, and Haley have described the new approaches to product segmentation, Alvin J. Silk and Robert N. Reitter, in the two remaining articles of this section, illustrate the basic concepts in a somewhat more analytical fashion. Silk explores a new approach to product development. Until recently, marketing analysts have relied upon methods of cluster and factor analysis[3] for discovering the patterns of values and benefits desired by consumers. What has been lacking, however, as Silk points out, is a valid and practical methodology based on a theory of how consumers respond to new products. At first glance, the monumental work of Everett Rogers on the diffusion of innovations appears to be such a theory. Silk finds this work offers very little insight into why people buy or what characteristics of the product are instrumental in causing people to react favorably or unfavorably once they have learned about it. At the end of the 1960s interest

---

[2] See Leslie A. Beldo, "Market Segmentation and Food Consumption," Reading 11 in this volume.

[3] See Part Four for a discussion of new analytical techniques.

in this area has been sparked by a theory and methodology of new product development, originally formulated by Volney Stefflre at the University of California, Irvine. Stefflre's method of "market structure analysis" is claimed to offer a means for developing new products that will fit into markets in predetermined ways. Silk reviews and assesses Stefflre's methodology in the context of the coffee market.

The final paper of Section A, "Product Testing in Segmented Markets," by Reitter, illustrates how modified semantic differential scales guide the researcher engaged in product and concept development work. Reitter suggests a solution to the problem of studying preference among relevant market segments.

In summary, the papers presented in Section A of Part Three deal with the critical questions of nondemographic market segmentation. More specifically, they treat in some detail questions of aligning product development to consumer preferences.

SEGMENTATION IN PROMOTIONAL PLANNING

It is abundantly clear from the previous readings that nondemographic modes of segmentation can offer the planner useful new insights into matching product attributes to consumer wants and thereby arrive at a more precise fit to the market. An additional and valuable aspect of the new methods is, therefore, a potential for creative direction in marketing communications tasks. In Section B we examine another aspect of promotional decision-making—the identification of media targets for promotional planning.

Norton Garfinkle in the opening paper of the section ("A Marketing Approach to Media Selection") illustrates the developments on the media selection side that have paralleled the new trends in product segmentation work. This early paper (1963) discusses an approach whereby marketing (product usage) data and media exposure patterns are collected and analyzed to permit greater efficiency in reaching selected market targets. It is now possible with the use of a variety of syndicated services—such as the Brand Rating Index, Nielsen Media Service, and Simmons Studies of Selective and Mass Magazines in the United States and the Markets and Media Study of Burke Marketing Research in Canada—to obtain both product usage and media exposure patterns for the same set of consumers. Garfinkle's article details several applications of the Brand Rating Index, a periodic survey of marketing and media behavior taken from a national probability sample of male and female adult product purchasers to questions of media selection.

The paper by Frank M. Bass, Edgar A. Pessemier and Douglas J. Tigert pursues the preceding concept further. The value of their paper to this section is easily demonstrated. Bass and his coauthors make the much needed point that bears repeating here:

The manager cannot change the audience of a medium or the media exposure profiles of consumers. Rather, he must select media. In turn, these media are read, viewed, and listened to by different kinds of consumers in various mixes. If there is strong matching of life-style, attitudes, interest, and consumption-related activities to consumer media exposure sets, segmentation by media market segments will serve the marketing manager well.[4]

While this is one of the more technical papers in the collection, it deals squarely with the issue that segments must be definable in terms of variables that management can manipulate. In addition, it demonstrates that media market segments are related to sets of descriptive variables; such sets of variables are perhaps uniquely related to each individual segment and may provide much useful information for the development of creative advertising strategy.

A different mode of media market segmentation that became popular in the early 1960s was the "heavy-half theory" proposed by Dik Warren Twedt. The theory, briefly stated, suggests that for a wide range of products 50 percent of the purchasers account for between 80 and 90 percent of the total volume. From this finding Twedt makes the assumption that efficient media selection demands a schedule that maximizes reach and frequency among the heavy-user segment.

The paper by William D. Wells and Douglas J. Tigert, "Activities, Interests and Opinions," is about another method of segmenting buyers and advertising to them. The authors call it "new motivation research." It has also been variously called such names as "psychographic" or life-style research. Its popularity is partly due to the fact that the data can be easily quantified and is typically collected from representative samples. Furthermore, the proponents of this technique suggest that it provides a useful insight into media segments by enabling the researcher to draw lifelike portraits of the medium's user. Consequently, psychographic profiles based upon activities, interest, and opinion data can help explain the linkages between a product usage and the medium in which it is advertised. To prove their point, Wells and Tigert offer two psychographic profiles for eye make-up buyers and heavy users of shortening. They then go on to discuss the data-gathering and analysis process and review some implementation problems.

"Market Segmentation: Group versus Individual Behavior," by Frank M. Bass, Douglas J. Tigert, and Ronald T. Lonsdale, bridges the gap between Section B and the paper by Ronald E. Frank and William F. Massy of the following section. Bass and his coauthors dispute the claim that socioeconomic

[4] Frank M. Bass, Edgar A. Pessemier, and Douglas J. Tigert, "A Taxonomy of Magazine Readership Applied to Problems in Marketing Strategy and Media Selection," in this volume, Reading 19.

variables do not provide a useful basis for the market segmentation of grocery products. Instead they claim that the proper focus of attention for would-be segmenters is the group, not the individual. The authors use simple cross-classification analysis to focus on the variation in group behavior which is associated with socioeconomic characteristics. They conclude that the previous inadequacy of these variables in explaining a substantial part of the usage rate variance of persons does not mean there are no substantial differences in the mean usage rates for different socioeconomic groups or segments. There is an obvious implication for advertisers: choosing a medium with a greater proportion of its audience in socioeconomic groups which exhibit a significant market potential relative to the number of households would be better than a medium with a lesser proportion of its audience in these segments.

In summary, Section B has dealt extensively with questions of media strategy in promotional planning. The fundamental point is that media and market segments should somehow be related to ensure maximum effectiveness in reaching the potential target group.

SEGMENTATION IN PRICING DECISIONS

It is appropriate that Ronald E. Frank and William F. Massy's paper, "Market Segmentation and the Effectiveness of a Brand's Price and Dealing Policies," is presented at this point. Most, if not all, of our selections have prefaced their discussions by citing the criteria usually required before a segment is identified. It has been seen, however, that the issue of customer response to changes in the marketing mix lies at the heart of any discussion on the topic. Frank and Massy dismiss the simple view of forming groups, irregardless of criteria used (for example, socioeconomic, life-cycle, age, and so on) on the basis of differences in the average purchase rate, as being insufficient as a guide for management strategy. This view is at odds with that presented by Bass, Tigert, and Lonsdale in the preceding section. In support of their case Frank and Massy present a conceptual framework for market segmentation which makes crucial the criterion that the different submarkets exhibit different elasticities with respect to the price and promotional policies of a firm.

To achieve these objectives, the authors report on a study for frequently purchased food products that (1) includes a model for estimating elasticities of price and dealing activities for a firm in selected market segments and (2) tests for the statistical significance of differences among segments. In addition, they deal with the subject of current and carry-over effects of the price and dealing activity. They thereby hope that the theory of market segmentation can be made more meaningful to the manager.

SEGMENTATION AND CHANNEL DECISIONS

We have found little on the topic of channels in our search of the literature that could justifiably be considered a proper selection for this particular collection. In large part, this reflects a lack of research interest due to the fact that marketing management is more apt to consider channel arrangements fixed in the short run. Consequently, it is easy to see how product, price, and promotion policy provide more immediate areas of concern to the manager. These are problem areas that simply occur much more frequently than questions of middlemen arrangements, type of outlet, or other facets of distribution. Because channel questions are of a longer-run nature and tend to be considered fixed in the short run, this view can blind marketers from innovation actions. For firms which are not blocked by lack of marketing vision, a successful distribution breakthrough is often the means of real marketing success.

William E. Davidson's interesting article, "Distribution Breakthroughs," starts with a discussion of basic channel concepts and continues with several provocative examples to show how a basic innovation helped a firm gain differential advantage by viewing the distribution process in a new way.

To further extend Davidson's paper, we have included Stuart U. Rich and Bernard Portis' "Clues for Action From Shopper Preferences." The growth of discount and self-serve operations in the last decade has been phenomenal and a significant trend in American retailing. The rapid growth of this and other forms of self-service has been spurred by the popularity of discount shopping among certain socioeconomic groups. Stuart V. Rich and Bernard Portis describe a study of department store shoppers in New York and Cleveland and analyze the reasons for the rapid rise of the discounter. Strategy implications are suggested for traditional department stores which find themselves competing against this new form of distribution outlet.

Readings for Part Three

Arndt, Johan, ed. *Insights Into Consumer Behavior*, Boston: Allyn & Bacon, Inc., 1968.

Bass, F. M., C. W. King, and E. A. Pessemier, eds. *Applications of the Sciences in Marketing Management*, New York: John Wiley & Sons, Inc., 1968.

Bliss, P. *Marketing and the Behavioral Sciences*, Boston: Allyn & Bacon, Inc., 1963.

Britt, S. H. *Consumer Behavior and the Behavioral Sciences: Theories and Applications*, New York: John Wiley & Sons, Inc., 1966.

Clark, L. H. ed. *Consumer Behavior: Research on Consumer Reactions*, New York: Harper & Row, Publishers, Inc., 1958.

Engel, J. F., D. T. Kollat, and R. D. Blackwell. *Consumer Behavior*, New York: Holt, Rinehart and Winston, Inc., 1968.

———, ———, ———. *Research in Consumer Behavior*, New York: Holt, Rinehart and Winston, Inc., 1969.

———, H. G. Wales, and M. R. Warshaw. *Promotional Strategy*, Homewood, Ill.: Richard D. Irwin, Inc., 1967.

Ferber, R., and H. G. Wales. *Motivation and Market Behavior*, Homewood, Ill.: Richard D. Irwin, Inc., 1958.

Fishbein, M., ed. *Readings in Attitude Theory and Measurement*, New York: John Wiley & Sons, Inc., 1967.

Foote, N. N., ed. *Household Decision-Making*, New York: New York University Press, 1961.

Howard, J. A., and J. N. Sheth. *The Theory of Buyer Behavior*, New York: John Wiley & Sons, Inc., 1969.

Myers, John G. *Consumer Image and Attitude*, Berkeley: Institute of Business and Economic Research, University of California, 1968.

Newman, J. W., ed. *On Knowing the Consumer*, New York: John Wiley & Sons, Inc., 1966.

Nicosia, F. M. *Consumer Decision Processes: Marketing and Advertising Implications*, Englewood Cliffs, N.J.: Prentice-Hall, Inc., 1966.

Zaltman, G. *Marketing: Contributions from the Behavioral Sciences*, New York: Harcourt Brace Jovanovich, Inc., 1965.

10.

New Criteria for Market Segmentation

Daniel Yankelovich

The director of marketing in a large company is confronted by some of the most difficult problems in the history of U.S. industry. To assist him, the information revolution of the past decade puts at his disposal a vast array of techniques, facts, and figures. But without a way to master this information, he can easily be overwhelmed by the reports that flow in to him incessantly from marketing research, economic forecasts, cost analyses, and sales breakdowns. He must have more than mere access to mountains of data. He must himself bring to bear a method of analysis that cuts through the detail to focus sharply on new opportunities.

In this article, I shall propose such a method. It is called *segmentation analysis*. It is based on the proposition that once you discover the most useful ways of segmenting a market, you have produced the beginnings of a sound marketing strategy.

UNIQUE ADVANTAGES

Segmentation analysis has developed out of several key premises:

In today's economy, each brand appears to sell effectively to only certain segments of any market and not to the whole market.

Sound marketing objectives depend on knowledge of how segments which produce the most customers for a company's brands differ in requirements and susceptibilities from the segments which produce the largest number of customers for competitive brands.

Traditional demographic methods of market segmentation do not usually provide this knowledge. Analyses of market segments by age, sex, geography, and income level are not likely to provide as much direction for marketing strategy as management requires.

From Daniel Yankelovich, "New Criteria for Market Segmentation," *Harvard Business Review,* Vol. 42 (March–April 1964), pp. 83–90. Copyright 1964 by the President and Fellows of Harvard College; all rights reserved. Reprinted by permission.

Once the marketing director does discover the most pragmatically useful way of segmenting his market, it becomes a new standard for almost all his evaluations. He will use it to appraise competitive strengths and vulnerabilities, to plan his product line, to determine his advertising and selling strategy, and to set precise marketing objectives against which performance can later be measured. Specifically, segmentation analysis helps him to—

direct the appropriate amounts of promotional attention and money to the most potentially profitable segments of his market;

design a product line that truly parallels the demands of the market instead of one that bulks in some areas and ignores or scants other potentially quite profitable segments;

catch the first sign of a major trend in a swiftly changing market and thus give him time to prepare to take advantage of it;

determine the appeals that will be most effective in his company's advertising; and, where several different appeals are significantly effective, quantify the segments of the market responsive to each;

choose advertising media more wisely and determine the proportion of budget that should be allocated to each medium in the light of anticipated impact;

correct the timing of advertising and promotional efforts so that they are massed in the weeks, months, and seasons when selling resistance is least and responsiveness is likely to be at its maximum;

understand otherwise seemingly meaningless demographic market information and apply it in scores of new and effective ways.

These advantages hold in the case of both packaged goods and hard goods, and for commercial and industrial products as well as consumer products.

Guides to Strategy

Segmentation analysis cuts through the data facing a marketing director when he tries to set targets based on markets as a whole, or when he relies primarily on demographic breakdowns. It is a systematic approach that permits the marketing planner to pick the strategically most important segmentations and then to design brands, products, packages, communications, and marketing strategies around them. It infinitely simplifies the setting of objectives.

In the following sections we shall consider nondemographic ways of segmenting markets. These ways dramatize the point that finding marketing opportunities by depending solely on demographic breakdowns is like trying to win a national election by relying only on the information in a census. A modern census contains useful data, but it identifies neither the crucial issues of an election, nor those groups whose voting habits are still fluid, nor the needs, values, and attitudes that influence how those groups will vote. This kind of information, rather than census-type data, is the kind that wins elections—and markets.

Consider, for example, companies like Procter & Gamble, General Motors, or American Tobacco, whose multiple brands sell against one another and must, every day, win new elections in the marketplace:

These companies sell to the whole market, not by offering one brand that appeals to all people, but by covering the different segments with multiple brands. How can they prevent these brands from cannibalizing each other? How can they avoid surrendering opportunities to competitors by failing to provide brands that appeal to all important segments? In neither automobiles, soaps, nor cigarettes do demographic analyses reveal to the manufacturer what products to make or what products to sell to what segments of the market. Obviously, some modes of segmentation other than demographic are needed to explain why brands which differ so little nevertheless find their own niches in the market, each one appealing to a different segment.

The point at issue is not that demographic segmentation should be disregarded, but rather that it should be regarded as only one among many possible ways of analyzing markets. In fact, the key requirement of segmentation analysis is that the marketing director should never assume in advance that any one method of segmentation is the best. His first job should be to muster all probable segmentation and *then* choose the most meaningful ones to work with. This approach is analogous to that used in research in the physical sciences, where the hypothesis that best seems to explain the phenomena under investigation is the one chosen for working purposes.

TEN MARKETS

In the following discussion we shall take ten markets for consumer and industrial products and see how they are affected by seven different modes of nondemographic segmentation. The products and modes are shown schematically in Figure 10–1. Of course, these segments are not the only ones important in business. The seven I have picked are only *examples* of how segmentation analysis can enlarge the scope and depth of a marketer's thinking.

I. Watches

In this first case we deal with a relatively simple mode of segmentation analysis. The most productive way of analyzing the market for watches turns out to be segmentation by *value*. This approach discloses three distinct segments, each representing a different value attributed to watches by each of three different groups of consumers:

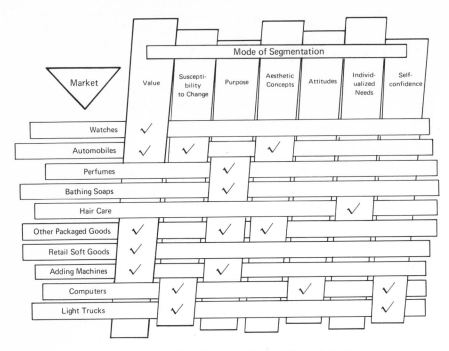

Figure 10–1. Example of Segmentation in Different Industries

1. *People who want to pay the lowest possible price for any watch that works reasonably well.* If the watch fails after six months or a year, they will throw it out and replace it.
2. *People who value watches for their long life, good workmanship, good material, and good styling.* They are willing to pay for these product qualities.
3. *People who look not only for useful product features but also for meaningful emotional qualities.* The most important consideration in this segment is that the watch should suitably symbolize an important occasion. Consequently, fine styling, a well-known brand name, the recommendation of the jeweler, and a gold or diamond case are highly valued.

In 1962, my research shows, the watch market divided quantitatively as follows:

Approximately 23% of the buyers bought for lowest price (value segment #1).

Another 46% bought for durability and general product quality (value segment #2).

And 31% bought watches as symbols of some important occasion (value segment #3).

Defining and quantifying such segments is helpful in marketing planning —especially if a watch company's product happens to appeal mostly to one segment or if the line straddles the three segments, failing to appeal effectively to any. Without such an understanding, the demographic characteristics of the market are most confusing. It turns out, for example, that the most expensive watches are being bought by people with both the highest and the lowest incomes. On the other hand, some upper income consumers are no longer buying costly watches, but are buying cheap, well-styled watches to throw away when they require servicing. Other upper income consumers, however, continue to buy fine, expensive watches for suitable occasions.

Timex's Timely Tactics.   The planning implications in value segmentation are very broad for the industry. For one thing, many of the better watch companies in the years between 1957 and 1962 were inadvertently focusing exclusively on the third segment described—the 31% of the market that bought a watch only as a gift on important occasions—thus leaving the bulk of the market open to attack and exploitation.

The U.S. Time Company took advantage of this opening and established a very strong position among the more than two-thirds of America's watch buyers in the first two segments. Its new low-price watch, the Timex, had obvious appeal for the first segment, and it catered to the second segment as well. At that time, higher-price watches' were making the disastrous mistake in their advertising of equating product quality with water-proof and shock-resistant features. The Timex also offered these low-cost features, at lower prices, thus striking at a vulnerable area which the competition itself created. When Timex pressed its attack, it was able within a few years to claim that "Timex sells more watches than any other watch company in the world."

Even the *timing* of Timex's watch advertising was involved. Much of the third segment was buying watches only during the Christmas season, and so most of Timex's competitors concentrated their advertising in November and December. But since buying by the other two segments went on all the time, Timex advertised all year round, getting exclusive attention ten months of the year.

Thus, nondemographic segmentation in the watch industry has directly affected almost every phase of marketing, including the composition of the product line. Major watch companies know that they must plan product line, pricing, advertising, and distribution within the framework of the three basic value segments of this market.

II. Automobiles

The nondemographic segmentation of the automobile market is more complex than that of the watch market. The segments crisscross, forming intricate patterns. Their dynamics must be seen clearly before automobile sales can be understood.

Segmentation analysis leads to at least three different ways of classifying the automobile market along nondemographic lines, all of which are important to marketing planning.

Value Segmentation. The first mode of segmentation can be compared to that in the watch market—a threefold division along lines which represent how different people look at the meaning of *value* in an automobile:

1. *People who buy cars primarily for economy.* Many of these become owners of the Falcon, Ford, Rambler American, and Chevrolet. They are less loyal to any make than the other segments, but go where the biggest savings are to be found.
2. *People who want to buy the best product they can find for their money.* These prospects emphasize values such as body quality, reliability, durability, economy of operation, and ease of upkeep. Rambler and Volkswagen have been successful because so many people in this segment were dissatisfied.
3. *People interested in "personal enhancement" (a more accurate description than "prestige").* A handsomely styled Pontiac or Thunderbird does a great deal for the owner's ego, even though the car may not serve as a status symbol. Although the value of an automobile as a status symbol has declined, the personal satisfaction in owning a fine car has not lessened for this segment of the market. It is interesting that while both watches and cars have declined in status value, they have retained *self-enhancement* value for large portions of the market.

Markets can change so swiftly, and the size of key segments can shift so rapidly, that great sensitivity is required to catch a trend in time to capitalize on it. In the automobile market, the biggest change in recent years has been the growth in segment two—the number of people oriented to strict product value. Only a few years ago, the bulk of the market was made up of the other segments, but now the product-value segment is probably the largest. Some automobile companies did not respond to this shift in the size of these market segments in time to maintain their share of the market.

Aesthetic Concepts. A second way of segmenting the automobile market is by differences in *style* preferences. For example, most automobile buyers tell you that they like "expensive looking" cars. To some people, however, "expensive looking" means a great deal of chrome and ornamentation, while to others it means the very opposite—clean, conservative lines, lacking much chrome or ornamentation.

Unfortunately, the same *words* are used by consumers to describe diametrically opposed style concepts. Data that quantify buyers according to their aesthetic *responses*—their differing conceptions of what constitutes a good-looking car—are among the most useful an automobile company can possess.

The importance of aesthetic segmentation can be pointed up by this example:

> When Ford changed from its 1959 styling to its 1960 styling, the change did not seem to be a radical one from the viewpoint of formal design. But, because it ran contrary to the special style expectations of a large group of loyal Ford buyers, it constituted a dramatic and unwelcome change to them. This essential segment was not prepared for the change, and the results were apparent in sales.

Susceptibility to Change.   A third and indispensable method of segmenting the automobile market cuts across the lines drawn by the other two modes of segmentation analysis. This involves measuring the relative susceptibility of potential car buyers to changing their choice of make. Consider the buyers of Chevrolet during any one year from the point of view of a competitor:

> At one extreme are people whose brand loyalty is so solidly entrenched that no competitor can get home to them. They always buy Chevrolets. They are closed off to change.

> At the other extreme are the open-minded and the unprejudiced buyers. They happened to buy a Chevrolet because they preferred its styling that year, or because they got a good buy, or because someone talked up the Fisher body to them. They could just as easily have purchased another make.

> In the middle of this susceptibility continuum are people who are predisposed to Chevrolet to a greater or lesser degree. They can be persuaded to buy another make, but the persuasion has to be strong enough to break through the Chevrolet predisposition.

The implications of this kind of a susceptibility segmentation are far-reaching. Advertising effectiveness, for example, must be measured against each susceptibility segment, not against the market as a whole. Competitors' advertising should appear in media most likely to break through the Chevrolet predisposition of the middle group. In addition, the wants of those who are not susceptible must be factored out, or they will muddy the picture. Marketing programs persuasive enough to influence the uncommitted may make no difference at all to the single largest group—those who are predisposed to Chevrolet but still open enough to respond to the right stimulus.

If the marketing director of an automobile company does not break down his potential market into segments representing key differences in susceptibility, or does not clearly understand the requirements of each key segment, his company can persevere for years with little or no results because its promotion programs are inadvertently being aimed at the wrong people.

III. Perfume

A segmentation analysis of the perfume market shows that a useful way to analyze it is by the different *purposes* women have in mind when they buy perfume.

One segment of the market thinks of a perfume as something to be added to what nature has supplied. Another segment believes that the purpose of fragrance products is to help a woman feel cleaner, fresher, and better groomed—to correct or negate what nature has supplied. In the latter instance, the fragrance product is used to *cancel out* natural body odors; in the former, to *add* a new scent. To illustrate this difference in point of view:

> One woman told an interviewer, "I like a woodsy scent like Fabergé. It seems more intense and lingers longer, and doesn't fade away like the sweeter scents."
>
> But another woman said, "I literally loathe Fabergé. It makes me think of a streetcar full of women coming home from work who haven't bathed."

These differences in reaction do not indicate objective differences in the scent of Fabergé. They are subjective differences in women's attitudes; they grow out of each woman's purpose in using a perfume.

Purposive segmentation, as this third mode of analysis might be called, has been of great value to alert marketers. For instance:

A company making a famous line of fragrance products realized that it was selling almost exclusively to a single segment, although it had believed it was competing in the whole market. Management had been misled by its marketing research, which had consistently shown no differences in the demographic characteristics of women buying the company's products and women buying competitors' products.

In the light of this insight, the company decided to allocate certain lines to the underdeveloped segments of the market. This required appropriate changes in the scent of the product and in its package design. A special advertising strategy was also developed, involving a different copy approach for each product line aimed at each segment.

In addition, it was learned that visualizations of the product in use helped to create viewer identification in the segment that used perfume for adding to nature's handiwork, but that more subtle methods of communication produced better results among the more reserved, more modest women in the second segment who want the "canceling out" benefits of perfume. The media susceptibilities of women in the two segments were also found to be different.

Thus, from a single act of resegmentation, the advertising department extracted data critical to its copy platform, communication strategy, and media decisions.

IV. Bathing Soap

A comparable purposive segmentation was found in the closely related bathing soap field. The key split was between women whose chief requirement of soap was that it should clean them adequately and those for whom bathing was a sensuous and enjoyable experience. The company (a new contender in this highly competitive field) focused its sights on the first segment, which had been much neglected in recent years. A new soap was shaped, designed, and packaged to appeal to this segment, a new advertising approach was evolved, and results were very successful.

V. Hair-Care Market

The Breck-Halo competition in the shampoo market affords an excellent example of another kind of segmentation. For many years, Breck's recognition of the market's individualized segmentation gave the company a very strong position. Its line of individualized shampoos included one for dry hair, another for oily hair, and one for normal hair. This line accurately paralleled the marketing reality that women think of their hair as being dry, oily, or normal, and they do not believe that any one shampoo (such as an all-purpose Halo) can meet their individual requirements. Colgate has finally been obliged, in the past several years, to revise its long-held marketing approach to Halo, and to come out with products for dry hair and for oily hair, as well as for normal hair.

Other companies in the hair-care industry are beginning to recognize other segmentations in this field. For example, some women think of their hair as fine, others as coarse. Each newly discovered key segmentation contains the seeds of a new product, a new marketing approach, and a new opportunity.

VI. Other Packaged Goods

Examples of segmentation analysis in other packaged goods can be selected almost at random. Let us mention a few briefly, to show the breadth of applicability of this method of marketing analysis:

In *convenience foods*, for example, we find that the most pragmatic classification is, once again, purposive segmentation. Analysis indicates that "convenience" in foods has many different meanings for women, supporting several different market segments. Women for whom convenience means "easy to use" are reached by products and appeals different from those used to reach women for whom convenience means shortcuts to creativity in cooking.

In the market for *cleaning agents,* some women clean preventively, while others clean therapeutically, i.e., only after a mess has been made. The appeals, the product characteristics, and the marketing approach must take into account these different reasons for buying—another example of purposive segmentation.

In still another market, some people use *air fresheners* to remove disagreeable odors and others to add an odor. A product like Glade, which is keyed to the second segment, differs from one like Airwick in product concept, packaging, and type of scent.

The *beer market* requires segmentation along at least four different axes— reasons for drinking beer (purposive); taste preferences (aesthetic); price/ quality (value); and consumption level.

VII. Retail Soft Goods

Although soft-goods manufacturers and retailers are aware that their customers are value conscious, not all of them realize that their markets break down into at least four different segments corresponding to four different conceptions of value held by women.

For some women value means a willingness to pay a little more for quality. For others, value means merchandise on sale. Still other women look for value in terms of the lowest possible price, while others buy seconds or discounted merchandise as representing the best value.

Retailing operations like Sears, Roebuck are highly successful because they project *all* these value concepts, and do so in proportions which closely parallel their distribution in the total population.

VIII. Adding Machines

In marketing planning for a major adding machine manufacturer, analysis showed that his product line had little relationship to the segmented needs of the market. Like most manufacturers of this kind of product, he had designed his line by adding features to one or several stripped-down basic models—each addition raising the model price. The lowest priced model could only add; it could not subtract, multiply, divide, or print, and it was operated by hand.

Since there are a great many features in adding machines, the manufacturer had an extremely long product line. When the needs of the market were analyzed, however, it became clear that, despite its length, the line barely met the needs of two out of the three major segments of the market. It had been conceived and planned from a logical point of view rather than from a market-need point of view.

The adding machine market is segmented along lines reflecting sharp differences in value and purpose:

One buyer group values accuracy, reliability, and long life above all else. It tends to buy medium-price, full-keyboard, electric machines. There are many banks and other institutions in this group where full-keyboard operations are believed to ensure accuracy.

Manufacturing establishments, on the other hand, prefer the ten-key machine. Value, to these people, means the maximum number of labor-saving and timesaving features. They are willing to pay the highest prices for such models.

Both these segments contrast sharply with the third group, the small retailer whose major purpose is to find a model at a low purchase price. The small retailer does not think in terms of amortizing his investment over a period of years, and neither laborsaving features nor full-keyboard reliability count for as much as an immediate savings in dollars.

Despite the many models in the company's line, it lacked those demanded by both the manufacturer and small retailer segments of the market. But, because it had always been most sensitive to the needs of financial institutions, it had developed more models for this segment than happened to be needed. Product, sales, and distribution changes were required to enable the company to compete in the whole market.

IX. Computers

One pragmatic way of segmenting the computer market is to divide potential customers between those who believe they know how to evaluate a computer and those who believe they do not. A few years ago only about 20% of the market was really open to IBM's competitors—the 20% who believed it knew how to evaluate a computer. By default, this left 80% of the market a virtual captive of IBM—the majority who did not have confidence in its own ability to evaluate computers and who leaned on IBM's reputation as a substitute for personal appraisal.

Another segmentation in this market involves differences in prospects' attitudes toward the inevitability of progress. Although this factor has been widely ignored, it is a significant method for qualifying prospects. People who believe that progress is inevitable (i.e., that change is good and that new business methods are constantly evolving) make far better prospects for computers than those who have a less optimistic attitude toward progress in the world of business.

X. Light Trucks

The market for light trucks affords us another example of segmentation in products bought by industry. As in the computer example, there are both buyers who lack confidence in their ability to choose among competing makes and purchasers who feel they are sophisticated about trucks and can choose knowledgeably. This mode of segmentation unexpectedly turns out to be a key to explaining some important dynamics of the light truck market:

Those who do not trust their own judgment in trucks tend to rely very heavily on both the dealer's and the manufacturer's reputation. Once they find a make that gives them reliability and trouble-free operation, they cease to shop other makes and are no longer susceptible to competitive promotion. Nor are they as price-sensitive as the buyer who thinks he is sophisticated about trucks. This buyer tends to look for the best price, to shop extensively, and to be susceptible to the right kind of competitive appeals, because he puts performance before reputation.

These ways of looking at the truck market have far-reaching implications for pricing policy, for product features, and for dealers' sales efforts.

CONCLUSION

To sum up the implications of the preceding analysis, let me stress three points:

1. *We should discard the old, unquestioned assumption that demography is always the best way of looking at markets.*

The demographic premise implies that differences in reasons for buying, in brand choice influences, in frequency of use, or in susceptibility will be reflected in differences in age, sex, income, and geographical location. But this is usually not true. Markets should be scrutinized for important differences in buyer attitudes, motivations, values, usage patterns, aesthetic preferences, or degree of susceptibility. These may have no demographic correlatives. Above all, we must never assume in advance that we know the best way of looking at a market. This is the cardinal rule of segmentation analysis. All ways of segmenting markets must be considered, and *then* we must select out of the various methods available the ones that have the most important implications for action. This process of choosing the strategically most useful mode of segmentation is the essence of the marketing approach espoused in this article.

In considering cases like those described, we must understand that we are not dealing with different types of people, but with differences in peoples' *values*. A woman who buys a refrigerator because it is the cheapest available may want to buy the most expensive towels. A man who pays extra for his beer may own a cheap watch. A Ford-owning Kellogg's Corn Flakes-eater may be closed off to Chevrolet but susceptible to Post Toasties; he is the same man, but he has had different experiences and holds different values toward each product he purchases. By segmenting markets on the basis of the values, purposes, needs, and attitudes relevant to the product being studied, as in Figure 10–1, we avoid misleading information derived from attempts to divide people into types.

2. *The strategic-choice concept of segmentation broadens the scope of marketing planning to include the positioning of new products as well as of established products.*

It also has implications for brand planning, not just for individual products but for the composition of a line of competing brands where any meaningful segment in the market can possibly support a brand. One explanation of the successful competing brand strategy of companies like Procter & Gamble is that they are based on sensitivity to the many different modes of market segmentation. The brands offered by P & G often appear very similar to the outsider, but small, marginal differences between them appeal to different market segments. It is this rather than intramural competition that supports P & G successes.

3. *Marketing must develop its own interpretive theory, and not borrow a ready-made one from the social sciences.*

Marketing research, as an applied science, is tempted to borrow its theoretical structures from the disciplines from which it derives. The social sciences offer an abundance of such structures, but they are not applicable to marketing in their pure academic form. While the temptation to apply them in that form is great, it should be resisted. From sociology, for example, marketing has frequently borrowed the concept of status. This is a far-reaching concept, but it is not necessarily the most important one in a marketing problem, nor even one of the important ones. Again, early psychoanalytic theory has contributed an understanding of the sexual factor. While this can sometimes be helpful in an analysis of buying behavior in a given situation, some motivation researchers have become oversensitive to the role of sex and, as a result, have made many mistakes. Much the same might be said of the concept of social character, that is, seeing the world as being "inner-directed," "other-directed," "tradition-directed," "autonomous," and so forth.

One of the values of segmentation analysis is that, while it has drawn on the insights of social scientists, it has developed an interpretive theory *within* marketing. It has been home-grown in business. This may explain its ability to impose patterns of meaning on the immense diversity of the market, and to provide the modern marketing director with a systematic method for evolving true marketing objectives.

11.

Market Segmentation and Food Consumption

Leslie A. Beldo

I shall attempt to define a number of conceptual and operational propositions concerning food consumption, based on experience with studies of various food categories, the most recent study being an extensive survey in the State of California on milk consumption.

The conceptual propositions concern an effort to expand market segmentation beyond demography, the classical and most typical mode of market segmentation.[1] The operational propositions represent an effort, incomplete as it is, to translate nondemographic market segmentation into the realities of new product concept development and product communications strategy.

The market propositions outlined here are not purported to represent a high order of generalization, causality, or predictive utility, which are basic requirements of scientific propositions. Instead, they are presented relative to a single category of consumer products, the food category, which may indeed be a restrictive parameter for generalizations about consumer behavior, and their value therefore is inherently pragmatic. They have a demonstrable utility in application to market and product planning.

TYPES OF MARKET SEGMENTATION AND RELATED CONCEPTS

The following conceptual propositions are offered concerning market segmentation:

Market Segmentation. A subset of a market universe that is physically or functionally homogeneous in one or more respects and is differentiated in these respects from other subsets within the market.

[1] Daniel Yankelovich, "New Criteria for Market Segmentation," *Harvard Business Review,* March–April, 1964, presents a similar approach to market segmentation.
From Leslie A. Beldo, "Market Segmentation and Food Consumption," in Joseph W. Newman, ed., *On Knowing The Consumer* (New York: John Wiley & Sons, Inc., 1966), pp. 90–106. Reprinted by permission.

Structural Segmentation.   A subset of a market universe that is differentiated by age, by sex, by geography, by physical environment, or by other physical characteristics that generate varying physical product *requirements*. For example, the Florida market for sun-tan products, the fall market for anti-freeze.

Functional Segmentation.   A subset of a market universe that is differentiated or differentiable by attitudes, life style, interests and values generating varying subjective *product requirements*. For example, a demand for satisfaction of a desire to be exotic by use of a cosmetic product, which may transcend physical characteristics of age, income, or geography.

Interpersonal Segmentation.   Segmentation among sets of individuals varying by physical or social characteristics. Interpersonal segmentation presupposes a consistency of product usage and a nonoverlapping of usage among market segments. Unfortunately, examples may sometimes represent a *reductio ad absurdum*. For example, women with straight hair use home permanents, women with naturally curly hair have no need for them.

Intrapersonal Segmentation.   Segmentation varying within sets of individuals. A given individual may shift from one segment to another in successive purchase of a product, or may simultaneously belong to two or more segments. Intrapersonal segmentation seems to be a more dynamic and viable concept than interpersonal segmentation. For example, a single family may own a Cadillac for prestige, a compact car for economy and efficiency, a sports car for *joie de vivre*. Or, as another example, a woman may buy a high-priced brand of cosmetics in a department store to satisfy exotic necessity, but subsequently, may buy a variety store brand for economy.

Corresponding to the propositions about market segmentation that have been advanced are certain marketing concepts, representing corporate behavior, the institutional parallels of consumer behavior:

Market Differentiation.   The development of a product or product communication to appeal to a defined functional or structural market segment with homogeneous physical or subjective product requirements.

1. *Product differentiation:* Price, quality, quantity, ingredients, components, style, packaging.
2. *Communication differentiation:* Basic product concept, product name, advertising appeals, media coverage.

Market Optimization.   Development of a single, uniform product and related product communication to appeal to the market at large, treating the market as invariant in terms of structural or functional segmentation.

Figure 11–1. Market subsets as defined by homogeneous structural or functional requirements, each unit representing a basic characteristic or requirement, or combination of requirements, and its relative importance.

HYPOTHETICAL MARKET SEGMENTATION

Figure 11–1 represents a graphic translation of market segmentation. Figure 11–2 represents a graphic translation of product differentiation.

HYPOTHETICAL MARKET SEGMENTATION AND PRODUCT OPTIMIZATION

Figure 11–3 is a graphic representation of market segmentation and product nondifferentiation. Although the market is segmented or segmentable, the product is undifferentiated, representing an optimal combination of qualities believed to have the broadest appeal. The Model T Ford, in its day, was an example of market optimization.

HYPOTHETICAL MARKET SEGMENTATION AND PRODUCT DIFFERENTIATION

Figure 11–4 is a graphic representation of perfect product differentiation and market segmentation. Product differentiation is adapted to varying consumer requirements. Figure 11–4 is a vast and categorical oversimplification, of course. Product differentiation and product communication can create segmentation, and examples of natural, spontaneous segmentation independent of institutional effects on consumer behavior may not exist, although their potential existence is often presumed, as for example, the predication by General Motors in the 1920's that the public was potentially segmentable according to variable requirements for automobiles in terms of style, price, and performance.

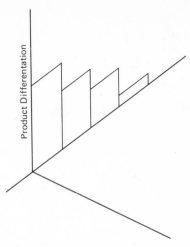

Figure 11–2. Product differentiation as defined by physical variation, each unit representing a varying combination of product qualities or features.

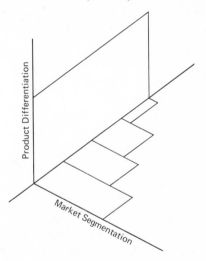

Figure 11–3.

FUNCTIONAL CONSUMER FOOD REQUIREMENTS AND MARKET SEGMENTATION

The application of functional market segmentation depends upon:

1. A definition of functional consumer requirements, in this case, consumer food requirements.
2. A measurement of food requirements in combination. It is practically impossible to measure all combinations of food requirements, and usually, the most workable procedure is to define the most salient requirements and attempt their measurement.

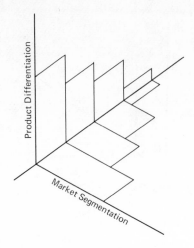

Figure 11—4.

A definition of basic consumer food requirements, as inferred from a series of food studies, and a partial measurement of certain relevant combinations with respect to milk consumption is here presented:

1. Nutritive/Health

> Sustenance
> Growth
> Maintenance
> Physiological Functioning
> Energy/Strength
> Weight Control
> Cholesterol Balance

This category includes basic sustenance, energy maintenance implicitly, and such emerging requirements as weight control and cholesterol control. In food product development and promotion, generally, the nutritive qualities of food may well be underpresented relative to flavor and convenience.

2. Sensory

> Aroma
> Taste
> Appearance
> Feel

Gratifications of aroma, taste, and textural stimulation comprise this category. The vocabulary of sensory satisfaction *vis-à-vis* food is extremely limited, defining our inadequate knowledge of the sensory correlates of food qualities.

3. Convenience

> Purchasing
> Storing
> Preparation
> Serving
> Consumption

This category represents a functional requirement, is quite complex, and is perhaps overestimated in importance to food marketing. Convenience of food preparation is a major area of food product innovation today, and ultimately the kitchen may become an artifact of the twentieth century. However, a substantial proportion of housewives still derive role satisfactions and a sense of accomplishment from the preparation of food, even though the sustained counterinfluence of convenience foods is gradually turning them toward other attainments. A substantial proportion of cakes baked in the home are made from basic ingredients; women still peel potatoes, bake apple pies, and scramble eggs, even though substitute convenience products are available at a reasonable price.

4. Social/Psychological

> Socioeconomic Status
> Life Style
> Anxiety Reduction

Foods *à la mode* are a sign of affluent times, when sustenance is taken for granted and food choice depends considerably on style of consumption. Extra-dry wine, medium-rare steak, French cuisine, and the outdoor barbecue are perhaps as much a matter of social taste as physical taste. Even though food may not be an object of conspicuous consumption, it is certainly a symbol of individual personality, life style, and social status. The person who goes to a restaurant and orders beer, bean soup, and a well-done steak is probably a different person socially than one who orders a martini, turtle soup amontillado, and sole almandine.

5. Value

> Price
> Price $\times$ Means
> Price $\times$ Nutritive, Sensory
> Convenience, and Social/
> Psychological Requirements

Value represents a consumer's qualitative assessment of a food's benefit times its price and times other basic food requirements, and as such, is more subjective than objective as a basic consumer requirement. It should be emphasized that very little is known about value, conceptually or operationally.

DYNAMIC INTERACTION OF CONSUMER REQUIREMENTS

In the foregoing description of food behavior, consumer requirements are posited as determining food choice, food preference, and food purchase by dynamic interactions. No single requirement is necessarily determinant of behavior, but the interacting of basic requirements resolves into choice of a particular food, into purchase decisions, into frequency and occasion of serving, and into overall volume of consumption.

Table 11-I illustrates that a substantial number of females in the age range 15 to 34 drink milk even though they dislike its taste. A requirement transcending taste accounts for their consumption of milk. For this age group, milk is perceived as being particularly important for nutrition (teenage girls, for growth, young mothers, for calcium intake).

Table 11-1
Per Cent Heavy Volume Drinkers (4 or More Glasses per Day)*

Taste Attitudes	Females		
	15–18	19–34	35–39
Like taste of milk	21.9	13.1	14.6
Dislike taste of milk	8.6	6.5	0
Total sample	22.0	11.2	8.0

* *A Study of Consumption of and Attitudes toward Milk in the State of California,* Dairy Council of California.

After 35 years of age, problems of weight control intensify and transcend a nutritional requirement for milk. If a woman over 35 dislikes milk, it is easy for her to eliminate it from her diet as a means to weight control in the context of her diminishing nutritional regard for milk.

SEGMENTATION OF CONSUMER REQUIREMENTS

Although the basic consumer requirements and their interactions that determine food behavior have been defined somewhat categorically, they are theoretically variable and continuous. Quantification of consumer requirements, classification by degree, and estimation of their frequency in the population are therefore necessary beyond primary definition and description. Any combination of requirements may exist among some proportion of the population, or, idiosyncratically, one consumer might theoretically differ from another by a unique combination of needs and motivations. The sometimes apparent contradictions of qualitative research based on small samples may simply represent reality segments, and more extended sampling with multi-dimensional measurement would lead to establishment of their true impor-tance and reconciliation of their contradictions. One motivation researcher may make one proclamation about prunes, and another motivation researcher may present a contrary interpretation. Polemically, the diverse conclusions make excellent trade journal copy, but scientifically, the diversity may only represent the reality of consumer segmentation.

As the total population increases, sample segmentation probably increases, in numbers of observable, definable segments, and in numbers of consumers within a given segment. Theoretically, an infinite number of combinations can be defined in terms of extensive measurement. Precise definition, however, cannot be matched with precise observation and measurement, or it may be impracticable to deploy or fragment marketing effort against precisely defined, but small, subsamples of the population.

CONSUMER FOOD REQUIREMENT SPACE

By projection of a combination of consumer elements and the fre-quency of occurrence for each class of combination, a kind of consumer "need space" can be structured, as shown in Figure 11–5, combining three of the basic consumer food requirements.

Four hypothetical constellations of consumer food requirements are plotted in Figure 11–5.

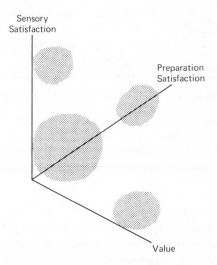

Figure 11–5. Consumer food requirement space. (Value, sensory satisfaction, preparation satis-faction for a given food class.)

1. A high value cluster
2. A high sensory satisfaction cluster
3. A high preparation satisfaction cluster
4. A cluster representing medium value, medium sensory satisfaction, medium preparation satisfaction

Clusters 1, 2, and 3 represent salient consumer requirement segments; cluster 4 represents an optimal combination of requirements.

APPLICATION OF FUNCTIONAL MARKET SEGMENTATION

The principles of market segmentation and functional food requirements have been applied recently to a study of milk consumption in the State of California, as a background for developing product and communications strategies for milk. Certain key findings are described here to illustrate the practical translation of market segmentation concepts.

In Figure 11–6 the three basic food requirements of nutrition, weight control, and taste are described for one demographic group, women 19 to 34 years of age.

From analysis of these salient reactions toward milk and their clustering in the context of basic food requirements it was concluded that:

1. A segment of women excludes milk from the diet because of problems of overweight and because of a perception of milk as fattening.
2. A segment excludes milk from the diet because of a distaste for milk.
3. A segment includes milk in the diet because of its perceived nutritional benefits; this segment includes some women who dislike the taste of milk.
4. A segment includes milk in the diet because they enjoy its taste, without having a strong nutritional involvement with milk.
5. A major segment likes the taste of milk, is nutritionally involved with milk, and does not consider it fattening.

Both structural segmentation and functional segmentation are qualitatively described in Table 11–2, illustrating a two-way segmentation of varying functional requirements by age segmentation.

Against these rather complex segmentations, marketing differentiation for milk involves:

1. *Product differentiation:* Development and improvement of lower-fat milks, with acceptable palatability, to position against market segments concerned with weight control, particularly stronger positioning of 2 per cent milks which combine calorie reduction and excellent palatability.
2. *Communications differentiation:*
   (a) Definition of target audiences (major segments).

(b) Definition of nutritional characteristics of milk compatible with nutritional requirements, to intensify *nutritional* involvement.

(c) Definition of product portrayal in terms of nutrients and nutritional benefits, taste connotations, social settings and situations that orient desired social perceptions of milk.

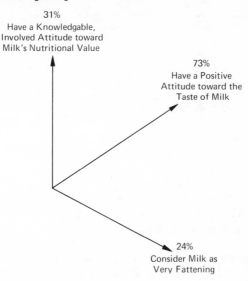

31%
Have a Knowledgable,
Involved Attitude toward
Milk's Nutritional Value

73%
Have a Positive
Attitude toward the
Taste of Milk

24%
Consider Milk as
Very Fattening

(*Taken from* A Study of Consumption of and Attitudes toward Milk in the State of California, Dairy Council of California.)

Figure 11—6.

SUMMARY

In this section, the research implications and the marketing implications of functional market segmentation are given general consideration.

Research Implications

The basic implications for observation and measurement of consumer requirements are twofold.

1. Measurement for a given food class should be multidimensional, translated perhaps into individual scales to classify levels of intensity for each requirement, and to estimate the proportion of consumers within each classification. Factor analysis, for example, could be applied to verify, redefine, or add basic requirements, and to purify measurement scales.

2. Analysis should accordingly be multidimensional, defining significant consumer segments and the dynamic combination of requirements influencing consumer behavior within a given food class.

Table 11–2
Basic Consumer Milk Requirements Among Females

Consumer Requirements	Age Groups	
	15–18	19–34, 35–49
Nutritive	Females restricting intake for weight control	Females restricting intake for weight control. Declining total food intake depresses milk consumption. Lessened nutritive importance of milk to diet
Sensory	Positive taste acceptance	Developing distaste for milk among females
Convenience	Inconvenience of milk consumption away from home	
Social-Psychological	Generally favorable status associations (vigorous, energetic, athletic), but perhaps somewhat too masculine	
Value		

Marketing Implications

A conceptual model of consumer food behavior has utility in three broad marketing areas: product development, product communications strategy, and overall marketing strategy.

Product Development. For a given product class, consumer requirement space can be examined for *vulnerability* to competitive entry by a new product combining qualities and features to satisfy consumer requirements heretofore not satisfied by existing products. For example, the fresh milk market may be highly vulnerable to a synthetic milk product that offers convenience, value, and palatability. Or, generalized consumer food requirements independent of a particular food class could be analyzed for opportunity to introduce a totally new food product class and create a new market, such as liquid food (Metrecal).

Fundamentally, such a model lends itself to the development of product concepts rather than specific product ideas. As abstractions, product concepts depend on feasibility and economics for concrete translation into physical prototypes. However, to editorialize, too much new product effort is economically wasted on minute food product variations and gimmickry, although competitively, such product variations are necessary to occupy shelf space and preempt competition. But competitive product development should be matched with basic new product exploration at conceptual levels independent of competitive brand shares, and should be aligned with dynamic interpretations of current and evolving consumer requirements.

Product Communications Strategy. Product communications strategy represents a plan to inform consumers, establish new attitudes, disestablish inhibiting attitudes, and persuade the public to buy a given food product.

The consumer requirement model can guide food product communication strategy in the areas of package design, advertising, corporate identification, etc., to correct any misimpressions of negative physical effects of product consumption, enhance product value, or create a more attractive social setting for a product. Whole milk, for example, could be defended against charges of excessive cholesterol (assuming this is physically and medically established); it could be advertised as an economic value, or could be depicted in attractive social settings.

Overall Marketing Strategy. A comprehensive definition of market segments and consumer requirements, as described, lends itself to conceptual strategies for new food product development and product communications. Total marketing strategy is dependent on corporate policies and capabilities, but within these parameters, a conceptual model of consumer requirements can guide the development of a well-modulated strategy that corrects vulnerabilities, avails itself of opportunities, reacts to consumer needs, and yet organizes consumers toward a demand for new food products that offer utility and value.

12.

Benefit Segmentation: A Decision-oriented Research Tool

Russell I. Haley

Market segmentation has been steadily moving toward center stage as a topic of discussion in marketing and research circles. Hardly a conference passes without at least one session devoted to it. Moreover, in March the American Management Association held a three-day conference entirely concerned with various aspects of the segmentation problem.

According to Wendell Smith, "Segmentation is based upon developments on the demand side of the market and represents a rational and more precise adjustment of product and marketing effort to consumer or user requirements."[1] The idea that all markets can be profitably segmented has now received almost as wide-spread acceptance as the marketing concept itself. However, problems remain. In the extreme, a marketer can divide up his market in as many ways as he can describe his prospects. If he wishes, he can define a left-handed segment, or a blue-eyed segment, or a German-speaking segment. Consequently, current discussion revolves largely around which of the virtually limitless alternatives is likely to be most productive.

Segmentation Methods

Several varieties of market segmentation have been popular in the recent past. At least three kinds have achieved some degree of prominence. Historically, perhaps the first type to exist was geographic segmentation. Small manufacturers who wished to limit their investments, or whose distribution channels were not large enough to cover the entire country, segmented the U. S. market, in effect, by selling their products only in certain areas.

However, as more and more brands became national, the second major

---

[1] Wendell R. Smith, "Product Differentiation and Market Segmentation as Alternative Product Strategies," *Journal of Marketing,* Vol. XXI (July, 1956), pp. 3–8.
From Russell I. Haley, "Benefit Segmentation," *Journal of Marketing,* Vol. 32 (July 1968), pp. 30–35. Published by the American Marketing Association. Reprinted by permission.

system of segmentation—demographic segmentation—became popular. Under this philosophy targets were defined as younger people, men, or families with children. Unfortunately, a number of recent studies have shown that demographic variables such as age, sex, income, occupation, and race are, in general, poor predictors of behavior and, consequently, less than optimum bases for segmentation strategies.[2]

More recently, a third type of segmentation has come into increasing favor—volume segmentation. The so-called "heavy half" theory, popularized by Dik Twedt of the Oscar Mayer Company,[3] points out that in most product categories one-half of the consumers account for around 80% of the consumption. If this is true, the argument goes, shouldn't knowledgeable marketers concentrate their efforts on these high-volume consumers? Certainly they are the most *valuable* consumers.

The trouble with this line of reasoning is that not all heavy consumers are usually available to the same brand—because they are not all seeking the same kinds of benefits from a product. For example, heavy coffee drinkers consist of two types of consumers—those who drink chain store brands and those who drink premium brands. The chain store customers feel that all coffees are basically alike and, because they drink so much coffee, they feel it is sensible to buy a relatively inexpensive brand. The premium brand buyers, on the other hand, feel that the few added pennies which coffees like Yuban, Martinson's, Chock Full O'Nuts, and Savarin cost are more than justified by their fuller taste. Obviously, these two groups of people, although they are both members of the "heavy half" segment, are not equally good prospects for any one brand, nor can they be expected to respond to the same advertising claims.

These three systems of segmentation have been used because they provide helpful guidance in the use of certain marketing tools. For example, geographic segmentation, because it describes the market in a discrete way, provides definite direction in media purchases. Spot TV, spot radio, and newspapers can be bought for the geographical segment selected for concentrated effort. Similarly, demographic segmentation allows media to be bought more efficiently since demographic data on readers, viewers, and listeners are readily available for most media vehicles. Also, in some product categories demo-

[2] Ronald E. Frank, "Correlates of Buying Behavior for Grocery Products," *Journal of Marketing,* Vol. 31 (October, 1967), pp. 48–53; Ronald E. Frank, William Massy, and Harper W. Boyd, Jr., "Correlates of Grocery Product Consumption Rates," *Journal of Marketing Research,* Vol. 4 (May, 1967), pp. 184–190; and Clark Wilson, "Homemaker Living Patterns and Marketplace Behavior—A Psychometric Approach," in John S. Wright and Jac L. Goldstucker, Editors, *New Ideas for Successful Marketing,* Proceedings of 1966 World Congress (Chicago: American Marketing Association, June, 1966), pp. 305–331.

[3] Dik Warren Twedt, "Some Practical Applications of the 'Heavy Half' Theory" (New York: Advertising Research Foundation 10th Annual Conference, October 6, 1964).

graphic variables are extremely helpful in differentiating users from non-users, although they are typically less helpful in distinguishing between the users of various brands. The heavy-half philosophy is especially effective in directing dollars toward the most important parts of the market.

However, each of these three systems of segmentation is handicapped by an underlying disadvantage inherent in its nature. All are based on an ex-post facto analysis of the kinds of people who make up various segments of a market. They rely on *descriptive* factors rather than *causal* factors. For this reason they are not efficient predictors of future buying behavior, and it is future buying behavior that is of central interest to marketers.

BENEFIT SEGMENTATION

An approach to market segmentation whereby it is possible to identify market segments by causal factors rather than descriptive factors, might be called "benefit segmentation." The belief underlying this segmentation strategy is that the benefits which people are seeking in consuming a given product are the basic reasons for the existence of true market segments. Experience with this approach has shown that benefits sought by consumers determine their behavior much more accurately than do demographic characteristics or volume of consumption.

This does not mean that the kinds of data gathered in more traditional types of segmentation are not useful. Once people have been classified into segments in accordance with the benefits they are seeking, each segment is contrasted with all of the other segments in terms of its demography, its volume of consumption, its brand perceptions, its media habits, its personality and life-style, and so forth. In this way, a reasonably deep understanding of the people who make up each segment can be obtained. And by capitalizing on this understanding, it is possible to reach them, to talk to them in their own terms, and to present a product in the most favorable light possible.

The benefit segmentation approach is not new. It has been employed by a number of America's largest corporations since it was introduced in 1961.[4] However, case histories have been notably absent from the literature because most studies have been contracted for privately, and have been treated confidentially.

The benefit segmentation approach is based upon being able to measure consumer value systems in detail, together with what the consumer thinks about various brands in the product category of interest. While this concept seems simple enough, operationally it is very complex. There is no simple straightforward way of handling the volumes of data that have to be generated. Com-

[4] Russell I. Haley, "Experimental Research on Attitudes Toward Shampoos," an unpublished paper (February, 1961).

puters and sophisticated multivariate attitude measurement techniques are a necessity.

Several alternative statistical approaches can be employed, among them the so-called "Q" technique of factor analysis, multi-dimensional scaling, and other distance measures.[5] All of these methods relate the ratings of each respondent to those of every other respondent and then seek clusters of individuals with similar rating patterns. If the items rated are potential consumer benefits, the clusters that emerge will be groups of people who attach similar degrees of importance to the various benefits. Whatever the statistical approach selected, the end result of the analysis is likely to be between three and seven consumer segments, each representing a potentially productive focal point for marketing efforts.

Each segment is identified by the benefits it is seeking. However, it is the *total configuration* of the benefits sought which differentiates one segment from another, rather than the fact that one segment is seeking one particular benefit and another a quite different benefit. Individual benefits are likely to have appeal for several segments. In fact, the research that has been done thus far suggests that most people would like as many benefits as possible. However, the *relative* importance they attach to individual benefits can differ importantly and, accordingly, can be used as an effective lever in segmenting markets.

Of course, it is possible to determine benefit segments intuitively as well as with computers and sophisticated research methods. The kinds of brilliant insights which produced the Mustang and the first 100-millimeter cigarette have a good chance of succeeding whenever marketers are able to tap an existing benefit segment.

However, intuition can be very expensive when it is mistaken. Marketing history is replete with examples of products which someone felt could not miss. Over the longer term, systematic benefit segmentation research is likely to have a higher proportion of successes.

But is benefit segmentation practical? And is it truly operational? The answer to both of these questions is "yes." In effect, the crux of the problem of choosing the best segmentation system is to determine which has the greatest number of practical marketing implications. An example should show that benefit segmentation has a much wider range of implications than alternative forms of segmentation.

An Example of Benefit Segmentation

While the material presented here is purely illustrative to protect the competitive edge of companies who have invested in studies of this kind, it is

[5] Ronald E. Frank and Paul E. Green, "Numerical Taxonomy in Marketing Analysis: A Review Article," *Journal of Marketing Research,* Vol. V (February, 1968), pp. 83–98.

based on actual segmentation studies. Consequently, it is quite typical of the kinds of things which are normally learned in the course of a benefit segmentation study.

The toothpaste market has been chosen as an example because it is one with which everyone is familiar. Let us assume that a benefit segmentation study has been done and four major segments have been identified—one particularly concerned with decay prevention, one with brightness of teeth, one with the flavor and appearance of the product, and one with price. A relatively large amount of supplementary information has also been gathered (Table 12–1) about the people in each of these segments.

Table 12–1
Toothpaste Market Segment Description

Segment Name:	The Sensory Segment	The Sociables	The Worriers	The Independent Segment
Principal benefit sought:	Flavor, product appearance	Brightness of teeth	Decay prevention	Price
Demographic strengths:	Children	Teens, young people	Large families	Men
Special behavioral characteristics:	Users of spearmint flavored toothpaste	Smokers	Heavy users	Heavy users
Brands disproportionately favored:	Colgate, Stripe	Macleans, Plus White, Ultra Brite	Crest	Brands on sale
Personality characteristics:	High self-involvement	High sociability	High hypochondriasis	High autonomy
Life-style characteristics:	Hedonistic	Active	Conservative	Value-oriented

The decay prevention segment, it has been found, contains a disproportionately large number of families with children. They are seriously concerned about the possibility of cavities and show a definite preference for fluoride toothpaste. This is reinforced by their personalities. They tend to be a little hypochondriacal and, in their life-styles, they are less socially-oriented than some of the other groups. This segment has been named The Worriers.

The second segment, comprised of people who show concern for the brightness of their teeth, is quite different. It includes a relatively large group of young marrieds. They smoke more than average. This is where the swingers are. They are strongly social and their life-style patterns are very active.

This is probably the group to which toothpastes such as Macleans or Plus White or Ultra Brite would appeal. This segment has been named The Sociables.

In the third segment, the one which is particularly concerned with the flavor and appearance of the product, a large portion of the brand deciders are children. Their use of spearmint toothpaste is well above average. Stripe has done relatively well in this segment. They are more ego-centered than other segments, and their life-style is outgoing but not to the extent of the swingers. They will be called The Sensory Segment.

The fourth segment, the price-oriented segment, shows a predominance of men. It tends to be above average in terms of toothpaste usage. People in this segment see very few meaningful differences between brands. They switch more frequently than people in other segments and tend to buy a brand on sale. In terms of personality, they are cognitive and they are independent. They like to think for themselves and make brand choices on the basis of their judgment. They will be called The Independent Segment.

MARKETING IMPLICATIONS OF BENEFIT SEGMENTATION STUDIES

Both copy directions and media choices will show sharp differences depending upon which of these segments is chosen as the target—The Worriers, The Sociables, The Sensory Segment, or The Independent Segment. For example, the tonality of the copy will be light if The Sociable Segment or The Sensory Segment is to be addressed. It will be more serious if the copy is aimed at The Worriers. And if The Independent Segment is selected, it will probably be desirable to use rational, two-sided arguments. Of course, to talk to this group at all it will be necessary to have either a price edge or some kind of demonstrable product superiority.

The depth-of-sell reflected by the copy will also vary, depending upon the segment which is of interest. It will be fairly intensive for The Worrier Segment and for The Independent Segment, but much more superficial and mood-oriented for The Sociable and Sensory Segments.

Likewise, the setting will vary. It will focus on the product for The Sensory Group, on socially-oriented situations for The Sociable Group, and perhaps on demonstration or on competitive comparisons for The Independent Group.

Media environments will also be tailored to the segments chosen as targets. Those with serious environments will be used for The Worrier and Independent Segments, and those with youthful, modern and active environments for The Sociable and the Sensory Groups. For example, it might be logical to use a larger proportion of television for The Sociable and Sensory Groups, while The Worriers and Independents might have heavier print schedules.

The depth-of-sell needed will also be reflected in the media choices. For

The Worrier and Rational Segments longer commercials—perhaps 60-second commercials—would be indicated, while for the other two groups shorter commercials and higher frequency would be desirable.

Of course, in media selection the facts that have been gathered about the demographic characteristics of the segment chosen as the target would also be taken into consideration.

The information in Table 12–1 also has packaging implications. For example, it might be appropriate to have colorful packages for The Sensory Segment, perhaps aqua (to indicate fluoride) for The Worrier Group, and gleaming white for The Sociable Segment because of their interest in bright white teeth.

It should be readily apparent that the kinds of information normally obtained in the course of a benefit segmentation study have a wide range of marketing implications. Sometimes they are useful in suggesting physical changes in a product. For example, one manufacturer discovered that his product was well suited to the needs of his chosen target with a single exception in the area of flavor. He was able to make a relatively inexpensive modification in his product and thereby strengthen his market position.

The new product implications of benefit segmentation studies are equally apparent. Once a marketer understands the kinds of segments that exist in his market, he is often able to see new product opportunities or particularly effective ways of positioning the products emerging from his research and development operation.

Similarly, benefit segmentation information has been found helpful in providing direction in the choice of compatible point-of-purchase materials and in the selection of the kinds of sales promotions which are most likely to be effective for any given market target.

GENERALIZATIONS FROM BENEFIT SEGMENTATION STUDIES

A number of generalizations are possible on the basis of the major benefit segmentation studies which have been conducted thus far. For example, the following general rules of thumb have become apparent:

It is easier to take advantage of market segments that already exist than to attempt to create new ones. Some time ago the strategy of product differentiation was heavily emphasized in marketing textbooks. Under this philosophy it was believed that a manufacturer was more or less able to create new market segments at will by making his product somewhat different from those of his competitors. Now it is generally recognized that fewer costly errors will be made if money is first invested in consumer research aimed at determining the present contours of the market. Once this knowledge is available, it is usually most efficient to tailor marketing strategies to existing consumer-need patterns.

No brand can expect to appeal to all consumers. The very act of attracting one segment may automatically alienate others. A corollary to this principle is that any marketer who wishes to cover a market fully must offer consumers more than a single brand. The flood of new brands which have recently appeared on the market is concrete recognition of this principle.

A company's brands can sometimes cannibalize each other but need not necessarily do so. It depends on whether or not they are positioned against the same segment of the market. Ivory Snow sharply reduced Ivory Flakes' share of market, and the Ford Falcon cut deeply into the sales of the standard size Ford because, in each case, the products were competing in the same segments. Later on, for the same companies, the Mustang was successfully introduced with comparatively little damage to Ford; and the success of Crest did not have a disproportionately adverse effect on Gleem's market position because, in these cases, the segments to which the products appealed were different.

New and old products alike should be designed to fit *exactly* the needs of some segment of the market. In other words, they should be aimed at people seeking a specific combination of benefits. It is a marketing truism that you sell people one at a time—that you have to get *someone* to buy your product before you get *anyone* to buy it. A substantial group of people must be interested in your specific set of benefits before you can make progress in a market. Yet, many products attempt to aim at two or more segments simultaneously. As a result, they are not able to maximize their appeal to any segment of the market, and they run the risk of ending up with a dangerously fuzzy brand image.

Marketers who adopt a benefit segmentation strategy have a distinct competitive edge. If a benefit segment can be located which is seeking exactly the kinds of satisfactions that one marketer's brand can offer better than any other brand, the marketer can almost certainly dominate the purchases of that segment. Furthermore, if his competitors are looking at the market in terms of traditional types of segments, they may not even be aware of the existence of the benefit segment which he has chosen as his market target. If they are ignorant in this sense, they will be at a loss to explain the success of his brand. And it naturally follows that if they do not understand the reasons for his success, the kinds of people buying his brand, and the benefits they are obtaining from it, his competitors will find it very difficult to successfully attack the marketer's position.

An understanding of the benefit segments which exist within a market can be used to advantage when competitors introduce new products. Once the way in which consumers are positioning the new product has been determined, the likelihood that it will make major inroads into segments of interest can be assessed, and a decision can be made on whether or not counteractions of any kind are required. If the new product appears to be assuming an ambiguous position, no money need be invested in defensive measures. However, if it appears that the new product is ideally suited to the needs of an important segment of the market, the manufacturer in question can introduce a new competitive product of his own, modify the physical properties of existing brands, change his advertising strategy, or take whatever steps appear appropriate.

Types of Segments Uncovered Through Benefit Segmentation Studies

It is difficult to generalize about the types of segments which are apt to be discovered in the course of a benefit segmentation study. To a large extent, the segments which have been found have been unique to the product categories being analyzed. However, a few types of segments have appeared in two or more private studies. Among them are the following:

The Status Seeker	. . . a group which is very much concerned with the prestige of the brands purchased.
The Swinger	. . . a group which tries to be modern and up to date in all of its activities. Brand choices reflect this orientation.
The Conservative	. . . a group which prefers to stick to large successful companies and popular brands.
The Rational Man	. . . a group which looks for benefits such as economy, value, durability, etc.
The Inner-directed Man	. . . a group which is especially concerned with self-concept. Members consider themselves to have a sense of humor, to be independent and/or honest.
The Hedonist	. . . a group which is concerned primarily with sensory benefits.

Some of these segments appear among the customers of almost all products and services. However, there is no guarantee that a majority of them or, for that matter, any of them exist in any given product category. Finding out whether they do and, if so, what should be done about them is the purpose of benefit segmentation research.

CONCLUSION

The benefit segmentation approach is of particular interest because it never fails to provide fresh insight into markets. As was indicated in the toothpaste example cited earlier, the marketing implications of this analytical research tool are limited only by the imagination of the person using the information a segmentation study provides. In effect, when segmentation studies are conducted, a number of smaller markets emerge instead of one large one. Moreover, each of these smaller markets can be subjected to the same kinds of thorough analyses to which total markets have been subjected in the past. The only difference—a crucial one—is that the total market was a heterogeneous conglomeration of sub-groups. The so-called average consumer existed only in the minds of some marketing people. When benefit segmentation is used, a number of relatively homogeneous segments are uncovered. And, because they are homogeneous, descriptions of them in terms of averages are much more appropriate and meaningful as marketing guides.

13.

Preference and Perception Measures in New Product Development: An Exposition and Review

Alvin J. Silk

INTRODUCTION

The subject of new products is one which has received a considerable amount of attention in the marketing research and management science literature in recent years. Most of what has emerged from this upsurge of research activity can be conveniently classified under two headings: normative decision models, and descriptive models and empirical studies. In order to place the work to be discussed here in perspective, it will be helpful to comment briefly on the orientation of other developments in the new product area.

In their review of what has been taking place on the normative side, Montgomery and Urban discuss new product decision making as a four-stage process of search, screen, analyze, and implement.[1] They describe models that have been developed to deal with each of these stages. That is, one way of looking at the firm's new product problem is to say that one starts out by identifying a relatively large number of possibilities and then subjects them to a sequential evaluation procedure. At each step, less desirable alternatives are discarded and the list is gradually honed down to a very small number which finally reaches the market. The models found in the Montgomery and Urban review represent attempts to formalize the various steps in this process. The benefits to be realized from such models need not be belabored here. It is also true, of course, that much of the firm's "new product problem" lies "outside" these models. Paralleling the sequential decision process of search, screen, and analyze are a whole series of developmental and testing activities through which product ideas on paper are given a physical form and plans for mar-

[1] [35], chapter 7.
From Alvin J. Silk, "Preference and Perception Measures in New Product Development: An Exposition and Review," *Industrial Management Review*, Vol. 2 (Fall 1969), pp. 21–37. Reprinted by permission.

keting them are formulated. The results of this testing and developmental work represent, directly or indirectly, the inputs for models like SPRINTER[2] and DEMON.[3] Let us consider for a moment the nature of the inputs required by such models. As we move from the beginning stages of the decision process, where we are dealing with product ideas, through the final stages of analysis, when we have the physical product in hand, the reliance on subjective or judgmental estimates as inputs diminishes while the use (and availability) of harder data increases. Compare, for example, the use of scaling techniques to elicit management's ratings of new products' "desirability" at the screening stage[4] with DEMON, an "analysis" model of the adaptive variety which is structured so as to utilize information from market studies of various kinds in a formal way.[5]

In effect, what is called for at each stage of the new product decision process in one form or another—and, of course, this is true whether or not one utilizes a formal model—is an estimate or prediction of consumer response. A variety of means, such as concept and product testing, is commonly used to obtain information relevant to this matter at various stages in the development of a new product.[6] For example, at a relatively early stage, lab tests may be used to gauge consumer reactions to a few versions of a product which differ from one another in some known way—in flavor or with respect to the amount of some ingredient. At later stages we have full scale market tests where the product is offered for sale with a supporting promotional program. The use of such studies is an attempt to learn something about consumer response by a cut-and-try empiricism. Some aspect of the product or its promotion is varied or altered and consumer response noted. Hopefully, one gets an idea of what works "best."

Measurement problems as well as time and cost considerations make this approach a less than satisfactory final solution to the problem of dealing with the uncertainty inherent in consumer response to new products. One widely discussed measurement problem that pervades virtually all consumer research is the question of external validity. Are measures of consumer response obtained under the kind of controlled or artificial conditions that permit us to isolate for study some variation in a particular feature of a product or its marketing plan indicative of what will happen in the market place? Even test marketing (itself a costly and uncertain activity) which may yield hard sales data (generally accorded high face validity)[7] obviously can only be

[2] See Urban [43].
[3] See [12].
[4] See [15].
[5] [12].
[6] See [1], [3], and [13] for a discussion of these techniques. A good illustration of their application may be found in [16].
[7] For some evidence of the low predictive accuracy of test market results, see Gold [18].

undertaken after the product exists and therefore necessitates that some, perhaps considerable, investment be made prior to having such results available.[8]

To supplant this raw empiricism, a workable and valid methodology based on a theory of how consumers respond to new products is needed. In particular, we need a theory that permits evaluation of consumer response to product possibilities at an early stage in their development—preferably while they are still ideas and before much sunk cost has been incurred to develop and produce the physical product. Our quest for such a theory naturally leads us to examine what the behaviorally oriented work that has been going on in the new product field has to offer.

The appearance of Everett Rogers' monumental review of the sociological research on the diffusion of innovations[9] provided marketing researchers with a structure for viewing the process whereby consumers come to accept or reject a new product. It offered valuable insights into the roles which the mass media and word-of-mouth communications play in that process. Tangible evidence of the impact of this viewpoint on marketing can be found in a series of published studies concerned with what factors characterize early adopters of new products and "opinion leaders," and how consumers use various kinds of information sources about new products.[10] A related step has been the development of aggregate market response models for new products which incorporate some of the behavioral aspects of the diffusion process into their structure.[11] While all of this has a certain value, diffusion research, as it presently stands, does not offer us much help as a theory or explanation of how consumers perceive and evaluate a new product. The innovation itself—be it a product, an idea, or some social object—is a variable that has not received much attention in research on the diffusion of innovations. Diffusion theory does give us some idea of *how* information about and acceptance of a new product spreads through a social system, but it says very little about *why*: what characteristics of the product itself lead people to react favorably or unfavorably once they have learned about it.[12] Recall that this was the kind of knowledge we identified earlier as being useful for the new product development problem. Having found diffusion theory deficient for such purposes, we must look elsewhere.

---

[8] For a discussion of the limitations of test marketing, see Hardin [24].

[9] [39].

[10] For a listing of some of this work, see King [25]. A comprehensive review of these studies is scheduled to appear shortly in Robertson [38].

[11] See [6], [7], [11], [37], and [43].

[12] Rogers [39], p. 121, draws attention to the fact that the "characteristics" of innovations that affect their diffusion has been a neglected area of study. Almost all diffusion studies have dealt with a single innovation, obviously precluding the treatment of the innovation itself as a variable.

THEORY

The approach to new product development to be discussed here was originally formulated by Volney Stefflre, a psychologist and linguist at the University of California, Irvine.[13] Stefflre purports to have developed a methodology, called "market structure analysis," for developing new products that will fit into markets in predetermined ways. More specifically, he claims that his method is capable of yielding:[14]

1. Estimates of the share of consumer choices that a brand which does or does not exist will receive when on the market.
2. Estimates of the patterns of substitution and competition among products or brands currently on the market, and predictions about the patterns that will exist after the introduction of specified new products.
3. Measurements of how closely a product matches the content of its advertising.
4. Indications of the opportunities for new brands in existing markets.
5. A means for the multi-brand firm to "position" new brands so that they will be substitutes for competitors' offerings but not for the firm's existing product line.

Let us begin by looking at the theory behind this methodology which promises so much. The basic premise is quite simple and has been stated by Stefflre as follows: "An individual will behave toward a new thing in a manner that is similar to the way he behaves toward other things he sees the new thing as being similar to."[15]

This is hardly a very complex idea, but it is a very powerful and practical one—if, as a hypothesis about human behavior, it can be shown to hold up. Here we have a statement that can be directly applied to the problem of predicting consumer reaction to a new product. In particular, it implies the following: for some product category presently consisting of say, three brands, A, B, and C, if we market a new brand, X, which consumers see as being similar to B, but unlike A and C, then those consumers who previously bought B will be just as likely to buy X as B. In other words, X should attain about one-half of B's previous market share (all other things being equal—price, distribution, promotion, etc.), but the entry of X will not affect the market shares of A and C. There are some additional implications of consequence to this line of reasoning. If we know *why* brands are judged similar or dissimilar—that is, we can identify the attributes or underlying dimensions

---

[13] This section borrows freely from the writings of Stefflre [41] and [42], and his co-worker, Barnett [4] and [5].
[14] [41], p. 252.
[15] [42], p. 12.

which consumers use to discriminate or differentiate among available brands —then this knowledge can be used to develop descriptions of new brands which will be perceived as similar or dissimilar to existing brands in predictable ways. Furthermore, Stefflre suggests that the *similarity judgments* which consumers can be asked to make *verbally* with reference to a *description* of a new product can be used to predict the manner in which they would *behave* toward the physical product itself if it were produced and placed on the market.

The foregoing may be summarized by the following set of hypotheses derived by Stefflre from the basic postulate stated previously.

1. *Verbal measures* of consumers' similarity *perceptions* about pairs of items allow prediction of the similarity of their behavior toward these items.
2. *Verbal measures* of similarity *judgments* made in response to descriptions of items allow prediction of the similarity of *behavior* toward the items *themselves*.
3. How items are perceived as similar or dissimilar, using either verbal or non-verbal measures, can vary in different situations, but as long as both measures are obtained in comparable situations, they will still correspond.[16]

Klahr has suggested an additional related hypothesis:

The number of dimensions required to represent the cognitive structure of brand perceptions will be relatively low.[17]

Previous studies of problem solving indicate that the information processing capacity of humans is limited. Noting this, Klahr conjectured that the cognitive structure of consumers for products could be characterized as a space of relatively low dimensionality— three or fewer dimensions. Alternatively, although a product or brand is a complex bundle of many attributes and qualities, consumers may be expected to pay attention to only a few in evaluating them.

To exploit these propositions for the managerial purposes mentioned previously requires that a series of measurements be obtained. Stefflre has developed a set of techniques which he indicates have proved satisfactory. In 1966, he reported having used this methodology in 12 studies conducted over a five-year period. The studies dealt with a variety of consumer products, including detergents, cigarettes, whiskey, coffee, and automobiles and other durables.[18]

---

[16] [42], p. 13.
[17] See [27].
[18] See [41], p. 252. Stefflre also suggests that his methodology may be used to guide the introduction of existing products into new markets and, therefore, is relevant to problems of international marketing. However, this topic will not be considered here.

More recently, some published accounts of new product development projects dealing with the problem in a manner that is similar but not identical to Stefflre's approach have appeared.[19] Although not specifically concerned with new product development, several other studies on related aspects of purchasing behavior have been carried out using the same types of perception and preference measurements employed by Stefflre. Of particular importance is the work of Paul Green and his collaborators in this area. Their recent monograph, prepared for the Marketing Science Institute, contains an excellent review of non-metric scaling and related techniques used in analyzing perception and preference data.[20] Also presented are the results of several pilot studies on the preference and similarity structures for such diverse objects as business schools, marketing journals, physicians' professional reading habits, women's panties, and computers. This work is an invaluable reference for anyone interested in the procedures used for collecting and analyzing these types of data.

In what follows, we summarize the research program Stefflre has prescribed for the complete development of a new product. Stefflre has made it reasonably clear what steps his approach to this problem entail,[21] but little in the way of technical detail or data have been publicly reported. The best source of such specific information known to the author is a Harvard case which describes some of Stefflre's work for General Foods on the coffee market.[22] Some materials taken from that source are used here for illustrative purposes.

A METHODOLOGY FOR NEW PRODUCT DEVELOPMENT

The sequential procedure advocated by Stefflre for developing a new product is outlined below.[23]

1. Define the relevant market in terms of existing patterns of substitution and competition.
2. Determine what products and brands are seen as similar to one another and why through studying small samples of consumers' judgments of similarity and difference.
3. Determine patterns of brand to brand and/or product to product substitution and competition through use of large-scale purchase panel data, when these are available, or through large-scale preference studies when panel data are not available.

---

[19] See [17], [36], and [40].
[20] See [19].
[21] See [41].
[22] [34].
[23] Based on [41], especially pp. 267–268.

4. Determine the relationships between the similarity judgment data and the brand switching or brand preference data.
5. Develop descriptions of possible new brands or products suggested by the results of steps 2 and 3.
6. Insert each description of a potential new product into a large-scale preference study to determine what share of choices it recieves and from what existing brands it draws these choices.
7. Build an actual physical product which consumers perceive as matching the new product description and which the results of step 6 indicate will be successful in terms of management objectives.
8. Use similar procedures to determine what brand name, packaging, and advertising copy "fit" the product.
9. Test market.

Defining a Market

Stefflre cautions against making a priori and/or implicit assumptions about what array of products and brands constitutes the relevant market. Patterns of substitution among brands and products are often not at all obvious. As an example, he notes that brandy competes with certain types of whiskies but not others.[24] To avoid being misled by one's intuition in this regard, it is highly desirable that some form of data on purchase or usage be examined to determine what is a set of substitute products and brands in the eyes of the consumer. For some product categories, existing information such as that derived from consumer panel data might be helpful. In other instances, a special consumer interview study may be required. At some point, however, judgment must be exercised to determine what range of items constitutes the relevant "market" of alternatives to consider. Defining the market is a crucial step because the set of brands and products identified becomes the inputs or stimuli for the similarity measurements.

Similarity Measurement

Given a set of products and/or brands which one has reason to believe are substitutes for one another and therefore represent competing alternatives, the next step is to determine which ones consumers perceive as similar and why. There are a number of ways of eliciting these similarity judgments. The methods differ in two important ways. First, the measurement may be a simple dichotomous one (similar or dissimilar) or a scale of several degrees of similarity or dissimilarity (most . . . least). A second difference is that the respondent may be either "forced" to make similarity judgments about all possible pairs of objects or, alternatively, he may be presented with

[24] [41], p. 254.

one object and asked to indicate which other objects on a list are similar or dissimilar in such a way that he is not forced to make a judgment on all possible pairs of items.

Choice of a similarity measurement technique is not an insignificant problem. If the number of objects being studied is at all large, requiring that judgments be made on all possible pairs can make the interview a long, boring, and highly repetitive task. Stefflre's technique seems to have certain advantages in this regard.[25] The respondent's attention is first directed toward a particular brand. He is then given a list of other brands and asked to indicate which ones he thinks are similar to the stimulus brand. The procedure is then repeated changing the stimulus brand on each round. By not insisting that respondents make judgments on all possible pairs, the length of time taken and repetitiveness may be reduced. Stefflre's procedure also does not force judgments about brands if the consumer is completely unaware of them. But this is a tricky matter, for we are interested in the content of even vague impressions and do not wish to discourage them. It is the author's own experience that asking consumers to make refined judgments about degrees of similarity or dissimilarity is likely to reduce the reliability of the measures obtained and increase the instance of intransitivities or inconsistent judgments. Studies need to be made of the test-retest reliabilities of these different measures.

The key information obtained from this stage of the research is an overall similarity score for all possible pairs of brands. These scores, obtained by aggregating the similarity judgments of individual respondents in the sample, are arranged in a matrix. The rows and columns of the matrix are formed by the brands and the main diagonal is empty. The cell entries are scores which reflect how similar two particular brands are judged to be by consumers. The manner in which these overall scores are calculated depends upon how the similarity judgments were measured. If, for example, respondents were asked to rate the similarity of each pair of brands on a seven-point scale, then the average for the entire sample (or perhaps some sub-group) would be used in the similarity matrix. For dichotomous measures, Stefflre determines an "index of similarity" which is defined as the ratio of the number of respondents who judge the two brands similar to an expected value. Because respondents do not necessarily make similarity judgments on all possible pairs of brands, brands will differ in the number of times they are judged similar to other brands. Presumably, the better-known brands (e.g., relatively large market share and heavily advertised) will receive more mentions than those less well known. To adjust for this he calculates an expected value in a manner similar to that used in determining a chi-square value for a contingency table. This value represents the number of times one would expect two brands to be

---

[25] For a sample questionnaire, see [34], Appendix II.

judged similar on a chance basis, given the total number of times each was judged similar to all brands considered. Hence, when the value of the index is 1, the actual extent of judged similarity is just equal to that which would be expected by "chance" as defined above.

Analyzing the Structure of Brand Perceptions

Much can be learned from an inspection of a matrix of similarity scores. It is possible to determine which brands are judged to be alike and which are perceived as different. The larger the value of the cell entry, the more similar brands have been judged. In order to get a clear picture of how *all* brands are "positioned" relative to one another in the minds of consumers, the similarity matrix can be analyzed by multidimensional scaling procedures. The basic idea is that consumers' perceptions of different brands may be conceived as a space of some unknown number of dimensions in which individual brands are positioned. The distances between brands reflect their degree of similarity: the more similar two brands are judged to be, the closer together they will be in this perceptual space. Multidimensional scaling techniques utilize similarity data to construct a map of this space.

The problem of multidimensional scaling is that of representing objects geometrically by n points so that their interpoint distances in some sense correspond to the dissimilarities of the n objects.[26] A simple example of multidimensional scaling would be a problem wherein one was given a set of cities and the task was to construct a map where the only information given was the distances between the cities. The technique used by Stefflre was developed by Kruskal.[27] Kruskal views multidimensional scaling as a problem of statistical fitting—the similarities or dissimilarities are given and the task is to find the configuration whose distances fit them "best." To accomplish this, he assumes that distances and dissimilarities are monotonically related. The dissimilarities need only be ordinal or rank-order measures. Kruskal has developed a program which computes that configuration of points (objects) which optimizes goodness of fit for a monotonic relationship between the similarity measures and the interpoint distances. "Goodness of fit" is evaluated by a quantity called "stress" that is *analogous* to a "residual sum of squares" or proportion of unexplained variance. The smaller the stress, the better the fit. For a space of a given number of dimensions, the Kruskal program finds that configuration of points which has minimum stress. The stress would be zero for a perfect relationship (perfect monotone relationship between dissimilarities and distances). The program starts with an

[26] For a good discussion of the basic concepts of multidimensional scaling and a comparison of alternative techniques, see [20].

[27] See [29] and [30]. Other approaches have been developed; see [21].

arbitrary configuration of points and proceeds iteratively to find the best (minimum stress) configuration in one dimension, then two, and so on up to $n-1$ dimensions, where n is the number of objects. It is always possible to get a perfect fit of n objects in $n-1$ dimensions. The lower the dimensionality, the more constrained the solution, and, hence, we are more apt to get poor fits in a small number of dimensions than with a larger number. At each stage the program prints out the minimum stress achieved and the (arbitrary) coordinates of the points and their interpoint distances. The coordinates can be used to plot positioning "maps." Choice of which configuration is the most appropriate representation of the data is a matter of judgment.

Figure 13–1 shows a three-dimensional map based on similarity data obtained for existing brands and descriptions of possible new brands of coffee.[28] Note that the location of the axes is purely arbitrary. The meaning of the dimensions is a matter of interpretation, and data on the reasons consumers

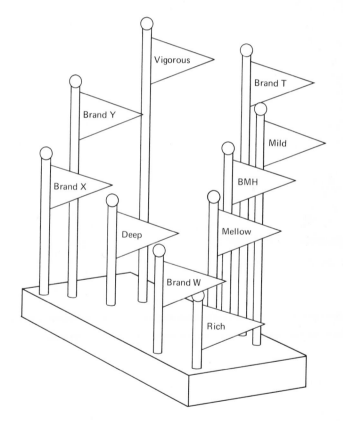

Figure 13–1. Perceptual Map for Coffee Brands. (Published in [10], p. 450.)

[28] [34], Appendix I.

give for their similarity judgments might be useful for this purpose.[29] Such data or ratings of brands on scales describing various prespecified attributes might be applied to various statistical procedures to try to "explain" the dimensions of this perceptual map.[30] In line with Klahr's hypothesis, it appears from the studies available that relatively few dimensions (2 to 5) are sufficient to obtain good fits of similarity perceptions for consumer products.

A word of caution is in order concerning the evaluation of the goodness of fit obtained from these multidimensional scaling results. Little is known about the statistical properties of these procedures. That is, no sampling theory has been developed which allows one to make inferences about the likelihood of obtaining a particular result. Klahr has done a most valuable study that bears on this point.[31] He applied Kruskal's scaling technique to similarity matrices generated from random numbers and observed the "relative frequency with which apparent structure was erroneously found in the unstructured data." He reports that "For a small number of points (i.e., six or seven) it is very likely that a good fit will be obtained in two or more dimensions when in fact the data are generated by a random process."[32] He also presents some estimates which can be used as a rough standard against which the statistical significance of results obtained in a particular study can be evaluated.

The Relationship Between Similarity Perceptions and Brand Switching

Stefflre makes use of very small samples (50 to 100) to obtain his similarity data. The explanation that he gives for being able to do so is that "there appears to be a surprising amount of homogeneity in a population of people about what is similar to what, and much less homogeneity about what is good."[33] However, other researchers have not consistently found similarity judgments to be markedly homogeneous. For example, after having conducted a number of studies among diverse groups in which similarity data were collected for a broad range of products, Green and Carmone noted that "homogeneity of preference has been the exception rather than the rule."[34] Quite likely, the amount of heterogeneity one observes is affected by the type of similarity measurement used. As mentioned earlier, some methods of obtaining similarity judgments appear to yield more reliable measurements than others. Aside from such methodological matters, it is difficult to see why,

---

[29] See [34], Appendix II, for some example of verbatum responses obtained with reference to coffee. In that study, two-thirds of all reasons consumers gave for similarity judgments dealt with flavor.

[30] See [21] and [23] for some suggested procedures and illustrative applications.

[31] See [26].

[32] [26], p. 1.

[33] [41], p. 256.

[34] [19], p. 31.

in general, perceptions should be homogeneous. Given the variability in what and how consumers learn about products, some heterogeneity in perceptions is to be expected.

To establish the validity of these similarity measures and justify the use of small samples to obtain them, Stefflre has correlated his index of similarity based on verbal responses with a similarity index calculated from brand switching matrices derived from consumer panel data.[35] Brand switching represents a behavioral measure of similarity—consumers will be more likely to switch among brands they regard as similar than among those they view as different. Stefflre reports that the verbal measures of similarity obtained from small samples of consumers have been found to correlate with measures derived from consumer panel data (based on much larger samples) from 0.50 to 0.80 in 12 different studies.[36] In the coffee example, correlations of 0.45, 0.64, 0.69, and 0.73 are shown for four different cities.[37] Stefflre also notes that the correlations between judged brand similarity and brand switching are about as high as those between switching measures obtained during different time periods.

A strong and simple relationship between similarity judgments may or may not exist. Whereas Doehlert reports high correlation between individuals' similarity judgments and their preferences with respect to automobile colors,[38] Klahr found only a relatively weak relationship between similarity and preference for cigarettes.[39] Other factors besides similarity perceptions can affect brand switching.

Stefflre points out that in addition to "psychological" similarity between brands, overlap in availability and overlap in the audiences of media in which competing brands are advertised account for the patterns of substitution observed in brand switching data.[40] Overlaps in availability and advertising increase competition. Stefflre's suggestion that there will be more brand switching among brands advertised in the same media than among those advertised in different ones is intriguing and, in principle, appears to be testable.

If a strong relationship between psychological similarity and brand switching could be assumed to hold generally, it would mean that patterns of brand substitution could be determined in situations where panel data are not available. As well, the cost of estimating market structures from small samples of similarity judgments is likely to be less than the expense involved in securing panel data. Here again, the question of the homogeneity of similar-

[35] See [34] for an example.
[36] [41], p. 255.
[37] [34], p. 31.
[38] See [14].
[39] See [27].
[40] [41], p. 256.

ity perceptions is involved. While the correlations Stefflre reports between aggregate measures of similarity and brand switching are encouraging, one would like to see this relationship demonstrated within the same sample.

From this first round of small sample studies, two types of data are obtained: measures of how similar consumers judge existing brands to be and their explanations of why. With the assistance of multidimensional scaling techniques, we are able to develop a picture of how brands currently being sold are positioned relative to one another in the minds of consumers. The qualitative data are used to identify what product features and attributes consumers utilize in making these similarity discriminations and what combination of product features or attributes accounts for each existing brand being positioned as it is in the similarity structure. One goal here may be to identify opportunities for new products that could be developed by combining salient product attributes in some way that would be unique in terms of existing brands and appealing to a substantial proportion of consumers. Alternatively, one might be interested in assessing the potential of some alternative new product ideas identified by other means. That is, similarity information may be helpful at either the "search" or "screen" stages of the new product decision process.

The use of similarity data for either of these two purposes depends a great deal upon the skill and judgment of the investigator. There are certain kinds of formal analysis that can be helpful. For example, if one has similarity and preference measurements for the same people, multidimensional scaling can be used to locate both existing brands and the "ideal" brand for different individuals or market segments.[41] In the Stefflre methodology, what comes out of this and other more informal analyses is a set of descriptions of possible new brands. Developing these descriptions in language that will be meaningful to the consumer is obviously no simple task.

Measuring Preferences for New Product Descriptions

Given a set of descriptions of potential new brands, the next step is to estimate what share of consumers' choices each would receive and for which existing brands the new ones would be substitutes. Stefflre stresses the importance of *not* using aggregate paired comparison data or average ratings of *just* the new product alternatives.[42] Using only information about which new product alternatives receive the largest number of choices or highest *average* rating can lead to what Kuehn and Day call the "majority fallacy— . . . assuming that every product must be acceptable to a majority of all consumers if it is to be successful."[43] Instead, what one needs to know

---

[41] See [21] for a discussion of these techniques and some examples.
[42] [41], p. 260.
[43] [31], p. 104.

is what share of choices a new item would receive if inserted into the array of existing brands. In addition, estimates are needed of the choices which will be drawn from existing brands. This latter information is especially important for the case of a manufacturer who already has a brand on the market and is considering adding another. Clearly, he would like to position a new brand so that it does not compete directly with his present brand but rather steals sales from competitors.

To obtain this information, a large-scale preference study would be conducted in which the descriptions of new items along with the names of existing brands are presented and respondents are asked to indicate their preferences.[44] From such a study carried out with a large sample (in the order of 1500 respondents), estimates are obtained of what market share each new product description would secure (if it alone were placed on the market) and how the market shares of existing brands would be affected by its entry. Such estimates allow management to select a new product alternative which will fit into the market in a predictable way and meet its goals with respect to market share and patterns of competition. This assumes, of course, that a new product can be produced which fits the description and that people will behave toward the actual product as they indicated they would when responding to the description in the preference interview.

One means of partially checking such predictions of future brand switching patterns is to conduct another similarity study using a new product description and existing brand names. The similarity judgments should correlate with the preference measurements—again assuming the basic theory is correct.

Development of Product and Supporting Promotion

The same basic techniques are used to develop the physical product, package, brand name, and advertising copy that will fit the new product description. Working with technical personnel, the researcher attempts to have a product "built" which fits the desired description. Consumer testing becomes a matter of presenting respondents with the actual product and asking them to describe it. The objective here is to develop a product which elicits the desired description from consumers. Next, the actual product is subjected to another preference or quasi-purchase test to see if it performs as did the description it was built to match. Again data are obtained which are used to estimate the new product's expected market share and how existing brands would be affected by its entry into the market. Unsatisfactory performance at any stage leads to a recycling of previous activities. Essentially the same procedures are used to select a name, package design, and advertising messages which match the physical product. When all of this is completed, the

---

[44] For the details of the procedure, see [34].

product is test marketed as a final check to assure that performance and goals coincide.

Stefflre's views about the role of advertising are worth repeating because they are unusually explicit and are relevant to established as well as new products. [45] He reports having encountered instances where there were marked discrepancies between what advertising said about a brand and how consumers described it and where, as a result, one brand's advertising seemingly helped rather than hindered a competing brand's sales. More specifically, he suggests that for products where repeat purchases are important, advertising should function to:

1. Bring into greater salience the attribute dimensions along which the brand occupies a favorable position;
2. State as euphemistically as possible the undesirable features of the brand which cannot be avoided;
3. Attempt to move the product along those dimensions where advertising is sufficient to place the product in an advantageous position; and
4. "Fit" the product so that, in the consumers' eyes, it does not contradict its advertising and play havoc with repurchase rates.[46]

SUMMARY

This paper has attempted to summarize and assess briefly a methodology that has been proposed for guiding the development and testing of new products. The approach is based upon a simple yet powerful theory of how people respond to new objects and consists of a series of reasonably well-defined steps. Successful applications have reportedly been realized. Barnett has recently presented an impressive set of results bearing on the predictive power of the methodology.[47] Using preference and similarity data obtained with reference to the description of a new consumer packaged good, Stefflre predicted how the product would actually perform in a test market. His pre-test market predictions of the market share that the product would actually achieve and how it would affect sales of existing brands turned out to be quite close to what was later observed in the test market. The approach is theoretically appealing and obviously has great practical value if it is capable of yielding such predictions of new product performance before test marketing. However, as has been noted, there are several methodological questions concerning the procedures used to collect and analyze preference and perception

---

[45] See [5] for a more detailed discussion of the application of Stefflre's methodology to advertising. His views bear some resemblance to certain other discussions of how advertising operates as an influence process; see [2], [9], and [28].

[46] [41], p. 262.

[47] [4], p. 164.

data that are unsettled. Work now in progress may help resolve some of these issues.[48]

It remains to be seen whether the methodology discussed here can be useful for many different types of new products. Most of the work done to date appears to have been in the area of low-priced, frequently purchased consumer goods where a "new product" is often a slight variation of an established product type. Can Stefflre's notions also be applied to a "truly" new product which has no close substitutes? What about the case of industrial products? Answers to these questions must await the outcome of imaginative efforts to adapt the approach to problems of these types. While the specific procedures described here may not be suitable in such situations, the basic concepts of how new objects are perceived may at least suggest an organized way for managers to think about new product planning. Given the vagaries of new product development, even a small step forward is not to be belittled.

References

1. Abrams, J. "Reducing the Risk of New Product Marketing Strategies Testing," *Journal of Marketing Research*, Vol. 6, no. 2 (May 1969), pp. 216–220.
2. Amstutz, A. *Computer Simulation of Competitive Market Response.* Cambridge, Mass., MIT Press, 1967.
3. Axelrod, J. N. "Reducing Advertising Failures by Concept Testing," *Journal of Marketing*, Vol. 28, no. 4 (October 1964), pp. 41–44.
4. Barnett, N. L. "Beyond Market Segmentation," *Harvard Business Review*, Vol. 47, no. 1 (January–February 1969), pp. 152–166.
5. Barnett, N. L. "Developing Effective Advertising for New Products," *Journal of Advertising Research*, Vol. 8, no. 4 (December 1968), pp. 13–20.
6. Bass, F. M. "A New Product Growth Model for Consumer Durables," *Management Science*, Vol. 15, no. 5 (January 1969), pp. 215–227.
7. Bass, F. M., and King, C. W. "The Theory of First Purchase of New Products." In: K. Cox and B. M. Ennis (eds.), *A New Measure of Responsibility for Marketing*, pp. 263–272. June 1968 Conference Proceedings, Series No. 27; Chicago, American Marketing Association, 1968.
8. Bass, F. M., King, C. W., and Pessemier, E. A. (eds.). *Applications of the Sciences in Marketing.* New York, John Wiley & Sons, 1968.
9. "Benton & Bowles, Inc.—Service Bureau Corporation: A Behavioral Simulation Model of the Advertising Communications Process." In:

---

[48] Readers interested in a technical discussion of these problems should consult [21] and [22].

R. D. Buzzell, *Mathematical Models and Marketing Management*, Ch. 9. Boston, Harvard University Graduate School of Business, Division of Research, 1964. Also see: *Proceedings of the Eighth Annual Conference of the Advertising Research Foundation* (October 1962), pp. 52–65.

10. Brown, M. P., Cardozo, R. N., Cunningham, S. M., Salmon, W. J., and Sultan, R. G. *Problems in Marketing*, 4th ed. New York, McGraw-Hill, 1968.

11. Burger, P. C., Bass, F. M., and Pessemier, E. A. "Forecasting New Product Sales: The Timing of First Purchase." Institute for Research in the Behavioral, Economic, and Management Sciences Working Paper No. 204; Lafayette, Indiana, Krannert Graduate School of Industrial Administration, Purdue University, 1968.

12. Charnes, A., Cooper, W. W., Devoe, J. K., and Learner, D. B. "DEMON: Decision Mapping Via Optimum Go-No Networks—A Model for Marketing New Products," *Management Science*, Vol. 12, no. 11 (July 1969), pp. 865–887.

13. Day, R. L. "Preference Tests and the Management of Product Failures," *Journal of Marketing*, Vol. 32, no. 3 (July 1968), pp. 24–29.

14. Doehlert, D. H. "Similarity and Preference Mapping: A Color Example." In: R. L. King (ed.), *Marketing and the New Science of Planning*, pp. 250–258. Fall 1968 Conference Proceedings, Series No. 28: Chicago, American Marketing Association, 1968.

15. Freimer, M., and Simon, L. S. "The Evaluation of Potential New Product Alternatives," *Management Science*, Vol. 13, no. 6 (February 1967), pp. B279–B292.

16. "General Foods-Post Division (A), (B), (C)." In: [10], pp. 720–804.

17. Golby, C. "New Product Development." In: D. Pym (ed.), *Industrial Society*, pp. 426–444. Baltimore, Penguin, 1968.

18. Gold, J. A. "Testing Test Market Predictions," *Journal of Marketing Research*, Vol. 1, no. 4 (August 1964), pp. 8–16.

19. Green, P. E., and Carmone, F. J. "Advertising Perception and Evaluation: An Application of Multi-dimensional Scaling." Marketing Science Institute Working Paper (August 1968).

20. Green, P. E., and Carmone, F. J. "Multidimensional Scaling: An Introduction and Comparison of Nonmetric Unfolding Techniques," *Journal of Marketing Research*, Vol. 6, no. 3 (August 1969), pp. 330–341.

21. Green, P. E., Carmone, F. J., and Robinson, P. J. *Analysis of Marketing Behavior Using Nonmetric Scaling and Related Techniques*. Philadelphia, Marketing Science Institute, 1968.

22. Green, P. E., Carmone, F. J., and Robinson, P. J. "Nonmetric Scaling Methods: An Exposition and Overview," *Wharton Quarterly*, Vol. 2 (Winter–Spring 1968), pp. 28–41.

23. Green, P. E., Maheshwarl, A., and Rao, V. R. "Dimensional Interpretation and Configuration Invariance in Multidimensional Scaling: An Empirical Study," *Multivariate Behavioral Research*, Vol. 4 (April 1969), pp. 159–180.

24. Hardin, D. K. "A New Approach to Test Marketing," *Journal of Marketing*, Vol. 30, no. 4 (October 1966), pp. 28–31.

25. King, C. W. "Adoption and Diffusion Research in Marketing: An Overview," In: R. M. Haas (ed.), *Science, Technology and Marketing*, pp. 665–684. Fall 1966 Conference Proceedings; Chicago, American Marketing Association, 1966.

26. Klahr, D. "A Monte-Carlo Investigation of the Statistical Significance of Kruskal's Nonmetric Scaling Procedure." Paper presented at the International Federation of Information Processing Congress, Edinburgh, 1968.

27. Klahr, D. "A Study of Consumers' Cognitive Structures for Cigarette Brands." Paper presented at the meeting of the Institute of Management Sciences, San Francisco, May 1968.

28. Krugman, H. E. "The Impact of Television Advertising: Learning Without Involvement," *Public Opinion Quarterly*, Vol. 29, no. 2 (Fall 1965), pp. 349–356.

29. Kruskal, J. B. "Multidimensional Scaling by Optimizing Goodness of Fit to a Nonmetric Hypothesis," *Psychometrika*, Vol. 29, no. 1 (March 1964), pp. 1–27.

30. Kruskal, J. B. "Nonmetric Multidimensional Scaling: A Numerical Example," *Psychometrika*, Vol. 29, no. 2 (June 1964), pp. 115–129.

31. Kuehn, A. A., and Day, R. L. "Strategy of Product Quality," *Harvard Business Review*, Vol. 40, no. 6 (November–December 1962), pp. 100–110.

32. Massy, W. F. "A Dynamic Model for Monitoring New Product Adoption." Stanford University Graduate School of Business Working Paper No. 95, March 1966.

33. Massy, W. F. "Stochastic Models for Monitoring New Product Introductions." In: [8], pp. 85–111.

34. "Maxwell House Division." Harvard Business School Case M266. Also in: [10], pp. 439–466.

35. Montgomery, D. B., and Urban, G. L. *Management Science in Marketing*. Englewood Cliffs, N.J., Prentice-Hall, 1969.

36. Morgan, N., and Purnell, J. M. "Isolating Openings for New Products in a Multidimensional Space," *Journal of the Market Research Society*, Vol. 11, no. 3 (July 1969), pp. 245–266.

37. Nakanishi, M. "A Model of Market Reaction to New Products." Unpublished Ph.D. dissertation; Los Angeles, University of California, 1968.

38. Robertson, T. S. *Innovative Behavior and Communication.* New York, Holt, Rinehart and Winston, [1971].

39. Rogers, E. M. *Diffusion of Innovations.* New York, The Free Press of Glencoe, 1962.

40. Rothman, L. J. "Research for Ranges, Assortments, and Multi-Brand Manufacturers," *Commentary: Journal of the Market Research Society*, Vol. 9, no. 1 (January 1967), pp. 1–11.

41. Stefflre, V. "Market Structure Studies: New Products for Old Markets and New Markets (Foreign) for Old Products." In: [8], pp. 251–268.

42. Stefflre, V. "Simulation of People's Behavior Toward New Objects and Events," *American Behavioral Scientist*, Vol. 8, no. 9 (May 1965), pp. 12–15.

43. Urban, G. L. "SPRINTER: A Model for the Analysis of New Frequently Purchased Consumer Products." Sloan School of Management Working Paper 364–69; Cambridge, Mass., MIT, 1969.

14.

Product Testing in Segmented Markets

Robert N. Reitter

STATEMENT OF PROBLEM

Marketers adopt a segmentation outlook when they recognize that consumers have different tastes. In reality perhaps all markets are segmented, but only some activities seem to call for recognition of taste differences among consumers. Entry into an already crowded, competitive category requires such an outlook. Here, an unsatisfied consumer segment represents a major opportunity. As more markets become competitive, the search for opportunities intensifies, and managements more frequently adopt the segmentation outlook.

Increased attention to such consumer differences should change thinking about two proven product research methods, paired comparison and monadic testing. Both methods are used to select the product or concept preferred by the greatest number of people. Such a testing process is appropriate in new markets when an optimal product has yet to be established. However, the process is quite inconsistent with the segmentation outlook. The traditional testing methods were designed to locate optimal products and concepts for markets as a whole. But these are by definition inappropriate for segmented tastes. In scanning the field for just this product and concept, the traditional testing methods necessarily ignore segmentation opportunities.

It might seem as though the segmentation outlook could be accommodated by simply altering the rules for interpretation of standard research techniques. Instead of approving only a product that won in a paired comparison test, a loss could be tolerated for a product directed at only one market segment. However, more modest targets would not solve the problem. There is no assurance that a minority vote signifies the presence of a cohesive market segment that would really prefer the test product if it were available. In a paired comparison test, some respondents only choose the lesser of two evils

From Robert N. Reitter, "Product Testing in Segmented Markets," *Journal of Marketing Research,* Vol. 6 (May 1969), pp. 179–184. Published by the American Marketing Association. Reprinted by permission.

when stating their preference. In reality, products not represented in the test but available in the market would better satisfy them. Still other respondents cannot discriminate between the two test products; their votes are arbitrary. Accordingly, one cannot determine to what extent a minority vote results from unenthusiastic preference or nondiscrimination and to what extent from special appeal to a particular market segment.

The problem is inherent in the traditional techniques themselves. Used consistently, paired comparison and monadic testing can help to achieve the probably unique mix of ingredients appealing to the greatest possible number of users. But these methods were not designed to help locate and satisfy groups whose tastes differ from those of the majority.

CHARACTERISTICS OF DESIRED SOLUTION

A testing method for segmented products should first be able to isolate the market segments in question. This should be accomplished directly, without using intermediate factors, such as demographic or psychological traits. Correlations between these factors and what people want in a product tend to be quite low [3], making their use as screening devices correspondingly inefficient.

A better and more direct approach is to *classify users by the features they desire in a product*. This way of looking at differences among consumers has been termed "benefit segmentation." The following hypothetical example will illustrate the advantages of the approach.

Example

A coffee manufacturer wishes to enter the market with a new blend of ground coffee. All of the blends he has tested have lost to the dominant established brand in blind preference tests. Realizing that the dominant brand must already maximize overall preference, he begins to think of finding a blend that is optimal for only one market segment—those who like a particularly strong, rich coffee.

Let us assume research has shown that upper-income people living in the East are more likely to prefer such a coffee. The next round of product testing is accordingly confined to this group. A blend produced to be especially strong and rich achieves 50 percent to 50 percent parity with the dominant brand.

It is not clear, however, whether this is the best blend for the marketer's purpose. Not everyone in the demographically screened sample desires a strong, rich coffee; perhaps some of the preference votes for the new blend come from people not in this market segment. These people would not be attracted by the concept of such a coffee and would be unlikely to try it in the marketplace; hence, their preference for it is of little practical value.

On the next round of testing, the manufacturer decides to use a subsample of respondents who describe themselves as preferring a strong, rich coffee. In effect, he decides to divide the sample by desired product attributes. This time, the new blend beats the dominant brand 60 percent to 40 percent among the strong, rich segment, and loses 35 percent to 65 percent among the rest of the sample. This result establishes that the test blend is at least suitable for the marketing purpose.

Classification by desired product attributes entails some additional advantages. The manufacturer can now obtain diagnostic information from his target market segment, which is isolated within the sample of respondents. He can determine whether the test blend is approximately optimal by comparing it with what the target segment ideally desires in a coffee. Perhaps an adjustment of its degree of strength and richness will further heighten preference for it. Moreover, he can compare reactions to the blend on a blind basis with reactions to a description of such a coffee, and thus determine whether the formulation and concept are compatible.

Testing Method and Objectives

Product and concept testing among market segments so defined allows the manufacturer to adjust formulation and concept to each other and to desires of the market segment in question. These adjustments can have great practical value. The formulation can be geared for compatibility with the communications about it and for superior performance as perceived by the target group. The effect is that those most likely to try the product are also most inclined to prefer it to other products once having tried it.

Ideally, the testing method would not require prior assumptions about market segmentation, but could scan the field for segmentation opportunities previously unknown.

The testing method should, therefore, accomplish these objectives:

focus on the segmentation inherent in the market
isolate segments in terms of desired product attributes
test the appeal of given formulations among such market segments
test the appeal of concepts or ads among the same segments
test the compatibility of the product and communication about it.

PRACTICAL SOLUTION

Antecedents

The technique to be described here has several published antecedents. A few years ago, Kuehn and Day [4] proposed a highly rigorous method for eliciting distributions of consumer preference along major dimensions of brand choice. The method is not intended, however, for repeated use in testing individual products, since the sample sizes required are very large and the developmental work prior to implementation is time-consuming and costly.

Benson [1] suggested the addition of this question to preference tests: "If you had to choose between a product with more of characteristic Q and a product with less of characteristic Q, which would you rather accept?" Provided that consumer preferences are known to be distributed normally, i.e. with one mode and little skewing, responses can be used to estimate the distribution of preferences. But this two-choice procedure does not yield enough information to discover market segments—secondary modes in the distribution not located at the central mean. Accordingly the procedure is not applicable when these market segments become the main focus of interest.

Eastlack [2], in looking at this problem with respect to the coffee market reports the successful use of a modified semantic differential scale, permitting a gradation of response. The scale is defined by labeling its extreme points; for example, "less bitterness" at the left end and "more bitterness" at the right end. The nine choices separating these extremes are unlabeled except for the central one, which is marked "the brand I prefer to use." Respondents are thus asked to describe the given product with reference to their favorite brand on the criterion of bitterness and are given a series of graduated choices to express degrees of satisfaction in this respect. A modified version of these scales is used in the technique described next.

Description of Technique

This method has been used to test coffee, beer, carbonated beverages, and canned food products. Sometimes respondents tasted products in a central location; other times they were given products to use over time at home. Most of the tests elicited response to four unidentified formulations and several concepts or names. In all instances concepts and names were disassociated from formulations actually tasted.

Before responding to any test products, respondents described their ideal in the category under consideration by marking a series of semantic differential scales at the point that best represented what an ideal coffee, beer, etc., would be like. The scales were developed to include the dimensions considered important by every market segment of appreciable size. A representative sample was asked to rate the importance of several attributes. When necessary, items rated as very important were selected for scaling after factor analysis had removed those among which high correlation existed.

Some of the scales used in testing coffee were:

Strong	Mild
Not rich	Rich
Bitter	Not bitter

Respondents first marked these lines to describe an ideal coffee; the marks of course represented purely verbal, approximate response. They continued to describe the taste of actual formulations using the scales on which the ideal had already been marked. The mark then functioned as a reference point, against which to evaluate given taste sensations. In effect the scales allowed nonverbal response to the implied questions, *Is this taste just as I like it, or is it too strong or mild? To what extent is it too strong or mild?* etc., for each of the scales used in the test.

Besides these qualitative taste ratings, respondents indicated preferences by ranking all blind products on an overall liking scale.

Product concepts were presented in the form of print ads or simply as brand names written on plain cards. Responses were again elicited on the semantic differential scales, which by this time contained marks for the ideal product and each of (usually) four unidentified formulations. Although each test was limited to four formulations to avoid taste fatigue in central location testing and excessive fieldwork in home use tests, there is no need to limit severely the number of concepts or brand names to be presented.

This interviewing method elicited great quantities of data. Each scale, marked by each respondent, often provided about 20 useful comparisons from ideal to formulation and concept judgments, and among and between formulation and concept judgments. Since 10 or 12 scales were used in each test and these were usually completed by at least two hundred respondents, the resulting data tended to defy thorough analysis. Indeed, the value of the scaling devices used proved to depend heavily on the techniques used to tabulate and analyze the data. Even the sketchiest analysis would not have been possible without use of a computer. Presently, a computer program has been developed which, though far from exhaustive, presents the data in all of the forms that have yielded valuable insights thus far.

The program presents the distribution of ratings, mean, standard deviation, and standard error for the ideal product, for each formulation and concept on each scale used, among the following subgroups:

> preferrers of each test formulation
> preferrers to each test concept
> brand usage
> heaviness of category usage.

A separate series of tables shows overall preference cross-tabulated by location of the ideal mark on each scale. Here, the bases tend to be small, resulting from the wide dispersion of ideal marks typically found. Accordingly, these tables are used as interim data solely for analytical purposes. The distribution of ideal marks provides clues concerning the combinations that will produce the most meaningful shifts in the preference data. The information is then presented in this form. Typically, on any one scale, two or three divisions are made to break up overall preference. These divisions are labeled for the scale in question; for example strong preferrers, medium preferrers, mild preferrers.

Inspection of the distributions guides the use of standard deviations to form the appropriate bands for statistical confidence. These simplify and shorten the analysis by screening out subsample comparisons that can reasonably be attributed to sampling errors. When the distributions deviate sufficiently from the normal so that nonparametric statistical methods must be used, few, if any, comparisons escape this screening. Accordingly, it is important that the scalar extremes be constructed to represent the real extremes of choice. The resulting distributions can still exhibit more than one mode but tend not to have the extremely non-normal forms requiring the use of less efficient statistical methods.

Examples of Results

Some examples, taken from actual test results, will illustrate these tabulations and their analytical uses.

An important but ambiguous tabulation is the distribution of ideal ratings (see Figure 14–1). Such findings reveal segmentation inherent in the market; the ambiguity lies in the unresolved distinction between consumer differences based on words and images, and those based on actual tastes. The fourth of the sample choosing an extreme rating near the word "strong" may or may not enjoy what the producing technologist would consider a really strong product; perhaps they would only like to believe that their tastes operate this way. Despite this ambiguity, the distribution of stated preferences provides useful marketing information. This example indicates an opportunity for a product marketed as "strong." Just how strong the formulation should actually be remains to be determined.

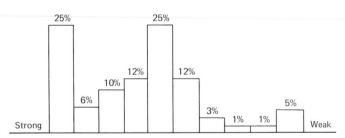

Figure 14–1. Distribution of Ratings for Ideal Product

Preference among the test products would then be examined using the distribution of ideal ratings for crosstabulation. Here, it might be most useful to contrast product preference among the 25 percent expressing an extreme desire for a strong product with the 75 percent distributed about the scale's midpoint (Figure 14–1).

With the distribution of ideal ratings as background, mean ratings can be plotted, showing reactions to the taste of the actual formulations tested (Figure 14–2). In this example, the four brands blind tested were considered fairly similar in strength; none appeared to have been formulated with the segment preferring a strong product as the target user group, although Brand A was the closest contender for this segment's choice.

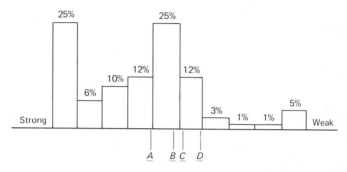

Figure 14–2. Mean Blind Product Ratings in Relation to Distribution of Ratings for Ideal Product

The blind product descriptions sometimes provide surprising contrast with the disassociated response to what are in fact the corresponding concepts or brand names (Figure 14–3). Brand D, perceived as the weakest of the four on the basis of formulation alone, is considered the strongest of the four in terms of brand image. (Here, there was reason to believe that the manufacturer of Brand D, a leading brand, acted on the premise that people enjoy a product weaker than they would like to believe.)

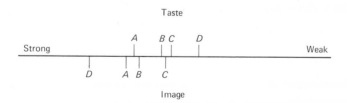

Figure 14–3. Mean Blind Product Ratings in Relation to Mean Concept Ratings

Comparison of blind product preference with the stated ideal product has proved particularly valuable. That those preferring a given blind taste should differ from others in what they consider an ideal product is especially meaningful because the two sets of responses are collected quite separately in the interview. Thus the subjects form associations that they need not be aware of to reveal. In one case, for example, preferrers of the unidentified taste of a new brand were more likely than others to term their ideal product "non-filling." The difference in mean ideal ratings between these subsamples represented 12 percent of the total scale length. Nonetheless, the difference proved to be significant at the 99 percent level. Accordingly, the idea of a nonfilling product was recommended as particularly appropriate in advertising the new brand.

One further analysis is useful to those responsible for the development of product formulations. This analysis is confined to preferrers of the formulation in question and compares ratings of the product against this group's stated ideal. On most criteria, it would be expected that the preferred product would deviate little from what is considered ideal. A study of the scales correlating most closely with overall preference can reveal the relative importance of the dimensions studied to this overall choice. Sometimes, however, the preferred product deviated from ideal on certain less critical dimensions (Figure 14–4). Here, Product Y, quite close to the ideal on other attributes, was judged too "tongue-tickling," a term interpreted by laboratory technicians as meaning excessive carbonation.

Flow of Information

Although the last analysis referred to is the only one specifically intended to provide information for the producing technologist, some of the other findings can also serve this function. Traditional product and concept tests have tended to produce summary scores. The preference rating is often followed by open-ended diagnostic questioning, but consumers' difficulty in articulating reasons for preference has often prevented the data from being useful. Hence, formulations and concepts are returned to those who devel-

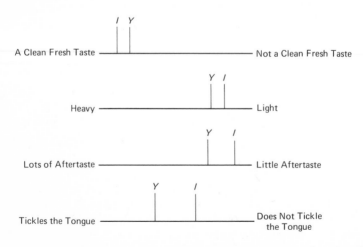

Figure 14–4. Ratings of Product Y and Ideal Product by Preferrers of Product Y

oped them, often with a single number representing their degree of success. The analyses described here tend to improve this flow of information.

The scalar terms represent a partial bridge between the terminology used by consumers and that used by developers of formulation and concept. To know that a product was liked by too few consumers because it was judged too "light" at least provides a clue for its developers. Although the clue tells neither the chemist nor the copywriter what elements to add or subtract, the finding may nevertheless suggest new directions. Subsequent tests will show how well the clues were interpreted. In the long run, the continued feedback process of diagnostic product research should improve the ability to match preferences as stated by consumer segments with products that will succeed in these segments.

CONCLUSION

Traditional tests of product concept and formulation ask,
How many prefer the test product?
In developing products for market segments, it is also useful to ask the following:
How close is the test product to the

> best possible product?
> product concept?
> formulations of other brands?
> image of other brands?

For how many people?

References

1. Purnell H. Benson, "Fitting and Analyzing Distribution Curves of Consumer Choices," *Journal of Advertising Research*, 5 (March 1965), 28–34.
2. J. O. Eastlack, Jr., "Consumer Flavor Preference Factors in Food Product Design," *Journal of Marketing Research*, 1 (February 1964), 38–42.
3. Russell I. Haley, "Benefit Segmentation: A Decision-Oriented Research Tool," *Journal of Marketing*, 32 (July 1968), 30–5.
4. Alfred A. Kuehn and Ralph L. Day, "Strategy of Product Quality," *Harvard Business Review*, 40 (November–December 1962), 100–10.

B. Segmentation in Media Decisions

15.

A Marketing Approach to Media Selection

Norton Garfinkle

One of the most important developments in advertising research during the past year has been the growth of syndicated services which relate marketing data to media data. These include the Brand Rating Index, the Nielsen Media Service, the Politz Media and Marketing Audit, Product and Media Q, the Simmons Studies of Selective and Mass Magazines, and SRDS Data, Inc.

Advertisers, advertising agencies, and media are allocating increasingly large shares of their research activity to these services. Fewer research dollars and fewer research man hours are being spent on independent research studies of specific problems. Is this tendency inhibiting the kind of creative research which seeks new answers to long standing marketing problems?

The answer is that the new services can lead in either of two directions. The enormous quantity of data they generate can be stifling if automatically applied. Or, the same data can afford unusual opportunities for solving marketing problems if analyzed in a creative fashion.

Which direction is taken will depend on the research practitioners who subscribe to the services. For too long, researchers have had to say: "We don't have the information." Now much of the information is available. The creative challenge posed by the new services is to apply it.

This paper reports several applications of the Brand Rating Index, a periodic survey of marketing and media behavior among a national probability sample of male and female adult product purchasers. These examples are drawn from the studies conducted in September and December 1962 among 3,631 women identified as the principal purchasing agents for their households.

METHOD

Marketing men have traditionally defined their target groups in terms of heaviness of product usage. Past studies have frequently shown that the

From Norton Garfinkle, "A Marketing Approach to Media Selection," reprinted from *Word of Mouth Advertising* by Johan Arndt. © Copyright 1967 by the Advertising Research Foundation.

one-third of the households that can be identified as heavy users of a specific product frequently account for two-thirds of the total product consumption. For this reason, the stated objective of many marketing campaigns has been to reach the "heavy user" households.

The Brand Rating Index starts with this concept. Interviews in 1962 were taken with a national probability sample of women having the primary purchasing responsibility for their households. The study obtained information on the frequency of use of 41 major types of products. This information provides a basis for identifying the heavy users of each of the 41 product categories studied. But this is only the first step. The modern marketing man is interested not only in the heavy product users, but also wants to isolate the best targets for *his own brand*.

Marketing men generally identify two groups as the prime targets of their advertising efforts. First, the current users of the brand. Advertising to these valued customers serves to confirm their commitment to the brand. Equally important are those consumers who consider the brand their second choice. These people are almost but not quite convinced; reaching them with advertising can convert them into users.

To meet the need for information on marketing targets, the Brand Rating Index gathered data on consumer usage and acceptance of all the major brands in each of the product categories studied. The data provide a basis for identifying the people who are current users of each brand and also those who consider it their second choice. These data can be used to identify the prime marketing targets for each of the 400 brands studied.

Traditionally media have been selected by matching the profile of product users derived from market studies with the profile of media audiences derived from separate media studies. This kind of matching could be done on the basis of only those few demographic characteristics which were covered in both the market and media studies. With the development of more sophisticated models of consumer behavior, marketing men have become dissatisfied with this old approach to media selection. They have been working toward techniques to select media in terms of their efficiency in reaching the best prospects for their specific brands.

To meet this need, the Brand Rating Index compiled media information to correlate with the data on brand usage and acceptance. Data were gathered on respondent exposure to 100 nighttime network television programs, 44 daytime programs, and 17 major consumer magazines, as well as general exposure to radio and newspapers. The same sample of women purchasers provided both marketing information and media information. Accordingly, the information can be used to describe the readers of individual magazines or the viewers of individual television programs in terms of their market potential for specific brands.

The media data are gathered so as to provide information not only on the total audience for a single issue of each magazine and a single telecast of each program, but also the cumulative audiences for two, three and four exposures to each vehicle studied. This permits an analysis of the cumulative reach and frequency of alternative media schedules utilizing as many as four episodes of each of any number of different programs and magazines.

Sampling

The universe for these studies was defined as all private households within the continental United States which include a female head. U.S. Census data indicate that these households represent the 93 per cent of all U.S. households which account for almost all purchases of the products studied.

The data were collected from a sample of households in such a way as to assure that every household in the defined universe would have a known probability of inclusion. The sample used for these studies is a multi-stage area probability sample, where the stages refer to selection of the primary sampling units, interviewing locations, specific sample segments, and the households where interviewing was to take place.

PSU's. The first step was to group the 3,100 counties in the U.S. into approximately 1,700 Primary Sampling Units—each generally consisting of one county or two or three contiguous counties. These 1,700 Primary Sampling Units were then grouped into 86 different classifications of strata so that PSU's with similar characteristics were grouped together. The stratification plan took account of such factors as geographic region, size of largest city, population density, and rate of growth. Because of their size, 22 major metropolitan areas were defined as unique strata. The remaining Primary Sampling Units were grouped into 64 distinctive strata.

One PSU was then selected from each stratum on the basis of probability methods. The 22 large metropolitan areas were automatically included in the sample as "self-representing" areas. Within each of the remaining 64 strata, the probability of selection of a PSU was directly proportionate to its total population. A total of 86 PSU's were thus selected to represent the 86 strata.

Interviewing Locations. Each of the 86 Primary Sampling Units was then divided into secondary sampling units or zones, containing approximately 800 households each. Census block statistics were utilized in this division for the major cities. Outside the major cities, Census Enumeration District data were employed.

Random methods were used to select specific interviewing locations from the total number of secondary sampling units in each PSU. The number of interviewing locations drawn from each PSU was directly proportionate to the population of the stratum represented by the PSU. For example, a major metropolitan area like the New York–Northeastern New Jersey Standard

Consolidated Area with eight per cent of the continental U. S. population also included eight per cent of the interviewing locations. Thus, interviewing locations were approximately equal in size and represented the same proportion of the total U. S. population.

Specific Sample Segments. A total of 180 interviewing locations were utilized in this study. Each interviewing location was subdivided into smaller units called sample segments. For urban areas, sample segments were defined as blocks or groups of blocks. For rural areas, sample segments were defined by recognizable physical boundaries, such as roads, streams and railroad tracks. Census Block statistics were used to estimate the size of sample segments in the major cities. In other areas, mapping materials were used as well as special field trips to subdivide Census Enumeration Districts into segments of equal size. One sample segment was selected for each of the 180 interviewing locations for the final sample. Within each interviewing location, the probability of selection of each sample segment was equal, since sample segments were units of equal size.

Households. Each interviewer was provided with a detailed map and instructions for listing all households within a specific sample segment. Every second household on the listing sheet was designated to be contacted in the September wave.

Recovery of Interviews with Designated Respondents

The sampling procedures outlined above were designed to assure that each household in the continental U. S. would have a precisely known opportunity of being included in the sample. The next problem was to provide for representation of the maximum number of households falling into the sample. This problem has two aspects: contacting and interviewing as many respondents as possible, and accounting for those not at home.

To secure the maximum response rate, provision was made in the first wave for three calls to each sample household and, in the subsequent wave, for six calls. Interviewers were instructed to interview the one female in each household who was primarily responsible for purchasing household products. Households having no female purchasing agent were dropped from the sample. Respondents received a gift necklace of DuBarry pearls, valued at $5.00, to encourage them to participate.

These efforts resulted in completed interviews with 3,067 female heads of household in the September study, representing 66 per cent of the assigned contacts for the September wave. The effective response rate was then increased to 87 per cent (or 4,032 interviews) by application of the "nights at home" weighting technique.

As a final step, the danger of bias due to the residual 13 per cent non-response rate was diminished by applying established statistical techniques of ratio estimation, in which the residual nonrespondents are represented in the total weighted sample by interviews from the same population groups (defined in terms of geographic area and size of household), rather than by interviews taken from the total population. This procedure is currently used by the major government agencies engaged in survey research, including the Bureau of the Census and the Department of Agriculture, as well as by other commercial survey organizations. The rationale for the procedure is outlined by Lansing and Eapen in "Dealing with Missing Information in Surveys" (*Journal of Marketing*, October 1959, pp. 21–27). Specific applications of the technique are described in the *Look National Appliance Survey 1961*, conducted by Audits and Surveys, and the *Life Study of Consumer Expenditures*, conducted by Alfred Politz Research, Inc.

The sampling and interviewing procedures in Wave I were designed to secure representation of the maximum number of households falling into the sample. The procedures developed for Wave II in December were designed to secure the maximum number of re-interviews. Three steps were taken to secure a high re-interview rate. First, personal letters thanked respondents for their participation in the first wave. Second, provision was made for up to six calls to each household. Third, respondents were given a bottle of Eau de Intoxication by D'Orsay. These procedures resulted in completed December interviews with 2,636 respondents—86 per cent of the original sample of 3,067 interviewed in September.

In addition to re-interviews with the original sample, first time interviews were conducted in December with a new sample of 995 respondents. These new respondents were drawn from a subsample of the alternate households skipped in the first wave of interviewing, and they thus constitute a national probability sample matched in characteristics with the first sample. The 995 new interviews represented 71.4 per cent of the assigned contacts for new interviews in the December study. The effective response rate for the sample of new interviews was increased to 95.0 per cent (or 1,324 interviews) by applying the "nights at home" weighting technique. Again, as a final step, the danger of bias due to the residual nonresponse rate was diminished by use of the statistical techniques of ratio estimation.

The procedures outlined above resulted in a final sample which closely paralleled the designated universe in its composition. Table 15–1 compares the Brand Rating Index sample with the total population of female heads of household on the critical demographic factors studied. The three columns show: (1) total respondents interviewed in September; (2) total respondents interviewed in December; and (3) the control sample interviewed in both waves. The three samples are closely matched with each other as well as with the total U. S. population of female household heads, giving added confidence in comparisons of brand preferences at the two points in time.

Table 15–1
Comparison of Sample with Total U.S. Population of
Female Heads of Household

Base: Total Households with a Female Head (51,153,000)	U.S. Total 100%	BRI Sept. 100%	BRI Dec. 100%	Control Sample 100%
Geographic Area				
Northeast	25	26	25	25
North Central	29	27	29	29
South	29	30	29	30
West	17	17	17	16
Size of Household				
1 person	10	10	10	9
2–3 persons	47	47	46	46
4–5 persons	31	30	31	32
6 or more	12	13	13	13
City Size				
1 million or over	29	28	28	28
500,000–999,999	9	9	8	8
Urban areas less than 500,000	32	35	35	35
Rural	30	28	29	29
Employment Status				
Employed outside household	33	33	32	33
Housewife, student, etc.	67	67	68	67
Marital Status				
Married	80	80	81	81
Single	4	5	5	5
Widowed, divorced or separated	16	15	14	14
Race of Household Head				
Negro	9	9	8	8
White or other	91	91	92	92

Sources: U. S. Census; BRI Report on Consumer Preferences for Major Brands, March 1963.

Interviewing Procedure

The Brand Rating Index studies are conducted through personal interviews but use a self-administered questionnaire to minimize the possibility of interviewer bias. For each product category studied, respondents are asked to indicate which brand they buy most often, which brand is their second choice, and then to specify their attitudes toward the other major brands in the product category. Finally, respondents specify their frequency of use of each product category in response to a specific question geared to the usage pattern within that category.

The media questioning procedure is designed to gather comparable information on respondent exposure to television and to magazines. Information is gathered on the exposure of the individual respondent to specific magazines and television programs. This is particularly important since so many comparisons utilize individual exposure for one medium and household exposure for the other medium. To ensure that the procedure would not favor one medium over another, the questioning procedure was developed in conjunction with and approved by, Brand Rating Index television and magazine clients prior to its use in the field.

The procedure developed utilizes a recall technique covering a four-exposure period for each vehicle—four weeks for weekly magazines and television programs, and four months for monthly magazines. A distinctive procedure serves to minimize overclaiming. Respondents first indicate whether they "Do not read the magazine" or they "Read the magazine now and then but have not read any issues in the last four weeks (four months for monthly magazines)." The second alternative effectively attracts respondents who normally overclaim in order to indicate that they are readers of a magazine or viewers of a program, though they have not been exposed during the period covered by the study.

Those respondents who indicate specifically that they were exposed to the magazine during the four issue period under study are asked to indicate how many issues of the magazine they read during that period. The same phrasing of the question and the same alternative responses are used for both television programs and magazines. The audience data produced are not only comparable for both television programs and magazines, but also produce results which fall directly into line with the data produced by studies in the magazine field using the "through-the-book technique."

Table 15–2 indicates the close relation between the December 1962 Brand Rating Index magazine audience figures for female heads of household and comparable figures derived from a major study conducted during the same period using the "through-the-book technique." This is particularly important, since there is nothing comparable to the "through-the-book technique" for television programs, while the Brand Rating Index procedure secures directly comparable data for both media.

Table 15–2
Comparison of BRI Average Issue Audience with
"Through-the-Book Technique"

	BRI Technique	"Through-the-Book Technique"
Base: Total Female Household Heads (Homemakers)	100%	100%
Life	22	22
Look	22	22
McCall's	26	24

Sources: BRI Technique—*Brand Rating Index Report, March 1963.* "Through-the-Book Technique"—Alfred Politz Inc., *The Female Audiences of McCall's, Look and Life, 1962.*

The tabulation of data for the Brand Rating Index studies is done by the National Cash Register Computer Processing Center. Information on the questionnaire is punched on IBM cards and then converted to magnetic tape. Some 15 different computer programs are utilized in the analysis of the data. Each program is geared to a specific kind of analysis. For example: one program computes the net reach and frequency of different media combinations; another computes the index of selectivity of different vehicles in reaching prime targets for specific brands; still another program computes the cost of reaching specific target groups through different media vehicles. The final tabulations are obtained by running the magnetic tape through the large scale NCR 304 computer, which records the data in percentaged form and prints out the tables presented in the Brand Rating Index reports.

RESULTS

One advertiser raised the general question: Which groups in the population should I try to reach most directly with my advertising? What is the best way to identify the prime targets for my advertising? This question was answered by a detailed analysis of brand switching behavior in a number of product categories among the Brand Rating Index control sample of women interviewed both in September and December 1962. We found that between 20 and 40 per cent of the regular purchasers of the brands studied (those who identified each brand as the one they buy most often) switched away from the brand within a three month period. The largest group of new customers came from those who previously considered the brand their second choice. The conversion rate from second choice to regular use was close to 20 per cent, as compared to less than five per cent for people who rated the brand lower than second choice. Equally significant, the conversion rate from second choice to regular use varied from as low as 10 per cent for some brands to as high as 30 per cent for other brands in the same product category.

These findings permitted the advertiser to identify his prime targets: *current customers*, to maintain their loyalty and to keep the switch-away rate to a minimum; and *customers who considered the brand their second choice*, to maximize the conversion rate and thereby gain the largest possible group of new customers.

This first question led directly to the question: How do I select media vehicles that will reach these prime prospects with greatest efficiency? This was answered by a detailed analysis of the extent to which the major television programs and magazines reach the people identified as prime targets for the specific brand (that is, the people who said it was their *regular brand* and those who considered the brand their *second choice*). We found for product after product that the prime marketing targets for different brands varied widely both in demographic characteristics and in media habits. Tables 15–3 and 15–4 illustrate this point with an analysis of three major toothpaste brands. Table 15–3 indicates that the prime targets for the three brands vary widely in their demographic characteristics. Brand A appeals largely to upper class and upper income families, while Brand C does very well among lower class families—despite the fact that the prime targets for each brand include a large segment of the total population. Table 15–4 shows how these differences in demographic characteristics are carried over in the way different media vehicles select out the prime targets for the three brands.

This analysis permits the advertiser to improve his media schedule by picking vehicles with increased brand potential. The data indicate that brand potential is an important factor to be taken into consideration along with the traditional cost and impact factors. Since there are sharp differences among vehicles in their ability to select out prime targets for specific brands, the cost savings in using the highly selective vehicles can be substantial.

Several advertisers have gone beyond comparisons of individual vehicles to comparisons of alternative media schedules in terms of net reach. Since the Brand Rating Index gathers marketing as well as media data for the same individuals, the reach and frequency of specific schedules can be analyzed for the population as a whole, among users of specific products, and among prime targets for specific brands. One advertiser with limited funds asked whether the addition of one vehicle to his schedule would make a substantial difference in reaching users of his product. Table 15–5 shows that the current schedule was efficient in the sense that it provided maximum weight against heavy product users and minimum waste among nonusers of the product category. But adding four insertions in the one major vehicle under consideration ideally complemented the current schedule. It increased net reach from 45 per cent to 72 per cent among heavy users and held waste among nonusers to its prior relatively low value.

These cases illustrate uses of the Brand Rating Index in selecting media for established products. One advertiser went on to consider vehicles for launching a new product. We developed an index of venturesomeness based not on verbal statements of attitude, but actual purchasing behavior. We analyzed 22 new brands introduced in the last five years and found that their average purchase level varied sharply among the audiences of different media vehicles. Readers of one vehicle had a new product purchase level that was 30 per cent higher than nonreaders. This was clearly an appropriate vehicle for the advertiser's new product.

Besides media selection, marketing and media data can be applied to other problems of advertising strategy. One advertising agency wanted to know: What happens when an advertiser sharply reduces his total advertising budget? After examining the advertising expenditure patterns of many brands, we found one advertiser who had sharply reduced his total expenditures in September–November 1962—from $244,000 a month to $72,000 a month. The reduction was due to media availabilities and budget balance

Table 15–3
How Demographic Groups Varied in Value as Marketing Targets
for Three Brands of Toothpaste

Ten Highest Ranking Demographic Characteristics	Per cent Prime Targets	Index of Target Selectivity	Ten Lowest Ranking Demographic Characteristics	Per cent Prime Targets	Index of Target Selectivity
BRAND A					
1. Incomes of $10,000 and over	66	131	26. Incomes $3,000–$4,999	47	94
2. Upper and upper middle class	65	130	27. 2–3 persons	47	94
3. Income of $7,000–$9,999	61	122	28. Lower middle class	46	91
4. Youngest child 6–17	60	119	29. Southern residents	44	88
5. 4–5 persons	59	118	30. No children under 18	40	79
6. Age 25–34	57	113	31. Lower class	36	71
7. Youngest child under 6	57	113	32. Negroes	33	65
8. Middle class	56	111	33. Age 55 and over	32	63
9. Age 35–44	55	110	34. Incomes under $3,000	30	60
10. SMSA's 500,000–999,999	55	110	35. One person families	29	58
BRAND B					
1. Under 25 years of age	53	131	26. No children under 18	38	94
2. 6 or more persons	49	123	27. Age 35–44	37	93
3. Incomes of $5,000–$6,999	48	120	28. Northeastern residents	37	93
4. North Central residents	46	114	29. Western residents	37	92
5. SMSA's of 500,000–999,999	46	114	30. SMSA's of 1 million or more	37	91
6. Youngest child under 6	45	112	31. Incomes under $3,000	36	90
7. Rural residents	45	111	32. Age 55 and over	35	86
8. Age 25–34	45	111	33. Upper and upper middle class	32	79
9. Lower class	41	110	34. Incomes of $10,000 and over	32	78
10. Lower middle class	44	109	35. One person families	29	71
BRAND C					
1. Negro	56	155	26. Middle class	32	89
2. Lower class	46	128	27. North Central residents	32	88
3. Northeastern residents	43	120	28. Income of $7,000–$9,999	31	86
4. Age 25–34	42	116	29. Age 55 and over	31	85
5. 6 or more persons	40	113	30. No children under 18	31	85
6. Youngest child under 6	40	110	31. SMSA's 500,000–999,999	30	84
7. Southern residents	39	110	32. Upper and upper middle class	30	82
8. Income of $5,000–$6,999	39	110	33. Income of $10,000 and over	27	75
9. Lower middle class	38	107	34. Western residents	26	72
10. Rural residents	38	106	35. One person families	18	50

Table 15–4

How 44 TV Programs and 15 Magazines Reached Marketing Targets
for Three Brands of Toothpaste

BRAND A

Ten Highest Ranking Vehicles	Per cent Prime Targets	Index of Target Selectivity	Ten Lowest Ranking Vehicles	Per cent Prime Targets	Index of Target Selectivity
1. American Home	60	119	50. Route 66	48	96
2. Ladies' Home Journal	58	115	51. Lucille Ball	47	93
3. Good Housekeeping	58	115	52. Rawhide	46	92
4. Woman's Day	57	114	53. Perry Mason	46	91
5. McCall's	57	113	54. I've Got A Secret	45	90
6. Life	57	113	55. True Story	45	90
7. Sat. Night at the Movies	56	112	56. Sing Along With Mitch	45	89
8. Family Circle	56	111	57. The Nurses	45	89
9. Better Homes & Gardens	55	110	58. To Tell The Truth	44	87
10. Look	55	110	59. Ed Sullivan	43	86

TOP 20 PER CENT IN EXPOSURE TO:

daytime TV	46	92
nighttime TV	48	95
magazines	58	116

BRAND B

1.	McHale's Navy	55	136
2.	Virginian	49	123
3.	77 Sunset Strip	49	121
4.	True Story	48	120
5.	The Eleventh Hour	48	119
6.	Sat. Night at the Movies	47	118
7.	Dick Van Dyke Show	47	117
8.	Beverly Hillbillies	47	116
9.	Ozzie & Harriet	47	116
10.	Ben Casey	46	115

#			
50.	To Tell The Truth	38	94
51.	Garry Moore Show	37	93
52.	Woman's Day	37	93
53.	Better Homes & Gardens	37	92
54.	Life	37	92
55.	I've Got A Secret	36	90
56.	Jack Paar	36	88
57.	Reader's Digest	35	88
58.	Ed Sullivan	35	87
59.	Redbook	35	86

TOP 20 PER CENT IN EXPOSURE TO:

daytime TV	47	113
nighttime TV	46	111
magazines	37	90

BRAND C

1.	True Story	45	126
2.	Parents	43	119
3.	Ed Sullivan	40	111
4.	The Nurses	40	110
5.	Gunsmoke	39	109
6.	Dr. Kildare	39	109
7.	Bonanza	39	108
8.	Lucille Ball Show	39	108
9.	The Flintstones	39	108
10.	Ben Casey	38	106

#			
50.	Woman's Day	32	90
51.	McCall's	32	89
52.	Ladies' Home Journal	32	89
53.	Better Homes & Gardens	32	88
54.	Look	31	86
55.	Redbook	31	86
56.	Good Housekeeping	30	85
57.	Eleventh Hour	30	85
58.	Family Circle	30	84
59.	American Home	29	81

TOP 20 PER CENT IN EXPOSURE TO:

daytime TV	38	107
nighttime TV	40	112
magazines	30	85

rather than a general policy decision. Whatever the reasons, the advertiser's major competitors maintained their spending at the same high level. The brand's share of expenditures among the three major brands declined from 41 to 15 per cent [Table 15–6].

Table 15–5
Media Schedule for Brand X With and Without Four Insertions in Vehicle A

Family Consumption of R.T.E. Cereals	Female Household Heads (000's)	Current Schedule		Plus Vehicle A	
		Reach	Freq.	Reach	Freq.
More than 15 Servings a week	6,394	45%	2.8	72%	3.9
7–15 Servings	14,118	39	2.8	67	3.9
4–6 Servings	10,845	36	3.0	68	3.8
1–3 Servings	11,459	36	2.7	62	3.8
None, don't use	8,337	27	2.7	55	3.5

This drop in share of advertising apparently had a marked effect on the brand's share of purchasers. By December, a total of 38 per cent of the September purchasers of the brand had switched to another brand, compared with an 18 per cent switchaway for the brand's major competitor. Equally significant was the conversion rate from second choice to regular use: 13 per cent for this brand, 29 per cent for its major competitor. The net effect was a drop in the brand's share of purchasers from 26 to 23 per cent.

General attitudes toward the brand also declined: 27 per cent expressed less favor in December than in September, compared with only 21 per cent whose attitudes toward the brand improved (Table 15–7).

Table 15–6
Average Monthly Advertising Expenditure for Three Major Brands of One Product

	Jan.–Aug., 1962		Sept.–Nov., 1962	
Brand A	$244,000	41%	$ 72,000	15%
Brand B	212,000	36	267,000	58
Brand C	138,000	23	126,000	27
Total Expenditures	$594,000	100	$465,000	100

Was the decline in brand acceptance due to the lower advertising budget or a poor copy platform? We dealt with this question by comparing changes in brand acceptance among those aware and not aware of the brand's advertising. Those who were aware of the brand's advertising theme (and associated it with the brand) tended to show improved attitudes toward the brand.

Table 15–7
Changes in Purchase and Acceptance of Brand A
and Its Major Competitor (September–December 1962)

	Brand A	Brand B
Change in Brand Share	−3%	+2%
Per cent of September regular purchasers who switched to other brands	38%	18%
Conversion rate from second choice to regular use	13%	29%
Index of Attitude Change	77	114
(Ratio of those whose attitudes improved over those whose attitudes worsened)		

The decline in brand acceptance occurred among those respondents who were not aware of or did not associate the theme with the brand. This suggests that it was not lack of force *in* the copy theme, but rather lack of weight *behind* the copy theme that produced a decline in brand acceptance. Additional evidence supports this conclusion. The decline in the brand's share of advertising expenditures occurred in nighttime television—the major medium used by the brand and its major competitors. The sharpest decline in brand acceptance occurred among those heavily exposed to nighttime television (Table 15–8).

Table 15–8
Changes in Purchase and Acceptance of Brand A
By Copy Theme Identification and Exposure to Nighttime TV

	Copy Theme Identification	No Copy Theme Identification	Heavy Exposure to Nighttime TV
Change in Brand Share	0	−4%	−5%
Per cent of September regular purchasers who switched to other brands	23%	45%	43%
Conversion Rate from second choice to regular choice	24%	12%	11%
Index of Attitude Change	104	75	55

In this case brand share was closely related to advertising weight. Other Brand Rating Index findings illustrate the same point. One researcher asked: What happens when an advertiser spends most or all of his money in one medium? Since the Brand Rating Index studied all major brands in many product categories, we could isolate several brands that had advertised exclusively or almost exclusively in one major medium: on *television* or in *magazines*. For each group of brands, we compared the share of purchasers among respondents most heavily exposed to the medium with that of those least exposed. The differences were quite sharp, both for brands heavily advertised in television and brands heavily advertised in magazines.

Results for hair shampoos and brassieres were particularly striking, since both categories included representative brands with opposite advertising patterns. Of the shampoos, Breck was the only brand putting a large portion of its budget into magazines. Among those heavily exposed to magazines, 21 per cent indicated that Breck was the brand they buy most often, compared with only 12 per cent for respondents with no exposure to magazines. Halo, Prell, Lustre Cream and VO-5, on the other hand, had advertised predominantly on television. The total purchase level for these brands was 43 per cent among the third of the population most heavily exposed to nighttime television, as compared with only 33 per cent among the third of the population that was least exposed.

The same pattern occurred for brands of brassieres. Playtex, which spent virtually all its money in nighttime television, had a 20 per cent purchase level among those heavily exposed to nighttime television, as compared with 14 per cent among those least exposed. Maidenform, which spent virtually all of its money in magazines, had a purchase level of 21 per cent among those most heavily exposed and only 15 per cent among those with no exposure to magazines.

Another question frequently raised: Which consumers are most aware of advertising? The December 1962 Brand Rating Index study examined the extent to which a sample of female heads of household recalled seeing or hearing some 30 major advertising themes and could recall unaided the appropriate brands. Respondents were grouped according to the total number of themes correctly associated with the advertised brands. Demographic groups varied widely on the proportion of respondents who correctly identified 13 or more of the 30 advertising themes. Recall was directly related to:

1. Age of housewife—54 per cent of housewives under 25 fell into the high advertising recall group, compared with only 19 per cent of those 55 and over.
2. Age of youngest child—41 per cent of housewives whose youngest child was under 6 years old were in the high advertising awareness group, compared with 23 per cent of housewives with no children under 18.
3. Family size—40 per cent of housewives with families of four or more fell into the high advertising awareness group, compared with only 21 per cent of female heads living alone.

These findings suggest that advertising performs a "professional" function for the housewife. Just as a professional journal provides the practitioner with information about his craft, so advertising provides product information sought by the young homemaker and the homemaker who serves as purchasing agent for a large family.

CONCLUSION

We have shown some ways in which comprehensive marketing and media information are used to understand purchase behavior. Further understanding is less dependent upon the development of new procedures than on the ability of sophisticated researchers to define the critical questions and analyze the comprehensive information now becoming available.

16.

Activities, Interests and Opinions[1]

William D. Wells
Douglas J. Tigert

In the early 1950s advertising and marketing were host to a galloping fad that came to be known as Motivation Research (MR). Armed with "projective techniques" from clinical psychology and some exciting notions from psychoanalysis, the most flamboyant of the MR practitioners penetrated deeply into the consumer's psyche, revealing for the first time to their astounded clients the "real" reasons people buy products.

The research establishment's reaction was predictable. Conventional researchers insisted that MR was unreliable, invalid, unobjective, too expensive, liable to be misleading, and altogether an instrument of the devil—and whatever was good about Motivation Research had long been standard practice anyway. To this the Motivation Researchers replied that conventional research was sterile, dull, shallow, rigid, and superficial.

The controversy rolled on through the 1950s until everything that could be said was said too often. As the contestants and the audience wearied, MR and the couch moved out of the spotlight to be replaced by Operation Research (OR) and the computer.

But MR left a legacy. Before MR, advertising and marketing research had in fact been a vast wasteland of percentages. The marketing manager who wanted to know why people ate the competitor's cornflakes was told "32 percent of the respondents said taste, 21 percent said flavor, 15 percent said texture, 10 percent said price, and 22 percent said don't know or no answer." The copywriter who wanted to know his audience was told: "32.4 years old, 12.62 years of schooling, 90 percent married with 2.1 children."

To this desert MR brought people. In addition to the exotic (and largely

[1] The data reported in this article were provided by Market Facts, Inc., and the Leo Burnett Company, Inc. The analysis was made possible by a grant from the Ford Foundation to the Graduate School of Business, University of Chicago.

unworkable) projective tests, Motivation Researchers employed long, free-flowing narrative interviews, and through these interviews marched a grand array of mothers who worried about getting the kids to school on time, old ladies whose feet hurt, fretful young housewives who did not know how to make good pie crust, fathers who felt guilty about watching television when they should be painting the porch, and skinny kids who secretly, but sincerely, believed that The Breakfast of Champions was the way to victory. For the first time research brought the marketing manager and the copywriter face to face with an audience or a group of customers instead of a bunch of decimals. The marketing manager and the copywriter thought they were, and they probably were in fact, aided in their task of communication.

The rise of OR and the computer did nothing to change this need to have some sensible contact with believable humans. As the mathematical models proliferated, percentages and averages turned into dots, arrows, brackets, boxes, asterisks, and squiggles. The humans who used to show up in Motivation Research reports disappeared into the computer and emerged as regression coefficients and eigenvalues. The copywriter and the marketing manager, especially the copywriter, still needed some way to appreciate the consumer.

It begins to appear that this need will be met, at least in part, by research that focuses on consumers' activities, interests, prejudices, and opinions. Variously called "psychographic" research, "life-style" research, and even (incorrectly) "attitude" research, it resembles Motivation Research in that a major aim is to draw recognizably human portraits of consumers. But it also resembles the tougher-minded more conventional research in that it is amenable to quantification and respectable samples.

This paper is about the new motivation research. It starts with a specific example. It mentions various uses. It describes some of the techniques of data gathering and analysis. And it ends with a discussion of some criticisms and problems.

AN EXAMPLE

One thousand questionnaires were mailed to homemaker members of Market Facts' mail panel. In addition to the usual demographics and questions about a variety of products, the questionnaires contained 300 "activity interest and opinion" statements to which the respondent indicated degree of agreement on a six-point scale. For instance, the first statement was, "When I set my mind to do something, I usually can do it," and the respondent answered on a scale that ran from 1 (definitely disagree) to 6 (definitely agree). The statements covered a wide variety of topics that will be described later.

Portrait No. 1: The Swinging Eye Make-Up User

One of the products on the questionnaire was eye make-up. Respondents were asked how often they use it on a seven-step scale ranging from "never" to "more than once a day."

The demographic questions showed that eye make-up users tend to be young and well-educated and to live in metropolitan areas. Usage rates are much higher for working wives than for full-time homemakers, and substantially higher in the West than in other parts of the country.

One way to add to this picture is to look at the products and the media the eye make-up user favors. Cross-tabulation with other products showed her to be a heavy user of other cosmetics—liquid face make-up base, lipstick, hair spray, perfume, and nail polish, for example. Perhaps less predictably, she also turned out to be an above-average cigarette smoker and an above average user of gasoline and the long-distance telephone.

On television, information from other studies showed that she likes the movies, the Tonight Show, and Run For Your Life; she does not like panel programs or Westerns. She reads fashion magazines, news magazines, and *Life* and *Look*; she does not read *True Confessions* or *Successful Farming*.

Thus, eye make-up is clearly not an isolated product. Instead it is part of a behavior pattern, a pattern that suggests an organized set of tastes and values.

Cross-tabulation of eye make-up with the activity, interest, and opinion questions adds significant detail. Compared with the nonuser of eye make-up, the user is much more interested in fashion. For instance, she was more apt to agree with statements such as: "I often try the latest hairdo styles when they change," "I usually have one or more outfits that are of the very latest style," "An important part of my life and activities is dressing smartly," and "I enjoy looking through fashion magazines."[2]

Second, she said in a number of ways that being attractive to others, especially to men, is an important aspect of her self-image. (Remember, all the respondents in this study were homemakers. The large majority were married.) More than the nonuser of eye make-up, the user said, "I like to feel attractive to all men," "Looking attractive is important in keeping your husband," "I want to look a little different from others," and "I like what I see when I look in the mirror."

She indicated that she is very meticulous about her person: "I comb my hair and put on my lipstick first thing in the morning," "I take good care of my skin," "I do not feel clean without a daily bath," and "Sloppy people feel terrible."

More than the nonuser she said, "I would like to take a trip around the world," "I would like to spend a year in London or Paris," "I enjoy going

[2] All relationships cited in this paper are statistically significant at the .01 level.

through an art gallery," and "I like ballet." She said, "I like parties where there is lots of music and talk," "I like things that are bright, gay, and exciting," and "I do more things socially than do most of my friends." Not surprisingly, she said "no" to "I am a homebody."

As far as household chores are concerned, she conceded that she is not a compulsive housekeeper. She said "yes" to "I would like to have a maid to do the housework" and "no" to "I like to go grocery shopping" and "I enjoy most forms of housework."

Her reaction to her home is style-conscious rather than utilitarian: "I like to serve unusual dinners," "I am interested in spices and seasonings," "If I had to choose, I would rather have a color television set than a new refrigerator." She said "no" to "I furnish my home for comfort, not for style," "I try to arrange my home for my children's convenience," and "It is more important to have good appliances in the home than good furniture."

Finally, she ascribed to a number of statements that suggest acceptance of the contemporary and rejection of traditional ideas. More than the nonuser she tended to agree with "I like to think I am a bit of a swinger," "I like bright, splashy colors," and "I really do believe that blondes have more fun." She rejected statements such as "Women should not smoke in public," "There is too much emphasis on sex today," "Spiritual values are more important than material things," and "If it was good enough for my mother, it is good enough for me."

Portrait No. 2: The Heavy User of Shortening

Another product produces another picture. The product is shortening, and both the product and its demographics suggest that the heavy user ought to be very different. Compared with the heavy user of eye make-up, the heavy user of shortening is not as young, has a larger family, and is much less likely to have a job outside the home. She is also much more apt to be living outside a metropolitan area, and to be living in the South, especially the Southeast.

The clues continue in the product use pattern. Heavy users of shortening tend to be heavy users of flour, sugar, laundry detergent, canned lunch meat, canned vegetables, cooked pudding, mustard, and catsup—all products that go with large families. They are not heavy users of eye make-up or any of the cosmetics that go with it.

In the activity, interest, and opinion questions the contrast deepens. Almost none of the items that correlated with eye make-up also correlated with shortening. When the same question did correlate with both products, the correlations were usually in opposite directions.

Compared with the light user of shortening, the heavy user expressed a much stronger interest in cooking and baking. With much greater frequency she said "yes" to "I love to bake and frequently do," "I save recipes from newspapers and magazines," "I always bake my cakes from scratch," and "The kitchen is my favorite room." She also said, "I love to eat" and "I love candy."

Instead of disliking the job of keeping house, she likes it: "I enjoy most forms of housework," "Usually I have regular days for washing, cleaning, etc. around the house," "I am uncomfortable when my house is not completely clean." She *disagreed* with "I would like to have a maid to do the housework" and "My idea of housekeeping is 'once over lightly.' "

She sews: "I often make my own or my children's clothes" and "I like to sew and frequently do."

She is heavily involved with her children and with the positive emotional tone of her family: "I try to arrange my home for my children's convenience," a statement that correlated *negatively* with eye make-up use. She also said, "Our family is a close-knit group," "There is a lot of love in our family," and "I spend a lot of time with my children talking about their activities, friends and problems."

An unexpected, and certainly nonobvious, finding was that she is unusually health conscious, and this frame of mind extends to a personal interest in fresh air and exercise: "Everyone should take walks, bicycle, garden or otherwise exercise several times a week," "Clothes should be dried in the fresh air and sunshine," "I love the fresh air and out-of-doors," "It is very important for people to wash their hands before eating each meal," and "You should have a medical checkup at least once a year."

Finally, she is not a party-goer, and she is definitely not cosmopolitan: "I would rather spend a quiet evening at home than go to a party" and "I would rather go to a sporting event than a dance." She said "no" to "Classical music is more interesting than popular music," "I like ballet," and "I'd like to spend a year in London or Paris."

These two sharply contrasting portraits—the eye make-up user and the shortening user—show how recognizable humans emerge from activity, interest, and opinion data.

USES

Portrait of Target Groups

Perhaps the most obvious use of this research is the one already mentioned—portraits of target groups in the advertising and marketing of products. The target group is often, but by no means always, the product's heavy user. It could be the light user or the nonuser. It could be some special segment, such as smokers of mentholated cigarettes. It could be some demographic segment, such as young married men with a college education. If a segment can be identified, a useful portrait is at least a possibility.

Media Values That Are Not in the Numbers

Media representatives insist that an audience's quality, as well as its size, should be considered. Activity interest and opinion questions can provide some insight into audience quality by drawing a portrait of the medium's user. The *Playboy* reader, for instance, turns out to be pretty much the male counterpart of the swinging eye make-up user, while the (male) *Reader's Digest* reader emerges as the soul of conservative middle-class values—pro-business, anti-government welfare, anti-union power, interested in politics, interested in community projects and activities. In the same study the *Time*-only reader, compared with the *Newsweek*-only reader, showed up as less concerned about job security, less worried about government and union power, less worried about the peril of communism and more favorably disposed toward advertising (Tigert, 1969).

Relationships Between Products and Media

Before Brand Rating Index, Simmons, and other syndicated product-media services it was customary to match media with products by demographic "profile": "Our product is used by young, upscale housewives, so we want to be in a book that appeals to such women."

While probably better than using a dart board blindfolded, this way of matching products and media left much room for error because the correlations between products and demographics, and demographics and media, are low. It was perfectly possible, for instance, that the young, upscale females who bought the product were not the young, upscale females who read the magazine.

It has been suggested that the psychographic profile be substituted for the demographic profile as a link between product and media: "Our product is used by women with a certain activity, interest, and opinion pattern; so we want to be in books that appeal to people who match that description." The flaw in this notion is the same as the flaw in the demographic equation. The correlations that link products to media through psychographics are no stronger than the correlations that link products to media through demographics. Thus a product and a medium can have similar activity, interest, and opinion profiles without bearing much relationships to each other.

Where psychographics can enter this picture usefully is in helping to explain product-medium linkages that are found through direct cross-tabulation. For instance, if direct cross-tabulation shows that many heavy users of home permanents are devoted readers of *True Story*, the activities, interests, and opinions of the women who *both use the product and read the magazine* may help the analyst understand the reasons.

Other Variables

Questions about activities, interests, and opinions can shed light on topics other than products and media. They can give additional meaning to the standard demographic classifications by showing how the executive's wife differs from the homemaker in a blue-collar household. They can further define the generation gap. They can add to what is known about sex differences. They can further describe the opinion leader, the new product trier, the television addict, the trading stamp saver, and the discount shopper. For almost any identifiable type of behavior there is at least the possibility of new insight when the behavior is viewed in the context of opinions, interests, and activities.

GETTING THE DATA

Mail or Personal Contact?

Since activity, interest, and opinion items are self-administering to literate respondents, data can be obtained through either personal contact or established mail panels. Personal contact permits probability samples. It can also, with enough effort, reach hard-to-find respondents like young single males, transients, hippies, and prisoners. For many purposes, however, established mail panels yield a satisfactory return at a good cost. Because activity, interest and opinion questions are in general so very interesting to respondents, mail questionnaires as long as 25 pages have yielded usable returns from 75 to 80 percent of mail panel samples.

True-False or a Scale?

Activity, interest, and opinion items can be set up to be marked "true" or "false," or to be answered on some scale of agreement. True-false items take less questionnaire space and are less cumbersome in analysis, but experience suggests that the scale approach is preferable because the *degree* of agreement or disagreement often provides meaningful discrimination.

Item Sources

Good items come from intuition, hunches, conversations with friends, other research, reading, head scratching, day-dreaming, and group or individual narrative interviews. Below is a list of items that came from Wilson (1966), Pessemier and Tigert (1966), a set of unpublished studies by Social Research, Inc., for the MacFadden-Bartell Corporation, and the sources noted above. The items have been grouped into "scales" through factor analysis. Some implications of the groupings will be discussed in the section that follows.

Price Conscious

"I shop a lot for 'specials.' "

"I find myself checking the prices in the grocery store even for small items."

"I usually watch the advertisements for announcements of sales."

"A person can save a lot of money by shopping around for bargains."

Fashion Conscious

"I usually have one or more outfits that are of the very latest style."

"When I must choose between the two, I usually dress for fashion, not for comfort."

"An important part of my life and activities is dressing smartly."

"I often try the latest hairdo styles when they change."

Child-Oriented

"When my children are ill in bed, I drop most everything else in order to see to their comfort."

"My children are the most important thing in my life."

"I try to arrange my home for my children's convenience."

"I take a lot of time and effort to teach my children good habits."

Compulsive Housekeeper

"I don't like to see children's toys lying about."

"I usually keep my house very neat and clean."

"I am uncomfortable when my house is not completely clean."

"Our days seem to follow a definite routine such as eating meals at a regular time, etc."

Dislikes Housekeeping

"I must admit I really don't like household chores."

"I find cleaning my house an unpleasant task."

"I enjoy most forms of housework." (Reversed scored)

"My idea of housekeeping is 'once over lightly.' "

Sewer

"I like to sew and frequently do."

"I often make my own or my children's clothes."

"You can save a lot of money by making your own clothes."

"I would like to know how to sew like an expert."

Homebody

"I would rather spend a quiet evening at home than go out to a party."

"I like parties where there is lots of music and talk." (Reverse scored)

"I would rather go to a sporting event than a dance."

"I am a homebody."

Community-Minded

"I am an active member of more than one service organization."

"I do volunteer work for a hospital or service organization on a fairly regular basis."

"I like to work on community projects."

"I have personally worked in a political campaign or for a candidate or an issue."

Credit User

"I buy many things with a credit card or a charge card."

"I like to pay cash for everything I buy." (Reverse scored)

"It is good to have charge accounts."

"To buy anything, other than a house or a car, on credit is unwise." (Reverse scored)

Sports Spectator

"I like to watch or listen to baseball or football games."

"I usually read the sports page in the daily paper."

"I thoroughly enjoy conversations about sports."

"I would rather go to a sporting event than a dance."

Cook

"I love to cook."

"I am a good cook."

"I love to bake and frequently do."

"I am interested in spices and seasoning."

Self-Confident

"I think I have more self-confidence than most people."

"I am more independent than most people."

"I think I have a lot of personal ability."

"I like to be considered a leader."

Self-Designated Opinion Leader

"My friends or neighbors often come to me for advice."

"I sometimes influence what my friends buy."

"People come to me more often than I go to them for information about brands."

Information Seeker

"I often seek out the advice of my friends regarding which brand to buy."

"I spend a lot of time talking with my friends about products and brands."

"My neighbors or friends usually give me good advice on what brands to buy in the grocery store."

New Brand Trier

"When I see a new brand on the shelf, I often buy it just to see what it's like."

"I often try new brands before my friends and neighbors do."

"I like to try new and different things."

Satisfied with Finances

"Our family income is high enough to satisfy nearly all our important desires."

"No matter how fast our income goes up we never seem to get ahead." (Reverse scored)

"I wish we had a lot of money." (Reverse scored)

Canned Food User

"I depend on canned food for at least one meal a day."

"I couldn't get along without canned foods."

"Things just don't taste right if they come out of a can." (Reverse scored)

Dieter

"During the warm weather I drink low-calorie soft drinks several times a week."

"I buy more low-calorie foods than the average housewife."

"I have used Metrecal or other diet foods at least one meal a day."

Financial Optimist

"I will probably have more money to spend next year than I have now."

"Five years from now the family income will probably be a lot higher than it is now."

Wrapper

"Food should never be left in the refrigerator uncovered."

"Leftovers should be wrapped before being put into the refrigerator."

Wide Horizons

"I'd like to spend a year in London or Paris."

"I would like to take a trip around the world."

Arts Enthusiast

"I enjoy going through an art gallery."

"I enjoy going to concerts."

"I like ballet."

Eater

"I love to eat."

"I eat more than I should."

Nervous

"I wish I knew how to relax."

"I'm just not the nervous type."

Mama's Girl

"I use many of the brands and products that my mother did."

"If it was good enough for my mother, it is good enough for me."

Individual Items vs. Scales

The user of activity, interest, and opinion material has the option of employing a large, highly diversified collection of statements that cover as many different topics as possible or of using a more limited number of multi-item scales. The multi-item scale approach is favored by psychometric tradition because properly constructed scales are invariably more reliable than individual items.

Unhappily, however, scales have four important disadvantages. First, they limit coverage because they reduce the number of topics covered by any given number of items, and the longer the scales, the greater the reduction. Second, the shorthand of the scale name (for example, "Credit User," "Fashion Conscious") encourages the analyst to think only in terms of the name rather than the richness of detail in the individual items. Third, since scale items are never exact duplicates of each other, there are times when the scale as a whole correlates with some other variable but individual items do not, and there are times when individual items correlate with some other variable but the scale as a whole does not. And finally, use of pre-established scales limits the findings to dimensions the analyst thought would be important, thereby precluding discovery of the unexpected.

The alternative is to throw a wide net and hope to catch something interesting, a practice sometimes disparagingly referred to as a fishing expedition. While this criticism should not be taken lightly, it should also be borne in mind that going on a fishing expedition is one of the best ways to catch fish.

There are strong arguments then, for large, diversified item sets. The items listed above, and the items cited in the examples, typify items that have worked well in past studies. An item library too large for reproduction here is available from the authors.

ANALYSIS

Condensing the Data

When the sample is large and responses are well scattered, the simplest way to look at AIO material is ordinary cross-tabulation. For instance, if the AIO scale has six steps and the product use scale has seven, the relationship between each AIO and the product would appear in an ordinary 6 × 7 table.

But when the sample is small, or when either AIO or product responses are highly skewed, a 6 × 7 table will have many empty or nearly empty cells. In these common situations it is best to condense the data beforehand by grouping scale steps to embrace reasonable numbers of respondents.

If many relationships must be considered, for instance 100 products × 300 AIO items, the analyst who orders a complete cross-tabulation will find 30,000 tables in his lap before he can shut off the computer. One alternative is to order a product's AIO's correlation matrix and to have only those product AIO correlations that are statistically significant cross-tabulated. This strategy may throw away some significant and potentially interesting curvilinear relationships, but it avoids the stupefying effect of 30,000 tables.

Once the significant relationships have been found, the problem is to organize and understand them. Here the analyst's skill, experience, and ingenuity come to work, just as they did in the analysis of Motivation Research interview data. In this case, however, the data are at least present, marshalled, tallied, and available for public inspection.

Some Examples

Here are three examples of the way relationships between products and AIO items can be turned into action. They are derived from real situations, but, for obvious reasons, they are heavily disguised.

A new car wax is a significant improvement over products now on the market. The plan is to present this new wax in the context of fantastic and futuristic space gadgetry, a product so much better than anything now available that it belongs in the twenty-first century. An examination of the AIO profile of the target group shows no special interest in the future, in fantasy, in science, or in space. Instead, the potential customer appears to be preoccupied with the here and now and to be most impressed by facts, by proof, by the testimony of others he trusts, and by demonstration. The campaign is reoriented to take account of this disposition.

A product traditionally advertised in folksy, homey, small-town settings is found to be most heavily used by young housewives with an AIO profile almost as swinging as that of the eye make-up user. This finding fosters consideration of new advertising and produces recommendations for changes in promotion and packaging.

The advertising for a heavy-duty floor cleaner has been emphasizing its ability to remove visible dirt such as mud, dog tracks, and spilled food. The AIO profile of the target group shows great concern about germs and odors and unusual preoccupation with the appearance of surfaces. The recommendation is to place special emphasis on the product's germicidal qualities and to feature the shiny surface that the product leaves when the job is finished.

CRITICISMS AND PROBLEMS

Relationships with Demographics

It has been said that the relationships between AIO's and products or media are merely surface manifestations of the more familiar, more "basic" demographics. The psychographic profile of the *Playboy* reader, for instance, might be thought of as merely a sign that *Playboy* readers are young, relatively well-educated males. While this assertion is in part correct, two considerations suggest that it would be wrong to depend on demographics only. First, two products with very similar demographic profiles sometimes turn out to have usefully different psychographic profiles. Fresh oranges and fresh lemons are one example. Canned soup and canned spaghetti are another. Second, a demographic bracket in itself means little unless one has a clear picture of its life-style implications. Everyone has some idea of what it means to be a young mother with a college education, or a middle-aged male with a blue-collar job, but such designations can be richly supplemented by information about the activities, interests and opinions that go with them.

Low Correlations

When expressed as product-moment correlations, the relationships between AIO items and products or media are low—often around .2 and seldom higher than .3 or .4. They thus do not "explain the variance" very well, even when put together in a prediction equation.

It should be remembered, however, that the variance "explained" is the variance in the behavior of individuals, not the variance in the average behavior of groups; thus a product-moment correlation of .2 is deceptively small. Consider cross-tabulation Table 16–1. The product-moment correlation is .2—4 percent of the variance "explained"—yet the relationship is obviously meaningful.

Table 16–1

Cross-Tabulation of Shortening Use and Degree of Agreement With "I Save Recipes From Newspapers and Magazines"*

	Once a Week or Less (286)	Few Times a Week (296)	Once a Day or More (204)
Definitely Agree	42%	52%	63%
Generally Agree	24%	25%	19%
Moderately Agree	20%	12%	14%
Moderately, Generally, or Definitely Disagree	14%	11%	4%

* To avoid small cell frequencies both variables are condensed by combining adjacent categories.

This point has been discussed in detail by Bass, Tigert, and Lonsdale (1968), so it will not be belabored here. Perhaps it is sufficient to say that anyone who refuses to look at the relationships between AIO's and products, or AIO's and media, must also—to be consistent—refuse to look at the relationships between products or media and demographics. Further, he must also refuse to look at the relationships between product use and media use because the product-moment correlations in all of these areas are of the same order of magnitude.

Overlapping Portraits

AIO portraits do not always differ as much as the portraits of the eye make-up user and the shortening user. Many cosmetics are very much alike. The heavy user of sugar looks like the heavy user of shortening and heavy user of flour. These overlaps occur because products themselves overlap, forming families that denote life styles (Wells, 1968).

But even similar portraits sometimes show useful differences, like the differences between heavy users of fresh oranges and heavy users of fresh lemons. Both groups of respondents show a strong interest in cooking and baking, especially with unusual recipes. Both also show unusual interest in community activities. However, the heavy user of fresh oranges, but *not* the heavy user of fresh lemons, is distinguished by a strong need for cleanliness: "A house should be dusted and polished at least three times a week." "It is very important for people to brush their teeth at least five times a day."

"Odors in the house embarrass me." The heavy user of fresh lemons, but *not* the heavy user of fresh oranges, is distinguished by an unusual interest in fresh air and exercise: "I love the fresh air and out-of-doors." "I bowl, play tennis, golf or other active sports quite often." And the heavy user of fresh oranges, but *not* the heavy user of fresh lemons, indicates she is a bargain hunter: "I usually watch the advertisements for announcements of sales," and "I'm not a penny-pincher but I love to shop for bargains."

Thus, the two groups are much alike, but they also differ in interesting and possibly actionable ways.

Are Heavy Users All Alike?

Certain products may be heavily used for two or more quite different purposes. For instance, mouthwash may be used as a precaution against colds or as a cosmetic. Should the cold user and the cosmetic user have very different life styles, the picture presented by "the heavy user" will be a jumble of the two. It is important to be aware of this possibility and to separate users into subgroups whenever there is reason to suspect that the product plays a variety of roles.

Thin Products

Not all products correlate significantly with a large number of activity, interest and opinion items. In one study, for example, of 127 products, 32 correlated significantly with fewer than 10 of the 300 AIO items, 67 correlated significantly with more than 10 but fewer than 30, and 35 correlated significantly with more than 30. Since portraits provided by fewer than 10 correlations are usually not very helpful, a general rule-of-thumb would be that the chances of drawing a blank are about one in four.

It is hard to know why some products are so "thin." It is not because "rich" products are used by small, way-out segments of the population, while "thin" products are used by people in general. Instant coffee, cat food, laxatives, and cold cereal have all shown few AIO associations; laundry detergent, stomach remedies, gasoline, and floor wax have shown many. It may be that the AIO items used so far simply do not contain material appropriate to the thin products. However, the items were made as diverse as possible, and it is hard to imagine what the missing item types might be.

Whatever the reason, the potential user should be aware that "rich" results are not automatic.

SUMMARY

This paper was about the value of using questions on activities, interests, and opinions in advertising and marketing research. It gave some specific examples of the portraits that such questions can provide. It described data-gathering and analysis techniques. In addition, it discussed some of the problems, criticisms, and precautions that the user should hold in mind.

References

F. M. Bass, D. J. Tigert and R. T. Lonsdale, "Market Segmentation: Group Versus Individual Behavior," *Journal of Marketing Research*, Vol. V, No. 3, August 1968.

E. A. Pessemier and D. J. Tigert, "Personality, Activity and Attitude Predictors of Consumer Behavior," in J. S. Wright and J. L. Goldstucker, eds., *New Ideas For Successful Marketing*. Chicago: American Marketing Association, 1966.

D. J. Tigert, "A Psychographic Profile of Magazine Audiences: An Investigation of a Media's Climate" Paper presented at the American Marketing Association Consumer Behavior Workshop, The Ohio State University, Columbus, Ohio, 1969.

W. D. Wells, "Backward Segmentation," in J. Arndt, ed., *Insights Into Consumer Behavior*. New York: Allyn and Bacon, 1968.

C. C. Wilson, "Homemaker Living Patterns and Marketplace Behavior—A Psychometric Approach," in J. S. Wright and J. L. Goldstucker, eds., *New Ideas for Successful Marketing*. Chicago: American Marketing Association, 1966.

17.

Some Practical Applications of "Heavy-Half" Theory

Dik Warren Twedt

It's certainly no news that some people buy more gasoline, drink more bourbon, use more paper napkins, eat more candy, chew more gum, and even use their credit cards more than other people. But what was news to us, when we began comparing purchase concentration for many different categories of products and services, was the extreme *skewness*, and the marked *similarity of slope*, of all these curves [see Figure 17–1]. Incidentally, the following discussion is limited to relatively mature product categories—it seems unlikely that the same rules would hold for new products.

One first step in the analysis was to eliminate the non-purchasers. Arraying the purchasers by amount consumed, and cumulating the percentage of total volume accounted for by purchasing deciles, it became apparent that for a very wide range of products, the "heavy half" of purchasers—those above the median of usage—account for 80 per cent to 90 per cent of total volume [see Table 17–1]. This relationship appears so consistently that it may be more appropriate to think of it as a marketing law rather than a theory to be proved.

The evidence for the next five propositions is not quite so well established as the heavy-half relationship, simply because the detailed analyses have not yet been made on all the product categories studied. They are, however, sufficiently well founded so that I urge each of you to apply the theory to those product categories in which you are most interested. The five propositions are these:

1. In general, demographic characteristics (age, education, income, race, etc.) are such poor predictors of heavy usage that it is usually much more efficient to measure consumption directly, and then cross-tabulate by measures of consumer preference or by advertising vehicle exposure.

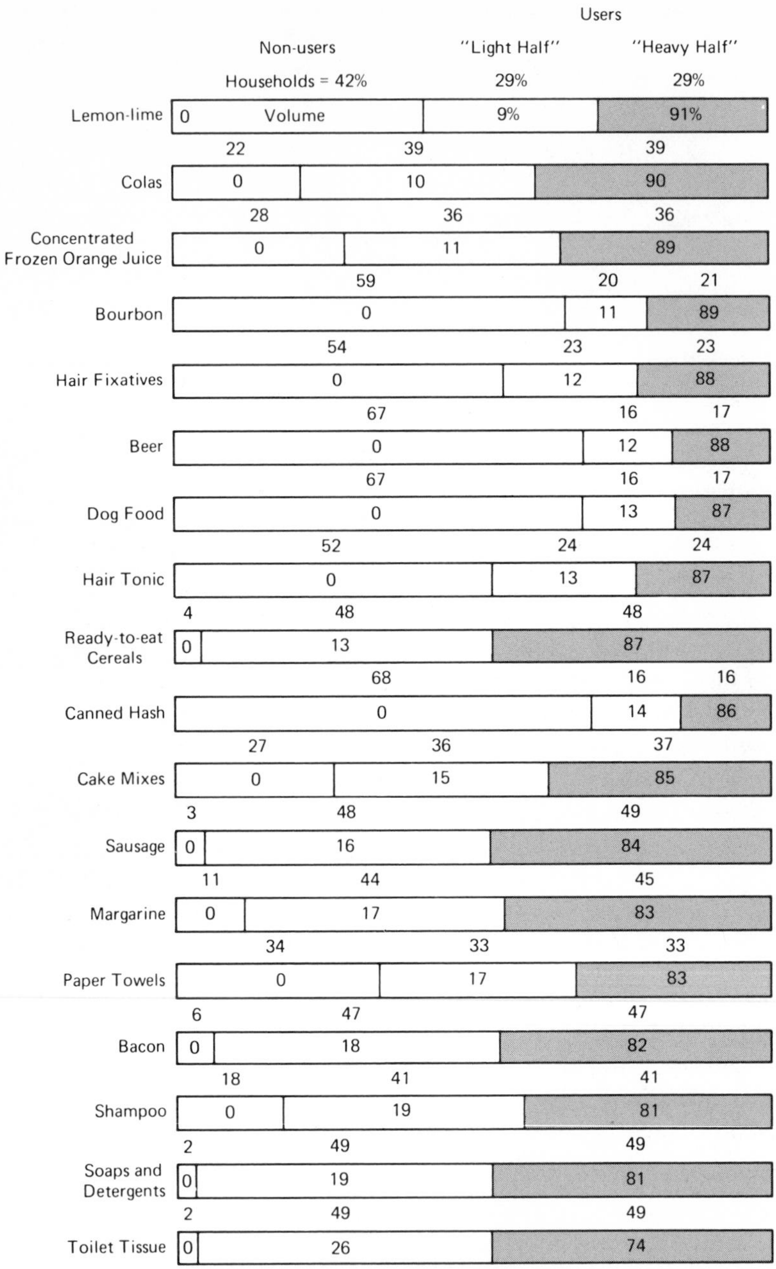

Figure 17—1. Annual purchase concentration in 18 product categories.
(Source: *Chicago Tribune* Consumer Panel, special analyses of 1962 data.)

Table 17–1
Purchase Concentration Deciles

% Buying		10	20	30	40	50	60	70	80	90	100
Concentrat'd Fruit Juice	72	39	58	72	82	89	94	97	99	99	100
Beer (Dec.)	33	42	62	74	82	88	92	95	97	99	100
Margarine	89	31	50	64	75	83	90	94	97	99	100
Dog Food	31	34	55	69	80	88	93	97	99	99	100
Cake Mixes	75	32	52	67	77	85	90	94	97	99	100
Hair Tonics	48	42	60	72	81	87	91	95	98	99	100
RTE Cereals	96	36	57	70	80	87	92	96	98	99	100
Soaps & Detergents	98	28	46	61	72	81	88	93	97	99	100
Toilet Tissue	98	24	40	53	64	74	82	89	94	98	100
Canned Hash	32	40	58	70	79	86	90	94	96	98	100
Cola Bev'gs (May–Aug.)	78	44	65	77	84	90	93	96	98	99	100
Lemon Lime	58	56	72	81	86	91	94	96	98	99	100
Hair Fixatives	46	52	68	76	83	88	92	95	98	99	100
Shampoo	82	32	50	63	73	81	87	92	96	98	100
Bourbon Whisky	41	48	66	76	84	89	91	92	95	98	100

(Source: *Chicago Tribune* Consumer Panel, special analyses of 1962 data.)

2. Heavy usage of different product categories is relatively independent—the fact that a household uses a lot of aluminum foil tells us nothing about how much canned dog food that family will buy. In a study completed last month, intercorrelations of 26 product categories by heavy-half usage were all quite low. The highest relationship was found between bacon and wieners, but even here the phi coefficient was only .37. These low relationships are not surprising when we remember that the more we spend for one product category, the less we have to spend for others.
3. Among the heavy users, there seems to be less, rather than more, brand loyalty. Not only do they buy more—they buy more often, and they buy more different brands.
4. The heavy users are not price buyers. They pay as much, or even a bit more, for a unit of purchase, than do the light users.
5. Although there are changes in consumption patterns as the family's position in the life cycle advances, these changes are usually not so abrupt or so pronounced as to impair the utility of direct consumption measures.

THE CUSTOMERS VOTE

We are now at a point where we can begin to let our customers "vote with their pocketbooks" by weighting their responses according to how much they buy. And this principle obviously holds for both product research and media research. Let's see how it applies to media.

The Consumer/Audience Profile Service of SRDS Data Division has provided us with a national probability sample of households. For each household, we know what magazines they read, what TV shows they watch, what radio stations they hear, what newspapers they read—and most important, how many pounds of bacon they bought during the previous month.

Our objective is a media schedule that maximizes reach and frequency among the heavy users. The computer program has three basic restrictions:

1. No media vehicle is to be placed on the schedule unless it contributes heavy users not delivered by any other vehicle on the schedule.
2. The schedule should, within limits of cost efficiency, approach complete coverage of heavy bacon users.
3. The schedule should maximize the total potential exposures while minimizing waste circulation.

Let's see how the system works:

The first column of Table 17–2 lists the total metro area audience of the four Chicago newspapers. The second column gives the total number of female heads of heavy bacon-using households by the Chicago papers they read. If we were only going to use one newspaper, we could calculate our cost-per-thousand heavy bacon-using households from this second column. But since we know from the Consumer/Audience Profile Service that there are 833,000 of these heavy bacon users in Chicago, no one of the papers is sufficient.

Table 17–2
Chicago Media Schedule for Bacon—Average Newspaper Readership (000)

Newspaper	Total Metro Audience*	First Iteration Total Female Heads of Heavy Bacon-Using HH's	Only One	Any Two	Any Three	Any Four
A	942	186	88			
B	1,683	308	162			
C	1,427	226	104			
D	865	137	58			
Total Exclusive Coverage			412	174	22	7
Total Coverage				615	(74%)	

* All "yesterday" readers 15 years and over of weekday (M-F) editions within the total metro area. Audience Profile.
Source: SRDS DATA, Division—Consumer/Audience Profile.

The third column shows the exclusive reach of each paper. For example, newspaper B has an estimated 162,000 of our target audience who read only that paper. The total in the fourth column represents the additional 174,000 who read any Chicago dailies. The fifth column shows that 22,000 read three of the four papers, and the sixth column says that 7,000 women in heavy bacon-using households read all four Chicago newspapers.

Table 17–2 tells us several things. First, we know the exclusive reach among our target audience provided by each medium, and we know what proportion of their audience is effective among our target group. Second, we know the potential frequency of exposure that advertising in all four papers will deliver. Third, by adding the sums of the last four columns, we know the total reach among our target audience provided by these papers; 615,000 (or 74 per cent) of the 833,000 target audience are covered by this newspaper schedule.

On the basis of this table, plus four others like it covering TV and radio by time segments, the number of media vehicles considered for the bacon schedule was reduced to the twelve shown in Table 17–3.

Table 17–3

Chicago Media Schedule for Bacon—Average Media Audience (000)

	Total Metro Audience	Total Female Heads of Heavy Using HH's	Second Iteration Only One	Third Iteration Only One	Fourth Iteration Only One	Fifth Iteration Only One	Sixth Iteration Only One	Seventh Iteration Only One
NEWSPAPERS:								
						Add Newspaper D→ 8		11
A	942	186	5	5	5	5	5	5
B	1,683	308	21	21	22	22	19	26
C	1,427	226	10	10	10	10	10	10
RADIO:								
E 6-10 pm	370	60	–	–	2	2	2	2
F 6-10 pm	697	123	3	3	3	3	–	Dropped
G 6-10 pm	441	62	5	5	5	5	5	11
TELEVISION:								
X 12-3 pm	806	245	6	6	6	10	10	10
X 6-7:30 pm	1,749	320	–	–	3	3	3	3
X 7:30-11 pm	3,405	623	14	14	56	61	46	58
Y 12-3 pm	389	94	–	–	–	Dropped	Dropped	Dropped
Y 6-7:30 pm	1,216	187	–	Dropped	Dropped	Dropped	Dropped	Dropped
Y 7:30-11 pm	2,875	496	–	–	Dropped	Dropped	Dropped	Dropped
	TOTAL (Exclusive Coverage)		64	64	112	121	108	136
	TOTAL COVERAGE		801	801	801	801	811	811
	COVERAGE GOAL		833	833	833	833	833	833

Source: SRDS DATA, Division—Consumer/Audience Profile.

This second iteration table was carried out to additional columns, showing the number of heavy bacon-using female heads who are reached by "any two," "any three," "any four," etc. of the vehicles on the list. The summation of these duplication columns added to the 64,000 reached by "only one" medium shows that of the 833,000 target audience in the Chicago market, these vehicles deliver 801,000—or 96 per cent.

This table also shows that we have some vehicles on this schedule that deliver *no* exclusive reach among our target audience, and thereby fail to meet the first restriction: "no media vehicle is to be placed on the schedule unless it contributes heavy users not delivered by any other vehicle on the schedule." There are five such vehicles on the list: radio station E—6 to 10 A.M.; TV station X—6 to 7:30 P.M., and all three of the remaining day parts for TV station Y.

MAY BE GOOD BUYS FOR OTHER PRODUCTS

It should be emphasized that this analysis does not imply that these five media vehicles are poor buys for other products. They may be just dandy for cigarettes, or instant coffee, or cake mix—but for our particular product, they seem to be relatively inefficient.

Since each of these five vehicles does deliver audience reach duplicated between them, no more than one can be dropped at each iteration. TV station Y—6 to 7:30 P.M. time segment was eliminated, and the third computer iteration yielded the distribution of exclusive audiences shown in the column headed "third iteration."

This third iteration shows that TV station Y—6 to 7:30 P.M. not only did not deliver any exclusive reach in combination with the other vehicles on this schedule, but that all of its audience was duplicated by at least two of the other vehicles—since none of the other exclusive audience courts changed.

For the fourth iteration, TV station Y—7:30 to 11 P.M. was eliminated, and the figures under "fourth iteration" were generated. Now we begin to see substantial changes. Newspaper B now delivers an additional 1,000 exclusive audience. Radio station E—6 to 10 A.M. delivers an audience for the first time. TV station X prime time now delivers a solid 56,000 not reached with the other vehicles. But TV station Y still does not deliver an exclusive audience.

On the basis of the one remaining blank in the column, the fifth iteration recomputed all audiences, eliminating TV station Y—12 to 3 P.M.

Throughout these iterations, the total reach of the schedule has remained constant. As you recall, this schedule delivers 801,000 of the 833,000 in our target audience. It still delivers this 96 per cent coverage, and now we have limited ourselves to one station for all of our TV advertising. The discount possibilities of this kind of buy are obvious. But still we are missing 4 per cent of our target audience, so we decided to start adding more possible buys. For the sixth iteration, we reintroduced newspaper D.

SOME RESULTS

Now some interesting things have happened. First, radio station F—6 to 10 A.M. exclusive audience was wiped out by newspaper D. Second, 3,000 of newspaper B's exclusive reach were duplicated by newspaper D, along with 15,000 of TV station X's prime-time exclusivity. But most important, our total reach among our target audience was increased to 811,000 —or 97 per cent of the 833,000 target. Since there is a point at which reiteration ceases to be profitable, we decided to iterate once more and quit. In the seventh iteration, radio station F—6 to 10 A.M. was eliminated. At this point of seven completed iterations, we had developed a media schedule that includes only nine media vehicles, delivers 97 per cent of our target audience of heavy bacon users—and tells us not only the maximum potential reach among heavy users, but also the maximum potential frequency of exposure through the computed duplications the schedule contains.

This application of the heavy-half relationship has exciting implications. This first experiment on the Chicago market was only a beginning, and work is now underway at SRDS Data on a series of iterations for national schedules. But a word of warning: as he proceeded with our bacon iterations, Phil Wenig, president of SRDS Data, Inc., also used the same rules of the game on heavy instant coffee users. The solution to the bacon problem is quite different from that of instant coffee. The media vehicles used to optimize our reach among heavy bacon users are not the right ones for reaching heavy instant coffee users.

It would seem that a unique schedule exists for each product category— again underscoring the point that heavy product users are different groups for different products. And while media analysis may be simplified by the elimination of demographic profiles, it is undoubtedly made more complex with the realization that a television program, for example, may have as many ratings as it has potential sponsors.

18.

Market Segmentation:
Group Versus Individual Behavior

Frank M. Bass
Douglas J. Tigert
Donald T. Lonsdale

This article is about market segmentation. Although most of this article is about the analysis of data and the measurement of market segments, it also focuses on those aspects of measurement that have a practical bearing on the managerial strategy of market segmentation. Though there are several possible bases for application of the selectivity principle in marketing [11], the specific concern here is the allocation of marketing effort, particularly advertising, to selective groups of potential customers. In current marketing management practice, there is probably no problem area of greater practical consequence than the question of how to define market segments. Despite extensive research in market segmentation, there is some uncertainty about the practical feasibility of defining market segments by socioeconomic measurements [15]. The authors will argue that such measurements are operationally feasible and demonstrate with empirical data.

SEGMENTATION STUDIES

Frank [4] reviewed the research literature on economic, demographic, personality, and purchasing characteristics as bases for segmenting the market for grocery products. His synthesis of the literature has yielded highly significant conclusions. In several cases reviewed by Frank, the almost universal conclusion appears to be that regression analysis—or some variant of regression such as discriminant analysis—of the quantity of grocery products purchased by individual families yields low R^2's when the independent variables are socioeconomic. Thus it would appear that these variables explain only a small part of the variance in purchasing rates by individual families. To

From Frank M. Bass, Douglas J. Tigert and Ronald T. Lonsdale, "Market Segmentation: Group versus Individual Behavior," *Journal of Marketing Research*, Vol. 5 (August 1968), pp. 264–270. Published by the American Marketing Association. Reprinted by permission.

illustrate, in the study by Frank, Massy, and Boyd [5] using *Chicago Tribune* panel data, quantities of 57 grocery products purchased by individual families were analyzed in relation to 14 socioeconomic variables. The highest R^2 obtained for any product category was .29, and about 50 percent of the regressions produced R^2's of less than .10.

There is evidence that the addition of psychological and sociological variables increases the "explained" variance somewhat [10, 13] but, even so, the unexplained variance remains high. The very low goodness of fit in cross-sectional studies of grocery products is not surprising, particularly considering the results of cross-sectional studies of consumer expenditures reported in economics journals. In a survey article in 1962, Ferber [3] indicated that in expenditure studies covering a wide range of products, including durables, the proportion of variance in individual household expenditures explained by socioeconomic variables is small, frequently less than .3. An extensive collection of cross-sectional expenditure studies is included in *Consumption and Savings* [6]. The evidence is overwhelming that R^2 is low when individual household purchase rates are related to socioeconomic variables.

The intuitive conclusion, perhaps, suggested by the evidence is that market segmentation based on socioeconomic measurements is infeasible. This is the conclusion of Twedt [14], Frank [4] and others. Frank concludes, "Based on the research reported in the preceding sections for the most part socioeconomic characteristics are not particularly effective bases for segmentation either in terms of their association with household differences in average purchase rate or response to promotion." Twedt said, "the heavy users usually account for 7–10 times the volume of light users. They buy more often and they buy more different brands. Furthermore, the heavy user is not readily identifiable in terms of any other characteristics."

Though we agree that multiple regression involving socioeconomic variables and quantities purchased by individual households of grocery products results in a low proportion of explained variance, we disagree with the conclusion that socioeconomic variables do not provide measurements that can be effectively applied in a strategy of market segmentation. In other words, the evidence is not disputed, but we argue that the conclusion does not follow from it. This shall be demonstrated with empirical illustrations, but before the analysis, some propositions about measurement and market segmentation will be examined.

MEASUREMENT THEORY AND MARKET SEGMENTATION

The two most important ideas to consider in market segmentation are the following fundamental propositions: (1) market segmentation is a management strategy and (2) implementation of the strategy of market segmentation involves postulates about the characteristics and the behavior of groups, not persons. Smith, in his pioneering article [11], expressly included these propositions in his definition of market segmentation. Smith's definition was "market segmentation consists of viewing a heterogeneous market as a number of small homogeneous markets in response to differing product preferences among important market segments. It is attributable to the desires of consumers or users for more precise satisfaction of their varying wants. Segmentation often involves the use of advertising and promotion. It is a merchandising strategy" [11]. Much of the confusion about market segmentation, we believe, stems from failure to recognize the two fundamental propositions. The absence of a satisfactory theory of individual behavior does not necessarily imply the absence of valid propositions about the groups' behavior. For marketing strategy, it is the behavior of groups, not persons, that is primarily important.

A hypothetical example illustrates the basic structure of the measurement problem in market segmentation as it applies to quantities purchased or usage rates. The analysis of segmentation considered here is restricted to usage rates although the principles generally apply equally well to other segmentation measurements like promotional elasticity and brand loyalty.

Table 18–1 shows the probabilities or proportions of families purchasing, on average, different quantities of some product. For market segmentation, the essential question is whether it is possible to identify groups of consumers with different mean purchase rates dependent on certain variables, such as income, age, and occupation.

Table 18–1
Probability of Low, Medium, and High Usage Rates

Usage rates	Probability
Low (amount purchased $= x_1$)	p_1
Medium (amount purchased $= x_2$)	p_2
High (amount purchased $= x_3$)	p_3

Table 18–2 shows the conditional probabilities of purchasing different quantities of a product given some measurement on a variable. If in each row of the matrix there is one number that is near one, maybe .8 or greater, it will be possible to predict fairly accurately the usage rates for individual consumers. The evidence from the regression and discriminant studies clearly indicates that it is impossible to predict usage rates very well on an individual basis with socioeconomic variables. For purposes of market segmentation, however, it is sufficient that the variables yield large differences in mean purchase rates. Thus in Table 18–2, if $E(x \mid Z_n) > E(x \mid Z_1)$, it may be possible to segment the market with this information. Even though the within-group variance is great, the fact that the choice is between groups not persons permits segmentation by group means.

Table 18–2
Conditional Probability of Low, Medium, and High Usage Rates
Given Measurement Z

Variable measurements	Low	Medium	High
Z_1	π_{11}	π_{12}	π_{13}
Z_2	π_{21}	π_{22}	π_{23}
.	.	.	.
.	.	.	.
.	.	.	.
Z_n	π_{n1}	π_{n2}	π_{n2}

The regression models applied in several studies of market segmentation have tended to focus on individual behavior, resulting in misleading conclusions. The propriety of the linearity assumption and noncontinuous observations on the dependent and independent variables bring into question the meaning of the regression results. This was essentially the point which Kuehn [8] made in his debate with Evans [1, 2]. Kuehn argued that simple cross-classification analysis of a single variable with the probability of ownership was more revealing than discriminant analysis.

It is not suggested that regression models are necessarily inappropriate for analysis of market segments. However, the results of these models should be interpreted in terms of group means. In succeeding sections of this article, these ideas will be illustrated with an analysis of survey data.

DATA SOURCE, MEASUREMENTS, AND PRODUCTS STUDIED

The grocery product data analyzed here were obtained by the *Milwaukee Journal* in its annual survey of consumer-purchasing behavior. The survey was conducted by mail in the Milwaukee area on a probability sampling basis in October, 1964. The sample return for two questionnaires in separate samples of 4,000 each was 6,264 or 81.2 percent [9]. The analysis here is restricted to the following product categories: catsup, frozen orange juice, pancake or waffle mix, candy bars, cake mix, beer, cream shampoo, hair spray, toothpaste, mouthwash or oral antiseptic. For the first six products, consumers were asked to state the quantities purchased in the past 30 days, but for the remaining four products the purchase period covered was 60 days.[1]

The socioeconomic variables analyzed and the measurement categories are:

[1] Although there is some question of the reliability with which consumers report quantity purchased and some bias in the unit of measurement for products in which there are a variety of sizes (the questionnaire calls only for a report on units, not sizes), it is not believed that either of these weaknesses is severe enough to destroy the usefulness of the data for the present purposes.

Age of male head	*Number of children under 18 years*
No man in household	0
18–24	1
25–34	2
35–49	3
50–64	4
65 and over	5
	6 or more

Family income	*Education of head*
Under $3,000	Grade school or less
$3,000 –$4,999	1–3 years of high school
$5,000 –$7,999	Graduated high school
$8,000 –$9,999	1–3 years college
$10,000–$14,999	Graduated college
$15,000 and over	

Occupation of head	*Television viewing yesterday, by head*
All other	0
Sales	0–1½ hours
Clerical	1½–3½ hours
Professional	Over 3½ hours
Manager	

REGRESSION ANALYSIS

The relationship between purchase rates and socioeconomic variables is analyzed by multiple regression, among other statistical techniques. To avoid the assumptions of linearity and continuity, dummy variables are used for the socioeconomic measurements [7]. Thus,

X_{ijk} is the value for the *k*th household on the *j*th discrete variable of the *i*th discrete classification and

X_{ijk} is one if the household is in the *j*th class, otherwise zero.

Therefore, least-squares regression provides estimates of cell means for a multiple cross-classification table using all of the socioeconomic variables.

If there are N classes of the *i*th discrete classification and if a household is not in the first $N - 1$ of these classes, then the household must necessarily be in the Nth class. In fact, the solution is indeterminate if all N variables are included [12]. Therefore, the first classification is omitted for each variable.

The Weighted Regression Analysis Program (WRAP), used to obtain the regression estimates, performs the multiple-regression calculations on all of the variables and then in a stepwise way deletes nonsignificant variables by a fixed F ratio or a fixed probability level. For the present analysis the probability was chosen such that all variables are significant at the .10 level.

The R^2 values are uniformly low—also true of previous studies—but the essential point is that all of the variables included in the final stage are significant by definition. The low R^2 values imply only that the variance within cells is great, not that the relationships are weak.

Table 18–3 shows the number of classifications for each variable and each product included in the final stage of the regression. Every variable appears in the final stage for some group of products. Number of children is included in nine of ten product categories, and age and income are included in eight of the ten. Occupation appears to be the weakest measurement since it is included only three times, and then with only one classification.

Table 18–3
Classifications for Each Variable for Each Product
in the Final Regression Stage

Product	Age	Children	Income	Education	Occupation	T.V. viewing	R^2
Catsup	2	6	0	2	0	1	.081
Frozen orange juice	2	3	2	1	1	1	.072
Pancake or waffle mix	0	4	0	2	0	0	.037
Candy bars	2	6	2	0	1	1	.080
Cake mix	4	6	4	0	0	3	.082
Beer	2	1	5	4	1	3	.092
Cream shampoo	0	2	4	2	0	0	.017
Hair spray	4	2	2	1	0	1	.058
Toothpaste	4	4	3	0	0	1	.093
Mouthwash or oral antiseptic	4	0	1	2	0	1	.032

The crucial test of whether it is possible to segment the market by socioeconomic measurements is whether segments can be described by socioeconomic measurements with widely varying mean purchase rates. For such a test, final stage regression estimates were used to estimate mean purchase rates for different segments by summing the appropriate regression coefficents using the vector description of socioeconomic measures for groups of households comprising that segment. Table 18–4 summarizes these estimates for various groups of segments, collected into light-buyer and heavy-buyer categories. The mean consumption rate ranges (see Table 18–4) have been computed from the final stage regression estimates by summing the regression coefficients included in the segment description and then summing over variables not included. It is clear from the range of variation of mean purchase rates between the segments that socioeconomic measurements provide a meaningful basis for segmentation. For example, married households whose heads are over 50 with no children under 18; the husbands are college

Table 18–4
Light and Heavy Buyers by Mean Purchase Rates
for Different Socioeconomic Cells

| Product | Description | | Mean consumption rate ranges | | Ratio of highest to lowest rate |
	Light buyers	Heavy buyers	Light buyers	Heavy buyers	
Catsup	Unmarried or married over age 50 without children	Under 50, 3 or more children	.74–1.82	2.73–5.89	7.8
Frozen orange juice	Under 35 or over 65, income less than $10,000, not college grads, 2 or less children	College grads, income over $10,000, between 35 & 65	1.12–2.24	3.53–9.00	8.0
Pancake mix	Some college, 2 or less children	3 or more children, high school or less ed.	.48–.52	1.10–1.51	3.3
Candy bars	Under 35, no children	35 or over, 3 or more children	1.01–4.31	6.56–22.29	21.9
Cake mix	Not married or under 35, no children, income under $10,000, T.V. less than 3½ hrs.	35 or over, 3 or more children, income over $10,000	.55–1.10	2.22–3.80	6.9
Beer	Under 25 or over 50, college ed., nonprofessional, T.V. less than 2 hrs.	Between 25 & 50, not college grad., T.V. more than 3½ hrs.	0–12.33	17.26–40.30	∞
Cream shampoo	Income less than $8,000, at least some college, less than 5 children	Income $10,000 or over with high school or less ed.	.16–.35	.44–.87	5.5
Hair spray	Over 65, under $8,000 income	Under 65, over $10,000 income, not college grad.	0–.41	.52–1.68	∞
Toothpaste	Over 50, less than 3 children, income less than $8,000	Under 50, 3 or more children, over $10,000 income	1.41–2.01	2.22–4.39	3.1
Mouthwash	Under 35 or over 65, less than $8,000 income, some college	Between 35 & 65, income over $8,000, high school or less ed.	.46–.85	.98–1.17	2.5

graduates, watch television less than one and a half hours a day, have an estimated mean purchase rate of .74 bottles a month for catsup. However, if heads are between 35 and 49, are not high-school graduates, have five children, and watch television between one and a half and three and a half hours per day; the households have an estimated mean purchase rate of 5.78 bottles per month for catsup, almost eight times as much.

The fact that the R^2 values are low implies only that the variance within segments is great, not necessarily that the differences in mean values between segments are not significant. Of course, even for large samples such as this one, sample measurements are small enough to raise questions about the reliability of estimates for cells sparsely represented in the sample. Later, the reliability of regression estimates will be examined in greater detail, and the possible application of regression measures of mean purchase rates to media analysis will be explored.

SIMPLE CROSS-CLASSIFICATION ANALYSIS

For greater focus on the variation in group behavior associated with socioeconomic characteristics, contingency tables were developed for each of the six socioeconomic variables with each of the ten products. This analysis thus provides a basis for measuring the ability of each variable singly to discriminate among group patterns of behavior for quantity purchased. Chi-square values have been calculated for each contingency table. The tables significant at the .05 level or less are listed in Table 18–5. Again socioeconomic measures effectively discriminate between patterns of group behavior. Number of children is significant for all ten products; age and income are significant for eight of ten products.

Table 18–5
Significant (S) and Nonsignificant (NS) Contingency Tables of Amounts Purchased for Each Product and Socioeconomic Measurements

Product	Age	Children	Income	Education	Occupation	T.V. viewing
Catsup	S	S	S	S	S	S
Frozen orange juice	S	S	S	S	S	S
Pancake or waffle mix	NS	S	S	S	S	NS
Candy bars	S	S	S	S	NS	NS
Cake mix	S	S	S	NS	NS	NS
Beer	S	S	S	NS	NS	S
Cream shampoo	NS	S	NS	NS	NS	NS
Hair spray	S	S	S	S	NS	NS
Toothpaste	S	S	S	S	S	S
Mouthwash	S	S	NS	S	S	NS

Although cross-classification analysis of a single independent variable with the dependent variable has the disadvantage relative to regression and other multivariate techniques of failing to measure the joint effects of several variables, it helps greatly in demonstrating the nature of the variation. In principle, of course, multiple cross-classification is possible and desirable; but as the number of variables increases, the number of cells becomes large enough to overwhelm even very large samples. However, several multiple cross-classification analyses (cross-classification with variable stacking) were performed, one of which is reported later.

It has been contended that the low R^2's obtained in regression analysis have led to false conclusions about the ability of socioeconomic variables to segment the market since R^2 is a measure of the model's ability to predict individual rather than group behavior. In addition, it has been argued that the relationships may be nonlinear. These points are demonstrated by conditional probability matrices of the character shown in Table 18–2. Development of these tables should be the first step in any segmentation study. To conserve space, only 4 of 42 significant tables for the ten products are presented here. Table 18–6 illustrates conditional probabilities, means, and standard errors. These conditional probabilities indicate clearly the strength of the socioeconomic variables. For example, the probability that a household with five or more children will buy three or more bottles of catsup in a month is more than three times as great as the corresponding conditional probability for a household with no children. There is a similar difference in the probabilities for toothpaste. The probability that a household in which the head is a college graduate will buy five or more cans of frozen orange juice in a month is about twice the probability for a household in which the head is a high school graduate.

The nonlinearity of beer consumption relative to age is also demonstrated in Table 18–6. When the analysis is extended to include two or more independent variables, the differences in conditional probabilities and means are further increased.

CROSS-CLASSIFICATION WITH VARIABLE STACKING

To study the simultaneous effects of two variables on mean usage rates, two variables were cross-classified with purchase rates for a subsample of 1,400 households. In addition, a regression analysis was done using only two variables, similar to the analyses with several variables discussed previously. This permits comparison of regression estimates of segment means with the sample estimates of these means determined from cross-classification. Table 18–7 shows the segment means, the standard error of these means, the regression estimates of segment means, and the sample sizes cross-classified into each segment for an analysis of education and income on beer purchases.

Table 18–6
Conditional Probabilities of Purchases of Four Products
by Selected Characteristics

Variable	Category	Conditional probability				Mean	Standard error
		Catsup					
		0	**1**	**2**	**3 or more**		
Children	0	.20	.32	.32	.16	1.76	.06
	1	.11	.23	.36	.30	2.45	.12
	2	.13	.17	.40	.30	2.47	.11
	3	.04	.12	.42	.42	3.06	.13
	4	.05	.14	.43	.39	2.95	.17
	5 or more	.08	.09	.29	.54	3.36	.19
		Frozen orange juice					
		0	**1**	**2–4**	**5 or more**		
Education	6 yrs.	.67	.12	.14	.07	1.18	.13
	10	.62	.16	.13	.09	1.37	.15
	12	.61	.13	.14	.12	1.65	.13
	14	.51	.16	.22	.11	1.83	.20
	16	.40	.17	.20	.23	2.87	.27
		Toothpaste					
		0	**1**	**2**	**3 or more**		
Children	0	.15	.33	.35	.16	1.77	.07
	1	.06	.26	.40	.28	2.36	.13
	2	.05	.20	.39	.36	2.65	.12
	3	.04	.19	.41	.36	2.68	.14
	4	.01	.19	.44	.37	2.79	.19
	5 or more	.04	.08	.31	.57	3.35	.19
		Beer					
		0	**1–18**	**19–24**	**25 or more**		
Not married	18–24	.45	.15	.17	.24	19.52	2.05
or age[a]	25–34	.33	.08	.24	.35	27.05	1.50
	35–49	.36	.09	.22	.33	25.50	1.10
	50–64	.42	.07	.23	.27	21.80	1.31
	65 or over	.61	.04	.22	.13	12.89	1.53

[a] Of head of household.

The differences in the segment means are again substantial. The mean consumption rate for households in which the husband is a high school graduate and has an annual income between $8,000 and $10,000 is five times as great as for households with the same education and less than $3,000 income. Furthermore, this group of households buys, on average, about 50 percent more beer than households with the same income but a college graduate head.

In general, the regression estimates are fairly good. In a few instances they are substantially inaccurate, but the larger errors tend to occur in those segments with a small sample. Fortunately, these segments are a small part of the population and represent a small proportion of the potential market. In developing segmentation strategy, regression analysis should be performed on several variables to determine which two or three are the more powerful. Estimates of segment means can then be made from cross-classification of the smaller number of variables. In practical terms these two or three variables will be sufficient to permit discrimination among groups.

Table 18–7
Cross-Classification Analysis of Beer Purchase of 1,400 Households, Education by Income

Annual family income			Years of education			
		6[a]	10	12	14	16
Under $3,000	$\bar{X}a$	10.01	6.53	6.18	12.27	15.21
	$\sigma\bar{x}$	1.64	2.38	1.74	7.78	13.17
	$\bar{X}c$	12.18	9.03	5.78	4.67	0.00
	n	124	36	38	7	4
$3,000– 4,999	$\bar{X}a$	27.74	20.27	11.70	17.40	1.79
	$\sigma\bar{x}$	3.93	4.03	2.98	9.51	1.65
	$\bar{X}c$	23.33	17.12	16.93	15.82	8.25
	n	48	38	45	14	7
$5,000– 7,999	$\bar{X}a$	25.23	26.03	22.63	24.27	16.80
	$\sigma\bar{x}$	2.62	2.45	1.85	3.48	3.85
	$\bar{X}c$	31.81	28.66	25.41	24.30	18.73
	n	115	122	196	57	35
$8,000– 9,999	$\bar{X}a$	27.72	24.21	32.14	21.78	23.23
	$\sigma\bar{x}$	4.62	3.38	2.13	4.41	4.93
	$\bar{X}c$	37.00	33.85	31.40	29.49	23.82
	n	30	56	88	32	30
$10,000– 14,999	$\bar{X}a$	34.24	24.05	21.54	20.63	24.18
	$\sigma\bar{x}$	6.47	4.51	3.07	3.92	3.78
	$\bar{X}c$	33.79	30.64	27.30	26.28	20.71
	n	15	37	61	45	50
$15,000 and over	$\bar{X}a$	36.58	12.50	28.49	34.17	17.86
	$\sigma\bar{x}$	10.68	0.00	6.93	8.52	3.80
	$\bar{X}c$	34.85	31.70	28.45	27.34	21.75
	n	7	1	15	10	37

[a] $\bar{X}a$ is the segment mean estimated by cross classification,
  $\sigma\bar{x}$ is the standard error of the mean,
  $\bar{X}c$ is the regression estimate of the segment mean,
  n is the sample size in the segment.

To study the overlap of the effectiveness of the segmentation structure suggested by Table 18–7, a weighted regression was performed in which the segment mean is the dependent variable and education and family income are independent variables. In this regression, R is equal to .65, and the regression coefficients for both variables are substantially larger than their standard deviations. Thus when the noise is eliminated from the data, it is even more obvious that variables effectively discriminate between groups with different mean purchasing rates.

MARKET POTENTIAL AND MEDIA SELECTION

In allocating marketing effort to market segments, the size and the mean usage rate of the segment must be considered. Other things being equal, a medium with a higher proportion of its audience in those segments with a large market potential relative to the number of households would be more valuable than a medium with a smaller proportion of its audience in these segments. If W_{mi} is the relative size of segment i in the total audience, A_m, of medium m, then

$$\overline{X}_m = \sum_i w_{mi}\overline{x}_i \text{ is the mean usage rate of medium } m \text{ and,}$$

$A_m\overline{X}_m$ is the market potential of medium m in units of the product. Media may then be ranked by order of cost per unit of market potential which they deliver.

An interesting area for future research would be a comparison of the mean usage rates for the audience of different media with the mean usage rates to be expected from the audience composition in socioeconomic segments. This comparison would provide a basis for evaluation of the media effect.

SUMMARY AND CONCLUSION

Although there is not yet a satisfactory theory to explain variations in usage rates of individuals of grocery products, this deficiency does not imply that a strategy of market segmentation is infeasible. The inability of socioeconomic variables to explain a substantial part of the variance of usage rates of persons does not necessarily imply that there are not substantial differences in the mean usage rates for different socioeconomic market segments. Differences in mean usage rates among segments is sufficient condition for the development of a strategy of market segmentation.

References

1. Franklin B. Evans, "Psychological and Objective Factors in the Prediction of Brand Choice: Ford versus Chevrolet," *Journal of Business*, 32 (October 1959), 340–69.

2. ———— and Harry V. Roberts, "Fords, Chevrolets and the Problem of Discrimination," *Journal of Business*, 36 (April 1963), 242–44.

3. Robert Ferber, "Research on Household Behavior," *American Economic Review*, 52 (March 1962), 19–63.

4. Ronald E. Frank, "Market Segmentation Research: Findings and Implications," in Frank M. Bass, Charles W. King, and Edgar A. Pessemier, *Application of the Sciences in Marketing Management*, New York: John Wiley & Sons, Inc., 1967.

5. ————, William F. Massy, and Harper W. Boyd, "Correlates of Grocery Products Consumption Rates," *Journal of Marketing Research*, 4 (May 1967), 184–90.

6. Irwin Friend and Robert Jones, eds., *Consumption and Saving,* Vol. 1, Philadelphia: University of Pennsylvania, 1960.

7. J. Johnston, *Econometric Methods*, New York: McGraw-Hill Book Co., 1963, 221–28.

8. Alfred A. Kuehn, "Demonstration of the Relationship Between Psychological Factors and Brand Choice," *Journal of Business*, 36 (April 1963), 237–41.

9. *The Milwaukee Journal Consumer Analysis*, 42nd ed., Milwaukee, Wis.: *The Milwaukee Journal*, 1965.

10. Edgar A. Pessemier, Phillip C. Burger, and Douglas J. Tigert, "Can New Product Buyers Be Identified," *Journal of Marketing Research*, 4 (November 1967), 349–55.

11. Wendell Smith, "Product Differentiation and Market Segmentation as Alternative Marketing Strategies," *Journal of Marketing*, 21 (July 1956), 3–8.

12. Daniel B. Suits, "Use of Dummy Variables in Regression Equations," *Journal of the American Statistical Association*, 52 (December 1957), 548–51.

13. Douglas J. Tigert, "Consumer Typologies and Market Behavior," Unpublished doctoral dissertation, Krannert Graduate School of Industrial Administration, Purdue University, 1966, 219.

14. Dik W. Twedt, "How Important to Marketing Strategy Is the Heavy User," *Journal of Marketing*, 28 (January 1964), 71–72.

15. Daniel Yankelovich, "New Criteria for Market Segmentation," *Harvard Business Review*, 42 (March–April 1964), 83–90.

19.

A Taxonomy of Magazine Readership Applied to Problems in Marketing Strategy and Media Selection

Frank M. Bass
Edgar A. Pessemier
Douglas J. Tigert

Broadly viewed, this paper considers the much discussed topics of market segmentation and media selection. The general literature on market segmentation has been reviewed by Frank [10], and Bass, Tigert, and Lonsdale have added new dimensions to the subject in recent papers [2, 3]. These matters will not be reviewed here. Furthermore, we will not discuss the large literature which has grown up around the media selection problem. The interested reader can find a good summary of current work in Little and Lodish [13].

In a recent paper, Frank and Green noted, "marketing managers and researchers alike frequently comment on the difficulty they experience in developing useful ways of classifying customers for the purpose of formulating marketing policy. The source of the difficulty frequently seems to stem more from the vast profusion of alternative ways of classifying customers than from a lack of possibilities" [11]. If the purpose in studying differences in behavior between market segments is managerial in character, it is important that the segments be defined in terms of variables that lend themselves to manipulation and choice. In the study reported here, our initial objective was the development of market segments in terms of media variables which typically constitute the set of alternatives available in the formulation of advertising strategy. Therefore the study first focused on locating *media market segments* or groups of consumers that display similar patterns of media exposure. Next, the remaining market-related behavioral characteristics of the individuals in each segment were studied. These qualitative and quantitative descriptions indicate the sales potential of the segments and suggest alternative advertising approaches. In turn, the data lead to a specific media selection model in which a media schedule can be examined in traditional terms. In our model, *reach* can be defined as the number of individuals in those media market segments that receive advertising exposure equal to or exceeding a stated threshold. *Frequency* can be defined as the total number of standard exposure values received by individuals in the segments that have been reached.

Given the above objectives and definitions, the results presented in this paper have been divided into the following parts: (1) review of the literature related to media market segments; (2) summary of the data and methodology employed; (3) results defining media market segments; (4) marketing descriptions of the media market segments; (5) definition of a media selection model; (6) application of the model, employing media market segments; (7) summary and notes on future work.

PREVIOUS RESEARCH

Research in the past aimed at investigating media reading has been based on a macro approach. Perhaps the most widely known work has been that of Agostini who developed a formula for examining the duplication of readership across a set of media [1]. The formula for Agostini's "K" requires knowledge of only the total audience for each vehicle and the pairwise duplication for each two vehicles. However, when the media set becomes large, the Agostini method loses accuracy. Bower indicated that Agostini's technique may not be acceptable as stated for estimating the unduplicated audience of combinations involving more than five or six vehicles [6]. Later work by other researchers has indicated that Agostini's "K" is a variable rather than a constant and that corrections in the formula can be applied depending on the size of the media set [7].

The problem of measuring the total audience for a single medium has plagued researchers for some time. Personal interviews using the "editorial-interest technique" and self-administered survey questionnaires represent two of the common approaches to the measurement problem [15, pp. 228–29]. Both techniques have their weaknesses. Marder reports that in the editorial-interest method "it is highly probable that the occasional readers of a magazine are not included in the audience estimates" [16]. On the other hand, Schyberger's [20] research indicated that the "direct question" approach leads to an overstatement of readership by heavy readers and an understatement of readership by light readers. Finally, McGlathery reported "discrepancies in audience measures appear to be related to the frequency of publication of an issue" [17].

The last three studies indicate direct questioning may be accurate enough for most practical purposes if appropriately adjusted for response bias. Therefore, we will not attempt to improve on the measurement methods for audiences of a single medium. Rather, it is the use of media readership data which concerns us, providing new insights into the analysis and interpretation of audiences once the measurement for a single medium has been obtained. Furthermore, when advertising programs are being analyzed, it appears relatively unproductive to start with profiles of prospective consumers based on traditional demographic variables. *The manager cannot change the audience of a medium or the media exposure profiles of consumers. Rather, he must select media. In turn, these media are read, viewed, and listened to by different kinds of consumers in various mixes. If there is strong matching of lifestyle, attitudes, interest, and consumption-related activities to consumer media exposure sets, segmentation by media market segments will serve the marketing manager well.*

DATA AND METHODOLOGY

The data reported here were obtained from a self-administered questionnaire completed by 540 housewives in the greater Lafayette, Indiana, area during October 1965 as part of a larger "Consumer Behavior Research Project" [19]. Data collection was completed in May 1966 and included, in addition to the questionnaire mentioned above, laboratory experiments, controlled store experiments, seven months of diary data, and a follow-up self-administered questionnaire completed by an expanded sample. For a sample of 344 housewives (student wives excluded), the data from the first questionnaire were analyzed as follows:

1. A set of forty-four magazines and newspapers was factor analyzed yielding five media groupings.
2. On the basis of the five factors, factor scores were obtained on each of the 344 subject housewives.
3. A stepwise multiple regression analysis was performed with both single media and media factor scores as the dependent variables included socioeconomic measures, activity-interest-and-opinion (AIO) factor scores, personality factor scores, and perceived occupational-skill factor scores.
4. A cluster analysis was performed using both the media factor scores and the single media readership level variables, in separate analyses. The factor analysis was a preliminary step in selecting the best magazines for the cluster process.
5. A multiple discriminant analysis was performed to measure the relative importance of each variable in the clustering process.
6. In order to determine additional characteristics of the clusters, differences in mean values for a set of socioeconomic and AIO variables were examined across the three clusters.
7. Finally, for the three principal clusters derived from the above analyses, differences in stated product-usage rates and scores on brand recognition questions were examined.

The media, AIO, personality, and occupational choice factor scores used in the analysis were all obtained on the basis of principal factor analysis (using the squared multiple correlation coefficient as a communality estimate) followed by oblique rotation using Carroll's OBLIMIN II [12][1] program. In addition, the media data were subjected to a principal components analysis followed by varimax rotation. The resulting ten factors included the five discussed here and, in addition, five other factors of less interest [18]. *The cluster program used correlation between subjects as the measure of similarity.* The stepwise regression program was BIMD 2R [5] and the discriminant analysis program was the one developed by Cooley and Lohnes [8].

RESULTS

Media Factors

The forty-four media variables that were factor analyzed are listed in Table 19–1. The media questions in the questionnaire were scaled on a 1–6 scale from "never read" to "read almost every issue." For all 344 subjects, the rank of the media from high to low readership compared very favorably with figures from Standard Rate and Data for Indiana.

The factor analysis was undertaken to investigate the extent to which the relative readership levels of various magazines were related and how well individual reading habits can be represented by scores on groups of print media. The resulting five factors are described in Table 19–2. These five factors accounted for approximately 50 percent of the total communality.

Our attempts to assign descriptive names to factors may suffer from faulty interpretation or an undesirable choice of words. At some risk of misinterpretation, the following names were assigned to the five factors:

1. Cultural, intellectual magazines and newspapers
2. Light reading news magazines and newspapers
3. Fashion magazines
4. Movie, romance, crime magazines (sensationalistic)
5. Homemaker magazines

This analysis reflects an attempt to simplify and describe the data, and we do not necessarily impute a model of an underlying process. The reader will undoubtedly conclude that the groupings overlap to some extent. Clearly, some people will have higher or lower than average reading levels in two or more sets. One method of examining overlap is through the correlation between factor scores on subject housewives. In Table 19–3, the largest correlation is between factors 2 and 5, the light reading set and the homemaker set (.57). In

[1] Harman [12, chap. 15, pp. 324–34] discusses the Carroll OBLIMIN criterion for rotation, using the OBLIMIN II computer program.

this case, *Ladies' Home Journal* loaded above .3 on both factors. Additional magazines not reported in table 2 also loaded on both factors, although the loadings were relatively lower. Factor 1 (cultural, intellectual) and factor 2 (light reading) were negatively correlated ($-.21$), indicating a rather wide separation between these two sets. Factors 3 (fashion) and 5 (homemaker) were also negatively correlated. Additional insights into these relationships will be provided later in the paper in the discussion of the cluster analysis. The dotted lines under the loading for factors 3, 4, and 5 in Table 19–2 indicate major breaks in the size of the loading on the particular factor.

Table 19–1
List of 44 Magazines and Newspapers
Factor Analyzed

1. Chicago Tribune	23. Look
2. Chicago Sun-Times	24. Mademoiselle
3. Indianapolis Star (weekdays)	25. McCall's
4. Indianapolis Star (Sunday paper)	26. Modern Romance
5. New York Times (weekdays)	27. Modern Screen
6. New York Times (Sunday paper)	28. National Geographic
7. Lafayette Journal & Courier	29. Newsweek
8. Atlantic Monthly	30. New Yorker
9. Better Homes & Gardens	31. Pageant
10. Business Week	32. Playboy
11. Consumer Bulletin	33. Post
12. Consumer Reports	34. Reader's Digest
13. Esquire	35. Redbook
14. Family Circle	36. Saturday Review
15. Field & Stream	37. Sports Illustrated
16. Glamour	38. Time
17. Good Housekeeping	39. True Story
18. Harper's Bazaar	40. True Confessions
19. Holiday	41. TV Guide
20. House Beautiful	42. U.S. News & World Report
21. Ladies' Home Journal	43. Vogue
22. Life	44. Woman's Day

Stepwise Regression Analysis

To examine the relationship between media reading, socioeconomic characteristics, and nondemographic variables, several stepwise multiple regression analyses were performed on the factor scores and on a selected set of the single media. The results are reported in Tables 19–4 and 19–5. In each case, the amount of variance accounted for is split to indicate the contribution of demographic and nondemographic variables. Also note that only eight demographic variables were included in the analysis contrasted to twenty-seven nondemographic variables. The twenty-seven nondemographic variables included: fourteen AIO factor scores, eight personality factor scores,

Table 19–2
Description of Media Reading Factors

Question	Loading	Commu-nality
Factor 1		
Tends to read New York Times weekdays	.7295	.68
Tends to read New York Times Sundays	.7290	.68
Tends to read Saturday Review	.6173	.48
Tends to read the New Yorker	.5819	.50
Tends to read Atlantic Monthly	.5597	.46
Tends to read Consumer Reports	.4579	.49
Tends to read Esquire	.4260	.39
Factor 2		
Tends to read Post	.4911	.36
Tends to read Reader's Digest	.4630	.25
Tends to read Indianapolis Star Sundays	.3977	.44
Tends to read Look	.3881	.36
Tends to read Indianapolis Star weekdays	.3782	.44
Tends to read Ladies' Home Jonrnal	.3366	.49
Tends to read Life	.3032	.28
Factor 3		
Tends to read Vogue	.7206	.64
Tends to read Harper's Bazaar	.6748	.64
Tends to read Glamour	.6234	.54
Tends to read Mademoiselle	.6068	.54
	. . .	. . .
Tends to read House Beautiful	.4362	.47
Tends to read Holiday	.3257	.42
Factor 4		
Tends to read Modern Romance	.8929	.82
Tends to read True Story	.8575	.82
Tends to read True Confessions	.8101	.71
	. . .	. . .
Tends to read Modern Screen	.4497	.40
Factor 5		
Tends to read Family Circle	.8262	.81
Tends to read Woman's Day	.8141	.81
	. . .	. . .
Tends to read McCall's	.4128	.49
Tends to read Good Housekeeping	.4095	.43
Tends to read Ladies' Home Journal	.3623	.49
Tends to read Better Homes & Gardens	.3301	.32

and five occupational choice factor scores. Thus, through chance alone and in a ratio of about three to one, the nondemographic variable set should have accounted for more of the explained variance than the demographic set if the two sets are equally potent.

Table 19–3
Correlations between Factor Scores on Individuals
for the Five Media Factors (344 Subjects)

	F1	F2	F3	F4	F5
F1		— .23	.03	.18	0
F2			.13	.04	.57
F3				— .18	— .21
F4					.12
F5					

None of the R^2's is particularly high. However, several interesting results are worth noting. First, the nondemographic variables outperformed the demographic variables about three to one in predicting the level of readership for a single medium, that is, in about the same ratio as the size of the two variable sets. Thus, the nondemographic variable "on average" explained about as much of the variance in readership as did the demographic variables. In the case of the first five media in Table 19–4, the nondemographic variables provided most of the explanatory power. Space does not permit a more detailed discussion of the regression results. It should be noted, however, that the AIO factor scores, which will be examined more closely later in the paper, were the dominant set of variables. For example, it was not surprising to find that the AIO factor score on fashion consciousness was the best predictor of readership of the fashion magazines.

The results in Table 19–5 are also of interest. For the cultural-intellectual and the movie-romance sets of magazines, explanatory power is about evenly split between demographic and nondemographic variables. However, the demographic variables provided almost no prediction of relative reading levels for the fashion, light reading, and home-maker magazine sets. The R^2's are also higher for the analysis of media factor scores compared to the single media. It is to be recalled that the five media factors represent groupings of media that accounted for only about 50 percent of the total variance in the communality of the forty-four media variables. Even so, the factor score variables are a richer representation of the readership for a single medium. Readers interested in a complete description of the AIO and personality factor scores should consult Tigert's dissertation [21]. Several AIO factor scores and the demographic variables are discussed later in this paper.

Table 19–4
Summary of Stepwise Regression Analysis of Media Reading Habits: Single Media

Media	N Significant Predictor Variables: Both Demographic and Nondemographic Variables Included in Run	Total R^2 (from Significant Predictor Variables): Both Demographic and Nondemographic Variables Combined	Increase in R^2 for Demographic Variables: Both Variable Sets Combined (%)	Total R^2: Only Demographic Variables Used	Increase in R^2 for Nondemographic Variables: Both Variable Sets Included (%)	Total R^2: Only Nondemographic Variables Used
1. Vogue	7	0.29	5.4	(11.1)	23.6	(29.2)
2. Glamour	7	0.23	1.5	(3.2)	21.5	(20.2)
3. Mademoiselle	7	0.22	2.4	(6.0)	19.6	(20.8)
4. Harper's Bazaar	7	0.19	3.0	(9.4)	16.0	(20.0)
5. House Beautiful	7	0.17	0.0	(3.7)	17.0	(17.9)
6. Modern Romance	7	0.15	8.6	(8.7)	6.4	(10.6)
7. True Confessions	6	0.14	7.2	(6.0)	6.8	(12.2)
8. TV Guide	7	0.14	6.6	(5.3)	7.3	(9.9)
9. Holiday	5	0.14	7.4	(12.7)	6.6	(15.0)
10. McCall's	7	0.14	0.0	(2.2)	14.0	(13.6)
11. Atlantic Monthly	6	0.14	7.0	(7.4)	6.0	(8.8)
12. Lafayette Journal & Courier	6	0.13	2.6	(4.7)	10.4	(11.1)
13. Better Homes & Gardens	7	0.13	4.7	(3.9)	8.3	(8.4)
14. Family Circle	7	0.12	1.7	(1.9)	10.3	(7.0)
15. Life	5	0.12	1.5	(3.6)	9.5	(4.5)
16. Consumer Reports	5	0.11	4.3	(8.2)	6.7	(10.4)
17. Good Housekeeping	7	0.11	0.0	(1.3)	11.0*	(8.3)
18. U.S. News & World Report	4	0.11	9.6	(11.8)	1.4	(9.6)
19. Esquire	5	0.10	4.5	(5.5)	5.5	(11.1)
20. Business Week	5	0.07	3.0	(1.9)	4.0	(1.2)
21. Consumer Bulletin	4	0.06	2.3	(1.4)	3.7	(2.6)
22. Field & Stream	4	0.06	0.0	(0.1)	6.0	(5.5)
23. Ladies' Home Journal	4	0.06	0.0	(1.7)	6.0	(7.2)
24. Look	4	0.05	0.0	(0.0)	5.0	(3.5)

* Of the 11 percent total variance explained in the dependent variable, the nondemographic variables accounted for 11 percent and the demographic variables for 0 percent.

Table 19-5
Summary of Stepwise Regression Analysis of Media Exposure Habits:
Dependent Variables for Factor Scores on Media Questions for Individuals

Dependent Variable *	N Significant Predictor Variables: Both Demographic and Nondemographic Variables Included in Run	Total R² (from Significant Predictor Variables): Both Demographic and Nondemographic Variables Combined	Increase in R² or Demographic Variable: Both Variable Sets Combined (%)	Total R²: Only Demographic Variables Used	Increase in R² for Nondemographic Variables: Both Variable Sets Included (%)	Total R²: Only Nondemographic Variables Used
1. First factor score: Cultural-intellectual media	10	0.31	14.3	(18.9)	16.7	(30.8)
2. Second factor score: light reading	7	0.16	1.0	(6.9)	15.0	(16.5)
3. Third factor score: fashion magazines	9	0.35	2.9	(10.6)	32.1	(36.1)
4. Fourth factor score: movie, crime, sensationalistic	6	0.14	8.0	(8.4)	6.0	(12.8)
5. Fifth factor score: homemaker magazines	7	0.14	2.5	(3.1)	11.5	(10.7)

* Of the 31 percent total variance explained in the dependent variable, the nondemographic variables accounted for 16.7 percent and the demographic variables 14.3 percent.

Cluster Analysis

The technique of cluster analysis is relatively new to researchers in marketing. In fact, cluster analysis is more accurately described as a family of techniques related to one another by general taxonomic objectives. Most of the widely used cluster programs are discussed in an excellent recent unpublished paper by Frank and Green [11]. The particular program we have used is discussed in more detail by Lorr, Bishop, and McNair [14].

In the Lorr et al., program, the index of similarity among respondents can be either a distance measure (D) or a correlation coefficient (r). A correlation coefficient reflects primarily similarity in the shapes of two profiles. However, in the process to be described, it is always possible to consider level (elevation) after groups have been assigned on the basis of shape. In contrast, a distance measure is more difficult to interpret. "It may reflect a large difference between two profiles on one score or dimension, or the sum of small differences on all dimensions. The 'D' measure also fails to take the direction of differences into account; it fails to differentiate between profiles with opposite slopes" [14].

The clustering process begins by listing with each subject the numbers of all other subjects whose profiles correlate with it, at or above a specified level. The one with the longest associated list is selected as a pivot subject. To this is *added a second subject with the highest average correlation with all members in* the pivot group. To the first pair is added the subject that correlates highest on the average with both. Subjects are continually added to the first group until none correlates on the average with the other group members at a specified level. The second group is formed in the same way. When a group of specified size cannot be formed from the residual subjects, the process is stopped. The final step involves computing the mean correlation between each member of a given group with all members of all other groups. If a subject from one group correlates at a certain level with another group, it is dropped from its own group. Each group is then characterized by examining the mean value and the range of values for each variable defining it. Thus defined, each group is mutually exclusive. The technique is by no means perfect, since a subject assigned to the first group in the first stage of the analysis has no chance to be admitted to any other group.

Because only 140 cases could be handled at one time by the computer program available, two subsamples of 140 each were selected from the sample of 344 housewives for the analysis. The cluster analysis was performed, first using the five media factor scores as the variable set and then using nineteen of the single media from the original set of forty-four magazines and newspapers.

The analysis using the five media factor scores provided only two clusters. In part, the small number of clusters was due to the information lost in factor analysis, the limited number of variables entering the cluster analyses, and the correlation among the variables. Given these limitations, the results are not reported here. However, as the number of raw variables entering into the calculation of the pairwise correlation coefficients increased to nineteen, more interesting results were observed. The nineteen single media were then chosen by selecting four or five magazines from each factor. No magazines were selected from the movie-romance factor, since preliminary analysis indicated that a cluster of minimum size could not be obtained. Those magazines chosen represented the highest loadings on each of the remaining four factors. The nineteen magazines and their mean values for the resulting three derived clusters are reported in Table 19–6. For thirteen of the ninteen magazines, there were significant differences in the mean values between the three clusters at the .05 level. The scaled discriminant coefficients and the F-ratios for the thirteen magazines used later in the discriminant analysis reported below are also listed in Table 19–6.

It is interesting to compare the three clusters with the previously discussed four media factors. Cluster I appears to be the cultural-intellectual set and also contains subjects with relatively higher (but not significantly) reading levels for the fashion magazines. Cluster II is the homemaker set, and the third cluster is similar to the light reading set. However, Cluster III scores highest on *TV Guide*, a magazine which did not load heavily on any of the five media factors. In total, 154 of the 280 subjects, or 55 percent, were clustered in the two initial split half-cluster analyses. The totals for the three principal clusters appear at the bottom of Table 19–6.

The remaining subjects' reading habits displayed sufficiently different profiles to exclude them in one of the three principal clusters. On the other hand, the remaining unclustered subjects were numerous enough to permit locating new cluster homogeneity and between-cluster heterogeneity. The 126 residual subjects, not clustered in either of the two split runs of 140 subjects each, were formed into a new group for a third cluster analysis. Two new secondary clusters of twenty-eight and twenty-three subjects each were formed. Although they represent potentially interesting clusters or segments, their descriptions are not reported here due to the small sample sizes. In total, 205 of the original 280 subjects were clustered in either primary or secondary clusters (72 percent).

Before leaving the interpretations of the clusters, it is important to note why clusters have been based solely on magazine readership. The qualitative aspects of the media data available here were far superior to the viewing and listening time measurements on radio and television. For purposes of forming media market segments, it is important to know program types, not just how much television or radio exposure occurred. Is the TV viewing concentrated on variety shows, current events, or adventure series? Was radio listening concentrated on FM music stations or AM disk jockey shows? Answers to these questions could provide qualitative information about consumers similar to the information contained in profiles displaying relatively high or low readership of *True Confessions, Consumer Reports, or Atlantic Monthly.*

Table 19–6

Mean Scores, Standard Deviations (in Parentheses), Scaled Discriminant Coefficients, and F-Ratios for Selected Magazines for Three Derived Clusters[a]

Magazine	Group I	Group II	Group III	Scaled Discriminant Coefficients		F-Ratio
				1st Function	2d Function	
New Yorker	**2.44**[b]	1.06	1.06	− 1.11	− 1.18	16.05
	(1.69)	(2.04)	(0.23)			
Atlantic Monthly	**2.00**	1.03	1.03	− .68	− 0.13	9.09
	(1.54)	(0.18)	(0.01)			
Consumer Reports	**2.07**	1.47	1.33	0.14	− 2.72	4.09*
	(1.41)	(0.67)	(0.48)			
Vogue	**1.89**	1.40	1.06	0.45	− 3.82	6.19**
	(1.19)	(0.56)	(0.23)			
Saturday Review	**1.78**	1.03	1.00	− 3.01	− 0.20	11.79
	(1.09)	(1.18)	(0.00)			
Woman's Day	2.59	**5.38**	2.17	2.19	− 1.00	42.25
	(1.62)	(1.26)	(1.25)			
Family Circle	2.41	**5.38**	2.33	3.90	− 2.81	50.96***
	(1.42)	(1.24)	(1.14)			
McCall's	2.04	**4.88**	3.22	2.41	1.85	26.11
	(1.19)	(1.62)	(1.73)			
Good Housekeeping	2.44	**4.59**	3.28	2.15	1.58	12.93
	(1.58)	(1.70)	(1.60)			
Reader's Digest	2.30	**4.59**	4.44	2.64	3.10	14.51
	(1.70)	(1.79)	(1.72)			
Ladies' Home Journal	2.37	**4.72**	2.17	3.61	− 4.12	27.48
	(1.36)	(1.61)	(1.10)			
TV Guide	1.78	3.19	**5.78**	1.03	5.90	32.31
	(1.31)	(2.19)	(0.55)			
Life	2.44	2.47	**3.94**	− 1.53	3.57	6.90
	(1.28)	(1.44)	(1.83)			

Nonsignificant Variables

Look	2.55	2.63	**3.17**
Post	<u>2.04</u>	**2.41**	2.33
Mademoiselle	**1.63**	1.47	<u>1.05</u>
Glamour	1.52	1.34	<u>1.28</u>
Harper's Bazaar	**1.89**	1.41	1.44
Esquire	1.48	<u>1.25</u>	<u>1.05</u>
N	45	64	45

[a] The three primary clusters from the split half analysis are pooled in these data. Separate analysis of differences in mean values for the two sets of three clusters across the nineteen magazines and the subsequent discriminant analysis reported later provided evidence that the two halves of the sample were sufficiently alike to warrant combining them.
[b] The highest value for each variable is in boldface type and the lowest value is underscored.
* p < .10.
** p < .05.
*** p < .01.

Other Cluster Characteristics—Socioeconomic and Attitudinal

As indicated earlier, additional information was collected for each respondent in the original questionnaire on numerous socioeconomic dimensions and various activity, interest, and opinion characteristics (AIO). For each of the three media clusters, means and standard deviations were computed for a set of eight socioeconomic variables and fourteen AIO factor scores. These are reported in Table 19–7. For four of the socioeconomic variables and four of the AIO factor scores, significant differences appear between at least two of the three clusters.

Table 19–7
Means and Standard Deviations (in Parentheses) for Selected Demographic and AIO Factor Score Variables Plus Three Media Clusters

Variable	Cluster I (N = 45)	Cluster II (N = 64)	Cluster III (N = 45)
Demographic:			
Number of children	2.14	**2.20**	2.11*
	(1.50)	(1.64)	(1.86)
Number of rooms in current residence	**3.79**	3.66	3.60
	(0.96)	(0.76)	(0.89)
Wife's age	3.09	3.05	**3.18**
	(0.95)	(1.06)	(1.19)
Wife's education†	**4.44**	3.47	3.27
	(1.05)	(0.96)	(0.89)
Wife's occupational status	1.86	1.72	**1.96**
	(1.30)	(1.03)	(1.33)
Husband's occupation†	83.26*	72.77	72.24
	(13.65)	(18.12)	(15.82)
Husband's education†	87.81‡	76.11	68.49
	(17.56)	(20.00)	(23.29)
Total family income†	90.09‡	81.73	83.89
	(10.15)	(18.10)	(12.74)
AIO factor scores:			
Health and social conformity	−0.23§	0.07	**0.14**
	(1.10)	(0.95)	(0.96)
Careful shopper, price conscious	−0.32	**0.08**	0.02
	(1.48)	(1.23)	(1.16)
Compulsive, orderly housekeeper†	−0.53	0.02	**0.12**
	(0.97)	(1.03)	(1.10)
Fashion and personal appearance conscious	−0.17	−0.21	**0.03**
	(1.12)	(1.05)	(1.10)
Careless, irresponsible†	−0.37	**0.26**	0.11
	(1.22)	(1.52)	(1.18)
Negative attitudes toward advertising's value†	**0.50**	−0.16	−0.10
	(1.42)	(1.45)	(1.39)
Conservative, mature, sociable	0.07	0.07	0.04
	(1.83)	(1.67)	(1.52)

Table 19–7 continued

Variable	Cluster I (N = 45)	Cluster II (N = 64)	Cluster III (N = 45)
Weight watcher, dieter	—0.02	**0.06**	—0.06
	(1.25)	(1.32)	(1.34)
Risk avoidance	—0.14	—0.11	**0.29**
	(1.56)	(1.52)	(1.42)
Outdoor, casual, activist†	**0.32**	—0.41	0.04
	(1.06)	(1.57)	(1.37)
Nonparticipating sports enthusiast	—0.17	—0.09	**0.03**
	(1.26)	(1.13)	(0.99)
Information seeker	—0.35	—0.18	**0.11**
	(1.61)	(1.83)	(1.61)
Do-it-yourself homemaker	—0.12	**0.18**	—0.24
	(1.10)	(1.30)	(1.05)
Husband oriented	—0.09	**0.09**	0.01
	(1.19)	(1.51)	(1.10)

* The highest value of each variable is in boldface and lowest value is underscored.
† These eight variables have means which are significantly different at the .05 level across at least two of the three clusters.
‡ These three demographic variables were coded according to the Bureau of the Census Classification for Socioeconomic Status. The remaining five demographic variables were arbitrarily coded on an integer scale.
§ The AIO factor scores for the original population of 344 housewives were normally distributed with mean (0) and variance approximately (1.0).

An examination of the differences in the mean scores for the eight significant variables in Table 19–7 indicated:

1. Cluster I represents the highest socioeconomic class. Clusters II and III are about the same except for husband's education, where Cluster II scored significantly higher.
2. On compulsive, orderly housekeeping, Cluster III subjects score highest, Cluster II subjects about neutral, and Cluster I subjects quite negative on this dimension.
3. Cluster I subjects are careful and responsible, Cluster II subjects are somewhat careless and irresponsible, while Cluster III subjects are close to neutral on this dimension.
4. Subjects in Cluster I have strong negative attitudes about the value of advertising, while Clusters II and III have positive attitudes about advertising.
5. Subjects in Cluster I are outdoor, active people; subjects in Cluster II are not active; and subjects in Cluster III are about neutral.

With perhaps one exception, the socioeconomic and attitudinal relationships are quite consistent with the types of media read by subjects in the three clusters. Based on the media readership characterizing the clusters, subjects in Cluster III, rather than subjects in Cluster II, were expected to score highest on the careless, irresponsible dimension. No particular explanation can be provided for the resulting relationship on this dimension.

Product Usage and Brand Recognition Across Clusters

In an attempt at relating market behavior to media reading, means and standard deviations were calculated for a set of eight brand recognition scores and twenty-eight stated product usage variables on the 154 subjects. Between at least two of the three clusters, significant differences were found for five of the eight brand recognition scores and eleven of the twenty-eight product-usage variables. These results are reported in Table 19–8. The brand recognition scores range from 30 to 0, and the product-usage variables range from 1 (regularly, e.g., once a week or more) through 4 (almost never). The clusters might be characterized as follows:

1. Cluster I subjects score high on brand recognition of expensive furniture, fibers, fabrics, and liquors. They are relatively heavier users of liquid cooking oil, instant coffee, liquor, wine, dehydrated soups, and cigarettes.
2. Cluster II subjects score high on brand recognition of medium-priced furniture. They are relatively heavier users of solid cooking fat and paste floor wax. They can also be characterized as being light users of cigarettes, dehydrated soups, wine, and liquor.
3. Cluster III subjects score relatively lower on all of the brand recognition questions. They are relatively heavy users of cold cereal, regular coffee, and cold remedies.

To further characterize the consumers in each cluster, mean scores on self-appraised occupation skill questions and TV viewing and radio listening time questions are displayed in Table 19–9. One set of interpretations is summarized below.

1. Cluster I subjects see themselves as relatively well equipped for occupations that have high intellectual content and influence over the behavior of others (lawyer, mathematician, labor organizer, psychologist). Also, they see themselves as artistically talented (artist, designer).
2. Cluster II subjects rate themselves relatively low on occupations with high intellectual content but higher than Cluster III subjects on occupations demanding artistic talents.
3. Cluster III subjects score relatively high on social service occupations (nurse, minister) but indicate the possession of little artistic talent and rather modest intellectual interests. Unlike subjects in Cluster II, they indicate stronger skill levels in the health related occupations.
4. Cluster II and III subjects display high viewing levels and modest radio listening levels as compared to those in Cluster I. Cluster I consumers view very little daytime TV.

Table 19–8
Mean Values and Standard Deviation (in Parentheses) for Eight Brand
Recognition Scores, Eleven Stated Product-Usage, Three Media Clusters

	Means			
Variable	Cluster I (N = 45)	Cluster II (N = 64)	Cluster III (N = 45)	p
Brand recognition:				
Expensive furniture	**13.8** (5.63)	12.6 (4.70)	10.9 (4.00)	< .01
Medium-priced furniture	16.3 (5.91)	**18.5** (5.18)	15.2 (5.81)	< .01
Artificial fibers	**19.1** (6.40)	18.5 (5.95)	16.2 (5.97)	< .03
Fabrics	**20.0** (6.26)	18.1 (4.98)	16.4 (6.04)	< .01
Liquors	**11.2** (5.72)	8.4 (3.80)	8.5 (4.22)	< .01
Product usage*				
Liquid cooking oil	**2.16** (0.80)	2.33 (0.82)	2.51 (0.89)	< .06
Solid cooking fat	2.52 (0.76)	**2.20** (0.78)	2.24 (0.80)	< .03
Paste floor wax	3.36 (0.57)	**3.34** (0.69)	3.62 (0.53)	< .02
Cold cereal	2.50 (0.98)	2.44 (1.09)	**2.13** (1.01)	< .06
Instant coffee	**2.57** (1.11)	2.64 (1.20)	3.00 (0.95)	< .01
Regular coffee	1.84 (1.12)	2.05 (1.21)	**1.69** (1.04)	< .08
Liquor	**2.48** (1.11)	3.06 (0.94)	2.96 (0.85)	< .01
Wine	**2.59** (0.99)	3.41 (0.73)	3.29 (0.81)	< .01
Dehydrated soup	**2.93** (0.82)	3.20 (0.67)	3.04 (0.88)	< .07
Cigarettes	**2.77** (1.29)	3.27 (1.21)	2.98 (1.21)	< .04
Cold remedies	3.07 (0.62)	2.92 (0.70)	**2.78** (0.73)	< .05

* The smaller the number on product usage, the higher the usage rate. Highest usage rates are in boldface type and the lowest are underscored.

Clearly, the number of characteristics of consumers assigned to media market clusters will depend on the problem at hand. What we have attempted to do is expand the range of descriptive variables which marketing and advertising managers may find useful.

DESCRIPTION OF AN ADVERTISING-BUDGET, MEDIA-SELECTION MODEL

We shall illustrate the possible managerial application of this method of defining market segments by developing a simple media allocation problem. Single time periods will be considered in which all of an advertisement's effects are concentrated. Furthermore, no formal allowance will be made for media discounts. To use our survey data and findings, market segments are media market segments of the type that has been described above. These restrictions were taken into account in drawing up the following definitions:

$$REV_i = \sum_{j=1}^{m} VC_j EE_{ij} VU_j$$

= rated exposure value per capita in market segment i,

where

VC_j = the relative value of jth media vehicle's "climate" for the advertising task,

EE_{ij} = exposure efficiency.

It is the product of (1) the fraction of the people in a market segment i who are in the medium j's audience; the proportion of the segment's population who will be exposed at any level to medium j during the year; (2) the average number of issues (shows, etc.) a member of the market segment will be exposed to during the year, given exposure to medium j: (3) the seasonal adjustment ratio for the period applied to the average in (2); (4) the probability of exposure to the jth vehicle under consideration, given exposure to an issue (show, etc.). In summary, (1) through (4) indicates who can be exposed and the probability of exposure to the medium *and* vehicle during the period of interest. (As used here, *Life* is a medium, and a four-color page is a vehicle. In TV, *Run for Your Life* is a medium, and the commercial time is a vehicle.)

VU_j = number of j media-vehicle units employed during the period.

This number can be constrained to lie within appropriate limits and

CU_j = the cost of a unit of media vehicle j.

The complete objective function to be maximized subject to the budget and related constraints is:

$$\sum_{i=1}^{s} (NC_i)(DSP_i)g(REV_i) = \text{total dollar sales over the planning period potentially produced } by \text{ the advertising as scheduled,}$$

where

NC_i = number of consumers in market segment i,

DSP_i = expected dollar sales per capita in segment i during the period which can be obtained *by* advertising,

and

$g(REV_i)$ = proportion of potential per capita sales achieved in market segment i by REV_i during the period.

To employ the above model, a series of estimates must be made. Some must be subjective. For example, although the degree to which editorial climate, mechanical capabilities, etc., fit a product may be relatively easy to grasp, the estimated value of a media vehicle's climate must be based largely on subjective judgment. Also, recall that the remaining data used to rate the effectiveness of a media-vehicle unit apply to groups or clusters of customers with similar media exposure patterns—the ones used to define market segment. The justification for this step is twofold: the consumers in the groups are reasonably homogeneous in regard to the marketing characteristics of interest, and the groups are not so numerous as to seriously encounter the computational procedures outlined below. Given media-cluster market segments, it is easy to estimate the number of consumers in each segment. Also, questionnaire data yield estimates of the total potential dollar sales per capita in each media-cluster market segment. The amount of this potential which advertising can influence in the period of interest is the sales that would go to competitors in the absence of an advertising program. In other words, the relative competitive ability of the product and the normal level of competitive promotions are assumed as a starting point.

Table 19–9
Means and Standard Deviations (in Parentheses) for Selected Variables on Occupational Choice, TV Viewing, and Radio Listening—Three Media Clusters

Variable	Cluster I (N = 45)		Cluster II (N = 64)		Cluster III (N = 45)	
Occupations:						
Nurse	3.47	(1.70)	3.11	(1.76)	4.07*	(1.76)
Lawyer	**2.89**	(1.50)	2.09	(1.52)	2.16	(1.31)
Elementary school teacher	**4.27**	(1.48)	3.76	(1.60)	3.82	(1.63)
Minister	2.11	(1.37)	1.81	(1.33)	**2.33**	(1.33)
Doctor	**3.33**	(1.73)	2.28	(1.60)	2.82	(1.68)
Artist	**3.04**	(1.89)	2.14	(1.60)	1.84	(1.57)
Labor organizer	**2.80**	(1.70)	1.91	(1.49)	1.76	(1.23)
Airline stewardess	**4.31**	(1.55)	3.67	(1.75)	3.82	(1.85)
Dress designer	**4.02**	(1.63)	3.42	(1.62)	3.33	(1.65)
Psychologist	**4.07**	(1.57)	3.19	(1.62)	3.29	(1.80)
Mathematician	**3.22**	(1.82)	2.55	(1.68)	2.96	(1.83)
TV watching:						
Daytime weekday (hrs/day)	0.56	(0.58)	**1.77**	(0.97)	1.69	(0.88)
Weekdays (hrs/day) 5/10 p.m.	1.62	(1.05)	**2.20**	(0.84)	2.11	(0.98)
Total hrs. per week	20.96	(12.47)	31.19	(16.01)	**32.47**	(14.35)
Radio total hrs. per week†	**16.47**	(15.26)	14.14	(13.34)	14.91	(11.65)

NOTE. The occupation choice variables were coded 1–6, from very poor to very good.
* The highest value for each variable in boldface type and the lowest underscored.
† No significant difference between three media clusters. For all other variables, there is a significant (.05) difference between at least two of the three groups.

To complete the data set for the model, the components of exposure effectiveness are required for each segment. The first component concerns the fraction of people in a market segment who are in the media's annual audience. The proportion of readers, viewers, etc., compared to nonreaders, nonviewers, etc., can be identified directly from the questionnaire data used to compute the mean exposure levels shown in Table 19–6. By segment definition, the variance by media is controlled and known. The second component, the average number of annual issues, shows, etc., that a member of the market segment will see or hear is also readily available from the same data source. It is computed by forming the product of the proportion of issues, shows, etc., viewed and the number appearing annually. When seasonally adjusted, it yields the average per capita exposure to the type media in the same time interval of interest. The third or seasonal adjustment factor can be obtained by questionnaire or from Starch, Nielsen, and allied sources. As a practical matter, questionnaire data can be supplemented or checked by a variety of commercial audience-measurement services. Fourth, the probability of exposure to the advertising message must be estimated by informal methods and sources such as Starch Reports. Also, a variety of specific studies have been made relating to attention and recall. The effects of vehicle units of different sizes (one page compared to one-half page) and of color compared to black and white have been the subject of several investigations.

Summarizing in more abstract form, the exposure effectiveness of media vehicle j in market segment i is: $EE_{ij} =$ (percentage of market segment in medium's audience at some time during the year) $\times$ (average number of issues, shows, etc., seen by those in the annual audience) $\times$ (a factor to adjust the average for seasonal or specific time period effects) $\times$ (probability of exposure to the message, given exposure to the issue, show, etc.)

In passing, note that the market segmentation method that has been suggested enjoys certain desirable characteristics:

1. The number of media market segments should remain relatively small in number, say less than a dozen for products bought by women. A somewhat larger number would be expected for products bought by men and women. (The number of segments is controlled by the number of media considered, the general heterogeneity of exposure patterns among members of the population being divided into segments, the tolerable heterogeneity of segments, and the minimum size of the groups or clusters that are labeled a media market segment.)
2. Both the sales and the cost of the sales expected from the segment can be readily determined for an optimal policy operating under any feasible potential budgets. (More will be said about costs in a later section.)
3. Much helpful quantitative and qualitative data are available to aid the advertisers in formulating an effective copy strategy.

With respect to formulating copy approaches, observe that a whole range of demographic measures can be made available. In addition, the data on AIO factor scores (Table 19–7), the brand recognition and product-usage variables (Table 19–8), and particularly the self-designating occupation skills (Table 19–9) make marked contributions to profiling activity, lifestyle, and motivational characteristics of consumers in each segment. The value of expanding the advertiser's insight beyond the usual socioeconomic measures should not be underestimated. Product-usage patterns, market-related activities, interests and opinions, and personal talents and aspirations may contain critical clues to specific campaign themes and copy appeals most suitable to each media market segment. For example, Table 19–9 indicated that subjects in Cluster I see themselves as relatively well equipped for positions of social, artistic, and intellectual influence, consumers in Cluster II see themselves as relatively ill-equipped for intellectually demanding work, and consumers in Cluster III indicate low artistic and intellectual skills but are oriented toward social and personal service activities. The copy appeals for a product which are directed to each media market segment could be specifically designed to allow for these consumer characteristics. Sophisticated appeals to Cluster II may be rejected, and pedestrian appeals to Cluster I may miss their mark. Appeals to artistic influentials may be successful with Cluster I and fail with Cluster III consumers. The rating of exposure effectiveness and media climate should allow for these facts. It also permits testing the effectiveness of various themes or copy approaches during the analysis of the media-selection problem.

ILLUSTRATIVE APPLICATION OF MEDIA MARKET SEGMENTS TO THE ADVERTISING-BUDGET, MEDIA-SELECTION PROBLEM

An illustrative application of media market segments can be developed from the data and model discussed in the preceding portion of the paper. To do so, assume that an importer of wines and liqueurs has placed a specialty liqueur in a test market and introduced it with the promotional effort required to achieve normal levels of distribution. The test market experience leads him to believe that wide acceptance and volume sales will depend on the degree to which it is accepted by women as an appropriate prestige after-dinner drink. Test market sales and questionnaire data obtained from package goods stores and consumers also indicate the item could be promoted as an appropriate Christmas gift item, especially as a gift from a woman to the men in her life: husband, father, and perhaps employer.

Based on these data and the advice of his advertising and marketing consultants, the importer decides to spend $140,000 in November and December on a gift promotion. His media decisions for this effort will be based on the data reported in the first half of this paper, augmented by the objective and subjective estimates required to employ the media-selection model which has been described.

The first step in the process was to estimate the number of household and the maximum per household purchases which could be expected from a two-month campaign for the gift-wrapped liqueur. This was done largely on the basis of questionnaire data of the type which has been described. The purchases per household were checked against general industry statistics to be sure they fell within reasonable limits and were then converted to sales per household at the importer's list price. On the basis of attainable national distribution and the above estimates, customers with Cluster I media and market behavior characteristics were judged to offer new potential gift sales of $320,000 = 4,000,000 × $0.08. The figures for Cluster II and III types, respectively, were $400,000 = 8,000,000 × $0.05 and $280,000 = 7,000,000 × $0.04. Therefore, for the period of interest and a given market segment i,

$$i = \quad 1 \qquad\qquad 2 \qquad\qquad 3$$
$$(NC_i)(DSP_i) = \$320{,}000 \qquad \$400{,}000 \qquad \$280{,}000.$$

The second step in the process was to make the estimates necessary to convert a unit vehicle in a medium to rated exposure values in each cluster or media market segment. Due to the prestige appeal of the product and its newness, the importer's advertising agency recommended the use of full-page, four-color advertisements. The importer agreed and indicated that *Look* magazine would be a suitable basis for assigning differential values to the "climate," a media offered in support of the copy theme and audience receptivity. Having assigned a value of 1.0 to *Look*, estimates were made of the appropriate values for other media. For example, *New Yorker* received a value of 3.0 (three times as effective as *Look*), and *Glamour* received a value of 0.5 (one-half as effective as *Look* and one-sixth as effective as *New Yorker*). Naturally, these values related specifically to the gift copy for the liqueur four-color display on a full page.

Starch readership data and the questionnaire measures of readership, demographic, and related characteristics of the audience in each cluster were available to aid the advertising agency estimate the proportion of each cluster population who would see the advertising copy in a vehicle unit of each medium. For example, about 14 percent of the women in Cluster I households and less than one-tenth of 1 percent of the women in Cluster II and III households were expected to see a one-page four-color *New Yorker* advertisement appearing during the two months before Christmas.

To complete the media effectiveness and sales potential data for the three media market segments, the product of the exposure efficiency (*EE*) and the media climate value (*VC*) was formed for the media vehicles. These figures, indicated the *REV*'s added to a cluster or segment by a unit of the media vehicle, are shown in Table 19–10. This table also shows the sales potential for each segment and the cost of a four-color page in each medium. When used in conjunction with the response function that converts a given level of *REV*'s to the expected fraction of potential sales, these data allow the importer to make the media selections for the liqueur advertising.

To establish the shape of the curve, for each cluster (media market segment), a base media vehicle was chosen. In this case, *Look* could be used. The question was then asked as to how many one-page units of *Look* would be required to achieve one-half (50 percent) of the potential sales. The importer and his consultants concluded that about seven would be needed in the case of Segments II and III and five to six would be needed in Segment I. Therefore, the curves were of essentially the same form for all segments so curve fitting by parameter adjustment was not required.

Table 19–10
Rated Exposure Values per Vehicle by Cluster of Media Market Segments, Media-Vehicle Costs and Sales Potential per Segment Included

Maximum N Available Vehicles	Media (Vehicle: One Page Four Color)	Rated Exposure Values of a Media-Vehicle Cluster or Media Market Segment			Cost per Page Four Color*
		1	2	3	
6	Saturday Review	.0872	†		$ 6,120
6	New Yorker	.4200			6,050
2	Atlantic Monthly	.1730			3,825
2	Esquire	.0880	.0176		12,130
3	Saturday Evening Post	.0541	.0648	.0648	41,375
3	Look	.1000	.1000	.1250	52,920
6	Life	.0900	.0900	.1125	54,250
2	Vogue	.1503	.1287	‡	6,500
2	Harper's Bazaar	.1216	.0570	.0570	6,450
2	Glamour	.0200	.0100	.0050	9,350
2	Mademoiselle	.0250	.0100		5,950
6	Family Circle	.0963	.2569	.0770	30,100
6	Woman's Day	.0963	.2569	.0770	30,415
2	McCall's	.0588	.1760	.1186	42,840
2	Good Housekeeping	.0704	.1760	.1186	27,440
2	Ladies' Home Journal	.0704	.1760	.0704	35,000
6	TV Guide	.0367	.0540	.2016	27,400
Potential dollar sales		$320,000	$400,000	$280,000	

* One-time rates used in this illustration.
† Substantially below .01 and not used in computations.
‡ The *REV* levels for *Vogue* and *Harper's Bazaar* may differ largely due to small size of sample used in this study.

The form of the response function is constrained mathematically to be concave downward and monotonically increasing. Therefore, it is convenient to specify

$$g_i(Z_{ij}) = [1 - \exp(-a_i Z_{ij})], a_i, \qquad Z_{ij} > 0$$

where

$Z_{ij} =$ the level of *REV*'s in market segment i resulting from a given media selection j.

In the present illustration, we can simplify by setting $a_i = 1$. As noted, subjective estimates of the shape of the response function are not difficult to make since they concern the percentage of potential sales which a given level of rated exposure values will yield. It is clear, however, that seldom will marketing and advertising personnel have extensive quantitative evidence about the form of the function. The cases where data are available tend to be concentrated in fields where sales are traceable to specific promotional activity, for example, mail-order sales solicited by direct-action advertising.

In computing an "optimal" media schedule, the following procedure is followed:

1. A list indicating the units of each media vehicle placed in the schedule is initialized with all elements set equal to zero.
2. Let

$$R_j^k = \sum_{i=1}^{s'} (NC_i)(DSP_i)g_i(REV_{ij}^k),$$

and

$$MR_j^k = (R_j^k - R_j^{k-1})/CU_j \qquad k = 1, \cdots, K.$$

3. The media vehicle for which MR_j^1 is a maximum enters the schedule, and a unit is added to the appropriate element in the media schedule. The REV_{ij}'s purchased by this action are added to the prevailing levels in each of the i segments.
4. Next, the margin return for each additional media vehicle j is computed. The media vehicle for which MR_j^2 is a maximum becomes the second entry in the schedule. The process is repeated for $K = L, \cdots, k$, where K is the analysis cycle in which the budget limit or all media constraints have been exceeded, or all media fall below some minimum acceptable level of marginal return.

The procedure insures that the highest marginal return found at any stage will be greater than the highest one found at the next stage (discount schedules being ignored in this illustration). Figure 19–2 illustrates the effect of the decreasing marginal return.

During the process of computing the solution at each step (optimal to that step), the manager and his analyst will want the following minimum level of summary data; (a) the schedule following the addition, and the associated expected sales and costs; (b) the media vehicle added and the associated expected sales and costs.

The reader interested in an introduction to the mathematical basis for the stepwise, nonlinear integer programming technique outlined above should consult a brief paper by Bennett Fox [9]. A time-dependent dynamic programming model of the media problem appears in Little and Lodish [13]. Finally, a working paper extending the current model to handle long-run effects and media discount schedules is being prepared by one of the authors (EAP).

In passing, the reader should observe that the media-selection advertising-budget model presented above offers a convenient way to test campaign themes. Each theme could profit by or suffer from a given medium's climate or the character of the vehicles in question. By selecting the media schedule which best suits each theme, the total dollar sales returned from a given number of advertising dollars could be measured for each theme. In this manner, the efficiency of several schedule-theme combinations could be measured.

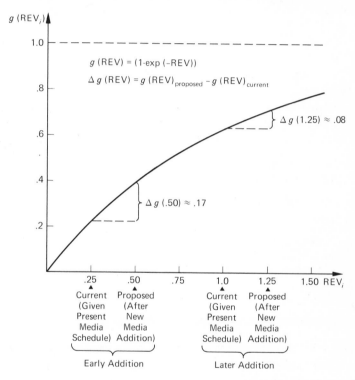

Figure 19–2. Proportion of potential per capita sales as a function of rated exposure values (all media) in a market segment.

Before moving on to review the solution to the liqueur importer's media-selection problem, we hope the above discussion has made clear the following general points about the problem:

1. The existence of media market segments clarifies the issues of motivation and copy strategies that should be part of a sound market segmentation strategy.
2. The form of the segmentation makes media allocation a good deal easier

to handle analytically. The one-period model does not appear to pose any serious data or data processing problems. Sequential incremental analysis handles the troublesome questions of nonlinearity in the response of consumers to various levels and qualities of exposures.

3. A multiperiod model which allows for allocations of media vehicles to time periods has been constructed. This extended version also permits media discount schedules to enter. The rate at which an exposure's effectiveness decays over time and the degree of discounting of cash flows should enter such a multiperiod model is a matter for further study. Further, it would be a great help if more empirical evidence about the relation of advertising expenditures and sales was available. The current work by Bass using simultaneous equation models may prove helpful [4]. Our computer program did not compute *reach and frequency* for each media schedule. It would, however, have been a simple matter to do so since the mean and variance of exposure had been computed for each medium and segment. The only unanswered question concerns what threshold level of exposure would be used for the purpose of defining reach.

MEDIA SCHEDULES FOR THE ILLUSTRATIVE GIFT LIQUEUR PROMOTION UNDER THREE MEDIA-SELECTION MODELS

In developing solutions to this media scheduling problem we have applied a variety of programming methods in order to compare the effects of programming techniques. Since the problem is formulated in terms of integer values of the variables, we have developed a stepwise, nonlinear, integer-constrained computer program which operates on the basis of simple marginal principles.

Before examining the solutions developed by this programming technique, we shall discuss alternative programming methods. A variety of nonlinear computer programs are available, many of which utilize gradient projection search principles. We have applied one of these gradient programs to the media scheduling problem. Since continuous variables are assumed in this computer program, integer constraints not being permitted, we have developed a solution in dollars for each vehicle. The results are shown in Table 19–11. The dollar solution has been rounded to the nearest integer number of solutions permitted by the technique. For purposes of comparison, a linear programming solution is also shown in Table 19–11. The effect of the linear objective function is to bring into the solution more vehicles which are efficient in only one segment, such as *Atlantic Monthly* and *Saturday Review*. The latter medium appears in the solution largely because of the constant, as contrasted to decreasing, increments of sales produced by successive increments of rated exposure values assigned to Segment I.

The solution and relevant by-product data produced by the stepwise, non-linear computer programming model are displayed in Tables 19–12 and 19–13.[2] It is of some interest to trace the order in which the media vehicles entered the solution, the total expected sales and media cost at each step, and the way in which average efficiency declines as the size of the media schedule grows. In addition, it is possible to follow a particular medium vehicle to the point where it clearly drops out as a contender, offering less sales revenue than the cost of obtaining the revenue, and to observe the efficiency of individual contenders that remain when the budget constraint has been reached.

Table 19–11
Solution to Continuous Programming Problems

	Linear Programming		Nonlinear Programming	
Vehicles	Dollar Solution	Integer Rounded Solution (Pages)	Dollar Solution	Integer Rounded Solution (Pages)
New Yorker	$36,720*	6	$33,087*	5
Vogue	13,000	2	13,000	2
Atlantic Monthly	7,650	2		
Harper's Bazaar	12,900	2	12,900	2
Good Housekeeping			35	1†
Family Circle	69,720	2	80,978	2
Saturday Review	12,240	2†		

* The actual dollar expenditures for six and five pages of New Yorker are, respectively, $36,300 and $30,250. Note that page solutions are rounded down.
† Last to enter, budget slightly exceeds $140,000.

Again, it should be emphasized that each iteration produces an optimal allocation for the budget spent and constraints met.[3] Therefore, the program could have been operated until all media dropped out as rational additions, by whatever criteria employed. All feasible optimal schedules would be visible to the manager and analyst. If it appeared desirable or necessary to use a different allocation and budget, good guideposts are available to indicate the likely result of the deviate schedule.

[2] The stepwise model should not be confused with the nonlinear programming solution shown in Table 19–11. The former stepwise procedure is integer valued, but the latter procedure is not.
[3] This program, like other algorithmic procedures for handling integer constraints, does not guarantee optimality. For conditions under which optimality is guaranteed, see Fox [9].

Table 19–12

Summary Data on Advertising Productivity Measures by Cycles in Stepwise Media-Selection Process: Sales Efficiency Criterion in Gift Liqueur Marketing Problem with $140,000 Budget Constraint Used as an Illustration

Maximum N Available Vehicles	Media (Vehicle: One Page, Four Color)	Dollar Sales per Dollar Medium Cost for Added Unit of Medium							
		Cycles of Analysis							
		1	2	4*	6	8	9	10	12*
6	Saturday Review	4.43	2.94	1.68	1.33	†	†	†	†
6	New Yorker	18.38	12.15	6.96	5.48	3.32	2.23	2.02	1.27
2	Atlantic Monthly	13.40	8.84	5.04	3.96	2.38	1.58	1.44	†
2	Esquire	2.82	2.05	1.35	1.11	†	†	†	†
3	Saturday Evening Post	1.44	1.30	1.10	†	†	†	†	†
3	Look	1.92	1.72	1.46	1.28	1.04	1.04	†	†
6	Life	1.69	1.51	1.29	1.13	†	†	†	†
2	Vogue	14.34	11.97	9.10	‡	‡	‡	‡	‡
2	Harper's Bazaar	11.52	9.56	7.51	6.47	‡	‡	‡	‡
2	Glamour	1.25	1.02	†	†	†	†	†	†
2	Mademoiselle	2.01	1.55	1.09	†	†	†	†	†
6	Family Circle	4.68	4.33	3.68	3.25	2.55	2.49	†	†
6	Woman's Day	4.63	4.29	3.65	3.21	2.52	2.46	2.00	†
2	McCall's	2.66	2.51	2.21	1.95	1.58	1.55	1.30	1.10
2	Good Housekeeping	4.29	4.01	3.49	3.08	2.49	2.44	2.04	†
2	Ladies' Home Journal	3.01	2.79	2.39	2.10	1.67	1.68	1.33	1.12
6	TV Guide	3.05	2.90	2.68	2.38	2.07	2.04	1.84	†

* Preceding cycle which brought in one of the two additional units of the added media vehicle (all full page, four color) has been omitted.
† Return of dollar sales remains below cost of media vehicle required to produce the sales.
‡ Constraint on vehicles in media has been reached.

SENSITIVITY ANALYSIS

In order to study the sensitivity of the solution to some of the more subjective inputs such as climate and probability of exposure, we have varied the *REV* values for groups of media, holding constant these values for the remaining media. The variations and the solution sequences produced by the computer program are displayed in Table 19–14. It is clear that in this case the solutions are not very sensitive to substantial variations in inputs. *New Yorker, Vogue, Harper's Bazaar,* and *Family Circle* appear in the solution in every instance. Circulation within segments and cost appear to be much more important in determining the solution than the more subjective variables.

Table 19–13
Solution Sequence of Stepwise Media-Selection Model

	Projected Percentage of Available Sales							
Segment I	0.34	0.57	0.68	0.75	0.89	0.90	0.91	0.96
Segment II			0.23	0.32	0.35	0.48	0.55	0.55
Segment III				0.11	0.14	0.19	0.29	0.29
Total sales	$111,172	$184,703	$311,467	$398,185	$448,268	$523,454	$579,223	$598,246
	Media Added							
New Yorker (6)*	1	1			2			2
Vogue (2)			2					
Harper's Bazaar (2)				2				
Family Circle (1)						1		
Good House-keeping (1)							1	
	Cumulative Spent							
	$6,050	$12,100	$25,100	$38,000	$50,100	$80,200	$107,440	$119,540
	Dollar Sales Increase per Dollar of Medium Spent							
	$18.38	$12.05	$9.10	$6.49	$3.32	$2.49	$2.04	$1.27

* Numbers in parentheses indicate total of media added.

SUMMARY

In conclusion, we note that the potential importance and/or irrelevance of variables to market segmentation problems depend strongly on individual cases. The simple illustration which was used here is a case in point. Classification of buyers as specialist or nonspecialist within a profession was all that was needed to deal effectively with both media readership and product usage. A large pool of additional socioeconomic variables could contribute little useful new information. In the media market segments which were discussed in the first section of this paper, consumers could be placed in groups which yielded a diffuse set of potentially useful descriptive variables. Some of these have been noted. In general, we would be surprised to find media market segments for consumer goods with very simple structures. More surprising would be segments that were most effectively defined exclusively by socioeconomic variables of the traditional type.

Sets of variables that can be related to potential marketing actions are needed. For this purpose, socioeconomic variables hold only modest promise since they are indirectly connected to market motivation and behavior. The arty, fashion-conscious consumer appears in many age and income levels. So do skiing buffs, weight watchers, and sports-car enthusiasts. It is not easy to deny the relevance of these activities and attitudes to selected types of

Table 19–14
Sensitivity Analysis, Variations in REV and Solution Sequences

	Group 1		Group 2		Group 3		Group 4		Group 5	
	+25%	−25%	+25%	−25%	+25%	−25%	+25%	−25%	+25%	−25%
Solution Sequences										
	New Yorker	New Yorker	New Yorker	New Yorker	New Yorker	New Yorker	New Yorker	New Yorker	New Yorker	New Yorker
	New Yorker	Vogue	New Yorker	New Yorker	Vogue	New Yorker	New Yorker	New Yorker	New Yorker	New Yorker
	Vogue	Vogue	Vogue	Vogue	Vogue	New Yorker	Vogue	Vogue	Vogue	Vogue
	Vogue	Harper's B.	Vogue	Vogue	Harper's B.	Vogue	Vogue	Vogue	Vogue	Vogue
	Harper's B.	Harper's B.	Harper's B.	Harper's B.	Vogue	Harper's B.	Harper's B.	Harper's B.	Harper's B.	Harper's B.
	Harper's B.	New Yorker	Harper's B.	Harper's B.	New Yorker	Harper's B.	Harper's B.	Harper's B.	Harper's B.	Harper's B.
	New Yorker	New Yorker	New Yorker	New Yorker	New Yorker	Harper's B.	New Yorker	New Yorker	New Yorker	New Yorker
	New Yorker	New Yorker	New Yorker	New Yorker	New Yorker	New Yorker	New Yorker	New Yorker	New Yorker	New Yorker
	Family Cir.	Family Cir.	Family Cir.	Family Cir.	Family Cir.	Family Cir.	Family Cir.	TV Guide	TV Guide	Family Cir.
	Good House.	New Yorker	Good House.	Good House.	Family Cir.	New Yorker	Good House.	Family Cir.	Family Cir.	Good House.
	Good House.	Family Cir.	New Yorker	New Yorker	Good House.	Good House.	Good House.	New Yorker	New Yorker	New Yorker
	Atlantic Mo.	New Yorker	New Yorker	New Yorker		New Yorker	Atlantic Mo.		New Yorker	
		Atlantic Mo.								
Unexpended Funds										
	$1,095	$13,775	$20,260	$20,260	$2,260	$20,260	$1,095	$20,300	$20,300	$20,260

NOTE. REV values were increased or decreased by 25 percent for the solutions shown above as follows: Group 1, for *Saturday Review, New Yorker, Atlantic Monthly, Esquire;* Group 2, for *Post, Look, Life;* Group 3, for *Vogue, Harper's Bazaar, Glamour, Mademoiselle;* Group 4, for *Family Circle, Woman's Day, McCall's, Good Housekeeping, Ladies' Home Journal;* Group 5, for *TV Guide.*

purchase and use patterns and to the marketing strategies designed to influ-ence buying decisions. Starting with thoughtfully developed media market segments, sets of allied descriptive variables should follow naturally from consideration of the product's characteristics and the relevant media exposure patterns. Furthermore, it is natural to assess the effectiveness of media in relation to the consumers in a media market segment. The subjective esti-mates of effectiveness and media climate will be more realistic, and relatively few estimates are required. The facts underline intuitive appeal and simplicity of the model and the data.

In the future, we hope that detailed readership, viewing, and listening data will be gathered in conjunction with market-related attitude, interest, and opinion data (AIO). Also, data on product usage, life-style, and market-connected personality and skill characteristics of consumers should be ob-tained along with the full range of demographic measures. It seems clear that analysts are now finding ways to process this broad information base in a way which will markedly assist managers in making more thoughtful strategic advertising decisions. The usual measures of media reach, frequency, dupli-cated audiences, demographic composition of audiences, cost per exposure, etc., disappear as critical dimensions of the allocation problem. Instead, re-sults are expressed, as they should be, in terms of dollars of new sales produced per additional dollar efficiently spent on media purchases.

References

1. Agostini, J. M. "How to Measure Unduplicated Audiences." *Journal of Advertising Research* 1, no. 3 (March 1961): 11–14.
2. Bass, Frank M. "A Simultaneous-Equation Regression Study of Adver-tising and Sales-Analysis of Cigarette Data." Working paper, Herman C. Krannert Graduate School of Industrial Administration, May 1967.
3. Bass, Frank M., Tigert, Douglas J., and Lonsdale, R. T. "Market Seg-mentation: Group versus Individual Behavior," *Journal of Marketing Research* (August 1968), pp. 264–70.
4. Bass, Frank M. "Simultaneous Equation Regression Analysis of Adver-tising and Sales." Working paper, Herman C. Krannert Graduate School of Industrial Administration, June 1967.
5. *Biomedical Computer Programs.* Health Sciences Computing Facility, Department of Preventive Medicine and Public Health, School of Medi-cine, University of California, Los Angeles, September 1, 1965, pp. 233–47.
6. Bower, John. "Net Audiences of U.S. and Canadian Magazines: Seven Tests of Agostini's Formula." *Journal of Advertising Research*, 3, no. 1 (March 1963): 13–20.
7. Claycamp, Henry J., and McClelland, C. W. "On Methods: Estimating

Reach and the Magic K." *Journal of Advertising Research* 8, no. 2 (June 1968): 44–51.

8. Cooley, William W., and Lohnes, Paul R. *Multivariate Procedure for the Behavioral Sciences.* New York: John Wiley & Sons, 1962.

9. Fox, Bennett. "Discrete Optimization via Marginal Analysis." *Management Science* 13, no. 3 (November 1966): 210–16.

10. Frank, Ronald E. "Market Segmentation Research: Findings and Implications." In *The Application of the Sciences to Marketing Management,* edited by Frank M. Bass, Charles W. King, and Edgar A. Pessemier. New York: John Wiley & Sons, 1968.

11. Frank, Ronald E., and Green, Paul E. "Numerical Taxonomy in Marketing Analysis." Working paper, presented at the Consumer Behavior Conference, Graduate School of Business, Columbia University, May 18–19, 1967.

12. Harman, Harry D. *Modern Factor Analysis.* Chicago: University of Chicago Press, 1960.

13. Little, John D. C., and Lodish, Leonard M. "A Media Selection Model and Its Optimization by Dynamic Programming." *Industrial Management Review* 8, no. 1 (Fall 1966): 15–24.

14. Lorr, Maurice, Bishop, Patricia F., and McNair, Douglas M. "Interpersonal Types among Psychiatric Patients." *Journal of Abnormal Psychology* 70, no. 6 (December 1965): 468–72.

15. Lucas, Darrell B., and Britt, Stuart H. *Measuring Advertising Effectiveness.* New York: McGraw-Hill Book Co., 1963.

16. Marder, Eric. "How Good Is the Editorial-Interest Method of Measuring Magazine Audiences." *Journal of Advertising Research* 7, no. 1 (March 1967): 2–6.

17. McGlathery, Donald G. "Claimed Frequency vs. Editorial-Interest Measures of Repeat Magazine Audiences." *Journal of Advertising Research* 7, no. 1 (March 1967): 7–15.

18. Pessemier, Edgar A., and Tigert, Douglas J. "Personality, Activity and Attitude Predictors of Consumer Behavior," *New Ideas for Successful Marketing.* Proceedings of the 1966 World Marketing Congress, American Marketing Association, pp. 332–47.

19. Pessemier, Edgar A., Teach, Richard and Tigert, Douglas J. *The Consumer Behavior Research Project.* Krannert Graduate School of Industrial Administration, Purdue University, August 1, 1965.

20. Bo Wilson Schyberger, "A Case against Direct Questions on Reading Habits." *Journal of Advertising Research* 6, no. 4 (December 1966): 25–29.

21. Tigert, Douglas J. "Consumer Typologies and Market Behavior." Doctoral thesis, Purdue University, August 1966.

C. Segmentation in Pricing Decisions

20.

Market Segmentation and the Effectiveness of a Brand's Price and Dealing Policies

Ronald E. Frank
William F. Massy

The marketing program of many firms is predicated on the assumption that their customers are heterogeneous with respect to purchasing habits. This assumption is often supported by data reporting that certain segments of customers buy more of a product than others. These customer segments are usually classified in terms of socioeconomic status, life cycle, location, and/or personality characteristics. The authors show that this simple view of market segmentation is not sufficient to provide an effective guide for management decisions. They advance a more precise conceptual framework for the evaluation of market segmentation as a strategy, based on estimates of the demand elasticities of individual market segments. In addition, they present the results of a research project aimed at estimating elasticities with respect to price and dealing activities for selected market segments for a frequently purchased food product. *Their work represents an attempt to make the concept of market segmentation more operational and managerially meaningful.*

INTRODUCTION

The strategy of market segmentation is defined as the development and pursuit of different marketing programs by the same firm and for essentially the same product but for different components of the over-all market.

The choice of segmentation as a strategy is predicated on the assumption that the market for a particular product is composed of segments of customers with somewhat different needs and wants. If these segments can be

From Ronald B. Frank and William F. Massy, "Market Segmentation and the Effectiveness of a Brand's Price and Dealing Policy," *Journal of Business.* Vol. 38 (April 1965), pp. 186–200. Copyright 1960 by the University of Chicago. Reprinted by permission.

identified, then it may be possible to develop a marketing program for each that corresponds to its requirements. For example, if a manufacturer knew that one identifiable group of his customers was more responsive to price changes than others, he might find it advantageous to charge them a different price. The same sort of tailoring might also be appropriate if it was found that customers reacted differently to changes in national advertising, packaging, product quality, etc.

The following are two of the most important and difficult decision problems that face marketing management: (1) Should the firm pursue a strategy of market segmentation? (2) Given that the market is to be segmented, upon what basis should it be divided?

It is normal to answer the first question in the affirmative if it can be shown that, on the average, certain groups of people buy more of the product under consideration than do other groups. These customer groups are usually classified in terms of socioeconomic, life cycle, or locational characteristics, although other dimensions such as personality variables may also be used. Groups for which the average purchase rate is high are identified as "target" market segments.

We shall see, however, that this simple view of market segmentation is not sufficient to provide an effective guide for management decisions. The next section of this paper will put forward a more precise conceptual framework for market segmentation. The subsequent sections report the results of an empirical research project designed to provide part of the information that would be required for a specific segmentation decision problem.

A Criterion for Segmentation

Management needs a criterion for determining the extent to which segmenting its market will place it in a more beneficial position than treating the market as a homogeneous entity. What should this criterion be? Presumably a firm desires to achieve increased profits via segmentation. Under what conditions can these be obtained?

If the incremental costs of serving different customers in a market are the same, then there is only one condition under which a firm can achieve greater profitability via market segmentation: Different groups of customers must have different responses to changes in the firm's marketing program. Consider, for example, a market in which some customers are very likely to switch brands in response to a cut in price while others are more sensitive to changes in national advertising. If one could identify these groups of customers and find a way to reach them separately, greater profits could probably be achieved by charging somewhat different prices and aiming different levels of advertising at each group.

This idea can be restated as follows: "In the language of economics, segmentation is *disaggregative* in its effects and tends to bring about recognition of several demand schedules where only one was recognized before."[1] A demand schedule is simply an expression for the quantity of a product that is demanded at each of the number of different price or promotional levels.

Suppose, for example, that a firm is spending the same amount of promotional funds on all its customers. Suppose further that it is trying to sell as much output as possible, given its promotional budget. An increase in promotional expenditures is contemplated. Should it extend the offer to all of its customers? If management knew that a particular, identifiable group of customers (a market segment) would increase its expenditures on the product by $10 per unit sold, whereas other customers would tend to increase their total expenditures by only $5 per unit, it clearly would be better off if it cut its prices to the first group, thereby selling an increased proportion of its output to that segment. This would continue until the incremental revenue associated with the sale of an additional unit was the same for the two groups. This is a well-recognized principal in the field of economics.

In other words, one crucial criterion for determining the desirability of segmenting a market along any particular dimension is whether or not the different submarkets have different elasticities with respect to the price and promotional policies of a firm.[2] An elasticity is simply a summary measure that relates a percentage change in quantity demanded to the associated percentage change in some causal variable such as price.

Where there are differences in the incremental costs involved in serving customers in the different submarkets, these cost differences should be matched against the effects of price and promotion upon demand in order to arrive at a criterion for judging the desirability of market segmentation. The treatment of costs in market segmentation is beyond the scope of this paper; the important point for our purposes is that, whether costs are equal or not, the degree to which the demand elasticities in the various submarkets are different from one another remains a crucial criterion for market segmentation.[3]

---

[1] Wendell R. Smith, "Product Differentiation and Market Segmentation as Alternative Marketing Strategies," *Journal of Marketing*, XXI, No. 1 (July 1956), 5.

[2] For a more detailed statement of the logic underlying this point see Joan Robinson, *The Economics of Imperfect Competition* (London: Macmillan & Co., 1954), pp. 179–88, and Kenneth E. Boulding, *Economic Analysis* (New York: Harper & Bros., 1955), pp. 608–15.

[3] For a discussion of the relationship between costs and promotional sensitivities see William J. Baumol and Charles H. Sevin, "Marketing Costs and Mathematical Programming," *Harvard Business Review* (September–October 1957).

Concept and Research: A Gap

In spite of the clear need for information about the demand elasticities of various submarkets, existing published research contains little information on this point.

Most studies provide data on the average purchases of different groups of customers. As previously stated, analysis is often based on the classification of customers by socioeconomic status, life cycle, location, and/or personality characteristics. For example, Martineau, in a discussion of social class, couches his evaluation of its usefulness for segmenting a market in terms of the fact that different classes have different levels of demand for appliances.[4] Similarly, Gottlieb argues that personality characteristics are an important basis for segmenting the market for a proprietary drug product, because customers with different personality scores tend to have different average levels of consumption.[5]

While these results are interesting and useful, our previous discussion has shown that measures of the *level* of consumption for a given submarket are not the crucial criteria for determining whether or not the market can be segmented fruitfully. What management needs to know is whether or not customers belonging to the upper class have a different set of price and promotional elasticities for the firm's products than do customers in the lower class, or whether customers with a dominant personality tend to have different elasticities than those with a different personality profile.

If the average consumption level for a market segment was almost always highly correlated with its price or promotional elasticities, then data such as that presented by Martineau and Gottlieb would have a much more immediate bearing on the problem of choosing the best basis to use for segmenting a market. Unfortunately, in most situations management has no information on the actual degree of correlation between measures of *level* and *elasticity* of demand. In fact, given their definitions, there is no reason that they should be correlated.

The Study

If the understanding and use of the concept of market segmentation are to be advanced, then what is needed is a system for developing estimates of the demand elasticities for particular submarkets facing an individual firm. The research system must be flexible so that one can examine results for a number of alternative bases for market segmentation. To paraphrase

[4] Pierre Martineau, "Social Classes and Spending Behavior," *Journal of Marketing*, XXIII, No. 2 (October, 1958), 126.

[5] Morris J. Gottlieb, "Segmentation by Personality Types," in Lynn H. Stockman (ed.), *Advancing Marketing Efficiency* (Chicago: American Marketing Association, 1958), pp. 148–58.

Yankelovich, it is seldom, if ever, safe to assume in advance that one knows the best way of looking at a market. Given our present state of ignorance, it is often desirable to consider many alternative bases for segmenting a market and then to choose the one that has the most important implications for action.[6]

We hope that the study to be reported here will provide a step forward toward making the concept of market segmentation operational and managerially meaningful.

The study represents an attempt (1) to build a model for estimating elasticities of price and dealing activities with respect to the market share of a firm in a frequently purchased food product market, and (2) to estimate these elasticities for selected market segments and test for the statistical significance of the differences among the segments. Estimates are made for both the current and carry-over effects of price and dealing activity. The first of these purposes is particularly important because of the general uncertainty about the nature of market responsiveness to dealing activity. The latter objective represents an attempt to demonstrate empirically a technique for measuring the differential responsiveness of different market segments.[7]

The next section contains a description of the data base for the study. This is followed by a delineation of the potential market segments for which analysis has been attempted. Next is a brief statement of the model, which is followed by a section reporting the current and carryover effects of price and dealing activity for the entire market. This is followed by a section that reports results for each market segment. The article concludes with a discussion of plans for future research.

The Data

Our analysis is based on data generated from 101 consecutive weeks of purchasing history, taken with respect to a single product class, for families who are members of the Market Research Corporation of America's Consumer Panel in a particular metropolitan area.

The data base for the investigation consisted of a record for each purchase in the product class under study as reported by each household in the panel during the relevant time period. Each purchase record included the household's code number, the date of purchase, the brand, the number of units, the

---

[6] Daniel Yankelovich, "New Criteria for Market Segmentation," *Harvard Business Review*, XLII, No. 2 (March–April, 1964), 89–90.

[7] For additional findings from this study, together with a technical treatment of the methods employed, see William F. Massy's and Ronald E. Frank's, "A Single Equation Model for Estimating Short Term Price and Dealing Effects in Selected Market Segments for a Frequently Purchased Consumer Product" (Research Report No. 5, Graduate School of Business, Stanford University, April, 1964), which is available from the authors upon request.

package size, the price paid, the store where purchased, and the type of deal involved, if any. As used in the panel, the deal measure is defined to include any special arrangement whereby the customer receives a price discount from merchandise at point of sale for the product. Two-for-one sales, special retail price cuts, and premiums made good by the grocer would be classified as deals, for example.

The Potential Segments

An overview of the potential market segments, for which analysis has been attempted, is presented in Figure 20–1. A set of weekly time series over the 101-week period, for each variable included in the analysis, was generated for each segment by means of a 7090 FORTRAN computer-programming system especially developed by the authors for the purpose. Three dimensions were studied:

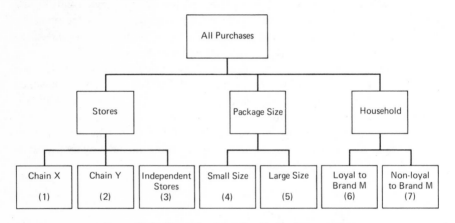

Figure 20–1. Alternative Bases for Market Segmentation

1. *Segmentation based on the type of retail institution in which the purchase was made (segments 1, 2, and 3).* All purchases made in chain store X were used as the basis for generating a weekly time series of the market share for Brand M (the code name of the brand used for illustrative purposes) and the relevant price and dealing information for that brand and its competitors. Similar time series were created for store-type Y and for the "Independent" store category, which consists primarily of smaller chains and independents. As shall be shown, dividing the data in this fashion permits one to develop separately for each store segment estimates of the price and dealing elasticities with respect to market share.

2. *Segmentation based on package sizes (segments 4 and 5).* This same procedure was used to create separate time series for the large and small package-size markets.

3. *Segments based on purchasing characteristics (segments 6 and 7).* Loyal customers were defined as those for whom Brand M was their favorite (the brand with the highest frequency of purchase during the period), while non-loyals were those for whom Brand M was not a favorite. The loyal versus non-loyal division is not based on entirely separate sets of data. Separate weekly market-share figures were generated for each of these groups, but the data were combined in order to arrive at a series for price and dealing activities. This procedure was based on the following assumption: Customers in each group might respond differently to changes in price and dealing activity, but the price and dealing opportunities in the over-all market, for a given store or for a given package size, would be the same for both types of customers.

Our analysis is concerned with whether or not different market segments, defined alternatively in terms of store environments, package sizes, and family characteristics, respond differently to the price and dealing activities of Firm M and its competitors. Cross-classification of the package-size loyalty and store-type segments was also attempted, but while the results were suggestive, the amount of data available was too small to permit unambiguous conclusions to be obtained.

The Model

The underlying model used as the basis for determining the extent and timing of the effects of price and dealing activity on market share evolved gradually as our thinking progressed. Over a period of two and one-half months, changes in the formulation of the problem led to the estimation of over five hundred multiple-regression equations. This number covers every equation used for the purpose of estimating the price and deal effects for each of the three bases for market segmentation; many of them differed from one another only to the extent that a variable or two was added or dropped. The ability to explore alternative-model formulations helped us to close in on the specification that best combined a priori plausability and empirical fit. The "final" regression model is given by

$$\log B_{M,\,t} = a + b_1 \log P^R_{M,\,t} + b_2 \log P^R_{M,\,t-1}$$
$$+ b_3 \log P^R_{M,\,t-2} + b_4 \log D^R_{M,\,t}$$
$$+ b_5 \log D^R_{M,\,t-1} + b_6 \log D^R_{M,\,t-2}$$
$$+ b_7 \log C_{M,\,t} + b_8 \log E_{M,\,t}$$
$$+ b_9 \log E_{M,\,t-1} + b_{10} \log b_{M,\,t-1}.$$

Before discussing the variable definitions, a note on the use of logarithms is in order. Economists have used log linear models in their empirical analyses of consumer demand for many years, and their reasons are applicable to the present study. The coefficients (b_1, b_2, etc.) in a logarithmic regression equation have a natural and extremely useful interpretation: b_1 equals the percentage change in the dependent variable associated with a 1 per cent change in the ith independent variable. In fact, the coefficients are the dimensionless quantities called *elasticities* that were discussed earlier. They are especially useful where regressions involving different average levels of demand, price, or other variables are to be compared, as is the case for the market-segmentaton analysis presented in this study.

The variables in the equation are defined as follows:[8]

$B_{M,\,t}$ = The market share of Brand M in week t;

$P_{M,\,t}^{R}$ = The average price of Brand M relative to a weighted average of the prices of competing brands in week t;

$P_{M,\,t-1}^{R}$ = Same as $P_{M,\,t}^{R}$ except for $t - 1$;

$P_{M,\,t-2}^{R}$ = Same as $P_{M,\,t}^{R}$ except for $t - 2$;

$D_{M,\,t}^{R}$ = The average price reduction associated with deals for Brand M relative to a weighted average of the price reductions associated with deals for competing brands in week t;

$D_{M,\,t-1}^{R}$ = Same as $D_{M,\,t}^{R}$ except for $t - 1$;

$D_{M,\,t-2}^{R}$ = Same as $D_{M,\,t}^{R}$ except for $t - 2$;

$C_{M,\,t}$ = The proportion of Brand M's purchases that were reported as made on a deal in week t;

$E_{M,\,t}$ = The expected share based on the distribution of loyal customers entering the market in week t;

$E_{M,\,t-1}$ = Same as $E_{M,\,t}$ except for $t - 1$;

$B_{M,\,t-1}$ = The market share of Brand M in week $t - 1$.

Effects of Price and Dealing Activity on Market Share

We have chosen to present the market's response in terms of the expected change in market share that would be associated with a hypothetical 1 per cent decrease in Brand M's price or a 1 per cent increase in the degree of its dealing activity, relative to competitive prices and levels of dealing activity. This has been done in order to obviate comparisons of the economic consequences of a change in price or in dealing activity and, at the same time, to reveal differences in sensitivities.

---

[8] For a detailed discussion of the operational definitions and rationales underlying each variable, see Appendix 1 [at end of article].

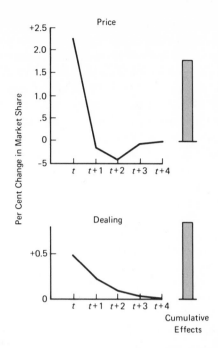

**Figure 20–2. Effect of a 1 Per Cent Change in Price and Dealing
Magnitudes on Market Share**

Figure 20–2 shows that a price change results in an immediate sharp increase in weekly market share over and above its long-run average (0 on the
scale), but that, in the four following weeks, market share is associated with
below-average demand.[9] The long-run effects, shown by the bars to the right,
are a simple summation of the effects as estimated for the weeks shown in the
figure.

According to Figure 20–2, (1) a price change has its greatest impact during the same period in which it was made; (2) in subsequent periods the
price change leads to *negative* offsets in share; (3) dealing activity tends to
have both an immediate *positive* effect as well as a cumulative *positive* effect
in subsequent periods (additional analysis also revealed that the effects of
both variables tend to become unimportant after the third or fourth week
following the change); (4) the relative ability of a price change to modify
market share decreases, therefore, as one takes carry-over effects into
account.

[9] The raw elasticity coefficients, which represent the percentage change in market share
associated with a 1 per cent change in the independent variables, are presented in Appendix 2. The elasticity of B_{t-1} can be used to trace the carry-over effects of price and dealing to weeks beyond those specifically included in the equation. The method is decribed in
the Massy-Frank reference cited in n. 7.

Comparisons of the effects of price and dealing activity cannot be made without further information as to the extent and effect of deal coverage in the market segment. This information is normally available as a by-product of the analysis. This is true of all the results reported in this article.

Any attempts by management to evaluate the profitability of a change in price or dealing activity that are based only on market responses in the current period will be biased, but the biases will be in the opposite direction for price and deals. The consequences of a price change will tend to be overstated, while those of a deal change would tend to be understated.

The differences in the time pattern of the effect described in points (2) and (3) above is consistent with the following assumptions as to customer behavior. An increase in dealing activity is apt to be regarded both as temporary and as having a higher probability than a decrease in price of being repeated in the future. Customers may come to expect that deals will be repeated with regularity, whereas real excitement may be generated by a cut in the "normal" shelf price. There may be some reason to believe that consumers do more "stocking up" upon seeing an unusually low shelf price than is the case for deals. Stocking up is, in effect, a transfer of demand in time so that, while the market share in the current period is unusually high, it partly represents sales borrowed from the future. This idea is consistent with the observed negative carry-over effects reported in Figure 20–2.

Retailers and national manufacturers are apt to respond in the same fashion as are customers. Dealing is a normal practice and thus leads to little, if any, extraordinary modification of retailer or competitive pricing policies, but a shelf-price change seems quite likely to induce immediate price adjustments on the part of other stores and for other brands. Two possible patterns of reaction of retailers and national manufacturers are: (1) a shelf-price decrease for Brand M in a given group of stores may lead to a similar reduction on the part of competitive stores in subsequent weeks; (2) a decrease in M's price may lead to cuts in the prices for other brands in the same or other stores.

If the first of these hypotheses is correct, then one would expect the subsequent price decreases to lead to positive carry-over effects, whereas if the second alternative holds, then negative offsets should occur. Our results support this second hypothesis. The evidence indicates that competitive retaliation is a more important phenomenon than price leadership among stores, at least with respect to the given brand in the market under study. This seems to be a reasonable conclusion, considering the fact that private brands are of some importance in the market. Stores might be expected to retaliate against a competitive price cut on Brand M by reducing the price of their own private brand. Price retaliation thus negates some of the favorable effects of a shelf-price decrease.

Elasticities by Market Segments

The objective of segmentation is to divide purchases on some basis that would make differences in price and promotional elasticities among the groups be relatively large. The discussion to follow analyzes the differences in price and dealing elasticities among the sets of stores, households with different purchasing characteristics, and package sizes given in Figure 20–2.

Store segments. There are a number of factors that might tend to generate differences in price and dealing sensitivities from one supermarket chain to another or between chains and independents. They include (1) differences in the number and quality of competing brands; (2) differences in the price and promotional policies of different groups of stores; (3) differences in the customer populations that tend to shop in different stores.

Three groups of stores were chosen for inclusion in the analysis: two major chains (called X and Y) and a category consisting of smaller chains and independents. The third category did not include data on a number of other major chains, to which the analysis may be extended in the future.

Figure 20–3 presents the response pattern for a 1 per cent decrease in relative price and a 1 per cent increase in relative dealing activity for each of the three groups of stores. There is a gross difference between the response patterns for price changes in the independents and the two chains. The carry-over effects of price on the market share tend to be positive for independents, whereas those for the chains are negative. Looking only at the current price effects will tend to understate the sensitivity of the independents relative to that for the other chains.

The observed differences in price sensitivity are consistent with the following rationale. The major chains have private brands of their own, whereas the independents and the smaller chains either do not have them or else have privates, which account for only a very small share of the product's sales in their respective stores. Chains, therefore, tend to react faster to a change of price of a national brand than do independents. In addition, the impact of chain's response tends to be felt at once, because often one individual or a closely knit group of individuals makes the decision to cut price for all stores in the chain; in the case of the independents there are many more decision-makers, some of whom wait longer than others before responding.

The fact that a price cut is associated with a long-run loss in market share for the chains probably means that the combined effect of stocking up by customers and competitive retaliation more than offset any short-run gains in market share. At first glance this result may seem somewhat peculiar, especially if one thinks in terms of the usually theoretical demand schedule where the quantity demanded is higher at lower prices. However, this theoretical model assumes that such things as stocking up and competitive retaliation are held constant, whereas they are not in the case of these results and, therefore, can cause a reversal in the direction of the effect from what one might initially expect.

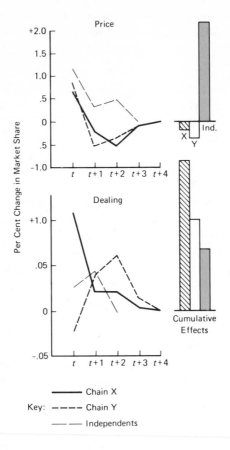

Figure 20–3. Effect of a 1 Per Cent Change in Price and Dealing Magnitudes on Market Share by Store Segments

The response to dealing activity does not form as clear-cut or as consistent a pattern as is the case for pricing. Chain store Y appears to have little sensitivity to dealing at time t but shows relatively large carry-over effects, whereas chain X exhibits the opposite pattern. This lack of consistency in the dealing-response patterns suggests that the small differences in long-run effects should not be taken too seriously.

The regression coefficients the table was based on were subjected to the multivariate statistical test for the significance of differences between regression equations generated by separate samples.[10] The F ratio calculated from the test was 5.68 as compared to the critical value of 2.32 at the 99 per cent confidence level for 11 and 270 degrees of freedom. Therefore, we may conclude that the observed differences among stores are statistically significant.

Purchasing characteristic segments. "Loyal" households would be expected to be less sensitive to changes in the relative price of Brand M than would households who rely on M for a smaller portion of their total purchases. Hypotheses with respect to the differential response to dealing activity are not as obvious. On the one hand, loyal families may be most aware of deal offers for the favorite brand and, therefore, tend to respond to a greater degree than non-loyal families. Conversely, non-loyal families may seek variety through the purchase of brands other than their favorite, but they may be willing to satisfy this desire only under special conditions, such as a deal. A second factor that would appear to make non-loyal families appear more sensitive to a deal than loyal families is that manufacturers tend to tailor their promotional programs to this group.

Figure 20–4 shows that non-loyal households tend to have a greater reaction to a change in price than do loyal households. Both the current and carry-over effects are more extreme. The differences in the time pattern of effects suggest that loyal households tend to do less stocking up than non-loyal households and, in this sense, are less responsive.

The time patterns of dealing response reveal less striking differences, although the cumulative effect is greater for the non-loyal households. This is consistent with the second set of hypotheses discussed above.

Though the direction and nature of these findings seem reasonable, given their context, the results were not statistically significant. The F ratio was 0.15 with 11 and 180 degrees of freedom, whereas the critical value for the 95 per cent confidence level is 1.8.

Product characteristic segments. There is some reason to believe that differences in price and dealing sensitivity are apt to exist between small- and large-size containers for the product under study. There is considerably more competitive activity with respect to the large-size market, for example. In addition, preliminary analysis of the socioeconomic characteristics of the panel members suggests that families who usually purchase smaller packages tend to have lower incomes, lower occupational status, and (other things being equal) have more younger children.

[10] For a discussion of the specific test used see J. Johnson, *Econometric Methods* (New York: McGraw-Hill Book Co., 1963), p. 136.

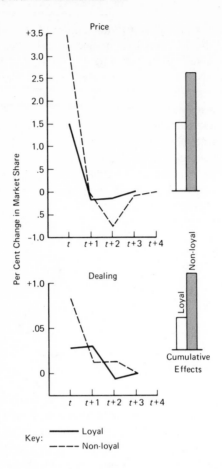

**Figure 20–4. Effect of a 1 Per Cent Change in Price and Dealing
Magnitudes on Market Share by Family Segments**

An attempt was made to develop separate elasticity estimates for the large and small package-size segments. While good results were obtained for the former, the response pattern for the small-package segment (for which our data are quite thin) was unsatisfactory. The signs of the coefficients for all of the price variables were contrary to expectation, and even after careful checking of the data and the underlying model we are unable to account for this result. The evidence does tentatively suggest that the long-run effect of deals is somewhat larger for small than for large containers.

Further analysis with additional data (mentioned in the following section) will be performed in order to obtain a better insight into the price and deal sensitivities and of segments based on package size.

PLANS FOR ADDITIONAL RESEARCH

The results reported in this article represent the first stage of one part of a large-scale research project on brand choice being conducted at Stanford University. The portion of the project represented here embraces a number of studies being conducted both by the authors and by doctoral candidates at the Graduate School of Business.

The next stage of our work will consist of breaking down our present model into two major components:

1. *A consumer demand model*, which will consist of submodels aimed at predicting brand choice and the purchase-timing of customers with varying degrees of loyalty to Brand M. These relationships would take the price and dealing activity at the retailer level as independent variables, as we have done in our present analysis. If possible, we shall also include the effects of short-term relative advertising expenditures (such as newspaper and spot radio commercials). The purchase-timing model will probably include the timing and quantity of the last purchase (or sequence of purchases) as explanatory variables.

2. *A retail behavior model* aimed at predicting retail price and advertising activity, given such things as manufacturer's prices, discount structures, advertising, and retail inventory level. The output of this model would serve as inputs to the consumer model.

APPENDIX 1

Variable Definitions

PRICING VARIABLES

$P_{M, t}^{R}$ is defined as the price of Brand M at time t (the current week) relative to the average price of competing brands, based on purchases not involving deals. Purchases involving deals were omitted from this index in order to permit separate estimates of the effect of changes in shelf price and dealing activities. (See the definition of the variable $D_{M, t}^{R}$.) The index is calculated by the following formula:

$$P_{M, t}^{R} = \frac{\bar{P}_{M, t}}{\sum_{j \neq M} w_j \bar{P}_{j, t}}.$$

The numerator of this index is the average price per unit for Brand M at time t. The denominator is a weighted average of the current average prices per unit of all brands except the Mth brand. The jth brand average price is given a weight (W_j), which is equal to the magnitude of its market share for the sample period relative to the shares of the other brands

$$(\sum_j W_j = 1.0).$$

If explicit weights had not been used, then each brand's price would have been of equal importance in determining the magnitude of the denominator of the price ratio. Since the brand with the smallest market share should not be allowed to affect the price index to the same extent as the brand with the highest share, we have used the convention of weighting the weekly average price by the brand's average market share. The same weights are used when calculating the index for each week, so only the raw prices are free to vary. Thus the weighting system has a further advantage: Changes in $P_{M,t}^R$ using this system reflect changes in price alone, whereas if the weights used were based on a shorter time period (such as a week) one could not be sure whether the change in $P_{M,t}^R$ from one week to the next was due to a change in price, a change in market share, or both. If the weights were based on weekly market shares, this would automatically build in a negative relationship between $P_{M,t}^R$ and $B_{M,t}$. This "accounting" relationship might then obscure the nature of any real underlying relationship between the variables.

$P_{M,t-1}^R$ and $P_{M,t-2}^R$ are the price relatives for the two weeks prior to time t. They make it possible to estimate the "longer-run" effects of a price change.[11] In this context, "long run" refers to the next two weeks as opposed to the current week. The coefficient of $P_{M,t-1}^R$, which is b_2, expresses the relation between it and $B_{M,t}$, given that the other variables are held at their average levels. It measures the effect of a brand's current price on its market share in the following week. The cumulative effect of any change in price is therefore given by the sum of the effects observed immediately and during each week subsequent to the event. Of course, there is no need for the cumulative, or "long-run," elasticity to equal its immediate, or "short-run," value.

DEALING VARIABLES

$D_{M,t}^R$ is a measure of the relative degree of dealing activity for Brand M versus competing brands. The dealing index is calculated in the same manner as the price index.

---

[11] The inclusion of these variables serves a function directly analogous to the function of a switch-over design in the field of experimentation. E.g., see R. J. Jessen, "A Switch-over Experimental Design to Measure Advertising Effect," *Journal of Advertising Research,* I, No. 3 (March, 1961), 15–22.

$$D_{M,t}^{R} = \frac{\overline{P}_{M,t} - \overline{P}\,\overline{D}_{M,t}}{\sum_{j \neq M} W_j(\overline{P}_{j,t} - \overline{P}\,\overline{D}_{j,t})},$$

where $\overline{P}_{M,t}$ is the average price per unit based on non-deal purchases at time t and where $\overline{PD}_{M,t}$ is the current average price based on deal purchases taken by themselves. The differences between these two numbers is, thus, a measure of the average size of the deals offered by Brand M. Therefore, $D_{M,t}^{R}$ represents the magnitude of Brand M's deal-offering relative to those of other brands.

The quantity $(P_{M,t} - PD_{M,t})$ probably underestimates the true average deal magnitude because of the likelihood that customers will forget to report the existence of deals or perhaps will not recognize their existence at all. This is more apt to occur than for consumers to "see" deals where none are present. If the incidence of the error is about the same for all brands in the market, however, the bias will tend to cancel out in the indexing process, making $D_{M,t}^{R}$ a valid measure of relative dealing activity. We adopted this assumption in the absence of any evidence to the contrary.

$D_{M,t-1}^{R}$ and $D_{M,t-2}^{R}$ serve the same purpose as do the lagged price variables. Differences between the short- and long-run effects are as likely for deals as for pricing activities.

$C_{M,t}$ represents the proportion of Brand M's purchases that were reported as having involved a deal. It can be looked upon as a proxy measure for the proportion of customers who were exposed to the deal. The more stores that carry a deal and/or the more customers that receive a coupon, the higher should be the percentage of Brand M's purchases that are associated with a deal, conditional on the magnitude of Brand M's deal relative to its competition (as well as on the magnitude of the other variables in the equation).

MARKET SHARE VARIABLES

$B_{M,t}$ is the market share for the Brand M at time t. It is the dependent variable in the analysis.

$E_{M,t}$ is called "expected market share." To understand its definition and the rationale for including it in the equation, we must consider again the objectives of this investigation. We are trying to make inferences about the effects of a brand's price and dealing policies by looking at the degree to which variation in these policies is associated with changes in market share. One of the basic assumptions in our analysis is that changes in share reflect changes in the desire of customers to buy the various brands during the week in question. Changes in share that are the result of other factors may distort our measures of price and deal effectiveness. The expected market-share variable was conceived in order to guard against this difficulty.

Assume that each family represented in the panel had a constant probability of buying Brand M and that this probability could be estimated by calculating the family's share of purchases for M over the entire sample period. If a given family's loyalty is high, the over-all market share obtained from the panel as a whole in a given week would tend to be higher if that family bought during that week than if it did not. If families enter the market in response to factors besides relative-price and deal levels, our effectiveness measures might be biased if we did not take explicit account of the phenomenon. $E_{M, t}$ is a proxy variable that masks all the factors that cause customers to enter or leave the market. It is defined as the market share for Brand M that would be obtained if all the families that actually bought any brand in week t did so in their "usual" quantities and according to their long-run purchase probabilities and if no one else purchased at all. The expected share $(E_{M, t})$ for Brand M in week t was then a weighted average of the $S_{M, k}$'s for each household that made at least one purchase during the week in question. The household weights (W_k) are defined as the total number of ounces purchased by the kth family during the 101-week period. The formula is as follows:

$$E_{M, t} = \frac{\sum_{k=1}^{N} \delta_{t, k} W_k S_{M, k}}{\sum_{k=1}^{N} \delta_{t, k} W_k},$$

where $\delta_{t, k}$ takes on the value of 1 if family k made at least one purchase in week t and is zero otherwise.

Figure 20–5 presents the weekly actual market share for Brand M and the expected share for the same brand given all purchases for all families. Twenty-two per cent of the total week-to-week variation in the actual share is associated with variation in the expected share. In other words, a substantial proportion of the week-to-week change in market share for a given brand can be explained by the fact that in some weeks there are proportionately more customers with higher long-run purchase probabilities than in other weeks. The crucial problem from management's standpoint is not to explain variation in market share alone but to explain the degree to which variations in relative price and dealing activity are associated with variation in the observed market share, given the level of the expected share. By including $E_{M, t}$ as a variable, the effects of price and dealing activity are measured independently of expected share and thus reflect the tendency of customers to depart from their long-run purchase probabilities as a function of the competitive behavior of firms in the market place. If this term had been left out of the analysis, these "spurious effects" would have been confounded with the findings reported above.

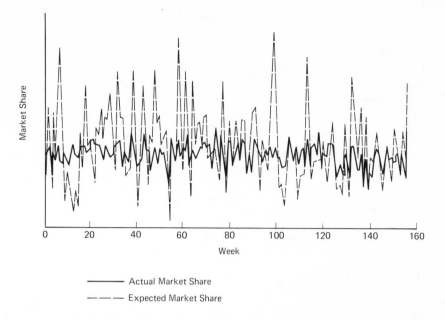

——— Actual Market Share

– – – Expected Market Share

Figure 20–5. Actual and Expected Market Share for Brand M

While the inclusion of $E_{M, t}$ facilitates the measurement of price and dealing effects, it opens up two additional questions: (1) What determines when (what week) customers with varying degrees of loyalty enter the market? (2) What process determines the level of the long-run probabilities for individual households? At present we are engaged in some exploratory work in relation to the first question. To our knowledge there have been no attempts to deal with the second issue. The span of data required for the reporting of household behavior is greater than that available from most sources, although a few panels are in a position to provide such information.

$E_{M, t-1}$ serves a function similar to that for the lagged-price and dealing-activity variables. At the start of our investigation we knew that most families tended to purchase the product on an average of less than once a week. If a family were in the market at time of t it would tend not to be in at $t - 1$. If there were a disproportionate number of highly loyal families in week $t - 1$, then one would expect the opposite to be true in week t. In other words, knowing lagged expected share for $t - 1$, one can explain even more of the variation in market share on the basis of the combined assumptions that the purchase probability for each household is constant; that the percentage of loyal families varies from week to week (as assumed when we introduced $E_{M, t}$); and that this variation is, to some extent, systematic.

$B_{M, t-1}$ and its coefficient b_{10} serve a special purpose. Our equation explicitly provides for estimating the carry-over effects of price and dealing activity for a three-week period. But what happens four weeks after a price change? Does the effect of that change go to zero after the third week? It does not seem reasonable to assume that there would be such a discontinuity in customer behavior. What we have assumed is that carry-over effects for price and dealing activity that operate beyond the third week decline to zero at a constant rate, starting from their level at that point. The coefficient of lagged market share provides an estimate of the rate of decline.[12]

[12] See Robert Ferber and T. J. Verdoorn, *Research Methods in Economics and Business* (New York: Macmillan Co., 1962), pp. 344–49.

APPENDIX 2

Regression Coefficients and *t* Ratios for Seven Main Market Segments*

	Over-all Market	Distribution Segments			Product Segments		Family Segments	
		Chain X	Ind.	Chain Y	Small	Large	Loyal	Non-loyal
P_t	−2.369	− .732	−1.223	− .835	.564	− .069	−1.620	−3.351
	(5.64)	(1.16)	(4.13)	(0.87)	(8.49)	(0.91)	(3.64)	(2.44)
P_{t-1}	.437	.306	− .329	.702	− .049	.148	.201	.091
	(0.93)	(0.53)	(1.03)	(0.75)	(0.54)	(2.05)	(0.45)	(0.07)
P_{t-2}	.434	.495	− .449	.276	.080	− .132	.162	.744
	(1.10)	(0.88)	(1.60)	(0.30)	(1.21)	(2.55)	(0.41)	(0.61)
D_t	.048	.113	.024	− .020	.048	− .003	.026	.085
	(2.48)	(2.82)	(1.13)	(0.26)	(1.61)	(0.17)	(1.22)	(1.26)
D_{t-1}	.022	.003	.042	.045	.015	.031	.029	.012
	(1.14)	(0.065)	(2.11)	(0.73)	(0.75)	(1.75)	(1.52)	(0.20)
D_{t-2}	.004	.018	− .002	.052	.042	.022	− .006	.014
	(0.21)	(0.55)	(0.10)	(0.86)	(2.12)	(1.20)	(0.29)	(0.23)
C_t	.027	.132	.115	.244	.008	.075	.046	.003
	(0.94)	(3.00)	(4.04)	(3.31)	(0.21)	(2.28)	(1.49)	(0.03)
E_t	1.014	.801	1.005	1.262	.376	1.261	1.384	1.165
	(5.74)	(4.99)	(6.85)	(6.40)	(3.47)	(7.29)	(3.82)	(2.10)
E_{t-1}	− .257	− .161	− .212	− .413	.206	− .195	− .456	− .591
	(1.23)	(0.91)	(1.23)	(1.80)	(1.76)	(0.89)	(1.02)	(1.17)
B_{t-1}	.124	.164	.057	.227	.031	.097	.174	.003
	(1.17)	(1.51)	(1.58)	(2.30)	(0.31)	(0.99)	(1.63)	(0.51)
R^2†	.59	.50	.57	.51	.58	.48	.40	.15

* Each of the equations presented in this table was tested for serial correlation among the regression residuals using the Durbin-Watson statistic. A value of 2 is expected if there is no serial correction. The actual values for these equations ranged from 1.82 to 2.15 which indicates that relatively little serial correlation is present.

† R^2 is the square of the multiple-correlation coefficient for the regression. It is known as the "coefficient of determination" and represents the proportion of the variation in weekly market share for Brand M that is accounted for by the particular equation.

D. Segmentation in Distribution Decisions

21.

Distribution Breakthroughs

William R. Davidson

Marketing management is often viewed as the task of optimizing the relationship between controllable variables in a firm's marketing mix and the noncontrollable or environmental variables. Among the noncontrollable items commonly accepted as given for a particular planning period are the nature of competition, industry demand, role of government, and the available structure of distributive outlets. In a manufacturing company the marketing effort is likely to be focused strongly upon product, price, advertising, and personal selling, these being the major marketing-mix ingredients that can be most readily adjusted to the state of the environment.

Frequently overlooked is the opportunity to make a breakthrough by applying the concept of marketing vision to distribution channels. While marketing channels are commonly regarded as a variable aspect of the marketing mix of the manufacturer, they often receive less attention than consideration of product, price, and promotion, simply because much of the channel, in the typical case, is "out there" where it is difficult to do much of anything about it, especially in the short run.

Upon reflection, almost any knowledgeable person would agree that the spatial and temporal availability of a product offering has a great deal to do with the profitable exploitation of opportunity. This is essentially the role of the distribution channel, and one too often neglected as higher priority is accorded to more highly variable matters.

Channel decisions are commonly analyzed from the standpoint of a manufacturer, with conventional discussions providing lists of pros and cons of common alternative arrangements. This conventionalism is likely to thwart a visionary approach. It will be apparent in the following discussion that real breakthroughs in distribution are likely to originate with any level of the channel, i.e., they may be the innovation of a retailer, a wholesaler, an agent or broker, as well as a manufacturer.

Since this is an area of much conceptual and semantical confusion, some clarification is in order.

CHANNEL CONCEPTS[1]

The term "channel of distribution" is part of the working vocabulary of every business executive, yet many would be hard pressed to define it. This is not surprising, because a wide variety of interpretations are available in the literature on the subject. The marketing manager should be well aware of the great diversity, for it emphasizes the great need for being very explicit about exactly what is meant in conversations, even with one's close associates.

For example, the channel has been defined by one author as "the pipeline through which a product flows on its way to the consumer. The manufacturer puts his product into the pipeline, or marketing channel, and various marketing people move it along to the consumer at the other end of the channel."[2]

Another authority states, "Marketing channels are the combination of agencies through which the seller, who is often, though not necessarily, the manufacturer, markets his product to the ultimate user."[3]

A third writer views marketing channels as consisting of "intermediary sellers who intervene between the original source of supply and the ultimate consumer." In his view, the number and character of such intermediaries "are determined primarily by the requirements of sorting and by the opportunity to effect economies by suitable sorting arrangements."[4] On another occasion, the same writer described a marketing channel as a group of firms that "constitute a loose coalition engaged in exploiting a joint opportunity in the market."[5]

Another well-known source states that "the trade channel is made up of the middlemen who move goods from producers to consumers" and that

---

[1] Portions of the following discussion have been adapted from material previously published by the author and his associates, especially William R. Davidson, "Channels of Distribution—One Aspect of Marketing Strategy," *Business Horizons,* Special Issue (February 1961), 84 ff; William R. Davidson and Alton F. Doody, *Retailing Management* (New York: Ronald Press Co., 1966), Chapter 2; and Theodore N. Beckman and William R. Davidson, *Marketing* (New York: Ronald Press Co., 8th ed., 1967), Chapter 9.

[2] Richard M. Clewett, "Checking Your Marketing Channels," No. 120 (Washington: U. S. Small Business Administration: *Management Aids for Small Manufacturers,* January 1961).

[3] John A. Howard, *Marketing Management: Analysis and Decision* (Homewood, Ill.: Richard D. Irwin, Inc., 1957), p. 179.

[4] Wroe Alderson, *Marketing Behavior and Executive Action* (Homewood, Ill.: Richard D. Irwin, Inc., 1957), p. 211.

[5] Wroe Alderson, "The Development of Marketing Channels," in Richard M. Clewett, ed., *Marketing Channels for Manufactured Goods* (Homewood, Ill.: Richard D. Irwin, Inc., 1954), p. 30.

"we usually think of the channel as being made up of those merchants who own the goods and of those agent middlemen who effect sales."[6]

In another source, it states that "a trading channel exists once the terms of the franchises or agreements spanning the whole gap from producer to consumer are concluded between concerns assumed to possess the necessary marketing capabilities."[7]

Still another says that "marketing channels are institutional configurations for directing and supporting the flows, from production to use, of things of value."[8]

This variety of viewpoints leads to lack of clarity on several points. Does the channel have to do primarily with the change of ownership of goods or with the physical movement of product? Is the nature of a given channel determined by the manufacturer, acting as a seller, or by middlemen and consumers, carrying out their role as buyers? Is the channel made up only of middlemen or intervening intermediaries, or does it include the manufacturer at one end and the consumer at the other?

THE CHANNEL FOR EXCHANGE

Given some product to be marketed, several jobs must be done. First, there is the question of arrangements for bringing about changes in ownership by performance of the functions of exchange, buying, and selling. Second, there is the logistical task of adjusting the physical supply of a product to the spatial and temporal aspects of demand. This involves the functions of transportation and storage, and related activities such as physical handling and control of inventories. Third, there is the necessity of various facilitating or auxiliary functions, such as the collection and dissemination of marketing information, management of market risks, financing of marketing activities, and standardization and grading.

Generally speaking, the functions of exchange may be considered as paramount because planning for physical supply and performance of facilitating functions do not become relevant in the typical marketing organization unless there is profitable opportunity for transfers of ownership.

It appears, therefore, most realistic to define the channel of distribution as consisting of "the course taken in the transfer of title to a commodity."[9] It is

[6] Paul D. Converse, Harvey W. Huegy, and Robert V. Mitchell, *Elements of Marketing* (Englewood Cliffs, N.J.: Prentice-Hall, Inc., 1958), p. 119.

[7] Ralph F. Breyer, "Some Observations on Structural Formation and the Growth of Marketing Channels," in Reavis Cox et al., eds., *Theory in Marketing*, 2nd Ser. (Homewood, Ill.: Richard D. Irwin, Inc., 1964), p. 164.

[8] F. E. Balderson, "Design of Marketing Channels," in Reavis Cox et al., eds., *op. cit.*, p. 176.

[9] Theodore N. Beckman and William R. Davidson, *Marketing* (New York: Ronald Press Co., 8th ed., 1967), p. 230.

the route taken in transferring the title of a product from its first owner (usually a manufacturer) to its last owner, the business user or ultimate consumer. Such a route necessarily includes both the origin and the destination; hence it should be viewed as including the manufacturer and the ultimate consumer, as well as any intervening middlemen, inasmuch as all three are originators and performers of much marketing activity.

The need for considering the manufacturer as part of the channel is perhaps more obvious than the case for the consumer. In a short or direct channel all of the marketing functions that are performed by any business unit are performed by the manufacturer rather than shifted to middlemen.

Less apparent is the role of the consumer as the initiator and performer of much marketing activity. Under conditions of self-service retailing, for example, the consumer is the active doer of functions such as selecting, transporting, storing, and financing, all of which were common retailing activities prior to self-service, and which are still the ordinary middlemen functions in some channels. Not only are marketing functions often shifted to the consumer, but they also form utility or manufacturing functions in some cases, as attested to by "in factory carton" marketing of many items that require home assembly.

Middlemen in the exchange channel include both merchants, who assume title and resell on their own account, and various kinds of agents or brokers, who do not take title but are nonetheless instrumental along the route taken to effect transfers of ownership. Broadly speaking, an exchange channel can also be viewed as including marketing establishments owned by vertically integrated companies, that is, those performing marketing functions on more than one plane or level of distribution. Examples are chain-store distribution warehouses and manufacturers' branch sales offices. There is no legal transfer of title between a chain-store warehouse and the retail units it serves; however, there are ordinarily intracompany transactions that have the nature of sales or shipments, and which are comparable in nature and accounted for in a manner similar to the transactions made by alternative suppliers or distributors performing similar functions on the same level or plane of distribution.

THE CHANNEL FOR LOGISTICS

The general tendency is for the physical flow of merchandising to accompany the route of exchange. This is not, however, universally the case, and there are indications that separate structural arrangements for logistics or physical distribution are increasingly important. A few examples will illustrate a variety of arrangements for providing logistical support apart from the exchange channel of distribution.

In the field of industrial marketing and in many lines of consumer goods, manufacturers' agents are used in lieu of manufacturers' sales branches. In combining the product lines of several manufacturers, the manufacturer's agent provides economical sales coverage of a given area, and often reaches certain customers who would be difficult to contact by other means. While such agents are links in the channel used to effect transfers of title, they do not ordinarily carry stocks. The physical flow of goods is another arrangement, one that is usually direct from the factory to the customer of the agent.

In the whole trade (as in many other lines of wholesaling), most transactions are handled from warehouse stocks owned and stored by the merchant. A large portion of the total dollar and physical volume of sales consists, however, of so-called "direct" sales. On individual orders of large size, the wholesale merchant buys from the manufacturer and takes title at the point where merchandise is loaded on cars, but the merchandise itself flows directly from factory to customer as a drop shipment, never coming near the establishment where the sale was negotiated.

Several retail mail-order companies have worked out arrangements to establish catalogue-order departments in retail establishments operated by supermarket chains. While the facilities of another retailing organization are used as part of the route through which sales contact is made with the consuming public, the merchandise is shipped directly from the mail-order establishment.

Several food-product companies with factories located in various parts of the country and wide product lines have established gigantic regional food distribution warehouses. Such warehouses consolidate in each region a reservior of all products in the line, permitting fast delivery of mixed cars at low freight rates to wholesalers and chain warehouses. This form of physical distribution tends to be separate from organizational responsibility for sales handled through branch offices or through food brokers, and the geographic flow of merchandise does not correspond to the location of establishments responsible for making sales contacts with customers.

In the appliance industry, some wide-line manufacturers have concentrated a physical supply of various items in the line, either by centralizing all manufacturing facilities or by providing for distribution warehouses. The wholesale distributor remains as the institution making sales contact with the retailer and assumes responsibility for developing the desired share of available market potential in the area of his operation. Many types of dealers at the retail level are able to purchase full cars containing a mixture of various items in the manufacturers' assortment, with the flow of goods direct from factory or manufacturers' warehouse. The retailer still has contact with the wholesaler as the next link in the distribution channel, but in many instances this is related to transfer of title, financing arrangements, and sales-promotion assistance, and has little to do with the physical flow of merchandise.

The last two examples, in particular, reflect a growing tendency to stream-line physical distribution by setting it apart from the complex of channel links used for obtaining sales. In some companies, a new department of logistics or physical distribution combines a number of previously scattered activities, including finished goods inventory control, transportation and traffic warehousing, order processing, container design, and sometimes even manu-facturing scheduling.[10]

While the flow of exchange activity and the flow of physical distribution still tend to coincide in many cases, it is increasingly recognized that this coincidence may be only one of a large number of theoretical possibilities. The concept of separability of exchange and supply activities, in instances of traditional coincidence, may comprise the vision for new breakthroughs.

The exchange channel is primarily concerned with those activities that increase demand and bring about changes of ownership, such as selling, advertising, display, product information, trade and consumer credit, etc.

The flow of logistical services includes those activities having to do with the location, movement, and size of the physical supply of a product, and the adjustment of it to demand.

Contrasted with promotional effort, which involves many personal, psycho-logical, and subjective considerations, logistics can be organized in a more systematic or scientific manner. Some reasons for this are:[11]

1. Personal contact is great, but not inherent, in carrying out logistics activities.
2. Logistics goals often can be more clearly defined than those for promo-tional efforts.
3. Alternative methods to achieve goals are becoming better known.
4. Logistics-systems alternatives lend themselves to quantification and mathematical analysis.
5. Mathematical tools to attack the more complicated logistics-systems prob-lems are becoming available.

Logistical considerations, while sometimes innovative, can also be destruc-tively apathetic. Consider the example of large meat-packing companies that remained married to branch houses located along the railroad tracks long after refrigerated trucks, chain supermarkets, centralized buying, prepackaged items, and new meat products had entirely changed the meat-distribution business.

---

[10] John F. Magee, "The Logistics of Distribution," *Harvard Business Review*, XXXVIII (July–August 1960), 89 ff.; Edward W. Smykay, Donald J. Bowersox, and Frank H. Mossman, *Physical Distribution Management* (New York; The Macmillan Co., 1961).
[11] J. L. Heskett, Robert M. Ivie, and Nicholas A. Glaskowsky, Sr., *Business Logistics* (New York: Ronald Press Co., 1964), p. 9.

STRUCTURE OF DISTRIBUTION

It is important to distinguish the concept of distribution channel from that of distribution structure. A *single* channel of distribution is brought into being when a particular set of exchange relationships is established linking a manufacturer with an ultimate consumer. For example, a single channel would be established when an insecticide manufacturer begins selling to a given hardware wholesaler, thereby establishing consumer contact through the retail stores served by the wholesaler. From the wholesaler's point of view, a single channel is formed by the establishment of trading relationships with any given store. Thus, any one manufacturer may actually be utilizing a large number of specific or single channels, even in one marketing area. This is true in the sense that there are many traceable or separable flows of exchange or ownership.

As indicated above, if the physical flow of product does not accompany the route taken in the transfer of title, there may be many additional specific logistical channels.

The structure of distribution for a product type is composed of all of the networks in use at a given time to connect all of the manufacturers of that product type with all the ultimate consumers or industrial users of that product class. It includes all of the exchange flows and all of the logistical flows when these are separate.

In marketing management, it is often said that the structure of distribution is a given environmental factor. The individual firm may make choices among the various routes or channels that are in the structure. The structure itself, however, is taken as a non-controllable variable.

While this may be a good assumption to make for various short-term practical purposes, it may make one blind to great opportunities that a more visionary approach would unfold. A real breakthrough in some cases is the successful discovery of a route not previously used by any firm in a given industry. Then the new channel arrangement would be new to the entire structure of distribution as well as to the first user of it. Such an innovation, as will be shown by later examples, may originate from visionary approaches taken at any level or plane of distribution, by manufacturers, wholesalers, or retailers.

CHANNEL CONTROL AND CHANNEL "COMMANDERS"

Much recent attention has been given to channel control, by which is meant the ability of one member of a marketing channel for a given product or brand to stipulate marketing policies to other channel members.[12] Chan-

---

[12] Louis W. Stern, "Channel Control and Inter-Organization Management," in Peter D. Bennett, *Marketing and Economic Development* (Chicago: American Marketing Association, 1965), 655 ff.

nel power may be achieved by the use of sheer economic power, political or legal means, superior knowledge, more effective promotional programs, or in other ways. The channel member who is able to use such means to achieve control over the bargaining process with other channel members obviously has a major advantage with respect to all aspects of relationships.

In many discussions of the subject, the manufacturer is cast in the role of "commander" of the channel situation. When introducing a new product or when making a major change in distribution policies, he examines a wide range of possible alternatives with respect to kinds and numbers of wholesale and retail outlets, weighs a number of factors that have a bearing upon sales volume, costs, and profitability, and selects the arrangements that best serve his purpose.

The types of decisions to be made by a manufacturer in choosing a channel may be divided into two classes: *vertical* considerations, which relate to the number of different levels or stages in the route used to effect transfers of title; and *horizontal* considerations, which pertain to the density or selectivity of distribution and the classes and number of outlets on a given plane (for example, wholesale or retail level).

Vertical choices may be illustrated by alternatives of the following kind that might be available to a manufacturer of home furnishings. He could choose (1) to sell direct to the consumer without use of any middlemen, perhaps by means of catalogs; (2) to sell to retail furniture stores by means of a manufacturer-employed sales organization; (3) to sell to furniture stores through wholesale merchants; (4) to sell to wholesale merchants by means of manufacturers' agents who also sell other related lines; (5) to use manufacturers' agents who call directly upon retailer; or (6) to use some combination of the above channels in order to reach different geographic markets or various classes of stores, perhaps differentiated on the basis of sales volume.

Horizontal choices may be illustrated by listing the channels open to a manufacturer of home furnishings who has his own sales organization calling directly upon the retail furniture trade. He must decide whether to (1) continue confining his distribution to retail furniture stores; (2) sell also to furniture departments in regular department stores; (3) offer his merchandise also to variety-department stores operated by certain variety chains that are expanding their merchandise offerings of this general type of merchandise; or (4) sell to various forms of discount houses.

Conventional discussions of channel problems have tended to devote more emphasis to questions of the vertical kind by stressing the factors that determine whether or when it is feasible for the manufacturer to move forward in the channel, assuming within his own organization the functions normally performed by various types of middlemen. He thereby carries his own marketing effort as close as possible to the final user. Among the various factors generally believed to contribute to the feasibility of short channels are a high unit value of product, a wide line of items marketed together, geographically concentrated markets, and financial strength and marketing know-how in the manufacturing company's organization.

In recent years several factors have tended to make decisions of the horizontal type appear as matters of greater decision-making significance. For one thing, various types of retail outlets have greatly diversified their merchandise offerings, thereby invading what was once considered the private province of establishments in other categories. As a consequence, there is a wider range of alternatives at the retail level, and each class has unique operating problems, buying procedures, and operating philosophies. Second, choices at the horizontal level are more likely to cause frictions and tensions in channel relationship. For example, antagonism among regular household-appliance stores and a possible withdrawal of sales support by them may occur when a manufacturer decides to solicit business aggressively from various types of discount houses. Similar frictions exist at the wholesale level when distributors in one line of trade find that new outlets in another trade classification are selling identical products formerly distributed in a more confined way. Third, decisions to use particular types of outlets at the retail level—a horizontal choice—may often dictate the kind of channel to be used in a vertical sense, since the retailer customarily uses certain sources of supply and a traditional outlook on buying arrangements.

As an illustration of a strategical horizontal channel choice, it has been reported that Armstrong Cork entered the household wax and polish business via the less competitive hardware and department store outlets, in order to gain something of a consumer franchise before engaging in shelf-space rivalry with S. C. Johnson and other well-established companies in supermarkets.

The Middleman

In numerous situations, the manufacturer can realistically be regarded as the channel commander, at least in the short run. It is rather common for the manufacturer to call the plays when he is large and powerful, when he has developed high public status by his demand-creation activities, when he finds it feasible to use a limited number of distribution outlets, and when distribution outlets operate under the terms of a franchise and would be seriously handicapped by the withdrawal of it. This tends to be the case with automobiles, some lines of household appliances, and major brands of automotive petroleum products sold through gasoline service stations.

In many other instances the manufacturer is channel commander not in any basic way but only in a derivative sense, owing to the strong position of middlemen in the channel. This circumstance stems from the twofold role of middlemen as distributors of manufacturers' goods and as suppliers of the purchasing requirements of their customers. When the middleman carries a variety of items drawn from many original sources, he tends to be more strongly oriented to the latter role than to the former.

Briefly, it may be noted that the manufacturers' freedom to select among conceptually available alternatives is practically limited by conditions and attitudes prevailing among middlemen. Many circumstances limit the potentialities for distribution in certain types of channel situations, whether the choice be of a vertical or horizontal nature. Examples of these circumstances follow:

The manufacturer finds that the most desirable types of outlets have already been pre-empted by strongly entrenched competitive organizations.

The middleman, already using his space and capital resources to the maximum, is reluctant to add additional items to his line, since such proliferation poses serious logistics problems, particularly in terms of available display space, warehousing space, catalog or stock control listings, capital required for inventory investment, and so forth.

The pricing or discount structure on the item is not sufficiently attractive to induce middlemen to devote promotional effort adequate to ensure movement to the consumer.

The manufacturer mishandles consumer packaging or shipping containers so that neither is acceptable under the conditions of selling or merchandise handling typical in a particular line of trade.

The manufacturer has created tensions or frictions in trade channels, either by using distribution techniques that place him in direct competition with some possible outlets or by distributing through various outlets in different lines of trade with varying margin and sales-supporting requirements. He thereby generates antagonism, which makes his products unacceptable or, at best, only marginally acceptable to certain types of potential outlets.

When the manufacturer encounters conditions of such a nature, he often learns that the middleman, in his role as a buyer and selector of sources of supply, really determines the nature of the channel of distribution.

The Consumer

Even when middlemen, whether they are wholesale distributors or retailers, are more strongly entrenched than manufacturers as channel commanders, their role too is more derivative than basic, owing to their need to adjust to constant changes. In a private-enterprise economy characterized by high levels of buying income per family, the consumer has a wide range of choices when it comes to satisfying those wants that can be met in the marketplace. The consumer can, for example, decide whether to use more of his purchasing power to eat better, to travel more, to buy more clothes, or to purchase new appliances for his home. If the choice is for appliances, he can satisfy his needs at a department store, an appliance store, a mail-order company, a furniture store, a discount house, an automobile-accessories store or, in some areas, a supermarket or consumers' cooperative organization. His choice will ordinarily be the outlet that has best harmonized its marketing mix with the buying interests of the group of consumers of which the individual purchaser is a member.

In the long run, therefore, the buying decisions of consumers determine the adjustments that occur in the relative importance of different kinds of channels of distribution. As adjustments occur at the retail level, they naturally have their impact in a vertical sense, by modifying the relative positions of various kinds of channel links between the manufacturer and the retailer.

HISTORIC BREAKTHROUGHS

The manner in which marketing vision has led to major distribution breakthroughs may be illustrated with several classic examples. From the many historic cases that might well be chosen, three have been selected because of their varying nature and because of the manner in which their long-standing effects are still apparent. Attention is given to A&P's cash-and-carry stores, to General Motors' dealer structure, and to several breakthroughs associated with Sears. It is observable in each instance how an innovative mind conceived the opportunity to achieve a differential advantage by viewing the process of distribution in a new way.

A&P's Cash-and-Carry Stores

The Great Atlantic & Pacific Tea Company, founded in 1859, developed originally as a service retailer, characteristic of its times. It had trading stamps, delivery service, charge accounts, and premiums for promotions. In 1912, John Hartford, a founder's son with marketing vision, observed an unusual New Jersey store that did a large volume of business on the basis of limited service and low prices. Sensing a possible distribution breakthrough, he got approval for an experiment at A&P. This involved a small unit that could be operated in many cases by one man. Services were cut to the bone by eliminating stamps, streamlining the inventory, and operating on a cash-and-carry basis. Traditional grocery-store gross margins at the time were about 25 per cent. With its new stores, A&P had a differential of about 10 to 15 per cent of sales, thus giving it a cost-protected price advantage over service competitors. So successful was this breakthrough that the company opened 7,500 stores of the new type within three years—about seven per day. John Hartford was quoted as saying, "We went so fast, hoboes hopping off trains got hired as managers."[13]

[13] "Pinching 500,000,000,000 Pennies," *Fortune* (March 1963), p. 172.

The Dealer Structure of General Motors

Prior to 1920, automobile distribution was largely from manufacturer to "distributor-wholesalers" who resold to dealers within their respective territories. Gradually manufacturers took over the wholesale function. During the 1920s, the prevailing manufacturer attitude was that the manufacturer was responsible for the product, the price, and the advertising, and the rest of marketing was up to the dealer. Under conditions of large untapped primary demand, this worked well for some. Henry Ford, by stressing continually enlarged production of standard models at lowered prices, brought Ford to a position of strong sales leadership.

At the same time, executives of General Motors realizing the growing complexities of marketing under conditions of increasing ownership saturation and trade-ins, began to give more attention to retail distribution. Alfred P. Sloan, Jr., as chief executive officer, fitted up a private railroad car as an office and traveled all over the United States, visiting five to ten dealers a day in their own towns. It was apparent to him that the economic position of dealers in the mid-1920s was deteriorating and that dealer franchises were less in demand. There were increasing problems of achieving market penetration, liquidating inventories at the end of model runs (then the financial responsibility solely of the dealer), of maintaining communication between manufacturers and dealers, and of preserving dealer financial solvency.[14]

Sloan and his General Motors associates decided that something drastic had to be done not only for the sake of dealers but also for the soundness of the enterprise as a whole. The decision was to involve the corporation, to an extent wholly unprecedented in the industry, in the retail distribution of its products, while still retaining independent franchised dealers. The resulting program involved, among other things, the following: (1) scientific local-area studies of market potential, to locate and establish dealers with respect to market opportunity; (2) shared manufacturer and dealer responsibility for year-end liquidation of old models; (3) the development of proper accounting systems on a departmental basis (new cars, used cars, service, parts) to permit internal and comparative analyses of financial position and operating results; (4) improved management and marketing approaches; and (5) the development of financing methods whereby able persons with inadequate capital could be assisted in the establishment of new dealerships.

Sloan has attributed much of the success and stability of General Motors in the years that followed to these early changes in relationships in the distributive organization.

---

[14] Adapted from Alfred P. Sloan, Jr., *My Years With General Motors* (Garden City, N.Y.: Doubleday & Co., 1964), Chapter 16, "Distribution and the Dealers."

Distributive Breakthroughs at Sears

Few indeed are the business organizations that could vie with Sears, Roebuck & Company with regard to outstanding visionary developments in distribution.

The two companies most prominently associated with the development of the mail-order business—Montgomery Ward & Company, Inc., and Sears, Roebuck & Company—date, respectively, from 1872 and 1893. In the early days the initial success of the enterprises founded by Montgomery Ward and Richard Sears is attributed to the failure of country merchants to adjust to changing conditions. In the post-Civil War period, country general stores and small-town merchants were characterized by high costs of operation, limited variety, frequent out-of-stock conditions, and high prices. Their failure to respond to rising income levels among farm families and industrial workers paved the way for mail-order pioneers. Sears won the confidence of customers by truthful descriptions of goods illustrated in catalogs and in a firm "money back" guarantee. Merchandise was bought in large quantities and priced to appeal to a rural target market.

The early success of the Sears pattern of mail-order distribution is an outstanding case of response to changing environmental conditions. The company took maximum advantage of the early availability of rail transportation to provide delivery to remote places. Rural free delivery service provided an opportunity for accelerated distribution of general and special catalogs, as well as bringing to rural America more information of all kinds which tended to make people more dissatisfied with offerings of inadequate small-town stores. Another impetus in 1913 was the inauguration of parcel post service, bringing small-package delivery right to the farmer's door.

Location became a major differential advantage of Sears as the mail-order business began to mature in the early 1920s, and more people had automobiles and access to city stores. Sears began to open retail stores in the 1920s, and 324 establishments were opened in the 1925–29 period.[15] General Robert E. Wood, then the principal Sears executive, was the only major department store executive with the vision to anticipate the future influence of the automobile and suburban living. While other merchants concentrated upon downtown locations that were oriented to public transit facilities, Sears expanded rapidly in newer outlying areas. At the time the company was often criticized or ridiculed by competitors for building stores upon "farmland." Once established, however, these stores often had a spatial monopoly that went largely unchallenged until the post-World War II era, and they had only to perform to Sears standards to grow substantially.

The nearly complete vertical integration of the channel of distribution

[15] "Sears Makes It Look Easy," *Fortune* (May 1964), 120 ff.

found in the contemporary Sears organization is often a subject of envy on the part of manufacturers who must devote considerable marketing effort to the obtaining of good will from thousands or tens of thousands of independent middlemen in their various channels.[16] A more recent chief executive officer, T. V. Houser, has contrasted the Sears method of distribution with the typical channel situation of the large manufacturer. According to Houser's account, the products of such a manufacturer are ordinarily distributed by a very large number of small retailers. There are likely to be independent or manufacturer-controlled wholesale functions in the channel. The manufacturer attempts to exert the marketing leadership in the channel, by preselling the product through advertising, and then to secure distribution on the basis of established demand.

The Sears type of system is just the reverse pattern of distribution. In Houser's account, the large retail distributor furnishes an outlet for great numbers of small manufacturers. Product determination becomes the responsibility of the retail distributor and marketing or channel leadership comes also from him through product advertising, display, direct sales effort, and customer-credit arrangements. The concept of channel commander is illustrated by Houser's statement: "So long as the customer is free to buy from competing sellers and producers, the function of the business closest to the customer must carry weight in influencing the decisions that determine the character and cost of the product."[17]

CONTEMPORARY ILLUSTRATIONS

Distribution breakthroughs need not bring into being new types or methods in the sense that they were previously unknown. The breakthrough may involve a new approach to working with a given type of situation, of utilizing a type of capability with reference to other products, or of applying concepts that have been perfected in some other field. Some contemporary cases are illustrated in the following paragraphs.

Coca-Cola as a Distribution Network

Depth of marketing vision has been explained as the successful seeking of the understanding of the essential being of a company, its distinctiveness of differential advantage with respect to ability to exploit profitable opportunities.

The Coca-Cola Company can be described as a remarkable distribution network. Distribution through more than 1,600,000 outlets of every kind,

[16] T. V. Houser, "The True Role of the Marketing Executive," *Journal of Marketing* (April 1959), 363 ff.
[17] *Ibid.*, p. 364.

type, and description, has, in the words of a former president, put the product "within an arm's length of desire." With 1,000 franchised bottlers supplying this myriad of retail outlets, the ability to gain rapid distribution of a new item in the product line is readily assured.

Programmed Merchandising at Scott's

The O. M. Scott & Sons Company of Marysville, Ohio, is the leading manufacturer and marketer of lawn products. The importance of distribution in the company's marketing mix is illustrated by the following statement: "There are three basic components for marketing success by a business such as Scott's: (1) Products must be those that build leadership because they satisfy the customer; (2) Advertising and promotion must be of the type that translates this leadership into buying interest; (3) Products must be available at the time and place required to convert favorable attitudes into sales."[18]

During a period of rapid post-World War II expansion, a policy of highly selective distribution was followed, with all but a very small proportion of sales made through hardware stores and garden and nursery stores that adhered closely to a standard Scott program. Each store was called upon directly by a company salesman, known as an account executive, and physical distribution was handled from company-controlled distribution centers direct to stores.

In the mid-1960s, consumer market research in a number of major market areas indicated that a large proportion of medium- to upper-income home-owning families did not use even one bag of lawn fertilizer in a year. This fact, along with other considerations, led the company to the decision to expand its distribution greatly, increasing the exposure of the product line to the nonusing segment of the general public.

While Scott's had significant distribution among department stores, the sales achieved in most such outlets were usually quite disappointing. In the summer of 1964, a careful study was made of selected typical department store cases.

The Scott lawn seed and chemical line was ordinarily merchandised as part of the housewares department. Top management of most such stores was oriented to fashion apparel or home furnishings, or both, often with minimal interest in lawn products. Thus there was little internal pressure upon the department manager to maximize his opportunity. In housewares the department manager or buyer sometimes had as many as 200 merchandise suppliers and several hundred merchandise items. The merchandising requirements of the Scott line, as developed with primary attention to hardware and garden

[18] O. M. Scott & Sons Co., Annual Report, 1965, p. 9.

stores, did not usually fit the operating method of department stores, thereby often generating friction between store and supplier.

Merchandising is commonly thought of as having the right merchandise at the right time at the right place in the right quantities and at the right price. A consultant to Scott's emphasized the concept of merchandising in terms of the opportunities to be wrong in the distribution channel, no matter how good the product or its promotion.

For example, a large department store was expected to have about 40 Scott items in stock. It had, in a typical case, a downtown and four branch stores, with five total locations. There were five distinct merchandising seasons with different quantity requirements to meet consumer needs. And there were at least ten key marketing activities to be handled at the retail level (dealer advertising, sales training, display, etc.). This is $40 \times 5 \times 5 \times 10$ or 10,000 opportunities to be wrong, assuming the variables are multiplicative, which was approximately the case.

Owing to the lack of top-management store interest and the buyer's orientation to different product classes, the "wrongs" were sometimes more numerous than the "rights."

The solution was for Scott's to become much more highly involved in department store merchandising activities. Special programs were worked out in detail for each major department store account that could be interested in substantially expanding its volume of lawn-products sales. Plans for monthly sales by product were developed by Scott account executives. These were projected to dollar totals and incorporated into the store's departmental plan well ahead of each six-month merchandising season, thereby automatically generating sufficient "open-to-buy" to cover planned sales. Promotional activities for each month (each week for the peak seasons) were detailed in advance, with responsibility clearly defined for each store location. All operating requirements were oriented to the conditions at the individual store. Some of these programs involved 50 or more pages of plans developed for an individual account. They were so comprehensive that the department manager rarely had to make a personal judgment that was not covered.

A fortuitous circumstance was that a trade magazine, *Department Store Economist*, featured prominently in its October 1964 issue the concept of *programmed merchandising*—something very much like the Scott department store program. This made it possible to popularize the new approach to department stores as programmed merchandising.

Many department stores were on this program of Scott-planned retail distribution activities within their companies in the fall of 1964. Sales increases were very large among this group. This provided the company with many success case histories for further expansion of the program among similar outlets in 1965 and 1966, and the extension of similar distribution approaches to other new classes of trade for the company, including mass outlets and supermarkets.

Total Supplier Distribution at Cotter

The retail hardware trade has long been dominated by the small independent merchant. According to Census of Business figures for 1958, single-unit independents accounted for more than 85 per cent of total hardware store sales and chains of more than ten units accounted for only 7 per cent. During the period 1948–58, the total number of hardware stores remained nearly stable at about 34,000, and the sales of such stores dropped from 1.9 per cent to 1.5 per cent of total retail trade.

Increasingly, the typical independent was finding it difficult to compete effectively with the pricing and often superior merchandising of branches of department stores in suburban centers, discount outlets, upgrading of units of variety store chains, general merchandise diversification in some supermarket companies and drug chains, and catalog retailing.

In the late 1940s and 1950s, distribution in the hardware trade was originally quite complex, with many contacts between retailers and the various agencies that supplied them. Much of the effort at the wholesale level was devoted to competitive activities, as one wholesaler vied with another, attempting to get a larger share of the dealer's business. This also meant that vast quantities of the retailer's time were taken up in contacts with order-taking salesmen of many suppliers.

For example, in a study supervised by the author in 1952, based on a sample of 10 Columbus, Ohio, independent hardware stores, it was found that the average (per store) number of suppliers included 7 general-line wholesalers, 10 specialty wholesalers, and 13 direct-selling manufacturers, for a total of about 30 regular or consistent suppliers.[19]

Perceiving the inefficiencies and competitive limitations of such a distribution pattern, a small group of hardware retailers had earlier banded together in Chicago. Under the guidance of John Cotter, a recognized leader in the hardware trade, they established a retailer-owned cooperative to serve as a complete supplier to members. It was named Cotter & Company. This program adapted various merchandising approaches and operating methods that had been developed earlier by chain stores and by voluntary chains in other lines.

As is the case with other retailer cooperatives, each member buys stock and receives patronage dividends from the wholesaler, in proportion to his volume of purchases during the year.

By getting a large proportion of the total business of each member dealer, and by handling this with a simplified mail-order method from catalogs, the order-taking salesman of the traditional wholesaler was eliminated. Savings in credit and bad debt expenses were also realized by concentrating on better-

---

[19] Harold Spielbert, *Purchasing Practices of Independent Retail Hardware Stores Located in Columbus, Ohio,* unpublished Master's thesis, deposited in library of Ohio State University, 1952.

financed dealers. These, plus other efficiencies associated with larger average order size, are claimed by Cotter to amount to direct savings in the range of 6 per cent to 8 per cent of sales at the wholesale level, as compared with traditional methods of hardware wholesaling.

Cotter executives feel that certain intangibles are even more important to the health of merchant members. Thus there are programs of store identification ("Value Service" or "True Value"), mass advertising by direct mail and in national media, bin-ticket stock-control systems, store-modernization counsel, pricing guidance for volume sales of key items, buying of promotional items in massive quantities for merchandise cost savings, and resource relationships with direct-shipping manufacturers.

For a small service fee, Cotter handles contacts with those manufacturers that normally sell direct to retailers, arranging for their participation in Cotter promotions, and handling the billing and collection for the manufacturer, who receives settlement in one sum for all outlets, without worry about bad-debt losses.

By utilizing some ideas and working with proven principles of closer integration of efforts between channel levels, Cotter has achieved fabulous growth in the fairly stable hardware trade. From 25 members in 1948, it grew to 1,885 in 1965. Wholesale volume increased from $385,000 in 1948 to a projected $106,000,000 for 1966.

With similar growth on the part of several other well-known hardware groups, distribution conditions have greatly changed. This has made it necessary for many manufacturers to realign their marketing effort accordingly.

Such changes have not, of course, been confined to retailer cooperatives. Many progressive, independent hardware wholesalers have also developed aggressive merchandising programs, thereby extending their influence forward in the distribution channel, and bringing about a more highly integrated relationship between wholesaling and retailing, often with some shifting of functions from the retail level to wholesale organizations.

EVALUATION OF CHANNEL-OF-DISTRIBUTION RELATIONSHIPS

The general discussion in the early parts as well as the more specific historic and contemporary examples just presented provide ample evidence that a channel of distribution is something more than a marketing choice that is made by a manufacturing company. It shows, moreover, why many manufacturers have had to modify their thinking about factors that influence channel choices. In any company that follows a program of modern, consumer-oriented marketing management, considerations relating to consumer requirements are elevated to paramount status, and factors relating to company situation are subordinated, at least in the sense that the latter must be adjusted to the former. This means that the manufacturer must look beyond his own circumstances and beyond the situation of intermediaries in the channel, so that he is attuned to the wants and interests of the consumer in the market segment he is trying to reach.

CHARTING THE CHANNEL

Too often channel relationships do not receive due attention, since they involve matters that are "outside" the company and hence are more easily taken for granted than other activities, such as marketing research, advertising, or personal selling. These "internal" functions come up for more frequent review or appraisal since responsibility for them tends to be fixed on the organizational chart or in job descriptions, and the cost of them is conspicuously identified on accounting statements.

In manufacturing companies, opportunities for more frequent and more realistic appraisal of channel problems and relationships might be provided by new approaches to charting the organization of marketing activities. An organization chart might well show not only the various departments within the marketing division of the company, but also all of the vertical links in the channel used to effect transfers of title to eventual users, and, moreover, the different types of outlets on each horizontal plane or state of distribution.

Another recommendation is to prepare operating statements that reveal sales performance and cost situations through the channels used. At the top of such a statement would be sales, stated in terms of prices paid by the ultimate user, and showing as expenses the costs of marketing through the various channels in use.

In any event, manufacturers will have made progress in solving channel-of-distribution problems when they recognize two considerations. First, channel activities must be thought of as only one aspect of the total marketing mix and one that must be coordinated with other ingredients, as these contribute to the objective of reaching a defined market; second, in the long run, the nature of channels is determined from "the bottom up" rather than from "the top down."

Finally, it may be concluded that the ability to achieve a differential advantage in distribution through marketing vision is related to ability to perceive the ways either in which wants are satisfied or in which satisfaction is being thwarted. By focusing attention upon values created through distribution, or upon values desired but remaining unfulfilled, some firms will look beyond the more readily controllable factors of product, price, and promotion, and achieve real breakthroughs by innovation in the flow of ownership transfer and product movement through distribution channels.

22.

Clues for Action
from Shopper Preferences

Stuart U. Rich
Bernard Portis

Eight years ago the nation's first full-line discount store, E. J. Korvette, Inc., opened in Westbury, Long Island. Since then, discount house sales have risen from meager amounts to an annual volume of over $6 billion. Despite recent signs of a shake-out of the marginal operators, one author estimates that by 1970 discount store sales could reach as high as $20 billion, or 30% of the general merchandise, apparel, and furniture and appliances market—as large a share as the department stores now enjoy.[1]

This projected growth pattern assumes that discount stores will continue to expand in the future as rapidly as they have in the past, and will go on drawing more and more customers away from the department stores. How valid is this assumption?

Our recent survey of 4,500 women shoppers in New York City and in Cleveland shows that *both* the discount stores and the department stores have strong distinctive appeals. Any projected growth of either type of store will depend on how successful that type is in exploiting its own strengths and avoiding its weaknesses in competing with the other one.

WHY DISCOUNTERS GROW

Before we present our findings, let us review what the experts have been saying about the reasons for discount house growth and about the best strategy for the department stores to follow in meeting the challenge of the discount stores. As we shall see, there are widely different opinions held on both of these subjects.

---

[1] Charles E. Silberman, "The Department Stores Are Waking Up," *Fortune*, July 1962, p. 143.

From Stuart U. Rich and Bernard Portis, "Clues for Action from Shoppers Preferences," *Harvard Business Review*, Col. 41, No. 2 (March–April), pp. 132–149. Copyright 1963 by the President and Fellows of Harvard College; all rights reserved. Reprinted by permission.

Lower Prices?

The appeal of lower prices has probably been the most common explanation of discount store success. After a study of the many characteristics of the stores listed in its 1961 Directory of Discount Houses, the publisher, *Chain Store Guide,* concluded:

> "Price is the major attraction of the discount store. . . . Some firms claim not to be discounters. Instead, they call themselves 'mass merchandisers' or 'promotional department stores.' Whatever the designation, though, price remains the deciding factor and the public shops these and other discount stores for price."[2]

Price attraction, of course, is nothing new, as there have always been price-appeal stores; in fact, the department stores themselves originally started out as price-cutters. What is different about the price appeal of the discount stores, it is said, is that it is not limited to the lower-income groups, but includes the huge new middle-income class who wish to economize on many types of household items and clothing. These families find that the savings they make in the discount stores help them to make payments on their suburban homes, to provide better education for their children, and to enjoy vacation travel and other leisure-time activities.

Furthermore, the sale of branded merchandise, particularly hard goods carrying manufacturers' list-price tags, has given these customers an assurance that they are getting value as well as lower prices. Finally, since many discount stores are located in the suburbs, they have been in a position to serve the price-conscious suburban shoppers whom the department stores neglected— at least until recently—through their failure to include basement operations in the suburban branches.

Convenience?

A second explanation for discount store success is that this new form of retailing has catered to the current demand for shopping convenience. Most women today, it is claimed, no longer regard shopping as a "day on the town," but as a household task that must be performed as expeditiously as possible, often in the evening when the family car is available. They find discount stores convenient places to shop for a number of reasons. Specifically:

They are easily accessible by car, offer ample parking, and are open evenings.

The location of desired merchandise is facilitated by single-floor layout, open displays, and self-selection.

---

[2] Quoted in "Understanding the Discount Store Industry," Market Study #1, *Discount Store News* (New York, Lebhar-Friedman Publication, December 1961), p. 2.

Purchase is speeded up by self-service and check-out (which is quicker than having to wait for uninterested salesclerks).

With the car in the parking lot nearby, it is just as easy to carry most packages as it is to have them delivered.

This emphasis on convenience rather than on price factors in discount store shopping was reported in a study which ranked store accessibility, parking, and self-service far ahead of price as advantages which customers attributed to discount stores.[3]

Emotional Appeal?

A third school of thought goes even further than the last group in stressing nonprice factors to explain the discounters' success. Not only do the discount stores offer convenience, some people claim, but also nonprice "psychological" satisfactions and emotional appeal.[4] They give thrills and excitement, and even provide their customers with an opportunity to "punish conventional department stores for years of poor service.[5]

DEPARTMENT STORE COUNTERATTACKS

The responses of the department stores to the challenge of the discount houses have been as varied as are the explanations for the discounters' success. Once they passed the stage of ignoring this new form of retailing, or decrying it as "illegitimate," the department stores have reacted to it in three different ways:

1. They have imitated the discounters, perhaps going so far as to convert to a discounting operation, with self-service, discount price promotions, and abandonment of such services as free delivery, phone orders, gift wrapping, and the like.
2. They have also moved in an opposite direction by emphasizing higher price fashion merchandise, by dropping some of the more competitive hard-goods lines sold by the discounters, and by offering more services than they had before.
3. The final strategy has combined the first two—operating self-service and discount departments and high-fashion departments under the same roof.

---

[3] Perry Meyers, *Profile of a New Market Place* (New York, Perry Meyers, Inc., 1961), p. 22.

[4] Robert D. Entenberg, "The Discount House: Panic or Panacea," *Georgia Business*, October 1961, p. 2.

[5] Ernest Dichter, Emanuel Demby, and others, quoted in "Department Stores Strike Back," *Barron's National Business & Financial Weekly*, September 4, 1961, p. 15.

Which of these three approaches is most likely to prove the most successful? Some insight into the probable success of each can be gained through an analysis of the results of a study we did of *who shops at the discount stores, why they do so,* and *how they react to the merchandise-price-convenience mix of the discount stores* as compared with that of the conventional department stores. This recently completed study formed a part of a larger research project dealing with the total shopping habits and behavior of women shoppers, with particular emphasis on their demand for department store services.[6]

Interviews conducted in the spring of 1962 with 4,500 women shoppers provide the data on which the study and this article are based. Interviewers were furnished by the Psychological Corporation of New York. The interviews lasted approximately one hour, were conducted in person, and took place in the New York–northeastern New Jersey metropolitan area and in the Cleveland metropolitan area. These two areas presented contrasting patterns in terms of size, geographical location, and demography. In addition, at the time of our survey, discount stores had been well established in New York for some years, whereas in Cleveland they were relatively new. Random samples were taken of women shoppers in these two cities, and similarities and differences in customer shopping behavior were noted. Our belief is that the results of this study will prove meaningful as guides to policy for department store executives in general and not merely for those in the two tested areas. It is not too early to mention, for example, that this article will suggest which of the three counteractions to discount store inroads seems most likely to be successful.

In the interests of economy we will present our findings essentially in a series of exhibits, with accompanying commentary to point out the highlights and key implications. In all of these exhibits, we will be concerned with shopping for clothing and household items as opposed to shopping for food and drugs. Furthermore, the "don't knows," averaging about 1.5%, are excluded from all tabulations; hence, the percentages sometimes total less than 100%.

WHO SHOPS DISCOUNT STORES?

"The objective of the better discount store today is to appeal to 85% of the public—those people who earn up to $12,000 or so annually," the president of one large discount chain remarked recently.[7] Most estimates of

[6] For a full report on the entire research project, see Stuart U. Rich, *Delivery Service and Telephone Ordering: Department Store Policies and Customer Demand*, to be published in the near future by the Division of Research, Harvard Business School.

[7] Sol W. Cantor, president of Interstate Department Stores, quoted in "Discounters: 20% of Retail Sales by 1972," *Women's Wear Daily*, October 26, 1962, p. 1.

the current and potential size of the discount store market, however, are somewhat less grandiose. Usually portrayed as furnishing the bulk of the discount house customers are the low- to lower-middle-income families.[8] The upper-middle and even high-income-group women are thought to be occasional shoppers at these stores, at least for certain lines of goods, such as major appliances and children's clothing. Now let us take a look at some specific facts we discovered in our study (see Figures 22–1 and 22–2).

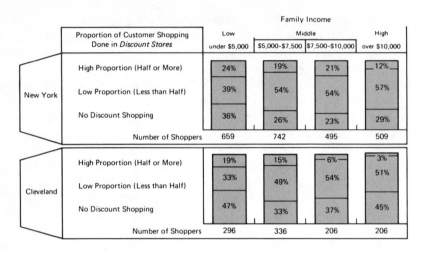

Figure 22–1. How Does Customer's Income Level Affect Discount Shopping?

Note that [in Figure 22–1] 70% of New York women and 60% of Cleveland women do at least some of their shopping in discount stores. In fact, 19% of the women in New York and 12% of those in Cleveland can be considered to be high-frequency discount shoppers, since they do half or more of their shopping in these stores.

Discount shopping also tends to be more popular among the lower- and middle-income women. The frequent discount shoppers are in these same income groups in both areas, although more than half of the high-income women do at least some of their shopping in these stores. There is, however, a sizable proportion of the low-income group who have not shopped in the discount stores. This is because of the tendency of the less mobile, low-income shoppers to go to small, low-price neighborhood stores.

As [Figure 22–2] shows, the discount stores have greater patronage in the New York area, where they have been established longer, than they do in the Cleveland area. This finding holds, even when family incomes are taken

[8] Perry Meyers, op. cit., pp. i, ii.

into consideration. Interestingly, although a few more of the high-frequency discount shoppers live in the city than in the suburbs, the over-all effect of place of residence on discount shopping is not as great as is the effect of income.

Figure 22–3 indicates the combined effects on shopping behavior of age and the presence of children in the home. To measure these factors, a "life cycle" code was used, which divided the women into those under 40 and those 40 or over, with and without children living at home.

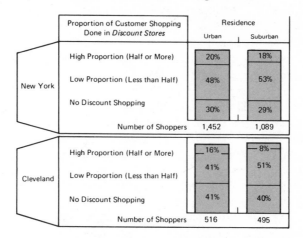

Figure 22—2. How Do Urban Dwellers Compare with Suburbanites in Their Discount Shopping?

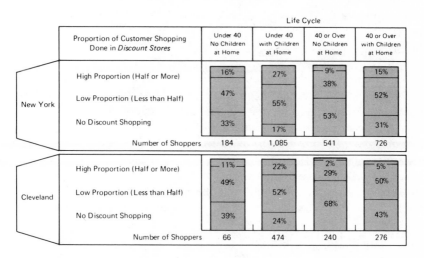

Figure 22–3. Does Life Cycle (Age and Children) Affect Discount Shopping?

The effects of life cycle [in Figure 22–3] on discount shopping are surprisingly similar in New York and Cleveland. Younger women patronize discount stores more than do older women. Women with children, regardless of age, do more discount shopping than do those without children. And so the best discount store customers are the younger women with children. This greater amount of discount shopping done by the younger women is not a function of their lower income; rather, the younger women at all income levels are heavier discount shoppers than are the older women.

These findings are significant for both department stores and discount stores. The popularity of the discount stores for the younger women suggests that there will be greater inroads made by these stores in the future, as these younger women grow older and as they replace today's generation of department-store-oriented older women.

The fairly high percentage of nondiscount shoppers in the under-$5,000 income group demands immediate attention from discount store executives. Those executives who are talking about upgrading and capturing a larger segment of the upper-middle-income, or even higher-income market, should be reminded that a large potential market still exists among the low-income women. If this group is neglected, then doubtless some new type of "super-discounter" will come along and make inroads into the broad low-income market on which the discount stores are now dependent.

Perhaps, as Malcolm P. McNair has suggested, this is the inevitable pattern of innovation and growth, with each new type of retailer starting out as a price-cutter.[9] However, it seems unwise at this point for discount stores to hasten this trend and leave their low-income customers behind by trying to upgrade too rapidly.

WHAT DISCOUNT SHOPPERS BUY

In projecting their future growth by means of gaining a greater share of the middle-to-upper-income market, many discount store executives say that to attain this goal they must upgrade the quality of their apparel lines. This view was reflected in *Modern Retailer*, one of the magazines of the discount trade. "If our industry is to show consistent growth within the next few years," the editorial said, "it must start to make larger inroads into the income levels of $7,500 and up."[10] The editorial pointed out that while the upper-income groups did come into the discount stores, they limited their purchases primarily to standard-brand hard goods. Finally, the article noted

[9] "The New Turn of the Wheel in Mass Merchandising," speech delivered to the National-American Wholesale Grocers' Association, 56th Annual Convention, Chicago, March 12th, 1962.

[10] "We Must Ask Ourselves If It Is Good Business to Look and Sell Alike," February 9, 1962, p. 5.

that the first step in making greater inroads into this "department store market" was to convince these customers that they were getting good quality for their money when buying personal apparel.

The limited attraction of the discount stores in apparel lines, at least in women's coats and better dresses, is evident in our study. However, there are still many kinds of merchandise which are purchased in the discount stores by all income groups. In Figure 22–4 discount shoppers categorized by income groups report which of a list of items they buy in these stores.

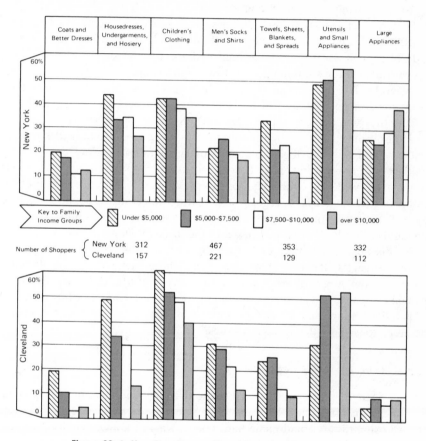

Figure 22–4. How Does Income Class Affect the Items Purchased?

The over-all purchases of the various types of merchandise are about the same in both cities, except for children's clothing and large appliances. The higher incidence in Cleveland of discount purchase of children's clothing and the much lower incidence of purchase of large appliances reflect the greater strength of the soft-goods discount houses in Cleveland, relative to those selling hard lines. At present there is no large, well-established discount company in that city with a reputation in major appliances comparable to E. J. Korvette, Inc., Masters, Inc., or Two Guys from Harrison, Inc., in the New York area.

The effect of income level on the types of items which discount shoppers purchase is evident. For hard-goods lines discount stores are just as well accepted among the high-income discount shoppers as among the low-income ones. Except for large appliance purchases in Cleveland, as noted earlier, the hard-goods lines are the most important types of merchandise which the high-income women buy in discount stores.

The purchase of all soft-goods lines goes down as income rises in both areas. This decline is less marked for children's clothing and for men's socks and shirts than for women's clothing and for towels, sheets, and the like. Except for children's clothing, bought by high-income women in both cities, the Cleveland higher-income women show less acceptance of the discount stores for soft goods than do the New York women. This finding probably reflects the presence of several "fashion" discount stores in New York. It could also reflect the fact that discount stores have been established longer in that city and that the higher-income women, who earlier had bought only appliances in these stores, have become accustomed to purchasing soft goods in them as well. (Interestingly, one-third of the high-frequency discount shoppers in both cities buy coats and better dresses in discount stores. In general, however, these items, where style and quality are important, are among the lines least often purchased in the discount stores.)

For the department store executive, Figure 22–4 (as well as the first three figures) suggests one important step: push those lines where the discount stores are the weakest. And it is particularly important to stay ahead in women's apparel, in view of the ambitions of the discounters in this direction —ambitions supported by the growing tendency of national brand manufacturers to sell to the discount stores.

COMPARATIVE ATTRACTIONS

Many department stores advertise that they will meet the discounters' low prices on the same items and offer free service besides. This policy is applied primarily to brand-name hard goods, where the merchandise in question is easily identifiable, and where installation and delivery services are needed. However, one president of a large regional department store chain, who was perhaps more candid than many of his colleagues, said to us, "Actually, we just try to give the appearance of meeting discount house prices." Appearance or not, the retail institution with the low-price image today is the discount house. Its appeal is not limited to price, however, but shows up on several broad fronts.

In our study we have explored the various reasons which women give for shopping at discount stores and at department stores. Price appeal is the major attraction of the discount stores. These preferences are brought out when women name the one store in which they do more shopping than in any other, and state what their reasons are for this preference.

In our analysis of interview results, the stores designated as being the respondents' "favorite" have been put into eight different categories: higher-price specialty stores, regular department stores, discount stores, medium- to low-price specialty stores, variety stores and junior department stores, mail-order stores, small local "neighborhood" women's stores, and "other" stores (including other local stores, men's clothing stores, hardware stores, and furniture stores).

We are concerned in this article only with the department store and discount store—the two types most frequently mentioned. This is not to deny that major inroads have also been made by the discount houses into the business of the variety and junior department stores, as well as the local "neighborhood" women's stores. It is just that the proportion of women who shop frequently in those stores is too small—under 4%—to permit comparative analysis of the attractions of these stores versus the discount houses.

In New York City 43% of the women have a "favorite" department store, and 20% have a "favorite" discount store. For Cleveland, these percentages are 69% and 8%, respectively. In this latter city, discount stores are much newer, and there are no "fashion" discount stores comparable to Alexander's and Ohrbach's in New York.

Respondents were then asked their opinion as to why they do more of their shopping in their favorite store than in any other. The replies they gave are classified under three main headings: merchandise (including store reliability), price appeal, and shopping convenience (including services).

Figures 22–5—22–8 reveal some reasons why women shoppers show such preferences.

It seems apparent that the main strengths of the department stores lie in the quality of their merchandise, their reputation and reliability, their salesclerk service, and other services. Price appeal stands out for the discount stores, in terms of both good value and lower prices, although the latter is by far the stronger reason of the two when it is compared with the store preference reasons for particular department stores. Remember that respondents are not making direct comparisons between discount and department stores, but rather are expressing their reasons for concentrating their shopping at particular stores of one type or another. As we shall see later when direct comparisons are made between discount and department stores in terms of shopping convenience, factors such as self-service assume more prominence as discount store advantages.

Although price remains the major factor among discount store attractions, other store preference reasons, notably merchandise selection, show up as important when certain subgroups among these "favorite" discount store respondents are analyzed. For instance, 42% of the New York discount shoppers under 40 feel merchandise selection is the main attraction, compared with 22% of the women over 40. In Cleveland, age comparison is not possible because an overwhelming majority (95%) of the women in this favorite discount store group are under 40. It is also interesting that as income rises, merchandise selection becomes more important and price relatively less important. Finally, merchandise selection in the discount stores receives greater mention by the suburban dwellers.

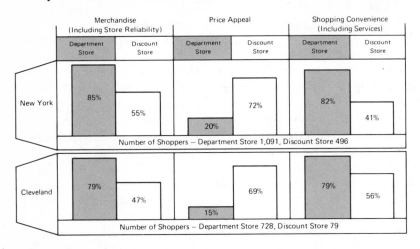

Figure 22–5. What Merchandise-Price-Convenience Mix Attracts Customers to a "Favorite" Store?

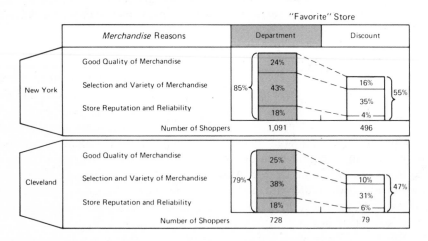

Figure 22–6. What Merchandise Reasons Attract Customers to a "Favorite" Store?

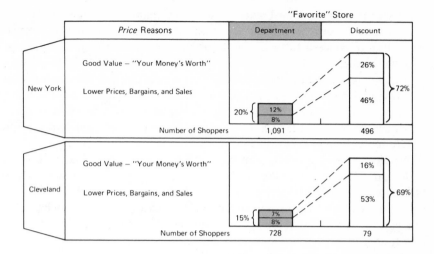

Figure 22–7. What Price Reasons Attract Customers to a "Favorite" Store?

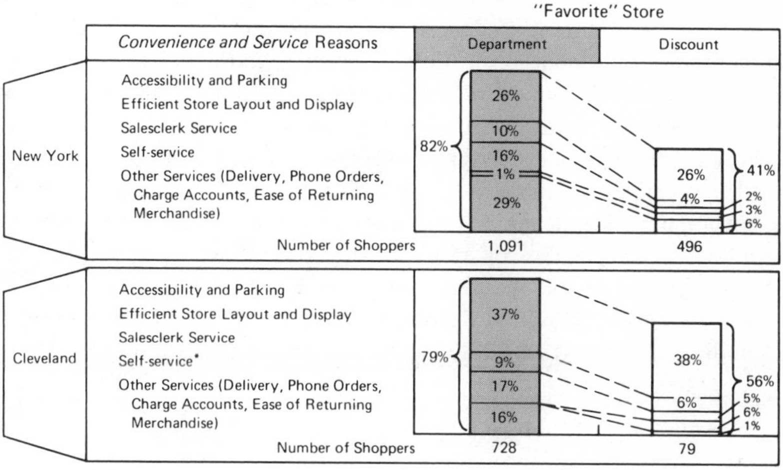

* Less than 1% for department stores.

Figure 22–8. What Convenience and Service Reasons Attract Customers to a "Favorite" Store?

When subgroups among the favorite department store respondents are analyzed, very little difference in the relative importance of the major department store attractions is found. Merchandise quality, store reliability, and salesclerk service are mentioned with equal frequency, regardless of income group or age of respondent. The one exception is in Cleveland, where salesclerk service receives less emphasis in the suburbs than in the city itself.

The fact that price appeal stands out as the major attraction of the discount stores will probably come as no surprise to department store executives. Of more concern to them should be the reason for this price appeal—discount shoppers think that they are getting good value in what they buy. Accompanying this value concept, however, is the reaction of some women that "you get what you pay for." But the counter to the value-for-your-money attraction of the discount stores is the feeling of many women who favor department stores that they are getting good quality merchandise, backed up by store reputation and reliability.

This latter feeling, in fact, appears to be one of the major advantages of the department stores over the discount houses. The department store which attempts to meet discount prices over any wide range of items and the discount house which tries to upgrade its merchandise on any extensive scale both appear to face major tasks in changing their store images. It seems unlikely that either type of store can convince customers that they will find both low prices *and* high quality there.

The frequency of mention of variety and selection of merchandise as an attraction of the discount houses, particularly by the younger women, might also warrant the attention of department store executives. In time they may find that their traditional dedication to great breadth of stock, in contrast with the discounter's policy of emphasizing a limited line of fast-moving items, may not give them much advantage over the discount stores after all, at least not great enough to warrant the high inventory investment required. One other possible explanation of the finding that wide merchandise selection does not appear to be a major advantage of the department stores over the discount stores is that the full range of department store stocks are not out on open display, as in the discount stores, and salesclerks, even when requested by customers, often do not make much of an effort to bring their merchandise out of its place of concealment under the counters.

SERVICE & CONVENIENCE

Department stores often advertise the fact that they are easier places in which to shop than are discount stores because of the services they offer—salesclerks, delivery, more liberal policies on credit and merchandise returns, and so on. At the same time, however, because of rising expenses they frequently tend to curtail some of these services or discourage their use, notably salesclerk service and delivery.

Some department store executives we interviewed express the opinion that "today's department store customer does not want the services we once thought all-important to her." Having grown accustomed to self-service and to carrying her own purchases in the supermarkets, the customer, they feel, would often be able to get along without salesclerks and delivery service when shopping in department stores. Other store executives, however, while admitting that shoppers might use self-service elsewhere, say, "When they come into *our* type of store, they expect salesclerk service and delivery; these are an important part of our appeal to them."

Rather than compare the service of the department stores with the self-service or nonservice of the discount stores, it may be more meaningful to examine which type of store offers greater *convenience* in shopping, and to define just what it is that constitutes convenience to various groups of shoppers. Convenience may mean shopping during evening hours when the woman is less encumbered with children and household duties and has a car available. It may even be more convenient for many women to dispense with certain services, to serve themselves rather than to wait for a salesclerk, or to carry their own packages rather than having them delivered.

Of the women who have shopped in discount stores, one-fifth of those in New York and one-third of those in Cleveland feel that these stores are easier places to shop in than are department stores. This finding is revealed when those women who say that they have shopped in discount stores are asked, "In which type of store is it easier for you to shop—regular department stores or discount stores?" Their answers to this question are shown in Figures 22–9—22–11.

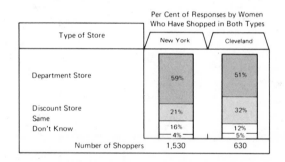

Figure 22—9. In Which Type of Store Is It Easier to Shop?

Younger women and lower-to-middle-income women are more likely to consider discount stores as easier places to shop. The most marked differences of opinion, however, are determined by income. Of the high-income New York women, for instance, 73% feel that department stores are easier places to shop, and 12% believe that discount stores offer easier shopping. Of the low-income women in this city, 51% vote for the department stores and 28% for the discount stores. In Cleveland, in contrast, among the high-income women, the split is 67% for the department stores and 17% for the discount stores. Among the low-income women, the discount stores come out ahead with 47% against 41% for the department stores.

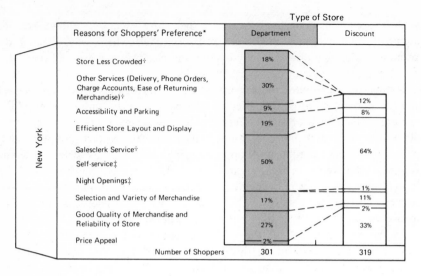

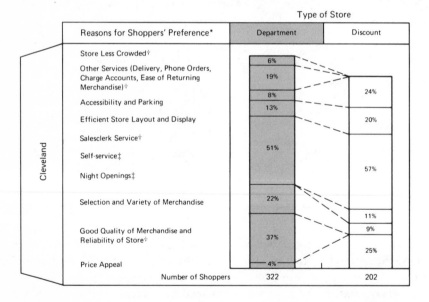

* Percentages exceed 100% because of multiple responses. The category "all other reasons," which includes trustworthy advertising, salesclerks (for discount stores), and so on, averaged about 7% and has been excluded from this exhibit.
† Only for department stores.
‡ Only for discount stores.

Figure 22—10. What Are The Shopping Convenience Attractions of Department Stores and of Discount Stores?

Salesclerk service and other traditional department store services such as delivery, charge accounts, and so on, are of major importance to the large proportion of women who say that department stores are easier places to shop in than are discount stores. As a counter to this attraction, however, the self-service of the discount stores is also of major importance to another sizable group of women who prefer the discount stores.

Quality and selection of merchandise are considered important dimensions of shopping convenience. Here again (as was true when respondents discussed the attractions of their favorite stores), merchandise quality and store reliability stand out as major advantages of the department stores over the discount stores.

In New York, women appreciate the less-crowded atmosphere of the department stores. They also view these stores as offering a more efficient layout, and providing a larger and more attractive display of merchandise. In Cleveland, however, the first of these advantages is considerably less, and the second—store layout and display—actually pulls more votes for the discount stores. This is probably because of the number of large, modern, single-story discount stores which have recently been built on the outskirts of that city. The location of these new discount stores attracts those shoppers who appreciate the "accessibility and parking" advantage there.

Discount stores in Cleveland receive greater mention for their night openings, probably because in that city, unlike New York, there are no department stores which attempt to match the five-nights-per-week policy of the discount stores.

A final strongpoint of the discount stores in both cities is price appeal; this receives considerable mention although not strictly for "convenience" reasons.

[In Figure 22–11,] salesclerk service is again ranked first in importance among the services, followed by delivery service, range and quality of merchandise, and ease of returning merchandise. Also considered as an important service by many respondents is the offering of suitable merchandise, backed by store reliability. Income level influences the frequency of mention of salesclerk service and delivery service in particular, and of the other services to a lesser degree. In New York, for instance, salesclerk service is noted by 82% of the high-income women and by 69% of the low-income women. In Cleveland, these percentages are 87% and 77%, respectively.

As for delivery service, 23% of the high-income New York women mention it, compared with 9% of the low-income women. In Cleveland, these percentages are 17% and 7%. Life cycle and residence have no bearing on the importance of the various services listed. We see, however, that the high-frequency discount store shoppers expect salesclerk service and delivery when they go to the department stores quite as much as do those women who have not shopped in the discount stores.

While services are an important element of department store shopping convenience, the more informal, nonservice atmosphere of discount stores, plus their greater emphasis on night openings, appeals to many customers. In both New York and Cleveland one-fourth of the women usually shop in the evening, and one-fourth do at least some of their shopping with their husbands. One-third of the women say that it is "always important" to them to shop quickly. And, as could have been predicted, it is among the younger, low-to-middle income, suburban women that these traits are found most often.

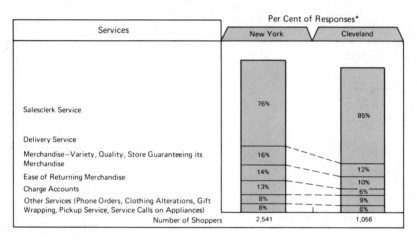

* Total exceeds 100% because of multiple response.

Figure 22—11. What Services Do Women Expect When They Shop in Regular Department Stores?

The evening shoppers, those who shop with their husbands, and the time-conscious shoppers are usually those women who are frequent discount shoppers. In New York, 31% of the frequent discount store shoppers, for instance, are evening shoppers, compared with 18% of the nondiscount shoppers who shop in the evening. In Cleveland, these percentages are 36% and 21%, respectively. Similar comparisons exist for the women who shop with their husbands and for the time-conscious shoppers in Cleveland, although the comparison is less marked in New York. Although the possession of these three shopping behavior traits is not necessarily a determinant of discount shopping, it does suggest a profile of the discount shopper as more than just a bargain hunter. Apparently, discount shopping fits well into the shopping convenience desires and buying behavior of significant segments of today's population.

Among department store executives, the proponents of more self-service, as well as those urging the retention of the full range of traditional services, can find arguments to support their positions in the findings just presented. The discount stores, mainly because of their self-service, are viewed as easier places to shop by a fairly large proportion of women, particularly by the younger ones and by those in the lower-to-middle income brackets. These women, presumably, can easily dispense with salesclerk service when they shop the department stores.

On the other hand, a majority of women interviewed still prefer salesclerk service and other services of the department stores. All women, in fact, including the high-frequency discount shoppers, expect to find a full range of services when they go to the department stores. Their acceptance of self-service at discount stores is no guarantee of their enthusiasm for it, on any large-scale basis, in the department stores.

A major consideration in any decision on converting to self-service is the type of merchandise sold. As shown earlier, the main strength of the discount houses lies in the more standardized lines of merchandise. Our survey shows that there is very low incidence of purchase of such things as women's coats, better dresses, and furniture—where fashion, style, fit, or individuality is important. For these lines of merchandise, then, salesclerk help still appears necessary.

At present, the degree to which a department store adopts self-service requires a careful appraisal of the type of customer served and kind of merchandise to be sold. Furthermore, even if salesclerk service is dispensed with in some departments, it does not follow that other services, such as delivery, liberal merchandise returns, and so on should likewise be curtailed. These other services are ranked high among the convenience attractions of the department stores and tend to differentiate them from the discount stores more than most other traits.

WHICH IS MORE ENJOYABLE?

At the beginning of this article three current explanations for discount house success were listed. The first two—price appeal and shopping convenience—are supported to some degree by the findings of our study. But what about the third possibility—the nonprice "psychological" satisfactions and shopping "excitement" of the discount stores?

The argument that discount stores provide excitement appears to conflict with the other belief that the discount stores appeal to convenience-minded customers who regard shopping as a chore to be performed as quickly as possible. It may be appropriate, therefore, to see first how women feel about shopping, and, if they do enjoy it, what particular psychological satisfactions, if any, can be isolated from their reactions.

Two-thirds of the women interviewed in New York and Cleveland report that they "really enjoy" shopping. The responses hover close to this average figure, regardless of whether the women are talking about shopping for their own clothes, for clothes for other members of the family, or for household items. One-fifth of the women interviewed "do not mind" shopping, and 10% to 15% dislike it.

Although perhaps they do not regard shopping as a "day on the town" quite so much as their mothers or grandmothers once did, the majority of today's shoppers still get real enjoyment out of it. Furthermore, when they are asked what they like and dislike most about shopping, their replies show that shopping still offers many recreational and other noneconomic attractions.

As a final check on these "psychological" satisfactions, we asked the women a number of questions about their behavior while on a shopping trip. Specifically, we wanted to know how often they shop around at different stores to compare merchandise and prices before buying; how often they spend time just browsing through the stores without buying anything; how often they spend time looking for bargains or special sales while shopping; and how often they buy extra things they had not intended to get when they started on their shopping trip. Their responses are summarized in Figures 22–12 through 22–14.

Among the many reasons women give for liking shopping [Figure 22–12], the first three categories of responses come closest to describing what might be termed nonprice, psychological satisfactions.

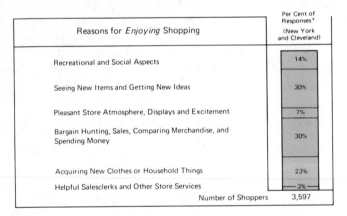

Reasons for *Enjoying* Shopping	Per Cent of Responses* (New York and Cleveland)
Recreational and Social Aspects	14%
Seeing New Items and Getting New Ideas	30%
Pleasant Store Atmosphere, Displays and Excitement	7%
Bargain Hunting, Sales, Comparing Merchandise, and Spending Money	30%
Acquiring New Clothes or Household Things	23%
Helpful Salesclerks and Other Store Services	3%
Number of Shoppers	3,597

* Percentages exceed 100% because of multiple responses. Since the percentages for New York and Cleveland are very similar, the results are combined. The category "all other likes," including convenient parking, evening openings, merchandise, and so on, total 5%, but is not included. Likewise, the "don't knows" and those who "liked nothing about shopping," who together total 16%, are excluded from this exhibit.

Figure 22–12. What Do Women Enjoy Most about Shopping?

These satisfactions, however, do not characterize the discount shopper with any greater exactitude than they do the nondiscount shoppers. For example, women who do not shop at discount stores mention recreational factors, seeing new things, and store atmosphere and excitement as often as do the high-frequency discount shoppers. Likewise, the women whose favorite store is a department store mention these psychological aspects of shopping with the same frequency as the women whose favorite store is a discount house.

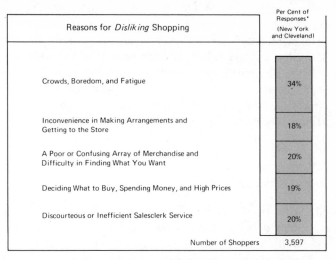

Reasons for *Disliking* Shopping	Per Cent of Responses* (New York and Cleveland)
Crowds, Boredom, and Fatigue	34%
Inconvenience in Making Arrangements and Getting to the Store	18%
A Poor or Confusing Array of Merchandise and Difficulty in Finding What You Want	20%
Deciding What to Buy, Spending Money, and High Prices	19%
Discourteous or Inefficient Salesclerk Service	20%
Number of Shoppers	3,597

* Percentages exceed 100% because of multiple responses. Since the percentages for New York and Cleveland are similar, the results are combined. The category "all other dislikes," including poor delivery, difficulty in making returns, untagged merchandise, and so on, totals 7%, but is not included. Likewise, the "don't knows" and those who dislike nothing about shopping, who together total 14%, are excluded from this exhibit.

Figure 22–13. What Do Women Dislike about Shopping?

In the case of dislikes about shopping [Figure 22–13], the first category of responses—"crowds, fatigue, and boredom"—comes closest to describing the "psychological dislikes." And, as was true in our analysis of the things which women liked about shopping, these psychological dislikes are mentioned with equal frequency both by discount store shoppers and by department store shoppers. In fact, this same relationship holds true for all of the shopping dislikes which are listed in Figure 22–13.

Comparison shopping and bargain hunting on a regular basis seem to characterize the frequent discount shoppers [see Figure 22–14], whereas browsing and impulse buying are found equally often among the women who do most of their shopping at discount stores and among those who go mostly to department stores. The attraction of the discount stores for the comparison shoppers and the bargain hunters is not particularly surprising, especially in view of the strong price image of the discount stores noted earlier in the article.

Shopping in the discount stores, then, does not appear to be any more "psychologically" satisfying to women than shopping in department stores, at least when the factors of bargain hunting and price appeal are excluded. However, if we do not limit ourselves to "psychological" satisfactions of a nonprice nature, then the discount stores appear to come out ahead of the department stores by virtue of their image of lower prices, "value for your money," and places to go for comparison shopping and bargain hunting.

On the other hand, as we saw earlier, many customers are attracted to particular department stores by the assurance that they are getting good quality merchandise in a reliable store with liberal return policies. In addition, the purchase of fashion apparel, which is done mainly in the department stores rather than in the discount houses, should also fulfill some of the shoppers' "psychological" needs. In summary, the "psychological" satisfactions of women shoppers are many and varied, and so neither the department store nor the discount store can claim any clear advantage in this type of shopping appeal.

DEPARTMENT STORE STRATEGY

With 70% of the New York women and 60% of the Cleveland women interviewed doing at least some shopping in the discount stores— and with many of these women doing *half or more* of their shopping in them— there appears to be no question that the discounters have established a strong position among retail customers. Of more concern to the department stores are the inroads of the discount houses among the younger women and among the fast-growing new middle-income groups. We saw that in New York, for instance, one-fifth of the middle-income women ($5,000–$10,000) do half or more of their shopping in discount stores.

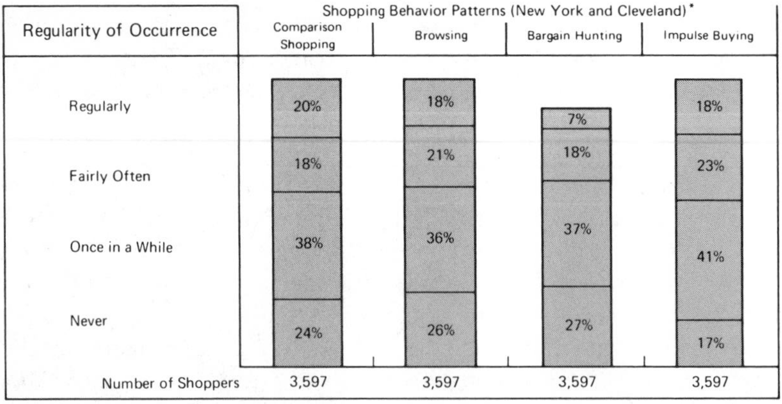

Regularity of Occurrence	Shopping Behavior Patterns (New York and Cleveland)*			
	Comparison Shopping	Browsing	Bargain Hunting	Impulse Buying
Regularly	20%	18%	7%	18%
Fairly Often	18%	21%	18%	23%
Once in a While	38%	36%	37%	41%
Never	24%	26%	27%	17%
Number of Shoppers	3,597	3,597	3,597	3,597

* Percentages do not total exactly 100% because of rounding and the exclusion of "don't knows," who average less than 1%. Since the percentages for New York and Cleveland are almost identical, the results are combined.

Figure 22–14. How Do Women Behave on a Shopping Trip?

The findings of our study paint the profile of the frequent discount shopper as a lower-to-middle-income woman, under 40 years of age, who has children. She may live in either the city or the suburbs. When on a shopping trip, she likes to shop around and compare merchandise and prices before buying, and often spends time looking for sales and bargains. She is likely to shop in the evening and may have her husband with her then. Although she enjoys shopping, she wants to get it done quickly.

What sort of merchandise-price-convenience mix is it that attracts this frequent customer to the discount stores? The strongest single appeal is price; however, this does not mean just lower prices but also good bargains and value for her money. Variety and selection of merchandise are likewise important, and so this customer buys a wide range of both hard goods and soft goods in the discount stores. For her coats and better dresses, however she is more likely to go to a department store. Finally, she finds discount stores convenient places to shop because of their accessibility and parking, night openings, self-service, and (in the newer, more modern units) general store layout and display of merchandise.

In discussing discount store attractions, we should not forget that the department stores, which after all serve considerably more customers than the discount houses, have some real strengths of their own. Of major importance is the quality of their merchandise, backed up by the reputation and reliability of the stores themselves. For many women, the traditional services offered by the department stores spell convenience in shopping. In order of importance these include: salesclerk service, delivery, ease of returning merchandise, charge accounts, and a variety of other services such as phone orders, clothing alterations, gift wrapping, and pick-up service on returned merchandise. The less-crowded atmosphere of the department stores also makes for easier shopping.

In the light of the comparative strengths of department stores and discount houses, which of the three basic strategies should the department stores adopt in order to compete most effectively with the discounters?

The first strategy—that of converting to self-service, dropping other services, and featuring discount prices—means leading from weakness rather than from strength. If a particular department store is second- or third-rate to start with (stressing price appeal and having no particular standing in the community anyway), then joining the ranks of the discounters will probably not harm its position, and may even boost its sales, at least temporarily. However, for the majority of department stores, to try to beat the discount houses at their own game in this manner appears to involve much risk and to promise little reward.

The second policy—that of trading up, dropping some of the more competitive hard-goods lines, emphasizing fashion, and offering more services— since it capitalizes on the distinctive attractions of the department store, does offer some benefits. However, except for a few of the top-line department stores, and also, of course, the high-price specialty shops, this policy carries a number of dangers. For one thing, it ignores the fact that self-service is well accepted by a large number of shoppers today, including the younger, middle-income women, a group certainly essential to the future growth of the department stores. Furthermore, this policy is poorly designed for the large department store which, while catering to the prestige market that demands the traditional department store services, must retain a broad base of middle-income customers to keep up sales volume.

The third approach (upgrading merchandise lines and emphasizing fashion, but at the same time adding certain features of the discounters on a limited basis) seems the most promising in the light of our findings about shopping behavior. For certain types of merchandise (such as fashion apparel), the great majority of women rely on the quality and reputation of the department stores to assure them they are getting the best buys. Such merchandise also requires salesclerk service and delivery. For other types of merchandise (such as kitchen utensils, small appliances, staple lines of household linens, men's socks, children's clothes, and so on), price is a major factor, and self-service may be quite as convenient as salesclerk service.

Converting some departments, such as the basement, to self-service does not mean that other services including delivery, liberal credit and return policies, phone orders, etc. should also be curtailed. This would result in an unnecessary erosion of some of the major shopping convenience appeals of the department store.

If management decides to convert some of its departments to self-service, it should remember that such a changeover entails more than just eliminating most of the salesclerks and putting merchandise on open display. Careful attention must be paid to fixturing, to traffic flow, and to the best way of educating customers, store buyers, and salesclerks about the reasons for, and expected benefits to be derived from, the change. A different merchandise mix may be called for, and the variety and selection of stock in the department may have to be trimmed; but, needless to say, too rapid a conversion to self-service for certain merchandise lines may tend to weaken management's efforts to strengthen the overall fashion image of its store.

As part of their strategy in upgrading their merchandise and emphasizing fashion, department store executives might well ask themselves what they can do to make shopping more enjoyable and exciting. We saw earlier that the recreational and social aspects of shopping and the fun of seeing new things and getting new ideas were important to many women. We also saw, however, that the department stores and the discount stores scored about evenly with their customers on these attractions. Certainly, the purchase of a new dress or coat in a department store should be a more exciting experience for the average housewife than would the purchase of kitchen wares or hosiery in a discount store! With indifferent or discourteous salesclerks mentioned as one of the major "dislikes" of shopping, better methods of recruiting and training sales help would seem to be a good place to start making the shopping experience more enjoyable. Finally, more attractive store layout and display of merchandise to invite browsing and impulse buying would also add to shopping excitement.

To combat the inroads of the discount houses, the department stores must emphasize their strengths, while at the same time recognizing that there are many types of merchandise for which personalized service is not needed by the mass of shoppers. A more flexible strategy is needed, that is, one which emphasizes quality and fashion merchandise, but at the same time adopts some of the self-service features of the discount stores in those departments selling low-price staple merchandise.

PART FOUR

NEW QUANTITATIVE TECHNIQUES IN MARKET SEGMENTATION ANALYSIS

F ROM THE preceding readings it is clear that new and exciting ways of conceptualizing customer behavior are being developed and used to guide marketing policy. More traditional, but now perhaps outworn, methods of simple conception in terms of the consumer's socioeconomic and demographic characteristics are being supplemented by measures which relate to the consumer's sociological and psychological make-up. The older approaches are being replaced in the realization that measures of buyer attitudes, preferences, and personality, for example, will relate more directly to the manager's decision-making requirements. There is a danger in this trend, however, as we witness a proliferation of techniques and approaches that may confuse rather than make clear the path to successful segmentation.

As Ronald E. Frank and Paul E. Green note in their paper "Numerical Taxonomy in Marketing Analysis: A Review Article," marketing managers frequently complain about the difficulty in finding useful ways of classifying customers. This is due partly to the "abundance of alternative classification methods rather than from lack of possibilities."[1] It is the purpose of this

---

[1] Ronald E. Frank, and Paul E. Green, "Numerical Taxonomy in Marketing Analyses: A Review Article," in this volume Reading 24.

section, therefore, to present a distillation of articles that describe, with a minimum of technical detail, the concepts and applications associated with some of the most promising of the newer techniques.

Richard M. Johnson, of Market Facts, opens the section with an article entitled "Market Segmentation: A Strategic Management Tool." The focus of Johnson's approach is the development of a model of consumer perceptions and preferences to represent the market structure and to show how various market brands fit into this structure. His approach is reminiscent of that taken by Silk in an earlier article.

The usefulness of the Johnson paper is in the comparisons that are made among the different techniques available to the research technician who wants to construct a model of consumer perception and preference. As we shall see, there are several possible ways of doing this, among them factor analysis, multiple discriminant analysis, and nonmetric multidimensional scaling. Use of any of these techniques, however, requires a grasp of the nature of the data used, the conceptual basis implicit in the model including its assumptions, and the desirable properties of the resulting model. This understanding is vital even to the manager who must eventually utilize output from these studies for policy decisions. Later in the article, Johnson illustrates several practical examples where the use of multiple discriminant analysis has aided management's understanding of the beer market. He also describes a study applying these techniques to data generated in the political sphere. The latter example is just one of the growing number of nonbusiness applications of segmentation theory, methods, and techniques.

A second review article, the one by Frank and Green mentioned above, examines in more detail two techniques that the reader will have encountered beforehand. In Haley's paper, "Benefit Segmentation" it was pointed out how factor and cluster analysis are used in determining the underlying characteristics of benefit segments. These two analytical approaches, usually termed "numerical taxonomy," show considerable promise for classifying customer benefits and groups. Another interesting example using factor and cluster analysis is found in the article by Bass, Pessemier, and Tigert in which the use of these techniques is described in arriving at a taxonomy or classification of magazine readership. The Frank and Green selection in the present section provides other illustrative applications of these techniques.

Use of the new techniques invites caution, however, because of limitations common to these and other taxonomic procedures. It is not, for example, clear what is the exact number of clusters that should be developed from any set of data, or for that matter, what their statistical properties are. Nor is it certain, as yet, how to deal with different units of measurement for different characteristics of the object studied. In addition, researchers wishing to explore these new developments must eventually be concerned with the choice of appropriate techniques. These and other questions remain for future work.

Where Johnson has examined multiple discriminant analysis in some detail, and Frank and Green review the uses and implications of factor and cluster analysis, Lester Neidell provides an overview of the use of nonmetric multidimensional scaling methods for the solution of market segmentation problems. Neidell emphasizes both the practical differences between this approach and other scaling methods while exploring the underlying theory. He discusses the relevance of various scaling approaches to marketing situations and presents several illustrative examples.

Finally, the paper by V. Parker Lessig and John O. Tollefson reports a study utilizing an aggregation approach to market segment identification and also makes extensive use of cluster analysis. The authors suggest that, in addition to showing a practical method for isolating segments, their results provide a positive test of the existence of relationships between buyer behavior and personal characteristics. Their results supplement the meager evidence now available which support the belief in such relationships. Consequently, they provide indirect empirical support for the segment identification process.

Readings for Part Four

Anderson, T. W. *Introduction to Multivariate Statistical Analysis,* New York: John Wiley & Sons, Inc., 1958.

Cooley, W. W., and P. R. Lohnes. *Multivariate Procedures for Behavioral Sciences*, New York: John Wiley & Sons, Inc., 1962.

Green, P. E., and F. J. Carmone. *Multidimensional Scaling and Related Techniques in Marketing Analysis*, Boston: Allyn & Bacon, Inc., 1970.

Harman, H. H. *Modern Factor Analysis*, 2nd ed., Chicago: University of Chicago Press, 1960.

Morrison, D. F. *Multivariate Statistical Methods*, New York: McGraw-Hill Book Company, 1967, pp. 152–153.

Sokal, R. R., and P. H. A. Sneath. *Principles of Numerical Taxonomy*, San Francisco: W. H. Freeman and Co., Publishers, 1963.

23.

Market Segmentation:
A Strategic Management Tool

Richard M. Johnson

Like motivation research in the late 1950's, market segmentation is receiving much attention in research circles. Although this term evokes the idea of cutting up a market into little pieces, the real role of such research is more basic and potentially more valuable. In this discussion *market segmentation analysis* refers to examination of the structure of a market as perceived by consumers, preferably using a geometric spatial model, and to forcasting the intensity of demand for a potential product positioned anywhere in the space.

The purpose of such a study, as seen by a marketing manager, might be:

1. To learn how the brands or products in a class are perceived with respect to strengths, weaknesses, similarities, etc.
2. To learn about consumers' desires, and how these are satisfied or unsatisfied by the current market.
3. To integrate these findings strategically, determining the greatest opportunities for new brands or products and how a product or its image should be modified to produce the greatest sales gain.

From the position of a marketing research technician, each of these three goals translates into a separate technical problem:

1. To construct a product space, a geometric representation of consumers' perceptions of products or brands in a category.
2. To obtain a density distribution by positioning consumers' ideal points in the same space.
3. To construct a model which predicts preferences of groups of consumers toward new or modified products.

This discussion will focus on each of these three problems in turn, suggesting solutions now available. Solutions to the first two problems can be illus-

From Richard M. Johnson, "Market Segmentation: A Strategic Management Tool," *Journal of Marketing Research*, Vol. 8 (February 1971), pp. 13–18. Published by the American Marketing Association. Reprinted by permission.

trated with actual data, although currently solutions for the third problem are more tentative. This will not be an exhaustive catalog of techniques, nor is this the only way of structuring the general problem of forecasting consumer demand for new or modified products.

CONSTRUCTING THE PRODUCT SPACE

A spatial representation or map of a product category provides the foundation on which other aspects of the solution are built. Many equally-useful techniques are available for constructing product spaces which require different assumptions and possess different properties. The following is a list of useful properties of product spaces which may be used to evaluate alternative techniques:

1. *Metric:* distances between products in space should relate to perceived similarity between them.
2. *Identification:* directions in the space should correspond to identified product attributes.
3. *Uniqueness/reliability:* similar procedures applied to similar data should yield similar answers.
4. *Robustness/foolproofness:* procedures should work every time. It should not be necessary to switch techniques or make basic changes in order to cope with each new set of data.
5. *Freedom from improper assumptions:* other things being equal, a procedure that requires fewer assumptions is preferred.

One basic distinction has to do with the kinds of data to be analyzed. Three kinds of data are frequently used.

Similarity/Dissimilarity Data

Here a respondent is not concerned in any obvious way with dimensions or attributes which describe the products judged. He makes global judgments of relative similarity among products, with the theoretical advantage that there is no burden on the researcher to determine in advance the important attributes or dimensions within a product category. Examples of such data might be: (1) to present triples of products and ask which two are most or least similar, (2) to present pairs of products and ask which pair is most similar, or (3) to rank order k-1 products in terms of similarity with the kth.

Preference Data

Preference data can be used to construct a product space, given assumptions relating preference to distances. For instance, a frequent assumption is that an individual has ideal points in the same space and that product preference is related in some systematic way to distances from his ideal point to his perception of products' locations. As with similarity/dissimilarity data, preference data place no burden on the researcher to determine salient product attributes in advance. Examples of preference data which might lead to a product space are: (1) paired comparison data, (2) rank orders of preference, or (3) generalized overall ratings (as on a 1 to 9 scale).

Attribute Data

If the researcher knows in advance important product attributes by which consumers discriminate among products, or with which they form preferences, then he may ask respondents to describe products on scales relating to each attribute. For instance, they may use rating scales describing brands of beer with respect to price vs. quality, heaviness vs. lightness, or smoothness vs. bitterness.

In addition to these three kinds of data, *procedures* can be *metric* or *nonmetric*. Metric procedures make assumptions about the properties of data, as when in computing a mean one assumes that the difference between ratings of values one and two is the same as that between two and three, etc. Nonmetric procedures make fewer assumptions about the nature of the data; these are usually techniques in which the only operations on data are comparisons such as "greater than" or "less than." Nonmetric procedures are typically used with data from rank order or paired comparison methods.

Another issue is whether or not a *single product space* will adequately represent all respondents' perceptions. At the extreme, each respondent might require a unique product space to account for aspects of his perceptions. However, one of the main reasons for product spaces' utility is that they summarize a larger amount of information in unusually tangible and compact form. Allowing a totally different product space for each respondent would certainly destroy much of the illustrative value of the result. A compromise would be to recognize that respondents might fall naturally into a relatively small number of subgroups with different product perceptions. In this case, a separate product space could be constructed for each subgroup.

Frequently a single product space is assumed to be adequate to account for important aspects of all respondents' *perceptions*. Differences in *preference* are then taken into account by considering each respondent's ideal product to have a unique location in the common product space, and by recognizing that different respondents may weight dimensions uniquely. This was the approach taken in the examples to follow.

Techniques which have received a great deal of use in constructing product spaces include nonmetric multidimensional scaling [3, 7, 8, 12], factor analysis [11], and multiple discriminant analysis [4]. Factor analysis has been available for this purpose for many years, and multidimensional scaling was discussed as early as 1938 [13]. *Nonmetric* multidimensional scaling, a comparatively recent development, has achieved great popularity because of the invention of ingenious computing methods requiring only the most minimal assumptions regarding the nature of the data. Discriminant analysis requires assumptions about the metric properties of data, but it appears to be particularly robust and foolproof in application.

These techniques produce similar results in most practical applications. The technique of multiple discriminant analysis will be illustrated here.

EXAMPLES OF PRODUCT SPACES

Imagine settling on a number of attributes which together account for all of the important ways in which products in a set are seen to differ from each other. Suppose that each product has been rated on each attribute by several people, although each person has not necessarily described more than one product.

Given such data, multiple discriminant analysis is a powerful technique for constructing a spatial model of the product category. First, it finds the weighted combination of attributes which discriminates most among products, maximizing an F-ratio of between-product to within-product variance. Then second and subsequent weighted combinations are found which discriminate maximally among products, within the constraint that they all be uncorrelated with one another. Having determined as many discriminating dimensions as possible, average scores can be used to plot products on each dimension. Distances between pairs of products in this space reflect the amount of discrimination between them.[1]

Figure 23–1 shows such a space for the Chicago beer market as perceived by members of Market Facts' Consumer Mail Panels in a pilot study, September, 1968. Approximately 500 male beer drinkers described 8 brands of beer on each of 35 attributes. The data indicated that a third sizable dimension also existed, but the two dimensions pictured here account for approximately 90% of discrimination among images of these 8 products.

The location of each brand is indicated on these two major dimensions. The horizontal dimension contrasts premium quality on the right with popular price on the left. The vertical dimension reflects relative lightness. In addition, the mean rating of each product on each of the attributes is shown by relative position on each attribute vector. For instance, Miller is perceived as being most popular with women, followed by Budweiser, Schlitz, Hamms, and four unnamed, popularly priced beers.

---

[1] McKeon [10] has shown that multiple discriminant analysis produces the same results as classic (metric) multidimensional scaling of Mahalanobis' distances based on the same data.

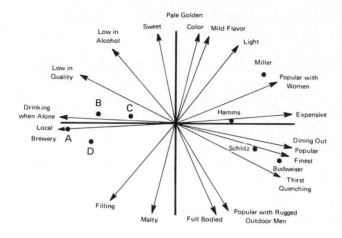

Figure 23–1. The Chicago Beer Market

As a second example, the same technique was applied to political data. During the weeks immediately preceding the 1968 presidential election, a questionnaire was sent to 1,000 Consumer Mail Panels households. Respondents were asked to agree or disagree with each of 35 political statements on a four-point scale. Topics were Vietnam, law and order, welfare, and other issues felt to be germane to current politics. Respondents also described two preselected political figures, according to their perceptions of each figure's stand on each issue. Discriminant analysis indicated two major dimensions accounting for 86% of the discrimination among 14 political figures.

The liberal vs. conservative dimension is apparent in the data, as shown in Figure 23–2. The remaining dimension apparently reflects perceived favorability of attitude toward government involvement in domestic and international matters. As in the beer space, it is only necessary to erect perpendiculars to each vector to observe each political figure's relative position on each of the 35 issues. Additional details are in [5].

Multiple discriminant analysis is a major competitor of nonmetric multidimensional scaling in constructing product spaces. The principal assumptions which the former requires are that: (1) perceptions be homogeneous across respondents, (2) attribute data be scaled at the interval level (equal intervals on rating scales), (3) attributes be linearly related to one another, and (4) amount of disagreement (error covariance matrix) be the same for each product.

Only the first of these assumptions is required by most nonmetric methods, and some even relax that assumption. However, the space provided by multiple discriminant analysis has the following useful properties:

1. Given customary assumptions of multivariate normality, there is a test of significance for distance (dissimilarity) between any two products.

2. Unlike nonmetric procedures, distances estimated among a collection of products do not depend upon whether or not additional products are included in the analysis. Any of the brands of beer or political figures could have been deleted from the examples and the remaining object locations would have had the same relationships to one another and to the attribute vectors.

3. The technique is reliable and well known, and solutions are unique, since the technique cannot be misled by any local optimum.

OBTAINING THE DISTRIBUTION OF CONSUMERS' IDEAL POINTS

After constructing a product space, the next concern is estimating consumer demand for a product located at any particular point. The demand

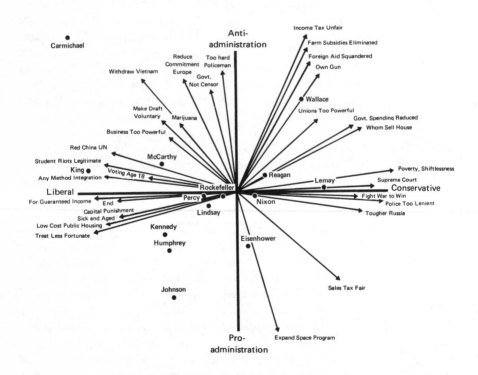

Figure 23–2. The Political Space, 1968

function over such a space is desired and can be approximated by one of several general approaches.

The first is to locate each person's ideal point in the region of the space implied by his rank ordered preferences. His ideal point would be closest to the product he likes best, second closest to the product he likes second best, etc. There are several procedures which show promise using this approach [2, 3, 7, 8, 12], although difficulties remain in practical execution. This approach has trouble dealing with individuals who behave in a manner contrary to the basic assumptions of the model, as when one chooses products first on the far left side of the space, second on the far right side, and third in the center. Most individuals giving rank orders of preference do display such nonmonotonicity to some extent, understandably producing problems for the application of these techniques.

The second approach involves deducing the number of ideal points at each region in space by using data on whether a product has too much or too little of each attribute. This procedure has not yet been fully explored, but at present seems to be appropriate to the multidimensional case only when strong assumptions about the shape of the ideal point distribution are given.

The third approach is to have each person describe his ideal product, with the same attributes and rating scales as for existing products. If multiple discriminant analysis has been used to obtain a product space, each person's ideal product can then be inserted in the same space.

There are considerable differences between an ideal point location inferred from a rank order of preference and one obtained directly from an attribute rating. To clarify matters, consider a single dimension, heaviness vs. lightness in beer. If a previous mapping has shown that brands A, B, C, and D are equally spaced on this one dimension, and if a respondent ranks his preferences as B, C, A, and D, then his ideal must lie closer to B than to A or C and closer to C than to A. This narrows the feasible region for his ideal point down to the area indicated in Figure 23–3. Had he stated a preference for A, with D second, there would be no logically corresponding position for his ideal point in the space.

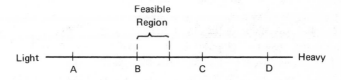

Figure 23–3. A One-dimensional Product Space

However, suppose these products have already been given the following scale positions on a heavy/light dimension: A = 1.0, B = 2.0, C = 3.0, and D = 4.0. If a respondent unambiguously specifies his ideal on this scale at 2.25, his ideal can be put directly on the scale, with no complexities. Of course, it does not follow *necessarily* that his stated rank order of preference will be predictable from the location of his ideal point.

There is no logical reason why individuals must be clustered into market segments. Mathematically, one can cope with the case where hundreds or thousands of individual ideal points are each located in the space. However, it is much easier to approximate such distributions by clustering respondents into groups. Cluster analysis [6] has been used with the present data to put individuals into a few groups with relatively similar product desires (beer) or points of view (politics).

Figure 23–4 shows an approximation to the density distribution of consumers' ideal points in the Chicago beer market, a "poor man's contour map." Ideal points tended somewhat to group themselves (circles) into clusters. It is not implied that all ideal points lie within the circles, since they are really distributed to some extent throughout the entire space. Circle sizes indicate the relative sizes of clusters, and the center of each is located at the center of its circle.

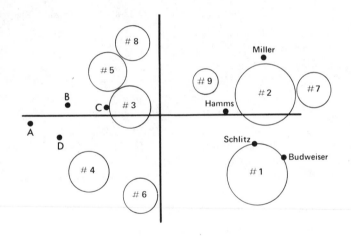

Figure 23–4. Distribution of Ideal Points in Product Space

A representation such as this contains much potentially useful marketing information. For instance, if people can be assumed to prefer products closer to their ideal points, there may be a ready market for a new brand on the lower or "heavy" side of the space, approximately neutral in price/quality. Likewise, there may be opportunities for new brands in the upper middle region, decidedly light and neutral in price/quality. Perhaps popularly priced Brand A will have marketing problems, since this brand is closest to no cluster.

Figure 23–5 shows a similar representation for the political space, where circles represent concentrations of voters' points. These are not ideal points, but rather personally held positions on political issues. Clusters on the left side of the space intended to vote mostly for Humphrey and those on the right for Nixon in the 1968 election. Throughout the space, the percentage voting Republican increases generally from left to right.

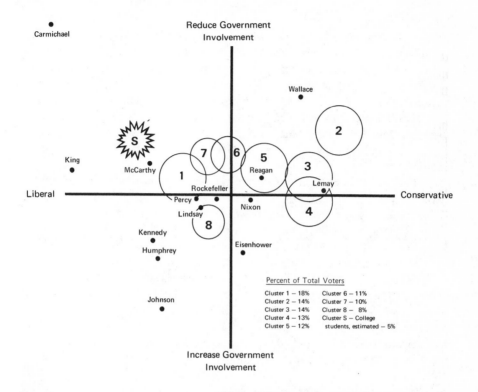

Figure 23—5. Voter Segment Positions Relative to Political Figures

It may be surprising that the center of the ideal points lies considerably to the right of that of the political figures. One possible explanation is that this study dealt solely with positions on *issues*, so matters of style or personality did not enter the definition of the space. It is entirely possible that members of clusters one and eight, the most liberal, found Nixon's position on issues approximately as attractive as Humphrey's, but they voted for Humphrey on the basis of preference for style, personality, or political party. Likewise, members of cluster two might have voted strongly for Wallace, given his position, but he received only 14% of this cluster's vote. He may have been rejected on the basis of other qualities. The clusters are described in more detail in [5].

A small experiment was undertaken to test the validity of this model. Responses from a class of sociology students in a western state university showed them to be more liberal and more for decreasing government involvement internationally than any of the eight voter clusters. Their position is close to McCarthy's, indicated by an "S".

STRATEGIC INTEGRATION OF FINDINGS

Having determined the position of products in a space and seen where consumer ideal points are located, how can such findings be integrated to determine appropriate product strategy? A product's market share should be increased by repositioning: (1) closer to ideal points of sizable segments of the market, (2) farther from other products with which it must compete, and (3) on dimensions weighted heavily in consumers' preferences. Even these broad guidelines provide some basis for marketing strategy. For instance, in Figure 23–4, Brand A is clearly farthest from all clusters and should be repositioned.

In Figure 23–5, Humphrey, Kennedy, and Johnson could have increased their acceptance with this respondent sample by moving upwards and to the right, modifying their perceived position. Presumably, endorsement of any issue in the upper right quadrant or a negative position on any issue in the lower left quadrant of Figure 23–2 would have helped move Humphrey closer to the concentration of voters' ideal points.

Although the broad outlines of marketing strategy are suggested by spaces such as these, it would be desirable to make more precise quantitative forecasts of the effect of modifying a product's position. Unfortunately, the problem of constructing a model to explain product choice behavior based on locations of ideal points and products in a multidimensional space has not yet been completely solved, although some useful approaches are currently available.

As the first step, it is useful to concentrate on the behavior of clusters of respondents rather than that of individuals, especially if clusters are truly homogeneous. Data predicting behavior of groups are much smoother and results for a few groups are far more communicable to marketing management than findings stated in terms of large numbers of individual respondents.

If preference data are available for a collection of products, one can analyze the extent to which respondents' preferences are related to distances in the space. Using regression analysis, one can estimate a set of importance weights for each cluster or, if desired, for each respondent, to be applied to the dimensions of the product space. Weights would be chosen providing the best explanation of cluster or individual respondent preferences in terms of weighted distances between ideal points and each product's perceived location. If clusters, rather than individuals, are used it may be desirable to first calculate preference scale values or utilities for each cluster [1, 9]. Importance weights can then be obtained using multiple regression to predict these values from distances. If explanations of product preference can be made for *existing products*, which depend only on locations in space, then the same approach should permit *predictions* of preference levels for new or modified products to be positioned at specific locations in the space.

Models of choice behavior clearly deserve more attention. Although the problem of constructing the product space has received much attention, we are denied the full potential of these powerful solutions unless we are able to quantify relationships between distances in such a space and consumer choice behavior.

SUMMARY

Market segmentation studies can produce results which indicate desirable marketing action. Techniques which are presently available can: (1) construct a product space, (2) discover the shape of the distribution of consumer's ideal points throughout such a space, and (3) identify likely opportunities for new or modified products.

In the past, marketing research has often been restricted to *tactical* questions such as package design or pricing levels. However, with' the advent of new techniques, marketing research can contribute directly to the development of *strategic* alternatives to current product marketing plans. There remains a need for improved technology, particularly in the development of models for explaining and predicting preferential choice behavior. The general problem has great practical significance, and provides a wealth of opportunity for development of new techniques and models.

References

1. Bradley, M. E. and R. A. Terry. "Rank Analysis of Incomplete Block Designs: The Method of Paired Comparisons," *Biometrika*, 39 (1952), 324–45.
2. Carroll, J. D. "Individual Differences and Multidimensional Scaling," Murray Hill, N.J.: Bell Telephone Laboratories, 1969.
3. Guttman, Louis. "A General Nonmetric Technique for Finding the Smallest Space for a Configuration of Points," *Psychometrika*, 33 (December 1968), 469–506.
4. Johnson, Richard M. "Multiple Discriminant Analysis," unpublished paper, Workshop on Multivariate Methods in Marketing, University of Chicago, 1970.
5. ————. "Political Segmentation," paper presented at Spring Conference on Research Methodology, American Marketing Association, New York, 1969.

6. Johnson, Stephen C. "Hierarchial Clustering Schemes," *Psychometrika*, 32 (September 1967), 241–54.

7. Kruskal, Joseph B. "Multidimensional Scaling by Optimizing Goodness of Fit to a Nonmetric Hypothesis," *Psychometrika*, 29 (March 1964), 1–27.

8. ———. "Nonmetric Multidimensional Scaling: A Numerical Method," *Psychometrika*, 29 (June 1964), 115–29.

9. Luce, R. D. "A Choice Theory Analysis of Similarity Judgments," *Psychometrika*, 26 (September 1961), 325–32.

10. McKeon, James J. "Canonical Analysis," *Psychometric Monographs*, 13.

11. Tucker, Ledyard. "Dimensions of Preference," Research Memorandum RM–60–7, Princeton, N.J.: Educational Testing Service, 1960.

12. Young, F. W. "TORSCA, An IBM Program for Nonmetric Multidimensional Scaling," *Journal of Marketing Research*, 5 (August 1968), 319–21.

13. Young, G. and A. S. Householder. "Discussion of a Set of Points in Terms of Their Mutual Distances," *Psychometrika*, 3 (March 1938), 19–22.

24.

Numerical Taxonomy in Marketing Analysis: A Review Article

Ronald E. Frank
Paul E. Green

Marketing managers and researchers often comment on their difficulty in developing useful ways of classifying customers for formulating marketing policy. The source of the difficulty frequently stems from the abundance of alternative classification methods rather than from a lack of possibilities. Changes in our concepts of customer behavior have more often been associated with the generation of new measures of behavior than with the integration of existing measures. In 50 years, researchers have stopped focusing almost exclusively on customer socioeconomic characteristics as a basis for policy formulation and have begun considering a wide range of measures of sociological and psychological phenomena (such as personality, preferences, buying intentions, perceived risk, interpersonal influence) and an increasing number of measures of actual buying behavior (such as total consumption and brand loyalty).

Much of customer behavior has many factors—it is multidimensional. Researchers often sidestep its complexity by picking some unidimensional attribute assumed to be an indicator of the more complex phenomena to be understood. For example, in studies of household brand loyalty (with respect to frequently purchased, branded food products), the researcher often finds variables used to measure brand loyalty such as the proportion of purchases spent on the most frequently purchased brand or the proportion spent on the brand that is of central interest to the researcher. For many purposes, however, these might be too limited a measure of loyalty since they fail to approximate a full description of a rather complex phenomenon. Customers do not typically buy a single brand or even two brands. Many households purchase three, four, or five brands of a product. In addition, the subset of brands chosen for consumption will vary from household to household.

From Ronald E. Frank and Paul E. Green, "Numerical Taxonomy in Marketing Analysis: A Review Article," *Journal of Marketing Research*, Vol. 5 (February 1968), pp. 83–98. Published by the American Marketing Association. Reprinted by permission.

What procedure could be used to study the clusters of brands that different households consume? All possible combinations of brands could be computed and households sorted into respective classes, but this approach presents a few problems. How many combinations are there in a market with only twelve brands? There are over four million if the number of partitions resulting from grouping twelve brands into two or more clusters is added.[1] Even worse, one may want to measure the similarity of brand purchasing behavior not only for the combination of brands but also for the relative proportion of money spent on each brand.

This kind of classification problem is not unique to brand loyalty. How are television programs classified for similarity of audience profiles? Here, too, practitioners often use a single category as the basis for classification, such as the modal audience group, (for example, teenagers loyal to "Rat Patrol"). How should market areas for choosing test markets be grouped? How can a potential purchaser compare the performance specifications of a wide range of computers? How should the readership characteristics of a number of alternative magazines be compared?

Almost every major analytical problem requires the classification of objects by several characteristics—whether customers, products, cities, television programs, or magazines. Seldom are explicit classification systems with some combination of attributes, such as those used for measuring a customer's social class or stage in life cycle, found. Such classification systems typically represent self-imposed taxonomies; that is, taxonomies the researcher believes to be relevant because of a theory or prior experience.[2] Although this approach can be useful, it has limitations. Regardless of the complexity of reality, it is difficult to classify objects by more than two or three characteristics at a time. If reality requires greater complexity, researchers are severely constrained by their conceptual limitations.

The difficulty of seeing through this often bewildering maze is not unique to marketing, (not to mention business problems) as indicated by Sokal, an entymologist:

---

[1] The general formula [29] for finding all possible partitions of a given set of entities is

$$P(n,m) = \left[m^n - \sum_{i-1}^{m-1} m_{(m-i)} P(i) \right] / m!$$

where

m is number of partitions; $m \geq 2$
n is number of entities in set to be clustered; $n \geq m$
$P(m)$ is number of distinct partitions containing exactly m clusters
$m_{(m-i)}$ is $m(m-1)(m-2) \cdots (m-i+1)$.

[2] Taxonomies can be distinguished from classifications since they denote interconnections (usually a hierarchy) among characteristics of the objects—a less generic term than classifications. In practice, however, the terms are often used interchangeably.

Classification is one of the fundamental concerns of science. Facts and objects must be arranged in an orderly fashion before their unifying principles can be discovered and used as a basis for prediction. Many phenomena occur in such variety and profusion that unless some system is created among them, they would be unlikely to provide any useful information [82].

A new technology, numerical taxonomy, has been developed, primarily in biology. It consists of a set of numerical procedures for classifying objects [83]. These taxonomic procedures may be called preclassification techniques since their purpose is to describe the natural groupings that occur in large masses of data. From these natural groupings (or clusters) the researcher can sometimes develop the requisite conceptual framework for classification.

Numerical taxonomy is still new, and to the authors' knowledge, only three articles in marketing have appeared [34, 50, 66]. This article introduces potential marketing applications of this set of techniques, giving some attention to their mathematical bases, current limitations, and assumptions. The following topics are discussed:

1. The nature of taxonomic procedures,
2. Illustrative applications of taxonomic methods to marketing problems,
3. The assumptions and limitations of the procedures.

The authors feel that taxonomic methods will be used increasingly to describe complex marketing data. Hopefully, this article will alert more researchers to the potential of these methods and to some of the cautions associated with use.

THE NATURE OF TAXONOMIC PROCEDURES

Assume that there is a set of objects, such as people, products, advertisements, and marketing channels, each of which can be characterized by a measurement (or more generally, by an attribute score) on each of a set of characteristics. The researcher has no external criterion for grouping the objects into subsets of similar objects; instead, he wants to identify natural groupings in the data, after which more formal models might be developed.

More formally stated, the problem is: How should objects be assigned to groups so there will be as much likeness within groups and as much difference among groups as possible? From this question four others arise: (1) what proximity measure is to be used to summarize the likeness of profiles, (2) after these likeness measures have been computed, how should the objects be grouped, (3) after the objects have been grouped, what descriptive measures are appropriate for summarizing the characteristics of each group, (4) are the groups formed really different from each other (the inferential problem)?

There are numerous taxonomic procedures for achieving the major objective. The following discussion illustrates the logic of one of them, followed by a brief overview of other kinds of procedures that have been developed. The purpose is to show the relevance of these techniques for establishing multidimensional classification systems, not to provide a definitive methodological statement.

An Example

Suppose that the objects of interest are television programs and the characteristics are (assumed independent) measures of the socioeconomic profile of each program. Let us start with measures of two characteristics, number of teenagers (X_1) and number of adult men (X_2), for each of ten programs. Our problem is to find a way of grouping the programs by the similarity of their audience profiles. Figure 24–1 plots the programs in two dimensions.

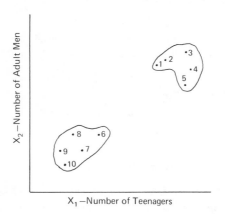

Figure 24–1. Illustration of Taxonomic Techniques (Hypothetical)

Assume that two clusters of five programs each are desired. A start is to compute Euclidean distances of every point from every other point with the usual formula:

$$\Delta_{jk} = [(X_{1j} - X_{1k})^2 + (X_{2j} - X_{2k})^2]^{1/2}.$$

Points 1 and 2 in Figure 24–1 appear to be closest together. The first cluster would then be formed by finding the midpoint between Points 1 and 2, the centroid of the point coordinates. Then the distance of each point from this average would be computed and the point closest to this average would be added (here, Point 3). Similarly, Point 4 and then Point 5 would be added, giving a cluster of five programs as desired.

Generalizing to More than Two Dimensions

In the previous illustration, only two measurements were considered for each point (television program). It is relatively easy to follow the procedure visually.[3] In practice there may be many measurements for each program; hence, the graphical procedure must be supplemented by a computational technique that can deal with several characteristics.

Several computer routines are available for this type of taxonomic analysis often called cluster analysis. For example, one computer routine used involves these steps:

1. Each characteristic is first converted to a standardized variate with zero mean and unit standard deviation.
2. Euclidean distances are then computed for each of all possible pairs of points.
3. The pair with the smallest distance is chosen as the node of the first cluster, and the average of this pair is computed.
4. Additional points are added to this cluster (based on closeness to the last-computed average) until:
   a. Some prespecified number of points has been clustered.
   b. The point to be added to the cluster exceeds some prespecified distance-cutoff or threshold number.
5. The program then proceeds to the next pair of points which are closest together of all unclustered points, and the above process is repeated.
6. If desired, the program can be modified to allow points to be in more than one cluster.
7. The program can be further modified to shift points from cluster to cluster to obtain final clusters which are best in the sense of having the lowest average within-cluster distance summed over all clusters at a given stage in the clustering.

OTHER CLUSTERING TECHNIQUES

Proximity Measures.   This program is only one way to cluster points in multidimensional space. Other proximity measures and clustering techniques have been proposed by researchers in the biological and social sciences. With some simplification, the proximity measures can be categorized as:

[3] The typical Euclidean distance measure can be easily generalized to more than two dimensions as:

$$\Delta_{jk} = \left[\sum_{i=1}^{n} (X_{ij} - X_{ik})^2 \right]^{1/2}.$$

1. Distance measures
2. Correlation measures
3. Similarity measures for attribute data

The input data—nominal, ordinal, interval, ratio, or mixed scales—often determines the proximity measure used to express pairwise relationships among the elements.

Distance Measures.   One kind of clustering technique based on Euclidean distance has already been described. Two problems exist with regard to this kind of measure: (1) correlated characteristics and (2) noncomparability of the original units in which the characteristics are measured [69]. The second problem is usually "solved" by standardizing all characteristics to mean zero and unit standard deviation. Thus it is assumed that mean and variance among characteristics is not important in the grouping process.

The first problem can be handled two ways. A principal component analysis may be run on the characteristics and factor scores computed for the objects. Each component score may then be weighted by the square root of the eigenvalue associated with that component before computing the distance measure. A second approach uses the Mahalanobis [60] generalized distance in which the squared distances between objects is measured as a linear combination of the correlated measurements expressed in units of the estimated population dispersion of the composite measure. If the characteristics are uncorrelated and measurements are first standardized (mean zero and unit standard deviation), the square root of the Mahalanobis measure is equivalent to the Euclidean measure discussed.

In practice, distance measures of the kind just described are usually used when data are at least intervally scaled. Kendall [54], however, proposed a distance measure requiring only ordinally scaled measurements. Also, Restle [75] and others have shown that even nominally scaled data may be characterized in distance terms, in the sense of obeying the distance axioms. The resulting metric, however, may not be Euclidean.

Correlation Measures.   Probably the most widely used proximity measure in clustering procedures involves the correlation coefficient.[4] Inverse factor analysis, the Q-technique, is a fairly widely used procedure in which objects replace tests in the computation of factor loadings. Clusters may then be formed by grouping subjects with similar factor loadings. Three problems are associated with this class of techniques. First, correlation removes the elevation and scatter of each object, thereby losing information. Second, in group-

---

[4] If the characteristics are expressed in standard scores, the Euclidean distance between two objects is a monotone transformation of their correlation [18].

ing objects by factor loadings, the analyst risks obtaining some objects that are split among clusters. Finally, the analyst must usually resort to an R-technique to interpret the clusters' characteristics according to their correlations with underlying factors.

Similarity Measures.   Similarity measures are often used in clustering when the characteristics of each object are only nominally scaled, for example, dichotomous or multichotomous. The usual notion of distance seems less applicable here (although it is still possible to use multidimensional scaling techniques to "metricize" such data before clustering). Typically, however, the analyst tries to develop similarity coefficients based on attribute matching.

For example, if two objects are compared on each of eight attributes, the following might result:

	Attribute							
Entity	1	2	3	4	5	6	7	8
1	1	0	0	1	1	0	1	0
2	0	1	0	1	0	1	1	1

The fractional match coefficient would be:

$$S_{12} = \frac{M}{N} = \tfrac{3}{8},$$

where M denotes the number of attributes held in common (matching 1's or 0's) and N denotes the total number of attributes. If weak matches (nonpossession of the attribute) are to be deemphasized, the Tanimoto [76] coefficient is appropriate:

$$\text{Tanimoto } S_{ij} = \frac{\text{No. of attributes which are 1 for both objects } i \text{ and } j}{\text{No. of attributes which are 1 for either } i \text{ or } j, \text{or both}}.$$

In this problem the coefficient would be $\tfrac{2}{7}$. Many other similarity measures have been developed that represent variations of the fractional match coefficient. (See [83].)

One interesting distance-type measure which can also be used for attribute matching is the pattern similarity coefficient, r_p, proposed by Cattell, Coulter, and Tsujioka [16]. In interval-scaled data, the coefficient compares the computed distance with that expected by chance alone:

$$r_{p(jk)} = \frac{E_i - \sum_{i=1}^{n} d^2_{(jk)}}{E_i + \sum_{i=1}^{n} d^2_{(jk)}},$$

where i is the number of dimensions, $d^2_{(jk)}$ is the squared Euclidean distance in standard units between entities j and k, and E_i is twice the median chi-square value for i degrees of freedom. Cattell's coefficient has the convenient property of varying from $+1$ for complete agreement, 0 for no agreement, to -1 for inverse agreement.

The coefficient may also be adapted for dichotomous items as:

$$r'_p = \frac{E_i - d}{E_i + d},$$

where d represents the number of disagreements on d items.

Finally, some mention should be made of the mixed-scale problem in which the characteristics are measured in different modes. One possibility is to degrade interval-scaled data into categories and use similarity coefficients. Another possibility is to upgrade nominally or ordinally scaled data. There seems to be no satisfactory solution to this problem although it is conceivable that some highly general measure of proximity, perhaps one derived from information theory, may be appropriate.

Clustering Routines

After the analyst has decided on some measure of pairwise proximity, he must still contend with the grouping process itself. A variety of approaches are possible. One major class of approaches to the clustering problem consists of hierarchical routines. For example, Edwards and Cavalli-Sforza [24] describe a clustering procedure (based on a least-squares technique) which first clusters the data into two groups. The procedure is repeated sequentially so that progressively smaller clusters are formed sequentially by splitting the original clusters. A hierarchical array is obtained. A variant of this procedure starts with clusters of one object each and builds new clusters hierarchically until one overall cluster results. This approach was described by Ward [93].

Other grouping routines use threshold or cutoff measures similar to the algorithm described earlier. Some procedures, for example, suggest selecting an object closest to the centroid of all the data to serve as a prime node around which other points are clustered until some threshold distance level is reached. An unclustered object farthest from the centroid of the first cluster may then be chosen as a new prime node. The process is continued, the third and subsequent prime nodes being selected on the basis of largest average distance from the centroids of clusters already formed.

Some grouping routines [24, 93] are highly metric since effectiveness measures involve the computation of within-cluster variance around the centroid of the cluster members. Others [83] use only the proximity between an unclustered object and some single member of the clustered set as a criterion for set inclusion.

In Q-technique, objects are often clustered by highest factor loadings, a simple approach; but it does not use all available information.

Finally, there is the possibility of clustering by systematic space-density search routines in which the n-dimensional space is cut into hypercubes and the computer program counts the number of cases falling into each region. Relatively little work, however, has been done on this taxonomic routine.

Descriptive Characteristics of the Groups

Even after objects are grouped, each cluster must be characterized by its representative profile. In some instances the cluster's centroid is used as a description of its members. In others the actual profile of the object closest to the group's centroid may be used. As in choice of proximity measure and choice of grouping routine, however, the criteria for describing each group are usually ad hoc, a main problem being that *cluster* is still not a precisely defined term. Some of these problems and the inferential problem will be reconsidered later in this article.

ILLUSTRATIVE MARKETING APPLICATIONS

Some appreciation for the versatility and unresolved problems of taxonomic methods can be gained from the following short review of studies conducted by the authors in the past two years. [1966 and 1967].

Clustering Analysis in Test Marketing

One of the earliest pilot applications involved the use of cluster analysis in the grouping of cities (standard metropolitan areas) for test marketing purposes [34]. Data for each of 88 cities were available on 14 measured characteristics, such as population, number of retail stores, percent non-white. A clustering program using the Euclidean distance measure grouped the cities into homogeneous five-point clusters. Centroids of each cluster in 14-space and average distances of each point from the grand centroid and from the centroid of its own cluster were obtained. As an alternative for comparison purposes, the original data matrix was factored, and cluster analysis was performed on the resultant (standardized) factor scores.

The cluster analysis yielded some interesting findings. First, the cluster of five cities closest to the grand mean of all 88—Dayton, Columbus, Indianapolis, Syracuse, and New Haven—agreed well with various lists of typical cities prepared by such magazines as *Sales Management* and *Printers' Ink* indicating results consistent with industry judgment. This method also provides homogeneous groups of cities with centroids quite distant from the grand origin. Second, the combined procedure of factor analysis (and subsequent clustering of factor scores) indicated that two major dimensions, a city size construct and a demographic construct, explained most of the variance in the data.

This study was only a pilot effort. In practice, the marketing manager would use those city characteristics most relevant to his product line. The clusters could then serve as homogeneous blocks from which individual cities could be chosen to serve as treatment and control units, that is matched units for various experimental purposes.

Television Program Audience Profile Analysis

Grouping of television programs into clusters having similar audience profile, which was used to illustrate the nature of taxonomic procedures, comprises still another exploratory investigation currently in progress. American Research Bureau data for both day and evening programs in October, 1965, are the bases for this analysis. For each, program measures of the number of adult men and women in different age categories and the number of children and teenagers viewing the program are available. The primary objective is to group programs by viewer characteristics so that their grouping is a function of viewer reaction to content and casting—not to the effects of time of day, day of week, and lead-in programs.

The analysis is divided into two stages. The first is the adjustment of raw data for the effects of time of day, day of week, and lead-in programs. The adjustment is roughly analogous to making a cyclical adjustment in a time series analysis to ensure a cleaner set of data for studying trend movements. When variations in audience profile from program to program are caused primarily by the effect of program content and casting, the adjusted data are subjected to a taxonomic analysis. The first stage of the study is complete, and the taxonomic work is about to begin. (It will soon appear as a working paper [30].)

Patterns of Customer Brand Loyalty

At the beginning of this article the study of brand loyalty was used to illustrate the tendency for letting unidimensional measures represent customer behavior that may be multidimensional. In this study cluster analysis and Kruskal's algorithm [56] is used to characterize customer brand purchasing behavior. The objective is to develop more comprehensive classification systems for analyzing brand choice.

Chicago Tribune panel data for three product categories (carbonated beverages, regular coffee, and ready-to-eat cereals) for 1961 were used in the analysis. For each product category for each of 480 households, the percentage of units (based on weight) purchased by brand was computed.

Two different approaches were then taken. A Euclidean distance measure was used to group households that had relatively similar percentage distributions of brand purchasing behavior within a product. This is equivalent to studying brand loyalty for the bundle of brands households purchase. The results showed that with only one exception in the regular coffee market each cluster of households bought only one brand at a rate greater than the brand's overall market share. Although other brands were purchased, none was given this degree of favor. The only exceptions are the clusters containing several private brands. Households that purchase one private brand at a greater rate than its overall share are likely to purchase another with a similar degree of concentration. Customers who buy them may be less sensitive to differences in product characteristics, or the products themselves may be more similar.

A second approach organized the data by brand instead of by customer. This part of the analysis started with the transpose of the data matrix used, that is the data were organized by brand and within brand, by household. For each brand the percentage of purchases devoted to that brand by each of about 100 households was available. Euclidean distance measures characterized brand similarity by pattern of purchase requirements over households.

Results so far have provided few surprises and have raised more questions than can be answered here. For example in the cereal market, evidence appears that old standard brands (Kellogg's Corn Flakes, Cheerios, Wheaties) tend to serve segments which overlap, yet many health-oriented cereals (Special K, All Bran, Grape Nuts) tend to serve a somewhat different group of customers.

An Experimental Gaming Application

Another application of clustering was prompted by experimental data obtained in studying the relationship between risk taking (in a no-information-improvement context) and the propensity to acquire uncertainty-reducing information in an information-buying context [35]. Data were available for 42 men and women subjects on a variety of behavioral and personality variables.

Preliminary analysis using a variety of multivariate techniques showed little support for the study's primary hypotheses. Part of the problem was thought to be that different subjects were using different behavioral models; these differences became obscured in the process of data aggregation. Accordingly, each subject's behavior in the experiment was viewed as a point in task performance space, the axes of which were represented by the situational and personality variables comprising the experimental situation. Subjects were then clustered by their similarities to each other over the whole experiment.

This procedure produced various clusters of subjects—some supported the hypothesis and others suggested other kinds of behavioral models. The potentialities of this approach appear provocative in the examination of experimental gaming data generally. Perhaps even more interesting, however, is the application of this kind of approach to the design of behavioral experiments. Alternative explanatory models are the rule rather than the exception in experimental games. Before collecting any data the researcher could characterize the play of ideal subjects (those whose behavior corresponded to each alternative model) by points in experimental performance space. Levels of the experimental variables might then be chosen to maximize the discrimination among alternative models before the experiment is conducted.

Operational Characterization of Inter-Brand Competition

In another pilot study, cluster analysis helped to characterize inter-brand competition in the computer field [38]. Performance data were obtained for over 100 different computer models with installation date used to categorize them at first- or second-generation models. For each computer model, data were available on 12 measured characteristics, such as word length, execution time, digital storage, transfer rate, and 10 categorical characteristics, such as whether the computer possessed Boolean operations, table look-up, and indirect addressing.

The data's mixed character (continuous variables and dichotomous features data) required a different approach from that typically used in cluster analysis. First, the attribute data were metricized by a multidimensional scaling technique [56]. A two-dimensional representation revealed that each computer model could be characterized by the dimensions of capacity (number of different features) and orientation (scientific versus business), as based on the particular pattern of zeroes and ones.

The resultant clusters, developed by a hierarchical grouping technique, displayed interesting characteristics from the standpoint of intermodel competition. For example, a machine's cluster of features appears to be idiosyncratic to the particular manufacturer, that is, each manufacturer tends to build all his machines with a particular set of features. Each manufacturer's complex, however, may vary from that of his competitors. It is interesting that only IBM had a model in each of the major clusters. However, the time period comparison—first- versus second-generation computers—indicated a trend toward all models having a greater number of features.

The measured variables were then analyzed separately, yielding two main dimensions—speed and size of computers. Finally, the measured data were dichotomized about the median of each characteristic (taken separately) and submitted to a combination multidimensional scaling and cluster analysis.

Figure 24–2 shows a two-space configuration derived from applying a nonmetric program to proximity measures developed from the above steps. After adjusting for intercorrelation of the characteristics [39], similarity measures were developed by tabulating the number of (weighted) matches for all computer pairs. The higher this number, the more similar each pair was assumed to be with respect to all 22 performance characteristics. For $n = 55$, there are 1,485 interpoint proximities as input to the program; only their rank order is required.

The two-space configuration of Figure 24–2 shows the boundaries of clusters formed (by another means) on a more precise configuration obtained in four-space. Such compression of results (into two-space) seriously distorts the makeup of Cluster 8; otherwise the clusters are fairly compact. It is interesting to note that Cluster 5 is composed of small, fairly slow, business-oriented machines, but Cluster 7 is characterized by large, relatively fast, scientific machines.

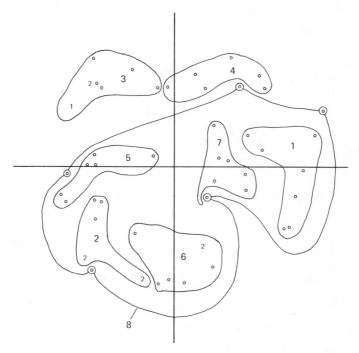

Figure 24–2. Two-space Configuration of Computer Models in "Performance Space"

The complete study on which Figure 24–2 is based revealed that four dimensions—speed, size, number of different features (qualitative characteristics), and orientation (scientific versus business)—appeared to adequately describe the computer market.

The possibilities of such performance-space analyses over time have potential for the study of product innovation and modification—particularly industrial products like electric motors and machine tools. In this approach a whole series of performance spaces could be viewed through time—their dimensions, number of points (models), and interrelationships among points could all be changing, reflecting changes in technology and inter-model competition. Such an approach would seem to indicate the data's fine structure better than the more traditional reliance on S-curves to describe product life cycles.

Physician's Media Reading Habits

In another study [41], numerical taxonomy was used to cluster reading profiles of both physicians and medical journals. The basic data consisted of zero-one matrixes in which each physician was classified as a light (zero) or heavy (one) reader of each of 19 medical journals. Each physician was also classified as one who lightly or heavily prescribed each of 29 therapeutic drug classes. Data were also available on the physician's specialty, age, and total weekly patient and prescription loads. The zero-one matrixes were again metricized by a multidimensional scaling program. Clusters of journals with similar, physician reading habits and clusters of physicians with similar journal profiles were developed.

Findings indicated that, within a given specialty, media reading profiles are not associated with such variables as physician age, total prescribing frequency, and product mix selection. However, the journal clusters provided an interesting output of the analysis by summarizing a diverse set of zero-one data. The marketing manager could use these clusters as a guide to media scheduling. For example, if he wishes to choose journals with high overlap of coverage, he can choose all journals within a given cluster. If, however, he wishes to emphasize diversity, he can choose one journal from each cluster.

From a methodological viewpoint, the interesting concept is the dual use of multidimensional scaling and cluster analysis. The first technique allows the researcher to make a concise description of the data—frequently interpretable in its own right—and the last allows him to organize the data into similar journal profiles that can then be subjected to further analysis.

Taxonomy in Psychometric Studies

Some mention should also be made of the usefulness of clustering procedures in psychometric studies involving perceptual and preference mapping. A recently completed study [36] involved the analysis of proximities data developed during a study of student perception of six graduate schools of business. Three modes of data collection—similarity triads, direct ratings, and the semantic differential—were used to collect proximity judgments.

In this study a hierarchical grouping method was used to develop clusters of respondents with similar perceptions of the six business schools. That is, although the main objective of this study was the development of perceptual maps, cluster analysis was useful in partitioning the respondents into homogeneous groups with similar perceptions.

The results indicated that a two-space solution adequately portrayed the respondents' perceptions. From other data collected in the study, the dimensions of the space could be characterized as prestige of school and quantitativeness of its curriculum. Not inconsequentially all three data collection methods yielded fairly similar perceptual maps, on an aggregate basis. Moreover, differences in perceptual mappings were not generally explainable by respondent personal data, such as undergraduate major, previous work experience, graduate major. Only one variable, home state of respondent, appeared to influence his perception of the business schools in any significant way.

A similar study [37] involved a multidimensional scaling of professional journals typically read by marketing academics and researchers. Perception and preference data were obtained for eight journals, and respondents were clustered on the basis of similarity of perception and preference.

Figure 24–3 shows the results of applying a nonmetric clustering routine to the perception data [37]. Note that this program is hierarchical. Respondents 4 and 7 are first clustered because they had the highest proximity measure of the group. Respondents 2 and 11 are next clustered at level two, and so on, until all points are eventually in one large cluster. On the left-hand side of Figure 24–3 one can see how the proximity measure declines as more disparate points are clustered.

The results of this study indicated that preferences and perception were independent over stimuli, that is respondents clustered by commonality of perception were unrelated to clusters formed by commonality of preference.

ASSUMPTIONS AND LIMITATIONS OF CLUSTERING METHODS

Cluster analysis is not a single, cohesive set of techniques but rather a variety of procedures, each having a kind of ad hoc flavor and certain advantages and disadvantages. Some of the limitations are shared by all these techniques to some degree, but specific procedures have both advantages and disadvantages.

General Problems in Cluster Analysis

All clustering techniques have certain general analytical inadequacies because the data are used to generate the groupings. Illustrative questions are:

1. How many clusters should be formed?
2. If, as is usually the case, the characteristics of the objects are measured in different units, how can equivalence among metrics be achieved?
3. If the objects' scores along several dimensions are intercorrelated, how should these interdependencies be handled?

Subject number

Proximity measure	09	10	01	08	06	02	11	03	04	07	05	12
1.8253	·	·	·	·	·	·	·	·	X	X	·	·
1.7745	·	·	·	·	·	X	X	·	X	X	·	·
1.7111	·	·	·	·	·	X	X	X	X	X	·	·
1.6871	·	·	·	·	·	X	X	X	X	X	X	X
1.5961	·	·	·	·	X	X	X	X	X	X	X	X
1.4724	·	·	X	X	X	X	X	X	X	X	X	X
1.3715	·	·	X	X	X	X	X	X	X	X	X	X
1.2901	·	·	X	X	X	X	X	X	X	X	X	X
1.1388	·	·	X	X	X	X	X	X	X	X	X	X
1.0558	·	X	X	X	X	X	X	X	X	X	X	X
0.8077	X	X	X	X	X	X	X	X	X	X	X	X

Figure 24—3 Illustration of Hierarchical Clustering Routine

4. Even if the number of clusters can be determined in some satisfactory way, how does the analyst decide on the appropriate boundaries for clusters, summary measures of the characteristics of each cluster, and their statistical significance?

In some of the illustrative applications described here, the number of clusters were decided in advance. Increasing the number of clusters will tend to reduce the average within-cluster distance but, obviously, one must stop short of ending with each point being a cluster.

In addition, all data including variables originally interval-scaled were standardized to zero mean and unit standard deviation. Although this step enables the analyst to work with common metrics, it is assumed that central tendency and variability among dimensions are not important.

The problem of dealing with intercorrelated characteristics was pointed out in the test marketing illustration. In this study an alternative procedure was used in which the set of characteristics was first reduced to independent constructs by a principal component analysis before the cluster analysis. This procedure can lead to different clusters from those obtained by the first procedure that ignored the intercorrelations among characteristics. Finally, the researcher might wish to use the Mahalanobis generalized distance measure discussed by Morrison [66].

Appropriate boundaries and descriptive statistics of clusters are usually determined by the specific technique used—in many instances by a generalized distance function, the computation of centroids, and the use of a preset number of points or cutoff distances. Even so, it is fair to say that good measures of cluster compactness are not available. In the test marketing illustration each dimension included in the analysis was given (manifest) equal weight in determining similarity. In a given situation one might choose to give a single dimension or some subset of dimensions more weight than others in defining proximity measures. Cluster analysis can be easily modified to take into account unequal weights, but this approach still largely varies with circumstances.

Still less is known about the inferential characteristics of clustering techniques. Unlike other multivariate techniques, such as discriminant analysis and principal component analysis, clustering techniques are much less structured, and little investigation has been made to date of their statistical proprieties.

Limitations of Specific Proximity Measures

In earlier sections of this article, the characteristics of specific proximity measures—distance measures, correlation techniques, similarity coefficients—were briefly described. Each measure suffers from certain specific limitations.

Distance measures are usually restricted to instances in which the objects' characteristics to be measured can be expressed as interval-scaled variables. This represents a limitation on the kind of variable meaningfully handled although Kendall's nonparametric measure (mentioned earlier) could be used to handle data that are scaled only ordinally and the researcher could develop non-Euclidean metrics.

In addition, the Euclidean measure suffers from the disadvantage that two objects may be viewed as different solely because their values on one variable differ markedly. Finally, it should be reiterated that the researcher would, in general, obtain different results by using original versus standardized data for the characteristics of the objects being clustered by this method.

Correlative techniques, such as Q-factor analysis, have an even more serious limitation because one must standardize over objects, thus losing mean and scatter information. That is, in this technique, each object is given the same mean and variance.

A second disadvantage is that rotation of factor axes (to get purer loadings) lends a certain arbitrariness to the procedure. Finally, also mentioned earlier, in this procedure objects may be split on factors, leading to uncertainty of the placement of an object into a specific group.

Similarity measures are flexible since they can be adapted to handle nominal, ordinal, and interval-scaled data. Furthermore, it can be shown that similarity measures can be metricized by multidimensional-scaling procedures. Moreover, similarity measures are generally less sensitive to the impact of a single characteristic on the resultant dissimilarity of two objects than are the Euclidean distance measures.

However, similarity measures have their set of limitations. First, if a group is to be formed on the basis of overall matches, two objects may not be grouped even if they match well on some subset of characteristics. Conversely, an object may be in a group because it is similar to different members of the group on different subsets of characteristics.

Second, if a large number of characteristics are involved, objects which match may do so for accidental reasons, reflecting the noise in the data; and third, if some variables are dichotomous and others are multichotomous, the two-state attributes will tend to be more heavily weighted in the similarity measures. For example, if one attribute were broken down into 100 states, we would rarely find matches. Hence this attribute would receive little importance in the overall similarity measure.

Finally, if continuous data are discretized in order to use similarity measures, valuable information can be lost. The analyst is thus plagued with the problem of deciding both the kinds of attributes to include in the analysis and the number of states to be associated with each.

Choosing Appropriate Techniques

Numerical taxonomy invites some ambivalence by the analyst wanting to use the techniques. On one hand, the procedures are designed to cope with a relevant aspect of marketing description—the orderly classification of multivariate phenomena. On the other hand, the varying character of various proximity measures and clustering techniques—and the basic lack of structure at either the descriptive statistic or inferential statistic level—suggests that the analyst be cautious in applying them.

Until more structure is introduced, it seems prudent to conduct analyses in parallel where alternative proximity measures and grouping procedures are used [40]. Moreover, sensitivity analyses on synthetic data might be helpful in exploring the various idiosyncracies of alternative techniques. If the data are well clustered to begin with, similar results over alternative techniques will usually be obtained—but how often will these pleasant states of affairs exist? Though the authors believe numerical taxonomy can be useful in marketing analysis, they would urge prudence in its application and the systematic study of similarities and differences among alternative procedures. (The references may help to facilitate this study.)

References

1. G. H. Ball, "Data Analysis in the Social Sciences: What About the Details?" *Proceedings Fall Joint Computer Conference*, 1965, 533–59.
2. B. M. Bass, "Iterative Inverse Factor Analysis: A Rapid Method for Clustering Persons," *Psychometrika*, 22 (March 1957), 105.
3. J. F. Bennett and W. L. Hays, "Multidimensional Unfolding: Determining the Dimensionality of Ranked Preference Data," *Psychometrika*, 25 (March 1960), 27–43.
4. A. Birnbaum and A. E. Maxwell, "Classification Proceedures Based on Bayes' Formula," *Applied Statistics*, 9 (November 1961), 152–68.
5. Jack Block, "The Difference Between Q and R," *Psychological Review,* 62 (1955), 356–58.
6. ———, Louis Levine and Quinn McNemar, "Testing for the Existence of Psychometric Patterns," *Journal of Abnormal Social Psychology*, 46 (July 1951), 356–59.
7. R. E. Bonner, "Some Clustering Techniques," *IBM Journal of Research and Development*, 8 (January 1964), 22–33.
8. A. D. Booth, "An Application of the Method of Steepest Descent to the Solution of Simultaneous Non-linear Equations," *Quarterly Journal of Mech. Applied Mathematics*, 2 (December 1949), 460–68.
9. G. E. P. Box, "The Exploration and Exploitation of Response Surfaces:

Some General Considerations and Examples," *Biometrics*, 10 (March 1954), 16–60.

10. S. H. Brooks, "A Discussion of Random Methods of Seeking Maxima," *Journal of Operations Research Society*, 6 (1958), 244–51.

11. ———, "A Comparison of Maximum Seeking Methods," *Journal of Operations Research Society*, 7 (1959), 430–57.

12. Cyril L. Burt, "Correlations Between Persons," *British Journal of Psychology*, 28 (July 1937), 59–96.

13. H. Cartwright, *Structural Models: An Introduction to the Theory of Directed Graphs*, New York: John Wiley & Sons, Inc., 1963.

14. Raymond B. Cattell, "r_p and Other Coefficients of Pattern Similarity," *Psychometrika*, 14 (December 1949), 279–98.

15. ———, "On the Disuse and Misuse of R, P, Q and O Techniques in Clinical Psychology," *Journal of Clinical Psychology*, 7 (1951), 203–14.

16. ———, M. A. Coulter and B. Tsujioka, "The Taxonometric Recognition of Types and Functional Emergents," in R. B. Cattell, ed., *Handbook of Multivariate Experimental Psychology*, Chicago: Rand McNally and Co., 1966, 288–329.

17. W. W. Cooley and Paul R. Lohnes, *Multivariate Procedures for the Behavioral Sciences*, New York: John Wiley & Sons, Inc., 1963.

18. C. H. Coombs, *A Theory of Data*, New York: John Wiley & Sons, Inc., 1964.

19. ———, "A Method for the Study of Interstimulus Similarity," *Psychometrika*, 19 (September 1954), 183–94.

20. Douglas R. Cox, "Note on Grouping," *Journal of American Statistical Association*, 52 (December 1957), 543–47.

21. Lee J. Cronbach and Goldine C. Gleser, "Assessing Similarity Between Profiles," *Psychological Bulletin*, 50 (November 1953), 456–73.

22. Frank M. duMas, "A Quick Method of Analyzing the Similarity of Profiles," *Journal of Clinical Psychology*, 2 (January 1946), 80–83.

23. ———, "On the Interpretation of Personality Profiles," *Journal of Clinical Psychology*, 3 (1947), 57–65.

24. A. W. F. Edwards and L. L. Cavalli-Sforza, "A Method for Cluster Analysis," *Biometrics*, 52 (June 1965), 362–75.

25. G. A. Ferguson, "The Factorial Interpretation of Test Difficulty," *Psychometrika*, 6 (October 1941), 323–29.

26. R. A. Fisher, "The Use of Multiple Measurements in Taxonomic Problems," *American Eugenics*, 7 (1963), 179–88.

27. W. D. Fisher, "On Grouping for Maximum Homogeneity," *Journal of American Statistical Association*, 53 (December 1958), 789–98.

28. Claude Flament, *Applications of Graph Theory to Group Structure*, New Jersey: Prentice-Hall, Inc., 1963.

29. J. J. Fortier and H. Solomon, "Clustering Procedures," Unpublished

paper, International Symposium on Multivariate Analysis, University of Dayton, June 1965.

30. Ronald E. Frank, "Television Program Audience Similarities: A Taxonomic Analysis," University of Pennsylvania, December 1967, mimeographed.

31. Eugene L. Gaier and Marilyn C. Lee, "Pattern Analysis: The Configural Approach to Predictive Measurement," *Psychological Bulletin*, 50 (March 1953), 140–48.

32. J. A. Generelli, "A Method for Detecting Subgroups in a Population and Specifying Their Membership," *Journal of Psychology*, 55 (1953), 140–48.

33. L. A. Goodman and W. H. Kruskal, "Measures of Association for Cross Classifications," *Journal of American Statistical Association*, 59 (September 1964), 732–64.

34. Paul E. Green, Ronald E. Frank and Patrick J. Robinson, "Cluster Analysis in Test Market Selection," *Management Science*, 13 (April 1967), 387–400.

35. ———, "A Behavioral Experiment in Risk Taking and Information Seeking," Working paper, University of Pennsylvania, January 1967.

36. Paul E. Green and P. J. Robinson, "Perceptual Structure of Graduate Business Schools—An Application of Multidimensional Scaling," Workpaper, June 1967.

37. ———, "Perceptual and Preference Mapping of Professional Journals," Working paper, May 1967.

38. ——— and F. J. Carmone, "Structural Characteristics of the Computer Market—An Application of Cluster and Reduced Space Analysis," Working paper, May 1967.

39. ———, "WAGS: An IBM 7040 Computer Program for Obtaining Weighted Agreement Scores for Multidimensional Scaling," Working paper, May 1967.

40. ———, "Cross Techniques Study—Computer Model Clustering," Working paper, August 1967.

41. ———, "A Reduced Space and Cluster Analysis of Physicians' Media Reading Habits," Working paper, September 1967.

42. H. H. Harman, *Modern Factor Analysis*, Chicago: University of Chicago Press, 1960.

43. C. W. Harris, "Characteristics of Two Measures of Profile Similarity," *Psychometrika*, 20 (1955), 289–97.

44. G. C. Helmstadter, "An Empirical Comparison of Methods for Estimating Profile Similarity," *Educational and Psychological Measurement*, 17 (1957), 71–82.

45. J. L. Hodges, Jr., "Discriminatory Analysis I: Survey of Discriminatory Analysis," USAF School of Aviation Medicine, Randolph, Texas, 1950.

46. Karl J. Holzinger, "Factoring Test Scores and Implications for the Method of Averages," *Psychometrika*, 9 (December 1944), 257–62.

47. Paul Horst, *Matrix Algebra for Social Scientists*, New York: Holt, Rinehart and Winston, 1963.

48. ———, "Pattern Analysis and Configural Scoring," *Journal of Clinical Psychology*, 10 (January 1954), 1–11.

49. K. J. Jones, *The Multivariate Statistical Analyzer*, Cambridge, Mass.: Harvard Cooperative Society, 1964.

50. J. Joyce and C. Charron, "Classifying Market Survey Respondents,"*Applied Statistics*, 15 (November 1966), 191–215.

51. H. F. Kaiser, "Formulas for Component Scores," *Psychometrika*, 27 (March 1962), 83–87.

52. M. G. Kendall, *The Advanced Theory of Statistics*, Vol. 1, New York: Hafner Publishing Company, 1958.

53. ———, *Rank Correlation Methods*, London: Griffin Publishing Company, 1948.

54. ———, "Discrimination and Classification," London: CEIR Ltd., 1965.

55. J. B. Kruskal, "Nonmetric Multidimensional Scaling: A Numerical Scaling Method," *Psychometrika*, 29 (June 1964), 115–30.

56. ———, "Multidimensional Scaling by Optimizing Goodness of Fit to a Nonmetric Hypothesis," *Psychometrika*, 29 (March 1964), 1–28.

57. E. O. Laumann and L. Guttman, "The Relative Association Contiguity of Occupations in an Urban Setting," *American Sociological Review*, 31 (April 1966), 169–78.

58. J. C. Lingoes, "A Taxonometric Optimization Procedure: An IBM 7090 Classification Program," *Behavioral Science*, 8 (October 1963), 370.

59. ———, "An IBM 7090 program for Guttman-Lingoes Smallest Space Analysis," Computer Center, University of Michigan, 1965.

60. P. C. Mahalanobis, "On the Generalized Distance in Statistics," *Proceedings National Institute of Science*, Vol. 12, India, 1936, 49–58.

61. F. Massarik and P. Ratoosh, *Mathematical Explorations in Behavioral Science*, Homewood, Ill.: Richard D. Irwin, Inc., 1965.

62. P. McNaughton-Smith, *et al.*, "Dissimilarity Analysis: A New Technique of Hierarchical Subdivision," *Nature*, 202 (June 1964), 1033–34.

63. Louis L. McQuitty, "Hierarchical Syndrome Analysis," *Educational and Psychological Measurement*, 20 (1960), 293–304.

64. ———, "Typical Analysis," *Educational and Psychological Measurement*, 20 (1960), 293–304.

65. ———,"Best Classifying Every Individual at Every Level," *Educational and Psychological Measurement*, 23 (July 1963), 337–46.

66. Donald G. Morrison, "Measurement Problems in Cluster Analysis," *Management Science*, 13 (August 1967), B-755–80.

67. Jum Nunnally, "The Analysis of Profile Data," *Psychological Bulletin*, 59 (July 1962), 311–19.

68. Charles E. Osgood and George J. Suci, "A Measure of Relation Determined by Both Mean Difference and Profile Information," *Psychological Bulletin*, 49 (May 1952), 251–62.

69. J. E. Overall, "Note on Multivariate Methods of Profile Analysis," *Psychological Bulletin*, 61 (March 1964), 195–98.

70. K. Pearson, "On the Dissection of Assymetrical Frequency Curves," *Contributions to the Mathematical Theory of Evolution, Phil. Trans. of Royal Society*, 1894.

71. ———, "On the Coefficient of Racial Likeness," *Biometrika*, 18 (July 1926), 105–17.

72. R. G. Pettit, "Clustering Program: Continuous Variables," Advanced Systems Development Division, IBM, Yorktown Heights, New York, 1964.

73. C. R. Rao, "Tests of Significance in Multivariate Analysis," *Biometrika*, 35 (May 1948), 58–79.

74. ———, "The Utilization of Multiple Measurements in Problems of Biological Classification," *Journal of Royal Statistical Society*, Section B, 10 (1948), 159–203.

75. F. Restle, *Psychology of Judgment and Choice*, New York: John Wiley & Sons, Inc., 1961.

76. D. J. Rogers and T. T. Tanimoto, "A Computer Program for Classifying Plants," *Science*, 132 (October 1960), 1115–22.

77. P. J. Rulon, "Distinctions Between Discriminant and Regression Analysis and a Geometric Interpretation of the Discriminant Function," *Harvard Educational Review*, 21 (June 1951), 80–90.

78. R. N. Shepard, "The Analysis of Proximities: Multidimensional Scaling With an Unknown Distance Functions: I and II," *Psychometrika*, 27 (June 1962, September 1962), 125–40, 219–46.

79. ———, "Analysis of Proximities as a Technique for the Study of Information Processing in Man," *Human Factors*, 5 (February 1963), 33–48.

80. G. G. Simpson, "Numerical Taxonomy and Biological Classification," *Science*, 144 (May 1964), 712–13.

81. P. H. A. Sneath, "The Application of Computers to Taxonomy," *Journal of General Micro-Biology*, 17 (August 1957), 201–27.

82. R. R. Sokal, "Numerical Taxonomy," *Scientific American*, 215 (December 1966), 106–16.

83. ——— and P. H. A. Sneath, *Principles of Numerical Taxonomy*, San Francisco: Freeman & Company, 1963.

84. William Stephenson, "Some Observations on Q Technique," *Psychological Bulletin*, Vol. 49 (September 1952), 483–98.

85. S. A. Stouffer, *et al., Measurement and Prediction,* Princeton, N.J.: Princeton University Press, 1950.

86. Robert L. Thorndike, "Who Belongs in the Family?", *Psychometrika,* 18 (December 1953), 267–76.

87. Warren S. Torgerson, "Multidimensional Scaling: Theory and Method," *Psychometrika,* 17 (December 1952), 401–19.

88. ———, "Multidimensional Scaling of Similarity," *Psychometrika,* 30 (December 1965), 379–93.

89. Fred T. Tyler, "Some Examples of Multivariate Analysis in Educational and Psychological Research," *Psychometrika,* 17 (September 1952) 289–96.

90. Robert C. Tyron, *Cluster Analysis,* Edwards Bros., 1939.

91. ———, "Cumulative Communality Cluster Analysis," *Educational and Psychological Measurement,* 18 (March 1958), 3–35.

92. J. W. Tukey, "The Future of Data Analysis," *Annals of Mathematical Statistics,* 33 (March 1962), 1–67.

93. J. H. Ward, "Hierarchical Grouping to Optimize an Objective Function," *Journal of American Statistical Association,* 58 (March 1963), 236–44.

94. Joe E. Ward, Jr., and Marion E. Hook, "Application of an Hierarchical Grouping Procedure to a Problem of Grouping Profiles," *Educational and Psychological Measurement,* 23 (1963), 69–82.

95. Harold Webster, "A Note on Profile Similarity," *Psychological Bulletin,* 49 (September 1952), 538–59.

96. Joseph Zubin, "A Technique for Measuring Like-Mindedness," *Journal of Abnormal Social Psychology,* 33 (October 1938), 508–16.

25

The Use of Nonmetric Multidimensional Scaling in Marketing Analysis

Lester A. Neidell

Within the past two years marketing analysts have made increasing reference to new methodology, loosely referred to as "scaling."[1] These references are often confusing to the marketing executive for they do not pertain to the scaling procedures such as rating scales, paired comparisons, semantic differentiation, and scalogram analysis, which have been utilized previously in marketing studies. Instead, many analysts are now referring to the set of techniques called nonmetric multidimensional scaling which seems to be admirably suited to the analysis of several problem areas in marketing.

The purposes of this paper are: (1) to explain, in a nontechnical fashion, the theory and procedures underlying nonmetric multidimensional scaling; (2) to present an example of its use; and (3) to speculate on further marketing applications.

THE PROBLEM OF MEASUREMENT

Measurement involves the assignment of numbers to objects or properties of objects according to a set of rules. The rules by which numbers are assigned during measurement define the properties of the scales which are a result of measurement.[2] For example, road mileages represent a *ratio* scale, so-called because the ratios of distances among cities have meaning. A

[1] Yoram Wind, "Mathematical Analysis of Perception and Preference for Industrial Marketing," in Keith Cox and Ben M. Enis, eds., *A New Measure of Responsibility for Marketing* (Chicago, Ill.: American Marketing Association, June, 1968), pp. 284–294; James R. Taylor, "The Meaning and Structure of Data as Related to Scaling Models," in Robert L. King, ed., *Marketing and the New Science of Planning* (Chicago, Ill.: American Marketing Association, August, 1968), pp. 309–315.

[2] Warren S. Torgerson, *Theory and Methods of Scaling* (New York: John Wiley and Sons, Inc., 1958), Chapter 1.

From Lester A. Neidell, "The Use of Nonmetric Multidimensional Scaling in Marketing Analysis," *Journal of Marketing*, Vol. 33 (October 1969), pp. 37–43. Published by the American Marketing Association. Reprinted by permission.

natural origin—zero point—exists from which all distances can be measured. In many instances of measurement, however, a natural zero does not exist yet the size of the distance between *pairs* of objects has meaning. These are called *interval* scales. A very obvious example is the measurement of temperature in which different arbitrary zero points are established according to the rules of the measurement process one is using. Thus, regardless of the temperature scale being used, it is correct to say that the temperature difference from 20° to 40° is twice that of 20° to 30°, but it is not correct to say that 40° is twice as warm as 20°.

Ratio and interval scales are both *metric* scales because they contain information about equality relationships (that is, *how much* larger or smaller) among the objects being measured. Explicit distance functions are defined by the rules of measurement. It is possible, however, to generate scales by rules of measurement in which inter-object relationships are described simply by inequality or *nonmetric* relationships (that is, *which one* is larger or smaller), as will be shown. The rules of the measurement process which produce nonmetric scales are (1) objects can be ordered, and (2) (sometimes) intervals among objects can be ordered.

RELEVANCE TO THE MARKETING SITUATION

People cannot ordinarily provide accurate and reliable data about equality relationships among objects such as competing brands, or about brand characteristics. Psychological evidence of this is overwhelming.[3] Yet because of the ease of manipulating metric data, and because of the lack of nonmetric analytical procedures, marketing analysts have invariably assumed the existence of a metric scale. For example, analysts using a *t* test of significance applied to different rating scale scores frequently assume an interval (metric) scale where it is not appropriate.

At this point, it is entirely proper to ask, "So what? What harm is being done? And, do you have a better method?"

The lack of recognition that different assumptions can be made about data may account for some of the disappointing results which have been reported in attempts to predict market behavior. By assuming interval data when neither data nor theory supports it, the marketing analyst, in interpreting (for example) the results of consumer product evaluations, is quite liable to postulate that unnecessarily strong relationships exist between the evaluations and subsequent consumer behavior. When a relationship is not verified by empirical evidence, the validity of the relationship is questioned, when the error may lie instead in the *strength* of the postulated relationship.

---

[3] Same reference as footnote 2, Chapter 4–10. Also Roger N. Shepard, "Metric Structures in Ordinal Data," *Journal of Mathematical Psychology*, Vol. 3 (July, 1966), pp. 287–315, at pp. 310–312; and Frank Restle, *Psychology of Judgment and Choice* (New York: John Wiley and Sons, Inc., 1961).

METRIC RESULTS FROM NONMETRIC INPUTS

The techniques of nonmetric multidimensional scaling require only nonmetric (ordinal) input measures, yet metric (ratio scale) results are ordinarily obtained. This result, metrically invariant output from only ordinal input, stems from the reduction in the number of constraints needed to represent a k dimensional nonmetric solution in a metric space of less than k dimensions. This can be demonstrated intuitively.

All order relationships among n objects can be depicted in a space of $n-1$ dimensions.[4] As an example, the distance between any two objects can be represented by a straight line which is a unidimensional space. Similarly the distance relationships among any three objects can be completely described by a triangle which requires only a two-dimensional space to represent the three order relationships. As the number of objects (n) becomes large, the number of order relationships (that is, nonmetric constraints) required grows approximately with the *square* of n (actually $[n(n-1)/2]$). *However, the number of metric constraints required for complete specification of* n *points grows only linearly with* n. Thus, 45 *ordinal* relationships $[10(10-1)/2=45]$ are required to show completely the structure among ten objects. If one were to plot these same ten objects in a two-dimensional space, only 20 coordinates ($n \cdot k$ or $10 \cdot 2$) would be needed. The net result is that with large n a metric solution involving a space of considerably fewer dimensions may be contained within the set of $[n(n-1)/2]$ relationships. In Shepard's words, ". . . the metric information was contained in the original numbers all along—only in such a dilute form that we did not recognize it. But when this same information is squeezed into a smaller set of numbers, it finally becomes concentrated enough to be recognized for what it is."[5]

THE ROADMAP PROBLEM—AN ILLUSTRATIVE EXAMPLE

A useful way of evaluating any new analytical procedure is to relate it to a problem with a known solution. In this case the problem to be considered was the placement of key cities on a map of the United States.[6]

In terms of nonmetric multidimensional scaling, the minimum data necessary to "solve" this problem are the rank orders of the inter-city distances. An atlas of the United States was used in calculating inter-city road mileages among all pairs of 15 cities. There are, therefore, 105 inter-city distances

[4] J. F. Bennett and W. L. Hays, "Multidimensional Unfolding: Determining the Dimensionality of Ranked Preference Data, *Psychometrika*, Vol. 25 (December, 1960), pp. 27–43.

[5] Roger N. Shepard, "Analysis of Proximities as a Technique for the Study of Information Processing in Man," *Human Factors* (February, 1963), pp. 33–48, at p. 35.

[6] Marshall G. Greenberg, "A Variety of Approaches to Nonmetric Multidimensional Scaling," Paper presented at the 16th International Meeting of the Institute of Management Sciences, New York (March, 1969).

$[n(n-1)/2]$. Conversion of actual inter-city distances into rank order data was achieved by assigning the number "1" to the shortest road distance, that is, Boston–New York; the number "2" to the next shortest distance, that is, Kansas City–St. Louis; and so on, until all 105 inter-city distances were assigned a number. Ties were given equal numbers. This data base of rank orders was then utilized as input to a nonmetric multidimensional scaling program.

Clearly, the solution to the problem of city placement is known. What is required is a two-dimensional figure, with the axes labeled north–south and east–west. The nonmetric multidimensional scaling result should indicate clearly a two-dimensional solution and should place the cities in their correct geographic location on a United States map.

In Figure 25–1 the two-dimensional result obtained from a nonmetric multidimensional scaling program[7] is compared to the actual geographic locations of the cities. The correct geographic locations are identified by a dot (·) and the scaling solution by an "x." The fit between the scaling positions and actual geographic locations is quite good, although errors of approximately 200 miles are evident in the South and West. However, a substantial part of the error can be explained.

The differences are due primarily to imperfect data. Road distances often are *not* the shortest straight line distances between any pair of cities, but reflect natural detours such as mountain ranges and lakes, and the intricacy of the road network in any section of the country. The imperfections in the mileage data base affected some of the rank order placements. Thus, cities which are more inaccessible due to terrain and/or to being in more sparsely settled sections of the country are more likely to be "out of place" on the nonmetric scaling solution. This is indeed the case as shown by the locations of Miami, New Orleans, Phoenix, and Los Angeles.

In other words, the data base used for nonmetric multidimensional scaling in this example was both systematically and randomly biased, not unlike the data often available to marketing practitioners.

This roadmap example has illustrated four aspects of nonmetric multidimensional scaling methods which must be understood in order to comprehend fully the novelty and the power of this set of techniques. These aspects are the nonmetric input, the metric output, the number of dimensions, and the interpretation of the dimensions.

The Number and Interpretation of Dimensions

In the roadmap example the true dimensionality of the solution was known. This is usually not the case in marketing analyses, as one of the

---

[7] The actual program used was TORSCA. See F. W. Young and W. S. Torgerson, "TORSCA, A Fortran IV Program for Shepard-Kruskal Multidimensional Scaling Analysis," *Behavioral Science*, Vol. 12 (July, 1967), pp. 498–99.

variables under study *is* the number (and interpretation) of dimensions necessary to represent the data. Currently there are programmed statistical techniques which will assist the analyst in determining the appropriate number of dimensions required.[8]

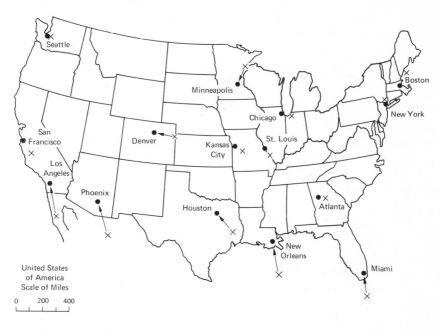

Figure 25–1. Comparison of Actual Geographic Locations of Fifteen Cities with the Locations Defined by the Two-dimensional Multidimensional Scaling Solution

Interpretation of the dimensions is a matter of the investigator's judgment, as is true in factor analysis. Multidimensional scaling does not inherently provide any clues, but inspection of the objects in the extremes of the solution space or inclusion in the analysis of an object with "known" attributes can provide clues. Referring again to the roadmap example, one might look for the cities Miami and Seattle, knowing that they represent the extremes of Southeast and Northwest.

In summary, the techniques described in this paper utilize only order relationships among data, but can often provide metric information about

[8] Same reference as footnote 7. Also Joseph B. Kruskal, "Multidimensional Scaling by Optimizing Goodness of Fit to a Nonmetric Hypothesis," *Psychometrika*. Vol. 29 (March, 1964), pp. 1–27, and "Nonmetric Multidimensional Scaling: A Numerical Method," *Psychometrika*, Vol. 29 (June 1964), pp. 115–29.

distance relationships. Moreover, a *multi*dimensional solution may result even though the input measures were merely unidimensional (that is, the rank orders of the inter-object relationships).

APPLICATIONS OF NONMETRIC MULTIDIMENSIONAL SCALING TO MARKETING PROBLEMS

Marketing analyses often involve two distinct types of data bases. In one case the data such as sales, profits, or the presence or absence of a particular product feature are objectively determined. In the second case the data are defined by the perceptual processes of individuals. Examples of this type of data are perceptions, attitudes, and preferences. In many cases analysis of the same problem utilizing the two types of data can yield disparate results. A hypothetical problem will make this clear.

Suppose it were desirable to determine if the Chevrolet Camaro is more similar to the Pontiac Firebird than to the Ford Mustang. Clearly, there are several characteristics or attributes associated with all of these specialty cars. Each attribute, however, may be "more" or "less" associated with any one car. In order to evaluate the similarity among the three cars, a *set* of attributes (assuming that a common reference frame or set of attributes is suitable) must be considered. This set of attributes can possibly be represented (or modeled) geometrically, so that the "distance" between any of the three automobiles represents the degree to which they possess similar "scores" on the common attributes. This attribute space for specialty automobiles might be developed either by (1) asking consumers for their estimates (perceptions) of similarity, or by (2) objectively deriving it from measurement of horsepower, weight, and braking of the three automobiles.

The two attribute spaces may not be the same. People may not perceive differences in some of the objective measures, or their perceptions of these measures may not be "correct." In order to distinguish between objectively measured and people-derived attribute spaces, it is convenient to call the former "performance spaces" and the latter "perceptual spaces."

Development of a Perceptual Space

For many products purchasing behavior is believed to be related more to perceived product features (including something called "product image") than to actual performance characteristics. This might be true perhaps in explaining consumer purchasing patterns with respect to frequently purchased grocery items such as detergent, coffee, and beer. Similarly, it has been suggested that perceptions, rather than objective analysis of laboratory reports, can "explain" physician selection of competing brands of ethical pharmaceuticals.

In a pilot study, physician perceptions of, and preferences for, brands of drugs within two classes of ethical pharmaceuticals were analyzed.[9] Figure 25-2 illustrates a typical perceptual space derived in this study. A composite space of only two dimensions based on a statistical goodness of fit measure and on interpretability appeared to be necessary to portray accurately inter-brand relationships.

To develop this perceptual space data were collected from a sample of general medical practitioners who were simply asked to render overall similarity judgments for all product pairs. Two methods of data collection were utilized successfully—triadic combinations and rating scales. These procedures are illustrated in Table 25–1. The critical aspect is that in neither method were the criteria for determining similarity stated. Individual response data were aggregated, and the aggregate or average perceptions were analyzed using a nonmetric multidimensional scaling program. Conceptually, the data used to develop this attribute space are vastly different from those used in performance space studies. However, after the similarity measures used for input are derived, the computational procedure is identical.

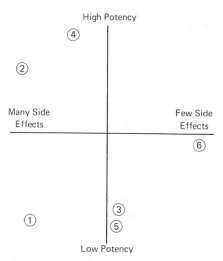

Figure 25–2. Perceptual Space of Brands of Ethical Pharmaceuticals

Figure 25–2 contains five "real" brands (Brands 1–5) which were identified during data collection, and one hypothetical brand (Brand 6) which was labeled the hypothetical "Ideal brand" during data collection. The concept of the "Ideal brand" is a simple one; it merely states that the closer a real

[9] Lester A. Neidell, *Physician Perception and Evaluation of Selected Ethical Drugs: An Application of Nonmetric Multidimensional Scaling to Pharmaceutical Marketing*, unpublished doctoral dissertation, University of Pennsylvania, 1969.

Table 25–1

Illustration of the Methods of Data Collection Used in the Physician Study

---

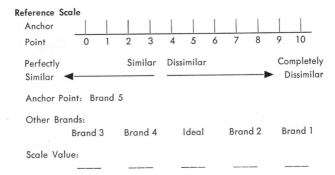

Method of Triadic Combinations

Instructions: Select the two most similar and the two least similar brands in each triple.

	Most Similar	Least Similar
Brand A	( )	( )
Brand B	( )	( )
Brand C	( )	( )

All possible combinations of triples $[(6!/3!3!) = 20]$ were included.

Rating Scale Method

Instructions: Compare the five remaining brands to the brand acting as an anchor point by assigning a number which reflects your assessment of their overall similarity to the anchor point brand.

Reference Scale

Anchor
Point

```
|  |  |  |  |  |  |  |  |  |  |
0  1  2  3  4  5  6  7  8  9  10
```

Perfectly   Similar   Dissimilar   Completely
Similar   ◄────────────────   ────────────────►   Dissimilar

Anchor Point: Brand 5

Other Brands:

Brand 3	Brand 4	Ideal	Brand 2	Brand 1

Scale Value:

___   ___   ___   ___   ___

Each brand in turn acted as an anchor point. While interval measures might be derived from this procedure only the ordinal results were utilized.

---

brand is to the "Ideal brand," the more preferred is the real brand.[10] By definition, the "Ideal brand" is the most preferred brand.

This use of the "Ideal brand" concept introduces another aspect of non-metric multidimensional scaling. *Preferences and/or preference distributions can be super-imposed on, or jointly derived with, most attribute spaces, for both performance and perceptual data.*[11]

The usefulness of this feature can be demonstrated by analyzing Figure 25–2. Suppose that this sample of physicians was actually a representative

[10] Clyde H. Coombs, *A Theory of Data* (New York: John Wiley and Sons, Inc., 1964), p. 141.

[11] See Paul E. Green, Frank J. Carmone, and Patrick J. Robinson, *Analysis of Marketing Behavior Using Nonmetric Scaling and Related Techniques* (Cambridge, Massachusetts: Marketing Science Institute, March, 1968).

national sample, and further, that the two dimensions were equally important to the sample. Since by definition the "Ideal brand" would be most preferred, this suggests that Brands 3 and 5 would have the largest market shares of the five brands. If a drug manufacturer were to introduce a new brand in this product class, he would attempt to place it close to the "Ideal brand."

Labeling of the axes of this perceptual space was achieved by analyzing other data collected during the study and by relying on the advice of knowledgeable people in the pharmaceutical industry. The two dimensions were identified as "potency" and "side effects." Thus, Brands 2 and 4 were perceived to be highly potent, but also to induce (undesirable) side effects. Brands 1, 3, and 5 were perceived to be considerably weaker than the other two brands, but despite this, Brand 1 still had associated with it undesirable side effects.

Market Segmentation Analysis

In terms of marketing strategy, the position of the "Ideal brand" (Brand 6) suggests that a more "ideal" brand might be introduced. This implies, however, that a single "Ideal brand" exists which will be the "most preferred" brand for all respondents. Alternatively, *different* "Ideal brands" might exist. For example, suppose that the similarities data were collected from two distinct sets of physicians, one group of which placed the "Ideal brand" near Brands 2 and 4, while the other perceived their "Ideal brand" to be similar to Brands 3 and 5. If this were true, then the single "average Ideal" would be one that satisfies neither of these groups very well.

To further complicate marketing strategy decisions, the perceptual spaces of the *real brands* may not be similar. For example, on the average Brands 2 and 4 were perceived as similar; however, there may be a subset of respondents who did not believe this to be true. For this particular product class the possibility that different perceptual maps existed was supported by clinical evidence. According to this evidence, the interbrand relationships of Brands 1, 3, 4, and 5 were accurately portrayed, but the positioning of Brand 2 was inaccurate. Brand 2 should have been midway between Brand 4 and Brands 3 and 5 in both potency and side effects. Was it possible that some of the respondent physicians did in fact perceive the relationships of Brand 2 to the other four brands "correctly"?

In summary, average perceptual maps may be a satsistical artifact. In order to decide among alternative strategies it is necessary to assess the scatter or variability of perceptions.

A procedure called cluster analysis was utilized to determine if the aggregate perceptual maps did in fact disguise the existence of different perceptual maps. The objective of cluster analysis is to delineate any natural groupings that exist in a set of data.[12] No clearly defined rules exist, however, to determine an "optimum" number of clusters to extract from any given data bank. In this particular product class, analysis of the volume of potential segments suggested that a maximum of two market segments could be profitably developed. Accordingly, only two clusters of respondents were developed. Similarities judgments were aggregated within each cluster, and again nonmetric multidimensional scaling was applied. The results are shown in Figures 25–3 and 25–4.

Figures 25–2 (aggregate analysis) and 25–3 (first market segment) are quite similar with respect to interbrand relationships. However, in Figure 25–4 (which represents a second market segment) Brand 2 was perceived as being medium in potency and side effects, as suggested by the clinical evidence. The "Ideal brand" for this subset of respondents also "moved"; it was very similar to Brands 3 and 5.

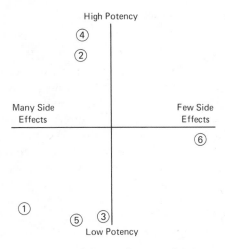

Figure 25–3. Perceptual Map of First Market Segment

In both market segments, Brands 3 and 5 were closest to the "Ideal," suggesting that a single "optimum" brand choice might resemble either of these two brands. Such a choice, however, would leave a company very vulnerable to competition in segment one, since there is room for a brand to be "more ideal" in terms of the needs of these physicians. This choice would also face extremely stiff competition in segment two where it would be difficult to move a new brand into a position closer to the "Ideal" than either Brands

[12] See R. R. Sokal and P. H. A. Sneath, *Principles of Numerical Taxonomy* (San Francisco: Freeman and Company, 1963); Stephen C. Johnson, "Hierarchical Clustering Schemes," *Psychometrika*, Vol. 32 (March, 1965), pp. 241–254; and Paul E. Green, Ronald Frank, and Patrick Robinson, "Cluster Analysis in Test Market Selection," *Management Science*, Vol. 13 (April, 1967), pp. B387–B400.

3 or 5. Thus, if this were a completely virgin market and if the brand placements were hypothetical entities, a brand resembling 3 and 5 might be considered optimum. Given the existing market structure, the preferred strategy would probably be to concentrate on segment one where the possibility of satisfying unfilled customer needs is much greater than in segment 2.

In summary, different preferences (that is, "Ideal brand" locations) rather than different "real brand" perceptions would be the major consideration in implementing a segmentation strategy for this particular product class. In both segments the "Ideal brand" is one with few side effects. Some physicians feel the "Ideal" should be medium in potency, perhaps in order to more easily control the dosage. Other physicians prefer a drug which is relatively ineffective, possibly because they feel this product is useful only as a placebo. Whatever the reasons for the different perceptual maps, it is clear that a strategy of market segmentation is feasible.

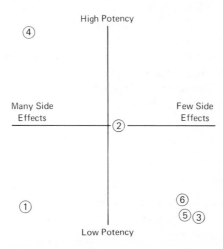

Figure 25–4. Perceptual Map of Second Market Segment

ADDITIONAL USES AND LIMITATIONS

This example has only hinted at the range of possible applications of nonmetric multidimensional scaling in marketing. In addition to market segmentation analysis and new product studies, the techniques of nonmetric multidimensional scaling might be applied to the study of product life cycle, vendor and advertising evaluation, test marketing, salesmen and store image studies, and brand switching research.[13]

---

[13] Paul E. Green and Frank J. Carmone, "The Performance Structure of the Computer Market: A Multivariate Approach," *Economic and Business Bulletin*, Vol. 21 (Fall, 1969), pp. 1–11, and same reference as footnote 11, Chapter 1.

This is not to say that there are no limitations or problems to this methodology. There are. First of all there is a practical problem—data availability. This is particularly true in developing *perceptual spaces*, because the data must often be specially collected. Therefore, these analyses can be expensive, as anyone involved in empirical research can testify.

Second, there are computational problems. How unique are the attribute spaces given noisy and/or missing data? How reliable, statistically, are the solutions? It is clear that additional empirical and analytical work is needed in this area.

Third, there are theoretical questions. One of these concerns distance measurement. In the results discussed above, the ordinary Euclidean distance measure was utilized. There are other distance measures, which if utilized, might change drastically some of the interpretations earlier suggested.[14] One distance measure suggested in psychological literature is the "city-block" measure, in which distance between any two objects is *not* the shortest straight line distance, but is instead a function of the absolute distance traveled in terms of corners or right angles.

This limited discussion of the possible pitfalls of these new techniques is intended to indicate that, as with *any* set of analytical procedures, there are unresolved issues. Nonmetric multidimensional scaling offers the possibility of new insights into analysis of market behavior. It cannot, however, be used indiscriminately.

SUMMARY

This paper has tried to introduce the reader to a set of new analytical procedures—nonmetric multidimensional scaling. An acquaintance with the specialized language of this technique is necessary to fully comprehend its possibilities. The central idea is that a multidimensional *attribute space* can be developed from a unidimensional data bank in which distances represent the degree of similarity among objects. Potential applications cover many facets of marketing. An example developed a *perceptual space* for competing ethical pharmaceuticals. Also in this example, the concept of a joint space, incorporating both perceptual and preference data, was introduced. In the example, the interpretation of the analyses, and their potential effects on marketing strategies, were stressed. The article concluded with a short discussion of some of the difficulties which might be encountered when utilizing these techniques.

[14] Roger N. Shepard, "Attention and the Metric Structure of the Stimulus," *Journal of Mathematical Psychology*, Vol. 1 (February, 1964), pp. 54–87.

26.

Market Segment Identification through Consumer Buying Behavior and Personal Characteristics

V. Parker Lessig
John O. Tollefson

INTRODUCTION

The study reported explores and demonstrates the application of an aggregation approach to market segment identification using cluster analysis. The research was motivated in part by the rather meager evidence of relationships between buying behavior and personal characteristics provided by previous studies. Thus, in addition to showing a practical method of finding market segments, the results of a cluster analysis are utilized to test for the existence of such relationships. The results of the test are generally positive and provide indirect empirical support for the market segment identification methodology.

PERSONAL CHARACTERISTICS AND BUYING BEHAVIOR

A number of studies over the past 12 years have attempted to show that a consumer's personal characteristics are related to his buying behavior [5, 6, 7, 10, 11, and 13]. For the most part, these studies used linear regression analyses in which socioeconomic and/or psychological measures were used as the independent variables, and a univariate characteristic of buying behavior was used as the dependent variable. The resulting coefficients of determination were very low. As a result, these studies provide little evidence of relationships between buying behavior and personal characteristics. Studies utilizing other methods to find relationships between personal characteristics and some univariate buying behavior characteristic have, in general, yielded similarly disappointing results [3, 4, 15, and 17].

This is a revision of a paper originally presented to the 1970 Fall Educator's Conference, American Marketing Association, August 31–September 2, 1970, Boston. The research was supported in part by a grant from the University of Kansas. Use was made of the facilities of the University of Kansas Computation Center.

Linear and Restricted Non-Linear Relationships

One limitation of most of these studies is that the statistical models employed would be appropriate only if the relationships existing between buying behavior and personal characteristics were linear. Some studies considered the possibility of nonlinearities and hypothesized a particular non-linear form [cf., 6, 10]. Transformations were made which would linearize the relationships if the hypothesized nonlinear form was correct. These transformations were found to be ineffective in increasing the coefficient of determination. If nonlinear relations do exist between buying behavior and personal characteristics, but in a form other than that hypothesized, this would explain in part why the coefficients of determination were low.

What Kind of Buying Behavior?

Another limitation of these studies arises from the theoretical basis for the selection of a measure of buying behavior. Typically, these studies have involved a search for relationships between a number of personal characteristics and a single buying behavior variable (for example, brand purchased, quantity consumed).

Decision process theories of consumer behavior [2, 8, and 14] lead one to select measures which differ substantially from those used in previous studies. These theories emphasize the process which generates buying behavior. Inferences from these theories suggest that: (1) relationships probably exist between a consumer's personal characteristics and his purchase decision process: and (2) individuals who have similarly structured purchase decision processes are likely to exhibit over-all similarity in buying behavior. Consequently, one would expect a relationship to exist between personal characteristics and buying behavior type rather than between personal characteristics and some single facet of buying behavior. Thus, in determining whether relationships exist between buying behavior and personal characteristics, a multivariate measure of behavior should be used.

This position gains some empirical support from Kernan [9], who investigated the relationship between personality and the usage of alternative choice criteria under conditions of uncertainty. He found no relationships between personality variables and univariate measures of the usage of choice criteria, but significant relationships were found between a multivariate measure of the usage of choice criteria and personality variables.

MARKET SEGMENTATION

An extension of the above argument provides the basis for an operational method of identifying market segments.

The Concept of Market Segmentation

Within the set of actual and potential buyers of a product, there are many consumers whose responses differ with respect to such stimuli as price, advertising, point of purchase displays, and type of retail outlet. For example, not all consumers in the market may have the same price elasticity of demand for the product, or they may differ with respect to their sensitivity to advertising stimuli. The differences in stimuli sensitivity also imply that the overt buying behavior of all the consumers in the market is not the same. Differences in buying behavior may be reflected in differences in brand purchased, degree of brand loyalty, store shopped, store loyalty, usage rate, and quantity purchased.

The concept of market segmentation as developed in economic theory shows how a firm can maximize profits when the market for its product may be divided into separable sub-markets having differing price elasticities. In this event, a monopolist (or other price setter) could maximize profits by charging different prices to groups of consumers who differ in their elasticity of demand.

Today marketers realize that within the mass market for a product differences exist among consumers not only in their response to price but also in responses to advertising, product design and style, and other merchandising variables. In attempting to maximize profits, a firm is not free to practice classical price discrimination. However a firm does have an opportunity to discriminate through the use of market stimuli such as advertising copy design, advertising exposure, price and product feature variation, and location of product distribution.

This point was brought out by Smith [16] who suggested that market segmentation can be used to increase a firm's profits when differences exist among consumers in their reaction to market stimuli. Smith said that these differences result in a heterogeneous market having a number of demand schedules for a given product. This heterogeneous market should be viewed, according to Smith, as consisting of a number of market segments. Since all the members of a given segment are somewhat similar to each other in their response to market stimuli, the demand functions of all the consumers in a given segment should be similar. Smith felt that a firm's strategy should be directed toward the satisfaction of one or more of these market segments by adjusting the marketing mix according to each market's elasticity on each market stimuli. This would result in a deeper sales penetration in each segment than would have been obtained had no differences been recognized among the consumers in their responses to various market strategies.

Claycamp and Massy [1] presented a relatively complete normative theory of market segmentation. This article made at least two important contributions to our understanding of the problem. First, it pointed out that market segmentation is an aggregation process. Since the objective of market segmentation, as pointed out by Smith, is to maximize profits by designing the product and selling effort to fit each individual's demand functions, segmentation must begin at the individual level. If no diseconomies exist in designing separate strategies for each individual, profits could be maximized by such an approach. However, because of diseconomies, consumers must be aggregated into larger groups. Second, the normative theory presented includes within its context the question of the optimum level of aggregation into market segments. By determining the marketing strategies which maximize profits at each level of aggregation, the firm should, in theory, be able to find that level of market segmentation and combination of strategies which will maximize profits.

Market Segment Identification

The problem for the marketer is one of determining how he should aggregate individual consumers into segments so that he can increase profits by designing strategies specifically for each segment. Ideally, this problem can be solved by aggregating into the same group all consumers having similar response functions. (A response function for a consumer expresses his buying behavior as a function of the level of the marketing stimuli, such as prices, advertising cues, and product alternatives. Obviously, the domain of the function must be the set of all possible levels of these marketing stimuli.) The members of such a group would be similar in terms of their response to all marketing stimuli, not just one. Because of the similarity in their response functions, all consumers in the same market segment should show similar overt buying behavior at a given point in time, and their overt behavior should change, but similarly, as market stimuli change.

The difficulty of measuring individual response functions prevents utilization of this basis for segmenting markets. Partial measurements can be made of these functions. Unfortunately, these measurements include only small portions of the function's domain and do not permit generalizations about the consumer's entire response surface. It is, therefore, necessary to develop substitute procedures for finding consumers having similar response functions if the concept of market segmentation is to be used.

Current Methods. One of the approaches often used has been to define segments on the basis of socioeconomic and demographic characteristics. For example, a segment would be defined as consisting of individuals in a certain age group, having a certain number of children, and having other shared characteristics. This approach was used for several reasons. First, information on consumer socioeconomic and demographic characteristics was relatively easy to obtain. Second, it was felt that there might be some relationship between an individual's purchase behavior and his socioeconomic and demographic characteristics. This method of identifying market segments has often been used in the selection of advertising media on the basis of the personal characteristic descriptions of the audience. The assumption was often made that individuals having the same personal characteristics were similar in behavior. The problem with this approach is that attempts were not made to see if the individuals having similar personal characteristics were also similar in their responses to market stimuli. Consumers having the same personal characteristics often differ in their purchase behavior. There is, therefore, little reason to believe that consumers aggregated only on the basis of personal characteristic information should have similar responses to the market stimuli directed toward them.

Other approaches to market segmentation have placed individual consumers into market segments on the basis of one overt buying behavior characteristic such as the brand purchased, usage rate for the product, or place of purchase. All individuals who were similar in the one characteristic of behavior were placed in the same segment. One objection to this approach is that consumers who are similar on one behavioral characteristic often differ on other characteristics of behavior. Consumers having similar response functions to market stimuli should be similar on many dimensions of behavior.

Even if it could be assumed that individuals who are similar on one behavioral characteristic are also similar on other behavioral dimensions (an assumption which can not be made), such a group still does not necessarily represent a market segment. Although the consumers in such a group would have the same overt buying behavior at a given point in time, they will not necessarily continue to behave similarly to each other when the stimuli change. This possibility can be illustrated by looking at the price elasticity of demand for two individuals. The demand curve for each of two individuals is represented in Figure 26–1. As shown, individual A has a more price elastic demand than does individual B. Therefore, it cannot be said that these two consumers have the same response to price changes. Yet at point P_0 both consumers have the same behavior with respect to price. When the price is at any level other than P_0, the individuals have different demands for the product.

A similar condition could exist where more general response functions are employed. If an individual's response behavior to several market stimuli is expressed as a function of several variables, the response function would be represented by a hypersurface in a multidimensional space. Individuals having the same behavior at a given point in time could actually belong to different market segments; but at this particular combination of stimuli, there is an intersection of their hypersurfaces.

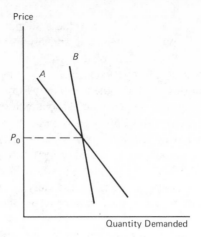

Figure 26–1. Intersecting Response Functions

A Proposed Method. It was stated *supra* that inferences from decision process theories of consumer behavior [2, 8, and 14] suggest that (1) relationships probably exist between a consumer's personal characteristics and his purchase decision process; and (2) individuals who have similarly structured purchase decision processes are likely to exhibit over-all similarity in buying behavior (for example, quantity purchased, relative frequency of buying various brands, relative frequency of shopping at various stores, and so on). Again, although similarity of purchase decision processes implies similarity in buying behavior, the implication flows in one direction only. Similarity of decision processes *cannot* be inferred from observations of similarity in behavior. However, by an extension of the argument above, consumers who exhibit similar buying behavior *and who have similar personal characteristics* are likely to have similar purchase decision processes, that is, they are likely to have similar response functions.

Thus, consumers can be grouped into probable market segments by a two-stage aggregation process. First, consumers are aggregated on the basis of similarity in buying behavior. Second, within each behavioral group, consumers are aggregated into subgroups on the basis of personal characteristic similarities. A subgroup thus found can be regarded as a probable market segment.

The substitute procedure to be used for the identification of market segments can be summarized as follows: Let B_i^j where $i = 1, \cdots, m$ represent a buying behavior characteristic for consumer j. Letting $X_1^j, X_2^j, \cdots, X_n^j$ represent consumer j's personal characteristics, given a certain exposure to market stimuli. The influence of these personal characteristics on each of j's behavioral characteristics can then be expressed by the following response functions:

$$B_1^j = f_1^j (X_1^j, X_2^j, \ldots, X_n^j, MS)$$
$$B_2^j = f_2^j (X_1^j, X_2^j, \ldots, X_n^j, MS)$$

$\bullet$ $\bullet$

$\bullet$ $\bullet$

$\bullet$ $\bullet$

(26–1) $\qquad\qquad B_i^j = f_i^j (X_1^j, X_2^j, \ldots, X_n^j, MS)$

$\bullet$ $\bullet$

$\bullet$ $\bullet$

$\bullet$ $\bullet$

$$B_m^j = f_m^j (X_1^j, X_2^j, \ldots, X_n^j, MS)$$

where MS represents the market stimuli. The series of equations in (26–1) are not intended to be operational. Rather, they are intended to indicate the theorized influence of market stimuli and personal characteristics on an individual's buying behavior. Let the set of buying behavior characteristics for consumers j and k, respectively, be expressed as

(26–2)
$$\beta_j = (B_1^j, B_2^j, \ldots, B_m^j)$$
$$\beta_k = (B_1^k, B_2^k, \ldots, B_m^k)$$

If j and k have similar response functions to market stimuli, then given that they have been exposed to the same stimuli

(26–3) $\qquad\qquad\qquad\qquad \beta_j \ s \ \beta_k$

where s means that the two sets of behavioral characteristics are similar. From decision process theories of consumer behavior, it follows that

(26–4) $\qquad\qquad\qquad\qquad \beta_j \ s \ \beta_k => [(a) \ v \ (b)]$

where (a) means that j and k have the same response functions and (b) means that j and k have different response functions which happen to intersect at the given set of market stimuli. Let PC_j represent j's set of classifications on the personal characteristics believed to be related to behavior. Decision process theories of consumer behavior imply that

(26–5) $\qquad\qquad [(\beta_j \ s \ \beta_k) \cap (PC_j \ s \ PC_k)] => [(a) \cap (\tilde{b})].$

Since consumers having similar response functions belong to the same market segment, (4) and (5) can be used in the identification of market segments.

Operationally, it is suggested that cluster analysis be used to aggregate consumers into these probable market segments. First, all consumers are placed in the same multidimensional space where each dimension represents a specific buying behavior activity. Cluster analysis can then be used to find those consumers who are similar in all of the characteristics of comparison.

Next, the members of a given behavioral cluster should be placed in a space having dimensions which represent personal characteristic variables. A cluster analysis is then performed. Clusters resulting from this second analysis are aggregations of consumers having similar buying behavior and personal characteristics. The personal characteristic cluster analysis should be performed separately within each behavioral cluster.

EMPIRICAL ANALYSIS

The empirical analysis consisted of: (1) a two-stage cluster analysis, first on buying behavior and then on personal characteristics, to demonstrate the market segment identification methodology; and (2) tests for relationships between personal characteristics and buying behavior type, or group membership. Panel data containing information on the personal characteristics and the coffee purchasing behavior of 212 households[1] were used in the study. The details of the empirical analysis will be presented following identification of the behavioral and personal characteristic variables selected from these data for use in the study.

Buying Behavior Characteristics

According to the method of market segment identification proposed above, consumers must first be aggregated into buying behavior similarity groups. If variation in behavior exists among consumers, such a behavioral characteristic is relevant in the identification of segments if an adjustment of a firm's marketing strategy in response to the variation along this characteristic could lead to an increase in the firm's profit.

Attempting to apply these criteria, the following overt buying behavior characteristics for coffee were selected for use in the study:

1. Distribution of purchases over brands
2. Distribution of purchases over stores
3. Average number of packages purchased each shopping trip
4. Size of packages purchased
5. Purchase rate

Substantial interpersonal variation existed among the panel members on each of these characteristics. It was also felt that variations in these behavioral characteristics would be relevant to the marketing strategy decisions of a coffee marketer.

---

[1] The data were made available through the courtesy of Professors Louis P. Bucklin, James M. Carman, and Francesco M. Nicosia, all of the University of California, Berkeley.

Personal Characteristics

After buying behavior similarity groups are found, the theory of market segment identification calls for the identification of consumers within each behavioral group who are similar in personal characteristics. A priori, twenty-four personal characteristics were selected for investigation in the study. Each variable measures a characteristic commonly included in a decision process theory model of consumer behavior [2, 8, and 14]. Also, many have been used as independent variables in previous studies. The variables, listed below, include common socioeconomic and demographic measures together with variables measuring social interaction and scores on the Myers-Briggs Type Indicator, a personality test.

1. Race
2. Church membership
3. Church attendance
4. Education of wife
5. Education of husband
6. Stated social class membership
7. Property value of home
8. Amount of rent (if home is not owned)
9. Income
10. Occupation
11. Political affiliation
12. Total household size
13. Wife's age
14. Portion of time wife works
15. Portion of time husband works
16. Number of contributors to family income
17. Frequency of visiting a friend
18. Frequency of entertaining or being entertained by relatives over a four-week period (wife alone plus wife and husband together)
19. Frequency of entertaining or being entertained by friends over a four-week period (wife alone plus wife and husband together)
20. Desired social class membership
21. EI score on the Myers-Briggs Type Indicator (introvert or extrovert in judgment and perception)
22. SN score on the Myers-Briggs Type Indicator (relies on senses or intuition)
23. TF score on the Myers-Briggs Type Indicator (preference between thinking or feeling)
24. JP score on the Myers-Briggs Type Indicator (relies on a perceptive or on a judging process)

DEMONSTRATION OF THE MARKET SEGMENT

Identification Methodology

Buying Behavior Clusters. A cluster analysis was used to identify buying behavior similarity groups. Each household was represented by a point in a multidimensional space. The coordinates of that point were the household's scores on each of the buying behavior variables. The following distance formula served as an inverse measure of the buying behavior similarity between households j and k.

$$(26\text{–}6) \qquad D_{jk} = \left[\sum_{i=1}^{n} (X_{ij} - X_{ik})^2 \right]^{1/2}$$

where n represents the number of dimensions and X_{ij} and X_{ik} are the scores on dimensions i for household j and household k, respectively. The smaller the distance between households, the greater their similarity on the dimensions of comparison. In the cluster analysis,[2] individual households were initially treated as separate groups. At each stage in the clustering operation, the two groups separated by the minimum intercentroid distance were merged. Following this merging, centroid locations and intercentroid distances were recomputed, as necessary, for each pair of groups and the process was repeated. Through such a continuing aggregation process it was possible to identify groups of households in which the members of each were similar in the given buying behavior characteristics.

Before the aggregation of households began, the distribution of households on each dimension was standardized to a mean of zero and a standard deviation of one so that the weights would not be distorted by differences in the variances between dimensions. One might argue that clustering should be performed after removing redundancy in the measures through factor analysis. However, the original dimensions were used in this study to permit interpretation of the results at several stages in the hierarchical clustering operation.

The characteristics of average number of packages purchased, size of packages purchases, and purchase rate were each represented by a single dimension. However, it was necessary to represent the information on the characteristic of distribution of purchases over brands through the use of 10 dimensions. Only seven brands of regular coffee were purchased by enough panel members to justify representation by separate dimensions. A household's score on each of these dimensions was the percent of its coffee purchases concentrated on the specified brand. A household's score on the 8th

---

[2] This program was written specifically for the needs of this study. It was developed after extensive consultation with F. James Rohlf, then Associate Professor of Entomology at the University of Kansas, now at the State University of New York at Stony Brook.

dimension was the percent of its coffee purchases concentrated on the "other" brand of regular coffee which it purchased most frequently. The 9th dimension showed the percent of the household's coffee purchases concentrated on the brand of instant coffee which it purchased most frequently. The 10th dimension represented the percent of coffee purchases which were made from brands of regular coffee.

Seven dimensions were used to represent distribution of purchases over stores. Six of these dimensions showed the percent of a household's coffee purchases made at a particular major supermarket. The seventh dimension represented the household's tendency to purchase coffee at neighborhood markets.

It was desired that all behavioral characteristics have the same weight of importance in the determination of cluster membership. However, if all dimensions were permitted to enter cluster analysis without adjustment, the characteristics of distribution of purchases over brands and distribution of purchases over stores would each have a greater influence in the formation of clusters than a characteristic such as purchase rate, which can be represented by one dimension. This problem was avoided by giving the combined dimensions on a given characteristic a weight of one. Equality of weights is achieved by dividing all of those terms in the distance formula (26–6) of the form $(X_{ij} - X_{ik})^2$ which pertain to a single characteristic by the number of dimensions used to represent that characteristic.

Eight relatively distinct buying behavior similarity groups consisting of 125 households were found from the cluster analysis. The characteristic behavior of each group can be described by the group centroids which are given in Table 26–1. Determination of the stopping point in a hierarchical clustering routine is essentially a judgmental problem. The average distance of entities from the cluster centroid within the most recently formed cluster (AWCD) was used as the measure of within cluster similarity. Aggregation was continued to the point where the number of clusters became small enough to permit interpretation and stopped when the AWCD measure began to increase rapidly.

Some light was cast upon the nature of the resulting clusters through an examination of the distances separating the centroids of the clusters in the buying behavior space. The clusters identified as A and B in Table 26–1 showed the greatest similarity. Even so, the members of these two groups differed considerably in their brand loyalties and size of packages purchased. The clear distinction between clusters is important in the identification of market segments because the greater the differences between clusters in overall buying behavior, the greater the likelihood that response function differences exist between members of different groups.

In addition to the eight distinct clusters, 52 additional groups were found. These 52 groups were small in size with most containing only one household

Table 26–1
Centroids of the Buying Behavior Clusters

Dimension Description	Value of the Centroid for the Respective Clusters							
	A	B	C	D	E	F	G	H
Purchases of Brands								
1 Edwards regular	1.4	0.0	0.0	0.0	42.0	0.0	11.4	0.0
2 COOP regular	41.8	5.1	2.4	0.0	5.3	0.0	11.4	0.0
3 Folgers regular	4.1	2.8	2.4	10.9	6.6	10.0	4.7	0.0
4 Hills regular	15.5	0.0	1.6	15.8	7.5	0.0	13.9	0.0
5 MJB regular	2.8	5.2	0.0	22.7	3.3	13.6	6.4	0.0
6 Maxwell House regular	1.1	1.4	1.6	6.7	5.3	0.0	1.0	0.0
7 Yuban regular	11.9	3.8	0.0	0.0	2.0	76.4	2.7	0.0
8 "Other" regular	9.9	36.4	2.4	36.5	22.0	0.0	30.1	0.0
9 Favorite instant	5.6	31.2	79.8	5.6	2.5	0.0	8.3	0.0
10 Percent regular	93.6	59.3	10.3	92.6	97.5	100.0	88.5	0.0
Purchases at Stores								
11 Safeway Stores	2.8	6.9	31.8	3.8	69.5	2.9	36.8	0.0
12 COOP Stores	86.8	83.6	30.9	0.0	7.4	78.1	36.0	0.0
13 Louis Stores	1.6	0.0	1.6	1.5	0.0	0.0	0.0	0.0
14 Park & Shop	0.0	0.7	2.4	7.6	3.3	0.0	6.8	0.0
15 Bonanza	0.0	1.7	24.6	0.0	5.3	0.0	9.9	0.0
16 U-Save	2.8	2.4	3.6	85.3	11.2	0.0	1.3	0.0
17 "Other" stores	6.1	4.0	5.2	1.8	3.3	19.1	8.4	0.0
Remaining Three Characteristics								
18 No. of purchases (during panel)	5.17	4.25	2.29	3.73	3.79	3.14	8.80	0.00
19 Avg. package size (in ounces)	21.2	12.6	7.3	29.2	30.9	26.8	20.0	0.0
20 Avg. no. purchased (each trip)	1.26	1.05	1.01	1.06	1.22	1.18	1.07	0.00

(only four of these groups contained more than three households). If the households in these extremely small groups were to be used in the remainder of the study, one of three alternatives had to be followed. The first of these was to treat each of these groups individually as potential market segments. The marketing and production costs of this approach would be too high for a product such as coffee. The second alternative was to collectively treat all of these households as one potential segment. This was rejected because the resulting group did not satisfy the condition of similarity in buying behavior. The third alternative was to continue the aggregation process until these groups merged with the eight distinct clusters. This would substantially reduce the buying behavior similarity within clusters. It was therefore decided to consider only the eight distinct clusters as potential market segments.

The decision to focus only on those households which were members of clearly defined behavioral groups is also appropriate in an applied context. Here, the marketing manager may decide that it would be profitable to design separate strategies only for the large and dominant market segments while ignoring the small scattered groups of consumers. This could prove to be more profitable than trying to include the small scattered groups through mass marketing or through attempts to reach each individually.

The question of whether different buying behavior similarity groups would have been found had different weights been used in the cluster analysis remains. One way of answering this question would have been to cluster the households using many different weight combinations. However, the costs involved eliminated this possibility. A priori, it was decided to perform a cluster analysis in which each of the characteristics distribution of purchases over brands and distribution of purchases over stores had a weight twice that given to each of the remaining three characteristics.[3] The objective of this analysis was to obtain information concerning the stability of the clusters when the characteristic weights are moderately changed. The membership of the resulting clusters had an almost one-to-one corespondence to the membership of the clusters found using equal weights; all but seven of the 125 households were in corresponding clusters. This observation leads one to believe that the identification of behavioral clusters is somewhat insensitive to moderate changes in weights. Thus, it appears that the eight major clusters are natural groupings with distinct buying behavior.

At this point it is not possible to say that each distinct behavioral cluster is a market segment. However, there is reason to believe that marketers should be interested in knowing that groups exist which differ in behavior at a point in time. Through this information the marketer can view the market as consisting of a small number of behavioral groups each of which is distinct from the others in behavior rather than as one large group having similar behavior or as a large number of entities having unique overall behavior.

Personal Characteristic Dimensions.   Before it can be said that all or part of the members of each buying behavior similarity group identified above constitute a market segment, personal characteristic similarities must be observed. Thus, a personal characteristic cluster analysis was performed within each buying behavior similarity group.

Because five of the personal characteristics were of nominal rank, 44 dimensions would have been required if all 24 personal characteristics were represented in the cluster analysis. Since misleading interpretations of the resulting clusters could result from the use of an unnecessarily large number of personal characteristics, an attempt was made to determine whether certain dimensions should be eliminated from the cluster analysis.

---

[3] This selection of weights should not be taken to mean that the authors feel that the characteristics Distribution of Purchases over Brands and Distribution of Purchases over Stores are of greater concern to either the consumer or the firm than are the other behavioral characteristics. These weights merely represent one of several weight combinations that could have appropriately been used to indicate possible instabilities in the clusters.

Sixteen dimensions were eliminated either because they were redundant or because little if any variation existed among the households on each of the characteristics. Twenty-eight dimensions remained. A separate chi-square analysis was performed for each personal characteristic dimension to see if it was related to buying behavior. For each, the null hypothesis was that a household's classification on the specified personal characteristic is independent of buying behavior cluster membership. (For the nominal characteristics, it was felt that the chi-square analysis should be constructed so that it would be possible to test the independence of buying behavior to each classification. Therefore, separate contingency tables were constructed for each classification of each nominal characteristic.) The results of the tests indicated that for 13 of the 28 personal characteristic dimensions the hypothesis of independence between a household's score on that dimension and its buying behavior cluster membership could be rejected at or well beyond the 0.1 level of significance. The levels of significance for these variables are listed in Table 26–2. These variables in addition to three others, also listed in Table 26–2, which showed possible relationships to buying behavior were used as dimensions in the personal characteristic cluster analysis.

Table 26–2
Personal Characteristics Differing Significantly Between Buying Behavior Clusters

Variable	Level of Significance
TF score on the Myers-Briggs	0.074
Household size	0.002
Age of wife	0.021
Occupation	0.003
Education of husband	0.01
Property value of home	0.02
Income	0.004
Portion of time wife works	0.05
Portion of time husband works	0.023
Political party (1 if no affiliation, otherwise 0)	0.002
Political party (1 if Republican, otherwise 0)	0.1
Political party (1 if Democrat, otherwise 0)	0.001
Frequency of entertaining or being entertained by friends	0.055

Personal Characteristics Showing Some Relationship to Buying Behavior

Variable	Level of Significance
Church membership (1 if other Protestant[a], otherwise 0)	0.15
Church membership (1 if no religious affiliation, otherwise 0)	0.3
Frequency of visiting a friend	0.285

[a] This value was 1 if the housewife was a member of a Protestant church other than Baptist, Mormon, Jehovah's Witness, or Seventh Day Adventist. If she was not a Protestant or if she was a Baptist, Mormon, Jehovah's Witness, or a Seventh Day Adventist, the value was 0.

In addition to indicating which dimensions should be used in the cluster analyses, the results of these chi-square tests, taken together, provide positive evidence in support of those portions of the decision process theories which state that relationships exist between buying behavior and personal characteristics. The probability of rejecting 13 or more of 28 statistical hypotheses at the 0.1 level by chance is less than 0.0001. Thus, rejection of the hypothesis of independence for 13 personal characteristic variables at or well beyond the 0.1 level leads one to believe that decision process theories of consumer behavior are correct in stating that relationships exist between buying behavior and personal characteristics.

Personal Characteristic Clusters and Relationships Between Behavioral Clusters and Personal Characteristic Clusters. A cluster analysis using the sixteen personal characteristic variables as dimensions was performed separately within each of the eight distinct behavioral clusters. Since three dimensions represented the characteristic political affiliation, the summation of the squared differences in equation (26–6) for these three dimensions was divided by three. The characteristic church membership was represented through the use of two dimensions; as a result, the summation of their squared differences in (26–6) was divided by two. The results of these eight analyses were ambiguous. That is, as groups were merged in the hierarchical routine, the AWCD dissimilarity measure increased quite uniformly throughout the analysis. Thus, it was not clear whether each behavioral cluster (1) was relatively homogeneous in terms of personal characteristics or (2) contained distinct personal characteristic subgroupings which could not be identified given the sample size.

Because of these ambiguities, additional analyses were performed to cast light on the proposed aggregation approach to market segment identification. First, a personal characteristic cluster analysis was performed in which all households in the eight buying behavior similarity groups were located in the same 16-dimensional personal characteristic space. Two analyses were then conducted to determine if a relationship exists between a household's position in the buying behavior space and its position in the personal characteristic space.

Based upon the results of the cluster analysis, each household, with the exception of two, was placed into one of four groups. A chi-square test was performed on the null hypothesis that a household's position in the buying behavior space is independent of its position in the personal charactertistic space. The contingency table for this analysis is given in Table 26–3. So that no more than 20 percent of the cells would have an expected value less than five, it was necessary to collapse some of the cells. Groups whose centroids were closest together were joined. The collapsed contingency table is shown in Table 26–4. The null hypothesis of independence was rejected at a significance level beyond 0.001.

The chi-square analysis required no restrictive assumptions about the structure of the underlying data. However, not all of the information in the data was utilized. Thus, a canonical correlation analysis was performed to measure the degree of linear relationship between a household's position in the personal characteristic space and the buying behavior space. The canonical correlation was found to be 0.729 between the maximally correlated linear compounds of the 16 personal characteristic variables and the 20 buying behavior variables used in the cluster analyses. This coefficient is significantly different from zero ($p = 0.01$). It should be recognized that the above analysis was based upon the assumption of linear relationships. Thus, if the actual relationships are nonlinear, which is a reasonable assumption, the canonical correlation coefficient above understates the degree to which buying behavior is related to personal characteristics.

Table 26–3
Contingency Table Showing Buying Behavior and
Personal Characteristic Cluster Membership

Buyer Behavior Cluster	Personal Characteristic Group				Row Total
	I	II	III	IV	
A	10	2	3	3	18
B	13	2	2	6	23
C	1	5	5	10	21
D	2	0	0	8	10
E	2	0	1	7	10
F	5	0	1	1	7
G	3	1	1	5	10
H	6	6	1	11	24
Column Total	42	16	14	51	123

Table 26–4
Collapsed Contingency Table Showing Buying Behavior
and Personal Characteristic Cluster Membership

Buying Behavior Cluster	Personal Characteristic Group			Row Total
	I	II–III	IV	
A–B	23	9	9	41
C	1	10	10	21
D–E–F	9	2	16	27
G	3	2	5	10
H	6	7	11	24
Column Total	42	30	51	123

The Prediction of Buying Behavior Cluster Membership
by Means of Discriminant Analysis

The results of the chi-square analyses and the canonical correlation analysis provide evidence in support of the position, derived from decision process theories, that buying behavior is related to personal characteristics. Further support for this position, and thus for the buying behavior and personal characteristic aggregation approach to market segment identification, is obtained if it can be shown that a household's buying behavior group membership can be predicted from information on its personal characteristics.

A discriminant model for the prediction of buying behavior group membership from personal characteristic variables was developed. A stepwise discriminant analysis program was used. Ninety-seven households were randomly drawn from the eight behavioral clusters to be used in the derivation of the discriminant model. This model was then used to predict the buying behavior cluster membership of the 28 remaining households based upon their personal characteristics; this group of 28 was a validation group. The performance of the discriminant model in classifying the validation group provides an unbiased estimate of the predictive validity of the model.

The personal characteristic variables used in the development of the model were the same 16 that were used in the personal characteristic cluster analysis. Characteristics of nominal data rank were introduced through the use of dummy variables.

An examination of each nonnominal personal characteristic variable showed that four were not normally distributed. Appropriate transformations were made which increased the homogeneity of the variances and made the data satisfactorily fit the normality assumption of the model. Nonlinearities were introduced into the model through the definition of additional variables. These variables represented the squares and cubes of the nonnominal personal characteristics.

The model that provided the best fit to the analysis sample of 97 households was developed through the stepwise discriminant analysis. This model incorporated 17 variables, which are listed in Table 26–5 in the order of their entrance into the model.

The 17 variables used represented, in one form or another, eight personal characteristics. Two of these characteristics were of nominal rank and were expressed using dummy variables. Of the remaining six characteristics, five were squared and/or cubed in the discriminant model. If this best-fitting model has predictive validity, this result strongly suggests that relationships between buying behavior and personal characteristics must be considered to be nonlinear.

Since the buying behavior group membership of the 28 households in the validation sample was already known, it was possible to test the predictive validity of the model. The discriminant model developed from the analysis

Table 26–5
Variables Entered into the Discriminant Model
(listed in the order of their entrance)

---

 1. Political party (1 if no affiliation)
 2. Myers-Briggs TF score—squared
 3. Education of husband
 4. Political party (1 if Democrat)
 5. Church membership (1 if other Protestant)
 6. Income
 7. Income—cubed
 8. Frequency of entertaining or being entertained by friends
 9. Political party (1 if Republican)
10. Household size
11. Frequency of entertaining or being entertained by friends—squared
12. Myers-Briggs TF score—cubed
13. Myers-Briggs TF score
14. Education of husband—cubed
15. Education of husband—squared
16. Frequency of visiting a friend
17. Household size—cubed

---

sample was used to predict the buying behavior group membership of each of the twenty-eight households in the validation sample. Table 26–6 shows the actual and predicted buying behavior group membership of each household. Membership was correctly predicted for 11, or roughly 39%, of the 28 households.

In testing the accuracy of the discriminant model it must be determined whether the actual number of correct classifications differs significantly from that which would have been expected had the households been randomly assigned to segments. Following Mosteller and Bush [12] it was determined that, under a random assignment of households, the number of households out of 28 correctly classified would be approximately normally distributed with a mean of 3.89 and a standard deviation of 1.82. From this it was possible to calculate the probability of getting 11 correct classifications under a random assignment; this probability was found to be 0.00005.

A question may be raised about the predictive power of this nonlinear discriminant model in comparison to the more parsimonious linear model. The best linear discriminant model developed in several attempts, using various subsets of the 16 variables listed in Table 26–2, correctly predicted the group membership of 2, or less than 8%, of a 28 household validation sample. The difference in predictive accuracy between the non-linear and linear models is statistically significant ($p < .004$). This apparent fivefold increase in predictive accuracy yielded by the non-linear model may also be considered operationally relevant.

Table 26–6
The Correct and Incorrect Classifications Obtained from the Discriminant Model
Containing 17 Personal Characteristics

| Actual Group | The Number of Households Classified into Group | | | | | | | | Row |
Membership	A	B	C	D	E	F	G	H	Total
A	1	0	0	0	1	0	1	1	4
B	1	3	0	0	0	0	0	1	5
C	1	0	1	0	1	0	0	2	5
D	0	0	0	1	1	1	0	0	3
E	0	0	1	0	1	0	0	0	2
F	1	0	1	0	0	0	0	0	2
G	0	0	0	1	0	0	1	0	2
H	0	0	1	1	0	0	0	3	5
Column Total	4	3	4	3	4	1	2	7	28

Thus, we may be quite confident that this discriminant model, which is intended to predict buying behavior type as a non-linear function of personal characteristic variables, performs significantly better than either a random classification mechanism or a strictly *linear* discriminant function. Although the prediction of behavioral group membership which it provides may not be accurate enough to be of immediate practical value, the above finding definitely supports the position that buying behavior type.is related to personal characteristic variables.

SUMMARY AND CONCLUSIONS

The intent of the study was to explore and demonstrate a method of market segment identification and to test for the existence of relationships between personal characteristics and buying behavior. The expectation that such relationships should exist and the rationale for the method of market segment identification were both drawn from a decision process approach to consumer behavior.

The results of four different, though not independent, empirical tests provided support for the inference from decision process theories that relationships exist between personal characteristics and buying behavior. In all of these tests a multivariate measure of buying behavior was employed. These empirical findings do not bear directly upon the market segment identification methodology which was demonstrated in the study. Yet, the credence of this methodology is indirectly strengthened by the above research findings since the proposed methodology receives its justification from these theories.

The cluster analysis approach to market segmentation resulted in the identification of eight behavioral clusters which were distinct in that the purchasing behavior of the households within a given cluster was similar while a great deal of difference in behavior existed between clusters. Since there was not a one-to-one correspondence between behavioral clusters and personal characteristic groups, it cannot be said that all of the households in a given behavioral cluster are members of the same market segment. Yet, the strength of the relationships between behavioral cluster membership and personal characteristic variables leads one to believe that many of the households in given clusters have similar responses to market stimuli. Also, it seems safe to conclude that households belonging to different behavioral clusters are not members of the same market segment.

The market segmentation methodology yielded groups which have substantial face validity from a marketing strategy point of view. This is shown in the fact that it was possible to meaningfully describe and contrast the eight behavioral groups in terms of personal characteristics and several dimensions of buying behavior which collectively distinguished the members of one group from the members of other groups. Such a description would be of value to the marketer since it shows him that within his market a number of groups can be found each differing from the others in overall buying behavior. The buying behavior description of each group could be of value to the marketer by indicating for that group the type of overt behavioral change which the firm should strive to create.

It should be noted that the cluster analysis approach to market segment identification does not indicate the type of strategy that should be used to bring about the desired change in behavior. However, the firm could obtain information on the relative effectiveness of the alternative strategies under consideration by conducting experiments on a sample of consumers randomly selected from the specified behavioral group. The buying behavior and personal characteristic descriptions of the distinct groups can be used to define the stratum from which each sample is drawn.

References

1. Claycamp, Henry J., and William F. Massy. "A Theory of Market Segmentation," *Journal of Marketing Research*, 5 (November 1968), 388–394.
2. Engel, James F., David T. Kollat, and Roger D. Blackwell. *Consumer Behavior*. New York: Holt, Rinehart and Winston, Inc., 1968.
3. Evans, Franklin B. "Psychological and Objective Factors in the Prediction of Brand Choice: Ford Versus Chevrolet," *The Journal of Business*, 32 (October 1959), 340–369.
4. Evans, Franklin B. "Ford Versus Chevrolet: Park Forest Revisited," *The Journal of Business*, 41 (October 1968), 445–459.

5. Ferber, Robert. "Research on Household Behavior," *American Economic Review*, 52 (March 1962), 19–63.
6. Frank, Ronald E., William F. Massy, and Harper W. Boyd. "Correlates of Grocery Product Consumption Rates," *Journal of Marketing Research*, 4 (May 1967), 184–190.
7. Hildegaard, Ingrid and Lester Krueger. "Are There Customer Types?" *Advertising Research Foundation*. New York, 1964.
8. Howard, John A. *Marketing Management*. Homewood, Ill.: Richard D. Irwin, Inc., 1963. Chapters 3 and 4.
9. Kernan, Jerome B. "Choice Criteria, Decision Behavior, and Personality," *Journal of Marketing Research*, 5 (May 1968), 115–165.
10. Kopenen, Arthur. "Personality Characteristics of Purchasers," *Journal of Advertising Research*, 1 (September 1960), 6–12.
11. Massy, William F., Ronald E. Frank, and Thomas M. Lodahl. *Purchasing Behavior and Personal Attributes*. Philadelphia: University of Pennsylvania Press, 1968.
12. Mosteller, Frederick, and Robert R. Bush. "Selected Quantitative Techniques," in Gardner Lindzey, ed., *Handbook of Social Psychology*. Reading, Mass.: Addison-Wesley Publishing Company, Inc., 1954. Vol. I, pp. 307–311.
13. Myers, John G. "Determinants of Private Brand Attitude," *Journal of Marketing Research*, 4 (February 1967), 73–81.
14. Nicosia, Francesco M. *Consumer Decision Processes*. Englewood Cliffs, N.J.: Prentice-Hall, Inc., 1966.
15. Rich, Stuart U., and Subhash C. Jain. "Social Class and Life Cycle as Predictors of Shopping Behavior," *Journal of Marketing Research*, 5 (Februray 1968), 41–49.
16. Smith, Wendell R. "Product Differentiation and Market Segmentation as Alternative Marketing Strategies," *Journal of Marketing*, 20 (July 1956), 3–8.
17. Westfall, Ralph. "Psychological Factors in Predicting Product Choice," *Journal of Marketing*, 26 (April 1962), 34–40.

PART FIVE

A LOOK TO THE FUTURE

27.

Segmentation: Prospect and Promise

As THE preceding readings make abundantly clear, market segmentation has found a permanent and significant place in the strategy of successful enterprises. There are, of course, many open questions regarding its application, such as determination of the appropriate segmentation base and introduction of optimum modification into the marketing mix given the existence of defined segments. There is no technological barrier, however, preventing profitable application of segmentation under a wide variety of circumstances.

What the future holds, therefore, seems a fitting conclusion to our overview of market segmentation. Discussion centers first on the impact of a changing environment, especially with respect to the effects of "consumerism" and governmental regulation, intensified competition, and increasing use of marketing techniques outside of the business community. The chapter ends with a review of certain managerial imperatives which underly the profitable use of market segmentation. These issues are of utmost importance since proper segmentation may hold the key to survival in the 1970s.

A CHANGING ENVIRONMENT

It seems certain that market segmentation will grow even more significant in the future. Three factors, in particular, lead to this conclusion: (1) the vitality of consumerism, (2) intensified competition, and (3) the mounting variety of nonbusiness applications.

Consumerism

One of the most remarkable phenomena of the late 1960s and early 1970's is the growth of consumerism—a movement designed to assert the consumer's voice collectively in an organized and effective manner.[1] The most visible spokesman, Ralph Nader, has given impetus to this movement through

[1] See Robert Moran, "Consumerism and Marketing" (working paper, Marketing Science Institute, May 1969) and "Consumerism—The Mood Turns Mean," *Sales Management* (July 1969).

his appeal for higher standards of automotive safety. He and others appear to have captured public sentiment and communicated it to business in such a manner that remedial action has been forthcoming.

One of the most persistent complaints on the consumer front is that substantial segments of buyers are poorly served. It is alleged that the range of alternatives frequently is so narrow that legitimate desires of many consumers cannot be served. One example is the virtual impossibility of purchasing a household blender offering only one or two speeds at a low price.[2] The great majority of blenders on the market have such a range of speeds and other options offered at higher prices that the simpler models are rapidly disappearing.

The critic is quick to point out that situations such as the blender example are indicative of calloused management whose only concern is to sell unnecessary frills at an excessive price. On closer analysis, it is doubtful that it is a deliberate attempt to be immoral or unethical; it is no doubt a fact that most buyers want the more complex and higher-priced models. On the other hand, there seems to be a neglected segment that warrants attention. Failure to capitalize upon this potential profit reflects poor management rather than a lack of ethics. Implementation of the philosophy inherent in market segmentation can do much to meet the valid complaints which are increasingly being heard.

The consumerism movement has been joined by government at local, state, and federal levels. Such agencies as the Federal Trade Commission, the Federal Communications Commission, and others are becoming increasingly suspicious of certain business activities. It seems inevitable that business will increasingly be called upon to demonstrate by its actions that it is truly meeting the expressed desires of consumers and in the most effective manner.

As a result of such pressures, business managers are becoming quite sensitive to the consumer's voice. The trend will continue to be manifested in greater adaptability to changing desires and hence will serve as an impetus to more careful market segmentation.

Intensified Competition

Not too many years ago, few firms worried much about a segmented market. The first manufacturer of an electric refrigerator, for example, was unconcerned whether or not consumers desired the item in a choice of colors, in different sizes, and with a left-hand door opening. The environment was such that there was an excess of demand over supply, and the firm was understandably more concerned about perfecting production practices than tailoring its product mix to varying buyer preferences.

[2] This situation was called to the attention of the authors through personal correspondence with a university home economist.

The competitive environment of the 1970s, however, presents quite a different situation; most markets are characterized by an excess of supply over demand. It is said, for example, that one refrigerator plant in Ohio can supply the entire national demand for this product. The presence of so many competing alternatives means that the buyer can be selective in his buying; the firm that most closely meets his preferences will be the winner. A great incentive, therefore, is placed on detecting untapped market segments so that a differential advantage can be gained over competitors.

There is no indication that the competitive climate will become less intensive in the future. Rather, the opposite situation will undoubtedly prevail, and the need for proper market segmentation will become even more pronounced.

Nonbusiness Applications

A philosophy of market segmentation is by no means confined to the business firm. It is equally applicable in any type of enterprise that offers a concept or service to the public.[3] While there are many potential areas of application, some of the more obvious lie in the areas of politics, religion and public issues.

Politics   Richard M. Johnson offered some interesting insights into the application of segmentation strategy in political campaigns.[4] Multiple discriminant analysis disclosed voter perceptions of the stands of various candidates on political issues. The individual candidate could then readily discern whether or not this perception map was consistent with his objectives. His planning could be further sharpened by undertaking such analyses within age, income, and other demographic segments. Clues thus are provided for ways in which his image might be strengthened or improved among those in strategic subgroups.

In the book, *The Selling of the President 1968*, author Joe McGinniss describes an insider's view of how sophisticated marketing research techniques and analysis were used in the 1968 presidential campaign.

> It was about this time that the results of the Semantic Differential Test came in. Treleaven and Garment and Shakespeare went into the big meeting room at Fuller and Smith and Ross watched a tall, thin, frowning man named John Maddox explain what all of it meant.
>
> "The semantic differential is the most sensitive instrument known to modern marketing research," he said. Then he pointed to a big chart on a slide screen on

[3] See Philip Kotler and Sidney J. Levy, "Broadening the Concept of Marketing," *Journal of Marketing*, Vol. 33 (January 1969), pp. 10–15.
[4] See Richard M. Johnson, "Marketing Segmentation: A Strategic Management Tool," in this volume, Reading 23.

the wall. Running down the chart were twenty-six pairs of adjectives or phrases such as weak–strong, wishy-washy–firm, stuffed-shirt–sense of humor, tense–relaxed, stingy–generous, and on like that. The bad description, like wishy-washy or stingy, was on the left side of the chart, the good one on the right. In between were the numbers one through seven.

John Maddox explained that he had gone all through the country asking people to evaluate the presidential candidates on the scale of one through seven, and also asking them to evaluate the qualities an ideal President would have. If they thought Humphrey, for instance, was very generous, they would give him a seven on the stingy–generous line; if they thought he was not much of either, they would give him a three or a four. Maddox had plotted what he called the Ideal President Curve, which was the line connecting the points that represented the average rating in each category as applied to the ideal. Then Maddox plotted curves for Nixon, Humphrey, and Wallace. The gaps between the Nixon line and the Ideal line represented the personality traits that Nixon should try to improve. It was considered especially important, Maddox said, that Nixon close the "Personality Gap" between himself and Humphrey.

"It is of substantial significance, we believe," Maddox wrote later in a report, "that the widest gap of all is the 'cold–warm.' We believe it highly probable that if the real personal warmth of Mr. Nixon could be more adequately exposed, it would release a flood of other inhibitions about him—and make him more tangible as a person to large numbers of Humphrey leaners."

Maddox had other charts which broke the responses down geographically and ethnically so people could see what kind of personality gap existed in the minds of southern Negroes or midwestern whites. The idea was, even if Nixon would not start to act warmer, Harry Treleaven could produce commercials that would make him seem so.[5]

Preference maps also are applicable in disclosing those segments of voters who currently find no candidate to be acceptable. This type of analysis appears to underlie the deliberate strategy of Nixon and Agnew to appeal to the "forgotten American" during the 1970 political campaign. Apparently a substantial segment of voters felt alienated from more liberal candidates and perceived that their traditional orientation toward patriotism and law and order was being overlooked. The hard-hitting approach of Agnew, in particular, has found receptive audiences within this segment.

Religion   It may be unfamiliar to some to refer to religion as a marketing problem, but the basic issues facing religion increasingly center around the communication of a religious message in a changing world.[6] Furthermore, the

[5] From Joe McGinniss, *The Selling of the President 1968* (New York: The Trident Press (division of Simon and Schuster Inc., 1969), pp. 77–78. Copyright 1969, Joemac, Incorporated. Reprinted by permission.

[6] James F. Engel and Roger D. Blackwell, "Communicating Religious Truth in a Changing World," paper delivered at the American Marketing Association meeting, Boston, September 1970.

market for religion is highly segmented, and this fact, in itself, goes a long way toward explaining the existence of a variety of denominations, many of which offer a varied approach.

One of the most interesting market segments is the college campus. Although the campus itself is characterized by diversity, college youth have much in common. For example, there is disenchantment with the materialistic striving of their elders, which, in their estimation, has not succeeded in conquering the survival imperatives facing the world today. As a result, the college youth is looking for a different purpose in life and is very responsive to a message which has as its essence a change for man's inner motivation and his outer behavior. Many are quite aware, for example, that racism and war can be viewed as symptoms of a deeper problem within man himself, and a religion that offers an answer to the problem and not the symptom finds a ready hearing. In addition, a desire for gratification and fulfillment are sought now, not at some point in the future. In other words, college youth are oriented toward a philosophy of life which effects everyday life. Thus, the appeal to an afterlife, while never to be denied, is of less significance than the demonstration of a practical faith; strong evidence of a changed life through Christian commitment has a potent appeal. Without this practical demonstration of faith, however, the message holds little meaning or significance. A Sunday morning sermon, in other words, is a decidedly inferior substitute for the layman who lives what he believes. This is a lesson that many in the church have failed to learn.

There is no doubt too that most college students will not go near a church. While the majority show receptivity to the historic Biblical message, the church as an institution is seen as being symptomatic of all the negative aspects of the "establishment." This means that there must be a new channel of distribution for this segment: individual to individual. The message must be taken to the individual since he no longer will come to a central distribution outlet. It is also apparent that the appeals cannot be couched in the language of a bygone era. Such terms as "saved" connote legitimate theological meaning but will be impotent in comparison with the equivalent term "personal relationship with Jesus Christ." The language used must be that which is meaningful to the market segment, another lesson which the church, broadly speaking, has been slow to learn.

In summary, college youth must be approached through new channels, with more relevant appeals, and with concrete demonstration of faith in action. Some groups have recognized the religious vacuum on the campus and have stepped in with programs to meet the need. Of special significance are Campus Crusade for Christ,[7] Intervarsity Christian Fellowship, Navigators, Young Life,

---

[7] For the marketing strategy of this organization see the Campus Crusade for Christ case in James F. Engel, W. Wayne Talarzyk, and Carl M. Larson, *Cases in Promotional Strategy* (Homewood, Ill.: Richard D. Irwin, Inc., 1971).

and Fellowship of Christian Athletes. All are interdenominational groups, evangelistic in purpose, who are succeeding in an exciting way to make the Christian message relevant to this segment.

Obviously, other markets must be approached differently from the college campus. Some, especially those in rural areas, are oriented to the institutional church and will respond to its program. The strategy to reach this group can thus rely on traditional means. The market for religion, then, is a classic example of segmentation along such multiple bases as age, attitude, personality, and geographic location. The churches and other groups which are succeeding are those which have recognized these differences and have adapted accordingly without compromising the basic historic Biblical message. Unfortunately, certain major demonations seem to pursue a single strategy built around the theme of social action. That this approach is alienating a substantial number is evidenced by membership downturns documented in the *1970 Yearbook of American Churches.*

Public Affairs   The public is bombarded with appeals of all sorts, but many of these fall short of maximum effectiveness because of the absence of careful market analysis. Marketing segmentation, in turn, may provide the key to success. For example, one of the authors was involved in open-housing efforts sponsored by a citizen's council in an affluent suburb. An objective was to encourage residents to list homes for sale on an open-occupancy basis. A general public relations campaign to persuade this type of action, however, would have failed because evidence documented the prevailing fear of neighborhood reprisals.[8] Therefore, it was necessary to find those whose attitudes and values would be consistent with this type of action. An attempt was made to use attitudes as the segmentation base.

Efforts were initially concentrated in churches where social action was a predominant theme. Many interested individuals were uncovered, and appeals for membership on the council soon attracted others. This generated a surprisingly large group who were pledged to open-occupancy, and they, in turn, spearheaded a number of person-to-person neighborhood education programs. When integration finally occurred, there was a minimum of difficulty. This success was due, at least in part, to the careful strategy of this citizen's group.

The Resulting Effects   It is apparent from our brief discussion that a number of nonbusiness enterprises are engaged in the processes of marketing, whether this fact is recognized or not. To the extent that there is an orientation toward goal attainment, it frequently becomes necessary to introduce a strategy of market segmentation in order to achieve optimum results. Hopefully the

[8] See James F. Engel and Roger D. Blackwell, "The Negro Neighbor in Affluent Suburbia," *Business Topics*, (September 1969), pp. 42–49.

mention of the word marketing in this context does not connote the image of manipulation or "hucksterism" because the essence of the marketing concept is to serve and satisfy human needs.

Conclusion

Is market segmentation, then, a passing fad, or has it found a permanent role in the strategy of enterprises offering a service to the public? We feel that it lies at the heart of successful management because it provides a concrete manifestation of consumer orientation. The changing environment, in turn, has intensified the pressures for consumer orientation and has made this approach even more necessary for survival. That it's application need not be confined just to the business firm has been confirmed by the examples given.

MAKING OPTIMUM USE OF SEGMENTATION

If market segmentation is to be used with greatest effectiveness, there are several managerial imperatives: (1) avoidance of managerial stagnation, (2) implementation of proper organizational arrangements, (3) active research orientation, and (4) capitalization on technological advances.

Avoidance of Stagnation

It is a fact of life that some human beings will go to almost any extreme to avoid change. They are adverse to risk taking and hence will pursue the route that appears to be least threatening. Maintenance of the status quo thus becomes the dominant operating philosophy, and this obviously militates against the benefits offered by market segmentation.

Successful management requires a willingness to take risks and to respond in a flexible manner to opportunities as they arise. The consequences of managerial stagnation can be devastating. For example, the marketing manager of a well-known firm proceeded for many years on the assumption that few changes were needed in his marketing program for the leading brand as long as sales increased. Sales did show a steady increase for a period of time, but, unknown to him, market share was declining rapidly as discounters made inroads. The declining market share finally was reflected in total sales, and a crisis arose which could have been averted much earlier had proper recognition been made of the growing segment who use price as their criterion for purchase. A second brand might have been introduced to fight the discounters, and it is probably that much of the damage could have been averted.

This unfortunate example illustrates the dangers that arise from an operating philosophy which assumes that the future will not be much different from the past. Such a *modus operandi* completely ignores the factor of competitive volatility. Maximum rewards go to those who detect opportunities and capitalize upon them through marketing mix variations before competitors can act.

Proper Organizational Arrangements

Organizational rigidities can militate against capitalization upon opportunities offered through market segmentation. In one large industrial goods firm, for example, the profit responsibility for many brands was concentrated in the hands of the marketing manager. There were a number of product managers, but they were responsible only for certain sales promotion activities. Neither product manager could, in effect, make the type of decision necessary to compete with innovative competitors. It was quite impossible, for the manager of a certain brand to move his product through a channel of distribution different from that employed to move other company products of a similar nature. Research, however, showed a clear need for developing a new approach to distribution for this particular product. Customer purchases had shown a distinct shift in the type of outlet in which the product in question was being purchased. Less constrained competitors were able to recognize and react to changing customer preferences and alter their distribution approach accordingly. Had the particular product manager mentioned above been able to undertake quick action, he likely could have prevented the loss of market share which actually occurred. From this example, it should be obvious that under such a rigid centralization, it is virtually impossible to undertake the kind of quick action that is frequently required.

The organization referred to was later changed so that the product manager, in effect, became responsible for his own company within the broader framework. He was held accountable for profit performance and was given free rein within certain policy guidelines to chart his own marketing course. This decentralization soon was reflected positively in profit and loss statements.

Active Research Orientation

The successful manager must continually scan the environment, for the underlying segmental structure of the market is a primary concern. Are we appealing to the youth market? What kind of response are we getting in the western region? Have our competitors discovered segments we have not detected? Management must expect continuous change and then find ways to adapt to such changes.

There are distinct limitations on individual observation and analysis. Marketing research, therefore, often must serve as the "eyes and ears" for the marketing manager. The emphasis here is not on "fire-fighting" research taken up when a problem becomes apparent but on environmental monitoring undertaken to detect problems and opportunities. Just collecting the information, however, is not enough. Management must also know how to utilize this input in planning. Because the demands for handling, sorting, and digesting the data are often so severe, few individuals have the capabilities to comprehend and use the full range of information which can be provided. Thus, we predict that the role of the marketing research department will evolve into that of planning consultants who provide factual input and assist in its proper utilization in marketing strategy. Such a team approach philosophy to decision-making can substantially narrow the risks of undertaking incorrect action.

Capitalization on Technological Opportunities

The readings in this volume have demonstrated that a substantial body of techniques exist for market segmentation. Such tools as multidimensional scaling, factor analysis, cluster analysis, multiple regression, multiple discriminant analysis, and other methods of numerical taxonomy each have areas of application.

Quite understandably this "technological revolution" is bewildering to many managers. Some feel threatened by "technological obsolesence." in reality, however, no one can be expected to be an expert in all things. This is yet another argument for a team approach to strategy determination in which a group of specialists are called upon as resources. It is not an admission of weakness; rather, it is realistic recognition that no one person can be sufficient for all necessary decision-making skills.

There is a danger, however, of becoming unduly "technique-centered." Multidimensional scaling, for example, is the "in" technique of the early 1970s, as was Bayesian analysis in the middle 1960s. Each of these tools has valid areas of application, but faddism must be avoided. Trade journals often contribute to this problem by ballyhooing a new technique as the panacea for all ills. An attitude of healthy skepticism is advisable until the potential for solving the problems of a particular firm is demonstrated. In the final analysis, decision-making success requires an ability to *fit the technique to the marketing problem*—not to fit the problem to the technique.

Some Dangers to Avoid

It is not unusual to find an unhealthy misunderstanding of the basic philosophy of market segmentation. When management looks for holes or niches in the market for existing products, such action is not a proper approach to consumer orientation and does not follow the tenets of market segmentation. If the management, on the other hand, isolates subgroups in the markets and introduces *changes* in the marketing mix to adapt to that segment, the segmentation governs the company's actions.

Another danger in market segmentation is the tendency to look upon it as a kind of panacea. If sales do not look especially bright, the natural tendency is to look for new segments and to hope for greater success there. The result often is abandonment of the company's position of strength in favor of a move into unchartered waters. Lee Adler mentioned the unfortunate consequences when this strategy was followed by a beer firm.[9] The best strategy may be to solidify one's position in the market core before branching out further.

Finally, most of the published examples in this volume and elsewhere lead to the impression that segmentation is primarily applicable to advertising and product policy. This, however, is not the case. The problem may well lie in price and/or channel strategy. An example was mentioned earlier in which a large firm should have introduced a price cut to capitalize upon a growing segment of price buyers—not an unusual situation. Furthermore, sales opportunities may be lost because products are not available in appropriate outlets. Motor oil is no longer bought exclusively through the service station because this market is segmented by channel preference. There are a growing number of "do-it-yourselfers" who prefer to purchase oil in a grocery store or discount house. Failure to provide products in these outlets can easily result in lost sales.

CONCLUSION

Market segmentation is a philosophy of management that reflects a consumer orientation. It will not work unless management is committed to attainment of specified objectives and is willing to be evalutaed in these terms. When the emphasis is placed upon accountability in terms of effectively serving the market, effective use of market segmentation is ensured.

[9] See Lee Adler, "A New Orientation for Plotting Marketing Strategy," in this volume, Reading 4.

References In Market Segmentation

CONCEPTS

Chamberlain, E. H. *Theory of Monopolistic Competition*, Cambridge: Harvard University Press, 1933.

Claycamp, Henry J., and William F. Massy. "A Theory of Market Segmentation," *J. Marketing Research*, Vol. 35 (November 1968), pp. 388–94.

Cox, R., W. Alderson, and S. Shapiro. *Theory in Marketing*, Homewood, Ill.: Richard D. Irwin, Inc., 1964.

Goldman, M. I. "Product Differentiation and Advertising: Some Lessons from Soviet Experience," *Political Economy*, Vol. 68 (August 1960), pp. 346–357.

Grether, B. T. "External Product and Enterprise Differentiation and Consumer Behavior," in R. H. Cole, ed., *Consumer Behavior and Motivation*, Marketing Symposium, University of Illinois, Urbana, October 1955.

Hise, R. T. "Have Manufacturing Firms Adopted the Marketing Concept?" *Marketing*, Vol. 20 (July 1965), pp. 9–12.

McKitterick, J. B. "What is the Marketing Management Concept?" *Proc. American Marketing Association*, Chicago: The Association, 1957, pp. 71–82.

Myers, John G. *Consumer Image and Attitude in Marketing*, Research Program in Marketing, Graduate School of Business Administration, University of California, Berkeley, 1968.

Robinson, Joan. *The Economics of Imperfect Competition*, London: Macmillan & Co., Ltd., 1954, pp. 179–88.

Smith, W. R. "Imperfect Competition and Marketing Strategy," *Cost and Profit Outlook*, Vol. 8, No. 10 (October 1955), p. 1.

———. "Product Differentiation and Market Segmentation as Alternative Marketing Strategies," *J. Marketing*, Vol. 21 (July 1956), pp. 3–8.

MANAGERIAL STRATEGY

Adler, Lee. "A New Orientation for Plotting Marketing Strategy," *Business Horizons*, Vol. 4 (Winter 1964), pp. 37–50.

———. "Phasing Research into the Marketing Plan," *Harvard Business Review*, Vol. 38, No. 3 (May 1960), pp. 113–122.

———, ed. *Plotting Marketing Strategy*, New York: Simon & Schuster, Inc., 1967.

Bowman, B. F., and F. E. McCormick. "Market Segmentation and Marketing Mixes," *J. Marketing*, Vol. 25 (January 1961), pp. 25–29.

Boyd, Harper W., Jr., and Sidney J. Levy. "New Dimension in Consumer Analysis," *Harvard Business Review*, Vol. 41, No. 6 (November–December 1963), pp. 105–113.

Brandt, S. C. "Dissecting the Segmentation Syndrome," *J. Marketing*, Vol. 30 (October 1966), pp. 22–27.

Bucklin, L. P., "Retail Strategy and the Classification of Consumers' Goods," *J. Marketing*, Vol. 28 (January 1963), pp. 50–55.

Bursk, Edward C., and John F. Chapman, ed. *Modern Marketing Strategy*, Cambridge: Harvard University Press, 1964.

Dommermuth, William P., and Edward W. Cundiff. "Shopping Goods, Shopping Centers and Selling Strategies," *J. Marketing*, Vol. 31 (October 1967), pp. 32–36.

Engel, J. F., H. G. Wales, and M. R. Warshaw. *Promotional Strategy*, Homewood, Ill.: Richard Irwin, Inc., 1967.

Foote, Nelson. "Market Segmentation as a Competitive Strategy," in Leo Bogart, ed., *Current Controversies in Marketing Research*, Chicago: Markham Publishing Company, 1969.

Holton, R. H. "The Distinction Between Convenience Goods, Shopping Goods, and Specialty Goods," *J. Marketing*, Vol. 23 (July 1958), pp. 53–56.

Kline, C. H. "The Strategy of Product Quality," *Harvard Business Review*, Vol. 33, No. 4 (July–August 1955), pp. 70–75.

Kolter, P. *Marketing Management: Analysis, Planning, and Control*, Englewood Cliffs, N.J.: Prentice-Hall, Inc., 1967, pp. 43–65. See especially Chapter 3.

———. "Marketing Mix Decisions for New Products," *J. Marketing Research*, Vol. 1 (February 1964), pp. 43–49.

Kuehn, A. A., and R. L. Day. "The Strategy of Product Quality," *Harvard Business Review*, Vol. 40, No. 6 (November–December 1962), pp. 100–110.

Levitt, Theodore. *The Marketing Mode: Pathways to Corporate Growth*, New York: McGraw Hill Book Company, 1969.

———. "Marketing Myopia," *Harvard Business Review*, Vol. 38, No. 4 (July–August 1960), pp. 55–68.

Mainer, R., and C. C. Slater. "Markets in Motion," *Harvard Business Review*, Vol. 42, No. 3 (May–June 1964), pp. 75–82.

Margulies, W. P. "Eight Ways to Segment a Market," *Advertising Age* (September 16, 1968), pp. 96–98.

Myers, J. G. "Advertising and Product Differentiation," working paper, Institute of Business and Economic Research, University of California, Berkeley, December 1965. Mimeographed.

Olsen, Robert M. "The Strategy of Market Segmentation," *Kansas Business Review*, Vol. 21, No. 9 (September 1968), pp. 13–18.

Roberts, A. A. "Applying the Strategy of Market Segmentation," *Business Horizons*, Vol. 4 (Fall 1961), pp. 65–72.

Wells, W. D. "Backward Segmentation," First Annual Buyer Behavior Conference, Columbia University, New York, May 1967. Mimeographed.

RESEARCH APPROACHES AND FINDINGS

Barnett, N. L. "Developing Effective Advertising for New Products," Vol. 8, No. 4 (December 1968), pp. 13–18.

Bass, F. M., E. A. Pessemier, and D. J. Tigert. "A Taxonomy of Magazine Readership Applied to Problems in Marketing Strategy and Media Selection," *J. Business*, Vol. 42, No. 3 (July 1969), pp. 337–363.

———, D. J. Tigert, and R. T. Lonsdale. "An Analysis of Socio-Economic-Related Market Segments for Grocery Products," unpublished working paper, Krannert School of Industrial Administration, Purdue University, 1967.

Beldo, L. A. "Market Segmentation and Food Consumption," in J. W. Newman, ed., *On Knowing the Consumer*, New York: John Wiley & Sons, Inc., 1966, pp. 125–137.

Frank, R. E. "Market Segmentation Research: Findings and Implications," in Frank M. Bass, Charles W. King, and Edgar A. Pessemier, eds., *The Application of the Sciences to Marketing Management*, John Wiley & Sons, 1968, pp. 39–68.

———, and H. W. Boyd, Jr. "Are Private-Brand-Prone Grocery Consumers Really Different?" *J. Advertising Research*, Vol. 5 (December 1965), pp. 27–35.

Garfinkle, N. "A Marketing Approach to Media Selection," *J. Advertising Research*, Vol. 3 (December 1963), pp. 7–15.

Green, Paul, Ronald Frank, and Patrick Robinson. "Cluster Analysis in Test Market Selection," *Management Science*, Vol. 13 (April 1967), pp. 387–400.

Haley, Russell I. "Benefit Segmentation," *J. Marketing*, Vol. 32 (July 1968), pp. 30–35.

Kishler, J. "New Comparative Segment Analytic Techniques in Pharmaceutical Marketing Now and in the Future," Yorktown Heights, N. Y.: Albert Shephard & Associates, 1967.

"The Marketing Man's Guide to Marketing Segmentation Analysis," *Advertising Management*, Vol. 54, No. 7 (August 1969), pp. 13–18.

Myers, J. G. and F. M. Nicosia. "New Empirical Directions in Market Segmentation," paper presented at the American Marketing Association Annual Meetings, Washington, D. C., 1967.

———, ———. "On the Study of Consumer Typologies," *J. Marketing Research*, Vol. 5 (May 1968), pp. 182–193.

Reynolds, W. H. "More Sense About Market Segmentation," *Harvard Business Review*, Vol. 43, No. 5 (September–October 1965), pp. 107–114.

Sherak, B. "Consumer Segmentation and Brand Mapping—A Methodological Study," *Market Facts*. Mimeographed. Market Facts, 1968.

Taylor, T. R. "Unfolding Theory Applied to Market Segmentation," *J. Advertising Research*, Vol. 9 (December 1969), pp. 39–46.

Twedt, D. W. "How Important to Marketing Strategy Is the Heavy User?" *J. Marketing*, Vol. 28 (January 1964), pp. 71–72.

———. "How to Select Media with Heavy Product Users," *Media Scope*, Vol. 8 (November 1964), pp. 95–100.

———. "Some Practical Applications of the 'Heavy Half' Theory," *Proc. Advertising Research Foundation* (October 1964).

Yankelovich, D. "New Criteria for Market Segmentation," *Harvard Business Review*, Vol. 42, No. 3 (March–April 1964), pp. 83–90.

———. "Psychological Market Segmentation," in J. Z. Sissors, ed., *Some Bold, New Theories of Advertising and Marketing*, Chicago, Ill.: Leo Burnett Co., Inc. and Northwestern University, 1963, pp. 21–32.

SEGMENTATION VARIABLES

Consumer Characteristics

Socioeconomic and Demographic

Alexis, M. "Some Negro-White Differences in Consumption," *Amer. J. Economics and Sociology*, Vol. 21 (January 1962), pp. 11–28.

Barban, Arnold M., and Edward W. Cundiff. "Negro and White Response to Advertising Stimuli," *J. Marketing Research*, Vol. 1 (November 1964), pp. 53–56.

Bauer, R. A., S. M. Cunningham, and L. H. Wortzel. "The Marketing Dilemma of Negroes," *J. Marketing*, Vol. 29 (July 1965), pp. 1–6.

Bell, J. E. F. "Mobiles—A Neglected Market Segment," *J. Marketing*, Vol. 33 (April 1969), pp. 37–44.

Bullock, H. A. "Consumer Motivations in Black and White," Part I, *Harvard Business Review*, Vol. 39, No. 3 (May–June 1961), pp. 89–104; Part II, *Harvard Business Review*, Vol. 39, No. 4 (July–August 1961), pp. 110–124.

Burk, M. C. "Ramifications of the Relationship Between Income and Food," *J. Farm Economics*, Vol. 44 (February 1962), pp. 115–125.

Callazo, C. J. "Effects of Income Upon Shopping Attitudes and Frustrations," *J. Retailing* (Spring 1966), pp. 1–7.

Carman, J. M. "The Application of Social Class in Market Segmentation," Institute of Business and Economic Research, University of California, Berkeley, 1965.

Coleman, R. P. "The Significance of Social Stratification in Selling," *Proc. American Marketing Association* (December 1960), pp. 171–184.

Ferber, R. "Brand Choice and Social Stratification," *Quarterly Review of Economic and Business*, Vol. 2 (February 1962), pp. 71–78.

Frank, R. E. "Correlates of Buying Behavior for Grocery Products," *J. Marketing,* Vol. 31 (October 1967), pp. 48–53.

————, P. E. Green, and H. F. Sieber, Jr. "Household Correlates of Purchase Price for Grocery Products," *J. Marketing Research,* Vol. 4 (February 1967), pp. 54–58.

Gibson, D. Parke. *The $30 Billion Negro,* New York: The Macmillan Company, 1969.

Goldstein, S. "The Age Segment of the Market, 1950 and 1960," *J. Marketing,* Vol. 32 (April 1968), pp. 62–68.

Jacobi, J. E., and S. G. Walters. "Social Status and Consumer Choice," *Social Forces,* Vol. 36 (March 1958), pp. 209–214.

Kassarjian, H. H. "The Negro and American Advertising," *J. Marketing Research,* Vol. 6 (1969), pp. 29–39.

Lansing, J. B., and L. Kish. "Family Life Cycle as an Independent Variable," *Amer. Sociological Review,* Vol. 22 (October 1957), pp. 512–519.

Levy, S. J. "Social Class and Consumer Behavior," in J. W. Newman, ed., *On Knowing the Consumer,* New York: John Wiley & Sons, Inc., 1966, pp. 146–160.

McNeal, J. U. "The Child Consumer," *J. Retailing,* Vol. 45, No. 2 (Summer 1969), pp. 15–22.

Martineau, P. D. "Social Classes and Spending Behavior," *J. Marketing,* Vol. 23 (October 1958), pp. 121–130.

Munn, H. L. "Brand Perception as Related to Age, Income and Education," *J. Marketing,* Vol. 24 (January 1960), pp. 29–34.

Namias, J. "Intentions to Purchase Related to Consumer Characteristics," *J. Marketing,* Vol. 25 (July 1960), pp. 32–36.

Petrof, J. V. "Customer Strategy for Negro Retailers," *J. Retailing,* Vol. 43 (Fall 1967), pp. 30–38.

————. "Reaching the Negro Market: A Segregated vs. a General Newspaper," *J. Advertising Research,* Vol. 8 (March 1968), pp. 40–43.

Rich, S. U. and Subhast C. Jain. "Social Class and Life Cycle as Predictors of Shopping Behavior," *J. Marketing Research,* Vol. 5 (January 1968), pp. 41–49.

Rotzoll, K. B. "The Effect of Social Stratification on Market Behavior," *J. Advertising Research,* Vol. 7 (March 1967), pp. 22–27.

Psychological

Advertising Research Foundation. *Are There Consumer Types?* New York: The Foundation, 1964.

Bayton, J. A. "Motivation, Cognition, Learning: Basic Factors in Consumer Behavior," *J. Marketing,* Vol. 22 (January 1958), pp. 282–289.

Blankertz, D. F. "Motivation and Rationalization in Retail Buying," *Public Opinion Quarterly,* Vol. 13 (Winter 1949–1960), pp. 659–668.

Britt, S. H. "The Strategy of Consumer Motivation," *J. Marketing*, Vol. 14 (April 1950), pp. 666–682.

Brody, R. P. and S. M. Cunningham. "Personality Variables and the Consumer Decision Process," *J. Marketing Research*, Vol. 5 (February 1968), pp. 50–57.

Brown, G. H. "Measuring Consumer Attitudes Towards Products," *J. Marketing*, Vol. 14 (April 1950), pp. 691–698.

Claycamp, H. J. "Characteristics of Owners of Thrift Deposits in Commercial Banks and Savings and Loan Associations," *J. Marketing Research*, Vol. 2 (May 1965), pp. 163–170.

Cohen, J. B. "The Role of Personality in Consumer Behavior," in H. H. Kassarjian and T. R. Robertson, eds., *Perspectives in Consumer Behavior*, Glenwood, Ill.: Scott, Foresman & Company, 1968.

Cunningham, S. M. "Perceived Risk as a Factor in Product-Oriented Word-of-Mouth Behavior: A First Step," *Proc. American Marketing Association* (1965), pp. 229–238.

————. "The Role of Perceived Risk in Product-Related Discussion and Brand Purchase Behavior," unpublished Ph.D. dissertation, Graduate School of Business Administration, Harvard University, Cambridge, 1965.

Dolich, I. J. "Congruence Relationships Between Self-Images and Product Brands," *J. Marketing Research*, Vol. 6 (February 1969), pp. 80–84.

Engle, J. F. "Are Automobile Purchasers Dissonant Consumers?" *J. Marketing*, Vol. 27 (April 1963), pp. 55–58.

————. "Motivation Research—Magic or Menace?" *Michigan Business Review*, Vol. 13 (March 1961), pp. 28–32.

Evans, F. B. "The Brand Image Myth," *Business Horizons*, Vol. 4 (Fall 1961), pp. 19–28.

————. "Correlates of Automobile Shopping Behavior," *J. Marketing*, Vol. 26 (October 1962), pp. 74–77.

————. "Psychological and Objective Factors in the Prediction of Brand Choice: Ford Versus Chevrolet," *J. Business*, Vol. 32 (October 1959), pp. 340–369.

————. "Reply: You Still Can't Tell a Ford Owner from a Chevrolet Owner," *J. Business*, Vol. 34 (January 1961), pp. 67–73.

————, and H. V. Roberts. "Fords, Chevrolets and the Problem of Discrimination," *J. Business*, Vol. 36 (April 1963), pp. 242–249.

Ferber, R. and H. F. Wales, eds. *Motivation Research in Marketing*, Homewood, Ill.: Richard D. Irwin, Inc.

Gardner, B. B., and S. J. Levy. "The Product and the Brand," *Harvard Business Review*, Vol. 33, No. 2 (March–April 1955), pp. 33–39.

Gottlieb, M. J. "Segmentation by Personality Types," *Proc. American Marketing Association* (December 1959), pp. 148–158.

Grubb, E. L., and G. Hupp. "Perception of Self, Generalized Stereotypes, and

Brand Selection," *J. Marketing Research*, Vol. 5 (February 1968), pp. 58–63.

Holloway, R. J. "An Experiment on Consumer Dissonance," *J. Marketing*, Vol. 31 (January 1967), pp. 39–43.

Kaish, S. "Cognitive Dissonance and the Classification of Consumer Goods," *J. Marketing*, Vol. 31 (October 1967), pp. 28–31.

Kamen, J. M. "Personality and Food Preferences," *J. Advertising Research*, Vol. 4 (September 1964), pp. 29–32.

Koponen, A. "Personality Characteristics of Purchasers," *J. Advertising Research*, Vol. 1 (September 1960), pp. 6–12.

Kuehn, A. A. "Demonstration of a Relationship Between Psychological Factors and Brand Choice," *J. Business*, Vol. 36 (April 1963), pp. 237–241.

Massy, W. F., R. E. Frank, and T. Lodahl. "Buying Behavior and Personality," unpublished working paper, *Graduate School of Business*, Stanford University, Stanford, Calif., 1966.

Pessemier, E. A., and D. J. Tigert. "Personality, Activity and Attitude Predictors of Consumer Behavior," *New Ideas for Successful Marketing*. Proceedings of the 1966 World Marketing Congress, American Marketing Association, pp. 332–347.

Robertson, T. S., and J. H. Myers. "Personality Correlates of Opinion Leadership and Innovative Buying Behavior," *J. Marketing Research*, Vol. 6 (May 1969), pp. 164–168.

Sheth, J. N., and M. Venkatesan. "Risk-Reduction Processes in Repetitive Consumer Behavior," *J. Marketing Research*, Vol. 5 (August 1968), pp. 307–310.

Shuchman, A., and M. Perry. "Self-Confidence and Persuasibility in Marketing: A Reappraisal," *J. Marketing Research*, Vol. 6 (May 1969), pp. 146–155.

Steiner, G. A. "Notes on Franklin B. Evans' 'Psychological and Objective Factors in the Prediction of Brand Choice,' " *J. Business*, Vol. 34 (January 1961), pp. 57–60.

Stone, G. P. "City Shoppers and Urban Identification: Observations on the Social Psychology of City Life," *Amer. J. Sociology*, Vol. 60 (July 1954), pp. 36–45.

Tucker, W. T., and J. J. Painter. "Personality and Product Use," *J. Applied Psychology* (October 1961), pp. 325–329.

Wells, W. D. "General Personality Tests and Consumer Behavior," in Joseph W. Newman, ed., *On Knowing the Consumer*, New York: John Wiley & Sons, Inc., 1966, pp. 187–190.

Westfall, R. "Psychological Factors in Predicting Product Choice," *J. Marketing*, Vol. 26 (April 1962), pp. 34–40.

Winnick, C. "The Relationship Among Personality Needs, Objective Factors and Brand Choice: A Re-examination," *J. Business*, Vol. 34 (January 1961), pp. 61–66.

Woods, W. A. "Psychological Dimensions of Consumer Decision," *J. Marketing*, Vol. 24 (January 1960), pp. 15–19.

Consumer Response Variables

Consumer Preferences, Attitudes and Perceptions

Assael, H., and G. S. Day. "Attitudes and Awareness as Predictors of Market Share," *J. Advertising Research*, Vol. 8 (December 1968), pp. 3–10.

Bell, G. D. "The Automobile Buyer After the Purchase," *J. Marketing*, Vol. 31 (July 1967), pp. 12–16.

Brown, G. H. "Measuring Consumer Attitudes Towards Products," *J. Marketing*, Vol. 14 (April 1950), pp. 691–698.

Brown, W. F. "The Determination of Factors Influencing Brand Choice," *J. Marketing.* Vol. 14 (April 1950), pp. 699–706.

Cook, V. J. "Group Decision, Social Comparison and Persuasion in Changing Attitudes," *J. Advertising Research*, Vol. 7 (March 1967, pp. 31–37.

Day, G. S. "Buyer Attitudes and Brand Choice Behavior," unpublished Ph.D. dissertation, Graduate School of Business, Columbia University, New York, 1967.

Day, R. "Systematic Paired Comparisons in Preference Analysis," *J. Marketing Research*, Vol. 2 (November 1965), pp. 406–412.

Eastlack, J. O., Jr. "Consumer Flavor Preference Factors in Food Product Design," *J. Marketing Research,* Vol. 1 (February 1964), pp. 38–42.

Fry, J. "Family Branding and Consumer Choice," *J. Marketing Research*, Vol. 4 (August 1967), pp. 237–247.

Ito, R. "Differential Attitudes of New Car Buyers," *J. Advertising Research*, Vol. 7 (March 1967), pp. 38–42.

Kollat, D. T., and R. T. Willett. "Customer Impulse Purchasing Behavior," *J. Marketing Research*, Vol. 4 (February 1967), pp. 21–31.

Lazer, W., and R. Wyckham. "Perceptual Segmentation of Department Store Markets," *J. of Retailing*, Vol. 45, No. 2 (Summer 1969), pp. 3–14.

Murray, J. A. "Utilizing Consumer Expectational Date to Allocate Promotional Efforts," *J. Marketing*, Vol. 33 (April 1969), pp. 26–33.

Myers, J. G. "Determinants of Private Brand Attitude," *J. Marketing Research*, Vol. 4 (February 1967), pp. 73–81.

Namais, J. "Intentions to Purchase Compared with Actual Purchase of Household Durables," *J. Marketing*, Vol. 24, (July 1959), pp. 26–30.

Osgood, C. E., G. J. Suci, and P. H. Tannenbourn. *The Measurement of Meaning*, Urbana: University of Illinois Press, 1957.

Rich, S. U., and B. Portis. "Clues for Action from Shopper Preferences," *Harvard Business Review*, Vol. 41, No. 2 (March–April 1963), pp. 132–149.

Sheth, J. N. "Are There Differences in Dissonance Reduction Behavior Between Students and Housewives?" working paper No. 15, Columbia University, New York, February, 1969.

————. "Attitude-Behavior Discrepancy in Buying Electrical Motors," workpaper No. 23, Graduate School of Business, Columbia University, New York, 1969.

————. "Cognitive Dissonance, Brand Preference and Product Familiarity," in John Arndt, ed., *Insights into Consumer Behavior*, Boston: Allyn & Bacon, Inc., 1968, pp. 41–54.

————. "Generalized Brand Preference of Durable Appliances," working paper No. 25, Columbia University, New York, April 1969.

————. "Influence of Brand Preference on Post-Decision Dissonance," *J. Indian Academy of Applied Psychology*, No. 3 (1968), pp. 73–77.

————. "Projective Attitudes Toward Instant Coffee in Late Sixties," working paper No. 18, Graduate School of Business, Columbia University, New York, 1969.

————, and L. W. Ring. "Correlates of General Attitudes," unpublished working paper, Graduate School of Business, Columbia University, New York, 1968.

Trier, H., H. C. Smith, and J. Shaffer. "Differences in Food Buying Attitudes of Housewives," *J. Marketing*, Vol. 25 (July 1960), pp. 66–69.

Twedt, D. W. "How Does Brand-Awareness-Attitude Affect Marketing Strategy?" *J. Marketing*, Vol. 31 (October 1967), pp. 64–66.

Udell, J. G. "Can Attitude Measurement Predict Consumer Behavior?" *J. Marketing*, Vol. 29 (October 1965), pp. 46–50.

Wells, W. D. "Measuring Readiness to Buy," *Harvard Business Review*, Vol. 39 No. 6 (November–December 1961), pp. 81–87.

Buyer Behavior Variables

Bass, F. M., E. A. Pessemier, and D. J. Tigert. "Complementary and Substitute Patterns of Purchasing and Use," *J. Advertising Research*, Vol. 9 (June 1969), pp. 19–27.

Brown, G. N. "Brand Loyalty—Fact or Fiction?" *Advertising Age*, June 9, 1952, pp. 53–55; June 30, 1952, pp. 45–47; July 14, 1952, pp. 54–56; July 28, 1952, pp. 46–48; August 11, 1952, pp. 80–82; October 6, 1952, pp. 82–86; December 1, 1952, pp. 76–79; January 26, 1953, pp. 75–76.

Carman, J. M. "Correlates of Brand Loyalty: Some Positive Results," working paper No. 26, Research Program in Marketing, Institute of Business and Economic Research, University of California, Berkeley, 1968.

————, and J. L. Stromberg. "A Comparison of Some Measures of Brand Loyalty," working paper No. 26, revised, Institute of Business and Economic Research, University of California, Berkeley, July 1967.

Cunningham, R. M. "Brand Loyalty and Store Loyalty Inter-relationships," *Proc. American Marketing Association* (June 1959), pp. 201–214.

————. "Brand Loyalty—What, Where, How Much?" *Harvard Business Review*, Vol. 34, No. 1 (January–February 1956), pp. 116–128.

————. "Customer Loyalty to Store and Brand," *Harvard Business Review,* Vol. 36, No. 6 (November–December 1961), pp. 127–137.

————. "Measurement of Brand Loyalty," *Proc. American Marketing Association* (1956), pp. 39–45.

Day, G. S. "A Two-Dimensional Concept of Brand Loyalty," *J. Advertising Research*, Vol. 9 (September 1969), pp. 29–35.

Demesetz, H. "The Effect of Consumer Experience on Brand Loyalty and the Structure of Market Demand," *Econometrica*, Vol. 30 (January 1962), pp. 22–23.

Du Pont. "The Shopper and the Supermarket," *6th Du Pont Consumer Buying Habits Study*, Wilmington, Del.: E. I. Du Pont de Nemours (1959).

Farley, J. U. "Brand Loyalty and the Economics of Information," *J. Business*, Vol. 37 (October 1964), pp. 9–14.

————. "Testing a Theory of Brand Loyalty," *Proc. American Marketing Association* (1963), pp. 308–315.

————. "Why Does Brand Loyalty Vary over Products?" *J. Marketing Research*, Vol. 1 (November 1964), pp. 9–14.

Frank, R. E. "Is Brand Loyalty a Useful Basis for Market Segmentation?" *J. Advertising Research*, Vol. 7 (June 1967), pp. 27–33.

————, S. P. Douglas, and R. E. Polli. "Household Correlates of 'Brand Loyalty, for Grocery Products," *J. Business*, Vol. 4 (February 1967), pp. 54–58.

————, and W. F. Massy. "Market Segmentation and the Effectiveness of a Brand's Price and Dealing Policy," *J. Business*, Vol. 38 (April 1965), pp. 186–200.

————, ————. "Short Term Price and Dealing Effects in Selected Market Segments," *J. Marketing Research*, Vol. 2 (May 1965), pp. 171–185.

Grahn, G. L. "NBD Model of Repeat-Purchase Loyalty: An Empirical Investigation," *J. Marketing Research*, Vol. 6 (February 1969), pp. 72–78.

Harp, J. "Socio-Economic Correlates of Consumer Behavior," *Amer. J. Economics and Sociology*, Vol. 20 (1961), pp. 265–270.

Kollat, D. T., and R. P. Willett, "Consumer Impulse Purchasing Behavior," *J. Marketing Research*, Vol. 4 (February 1967), pp. 21–31.

McConnell, J. D. "The Development of Brand Loyalty: An Experimental Study," *J. Marketing Research*, Vol. 5 (February 1968), pp. 13–19.

Myers, J. N., and M. I. Alpert. "Determinant Buying Attitudes: Meaning and Measurement," *J. Marketing*, Vol. 32 (October 1968), pp. 13–20.

Paranka, S. "Marketing Predictions from Consumer Attitudinal Data," *J. Marketing*, Vol. 24 (July 1960), pp. 46–51.

Perry, M. "Discriminant Analysis of Relations Between Consumers' Attitudes, Behavior, and Intentions," *J. Advertising Research*, Vol. 9 (June 1969), pp. 34–39.

Pollay, R. W. "Customer Impulse Purchasing Behavior: A Re-examination," *J. Marketing Research*, Vol. 5 (August 1968), pp. 323–325.

Sheth, J. N. "A Behavioral and Quantitative Investigation of Brand Loyalty," unpublished Ph.D. dissertation, University of Pittsburgh, Pittsburgh, 1966.

―――. "A Factor Analytic Model of Brand Loyalty," *J. Marketing Research*, Vol. 5 (November 1968), pp. 395–404.

―――. "Heavy Users and Early Adoption of Innovations," working paper No. 17, Graduate School of Business, Columbia University, New York, 1969.

―――. "How Adults Learn Brand Preference," *J. Advertising Research*, Vol. 8 (September 1968), pp. 25–38.

―――. "Measurement of Multi-Dimensional Brand Loyalty of a Consumer," working paper No. 24, Graduate School of Business, Columbia University, New York, April 1969.

Tate, R. S. "The Supermarket Battle for Store Loyalty," *J. Marketing*, Vol. 25 (October 1961), pp. 8–13.

Twedt, D. W. "How Important to Marketing Strategy is the Heavy User?" *J. Marketing*, Vol. 28 (January 1964), pp. 71–72.

Webster, Frederick, Jr. "The 'Deal-Prone' Consumer," *J. Marketing Research*, Vol. 2 (May 1965), pp. 186–189.

SUPPLEMENTARY READINGS

Comprehensive Models of Buyer Behavior

Engel, J. F., D. T. Kollat, and R. D. Blackwell. *Consumer Behavior,* New York: Holt, Rinehart and Winston, Inc., 1968.

Howard, J. A., and J. N. Sheth, *The Theory of Buyer Behavior*, New York: John Wiley & Sons, Inc., 1969.

Kotler, P. "Behavioral Models for Analysing Buyers," *J. Marketing*, Vol. 29 (October 1965), pp. 37–45.

Myers, J. G. "An Operational Framework for the Study of Consumer Typology and Process," working paper No. 39, Graduate School of Business Administration, University of California, Berkeley, July 1968.

―――, and F. M. Nicosia. "Time-Path Types: From Static to Dynamic Typologies," working paper No. 43, Graduate School of Business Administration, University of California, Berkeley, September 1968.

Nicosia, F. M. *Consumer Devision Processes: Marketing and Advertising Implications*, Englewood Cliffs, N.J.: Prentice-Hall, Inc. 1966.

Sheth, J. N. "A Review of Buyer Behavior," *Management Science*, Vol. 13 (August 1967), pp. 718–756.

Studies in New Product Diffusion

Arndt, J. "Role of Product-Related Conversations in the Diffusion of a New Product," *J. Marketing Research*, Vol. 4 (August 1967), pp. 291–295.

Barnett, N., and V. J. Stefflre. "An Empirical Approach to the Development of New Products," Cambridge, Mass.: Market Structure Studies Inc., 1968.

Bauer, R. A. "Risk Handling in Drug Adoption: The Role of Company Preference," *Public Opinion Quarterly*, Vol. 25 (Winter 1961), pp. 546–559.

Bell, W. E. "Consumer Innovators: A Unique Market for Newness," *Proc. American Marketing Association* (December 1963), pp. 85–95.

Brooks, R. C., Jr. "Word-of-Mouth Advertising in Selling New Products," *J. Marketing*, Vol. 22 (October 1957), pp. 154–161.

Coleman, J. S., E. Katz, and H. Menzel. *Medical Innovation: A Diffusion Study*, Indianapolis: The Bobbs-Merrill Company, 1966.

Cunningham, S. M. "Perceived Risk as a Factor in the Diffusion of New Product Information," *Proc. American Marketing Association* (Fall 1966), pp. 698–721.

————. "The Role of Perceived Risk in Product-Related Discussion and Brand Purchase Behavior," unpublished Ph.D. dissertation, Graduate School of Business Administration, Harvard University, Cambridge, 1965.

Dichter, E. "How Word-of-Mouth Advertising Works," *Harvard Business Review*, Vol. 44, No. 6 (November–December 1966), pp. 147–166.

Engel, J. F., R. J. Kegerreis, and R. D. Blackwell. "Word-of-Mouth Communication by the Innovator," *J. Marketing*, Vol. 33 (July 1969), pp. 15–19.

Fourt, L. A., and J. W. Woodlock. "Early Prediction of Market Success for New Grocery Products," *J. Marketing*, Vol. 25 (October 1960), pp. 31–38.

Frank, R. E., and W. F. Massy. "Innovation and Brand Choice: The Folgers Invasion," in Stephen Greyser, ed., *Toward Scientific Marketing*, Proceedings of the Winter Conference of the American Marketing Association (1963), pp. 96–107.

Friedson, E. "Communications Research and the Concept of the Mass," *Amer. Sociological Review*, Vol. 18 (June 1953), pp. 313–317.

Katz, E. "The Two-Step Flow of Communication: An Up-to-Date Report on an Hypothesis," *Public Opinion Quarterly*, Vol. 21 (Spring 1957), pp. 70–82.

Mancuso, J. R. "Why Not Create Opinion Leaders for New Product Introductions?" *J. Marketing*, Vol. 33 (July 1969), pp. 20–25.

Myers, J. G. "Patterns of Interpersonal Influence in the Adoption of New Products," Research Program in Marketing, Graduate School of Business Administration, working paper No. 22, Institute of Business and Economic Research, University of California, Berkeley, August 1966.

————. "References on Advertising and Mass Communications Research," Graduate School of Business Administration, Institute of Business and Economic Research, University of California, Berkeley, 1966.

————. "Reference on Diffusion Research in Sociology and Marketing," Graduate School of Business Administration, Institute of Business and Economic Research, University of California, Berkeley, 1966.

Nicosia, F. M. "Opinion Leadership and the Flow of Communication: Some Problems and Prospects," in L. George Smith, ed., *Reflections of Progress in Marketing*, Educators Conference of the American Marketing Association (1964), pp. 340–358.

Rogers, E. M. *Diffusion of Innovations*, New York: The Free Press, 1962.

Robertson, T. S. "The Process of Innovation and the Diffusion of Innovation," *J. Marketing*, Vol. 31 (January 1967), pp. 14–19.

———. "Purchase Sequence Responses: Innovators vs. Non-Innovators," *J. Advertising Research*, Vol. 8 (March 1968), pp. 47–54.

———, and J. N. Kennedy. "Prediction of Consumer Innovators: Application of Multiple Discriminant Analysis," *J. Marketing Research*, Vol. 5 (February 1968), pp. 64–69.

———, and J. R. Rossiter. "Fashion Diffusion. The Interplay of Innovator and Opinion Leader Roles," undated, unpublished manuscript.

Schramm, W., ed. *Studies of Innovation and Communication to the Public,* Stanford, Calif.: Stanford University Press, 1962.

Sheth, J. N. "Importance of Word-of-Mouth in the Diffusion of Low Risk and Highly Advantageous Innovations," working paper No. 16, Graduate School of Business, Columbia University, New York, 1969.

———. "Perceived Risk and Diffusion of Innovations," in John Arndt, ed., *Insights Into Consumer Behavior*, Boston: Allyn & Bacon, Inc., 1968, pp. 173–188.

Shibutani, T. "Reference Groups as Perspectives," *Amer. J. Sociology*, Vol. 60 (May 1955), pp. 562–569.

Steffire, V. "Simulation of People's Behavior Toward New Objects and Events," *Amer. Behavioral Scientist*, Vol. 8, No. 9 (May 1965), pp. 12–15.

Venkatesan, M., and J. N. Sheth. "An Experimental Study in Risk Reduction," (mimeograph), no date.

Yale Studies in Attitude and Communication, New Haven: Yale University Press: C. I. Hovland, I. L. James, and H. H. Kelley, *Communication and Persuasion, Psychological Studies of Opinion Change* (1957); C. I. Horland, ed., *The Order of Presentation in Persuasion* (1957); I. L. Janis, et al., *Personality and Persuasibility* (1959); M. Rosenburg, et al., *Attitude Organization and Change: An Analysis of Consistency Among Attitude Components* (1960).

Quantitative Techniques

Carman, J. M. "Brand Switching and Linear Learning Models: Some Empirical Results," working paper No. 20, Research Program in Marketing, Graduate School of Business, University of California, Berkeley, August 1965.

Claycamp, H. J., and A. E. Amstutz. "Behavioral Simulation in Evaluating Alternative Marketing Strategies," in S. M. Bass, *et al.*, eds., *Applications of the Sciences in Marketing Management,* New York: John Wiley & Sons, Inc., 1968.

Cronbach, L. J., and G. C. Gleser. "Assessing Similarity Between Profiles," *Psychol. Bulletin,* Vol. 50 (November 1953), pp. 456–473.

Day, R. "Simulation of Consumer Preference," *J. Advertising Research,* Vol. 5 (1965), pp. 6–10.

Duhammel, W. F. "The Use of Variable Markov Processes as a Partial Basis for the Determination and Analysis of Market Segments," unpublished Ph.D. dissertation, Graduate School of Business, Stanford University, Stanford, Calif., March 1966.

Frank, R. E. "Brand Choice as a Probability Process," *J. Business,* Vol. 35 (January 1962), pp. 43–56.

————, A. A. Kuehn, and W. F. Massy. *Quantitative Techniques in Marketing Analysis,* Homewood, Ill.: Richard D. Irwin, 1962.

Green, Paul E., and Frank J. Carmone. *Multi-Dimensional Scaling and Related Techniques in Marketng Analysis,* Boston: Allyn & Bacon, Inc., 1970.

Kuehn, A. A. "Consumer Brand Choice as a Learning Process," *J. Advertising Research,* Vol. 2 (December 1962), pp. 10–17.

————, and R. L. Day. "Probabilistic Models of Consumer Buying Behavior," *J. Marketing,* Vol. 28 (October 1964), pp. 27–31.

Morrison, D. G. "Measurement Problems in Cluster Analysis," *Management Science,* Vol. 13, No. 12 (August 1967), pp. 775–780.

Myers, J. G., and F. M. Nicosia. "A Marketing Research Application of the Latent Class Model," working paper No. 37, Graduate School of Business Administration, University of California, Berkeley, November 1967.

————, ————. "New Empirical Directions in Market Segmentation: Latent Structure Models," reprinted from *Proc. American Marketing Association* (December 27, 1967), pp. 247–252.

————, ————. "Some Applications of Cluster Analysis to the Study of Consumer Typologies, and Attitudinal-Behavioral Change," working paper No. 31, Graduate School of Business Administration, University of California, Berkeley, October 1967.

Robinson, P. J., and C. F. Hinkle, eds. *Sales Promotion Analysis: Some Applications of Quantitative Techniques,* Philadelphia: Marketing Science Institute, 1971.

Sheth, J. N. "Applications of Multivariate Methods in Marketing," in Robert L. King, ed., *Marketing and the New Science of Planning, Proc. American Marketing Association,* 1968, pp. 259–265.

————. "Factor Analysis of Classifactory Data," working paper No. 21, Graduate School of Business, Columbia University, New York, 1969.

————. "Multivariate Analysis of Marketing Data," working paper No. 14, Graduate School of Business, Columbia University, New York, 1968.

————. "Recency Effect and the Linear Learning Model," working paper

No. 22, Graduate School of Business, Columbia University, New York, 1969.

————. "Using Factor Analysis to Estimate Parameters," *J. Amer. Statistical Association* (1969).

Tigert, D. J. "Consumer Typologies and Market Behavior," unpublished Ph.D. dissertation, Krannert School of Industrial Administration, Purdue University (1966).

Tryon, R. C. "Cluster and Factor Analysis: General Exposition," unpublished manuscript, Department of Psychology, University of California, Berkeley, 1967.

Wirth, E. D. "Developing Marketing Strategy Through Multiple Regression," *J. Marketing Research*, Vol. 4 (August 1967), pp. 318–320.

Index of Authors